Treasurer's and Controller's Desk Book

Third Edition

Daniel L. Gotthilf, CPA

AMACOM
American Management Association

New York • Atlanta • Chicago • Kansas City • San Francisco • Washington, D.C.
Brussels • Mexico City • Tokyo • Toronto

This publication is designed to provide accurate and authoritative information in regard to the subject matter covered. It is sold with the understanding that the publisher is not engaged in rendering legal, accounting, or other professional service. If legal advice or other expert assistance is required, the services of a competent professional person should be sought.

Library of Congress Cataloging-in-Publication Data

Gotthilf, Daniel L., 1924—
    Treasurer's and controller's desk book / Daniel L. Gotthilf. —3rd ed.
        p.   cm.
    Includes indexes.
    ISBN 0-8144-0647-5
    1. Finance—Handbooks, manuals, etc.   2. Business enterprises—
Finance—Handbooks, manuals, etc.   3. Controllership—
Handbooks, manuals, etc.   I. Title.
HG4027.3.G68   2001
658.15—dc21   2001022761

Printing number

10   9   8   7   6   5   4   3   2   1

To
Lo
with love

Contents

Foreword to the First Edition

As I read the manuscript of Dan Gotthilf's *Treasurer's and Controller's Desk Book*, I became more and more impressed with the title of his book. Whether you are a treasurer or a controller or on your way to becoming one or the other, this is the book you should have on your desk.

Here is a book that is not intended to be read at one sitting. It is based, to a large extent, on the author's own business experiences, and trying to read it straight through would be like trying to live your lifetime in one day.

This book is a practical, how-to-do-it working tool, full of procedural guidelines, helpful hints, and warnings of pitfalls to avoid. It devotes a chapter to each major responsibility of the treasurer or controller, each supported by numerous forms and workpapers showing just how to get each job done.

Mr. Gotthilf has covered critical functions—providing an encyclopedic volume answering key questions that a treasurer or controller might be called upon to meet in his or her day-to-day challenges. It is an excellent guide to the performance of a financial executive's everyday duties, and I recommend that this book be kept right at the reader's fingertips. It belongs in every financial library.

Ted Reynolds
Treasurer
Hazeltine Corporation

Preface to the Third Edition: What This New Edition Will Do For You

The original manuscript of *Treasurer's and Controller's Desk Book* was published twenty-four years ago, in 1977, and was three years in the writing prior to that, bringing the book back to 1974. During the two and a half decades since publication, it has served as the definitive guide on how to be a treasurer or controller and has kept upper management and operating officers aware of what the treasurer or controller is supposed to do and why.

CHANGES OVER THE YEARS

In the intervening years, the world has changed, politically and economically. Senior management is utilizing new tools such as functional reengineering, materials requirement planning, just-in-time inventory management, global strategic planning, zero defect quality control, information technology, and human resources accounting. (In fact, the personnel director no longer exists. He or she is instead called the director of human resources.) These functions, however, are not normally within the province of the treasurer or controller, although on occasion that person may assume direct or dotted-line responsibility for them. Unlike these functions, the job of the corporate treasurer or controller as defined by the Financial Executives Institute (FEI) in Appendix A, has remained unchanged. What has changed are tax laws and accounting principles, and the tools to perform the job functions.

UPDATES FOR CONTROL DISRUPTIONS

I undertook to revise the book throughout, adding more than 15% new text and deleting noncurrent text, updating it completely for changes in tax and accounting principles to make it current in the new millennium, because to-day's ethical climate requires that the controller have in place a system to eliminate *control disruptions.* PricewaterhouseCoopers recently conducted a landmark internal control study, commissioned by the FEI and initiated by the group of private-sector organizations that originally sponsored the National Commission on Fraudulent Financial Reporting, known as the Treadway Commission. This group consists of the American Institute of Certified Public Accountants (AICPA), the American Accounting Association, the Institute of Internal Auditors, and the National Association of Accountants. My book addresses the major causes cited by the study for control disruptions: a weak control environment (Chapter 7); identifying change and analyzing its impact (Chapters 8 and 10); communications throughout the organization (Chapters 7 and 13); linkage of objectives throughout (Chapter 8); and ownership, meaning involvement of top management (Chapter 6). This study has yielded a consensus source to serve as a tool for determining how well such systems operate. Its findings will affect controllership for years to come. This book, with its tax and accounting principle revisions, is on the leading edge in ad-dressing these problems.

The Securities and Exchange Commission (SEC) has also taken the lead in identifying reporting practices that result in the misuse of materiality con-cepts to explain departures from generally accepted accounting principles, for the purpose of managing earnings. These reporting deficiencies are examined with a view to presenting more reliable financial statements. In a related action, the SEC and the AICPA's Auditing Standards Board have adopted rules re-quiring independent auditors to discuss with audit committees the auditors' judgment about the quality of the company's accounting principles as applied in its financial reporting. Further, the New York Stock Exchange, the American Stock Exchange, and the National Association of Securities Dealers have adopted rules that define independence more rigorously for audit committee members, and require audit committees to include at least three members and be composed solely of independent directors who are financially literate, re-quire companies to adopt written charters for their audit committees, and require at least one member of the audit committee to have accounting or financial management expertise. This revision examines these new require-ments.

NEW CHAPTERS AND SIGNIFICANT ADDITIONS

I have added two completely new chapters, both in keeping with changes and perceptions over the past decade, covering ways to improve cash flows through dealing with the Internet, information technology, and electronic business (Chapter 18, Today's Treasurer and Controller) and utilizing electronic aids to perform the job functions of the treasurer and controller (Chapter 19, Today's Management Tools). These chapters examine web site development accounting, increasing cash flow with improved systems for receivables and payables, implementing e-commerce and enterprise resource planning, measuring the performance of these new e-systems, creating the business plan, going public, and other cash flow improvement devices.

REFERENCE BOOK ON RESPONSIBILITIES OF TREASURER AND CONTROLLER

The responsibilities of the treasurer and controller have been defined by the FEI. These duties encompass the management and direction of the enterprise, and they are, in effect, the province of any overall business owner, manager, generalist, financial executive, or entrepreneur. This new addition will be of interest to successful and proven treasurers and controllers, as well as those on the way up, as a reference book on the requirements of the job and how to acquit those requirements.

PROBLEM-SOLVING FORMAT

This book was written to provide the practical methods, procedures, and systems for the acceptance and successful performance of all financial responsibilities—to present them in one place, in one handy desk book. The desk book is an "idea bank" of fingertip answers to everyday firing line challenges. The narrative is followed by an Index of Working Aids, a listing of the well over 100 exhibits illustrating the key points. This permits successful researching of problems in seconds. You will want to keep this desk book close at hand for instant reference, as well as to reacquaint yourself with the ever-widening scope of your responsibilities. In one illustrated source book, you now have set forth all the many and varied facets of the treasury and controllership functions—for example, in chapter order, the key subjects are:

- ✧ Banking and short-term borrowing arrangements
- ✧ Long-term borrowing
- ✧ Credit and collection
- ✧ Insurance coverage
- ✧ Cash forecasting
- ✧ Formulating the operating plan
- ✧ Controlling operations
- ✧ Reporting the results of operations
- ✧ Tax policies

❖ Operational audits
❖ Special areas of responsibility
❖ Mergers and acquisitions
❖ Record retention and filing
❖ Data processing control
❖ Stock option planning
❖ Employee benefit programs
❖ Economic appraisal
❖ Today's financial officer
❖ Today's management tools

INDEXED AND CROSS-REFERENCED

This book gives you practical, no-nonsense approaches to handling the pertinent responsibility. The book is conveniently indexed and cross-referenced to enable you to look up any subject and find the right chapter and page number for the precise schedule, exhibit, or graph that you need. Problems are a part of management. Solving them quickly is a part of good management. The *Treasurer's and Controller's Desk Book* is the manager's everyday tool for achieving this.

SUMMARY OF CHAPTER CONTENTS

Here are some examples of what you will find:

Chapter 1—How to set up most of your bank accounts to avoid the need for reconciliations monthly, through *color coding and imprest accounts*. How to apply for and get bank loans by supplying the right information, in advance. International cash management and hedging is explored. You'll also find a simple, accurate, and proven accounts payable "jacket" control system—a supervisor to ensure prompt payment to your vendors.

Chapter 2—A critique of the various borrowing devices and methods to compare the alternatives of short-term or *long-term borrowing*, through mortgages, sale and leasebacks, the captive finance subsidiary, the leasing partnership, straight debt, debt with "kickers," or equity. A term sheet on a typical long-term loan is presented. Eight different types of off-balance-sheet debt techniques are examined. All the alternatives are presented here in one section for simple comparison.

Chapter 3—Four unique methods of credit granting to customers, to enable you to broaden your sales base with very little risk or cost.

Chapter 4—Four types of catastrophe insurance with a view to a 25% premium savings. A typical schedule of *all required insurance coverage* to completely protect the enterprise is submitted. You may not be adequately covered now, or you may be overinsured. The exhibited insurance schedule is a checklist to be used to compare your present coverage.

Chapter 5—A working illustration on projecting cash requirements, focusing on the details of accounts receivable collections. Longer-term cash requirements are related to the operating plan, with illustrations of the technique used, showing the statement of cash flows. Techniques to meet unexpected cash shortages are outlined, and practical tips are presented to ensure that your cash forecasts are accurate.

Chapter 6—Step-by-step detail and building blocks for constructing the operating plan. You will find here all the basic rules to construct the budget and profit plan and to tie it in to the operating plan. The detailed *working tools of the budget* are presented, together with the ways to make them work. These ways include lines of authority and proper division of responsibilities. A successful operating plan depends on these. If you employ these techniques, you can build a solid framework for the entire corporate structure.

Chapter 7—The veritable framework of the company. This consists of the definitions, uses, and examples of the *policy manual, procedures manual, organization charts, and position descriptions*. No organization can operate efficiently, and some cannot operate at all, without them. They delineate the place and responsibilities of the individual within the corporate structure. These are the tools required to eliminate the weak control environment referred to in the PricewaterhouseCoopers study.

Chapter 8—Twenty-five *reports and graphs* for getting the story of the results of operations across to top management. Each report speeds up the transmission of clearer, more concise information to the user, allowing for corrective action based on realistic data. Reports are designed to present information by exception, rather than masses of detail.

Chapter 9—The financial and tax accounting aspects of five major *tax shelter areas* as they relate to most businesses—the foreign sales corporation, the Domestic International Sales Corporation (DISC), capital gains versus sales, not "effectively connected," and the captive finance subsidiary. One or more may give you a real tax-saving payoff of significant proportions.

Chapter 10—How to identify those headquarters departments requiring audit. An actual *field operational audit procedure* and a reporting system are illustrated. These procedures prevent fraud and ensure that your operating plan is not subject to mechanical failure.

Chapter 11—How to supervise special areas of responsibility, including activity-based costing; human resource accounting; how to monitor and report on employee performance; how to monitor loans to employees; how to hire your replacement; and the use of analytical tools like operations research, operations analysis, linear programming, and quality control evaluation. A system for product pricing control, with illustrated forms and a detailed procedure, is explained, and a *philosophy of management* is described, to set the tone for the company; checklists are given for control of external audits, inventories, and cost reduction programs.

Chapter 12—How to make tax-free *mergers and acquisitions.* This presents a mathematical evaluation formula for judging the feasibility of such acquisitions. Once having decided to acquire, you have a checklist to help you evaluate the operations and finances of the acquiree. A proven motivational device is presented to encourage the acquired owner, and an actual letter memorandum of acquisition agreement is illustrated.

Chapter 13—*Records* that you must retain, and for how long. This explains how to establish a good current filing system and explores a microfilm retrieval system that is inexpensively implemented. A new computer disk storage filing system is discussed.

Chapter 14—The entire *data processing* function, in both large and small business, is explored. An organization chart of the typical department is exhibited as well as status reports to control the flow of work coming out of the data processing department. Management by objectives to evaluate data processing performance is reviewed and exhibited. Whether to automate or not is examined. Security safeguards against theft and fire are explained. Management of microcomputers throughout the organization is discussed, involving selection of equipment and software, implementation, and follow-up of results.

Chapter 15—Three innovative *nonqualified stock option plans* and a qualified *incentive stock option plan* are reviewed in the light of tax and stock market dictates. These will motivate and induce managers to remain with the company. Both the financial and tax aspects of each plan are examined. A stock purchase plan for all employees is examined. It gives everyone a real stake in the operation and makes the lowest-level employee profit-conscious.

Chapter 16—How to develop and administer benefit programs for employees and key executives. The various benefit programs are identified, and management reports are exhibited.

Chapter 17—An identification of the world and domestic economic factors that affect every business and how to interpret their impact on the different operating departments of the company.

Chapter 18—A description of the functions of the treasurer and controller in today's new economy, explaining the attributes required to be successful and how to utilize e-systems to perform the job functions and improve cash flows.

Chapter 19—An explanation of the latest management tools, including e-commerce, application service providers, e-purchasing, enterprise resource planning, strategic risk management, treasury workstations, and cash shortfall analysis. The means of measuring the performance of these electronic systems is described. How to create effective business plans and going public are detailed.

THE PURPOSE OF OWNING THIS BOOK

This desk book is a guide to have at your fingertips, giving you access, updated for the latest tax and accounting rules, to those functions that the treasurer or controller needs to know in order to handle the responsibilities of either of those positions. Today's treasurer and controller is responsible to his or her company, its stockholders, the SEC, the public, and creditors (users of financial statements). He or she must establish an operating control environment that eliminates control disruptions and ensures that internal control procedures are such that the operating plans and published financial statements have integrity, that specified objectives are being obtained, and that no material, uncorrected weakness exists. This book provides the tools to accomplish those objectives.

1

Maintaining and Administering Banking and Financial Arrangements

Specifying which banks and financial institutions to use, maintaining relations with them, and handling and controlling the actual flow of cash through the company, involving accounts payable, payrolls, petty cash, interest, and dividends, are elements of the concepts of budgeting and cash planning, the control over collections, and provision for the prevention of fraud involving cash. The controller usually develops the budget and is responsible for operational disbursements involving payrolls and trade accounts payable. The treasurer retains banking liaison and overall control of company funds. They must work in close collaboration to ensure that all the responsibilities are being acquitted as called for in the company position descriptions, with nothing falling through the cracks because tasks are undesignated. This is a chapter on the source and control of "money," the life plasma of any business organization.

BANKING AND INSTITUTIONAL RELATIONS

The financial relationship is concerned with the company's banks, investment bankers, and institutional lenders such as insurance companies.

The financial officer of the company must develop a relationship of informality, trust, knowledge, and confidence with the suppliers of funds. All of the following should be used to achieve this relationship:

1. Once-a-month business meetings, sometimes at company head-quarters, sometimes at the bank
2. Semiannual meetings involving all major financial lenders, both long- and short-term
3. Special group meetings, as required, to present new programs
4. Luncheon meetings for discussion of one or two brief subjects, monthly or as the need arises
5. Social meetings, evenings, with spouses included, usually at dinner or some sporting event, for brief discussions on one or two business topics

Helpful Hint: Always return phone calls within two or three hours, no matter where you are in the world. Longer than that is inattentive and, perhaps, rude. You can't do business with someone who doesn't respond promptly. This applies to everyone, not just bankers.

A warm and friendly business relationship, and no more, can be developed using these approaches. Any further fraternity, such as invitations to cocktail parties or weekend home visits, is not appropriate unless it is sought by the lender. Even in such cases, it should be kept to an occasional meeting. This type of additional intimacy can place an unnecessary strain on the relationship, which could have the opposite effect to that one is seeking. The association is better built on a social engagement.

Your lender should never be made to feel that you are seeking her or him out, currying favor, or using any other blandishments to gain your own ends. On the contrary, your frequent meetings and lunches and occasional social evenings, always involving a business discussion, will impress your lender with your devotion to your company and your attention to the responsibilities of your job. To what end? Why all this? If the relationship is handled right, you will accomplish a great deal:

1. Your banker, through these frequent meetings, will practically become another member of your management team, at no cost to the company. You are effectively expanding the depth of your management.

2. The time required to explain your program is considerably shortened, since your lender already has a detailed, intimate knowledge of your company. Your own time, therefore, may be utilized more efficiently.

3. The lender, because of the frequency of these meetings and the sometimes social aspect of them, has an opportunity to assess your own competence and intelligence, and your ability to react to varied situations. This, in turn, will permit him or her to rely on that competence and intelligence in making commitments to your company.

4. At monthly and group meetings, your bankers will meet your entire management team. These meetings will have been structured to allow all sections of management to participate. The bankers will appreciate the involvement of all of management in the financial affairs of the company.

5. The company's bankers, through their frequent and total involvement in company affairs, will be of great assistance in long-range planning, acquisitions, and alternative marketing strategies. They can better recommend their total banking services, which are considerable, to a company they understand well.

6. Your bankers, in essence, will become experts in your business or industry, because of your assistance. Their own career paths will be eased, and you will have invaluable financial colleagues who can help ease your way—within your own company or at another with which you may become associated in the future.

The cultivation of this association should be an ongoing thing, whether or not the firm is currently borrowing or anticipates raising additional equity. There may be no need for banking services today, but there surely will be in the future. The banking relationship may be almost impossible to establish on short notice when it is needed. Therefore, it must already be in place.

Bankers develop confidence in a company when detailed financial information is presented to them on a continuing basis. This provides support for loans they have made or will make, keeps them continually informed, permits them to monitor progress, and gives them confidence in the integrity of the company. Bank credit agreements frequently call for quarterly internal financial statements and year-end certified audit reports. Monthly statements are better, however, to achieve the above ends, and they should be offered to banks even though they are not specified in any agreements. At a minimum, the following financial data should be submitted:

1. Monthly operating statement (P&L), compared to budget
2. Monthly balance sheet
3. Monthly narrative report consisting of a brief, few lines explanation for any significant changes in key balance sheet items or variation from budgeted operations
4. Monthly cash flow statement, or some variant thereof, showing cash receipts and disbursements by major categories
5. **Schedule of limitations under bank agreement** (see Exhibit 1-1), showing restrictions and limitations set by the bank and the company's performance vis-à-vis them

Exhibit 1-1.   Schedule of limitations under bank agreement.

SCHEDULE OF LIMITATIONS UNDER BANK AGREEMENT
FYE 4/30/
$000 omitted

	LIMITS	5/31/	6/30/	7/31/
Aggregate credit including L/C's	18,000	15,175	15,829	16,547
Letters of credit	6,000	1,802	1,205	1,289
Notices of litigation required - minimum	500	--	--	--
Secured indebtedness excluding mortgage	725	291	261	249
Working capital - minimum	10,000	10,300	10,135	10,153
Tangible net worth - minimum	9,000	10,654	10,690	10,807
Debt to equity	1.5 to 1	1.44 to 1	1.50 to 1	1.49 to 1
R & D and capital expenditures (excluding rental equipment)	1,000	23	47	78
Aggregate guarantees	250	--	--	--
Lease rental payments - annual	1,500	800	800	800
Dealer acquisitions for stock	400	--	--	--
Undischarged judgments	500	--	--	--

Most companies prepare most of this data monthly as a matter of routine, so that no extra effort need be expended to supply it to the banks. The availability of it will satisfy the most stringent requirements. Additional schedules may be made available on request, to suit the type of loan being made. These could include inventory schedules, 90-day cash forecasts, 12-month cash requirements projections, and 12-month operating statement projections.

SUMMARIZING AND SCHEDULING CREDIT AND LOAN ARRANGEMENTS

Bank agreements, credit and security agreements, and debt arrangements are generally lengthy documents, replete with representations, warranties, and restrictive covenants. An agreement, itself, is not a working document, and it needs to be reduced to a manageable form so that workers involved in administering the agreement can find their way through it. Usually, a 100-page document can be outlined and summarized in 5 or 6 pages. Article and section numbers of the agreement can be referenced to page numbers and a brief summary given of pertinent paragraphs. A **credit and security agreement summary** is illustrated at Exhibit 1-2. Its use will save hours of searching out the clauses needed for ready reference.

Similarly, the schedule of limitations or restrictions under the agreement, Exhibit 1-1, should be circulated to all executives and decision makers, to be used as a gentle reminder of prior commitments when negotiating new contracts and commitments. The treasurer will monitor this schedule monthly and will alert other officers of approaching limits.

An overview should also be taken of **cash in major bank accounts** and of **current short-term borrowings from banks** under the terms of existing bank agreements. These schedules are maintained on a daily basis and present a running history of bank balances and daily borrowings. They are illustrated in Exhibits 1-3 and 1-4. The treasurer utilizes them in maintaining balances requirements, transferring funds between banks, and limiting borrowings to obtain maximum utilization of the float. Each column on the bank borrowings schedule is supported with

(*text continues on page 9*)

Exhibit 1-2. Credit and security agreement.

Credit and Security Agreement

20xx

PG.	ART.	
1		Whereas (Purpose)
2	1	Defined Terms (See Schedule)
17		1.2 Use of Defined Terms
17	2	Amount and Terms of Credit
17		2.1 Commitments
20		2.2 Notice of Borrowing & Request for L/C's
20		a) 2 days notice - $250,000 multiple (except for L/C's)(oral & writing)
21		b) 2 days notice for L/C's
22		c) Officers' Certificate with Notice (Exh. F)
25		2.3 Reduction of Commitments for Outstanding L/C's
25		2.4 The Notes - 1 1/2% over prime, on demand, interest quarterly
26		2.5 Letters of Credit - 1/8% to MHCC, 1/8% to each Bank
26		2.6 Fees for Letters of Credit
27		2.7 Computation of Interest - 365 day basis
28		2.8 Pro Rata Treatment & Payments
29		2.9 Borrowing Base
29	3	Use of Proceeds
29		3.1 Proceeds of Initial Borrowing
30		3.2 Proceeds of Subsequent Borrowing
30		3.3 General Prohibitions on Use of Proceeds
30	4	Collateral Security
30		4.1 Collateral Security (Initial Borrowers Certificate, Exh. B & C)
31		(As needed - Assignment - Exh. B-1)
31		(45 days monthly - Assignment - Exh. C-1)
32		4.2 Collections - Lock Boxes Named "Cash Collateral Account"
34		4.3 Application of Collections - M, W, F of each week
35		4.4 Officers' Certificate with reference to receivables -
35		15th & 30th of each month - Certificate
35		Supplement to Exh. E
36		4.5 Notation on Books of Company - on C.L. accounts
37		4.6 Information regarding collateral
38		4.7 Receivables from Government & Agencies thereof
39		4.8 Communicating with Account Debtors, etc.
40		4.9 Waiver by the Company
40		4.10 Provision with respect to collateral in event of default
43		4.11 Power of Attorney
45		4.12 Financing Statements
46		4.13 Reimbursement of Expenses
47		4.14 Agent & Banks not liable with respect to collateral
47		4.15 Agent on premises
48	5	Conditions of Borrowing
48		5.1 Conditions of Initial Loans
48		a) Note b) Assignments c) Officers' Certificate
49		d) Senox Guarantee, Exh. I (e) Senox Security Agreement, Exh. J
49		f) Guarantee of Subs, Exh. K g) Guarantee of Sofax, Exh. 5
50		h) Guarantee of Savin-Canada, Exh. L i) Security Agreement
50		of Diversified, Exh. L; Security Agreement of Savin
50		World Trade, Exh. J & L; k) Notice to Equilease
51		l) Certificate of Swift, Florida, m) M. Low subordination
51		n) Ricoh subordination o) Secretary's Certificate - Savin

Exhibit 1-3. Daily cash summary.

Daily Cash Summary
February, 20 __

| Date | Sterling National Bank | | | Chase | | Trust Co. |
	General	Accts Pay.	SBMCL	General	Accts Pay.	Lock Box
1-31	19322955	122373	<14368076>	45237460	<84046657>	9541396
2-1	19322955	122373	<14368076>	58769077	<84046657>	13600099
2-4	19322955	122373	<14397793>	36047186	<64046657>	5903451
2-5	29322955	122373	602207	47260664	<64046657>	11855010
2-6	29322955	122373	584106	49812245	<64046657>	14541090
2-7	29322955	122373	584106	60977102	<49862177>	5862009
2-8	29322955	122373	584106	68350429	<49362177>	13009276
2-11	29322955	122373	584106	50053348	637823	7505718
2-12	29293438	122373	532439	22445225	637823	3383475
2-13	29893438	122373	532439	30824461	637823	9915479
2-14	29293438	122373	532439	8379784	637823	9270865
2-15	19293438	122373	532439	135148039	637823	13181353
2-19	19293438	122373	519375	129213787	637823	7425275
2-20	30293438	122373	156884	57213787	637823	13987395
2-21	30283510	122373	90156884	83773440	637823	6996445
2-22	29415209	122373	90156884	83773440	637823	10915370
2-25	29415209	122373	156884	110006202	637823	6611420
2-26	29415209	122373	92352	78295282	637823	11274767
2-27	29372425	122373	258767	86243733	637823	16121802
2-28	29372425	122373	258767	144116148	637823	6419843

Exhibit 1-4.   Bank borrowings.

Schedule of Borrowing From Banks
August, September 20 __

Date	Activity Borrowed	Payments	Total Borrowed	Chase 27.77% Activity	Balance
Bal 7-30			15254959		42363019½
8-1		(358800)	14896159	(9963876)	413666318
8-5	1000000		15896159	277700	441436318
8-6		(577100)	15319059	(160260)	425410318
8-8		(333900)	14985159	(9272403)	416137915
8-9	844900		15830059	234620	439599915
8-12	1250000		17080059	347126	474312515
8-13		(671500)	16408559	(186476)	455664915
8-15	106400	(388600)	16126359	(78367)	447808215
8-19	1000000		17126359	277700	475598215
8-20		(517400)	16608959	(14368198)	461230017
8-22		(412900)	16196059	(11466233)	449763784
8-26	793700		16989759	220411	471804884
8-27		(432900)	16556859	(120216)	459783284
8-29		(723100)	15833759	(200794)	439703884
9-3	1297300		17131059	360262	475730084
9-4		(754800)	16376259	(209608)	454769284
9-6		(274800)	16101459	(76312)	447138084
9-9	752600		16854059	208997	468037784
9-10	3	(643300)	16210762	(178644)	450172384
9-12		(738100)	15472662	(204970)	429675384
9-13		(1417700)	14054962	(393695)	390305884
9-16	1052700		15107662	292335	419539384
9-17		(530500)	14577162	(147320)	404807384
9-19		(264900)	14292262	(79118)	396895584
9-23	2000000		16292262	555400	452435584
9-24		(357700)	15934562	99333	442502284
9-26		(361800)	15572762	(100472)	432455584
9-30	1422700		16995462	395084	471963484

a **detailed page showing all deposits and disbursements** into that bank, summarized on a daily basis, which enables a better estimate of outstanding checks that affect the float. The supporting page is shown in Exhibit 1-5. Note that the total ties into the appropriate column of Exhibit 1-3. Additional supporting schedules can be prepared to supplement Exhibit 1-5, showing areas of the country to which checks have been mailed—an indicator of how quickly they will be returned through the Federal Reserve System.

These summary schedules should be posted with all bank reconciliation adjustments and agreed-to financial statement balances for cash and bank debt at month-end. When this is done, they serve as a valuable audit trail at fiscal year-end and are useful in composing the footnote to financial statements relating to bank balances and/or bank debt.

Increasing Cash Flow Through Banking Arrangements

Having established the basic bank borrowing agreements and the summary schedules to monitor cash and bank debt, you may now devote your attention to maximizing cash utilization. The schedules in Exhibits 1-3 and 1-4 are merely starting points. There are at least six additional methods of increasing cash flow through unique banking arrangements:

1. *Lockbox banking*. Companies with customers outside their immediate metropolitan area should explore the flow of customers' checks from the mailing point through the Federal Reserve Banking System. Most banks perform lockbox services or will refer you to a bank that does. Setting up a lockbox usually involves giving the bank an entire month's receipts, either checks or data processing runs, showing amounts and dates received by territory. If your system does not provide for territory coding, envelopes may be saved for an entire month, date-stamped with receipt and check amount. The bank will process them through its lockbox computer program and will output a **report showing the optimum locations for lockbox accounts**. This report allows for mailing time and the lag in clearance through

Exhibit 1-5.   Bank borrowings—detail.

Lock Box   Chase TRUST Company   A/c # _____

February 20__

	DATE	Receipts		Disbursements		Balance	
1	1-31					9541396	1
2	2-1	4058703	1-31			1360099	2
3	2-4	2533615	2-1	2-1	10230263	5903451	3
4	2-5	8470535	2-4	2-4	2518976	11855010	4
5	2-6	2686080	2-5			14541090	5
6	2-7	2478534	2-6	2-6	11157615	5862009	6
7	2-8	7147267	2-7			13009276	7
8	2-11	4122243	2-8	2-8	9625801	7505718	8
9	2-12			2-11	4122243	3383475	9
10	2-13	6532004	2-11			9915479	10
11	2-14	5887390	2-13	2-13	6532004	9270865	11
12	2-15	3910488	2-14			13181353	12
13	2-19	4040900	2-15	2-15	9796978	7425275	13
14	2-20	6562120	2-19			13987395	14
15	2-21	3612070	2-20	2-20	10514814	7084651	15
16				—	88206	6996445	16
17	2-22	3918925	2-21			10915370	17
18	2-25	3227045	2-22	2-22	7530995	6611420	18
19	2-26	7925382	2-25	2-25	3263035	11274767	19
20	2-27	4847035	2-26			16121802	20
21	2-28	3070456	2-27	2-27	12772415	6419843	21
22							22
23							23
24							24
25							25
26							26
27							27
28							28
29							29
30							30
31							31
32							32
33							33
34							34
35							35

the Federal Reserve System. Such a report is reproduced in Exhibit 1-6; for the company in the exhibit, lockboxes in San Francisco, Chicago, and New York provide the fastest clearance of funds. Customers are then instructed, at the time they are invoiced for merchandise, to remit to a special lockbox account number at a particular post office address. The bank is authorized to pick up checks at the lockbox post office and deposit them in a special lockbox bank account. Funds are then cleared from this special lockbox bank account in the company's regular general account on a routine basis. (A complete set of **lockbox instructions** is given in Exhibit 1-7.) These instructions provide not only the mechanics of the operation but the internal accounts receivable control needed.

Lockbox banking, in addition to clearing funds more quickly, offers the following advantages:

- ✧ The bank picks up checks at the post office on Saturdays, which companies do not normally do.
- ✧ The possibility of employee fraud is eliminated. Only bank employees handle checks, and the bank is responsible for defalcations. The company can save the cost of employee dishonesty bonds or similar insurance.
- ✧ The company saves the cost of establishing internal control procedures between the accounts receivable and accounting departments, since there is no actual handling of cash or checks.
- ✧ Checks are deposited on a timely basis. The company is not concerned with key employee illness or other factors that could delay timely deposits.

These lockbox banking advantages may usually be obtained without cost to the company. The cost of the bank's services will usually be met by the balances in the lockbox account. Thus, the company can obtain greater balances utilization overall, plus the above advantages.

2. *Zero-balance accounts.* These are usually ancillary accounts, in addition to the company's principal or general account, used for petty cash, freight payments on a weekly basis, travel expense accounts, municipal tax payments, payrolls, and other frequently used special accounts. They are, therefore, working bank accounts that are not used

(*text continues on page 16*)

Exhibit 1-6. Lockbox banking report.

LOCKBOX IN CHICAGO   RECEIVES A TOTAL OF $ 981657 FROM THE FOLLOWING CITIES

ATLANTA	BTNROUGE	BUFFALO	CHICAGO	CINCINNA	CLVELAND	CORPCHRI	DALLAS	DENVER	DETROIT
HOUSTON	INDIANAP	JACKSON	KAN CITY	MEMPHIS	MIAMI	MINNEAPO	MOBILE	MONTGMRY	PHILADEL

LOCKBOX IN SAN FRAN   RECEIVES A TOTAL OF $ 557483 FROM THE FOLLOWING CITIES

HUNTSVIL	LOS ANGE	OAKLAND	SAN FRAN

LOCKBOX IN NEW YORK   RECEIVES A TOTAL OF $ 747764 FROM THE FOLLOWING CITIES

ALBANY	BLTIMORE	BOSTON	BRATBORO	HARTFORD	MANCHSTR	NEWARK	NEWHAVEN	NEW ORLE	NEW YORK
PROVIDEN	SPGFLDMS	SYRACUSE	WASH DC						

IF DOLLAR DELAY CONSIDERS MAIL TIME + CLEARANCE TIME + CHECK PROCESSING TIME, AND CONSIDERS HOLIDAYS, THEN
DOLLAR DELAY IS   7800376.00 DOLLAR–DAYS FOR LOCKBOXES IN
                                  CHICAGO   SAN FRAN   NEW YORK

DOLLAR DELAY BASED ON MAIL TIME + CLEARANCE TIME, WEIGHTED BY DOLLAR AMOUNTS IS   6337736.00 DOLLAR–DAYS

SURVEY RESULTS

Total Dollars   : $2,286,904.00
Number of Cities: 41

More than half (57.5%) of the total dollar amount was
received from only 7 of the remitting areas. Totals by area
drop sharply after that.

Delays generated by one lock box city, two lock box
cities, and three lock box cities are shown below. These
are the best locations as chosen by the program. The Summary
Page shows the delay for these solutions as well as for
those which had locations pre-specified.

LOCK BOX CITY	COLUMN I DELAY (Including holidays, processing, mail & clearance time expressed in dollar days)	COLUMN II DELAY (Including mail & clearance time only, expressed in dollar days)
Chicago	8,423,028	7,576,777
Chicago, San Francisco	8,225,615	6,933,345
Chicago, San Francisco, New York	7,800,376	6,337,736

The figures which are of the most immediate interest are those
in Column II (shown again on Summary Page), which show absolute
delay based on mail and clearance time only (weekends and
holidays which fell during the survey period do not affect
this figure).

Exhibit 1-7. Lockbox instructions.

September 9, 20___

Mr._____
        Trust Company
        Avenue
New York, N.Y. 10022

Dear Mr._____ :

Confirming our telephone conversation of August 30, I am enclosing a
copy of our statement and invoice, for your review.

This letter will confirm the arrangements for our use of your Lock Box
Service, which we look forward to inaugurating on receipt of this letter.
We will instruct our customers to send remittances to _____
Corporation, c/o P. O. Box _____, Church Street Station, New York,
N.Y. 10049.

You will charge our account approximately $40 annually, to cover the post
office box rental. We have not discussed this charge, but I assume it
will be in this range.

Your Lock Box Department will open the envelopes, remove contents, inspect
and process remittances, as follows:

1. Checks will be inspected for correct payee.

2. Undated checks will be dated to correspond with envelope post
    office cancellation date.

3. Postdated checks which would not reach the drawee bank on or before
    the date on the check will be processed. All other postdated checks
    will not be processed, but will be forwarded to _____ without entry,
    together with the accompanying remittance data.

4. Checks with alterations and erasures and checks bearing typed or
    handwritten restrictive notations, such as, "Payment in Full," will
    not be processed and will be forwarded to _____ with the attached
    envelope and all other accompanying remittance data.

5. When remittances are received and the accompanying statements and the
    check amounts differ, you will lightly rule out the statement amount
    and inscribe the check amount and process the check.

6. One copy of each check will be provided - it will accompany the
    remittance details and envelopes forwarded to _____, New York,
    attention Mr. _____.

7. When an invoice accompanies a payment and the check coincides with
    the invoice total, the amount of the total will be circled. Copies of
    checks and invoices will be segregated and batched separately. All other
    payment copies and remittance details will be grouped and batched.

8. Unsigned checks will be processed with proper notification of the drawee
    bank requesting that the signature be obtained.

9. We will guarantee and process checks that reflect a difference between
    the written and numerical amounts provided the correct amount can be
    determined from any enclosed statement.

Mr._____
September 9, 20__
Page Two

10. Checks which are in order for deposit will be endorsed "Credited to the
     Account of the Within-Named Payee. Lack of Endorsement Guaranteed."

11. All "unprocessed items," with each check's envelope and any accompanying
     enclosures, will be separately batched for delivery with other processed
     items.

12. Checks returned unpaid because of insufficient funds will automatically
     be re-presented. On second refusal, items will be charged back and
     mailed to the customer's office with advice of debit. Items returned
     for "no account," "account closed," or other reasons implying inability
     of re-presentment, will be charged back immediately. Items for $1,000
     or over will be charged back with telephone and debit advice of nonpayment,
     to Mr. _____, at the address above.

13. At the close of the processing day, posting media will be mailed to us,
     together with duplicate credit advices, adding machine tapes of individual
     items, unprocessed items batch and any miscellaneous mail, and deposit
     tags and duplicate checks to _____ Corporation, _____, N.Y.
     10595, Attention Credit/Collection Department.

14. On Monday, Wednesday and Friday of each week, any federally available
     funds in our account, in excess of $20,000, should be transferred to
     our General Account, No. _____, _____ Trust Company,
     _____ Avenue, New York, N.Y. 10018.

     If there are any questions concerning the transfer, please contact
     Mr. _____, Assistant Vice President, at that office.

     A copy of the transfer advice should be sent to us on each Monday,
     Wednesday and Friday, at _____, New York 10595, attention
     Accounting Department.

15. Monthly bank statements should be sent to us at _____, New
     York 10595, attention Accounting Department.

16. You are directed and authorized to pick up mail from our post office
     box, Monday through Saturday, at frequent intervals. Enclosed is a
     copy of our letter of authorization to the Postmaster, Church Street
     Station, covering Post Office Box _____.

Thank you for your cooperation in establishing this Lock Box Account.

Very truly yours,

DANIEL L. GOTTHILF
Treasurer

DLG:R

Enclosure

sc:

to carry balances but are kept at zero. A letter of instructions is given to the bank, authorizing it to make transfers before the close of banking business each day, in an amount sufficient to cover the checks returned for payment to the zero-balance account. A limit is usually placed on the amount that may be transferred, say $5,000, and any larger transfers must be approved by a signatory. Transfers are made from the general account, where balances are normally maintained, and advice of such transfer is forwarded to the treasurer's department on a daily basis. Maximum utilization of cash is the result, as small balances need not be carried in these operating accounts in anticipation of checks being returned.

3. *Imprest and color-coded accounts.* Imprest accounts are similar to zero-balance accounts in that the amount of the deposit exactly equals the checks written. The difference, however, is that imprest account deposits are made at the time checks are written, or a few days after, when they are expected to be returned for payments. They do not provide quite as much cash utilization as zero-balance bank accounts, but in those cases where the bank is not equipped or prepared to make preauthorized zero-balance transfers, the imprest method gives the nearest result.

Imprest bank accounts are frequently used with color-coded checks. Bank reconciliations are completely unnecessary with imprest or zero-balance accounts, since the daily deposit exactly equals the daily disbursements. When these accounts are used in conjunction with color-coded checks, the amount outstanding from any given month may be easily calculated. Normally, six different color codes will suffice for an account without too much activity, with the color changing each month. A large national payroll account, serving many branch office locations, could use nine colors to allow for lost checks and late stragglers beyond the six-month period. Each month, the canceled checks are totaled by color, and the total for each color is subtracted from the total of checks originally written. The difference is the amount outstanding to be carried forward to next month. Color-coded checks may then be arranged in numerical order and filed. After two months of no activity in a particular color, the outstanding checks may be canceled, stop payments issued, and the bank balance adjusted. Each individual outstanding check should then be investigated to determine why it hasn't been returned. In the case of payroll checks, this may indicate some flaw in the system for handling checks sent to terminated employees at remote offices. The color-coded check, therefore, serves to eliminate the traditional bank reconciliation, substituting instead adding machine tapes, and also provides an internal control system review.

4. *Petty cash accounts.* These accounts are best handled on an imprest or zero-balance basis. Maximum cash utilization is obtained by well-documented procedures on when to use petty cash and when to pay through the company's general account. When petty cash is used as a checking account, rather than as a true cash box, bills tend to be paid more promptly than they would be through the general account. In the case of a company with a great many field offices and remote locations, there can be hundreds of petty cash checking accounts, all paying vendors' bills more quickly than necessary. Here are a few simple rules for controlling petty cash payments, which may be adapted to suit any particular company:

✧ Invoices in amounts over $100 may not be paid through petty cash fund checks (to avoid too prompt payment of larger invoices).

✧ Invoices in amounts under $100 *must* be paid through petty cash fund checks (to avoid the unnecessary expense of purchase requisitions, purchase orders, receiving reports, and vouching for payment).

✧ Collect freight bills may not be paid through petty cash funds. Vendor shipments should be made freight prepaid and billed back on the vendor invoice. Interbranch shipments should be freight prepaid by the shipping branch. All this avoids duplicate freight payments and the need for checking every freight bill to determine whether it is a proper charge or whether it has been paid by another branch or the headquarters office.

✧ Expense reports that require higher approvals (above that of the office administering the petty cash fund) may not be paid through petty cash. This keeps proper controls on excess travel and entertainment expense spending.

✧ A petty cash voucher must be made out for each disbursement, and this must be supported by a vendor's receipt. Hence, two documents are needed, one from the approver and one from the vendor.

✧ Petty cash reconcilations must be submitted with each reimbursement request, and these should be audited by the home office to verify conformity to procedures.

✧ Petty cash reimbursements must be made at least once a month (to avoid a requirement to establish a larger fund than necessary. As with inventory, a faster turnover requires less investment).

5. *Accounts payable imprest accounts.* The company's principal account for bill payments is the accounts payable bank account. The volume of activity is such that it may not be operated as a zero-balance account. However, operating it on an imprest basis, making daily deposits in the same amount as daily disbursements, will provide maximum cash flow. This can be further increased by using the schedule of bank borrowings in Exhibit 1-4 and the detailed support in Exhibit 1-5. Deposits into the imprest account can be written and timed, based on the section of the country to which the disbursement was sent.

6. *Online treasury workstations* (see Chapter 19).

FINANCIAL ARRANGEMENTS WITH VENDORS AND PAYMENTS CONTROLS

Payments to vendors are most frequently made in accordance with the terms on the vendor's invoice—in short, to accommodate the vendor. This is not the best way. Vendors' terms are myriad. This means an assortment of data processing runs and different check-writing dates during any month. Instead, the company as the buyer can generally set its own terms of payment to suit its own data processing or accounts payable system. If the method of payment is consistent, the vendor will usually accept it. If not, the purchasing department can usually educate the vendor to acquiesce. On occasion, it may find it necessary to replace the vendor.

A good company method is one that provides for two general payment periods per month. Bills for net payment (no discount) are paid on the 25th of the month following receipt in the accounts payable department. Bills with discounts are paid on the 10th of the month following receipt. Note that the controlling date is not the date of the vendor's invoice but, rather, the date received in the accounts payable department for processing. This schedule can be varied somewhat in the vendor's favor by using a 5th-of-the-month cutoff date—invoices received in accounts payable by the 5th of the month are considered as received in the prior month. This type of variation, though, is not at all necessary to gain vendor acceptance unless the company deals with many vendors who traditionally complete heavy shipments during the last few days of each month, thereby throwing their billings into the first of the following month.

The results of such a payment system are to translate 30-day terms from the vendor into payments in 25 to 55 days, and 10-day discount terms into 10- to 40-day discount terms, plus the added savings of only two processings per month. There are also considerable time savings in tracing unpaid invoices through the system using a two-payment system.

An adjunct to a two-payment system usually would provide for a payments run every Friday. This would handle freight bills that carry an ICC payment requirement of seven days, and expense reimbursements to employees who need prompt payment. Certain classes of trade accounts payable may also be coded to fit into the Friday payment runs. These might be utility bills or personnel recruitment agency bills, which usually require more immediate payment.

At any rate, it is obvious that with a firmly established payment schedule, suited to the company's own data processing or accounts payable system, significant extra cash utilization may be obtained. This will, of course, require the support of the purchasing department in establishing these terms with vendors. But even where these terms have not been preestablished, vendors will rarely complain if the method is consistently followed.

The purchasing department can contribute even more to additional and repetitive cash savings by specifying discount terms with all new vendors and insisting on them in renegotiating contracts with old vendors. Once the discount terms are negotiated, the vendor may very well consider that it has given the customer a price discount, but the vendor tends to forget about this on subsequent reorders or on new jobs. The effect is the same as if the company had received a permanent price reduction. Purchasing may take a firm stance in this regard, even refusing to do business with those vendors who do not allow such cash discounts.

The vendor's arguments against allowing discount terms can be easily overcome, provided the controller has educated the purchasing manager on the advantages to the seller of allowing such discounts. Breathes there a financial officer who has never agonized over whether or not to allow such discounts to the company's own customers? Here are some of the arguments in favor of allowing discount terms of, say, 2/10/30:

1. Customers who can afford to pay sooner do not, unless discount terms are made available to them.
2. Customers who cannot afford to pay sooner will do so, diverting funds from other vendors not offering discounts.
3. A 2% discount for payment within 10 days gives the vendor the use of 98% of the money for an extra 20 days.
4. While this has a cost of 37% per annum ($2 for 20 days = $36 for a 360-day year, or 37% on $98), the company probably earns close to this on its invested capital.
5. A faster turnover on trade accounts receivable gives the balance sheet a better look and is the mark of a well-managed company. Banks and investors have more confidence.
6. Less credit need be used to carry receivables, allowing the company to borrow for more important needs, such as capital expenditures or research and development.
7. Vendors' sales are probably increased when discounts are allowed, as customers tend to purchase in larger amounts to achieve greater savings. This is valid at least in the first fiscal period in which the discount is initiated.
8. In the case of customers who are able to take discounts but do not, there is no certainty that payment will be made on the net due date, 30 days after shipment. There is no incentive to make payment on the net due date, and no penalty for failure to do so. Consequently, if a more attractive alternative appears, funds may be diverted.
9. On an after-tax basis, the 2% discount is really a 1.2% discount for most companies, assuming a 40% tax rate, and the 37% effective rate is really 22% after tax.

Compromises will occasionally have to be made in the two-payment system described above, probably with a few key vendors. In these cases, the responsibility for such special payment terms is a treasury function. When payment methods are varied, an attempt should be made to fit the new method into the existing accounts payable system. For example, if a key vendor will not permit payments on the 25th of the month following, but offers instead that shipments of the preceding month be paid twice during the following month, a good compromise would be to pay on the 10th and 25th of the following month, as these are regular data processing run dates. Shipments from the 1st to the 15th could be paid on the 10th of the following month (a 25- to 40-day payment span), and shipments from the 16th to the 31st could be paid on the 25th of the month following (again a 25- to 40-day span).

Improper planning or unforeseen circumstances will sometimes dictate a change in some key vendor payment terms. When this happens, the vendor should be contacted personally by the treasurer and advised, with complete candor, as to the reason for the delay, how long it will last, and whether it will recur next month. Advance notice to the vendor is a courtesy to permit proper cash planning on the vendor's part.

With banking and other borrowing relationships established to provide for the ebb and flow of funds required to operate your company, an accounts payable system must be defined to provide for payments to vendors on a prompt and accurate basis. Any accounts payable system, whether manual or automated, will provide for the following controls:

1. Date-in stamp the receipt of the vendor's invoice.
2. Require a receiving report for all invoices except repetitive utilities or services.
3. Agree bills of lading, packing slips, and receiving reports as to quantities and whether freight is prepaid or collect to each other and to purchase orders.
4. Agree vendor's invoice to purchase order as to quantity, price, freight, terms of payment, and extensions.
5. Indicate initialed approval of the above audits through an approval stamp.
6. Provide for a schedule of payments within the defined payment system, say on the 10th and 25th of the month following.

7. Provide for two-signature check-signing control, at specified dollar levels.

8. Reconcile key vendor statements monthly to avoid unrecorded liabilities.

9. Research unmatched receiving reports monthly to avoid unrecorded liabilities.

10. Research unmatched invoices monthly to ensure vendor payment in accordance with terms.

11. Provide for routine duplicate invoice payment checks, using a computer edit and/or a manual checkoff list showing that the invoice has not been previously paid. The checkoff list would include:
    - Petty cash vouchers
    - Paid bill file
    - Unmatched invoice file
    - Invoices in process of payment
    - Purchase order files—completed and open
    - Original approver—does he or she recall invoice?
    - Receiving report records

12. Maintain a payment history file for key vendors, to include all non-receiving-report repetitive utility and services vendors.

13. Provide a chart of accounts code for all accounts payable vouchers to allow easy manipulation of data.

Computer-oriented systems maintain payment history files easily, on tape or disk. The problem is more complex in a manual system. Some sort of record control is necessary to verify that payment has been made for the variety of repetitive services that are intangible in nature—rent, financing payments, utilities, repairs, medical services, personnel recruitment agencies, and a host of others. The problem can be extremely severe in the case of an installment obligation, say 60 payments of $100 each, monthly. An example of this type of payment could be rent for premises, a premises cleaning and maintenance service, or an installment loan to finance a delivery truck. The company may have a coupon book to use for each monthly payment; the landlord may bill monthly for rent, and so, too, may the cleaning service. Even with such billing by the vendor, there is usually no receiving report for such services rendered, no purchase requisition or purchase order, no inventory control, and generally no positive way to determine that a duplicate payment is not being made, or that one of the repetitive payments has not been missed. A good manual historical record is an accounts payable "jacket," simply a manila folder in which each payment is recorded that accompanies the check to the check signer as proof that proper payment is being made. This may be created as well using a Lotus or Excel Spread Sheet. A **jacket page** is shown in Exhibit 1-8. The elements and advantages of the jacket system are as follows:

1. A brief, one-paragraph description heads up the jacket page, explaining the service being rendered, showing the requirements for monthly payments, and bearing the original approver's signature. The criteria for using a jacket are: (a) the services are repetitive, even if not in the same dollar amount; (b) the services are intangible, and hence no product has been delivered and no receiving document will be prepared; (c) an invoice may not be rendered by the vendor (even if it is, when criteria a and b are met, the jacket system is to be utilized).

2. If there is a predetermined contract amount, a declining balance column is used to show the remaining contract amount and to ensure that payments beyond the final one are not made.

3. Payment information is shown each month—month being paid, date paid, check number, amount, remarks. Payments are serially numbered.

4. Supporting documentation, such as a contract copy or original purchase order copy, is stapled on the left-hand side of the jacket.

5. The jacket is forwarded, monthly, with the check request, as authority for payment of a service without an invoice and/or a receiving report.

6. Jackets are scheduled for payment on the first of each month. A master listing of all jackets is maintained. Jackets pulled for monthly payment are compared to the monthly listing to ascertain that none are missed.

These elements will be included in any automated system as well, in the form of computer edits and maintenance of a history file that may be recalled on request.

Exhibit 1-8.   Accounts payable jacket.

Bank Loan for Forklift Truck

Purchased from Eastern Motors for $5,200. Financed through
Chase Bank, Thornwood. Garaged at Portchester warehouse.
Financed over 24 months, after $1,000 down payment
(Ch. #1072 Chemical of 2/1/ , net of $4,200). Payments
of $197.71/mo. Lease capitalized -- see JE 2-6 of
2/14/ . Original P.O. #16723 approved by RWB. Payments
due 1st of each month with coupon book receipts.

Declining
Balance
$4,745.04

Amount financed - $197.71 x 24 months.

Payment No.	Date Pd.	Amt. Pd.	Ck. No.	Bank	Approval & Remarks	
1	3-01	197.71	1920	CB	JDR	454733
2	4-01	197.71	80004	ST	DG	434961
3	5-01	197.71	2430	CB	JDR	415791
4	6-01	197.71	12006	MH	JDR	395420
5	7-01	197.71	33002	CB	JDR	375649
6	8-01	197.71	44809	CB	JDR	355878
7	9-01	197.71	81516	ST	JDR	336107
8	10-01	197.71	63922	CB	JDR	316336
9	11-01	197.71	74500	CB	DG	296565
10						
11						
12						
13						
14						
15						
16						
17						
18						
19						
20						
21						
22						
23						
24						

Control Procedure for the Financial Aspects of Contracts

All contracts will have financial aspects that are the responsibility of the treasurer or controller. Some contracts are directly financial in nature and will not directly concern other departments—insurance policies, bank credit agreements, leases for premises. Other contracts are working tools for other departments, such as a manufacturing contract, but will be used by financial officers to establish terms of payment or to audit costs.

Proper contract administration will therefore require the following steps:

1. The originals of contracts should be retained in permanent files by the chief executive officer, usually the president of the company. Copies should be retained by the general or in-house counsel and the chief financial officer, with other copies being distributed to concerned parties, including the treasurer and controller.
2. These copies should be maintained in working files, in alphabetical order, by the treasurer or controller.
3. Working summaries (see Exhibit 1-2) should be prepared for operating personnel.
4. Pertinent dates, including renewal or termination dates, should be "tickled" for proper review.
5. Completed contract copies should be removed from the open files and refiled in an alphabetical closed contracts file, kept as a permanent record.
6. Corporate policy should be written specifying which corporate officers may sign contracts. This should be published in the policy manual (Chapter 7).
7. Contracts should be reviewed for payment requirements and a determination made whether to include them in the accounts payable "jacket" system.

Contracts that are similar in nature, numerous, and special-purpose should be separately filed and administered. This would include insurance policies (see Chapter 4) and landlord/tenant leases for premises.

Exhibit 1-9. Leased premises summary.

DESCRIPTION CODE: O - Office   W - Warehouse   T - Total   B - Combined (No Breakdown)

R - Lease in Renewal or extension period

LEASED PREMISES

WESTERN ZONE	DESC.	FOOTAGE	MONTHLY RENTAL	COST PER SQ. FT.	LESSOR	PERIOD	OPTIONS
1016 So. 23rd Ave. ARIZONA, PHOENIX	O W T	4500 1800 6300	$2392	$4.56	Meyer Turken Realty	8/1/ - 7/31/	8/1/ - 7/31/ $2496 per mo.
816 E. Evans Blvd. ARIZONA, TUCSON	O W T	2000 1500 3500	$1072.04	$3.68	Vic Edelbrock	4/15/ -2/15/	
43 Park Lane CALIFORNIA, BRISBANE (San Francisco Branch)	O W T	4400 7200 11600	$5078 +80 $5158	$5.32	Hogland & Bogard/ Crocker Land Co.	3/27/ -3/26/	
13811 Artesia Blvd. CALIFORNIA, CERRITOS (Warehouse & Tech Ctr)	W B T	10032 4752 14784	$3630	$2.94	Cerritos-Pacific Development Co.	9/1/ -7/31/	5 yrs. - CPI increase in rent
19433 East Walnut Drive CALIFORNIA, CITY OF INDUSTRY	O	4158	$1700	$4.90	L & M Plaster	12/8/ -11/30/	First refusal on additional space
3303 Harbor Blvd. CALIFORNIA, COSTA MESA (Santa Ana Branch)	O	4200	$2505	$7.14	Koll Income Prop.	11/15/ -7/31/ (Possession 8/1/)	5 yrs. at prevail-ing rate
7668 Telegraph Road CALIFORNIA, LOS ANGELES	O	5000	$3105	$7.46	Ruby H. Price	9/1/ -8/31/	$3213.68 effective 9/1/
731 South Main St. CALIFORNIA, SALINAS (San Jose Sub-Office)	(	225	$ 150	$8.00	Frank E. & Judith M. Cosco	7/17/ -7/16/	Thereafter mo. to mo. @ $175/mo.

26

If the company maintains a great many premises locations, leases may be filed separately by the real estate administrator or by the accounts payable supervisor, since monthly payments are the responsibility of that department under the jacket method of payment. The controller, however, should maintain a checklist in processing each lease, to include the following:

1. Insurance coverage is provided in accordance with the terms of each lease, as to both property damage and liability. This usually requires that a copy of the lease be sent to the insurance department or the company's insurance broker.

2. Dates for termination of lease, or exercise of renewal options, are "tickled." Termination dates should be tickled 120 days prior to the end, to allow time to search for new premises, if necessary.

3. An accounts payable "jacket" is established to provide for repetitive monthly rental payments, with a copy of the lease filed in the jacket. It is best to pay the initial rent from the date of signing to the end of the calendar month, say from March 18 to March 31, thereafter paying on the first of each month on a calendar basis. (See Exhibit 1–8.)

4. The lease is recorded on a special **leased premises summary sheet**, showing all pertinent information, such as location, square footage, cost per foot, monthly rent, landlord's name, lease period, and any renewal options. This is seen in Exhibit 1-9. It is a convenient summary to use for a great many locations and is also useful in calculating the company's amounts payable under lease obligations (long-term indebtedness) for the annual report and 10K, annually for the next two years and thereafter through five years.

INVESTING SHORT-TERM FUNDS

Proper cash management will occasionally produce excess cash. This may arise because of the timing of long-term debt offerings or equity issues, or simply because of the cyclical nature of the business. Excess short-term funds may be invested in a variety of ways to produce income or reduce costs for the company:

1. Short-term bank debt may be temporarily reduced to save on interest costs.

2. Heavier purchases of inventories may be made if there is an expectation of inventory cost increases. This should be examined in the light of the cost of carrying additional inventories. These excess inventories should be planned to liquidate themselves in 90 days.

3. Marketable securities may be purchased, consonant with the degree of risk you are prepared to assume. This may include tax-free municipal bonds and other Moody's-rated industrial bonds. Commercial paper is also issued by rated businesses at somewhat higher rates of return, with little risk.

4. Short-term interest-bearing certificates of deposit are available from banks for 30-, 60-, and 90-day periods.

5. If the company purchases from overseas markets, excess dollars may be used to purchase currency in forward markets at today's prices, thereby hedging against currency fluctuations.

6. Link-financing transactions may be negotiated with other companies. You establish an interest-bearing certificate of deposit with a bank specified by the other company. The bank makes prime-rate loans to the other company, using your deposit in times of tight money conditions. You receive points or a fee from the other company, which, combined with your interest on the CD, gives you a higher rate of return than you could normally obtain. When negotiated with a customer, the device cements a selling relationship. When done with a vendor, it assures a supply of the merchandise you buy and provides additional surety of the receipt of your points or fee through your right to offset against payments due to the vendor.

7. Excess bank balances may be carried with your working banks, at no interest income to you, to compensate them for those times when you may have to operate with less than the required balances.

8. The company may purchase its own securities and resell them at a later date, subject to meeting SEC requirements. The shares may also be issued to employees under incentive or stock option programs. Such a purchase reduces the number of outstanding shares and thus increases earnings per share.

OTHER SHORT-TERM BORROWING TECHNIQUES

In addition to usual bank financing and the maximum utilization of cash within the company, there are a number of other techniques that may be explored to raise short-run monies. When used in this context, short-run is intended to mean for periods of one year or less. Some of the methods below may also be translated into long-term arrangements with proper contract provisions.

1. *Equipment lease financing.* This may be done with a variety of equipment lessors to finance furniture and fixtures, materials handling and manufacturing equipment, with monthly payments for from one to five years. Financing rates are quoted as "add-on" rates and range from 6% to 10% add-on, which translates to almost double the rate for simple interest. The yield to the lessor is highest on a shorter-term lease. The obligation is not reflected on the balance sheet and may usually be in addition to existing bank credit lines. This is discussed further in the chapter on long-term borrowings.

2. *Commercial financing.* This may usually be done for periods of at least one year, and thereafter may be terminated with little notice. This involves borrowing on trade accounts receivable, usually 80% advances on those receivables that are not more than 90 days past due, at a cost that is 150% to 200% of bank prime interest rates. Such a rate can work out to 1% on net sales. Added features of financing can be revolving inventory loans to provide greater borrowing capability.

3. *Factoring.* This is a variant on commercial financing, with the major difference being that the receivables are actually sold to the factor and collected by the factor, and rates are somewhat lower than those charged by commercial finance companies. Since the receivables are sold with recourse, factoring works best when the receivables are of high quality.

4. *Commercial paper.* This may be issued by the company to obtain funds to supplement bank borrowings. This is generally confined to companies above the $100 million sales level, issuing paper aggregating $10 million in lots of $100,000. The paper may be issued for any number of convenient months, and the rates paid depend on the credit of

the issuer and the length of time for which the paper is issued, but they are traditionally in the area of prime.

5. *Letters of credit.* These are guarantees of payment by a bank on submission of proof of shipment or other performance. They avoid the necessity for the company to pay cash in advance of shipment and tie up funds that could be used to better advantage in the business. Banks charge a fee and a rate for bankers' acceptances arising after shipment, and the combined result is always approximately the same as prime.

6. *Link financing.* As described above, this may be used on the other end of the transaction, to borrow money based on the credit of a customer or supplier. The cost is always in excess of prime, because of the points or fee paid to the supplier of the certificate of deposit.

7. *Inventory reductions.* These may be planned for limited periods of time to free funds for short periods of time. A comparison must be made of the risk associated with short inventories and the cost of other short-term fund-raising alternatives.

8. *Bank balances.* These may be worked down, provided that banks understand that the shortfall will be made up with excess balances at a later date.

9. *Treasury stock.* Previously acquired treasury stock may be resold, subject to SEC regulations, or issued under incentive or stock option programs.

10. *Money market credit.* This may be established with banks for major creditworthy customers. The bank will borrow 30-day Eurodollars in the London Interbank market at a specific rate, with interest due at maturity. The bank will then relend these funds at, say, 50 basis points ($\frac{1}{2}$%) above its Eurodollar rate. The quoted rate normally does not require compensating balances or fees.

11. *Revolving credit/term-loan agreement.* This is a bank credit line that is normally used to fund gradual increases in permanent working capital requirements or to fund capital expenditures. Credits are for two or three years, enabling paydown based on cash flow, while at the same time retaining the availability of the total line for contingent purposes. Upon the end of the term, the term loan is funded for four or five years, usually payable quarterly. Rates run in excess of prime, based on credit, with formal commitment fees of $\frac{1}{4}$% to $\frac{3}{8}$% and compensating balances of 5% to 10%. These loans are often structured as revolving

credit loans, based on 80% to 85% of eligible receivables (usually not over 90 days from date of invoice) and, on occasion, 50% to 65% of inventory value.

12. *Bankers' acceptances.* These are based on inventory or trade-related transactions. The bank's creditworthiness is substituted for that of the borrower. An import or export transaction is financed by the company's issuance of a sight or time draft, which is then rediscounted in the bankers' acceptance market. Shipping documentation must meet rigorous bank requirements and is subject to bank audit. Discounts are usually at the prime bankers' acceptance rate plus ½% to 1%, depending on the maturity.

13. *Accounts payable.* Management includes creativity in the payment of vendor invoices, zero-balance disbursing accounts, electronic funds transfer of collected balances from lockbox accounts, and daily cash balance reporting systems to monitor bank compensation.

14. *Derivatives.* See Chapter 2 for a discussion of interest-rate swaps and hedging.

There are other short-run management expedients that may be employed to increase cash availability. These involve the proper deployment of the resources of the company in any given department. Accounts receivable turnover may be increased by mounting a special-effort collection campaign with past due customers owing in excess of specific amounts. A national service department may embark on an over-time program to repair and make salable the company's product, thereby increasing inventory turnover and freeing up cash. The customer service department may "blitz" the issuance of credit memos to customers for returned merchandise and billing adjustments, thereby making it easier for the collection people to enforce prompt payments of trade accounts receivables. Proper cash flow, in other words, is directly affected by the total management approach, which is concerned with all facets of the operation of the company.

INTERNATIONAL CASH MANAGEMENT

International cash management involves the management of foreign exchange risk. It includes not only the management of cash but the management of all balance-sheet assets that will eventually be converted into cash. The treasurer's functions as defined by the FEI in Appendix A contemplate this responsibility through the provision of capital and banking and custody functions. The position description of the treasurer in that exhibit specifies the "plan for the provision of capital." The controller's functions include reporting and interpreting and evaluating and consulting with regard to these treasury functions.

Foreign exchange markets are characterized by volatility and risk. Most of these exposures arise as a result of the mismatching of asset and liability maturities on the balance sheet and cash inflow and outflow transactions on the cash flow statement. Risks arise as a result of the mismatching of the currencies denominating these factors, called translation and transaction exposures, respectively. This mismatching is exacerbated by the nature of international companies, which have branches and subsidiaries in various countries with differing currencies, tax laws, and accounting rules. The measure of risk is usually achieved through the net working capital method—the exposure is equal to current assets minus current liabilities valued in local currency. If there are net current assets, devaluation causes a loss and revaluation a gain. A variation of this, called the net financial method, adds long-term debt to the current liabilities, which usually reduces the exposure. Another method, the monetary/nonmonetary method, separates the monetary balance-sheet items from physical ones such as inventories, which are translated at their initial value.

Techniques for reducing these currency risks may be used as follows:

1. *Forward exchange hedging.* A net balance-sheet position is sold forward against the parent's currency on the expectation that the local currency will depreciate against the parent's. If the cost to hedge is less than the actual amount of the local currency depreciation on the balance-sheet date, compared to the initial contract date, a gain results. If the local currency appreciates, a loss results. This balance-sheet hedge is accomplished through a currency swap. Delivery of the forward currency is not taken. Instead, the contract is swapped back in the spot market on its maturity date. These contracts are easily obtained, are flexible, and may be cancelled or closed out quickly. Capital gains rates may apply, and they may be assigned to offshore companies for tax

advantages. Forward exchange hedging is a naked hedge with large potential risk. It requires careful forecasting of foreign exchange movements by experts and should have board of directors approval (see the discussion of derivatives in Chapter 2).

2. *Local currency borrowing.* This is the creation of a liability to offset an asset. The effect is the same as that of forward exchange hedging without the cash risk of currency depreciation. The cash risk in such borrowing is limited to a widening of interest differentials over time. Local borrowing requires that a productive use be found for the borrowed funds. As with any bank loan, there will be agreements, covenants, and legal costs. If the local currency does depreciate, the borrowing may be repaid with cheaper local currency.

3. *Cash reduction.* Cash levels are kept low to avoid the risk of a devaluation of the local currency. Excess cash is moved to a central location outside the country by wire transfer or lockbox, and customers may remit directly to another country. Excess funds can be pooled through banks, thereby providing funds to other companies in the group that are less liquid. Excess cash can be remitted to the parent.

4. *Accounts receivable.* The idea here is to avoid exposure by carrying receivables for as short a time as is possible. Invoices may specify payment in a strong currency. The cycle time for order processing, shipping, and billing should be reduced to avoid exposure. Discounts for fast payments may be offered, and penalties, such as late charges and interest, may be invoked for slow payments.

5. *Inventories.* As with receivables, inventories should be as low as possible, and the turnover as fast as possible. If the local currency is apt to be devalued, however, the sale prices of the products sold may be marked up after devaluation, resulting in a large profit margin that will offset the losses incurred through the devaluation.

6. *Accounts payable.* The situation here is the opposite of that for receivables. If the currency is weak and devaluation is a possibility, payments should be delayed, if possible, to make payments with a cheaper currency. If a revaluation is forecasted, purchases can be prepaid and merchandise can be ordered before it is needed.

7. *Long-term debt.* The need to forecast long-term interest and tax rates makes the utilization of long-term debt as a devaluation hedge very difficult. If such debt already exists, it is best to hedge against a

revaluation, which would require repayments with a dearer currency, by holding long-term assets that will appreciate in value with a revaluation. Another strategy would be to incur weak-currency debt, particularly if the local currency is under pressure. This can usually be done quickly and at a lower cost than formal currency hedging. Once again, if this is a naked or one-way hedge, it should be properly approved and disclosed in financial statements.

8. *Parallel loans and swaps.* These can be arranged among sister locations or independent companies, each of which has a need for the other's local currency. This results in a hedge for the long term, without entering the forward exchange market. It is also used when local borrowing as a hedge is not available. Instead, a liability is created in a weak currency to offset an asset position. Since these are long-term commitments, there is added credit risk of a default by the counter party. The parallel swap is considered a forward exchange contract. One company buys or sells the target currency to the counter corporation and agrees to buy or sell the currency on a forward date at an exchange rate set at the present time.

9. *The natural hedge.* This occurs when no hedging is necessary, as exposed assets equal exposed liabilities. The treasurer does nothing. If this equality of exposure results from natural forces, the do-nothing strategy is a good one. However, if the asset and liability positions are manipulated to obtain equality, this may work to the detriment of normal business operations and may reduce profitability.

10. *Self-insurance.* This is also a do-nothing strategy, but it may result in a gain or loss, depending on the movement of the local currency. This may be a good option if the company enjoys high profit margins, in which case devaluation is treated like any other cost of operations.

Managing Foreign Currency Exposure

The forecasting of foreign exchange movements and the hedging activities utilized to minimize risk require careful planning and supervision, similar to that required when dealing with derivative activities (see the section on derivatives in Chapter 2).

The treasury functions of financing and cash management may be managed centrally, by the parent, or decentrally, by the branch or subsidiary. Smaller companies tend to operate completely centrally, as they generally have little international experience. However, few companies operate in a completely decentralized mode, as they are leery of abandoning all control to the decentralized operation. Most operate somewhere in between. Often, very large corporations have decentralized marketing and management but are required to exercise centralized review over borrowings, as the very financial viability of the parent can be affected.

Regardless of which mode is selected, centralized or decentralized, the corporate treasurer should ask the six AICPA questions about derivatives delineated in Chapter 2, including off-balance-sheet or on-balance-sheet activities, and the audit committee and board of directors should review the answers and approve the activities.

Financial Accounting Considerations

SFAS 52 (statement of financial standards of the FASB), Foreign Currency Translation, specifies that (1) exchange-rate changes on integrated, self-contained operations within a foreign country do not affect cash flows and are not included in net income; (2) economic effects of an exchange-rate change on a foreign operation that is an extension of the parent's domestic operations do affect the parent's cash flows directly, and such exchange gains and loss are included in net income; and (3) contracts and transactions that are in fact effective hedges of foreign exchange risk are accounted for as hedges, without regard to their form. Effects are measured in the primary, or functional, currency in which the entity conducts its business. Normally, this is the currency of the economic environment in which cash is generated and expended by the entity. The entity can be any form of operation, including a subsidiary, division, branch, or joint venture. A currency in a highly inflationary environment, one with a three-year inflation rate of approximately 100 percent or more, is not considered stable enough to serve as a functional currency, and the more stable currency of the reporting parent is used instead. Deferral hedge accounting is used to defer recognition of gains and loss on hedges from the period in which they arise to the later period when the contracts are closed and the gains and losses are recognized.

SFAS 80, Accounting for Futures Contracts, deals with the accounting aspects of one type of hedging instrument, the futures contract. This also requires deferral hedge accounting. Futures contracts that are not used as hedges and do not qualify for hedge accounting must be marked to market.

SFAS 105, Disclosure of Information About Financial Instruments With Off-Balance-Sheet Risk and Financial Instruments With Concentrations of Credit Risk, requires disclosure of contract amounts, the nature and terms of the instrument, the potential loss that could be incurred, and any collateral held.

SFAS 107, Disclosures About Fair Value Financial Instruments, requires the fair market values of hedging instruments, both assets and liabilities, to be disclosed, whether recognized or not recognized on the balance sheet.

Tax Accounting Considerations

IRS regulations treat gains and losses from most hedging transactions as ordinary income or losses rather than as capital gains. Hedges of interest-rate, currency, and price risk result in ordinary gains or losses. Tax citations are: TD 8493; FI-46-93; FI-54-93.

PRACTICAL POINTERS

Banking and financial arrangements are concerned not only with establishing credit lines and relations with bankers but with methods to obtain maximum utilization of cash through the use of special bank accounts and vendor payment systems. The company's cash is affected by its contractual relationships, which are administered by the treasurer and controller. Short-term borrowings are often necessary to augment normal bank credit lines, and, occasionally, temporary imbalances create extra funds that need to be employed effectively. A solid measure of the level of performance of the treasurer and controller is the efficacy with which these functions are handled.

2

Long-Term Borrowing
Techniques

The treasurer's primary function, the first one listed in the FEI's definition, is the provision of capital: "To establish and execute programs for the provision of the capital required by the business, including negotiating the procurement of capital and maintaining the required financial arrangements." The need for capital is usually considered to be short-term or long-term, although some organizations identify a medium-term need. Short-term capital requirements, those needed to supply the company for the coming year, were discussed in Chapter 1. Anything longer than one year, we shall consider as a long-term need. A medium-term need may be defined as one to three years; this distinction is usually made by stable companies that utilize long-range planning techniques of five years or longer. Some of the short-term devices discussed in the first chapter, such as equipment lease financing and the use of commercial paper, are often continuing and revolving in nature and so may be considered to be long-term. This chapter will discuss the various capital alternatives, their advantages and disadvantages, their cost, accounting considerations, and how to choose the best alternative.

Types of long-term borrowing include the following:

1. Equity
2. Bank debt
3. Straight debt
4. Debt with equity

5. Installment loans and leases
6. Acquisitions
7. Off-balance-sheet financing

EQUITY

Equity tops the list. You may not ordinarily think of it as long-term debt, but it really is the ultimate and longest-term debt, and usually the lowest-cost. Unlike holders of other debt, shareholders do not acquire the right to the repayment of a fixed amount of principal and interest; rather, shareholders have the right to share in the company's fortunes, whatever they may be. If the company is successful, their share in that success will be much greater than the lender's fixed interest. If the company fails and is liquidated, they will suffer a much worse fate, since shareholders stand behind, or junior to, the lender's principal and interest, which must be paid before the shareholders can be paid whatever remains of the company's assets, if anything.

Stream of Earnings Approach

When viewed from a cash flow standpoint, equity has the lowest cost of any capital available. This cost includes the underwriting spread and legal, accounting, and printing costs, as well as the cost of future cash dividends. In a growth company, or one that stresses the price of its publicly traded shares, dividends may never be paid and equity is veritably the cheapest capital, its issuance costs being minimal.

Conceptually, however, all of the earnings belong to the shareholders, and the cost of equity is equal to the minimum rate of return that the company must earn on the equity funds to avoid any fall in the market price of the company's stock. Expressed as a formula, the cost of equity capital is

$$\frac{E}{P}$$

in which E is expected earnings per share and P is current stock price. This concept is acceptable when you view the value of any share to its owner as a claim on a stream of company earnings, rather than a claim upon cash flows from the company in the form of dividends. Using the claim on earnings concept, let us compute the cost of raising capital in an example:

> A company decides to raise $1 million of new equity at a time when its stock is selling for $12 per share, it has 1 million shares issued and outstanding, and it earns $1 per share after taxes (its price/earnings ratio is therefore 12). The new shares will probably have to sell at a more attractive price than the current $12, say $10, and so 100,000 new shares must be issued to raise the required $1 million.
>
> There will now be 1,100,000 shares outstanding, and if earnings remain at the same $1 million, the earnings per share will fall from $1 to $0.91 ($1,000,000 ÷ 1,100,000), and the price of the stock will fall from $12 to $10.92 (12 × $0.91). The cost of this equity may then be said to be 8.3% ($0.91 ÷ $10.92) (using the formula E/P).

In the calculation above, note that we have used the old reported earnings of $1 million, although our formula calls for anticipated earnings. One must assume that the company would have no need to raise $1 million of additional equity if it did not have a productive use for that capital, one that will produce additional earnings for the company. The effect on earnings per share of these new earnings will offset the fall in earnings per share that results from selling the additional shares. If the earnings on the new capital are high enough, they will fully offset the effects of the dilution caused by selling the new stock, and shareholder wealth will be unaffected. Therefore, E, or expected earnings, may be assumed to be those earnings that will cause zero dilution in the price of the shares held by existing stockholders. Using this assumption, the cost of equity may be determined to be:

> Earnings per share continue at $1, or $1,100,000, the price of the stock remains at 12 times earnings, or $12, and the cost of this equity may then be said to be the same 8.3% as before ($1 ÷ $12). Obviously, the price per share has increased in proportion to the

earnings per share, and the cost of equity remains constant. The cost of this capital would rise only if earnings continued at $1 million, so that earnings per share of $0.909 would result ($1,000,000 ÷ 1,100,000). The capital cost would then be 9.1%, assuming a stock price of $10 per share, based on the market price at which the new shares were sold.

The price/earnings ratio expected, then, is the determinant of the cost of capital, based on the expected stream of earnings. Examining this further, you may determine whether this is the least costly alternative, depending on that P/E ratio when compared to the cost of other debt. If long-term institutional debt is available at 7%, this would be preferred to an 8.3% cost of equity. On the other hand, if the P/E ratio were 20, the cost of equity would be 5% ($1 per share ÷ $20 per share), and this would appear to be the most desirable alternative.

Cash Flow From Dividends Approach

Another approach, as inferred above, for dividend-paying companies, or those that are expected to pay dividends, is to cost the equity based upon the cash flows expected from dividends, using the formula

$$V = \frac{D}{k - g}$$

in which:
- V is the present value of the stock
- D is the current annual dividend
- k is the investor's required rate of return
- g is the rate of earnings growth, which is less than k, say 6%

Then, in the example above,

E/P equals 8.3%. Assuming a dividend of 10¢ per quarter were paid:

$$k = \frac{D}{V} + g = \frac{0.40}{12} + 6\% = 3.3\% + 6\% = 9.3\%$$

Either approach to the cost of equity may be used, depending on whether or not dividends are expected.

Cost of Retained Earnings

A subset of equity is retained earnings, after-tax profits that have been plowed back into the company, rather than distributed to shareholders through cash dividends. The cost of these funds is the same as that of externally raised equity, except that earnings paid out in dividends are subject to double taxation. The company pays a tax on the predividend income, and the individual pays a tax on the dividend. Retained earnings, however, avoid this double tax. Thus, the cost of retained earnings (which may be considered to be internal equity, as distinguished from external equity) is the cost of raising external equity times the reciprocal of the average tax rate of the company's stockholders. For example, if the cost of raising equity is 8.3% as in previous examples, and average shareholders are in a 30% tax bracket, then the cost of retained earnings is:

$$8.3\% \times (1.0 - 0.30) = 8.3\% \times 0.70 = 5.8\%$$

This method may not be used for single proprietorships, partnerships, or corporations that elect to be taxed as partnerships, as they are not subject to the double tax.

BANK DEBT

Demand loans, short-term bank borrowings, are the most common form of bank debt. Banks generally initiate their borrowing relationships with short-term debt. As confidence is built, banks will participate in longer-term relationships, usually two- or three-year revolving credits. By revolving credit, I mean those loans that have a debt ceiling in dollars, with funds being lent according to a formula, say total dollar value of receivables and inventory. The loan fluctuates, up or down, based on the formula and subject to the lending limit, and the overall agreement may run for a year, or two, or three. This is a term loan by any definition, despite the revolving nature of the collateral, since the company's borrowings will tend to remain the same from year to year. At any rate, given constant collateral conditions, the loan will remain approximately the same, being reduced only by profits that are turned back into the operations.

Even short-term bank debt may be considered long-term under certain conditions. Demand notes may not be called, and 30- or 60-day notes are continually revolved. If the loan is outstanding for more than a year or is contemplated to be, then it is term in nature. Many banks lend short-term for 11 months, with a requirement that the loan be paid off for 30 days and then renewed. The payoff may come from corporate working capital or from another bank. Cash may be generated internally, using the inventory and accounts payable methods described in Chapter 1, in anticipation of the payoff. Or, a line of credit may be established with another bank or two, but not used until the paydown. In this event, the short-term debt is extended beyond a year, almost indefinitely, and the loan may be characterized as long-term for all practical purposes. Your accountants will, of course, continue to classify it as short-term.

Short-term debt of this nature is usually available only when a good credit rating is presented. The debt carries a favorable interest rate and may not be secured. The revolving credit, on the other hand, is secured and, unlike most long-term debt, carries a higher rate than short-term borrowings. The revolving credit also is subject to specific operating constraints, which may be onerous to the management but which bankers will generally consider to be prudent restrictions necessary to protect their secured interest. These include requirements to maintain net worth and working capital at predetermined levels, debt-to-equity limitations, and limits on capital spending. An example of these constraints is shown in the schedule of limitations under bank agreement in Exhibit 1-1.

The cost of this type of long-term bank debt is simply the interest rate, expressed as the formula:

$$k = I/P$$

where k is the rate of return, I is the annual interest cost, and P is the total value of the debt—in short, the simple interest rate. This cost, and this formula, may be considered to be valid when the company maintains a stable amount of debt; as one bank loan is paid off, it is replaced with another. If the debt is one-time—that is, not replaced—its true cost is not the simple interest rate but must take into account the expected outflows and the discount rate that makes these outflows just equal to the net proceeds obtained from the lending source. In short, the outstanding loan balances must be discounted to a present value basis.

From an accounting standpoint, revolving loans may usually be treated as long-term liabilities if they have a maturity of more than one year and the borrower has the right and a clear intention to renew or revolve the loan.

STRAIGHT DEBT

Straight debt refers to long-term borrowing in the form of bonds, notes, or debentures, without options, warrants, stock, or other equity features attached to it. Straight debt is available from private individuals, funds, institutions, or insurance companies. It may be new debt or a refunding of an older bond issue.

Features of Straight Debt

A bond is, in essence, an interest-bearing IOU. The IOU contains stipulations as to the principal sum to be repaid, dates of repayment, specific claims or liens against assets, and protective covenants. The protective covenants are a normal feature, since the bond is a long-term investment, with the risk presumed to increase as the time span of the investment increases. Typical covenants are:

1. Duties of the trustee
2. Limitations on further borrowing
3. Minimum financial ratios
4. Limitations on cash dividends
5. Sinking fund requirements
6. Callable features
7. Public registration

A **term sheet** containing typical restrictive covenants is illustrated in Exhibit 2-1. This exhibits the terms, conditions, and covenants for convertible senior subordinated notes. While there are additional features that relate to the convertibility, straight debt carries the same type of covenants.

The above general terms are characteristic of all long-term debt. There are, though, distinct features to various types of bonds, as discussed below:

1. *Mortgage bonds.* These give the lender a specified claim against stipulated real assets of the borrowing corporation, presumably reducing the risk to the lender. Such bonds may be open-end (more bonds of the same priority may be issued against the specified assets) or closed-end. Open-end bonds imply that the borrower was in a strong borrowing position at the time of original issuance. When closed-end bonds are issued, if the corporation needs to raise additional long-term debt, it must issue bonds against different assets or must subordinate them to the original issue. If the borrower was in a weak borrowing position, such bonds may contain an "after-acquired property clause," meaning that the lenders receive a claim against the specified assets in existence when the loan was made and all other assets of the specified type acquired at a later date as long as the bond issue is outstanding.

2. *Collateral trust bonds.* These are similar to mortgage bonds in that they give the lender a claim against specified assets. The difference

Exhibit 2-1.   Term sheet—convertible subordinate notes.

7 1/2% Convertible Senior Subordinated Notes

General Outline of Principal Terms

Amount:	$11,000,000
Interest Rate:	7.50% per annum payable quarterly
Maturity:	15 years
Conversion:	The Notes will be convertible into 637,681 shares of its Common Stock at $17.25 per share. Customary anti-dilution provisions will be included.
Fixed Sinking Fund:	Level payments of $1,100,000 per annum at the end of each of the last 10 years to retire 100% of the issue by maturity. The company may make an optional prepayment on a non-cumulative basis in the amount of $1,100,000 in any year that a principal payment is due. In all cases, the holders will have adequate opportunity to convert the amount of any principal payments.
Redemption:	The Notes will be non-callable for any reason for the first three years; from the fourth year through the average life of the issue, the Notes will be callable only if the stock price is at least 200% of the conversion price for at least 45 consecutive trading days; thereafter, the Notes will be callable at the company's option at a premium of 7 1/2%, declining evenly over the remaining life of the issue to par in the final year. In all cases, ample opportunity for conversion will be afforded to the Noteholders. The Notes will be non-refundable to the average life of the issue from the proceeds of an issue having an effective interest cost of 7 1/2% or less.
Registration:	Holders of not less than 40% of the Notes (including, in any event, holders of outstanding Notes convertible into not less than 100,000 shares of common stock) will have the right to request (a) a registration of the underlying stock at the company's expense where audits exist that are acceptable for purposes of the registration; and (b) an additional registration at the company's expense whether or not acceptable audits are available. In addition, Noteholders will have unlimited "piggyback" rights (subject to approval of underwriters, if any). Lenders will have one registration right at their own expense.

(continued)

Exhibit 2-1.   *(continued)*

-2-

Condition:

The company and applicable subsidiaries shall have substantially completed the contemplated sale of receivables to the Independent Finance Corporation, and Captive Finance Subsidiary Corporation shall not then be accepting the new receivables and shall accept none thereafter, except to the extent that the customer's second payment has not yet been received, as provided in the agreement with Equilease. This is in addition to other normal conditions of closing, including the absence of any material adverse change.

Permitted Current
Borrowing:

Current unsecured borrowing from banks, together with letter of credit and acceptance financing (secured as customary in the trade) will be permitted in the normal course of business for the purpose of financing import transactions. Other current unsecured borrowing shall be limited to $1,000,000 provided that no such debt is outstanding for at least 60 consecutive days in each 12-month period.

Permitted Additional
Funded Debt:

(a) Up to $10 million revolving credit, convertible into not less than 3-year Notes, incurred for the purpose of financing rental machines.
(b) Additional amounts of senior and subordinated debt if, after giving effect thereto, consolidated funded indebtedness does not exceed 60% of book capitalization plus deferred income taxes (if any) and provided that pro forma interest charges on all funded debt are earned at least three times on the average over the most recent three fiscal years.

Working Capital:

Consolidated working capital is to be maintained at least equal to the greater of $11 million or 100% of funded indebtedness.

Seniority:

The Convertible Senior Subordinated Notes will be subordinated in insolvency to existing senior debt and existing and future indebtedness held by banks and other senior debt (if any) held by institutions. The Notes will be senior to other junior securities, including public debenture issues, if any.

Dividends:

Dividends and net stock repurchases are to be limited to net income earned after April 30, 20__, plus $1,000,000, less any payments on indebtedness owed to First Subordinated Lender.

-3-

Loans, Investments, Advances & Guarantees:	(a)　Additional investments in Rapifax and Delco (after the contemplated sale of 80% of receivables to X Corp.) and other non-consolidated partnerships and other persons will be limited to amounts available for dividends. (b)　Securities or other assets received from sale of Docustat. (c)　U. S. Government securities, prime commercial paper, certificates of deposit in banks having capital funds of at least $100,000,000.
Merger & Consolidation:	The company may merge and consolidate provided that it is the surviving corporation and that the survivor is in compliance with the Note Agreement.　The company may not sell, lease or dispose of any substantial portion of its assets.
Leases:	The company will not enter into any sale-leaseback transaction without the consent of the lenders, except to the extent of sale-leaseback of non-revenue-producing assets carrying annual fixed charges not to exceed $500,000.
Financial Statements:	(1)　Within 45 days after each of the first three quarterly periods, the company will furnish comparative consolidated income statements and balance sheets in duplicate, accompanied by a breakdown showing sales and profit contribution by product category.　Also, a certificate from a responsible officer indicating compliance with the Note Agreement will be provided. (2)　Within 90 days after the end of each fiscal year, the company will furnish comparative consolidated income statements and balance sheets certified by auditors, as well as unaudited sales and profit breakdown by product category.　A certificate of compliance with the Note Agreement signed by the auditors and responsible company officers will also be provided.
Other Terms:	Other terms normally included in a transaction of this character will be included.
Special Counsel, etc:	Necessary legal documents will be prepared by counsel approved by the lenders.　All legal expenses and other expenses incurred in connection with this financing will be paid by the _____ Corporation whether or not the loan is consummated.

jck

　　　　　　　　Lawrence _____
　　　　　　　　　　　for
　　　　　　_____ Insurance Co.

is that collateral trust bonds secure financial assets, stock, and bonds, whereas mortgage bonds secure physical plant and equipment.

3. *Equipment trust certificates.* These are like mortgage bonds in that they give the lender a claim against equipment, such as rolling stock (used mostly by the railroads). The main difference is that title to the equipment belongs to the lender, rather than the corporation, until the debt is finally paid off. To this extent, they may be considered to be lease financing. This variant on mortgage bonds arose as corporations found a need to raise new funds to finance the purchase of new equipment without having the property come under the after-acquired clause described above.

4. *Debentures.* These are unsecured bonds that carry no claim against any specific assets. The lender may look only to the earning power of the corporation for repayment. Such bonds are usually issued by firms with strong earnings and low risk ratings. They also usually carry more restrictive covenants than mortgage bonds, although not always, if the issuer is in a strong bargaining position.

5. *Subordinated debentures.* These are also unsecured and carry only a secondary claim against the corporation's earnings or its assets in liquidation. Such bonds carry an increased risk to the lender and, hence, usually give a greater rate of return. The corporation views these as near equity, ranking ahead of preferred and common stock, but behind all other secured and unsecured debt. These are usually issued when existing bond indenture agreements prohibit the issuance of additional debt having an equal claim against the corporation's earnings and assets. Several stages of subordination may be used, resulting in layers of subordinated debt with titles like "second subordinated debentures" and "third subordinated debentures." Successive subordination usually results in higher interest rates. Rates are often reduced on subordinated debentures by combining them with a convertible feature.

6. *Income bonds.* These are debt securities wherein the interest payment depends on earnings. There is no legal obligation for interest payments unless earnings are adequate enough to permit such payments. These bonds are appropriate for companies with large fixed-capital investments and large fluctuations in earnings, or for emerging companies with the expectation of low earnings in the early years. Railroads, hotels, and motels have used income bonds for these reasons. The interest on

such bonds, like the dividend on preferred stocks, may be cumulative or noncumulative. Because of the added flexibility such bonds give to the corporation, they usually carry a higher interest rate than all other bonds. Many corporations have used income bonds to retire preferred stocks, since the interest paid on the bond is tax-deductible but the preferred dividend is not.

7. *Creative notes and bonds.* These have been created to accommodate marketing needs in a competitive environment:

 ❖ TIGRS and CATS are zero-coupon bonds backed by Treasury notes and certificates.

 ❖ Tax-deductible preferreds (really debt) are created through a subsidiary company, which forms a trust to borrow funds. These funds are then used to purchase an entire new preferred stock issue. The preferred is used as collateral for the trust's bonds. The SEC requires that the debt be booked, not kept off-balance-sheet.

 ❖ Collateralized mortgage obligations (CMOs) and certificates of automobile receivables (CARs) are backed by mortgages and automobiles, respectively. Some companies have attempted to treat this transaction as sales of collateral, rather than as recorded borrowings. The FASB has urged accountants to evaluate these instruments on a case-by-case basis.

 ❖ Index-linked bonds are those that index the principal to an inflation index or the value of a commodity (oil, silver, real estate). In some cases, the coupon is indexed as well. When this is done, the investor is assured of a "real" rate of return if the bond is held to redemption.

Perhaps the most innovative security was created by Lexington (Kentucky) Central Bank & Trust Company, which offered certificates of deposit with an interest rate tied to the University of Kentucky basketball team victories. For each game the Wildcats won, the CDs' 7.25% interest rate increased 0.01%. For each NCAA tournament game won, the CD rate increased 0.05%. If UK won the NCAA championship, the rate jumped to 8.25%. That is creative "indexing."

8. *Industrial revenue bonds.* These are generally no longer available to businesses as a device to borrow funds at below prime rate, since the interest the issuing municipality pays is tax-free. Such bonds continue to

be available for projects involving student loans, multifamily residential rental projects, airports, and hazardous waste disposal facilities.

The Cost of Debt

This is not simply the interest rate paid for funds, nor even the after-tax rate, but rather is based on the expected costs, or outflows, and the discount rate that makes these outflows exactly equal to the net proceeds of the loan. This is a discounted cash flow concept and may be expressed by:

$$P_0 = \frac{C_1}{(1 + k)^1} + \frac{C_2}{(1 + k)^2} + \cdots + \frac{C_n}{(1 + k)^n}$$

where:

P_0 = net proceeds in year
C_1 = total cost in year 1 and so on
k = the discount rate; the pretax cost of the debt funds

For example:

Assume a $1 million bond issue, for 20 years, with a sinking fund of $50,000 per year, a 7% interest rate, and an annual cost of mailing, administering, and handling the bonds of $30,000 (total cost of the bonds is $70,000 interest + $30,000 handling, or $100,000). Then the cost of the bonds will be the discount rate, k, determined from the above equation, or:

$$\$1,000,000 = \frac{\$100,000}{(1 + k)^1} + \frac{\$100,000}{(1 + k)^2} + \cdots + \frac{\$100,000}{(1 + k)^{20}}$$

which is 7.5%.

This type of discounted cash flow (DCF) calculation is readily available from spreadsheet programs such as Lotus, Excel, and PFS First Choice. Such calculations are also available on electronic calculators, hand models, like the Hewlett-Packard HP 12c selling at about $100. A variety of financial software vendors, particularly those serving the insurance industry, offer discounted cash flow applications for personal computers (PCs) at low cost. The calculation can be done in minutes with these aids.

On the other hand, if it is assumed that the company has perpetual debt, or revolves its debt by paying off one issue and replacing it with another, or does not use sinking funds, or pays off a final balloon amount with another issue's proceeds, then the cost of debt is simply the interest rate using the formula $k = I/P$ as set out on page 43, which is a pretax expression. This may be translated to an after-tax amount as follows:

- ✧ For large firms in a 48% bracket, $k \times (1 - 0.48)$
- ✧ For firms earning under $25,000, $k \times (1 - 0.26)$

The above rates assume bonds sold at par. If the bonds are sold at a premium or discount, then P, the total value of the debt, must be adjusted by the average of the bond's current sale price and its maturity value, and I, the annual interest cost, must be adjusted by adding or subtracting the effect of the difference between the proceeds of the debt and the amount of principal that will eventually have to be refunded.

DEBT WITH EQUITY

Subordinated debentures, as described previously, are near equity in that they rank just ahead of preferred and common stock, but behind all other debt as to a claim on the corporation's earnings or assets in liquidation. Income bonds, too, are close to preferred stock in nature, but neither income bonds nor subordinated debentures create or eventually result in the lender's having equity in the corporation. There are types of debt that do give this result.

1. *Convertible bonds.* These are the debt equivalent of preferred stock, differing from preferred in that before conversion they have the characteristics of debt. The conversion feature sets out circumstances under which, at the option of the holder, the bonds may be converted into common shares. Convertibility is expressed as a price (say, $20 a share, meaning that a $1000 bond may be converted into 50 shares) or as a ratio (say, 50 common shares per $1000 of face value of the bond issue). The conversion price may vary over the life of the security, specifying a higher conversion price or a declining conversion ratio, reflecting the expectation of a higher common stock price over the years as corporate earnings increase. The value of a convertible bond may be based only on its interest rate and the current rates of interest in the capital market; this is the bond's value on a yield basis. This value usually provides a downside floor on the value of the bond. The bond also has an alternative value based on its conversion price; a bond convertible into 50 shares with a market value of $15 equals $750. The two values are not the same, and the bond will tend to sell for close to the higher of the two. If the bond sells on a conversion basis and the price of the common stock falls, the bond price will fall, too, but not below its yield basis. In the absence of a call provision, the bond probably will not be converted, as its value will rise whenever the common stock rises. Thus, the lender enjoys all the capital appreciation on the common, without converting and without even losing the convertible's limited downside risk. In this case, the bondholder would convert only if the dividend yield on the common were to be greater than the interest yield on the bond—an unlikely circumstance. When the company calls the bond for conversion, the holder's decision is based on the comparison of the current call price and the market value of the stock, plus taxes and transaction costs. A corporation will consider the use of convertible bonds when:

   ✦ Increased debt is desirable but difficult or expensive. It may be difficult because of existing indenture restrictions in previous bond issues or simply because interest rates are too high. The equity feature and the possibility of capital appreciation because of the convertibility make a lower interest rate possible.

   ✦ The corporation wants to sell common stock, but the price of the common is too low or market conditions do not permit the sale of straight equity. The company is willing to pay the interest cost on the bond temporarily, as it believes that all the bonds will eventually be converted into common. The use of a call feature may force such conversion. The effective cost of this type of equity is reduced prior to conversion, as the interest paid is tax-deductible.

The conversion price must be set carefully if the company desires to attain its objectives of converting its bonds into common stock at the appropriate time. This requires a sensitivity to the technical aspects of the bonds as well as the capital and money markets, which is usually best provided by a competent investment banker. A miscalculation will have the following consequences:

- ✧ If the conversion price is too high, the conversion value of the bond may never reach its call price and the issue will be uncallable. The company is then saddled with continuing debt.
- ✧ If the conversion price is set too low, the corporation will not achieve its objective of selling its common stock significantly above the current depressed market price. The cost of this type of equity may be too high.

2. *Debt with warrants or options.* This is a bond issue with an option to buy common stock in the corporation at a stated price. The bond may be any of several types, and the warrant may be for a fixed period of time or indefinite. The warrants may also be at a single stated price or varying on an increasing scale, based on the company's expectation of higher prices. They usually are exercisable at 10% to 25% above the present market price of the stock. The warrants may be detachable from the bond and therefore separately tradable, or they may be permanently attached and not separable from the bond. This should not be confused with a convertible security, which gives the right to change or exchange the bond for stock under certain conditions. The warrant gives a right to buy, not to exchange.

Debt with warrants offers certain advantages:

- ✧ The investor has greater flexibility than with convertibles, as the warrants may sometimes be detached and traded separately.
- ✧ The exercise of the warrant produces additional cash for the company; the conversion of convertible debt does not. As with conversion, exercise of the warrants presupposes a rise in the stock price above the warrant price.
- ✧ The use of warrants may permit a company to issue bonds

when it would not otherwise be considered strong enough to do so.

✧ The use of warrants may offset the higher rate the corporation might have to pay without the warrants in view of a weak financial position.

Debt with warrants, however, has the following disadvantages:

✧ The stock price may have a ceiling while there are outstanding warrants. If the stock price rises above the warrant price, warrant holders will exercise. The resultant exercise dilutes total holdings and tends to depress the price of the stock. Hence, a market value of the stock tends to be established at a level slightly above the exercise price, not higher, until all the warrants are exercised.

✧ It is more costly to issue new stock while there are outstanding warrants, since the market price of the stock is depressed as a result of the warrants.

3. *Hybrid securities.* These are variants on convertible debt. Often, they have been created to attempt to keep the debt off-balance-sheet, or, at least, to show the borrowings as equity, rather than debt. (See the section on off-balance-sheet financing in this chapter.) In most cases, the FASB and/or the SEC have required that the debt be recorded and that the debt and equity elements be separated and properly accounted for. In the case of mandatory redeemable preferred stock, the SEC requires that this be shown on the balance sheet in a separate section, between long-term liabilities and equity—hence the oft-used name "mezzanine" financing. For accounting purposes, however, SFAS 47, section 9, requires that standard liability treatment be used.

Subordinated exchangeable debentures are issued by Company A and exchangeable into Company B's stock. This is in reality two instruments; it should be recorded as both straight debt and a call on B's stock. The value of the call should be deferred, rather than amortized, until the option is exercised or expires. It should not be offset to interest expense.

DARTS, Dutch auction-rate transferable securities, are securities with dividends that fluctuate based on periodic auctions. These securities are marked as notes but are true preferreds with a variable dividend.

LYONs, liquid yield option notes, are zero-coupon bonds that may be converted into common stock. As with any zero-coupon bond, interest is imputed and is taxable, even though it is not received until maturity. This product, therefore, is well suited for tax-free retirement funds, IRAs, and Keoghs. To the issuer, the interest is tax-deductible annually, without any cash outlay. From an accounting standpoint, if the imputed yield is less than two-thirds that of an average AA-rated bond, most of the value of the security is deemed to lie in the conversion right, rather than the bond, making it a common stock equivalent, which would reduce earnings per share. If the yield is more than the two-thirds standard, then only fully diluted earnings per share would be affected. (See SFAS 85.)

Tax-deductible equity is usually preferred stock issued to a trust. The trust issues bonds to outsiders in the amount of the preferred. The corporation makes an equity investment in the trust and becomes its sole shareholder. The IRS considers the preferred dividends to be intercompany, and so they are eliminated. The interest to the bondholders is deducted on a consolidated tax return. From an accounting standpoint, the agreements must be scrutinized carefully. If the bonds are not a liability of the corporation, and if the bondholders have no claim against the corporation, this should meet FASB requirements for equity treatment—the best of both worlds, tax-deductible debt for IRS purposes and equity for accounting purposes.

Word of Caution: SFAS 115, issued by FASB, addresses the accounting and reporting for investments in debt and equity securities. It expands the use of fair value accounting for those securities but retains the use of amortized cost for debt security investments that are intended to be held to maturity.

Additional Caution: The FASB is presently deliberating proposals on Distinguishing Between Liability and Equity Instruments and Accounting for Instruments With Characteristics of Both. These will consider when such instruments should be recognized on the balance sheet and how financial instruments that have both liability and equity elements should be treated by the issuer. FASB has stated its intention to issue a final statement in 2001.

Accounting for Convertible Debt and Debt With Stock Purchase Warrants

Accounting Principles Board (APB) Opinion No. 14, SFAS 84 (Statement of Financial Accounting Standards of the FASB), and a variety of EITFs (Emerging Issues Task Force of the FASB)—Nos. 84–3, 85–9, 85–17, 85–29, 86–35, 88–9, and 90–19—set forth the accounting principles and rules for dealing with convertible debt and warrants.

No portion of the proceeds from the issuance of convertible debt securities should be accounted for as attributable to the conversion feature. This is a different position from that originally taken under paragraphs 8 and 9 of Opinion No. 10, since suspended, which advocated that the conversion feature be given accounting recognition. Since Opinion 10, experience has indicated that the debt and the conversion option are inseparable, and so Opinion 14 and its new requirements better reflect both the theoretical situation and the practical considerations. Expressed simply, this means that since there is no discount set up on the issuance of the convertible, there is no loss in profits in later years through amortization of this discount as a charge to earnings.

The board also reaffirmed in this opinion its previous position regarding debt issued with detachable stock purchase warrants. The proceeds should be allocated to the debt *and* to the warrants based on their respective values at the time of issuance or shortly thereafter. The value attributable to the warrants is to be accounted for as paid-in capital, with the resulting discount, or reduced premium, treated as debt discount. Once again, any debt discount must be amortized as a charge against future earnings and will serve to reduce earnings per share.

However, when warrants are not detachable from the debt, and the debt security must be surrendered in order to exercise the warrant, the two securities are taken together and are the equivalent of convertible debt—hence there is no attribution to the warrant. If there is a choice and market conditions and interest rates permit it, the warrants should be attached to avoid a future reduction in earnings per share resulting from amortization of debt discount.

It is not always possible to clearly identify the broad classification of every type of debt security. There are many types of debt with varying conversion features, stock purchase warrants, or a combination of such features. In such cases, proper accounting dictates looking to the substance of the transaction. For example, if convertible debt is issued at a substantial premium, there is a strong presumption that the premium represents paid-in capital and that a portion of the proceeds should be accounted for as being attributable to the conversion feature.

INSTALLMENT LOANS AND LEASES

Installment loans are those obligations payable over a period of years, usually one to five, on a periodic basis, usually monthly or quarterly. While such loans may require payments during the current 12-month period, they are included in the discussion in this chapter on long-term borrowings because the major part of such loans is given long-term classification on the balance sheet.

As used in this context, installment loans would include equipment trust certificates (discussed on page 48), equipment lease financing (see page 29), and any other type of capital equipment purchasing that would include a payment schedule with installments.

The most common type of installment financing is equipment leasing. It offers these decided advantages:

1. Leasing is available to companies of any size, and particularly to smaller companies that are not large enough to do bond issues and to newer companies that have not established a track record that would enable them to sell bonds.
2. The lease liability need not necessarily be shown on the balance sheet. When it is not, the corporation's debt capacity is increased. Present accounting principles require that the lease be capitalized if it is, in fact, an installment purchase. Leases, however, are so varied in their terms, nature, and purchase options that they can readily be constructed so as to preclude capitalization and balance sheet presentation.
3. Lease payments are fully tax-deductible. If the lease period is shorter than the useful life of the equipment, this will supply

greater tax deductions than would depreciation if the asset were purchased outright with proceeds from a bond issue.

4. One hundred percent financing of the equipment, usually with little or no down payment, is available on terms tailored to the user.

5. Most loan indenture agreements and restrictive covenants do not prohibit debt created through leasing, or if they do, a ceiling is set to permit significant amounts of such leasing.

6. Debt financing through the use of leasing does not normally contain restrictive covenants. There are rarely limitations on debt to equity, working capital, or dividends.

7. There is no tax problem at audit time over lease payment deductions, as there well might be over useful life and the amount of depreciation claimed.

8. The lease may be structured to provide higher book income in the early years than under outright ownership. The early years' rental payments are generally less than the combined interest expense and depreciation under ownership.

9. State and city franchise and income taxes may be reduced, as the property factor, one of three, is reduced.

There may be some disadvantages to leasing, including the following:

1. Residual rights to the property may be lost at the end of the lease period. In a pure lease, the lessee may have renewal rights or the right to purchase, but these rights require the payment of additional sums.

2. Rentals under the lease may exceed comparable debt service. The lessor probably had to borrow the financed amount and tacked on a profit, structuring the required lease payments to meet this total. If the corporation borrowed its own funds for the purchase, it could avoid the profit factor.

3. There is a loss of operating flexibility and less protection against obsolescence. If a new and better piece of equipment were to become available, it might not be possible to sell or exchange the old equipment. This can be avoided if the lessor will allow a trade-up to newer equipment and will execute a new lease.

4. The lease payment is based on a fixed interest rate. If the cost of money declines, and with it interest rates, the lessee continues to pay the same amount. If, on the other hand, the asset had been purchased outright and financed, the debt could probably be refinanced at a lower rate in a declining money market.
5. There may be a loss of tax benefits that would accrue as a result of using accelerated depreciation and high interest deductions on the debt in the early years. This would produce a short-term cash advantage if the equipment were bought instead of leased.

Leveraged Leasing

The leveraged lease is a major financial vehicle for companies involved in making significant capital investments. Such leases are those in which the funds for the purchase of the leased property are provided in part by one or more third parties (loan participants) in addition to the financing institution (the owner or equity participant). Under these leases, a major portion of the lease payments may be typically assigned to these third parties as repayment of their investment, together with interest thereon. If the lessee defaults, the loan participants generally have no right of recovery against the owner participant. The loan participant must look only to the lessee and its first lien on the property. The owner participant's return on its investment usually includes some portion of the lease payments, in addition to the income tax benefits during the lease period, as well as proceeds from the sale or re-lease of the property during or at the end of the lease period. The income tax benefits, obviously, are any available investment tax credit, depreciation using current IRS fast methods, and the related high cash flow in the early years.

Structuring a leveraged lease is a complicated process, requiring thorough familiarity with legal, tax, and accounting details. Because of these complexities, firms have come into being that specialize in structuring this type of lease. The leveraged lease offers a good return to the investor through the utilization of tax benefits, and a lower than normal cost to the lessee. Accounting for leveraged leases follows the general rules for lease accounting, discussed below.

Accounting for Leases

SFAS 13, issued by FASB, entitled Accounting for Leases, sets forth the accounting rules for treatment of leases in the balance sheets of the lessees, and other statements.

Effectively, these require complete disclosure of the following:

✧ *Capital leases.* The gross amounts of assets capitalized by major function; future minimum lease payments in the aggregate and for the next five years, and the amount of imputed interest necessary to reduce the net minimum lease payments to present value; total sublease rentals to be received under noncancelable subleases; total contingent rentals in each income statement period; separate identification of capital leases on the balance sheet or notes thereto; separate identification of related liabilities on the balance sheet; separate amortization or depreciation disclosures.

✧ *Operating leases.* For terms in excess of one year, future minimum rental payments in aggregate and for the next five years; the same sublease disclosures as for capital leases; rental expense for each income statement period, with separate amounts for minimum rentals, contingent rentals, and sublease rentals; a general description of the lessee's leasing arrangements, including the basis for contingent rental payments, the existence and terms of renewal, purchase options, and escalation clauses; and restrictions, if any, imposed by lease agreements on dividends, debt, and further leasing.

SFAS 13 further specifies the rules for capitalization of leases, if any one of the following is met:

1. Ownership is transferred to the lessee by the end of the lease term.
2. The lease contains a bargain price purchase option.
3. The lease terms equal or exceed 75% of the estimated useful life of the property.
4. The present value of the minimum lease payments is 90% or more of the fair value of the leased property.

If none of the above criteria is met, the lease is an operating lease, and neither the asset nor the obligation is recorded by the lessee. Rental payments would be recorded as rental expense, usually on a straight-line basis.

> *Helpful Hint:* If an operating lease includes scheduled rent increases, these should generally be recognized on a straight-line basis over the lease term, thereby smoothing the annual rental payments.

Obligations that consist of short-term debt on the balance sheet, usually revolving loans and installment purchases, may receive long-term debt presentation, below the line, if the lender is financially able to renew the obligation and the borrower intends to so renew (see SFAS 6, paragraphs 10 and 11).

Sale and Leaseback

A form of leasing is the sale and leaseback. In nature, it is similar to the mortgage bond or the equipment trust certificates described previously. It is, however, often accomplished quickly, with little cost, and without any elaborate bond indenture.

Owned property, such as land, buildings, or equipment, may be sold to an independent finance company at a high percentage of its appraised value, say 80% (subject to negotiation and often contingent on the credit of the owner); the resultant cash received may be more than the original cost if the property has appreciated in value as a result of either inflation or economic utility. The property may then be leased back, usually for terms of three to eight years.

This is an excellent device to use in inflationary times. The property will usually have appreciated far over its cost, providing windfall cash on the sale. If the property has a long future life or is not expected to be replaced, then the debt incurred on the sale may be paid over future years of the lease with inflated dollars.

Such leases are as varied as the parties desire to have them. Factors receiving particular attention in negotiation are the term of the lease, the rate, and the residual value or renewal option at the end. The rate will be determined by the utilization either party may have of the investment tax credit, if any, and depreciation. Sale and leasebacks may be structured as leveraged leases and, on occasion, may even be structured as straight debt.

When a sale and leaseback is structured as straight debt, a tax-oriented partnership is usually found to purchase the equipment. The equipment is sold for 8% to 10% cash, the balance due on two notes. One of the notes is amortizing; the other is a nonrecourse balloon note. The amount of the monthly rental is set at a level exactly sufficient to pay for the interest and amortization on both notes. At the end of the leaseback period, usually five years on this type of program, the balloon note is canceled, and since it is nonrecourse, the equipment reverts to the company. The company may account for this as a straight long-term loan, at an interest rate substantially below bank prime, not even accounting for the sale and leaseback for financial accounting purposes. For tax purposes, the company will pay a capital gain on the sale and will lose the depreciation advantages of owning its equipment. It may also have an investment tax credit and depreciation recapture. These tax disadvantages will be offset by the higher monthly rental, which is a tax-deductible charge. The entire transaction can be structured with no unfavorable tax aspects.

The lenders, on the other hand, receive the full tax benefits and cash flow advantages of the tax-sheltered partnership, including depreciation, any available investment tax credit, and other benefits depending on the structure of the transaction.

The Captive Finance Subsidiary

Companies that manufacture equipment may find it advisable to establish a wholly owned finance subsidiary. The parent will sell the equipment to the subsidiary, taking full accounting sale treatment. The finance subsidiary will then lease the equipment to the ultimate user, with these advantages:

1. The finance subsidiary can support a debt-to-equity ratio greater than the parent's.
   a. Finance subsidiaries do not report traditional balance sheets showing current assets and liabilities. Instead, all assets and liabilities are lumped in a group, without the current classification.
   b. Banks and institutions will traditionally lend at least 2 to 1 on debt to equity, since the subsidiary's assets are always accounts receivable (leases receivable) and are usually secured by the equipment underlying the lease.

2. The customer receives terms of payment in accordance with the lease, from one to five years. This is a strong marketing device that the parent would not ordinarily supply.

3. The finance subsidiary usually has an independent name, which facilitates its collection activities against slow-paying lessees.

4. The parent treats the sale to the subsidiary as a sale, taking into income the full profit on the sale. This usually requires that the parent's sales representative has negotiated a full-payout lease with a third-party customer, using the subsidiary's lease document.

5. The finance subsidiary must be consolidated with the parent for both financial accounting and tax purposes. While this will require consolidation of the long-term receivables and debt, all details of these transactions will be footnoted in the financial statements. Moreover, separate financial statements for the subsidiary will be prepared and made available to banks and other lenders.

6. The finance subsidiary may utilize finance lease accounting for financial accounting purposes, which would permit it to reflect higher earnings in the early years.
   a. Sum-of-the-years'-digits accounting methods are proper, to match income in the early years to the higher debt balances. (See formula on page 305.)
   b. The subsidiary may reflect acquisition costs of new leases by front-loading income with a portion of the unearned interest income. (See SFAS 91.)

7. The finance subsidiary may utilize operating lease accounting

for tax purposes, reflecting less income and taxes in the early years.

8. The subsidiary will file a consolidated tax return with its parent. This will permit the consolidated group to use the tax losses of the subsidiary, which usually result in the early years, and any available investment tax credit may be utilized, it otherwise being lost to the parent.

9. The subsidiary's lease receivables may be "securitized" more easily than if they were carried by the parent. These receivables could be sold on a slightly discounted basis to an institution or financial house, which would issue securities backed by these leases—the same concept used by Fannie Mae in issuing government-guaranteed instruments backed by qualified mortgages. This type of transaction is more doable through the subsidiary, as its liabilities and creditors' claims are more clearly defined and subject to waiver.

The captive finance subsidiary, then, if properly structured, offers immediate cash flow, tax advantages, and financial benefits, while providing long-term financing to the company's customers. The use of a subsidiary permits the company to obtain bank financing and long-term institutional money more readily than through the parent. A word of caution, however: Such a subsidiary is "capital-intensive," requiring increasing amounts of borrowings each year to continue to finance the installment sales to the parent's customers. This requires a constant and inexorable fund-raising effort on the part of the subsidiary, year in and year out. This is difficult to accomplish in tight money times and requires careful long-range planning to provide advance funds to weather the tight money times. A way out of this eventuality is participation on a 50–50 partnership basis with an independent finance company, preferably a public company, that is in the business of raising funds in the public markets on a continuing basis. In any event, the wholly owned finance subsidiary could be set up for as short a period as three or four years to obtain the significant advantages offered, and then discontinued if tight money markets persist.

The American Management Association has developed a course for the American Institute of Certified Public Accountants (AICPA) entitled "How to Make the Right Leasing Decisions." This course guides you through a complex maze of leasing options, techniques, and regulations. You'll get an historical perspective on leasing; an overview of accounting, IRS, and industry viewpoints; and a complete set of quantitative tools for analyzing leasing options and methods of accounting and reporting. Since it is so highly specialized a field, the responsibility for the project should be placed in the hands of the treasurer or controller, who should personally supervise the project and be prepared to devote most of his or her time to establishing the project, including:

1. Formation of the corporation and qualification in required states
2. Design of the lease, guarantees, and other legal documents
3. Establishment of the format for tax and financial accounting
4. Creation of the marketing plan and promotional literature
5. Setting of appropriate and competitive rates
6. Structuring of the debt and equity aspects
7. Preparation of short- and long-term operating and cash projections
8. Establishment of the short- and long-term lending relationships

The Leasing Partnership

A 95%-owned leasing partnership may be formed, with most of the advantages of the captive finance subsidiary, and more:

1. If a valid business purpose exists for the partnership (say, additional credit availability through the 5% partner), and if the corporation controls 95%, the IRS will allow a step-up in the basis of the product sold by the corporation to the partnership. For example, a corporation manufactures a product at a cost of $2,000. The product lists at $5,000. It may be sold to the partnership for $5,000, simultaneously with the partnership's sale of the product to an end user on a full-payout, sales finance–type lease. The basis to the partnership is $5,000.

If the lease is properly structured with a fair market value option at the end of the lease, the partnership may use operating lease treatment for tax purposes, with depreciation based on the stepped-up $5,000. In effect, 95% of this step-up is passed back to the corporate partner. The same step-up would apply to any available investment tax credit. Because this is a partnership, tax returns would not be consolidated with those of the corporation.

2. For accounting purposes, present rules would not require consolidation. The FASB is currently studying the accounting treatment of controlled partnerships. For the moment, equity accounting controls. In any event, full disclosure must be made in the notes to the financial statement. The investment is recorded on the balance sheet, and the corporation's share of partnership income is a one-line income statement pickup. This accounting treatment is akin to nonconsolidation. The partnership financial statements will carry all of the long-term receivables and long-term debt, thus protecting the current ratio of the corporation.

> *Use Caution:* These agreements must be structured carefully, with a valid business purpose, to avoid having the IRS take the position that the partnership is really a corporation that must be consolidated.

ACQUISITIONS

Acquisitions are usually thought of as being made to increase earnings, to diversify products, to vertically integrate, to acquire assets, and, sometimes, even for the sake of creating excitement in a company's stock. Rarely are they considered as an alternative to the issuance of long-term debt, but this effect often results and, indeed, is often sought by the purchaser. Long-term debt may be acquired through acquisitions if:

1. The acquired company is in the business of obtaining long-term debt on a continuing basis. Examples are a fixed-asset company—say steel or rail—that makes major investments in fixed assets through such borrowings, or a finance company, which is capital-intensive and constantly raising funds to operate. The acquirer may use these relationships to obtain direct debt or debt funnelled through the subsidiary.

2. The acquired company may manufacture a product that is marketed or used in manufacturing by the parent. If such a product has been long-term financed by the subsidiary, the parent has, in effect, obtained long-term financing for its product, because of the intercompany eliminations in consolidation.

3. The parent, by issuing stock at the cost of equity previously described in the Equity section, has obtained all of the assets and liabilities, including the long-term liabilities of the acquired company.

Acquisitions may be treated as purchases or poolings of interest, for accounting purposes, in accordance with APB Opinion No. 16. In a pooling, an acquiring company takes the assets of a merged company onto its own books at their original cost. This has sometimes allowed a company to issue stock at a worth much more than the original cost of the acquired assets and then to sell the assets at present value and take the difference as a profit. It has also been possible to include the profit of an acquired company in an annual report, even though the pooling occurred at the end of the fiscal year reported on. Opinion No. 16 requires that either the pooling or the purchase method be used, not a combination; pooling may be used only if companies combine through an exchange of common stock, subject to certain restrictions. All other business combinations must be accounted for as purchases. In purchase accounting, any difference between the price paid and the value of tangible and identifiable intangible assets acquired, as goodwill, must be systematically written off against future earnings over a period not to exceed 40 years. Moreover, under Opinion No. 16, it is not possible to include the profits of an acquired company in net income reported to stockholders if the pooling took place after the end of the year reported on.

OFF-BALANCE-SHEET FINANCING

Debt may be incurred in various ways without carrying it on the balance sheet, in accordance with existing accounting principles.

Hybrid securities, leases, and sale and leasebacks, previously discussed, if properly structured, may be given off-balance-sheet treatment.

To receive such treatment, leases must generally be structured as operating leases, for accounting purposes, rather than sales-type or direct financing leases. If the lease transfers substantially all benefits and risks of ownership, the economic effect is similar to that of an installment purchase. If at its inception the lease meets one or more of the following four criteria, it shall be classified as a capital lease by the lessee. Otherwise, it shall be classified as an operating lease (off-balance-sheet):

1. The lease transfers ownership of the property to the lessee by the end of the lease term.
2. The lease contains a bargain purchase option.
3. The lease term is equal to 75% or more of the estimated economic life of the leased property.
4. The present value of the lease payments at the start of the lease term equals or exceeds 90% of the fair value of the leased property.

APB Statement 13, Accounting for Leases, provides complete details on the required accounting.

The advantages of off-balance-sheet financing stem from the fact that liabilities may be kept off the company's balance sheet, but the company may still achieve its operating and financial objectives, at the same or even less cost. This technique allows the company to:

1. *Improve its debt-to-equity ratio.* This allows it to conform to borrowing agreements and to give the appearance of having less debt, and hence a less risky stock. The market value of the stock could actually improve as a result.

2. *Limit risk and increase tax deferrals.* Some arrangements, such as sale and leasebacks, limited research and development partnerships, and debt defeasance, allow the company to share risk with the participants and to defer taxes.

3. *Increase borrowing capacity.* Many long-term borrowing agreements contain covenants limiting additional borrowing to formulas based on what is on the balance sheet. In addition, off-balance-sheet lenders are often additional sources of credit that would not be available from the company's standard long-term lenders.

4. *Decrease its cost of debt.* A better balance sheet with better current and debt-to-equity ratios can result in lower costs on borrowing from standard lenders. Also, traditionally, lower costs result from project financing and interest-rate swaps.

5. *Increase key management's compensation.* When compensation is tied to earnings or ratios that are improved by off-balance-sheet debt, managers can benefit directly.

The following are some off-balance-sheet arrangements that can provide the enumerated benefits:

✧ *Hybrid securities, leases, and sale and leaseback arrangements.* These were previously discussed.

✧ *Trusts, partnerships, and joint ventures.* Avis Rent-a-Car structured a trust to borrow funds to purchase automobiles, which were then leased to Avis's car rental fleet. Since the trust was a separate entity from both Avis and its parent, Norton Simon, Inc., neither company reported the debt incurred by the trust. Generally, partnerships and joint ventures would be accounted for using the equity method of accounting (APB Opinion No. 18) (a one-line income pickup and the investment carried on the balance sheet at cost plus income or minus losses). Debt incurred by the partnership or joint venture would not be carried on the investor company's balance sheet.

Caution: The equity method applies to common stock investments and investments in corporate joint ventures. However, for investments in unincorporated joint ventures wherein the investor-venturer owns an undivided interest in each asset and is proportionately liable for its share of each liability, the investor-venturer may be required to account in its financial statements for its pro rata share of the assets, liabilities, revenues, and expenses of the venture.

✧ *Limited partnerships.* Off-balance-sheet debt is created through a limited research and development partnership by bringing in outside investors who receive a return on their investment, plus a payment on liquidation of the partnership for their rights to the developments. The partnership borrows funds to finance the development. The debt may not be guaranteed by the sponsoring company, but that will not usually be necessary, as the partnership has a development contract that underlies the debt. The company transfers basic technology to the partnership and manages its affairs. The partnership contracts out the development work, usually back to the company. The partnership payments for the contract work generate tax losses to the partnership that are passed through to the partners—that is, the company and the investors. The company avoids showing book losses for R&D work in the early years, as well as recording the debt. SFAS 68, Research and Development Arrangements, clarifies the accounting issues involved.

❖ *Project financing.* This involves contracts for goods or services that are to be delivered in the future. The most common forms of these arrangements are known as take-or-pay contracts (for product) or throughput contracts (for services). These contracts allow the company to finance a major capital project off-balance-sheet. The company must pay for a minimum number of units of the unrelated supplier's product or service, even if delivery is not taken. The supplier uses the earnings from the contracts as security for the debt that will fund the construction of the project. The company's noncancelable purchase obligation is not a recorded liability, as it represents an executory contract for future goods and services. The accounting rules require footnote disclosure of these arrangements, as set forth in SFAS 47, Commitments: Long-Term Obligations.

❖ *Sale of accounts receivable with recourse.* Receivables, both notes and accounts, may be sold with recourse. If such a sale is not in essence a loan, it may be recorded as a sale with no liability for the proceeds being recorded on the balance sheet. SFAS 77, Reporting by Transferors for Transfers of Receivables With Recourse, governs the accounting for such transactions. Control of the receivables must be transferred, the cost of the recourse provision must be able to be reasonably estimated, and the transferee cannot force the transferor to repurchase the receivables except through the recourse arrangement. A contingency footnote for the recourse arrangement would need to be disclosed in accordance with SFAS 5, Accounting for Contingencies.

❖ *Defeasance.* Through the use of in-substance defeasance of debt, a company with long-term debt can extinguish it before maturity, without legally retiring the original debt issue. This may be desirable because of the high fees for bond redemption, the onerous call provisions on the original issue of debt, or unsatisfactory current market conditions. Moreover, there are substantial advantages to removing the debt from the balance sheet in the form of improved debt-to-equity or return on assets ratios. Earnings per share may be increased by recording the gain on the defeasance in the current period. The device involves transferring risk-free assets such as cash or marketable securities to an irrevocable trust, with such trust assets to be used solely to service the principal and interest on the debt. SFAS 76, Extinguishment of Debt, governs the accounting for these transactions.

✧ *Employment benefits.* Under present accounting rules, many postemployment benefits, such as life insurance, health care, and pension costs, are accounted for on a cash basis, with no accruals for future cost being required. While pension cost accounting does require that prior service cost be recognized, FASB requires that such cost be amortized over the remaining future service periods. Even when a minimum liability must be recorded, it is understated, as the liability does not anticipate future salary increases in calculating the present value of the future benefit payments. The accounting rules and disclosure requirements are found in SFAS 87, Employers' Accounting for Pensions. However, SFAS 112, Employers' Accounting for Postemployment Benefits, established standards for employers who provide benefits to former or inactive employees after employment, but *before* retirement (defined as postemployment benefits). This standard requires employers to recognize the obligation to provide postemployment benefits, in accordance with SFAS 43, Accounting for Compensated Absences, if the obligation is attributable to services already rendered, the rights to those benefits accumulate or vest, payment of them is probable, and the amounts can be reasonably estimated in accordance with SFAS 5, Accounting for Contingencies.

✧ *Interest-rate swaps (derivatives).* This technique involves the swapping of debt by two companies, one of which holds fixed debt, the other variable. While the debt continues to remain on the balance sheet, the additional cost of the swap may well exceed the interest cost that is presently reflected on the balance sheet or in the notes. The present value of this additional cost is not required to be recorded and, as such, represents off-balance-sheet financing. Companies swap debt to gain more control over interest-rate risk. For example, companies with cash inflows that are rate-sensitive attempt to lower interest-rate risk by arranging their cash outflows so that they are also interest-rate-sensitive.

Interest-rate swaps are, in effect, hedging instruments that are financial instrument derivatives. A derivative is a contract whose value is "derived" from the value of some underlying asset, index, or other reference rate. A call option, for example, derives its value from the value of the underlying stock. As the stock price rises, the option rises in value. As the stock price falls, the option decreases in value.

Most of the accounting guidance for handling derivatives comes from FASB SFAS 80, Accounting for Futures Contracts; SFAS 105, Disclosure of Information About Financial Instruments With Off-Balance-Sheet Risk and Financial Instruments With Concentrations of Credit Risk; SFAS 107 and 126, Disclosures About Fair Value of Financial Instruments; SFAS 119, Disclosure About Derivative Financial Instruments and Fair Value of Financial Instruments; and SFAS 133, 137, and 138, Accounting for Derivative Instruments and Hedging Activities. Generally, the disclosures require information about financial instruments with off-balance-sheet risk of accounting loss, to include the principal amount of the contract; the nature, terms, credit risk, market risk, and cash requirements; the accounting loss that could occur in the event of nonperformance; and the collateral required. In addition, the fair value of assets and liabilities, whether or not recognized, must be disclosed, along with the purpose for which the derivatives are held or issued. It is interesting to note that the definition of derivatives in SFAS 119 excludes all on-balance-sheet receivables and payables, including those that derive their values or contractually required cash flows from the price of some other security or index, such as mortgage-backed securities, interest-only and principal-only obligations, and indexed debt instruments. It also excludes optional features that are embedded in an on-balance-sheet item, such as the conversion feature and call provisions embedded in convertible bonds. Basically, this statement says that on-balance-sheet items, by definition, are disclosed to the reader. It is the off-balance-sheet items that need disclosure and scrutiny. Therefore, SFAS 119 seeks not only to appropriately measure financial assets and liabilities but to assist users in assessing the risks that are present and the effect of various possible outcomes.

The AICPA has developed six common-sense questions that may be used by boards of directors and audit committees to inquire about their company's activities in derivative financial instruments. The answers to these questions are needed to assess whether the derivatives activities are well managed and controlled. They are:

1. Has the board established a clear and internally consistent risk management policy, including risk limits (as appropriate)? For example, are the objectives for derivatives communicated to those who need to know? Do derivatives mitigate risk or create additional risk? If risk is being assumed, are the limits established? What is the purpose of the derivative activity?

2. Are management's strategies and implementation policies consistent with the board's authorization? For example, is the purpose of granting authority for derivative activity clearly understood by the recipients of that authority? Is compliance with these policies evaluated regularly? Does Treasury view itself as a profit center? (If so, beware.)

3. Do key controls exist to ensure that only authorized transactions take place and that unauthorized transactions are quickly detected and appropriate action is taken? For example, who evaluates the controls, and does the evaluator have the technical competence to do so? Is the derivative activity separate from other duties, such as accounting and internal audit functions?

4. Are the magnitude, complexity, and risks of the entity's derivatives commensurate with the entity's objectives? For example, internal analysis should include quantitative and qualitative information about the derivatives activities, including credit risk (financial loss from a counterparty's failure to perform), market risk (loss from adverse movements in the price of a financial asset or commodity), legal risk (loss from a legal or regulatory action that could invalidate a financial contract), and control risk (possible financial loss from inadequate internal controls). Are derivatives standard (plain vanilla), or are they more complex? Is the complexity inconsistent with the risks being managed?

5. Are personnel with authority to engage in and monitor derivatives transactions well qualified and appropriately trained? For example, who are the key players? Is the knowledge vested in only one individual or a small group? Have personnel been properly developed to undertake these activities? Do they have appropriate technical and professional expertise? Are people cross-trained? Are there sufficient backup person-

nel? How have we ensured the integrity, ethical values, and competence of the personnel involved?

6. Do the right people have the right information to make decisions? For example, are both internal and external information being identified, captured, and communicated, such as market changes affecting derivative transactions and changes in our strategy for the mix of assets and liabilities that are the focus of risk management activities? Are the analysis and internal reporting of the risks the company is managing and the effectiveness of its strategies comprehensive, reliable, and well designed to facilitate oversight? Does this analysis relate to the achievement of the entity's objectives—economic, regulatory, industry, or operating? Might the derivatives activities increase our exposure to risks that might frustrate the achievement of those objectives? Do we mark derivatives transactions to market regularly (and if not, why not)? Are we publishing financial information about derivatives in accordance with GAAP?

> *Word of Caution:* Appendix A sets forth the controller's responsibility for protection of assets, reporting and interpreting, and evaluating and consulting, and the treasurer's responsibility for short-term financing, banking and custody, and investments. Both the treasurer and the controller are, therefore, both very involved in the derivatives activities process. The protection of assets and investments responsibilities should avoid risks. Interest-rate swaps and currency hedges can be pure hedges for risk avoidance (in the nature of insurance). There should be no naked hedges without consideration of all the risks, board of directors approval, and complete financial statement disclosure.

INTEGRATION OF LONG-TERM BORROWINGS INTO THE LONG-RANGE CASH FORECAST

Forecasting cash requirements is discussed in Chapter 5. One of the considerations used in preparing the long-range forecast is a determination of the long-term debt required to support the company's operating programs over the period of years studied. That chapter discusses long-range planning techniques that translate themselves into financial statements, including statements of operations, balance sheets, and statements of changes in financial position. These statements give the absolute amount of cash required. The treasurer must determine the mix between short- and long-term debt and the different types of each.

For the financially strong company, the choices are varied, and the treasurer's decision is based on a mix that results in the lowest borrowing cost over the period, or if not the lowest cost, a mix that will ensure a reasonably low cost and provide open avenues for future financing. For example, some short-term debt, at higher than long-term rates, may be desirable to protect short-term bank commitments that may be required to meet contingent cash shortages.

For the company that is not the highest credit rated, the choice is not so much a choice as it is a dictum of market conditions. The weaker company may not be strong enough to negotiate institutional debt over an eight- to ten-year period; stock market conditions may be wrong for an equity offering, and the clear choice would then be a convertible debenture. Or, under these same conditions, the company may be too small to negotiate a convertible or debt with warrants. In this case, revolving bank debt would be the appropriate answer. A revolver could be augmented with leasing to acquire new equipment, or a sale and leaseback, and some of the continuing or revolving devices described in Chapter 1—commercial financing, factoring, inventory reductions, and accounts receivable reductions. The point is, despite market fluctuations, a thorough understanding of the avenues for creation of debt will provide the path to successful, low-cost financing for the enterprise.

3

The Direction of Credit Granting and Accounts Receivable Collection

The FEI treasurership functions listing in the "Treasurer's and Controller's Functions Defined by the Financial Executives Institute" describes the credit and collections function as "to direct the granting of credit and the collection of accounts due the company, including the supervision of required special arrangements for financing sales, such as time payment and leasing plans." Closely juxtaposed to this function is that of applying accounts receivable collections to the accounts, creating the aged trial balance of accounts receivable and associated accounts receivable reports. The latter function, relating to receivables application and related reports, is the responsibility of the controller, as part of the protection of assets and reporting and interpreting function. The position description of the treasurer, addended to the above, includes this function of credit and collection (the seventh major duty listed), and the controller's position description, likewise, includes the responsibilities for protecting assets and reporting results.

This chapter will examine these functions, with emphasis on:

1. Credit-granting procedures
2. Collection procedures
3. Special arrangements for credit

4. Internal control (fraud and asset protection)
5. Essential reports to monitor performance

CREDIT-GRANTING PROCEDURES

Any good credit-granting system is inextricably combined with a good order-writing discipline. The order, after all, contains the key elements that will later be necessary to ensure collection, as well as the key information needed to analyze the order to determine whether credit may even be granted. Such a system also provides for automatic approvals or rejections, based on standard criteria. This makes it possible for line employees to pass most of the orders without review by a manager.

A **procedure applicable to retail (ultimate consumers) accounts and to dealers (distributors)** is shown in Exhibit 3-1. This contains the following features:

1. The order must be in writing, legible, legally signed, with an accurate address, and must have a purchase order number in certain cases (large companies and institutions).
2. A letterhead order blank from the customer is required, and for new accounts, our company's own order form must be signed. This assures that our special terms and conditions are agreed to.
3. Special order forms supplied by us may be needed for special products to obtain conformity to their unique features.
4. Some orders require telephone confirmation. These are usually large dollar orders. The confirmation nails down the order, making certain that there are no salesperson's misrepresentations and that the customer clearly understands his or her obligations. A **confirmation call procedure and checklist** are shown at Exhibit 3-2.

Try This Helpful Hint: The confirmation call is ostensibly made under the guise of asking to obtain marketing

(*text continues on page 91*)

Exhibit 3-1. Order acceptance procedure.

Branch Office Procedure

Title		B.O.P Number: 1.01
	ORDER ACCEPTANCE	Page 1 of 11

Vol. No.	1	Vol. Name:	Order Processing

PURPOSE:

To provide a procedure governing the verification of the acceptability of all orders received.

GENERAL NARRATIVE:

Acceptance of orders is based on review of all information required for all new and repeat sales of machines, supplies and service.

RESPONSIBILITIES:

Sales: For the proper preparation of sales orders.
Field Engineering: Preparation of Maintenance Agreement forms and Service Call Reports.
Administration: Determines acceptability by: Verification, Credit Checking & Telephone Confirmation of Orders.

Table of Contents:

Section:

Supersedes		Orig. Code	Release No.	Effective Date
B.O.P. No.(s).	Page No.(s).	AP2	B-004	10/1/
Related Publications		Inquiries: Corporate Credit Manager		

(continued)

Exhibit 3-1. *(continued)*

Branch Office Procedure

Title	B.O.P Number: 1.01
ORDER ACCEPTANCE	Page 2 of 11

Vol. No. 1	Vol. Name: Order Processing

VERIFICATION OF ORDERS

Section A

Responsibility

Administration: to ensure that all required information pertaining to
an order is available.

Procedure:

1. Receives orders from following sources:
    a. Sales Order Form (#0-16-7) (Exhibit A) from Sales Representative
    b. Written requests or Purchase Orders from customers
    c. Telephone Orders - from Administration or sales
    d. Service Calls & Maintenance Agreements - Field Engineering

2. Checks order forms to ensure completion as follows:

    A. Sales

        1. Name and Address
        2. Purchase Order number or name of individual placing order
            A. Purchase Order number is required and must be included on
                invoices for all Government Agencies, banks, utilities,
                hospitals and large corporations
        3. Product and quantity (clearly defined)
        4. Pricing (in accord with current marketing programs and trade-
            in schedules) on telephone orders, confirm current pricing
            with customer
        5. Credit references (one bank, two trades) if new or inactive
            customer
        6. Special terms/conditions (must comply with current
            policy)
        7. Signature and title of individual who is authorized to make the
            purchase; Office Manager, Purchasing Agent, Branch Manager,
            Regional Director, etc.

    B. Leases

        1. Lessee name and address.
        2. Product and quantity (clearly defined).

Supersedes		Orig. Code	Release No.	Effective Date
B.O.P. No.(s).	Page No.(s).	AP2	B-004	10/1/
Related Publications		Inquiries: Corporate Credit Manager		

Branch Office Procedure

Title	B.O.P Number: 1.01
ORDER ACCEPTANCE	Page 3 of 11

Vol. No. 1	Vol. Name: Order Processing

3.   Pricing (in accord with sales order form)
4.   Term of Lease
5.   Monthly Payment Schedule
6.   Security deposit check received
7.   Type of business
8.   Length of time in business
9.   Credit reference (See "Credit Checking Procedure")
10.   If corporation in business for less than one year, must have personal guarantee and personal bank reference on guarantor.
11.   Duly authorized corporate officer signature - president, vice president, treasurer, corporate secretary, purchasing agent, partner, proprietor or owner.
12.   If a parent company is involved, a letter of authorization or corporate guarantee is necessary.

MAINTENANCE AGREEMENTS

1.   Name and Address
2.   Model & Serial Number of Equipment
3.   Period covered by Agreement
4.   Authorized Customer Signature
5.   Pricing must be in accordance with current price schedule.

SERVICE CALL REPORTS

1.   Name and Address
2.   Customer Signature (Verifying receipt of service)

Supersedes		Orig. Code	Release No.	Effective Date
B.O.P. No.(s).	Page No.(s).	AP2	B-004	10/1/
Related Publications		Inquiries: Corporate Credit Manager		

(continued)

Exhibit 3-1. *(continued)*

Branch Office Procedure

Title ORDER ACCEPTANCE	B.O.P Number: 1.01
	Page 4 of 11

Vol. No. 1   **Vol. Name:**   Order Processing

Section B Credit Checking

PURPOSE: B

Provide criteria to enable the company to determine ability and willingness of a customer to pay for products purchased.

GENERAL NARRATIVE:

Attempt to verify criteria by using credit references provided by customer on sales order. Determination is based on information received from references.

RESPONSIBILITIES:

SALES:

  Sales order submitted must provide one of the following:

  1. Credit references (one bank, two trades),
  2. D & B rating of DC2 or better, or
  3. States present account.

ADMINISTRATION:

Checks all references provided and determines acceptability.

PROCEDURE:

A. Retail Outright Sales (Non-lease)—all machine placements, supplies and service.

  1. New Customers

Administration:

      a. Receives orders from sales representative or customer.
      b. Phone Orders — Administration requests by phone, required bank and trade references.

Supersedes		Orig. Code	Release No.	Effective Date
B.O.P. No.(s). Page No.(s).		AP2	B-004	10/1/
Related Publications		Inquiries: Corporate Credit Manager		

Branch Office Procedure

Title		B.O.P Number: 1.01
	ORDER ACCEPTANCE	Page 5 of 11

Vol. No.	1	Vol. Name:	Order Processing

    c.   Calls and/or writes each reference and verifies past history and present standing (Check form based on credit Exhibits B & C); if the bank refuses to supply information, Branch Administration Manager should address a letter to the bank, attention of the officer in charge of the customer's account, authorizing release of information concerning the account, and this should be signed by the customer and mailed by the BAM. A copy of the completed letter is attached to order as backup documentation.

    d.   Retail Credit Bureau (contract #131593 plus branch code) may be used to gather credit info if other sources are not available.

    e.   D & B rating DC2 or better automatically qualifies customer as an acceptable credit risk, except any business involved in financing or the credit field. If the digit in the rating (i.e., the 2 in DC2) is 3 or 4, in any category, then the references are to be obtained.

    f.   Political orders can only be sold on a cash in advance or C.O.D. basis. Never on open account.

2. Evaluation of References

    a.   Bank Reference
       1.   The potential customer must have a minimum average balance of four figures unless the sale is for new products to a service type company or a funded organization and then additional payments may be required up front and the lease term shortened.
       2.   Account must be open for a reasonable length of time.
       3.   No overdrafts or returns.
       4.   Paying habits on past loans must be satisfactory.
       5.   If sales order has 30 day option to lease there must be a minimum average balance of four figures and the account must be at least one year old.

    b.   Trades
       1.   These should indicate applicant's willingness to pay. Do not include those vendors vital for customer's operation (i.e. telephone, electricity, etc.).
       2.   Paying habits should be prompt. References indicating 60 days and slower are unacceptable.

Supersedes		Orig. Code	Release No.	Effective Date
B.O.P. No.(s).	Page No.(s).			
1.01	5,9,10,11	AP3	B-039	2/21/
Related Publications		Inquiries: CORPORATE CREDIT MANAGER		

(continued)

Exhibit 3-1. *(continued)*

Branch Office Procedure

Title	B.O.P Number: 1.01
ORDER ACCEPTANCE	Page 6 of 11

Vol. No. 1	Vol. Name: Order Processing

B. Leases

1. Retail Sales - Financed on <u>Lease</u> thru Home Office
   a. <u>Bank References</u>
      1. All judgments in compliance with paragraph 2a are applicable.
      2. Check how long the applicant has been an account of the bank against how long the applicant has been in business. There must be a reasonable relationship between the two. If not, previous bank reference(s) must be obtained.
   b. <u>Trade References</u>
      1. All judgements in compliance with paragraph 2b are applicable..
      2. Another leasing company or some other installment purchase would be acceptable as one reference, while the second reference should be a major supplier so that insight may be gained into the size and scope of the applicant's business.
   c. <u>Additional Requirement for Leases</u>
      1. Advance rentals, Security Deposits, length of lease and personal guarantees.

         -Four-year (48-month) and five-year (60-month) leases must be accompanied by a check in an amount equal to three months rental; which will be applied to the first and last two months' rent.

         Lease applications for four- & five-year leases submitted on behalf of applicants in business for less than five years will be subject to a more intensive credit review than other shorter term leases. Based upon this review, additional advance rentals may be requested as an alternative to outright rejection.

         -Two-year (24-month) and three-year (36-month) leases must be accompanied by a check in an amount equal to two months rental; which will be applied to the first & last months' rent.

         -One-year leases need only be accompanied by a check for the first month's rent.

Supersedes		Orig. Code	Release No.	Effective Date
B.O.P No.(s).	Page No.(s).			
1.01 Rel. B-004	6	AP3	B-048	4/1/
Related Publications		Inquiries:		
		Corporate Credit Manager		

Branch Office Procedure

Title		B.O.P Number: 1.01
ORDER ACCEPTANCE		Page 7 of 11
Vol. No. 1	**Vol. Name:** Order Processing	

These advance rental rules may be waived where the lease applicant has a D & B rating of 1A1. In this instance the purchase order must accompany the lease.

    d. The following maximum lease terms are available with regard to low dollar sales.

        1. Where the "total cost to lessor" is at least $800.00, will accept a lease up to 36 months.
        2. Where the "total cost to lessor" is less than $800.00, will accept a lease up to 24 months.
        3. Where the "total cost to lessor" is less than $600.00, but more than $300.00, will accept a lease for a 12-month period only.
        4. Four- & five-year leases for dollar amounts under $800.00 are not acceptable under any condition.

    NOTE: A corporation in business 12 months or less or a service type organization (selling a service with little or no investment in inventory, machinery, equipment, etc.) in business less than three years must provide a personal guarantee from one of the principal officers.

        Additionally, a bank reference is required from the personal guarantor.

Fiscal Funded Leases

Leases may not be written for GSA nor for Municipal, County and State governments to whom we have generally extended GSA provisions.

    Institutional Agencies (Universities, Hospitals, etc.) may be on fiscal funded lease but under the following conditions:

    A. Price must be retail list.
    B. Maximum lease term 36 months.
    C. Only 1/3 commission to be given annually when renewal Purchase Order received.
    D. Purchase Order should be made out to Equilease covering monthly payments.

Supersedes		Orig. Code	Release No.	Effective Date
B.O.P. No.(s).	**Page No.(s).**			
1.01 Rel. B-004	7	AP3	B-048	4/1/
Related Publications		**Inquiries:** Corporate Credit Manager		

(continued)

Exhibit 3-1. *(continued)*

Branch Office Procedure

Title	B.O.P Number: 1.01
ORDER ACCEPTANCE	Page 8 of 11

Vol. No. 1	Vol. Name: Order Processing

Funded Organizations - Neighborhood type of organizations that are primarily dependent upon government allotment or charitable contributions for existence have proven to be too vulnerable to extinction and are not acceptable.

3. <u>Present Customer</u>

    a. Receives the following Customer Credit Data from Home Office:

        -Copies of Statement of Account for all active customers of the branch (Exhibit "D")
        -"Turn-Over Notice" (Exhibit "E")
        -"Doubtful Account" Statements (Exhibit "F")
        -Copy of the final "Dun Letter" (L-3) (Exhibit "G")
        -Dun-Master List (Exhibit "H")

    b. Refers to the above data on all incoming orders from present customers, and checks to determine if there is a past due balance.

    c. Upon checking credit status, proceeds as follows:

        1. In all instances when the statement balance plus the order on hand exceeds $7,500.00, contact Credit Department for approval.

        2. If amounts due are within 1-40 days from invoice date, Okay to ship.

        3. If amounts due are within 41-70 days from invoice date, call customer and request payment for past due amount. The order may be shipped with customer's assurance that payment will be or has been made. Notify Credit Department of the transaction.

        4. If amounts due are 71 days and over from invoice date, do not ship and advise customer that the matter has been referred to the Credit Department.

Supersedes		Orig. Code	Release No.	Effective Date
B.O.P. No.(s).	Page No.(s).			
1.01 Rel. B-004	8	AP3	B-048	4/1/
Related Publications		Inquiries:		
		Corporate Credit Manager		

Branch Office Procedure

Title		B.O.P Number: 1.01
	ORDER ACCEPTANCE	Page 9 of 11
Vol. No. 1	**Vol. Name:** Order Processing	

5. "Doubtful Accounts" - Upon receipt of order, advises customer that the account has been placed for collection. Should shipment, or invoice, be deemed essential, the Branch Administration Manager contacts Credit Department's Third-Party Collection Supervisor for approval.

6. If the customer has our equipment on lease at present, and wishes to lease additional equipment, all payments on existing lease must be current and a current bank reference obtained. In the event the customer has changed banks, completed new bank reference is required.

7. When a machine sale is made to a present customer, a complete credit check must be performed as for New Customers. This includes conversion from rental to sale.

4. Multiple Machine Orders

   a. Total sales in amounts up to $7,500.00 may be credit approved by Branch Administration Manager.

   b. Sales in amounts over $7,500.00 must be submitted in writing to Corporate Credit Manager for final credit approval, prior to shipping the equipment.

5. Special Terms

   Any terms other than those standard terms listed below must be approved in writing in advance by the Corporate Credit Manager.

   Machines: Net 10 days
                  1/3 with order, 1/3-30, 1/3-60
                  1/2 with order, 1/2-60

   Cpn. Books: Net 10 days
                  1/3 with order, 1/3-30, 1/3-60
                  1/2 with order and 1/2-60

   When extended terms are granted, they should appear on the invoice exactly as above.

   All other billing net 10 days — no exception.

Supersedes		Orig. Code	Release No.	Effective Date
B.O.P. No.(s).	**Page No.(s).**	AP3	B-048	4/1/
1.01 Rel. B-039	9			
Related Publications		**Inquiries:** CORPORATE CREDIT MANAGER		

(continued)

Exhibit 3-1. *(continued)*

Branch Office Procedure

Title	B.O.P Number: 1.01
ORDER ACCEPTANCE	Page 10 of 11

| **Vol. No.** 1 | **Vol. Name:** Order Processing |

6. <u>Cash Discounts</u>

<u>Equipment Sales</u> (Non-Lease) including conversions to sale
(Not applicable to typewriter sales)
5% for payment in full with order.
2% for payment in full within 10 days of the invoice date.

<u>Coupon Book Sales</u>

5% for payment in full with order.

GENERAL INFORMATION

Credit approval of orders is the Branch Administration Manager's
responsibility. If after analyzing the facts gathered about a
specific order, a credit decision cannot be made, all information
should be submitted to the Corporate Credit Manager for a final
decision.

Even though the equipment may be sold for cash, bank & trade references
are still required and should be checked. This is necessary to
establish credit for ensuing supply & service business.

In such instances, shipment should not be delayed pending completion of
the credit check.

An order accepted for future delivery should be credit checked at
delivery time.

SECTION C

Telephone Confirmations:

<u>Purpose:</u>

To insure validity of new orders through phone contact by Administration to each customer placing a new machine or coupon book
order to insure agreement on general terms and conditions of the order.

Supersedes		Orig. Code	Release No.	Effective Date
B.O.P. No.(s).	**Page No.(s).**	AP2	B-059	8/5/
B.O.P. 101 Rel. # 039 10				
Related Publications		**Inquiries:** Corporate Credit Manager		

Branch Office Procedure

Title		B.O.P Number: 1.01
ORDER ACCEPTANCE		Page 11 of 11
Vol. No. 1	**Vol. Name:** Order Processing	

Responsibility:

Administration

Procedure:

A. After receipt of the Sales Order Form for machines or coupon book sales, using that form for reference and with the use of Telephone Confirmation form (See Exhibit I) a phone call is made to the customer. This call is to be made only after the order and credit have been determined to be acceptable.
B. Speak only to the person who signed the Sales Order Form.
C. Ask all applicable questions on the Telephone Confirmation Form (See Exhibit I). Refer to the Sales Order Form as a cross reference.
D. Fill in form (See Exhibit I) as each question is discussed.
E. If any part of the confirmation is not in agreement with the Sales Order Form, advise the customer that you will get further information. Then hold order and advise the Sales Manager. Upon advice from Sales Manager of correction, reconfirm the order.
F. Sign and date the Telephone Confirmation.
G. Attach to invoice along with other backup paperwork on the order.

SECTION D **APPENDIX OF EXHIBITS**

Exhibit	Description
A	Sales Order Form
B	Trade Reference Letter
C	Bank Reference Letter
D	Statement of Account
E	Turnover Notice
F	Doubtful-Statement of Account
G	"Final" Dun Letter (L-3)
H	Dun Master List
I	Confirmation Telephone Call

Supersedes		Orig. Code	Release No.	Effective Date
B.O.P. No.(s).	**Page No.(s).**			
1.01	5, 9, 10, 11	AP3	B-039	2/21/
Related Publications		**Inquiries:** CORPORATE CREDIT MANAGER		

Exhibit 3-2.   Confirmation phone calls.

STANDARD OPERATING PROCEDURE			
Subject:			Number
			C-4d
			Page of
	CONFIRMATION PHONE CALLS		2 2
			Effective Date
Supersedes Cor. No.	Page	Dated	Related
	199		S.O.P./H.O.F

1. Give Speech (reason for call is marketing information)
2. Check:
   a. Their Purchase Order Number
   b. Price of Machine
   c. Terms
   d. Quantity of Machines and/or Supplies
   e. Price of Supplies (first order and reorders)
   f. Price of Future Supplies from **Salesperson, if these are No Charge**
   g. *Marketing Questions—Complete form
   h. Authority of Signer—If Not Obvious
   i. If Lease—Payments required per month terms; number of months on lease; options available on Lease/Purchase Plan; if interest-free rental:
      1. Is it clear that you have one of four options which may be exercised at the end of 36 months, but that until this option is exercised, title to the machine remains with us?
      2. Were you advised that your monthly payments will be payable to an outside Equipment Leasing Corp., but options at the end of 36 months are payable to this company?
      3. Were you handed a printed sheet showing the various options available to you? If not, we'll send it to you now.
   j. If a Trade-In-Machine, request an appointment for pickup.
   k. *Any Branches or Subsidiaries – Names and Addresses – Name of Contact
3. Conclude by asking "are there any other conditions I have omitted?"
4. Sign Form—Send original with Bill Only—Date it. File Duplicate with Pink awaiting Green Invoice Copy.
5. Party Spoken To: _____

*Send to Home Office Marketing Division   _____

SIGNED

_____

DATE CALL MADE

Correction No. 242
Date Prepared 4/8

(*text continued from page 78*)

information—why this particular machine was bought; did it replace another; what application will it be used for; are you satisfied with its potentials?—then a segue into the details of the confirmation.

Key Point: The confirmation phone call checklist can serve as a valuable collection tool in the event of future misunderstandings or disputes. You have the date, the person spoken to, and a record of the points you have confirmed to the buyer.

5. The customer's purchase order number is important; this is again stressed, as it was in item 1.
6. Merchandise returns result in credits and must be handled promptly to keep the customer's account clean and to avoid unnecessary collection action.
7. Returns that are accepted result in credits, and this is akin to signing a check in favor of the customer. Therefore, such returns require special authorization procedures.
8. Freight policy and FOB points control the passing of title—an important point in any collection action. Proper billing of freight and conformity to company policy are important sources of revenues.
9. Even exchanges are inevitable in any company that vends a product that is not immediately consumed. Even exchanges require tight control to prevent the shipment of unbilled merchandise. The danger, of course, is that a replacement shipment may be made at no charge, without the defective product ever being returned. This is best controlled by requiring that all even exchanges be both billed and credited. As a matter of convenience, even exchanges can be allowed without billing, but with adequate documentation, for limited amounts, say up to $500. For higher-priced items, every shipment should be invoiced. When the authorized defective product is returned, a credit may then be issued. A separate procedure should be published to set forth the governing rules.
10. Companies selling products nationally are subject to a multi-

tude of diverse and sometimes confusing state tax laws. Laxity in obtaining sales or use tax exemption certificates can cost the company dearly years later, when the state performs a tax audit. In some states, labor services are taxable; in others, they are not. In some, the value of traded-in equipment is a deduction from sales; in others, it is not. Specific instructions must be issued to those responsible in each state, and conformity to the instructions must be periodically monitored. Obtaining the proper exemption certificates must be an ongoing program to avoid losses through future state tax audits.

11. Orders from ultimate users are shipped if credit is approved after referring to a current statement of account. If the account has no past record, credit is not checked, in this example, for amounts up to $150. This avoids the expense of checking credit on a vast number of small orders. The risk of loss is spread among many small accounts. Orders are carefully checked by a bank and two trade references.

Note This Important Point: Good trade references cannot overcome a bad bank reference. A good bank reference is normally enough to blunt trade references that are not the best. A good bank reference cannot offset bad trades.

Helpful Hint: The trade references should not be a utility or landlord. These must be paid on time every month. Good references are the printer, stationer, or major supplier.

Avoid This Pitfall: Be selective and careful about accounts in business less than a year (50% fail within the first year). Moreover, an account in business exactly one year is to be evaluated differently from an account one to five years old.

12. Contracts that renew automatically, from year to year, may require special procedures. For example, if your product is one that requires periodic service or maintenance, do you want to hold up such maintenance if the customer is delinquent on

supply account payments? Perhaps the customer forgot that the contract renewed automatically and was questioning your invoice.

Watch Out for This: You may turn a customer over to a collection agency because of nonpayment. But if you have a service contract that automatically renews at the end of a year, the customer will receive a billing for the renewal that will age as current in your trial balance. Be sure to stop automatic renewal billings on collection accounts.

13. Large accounts require special attention and should be handled by exception.

14. Special types of customers present special problems in various industries. Any special terms must be handled by exception.

Avoid This Pitfall: Do not permit *anyone* to set special terms or change standard terms. If you do, you will find every salesperson or division selling on a different basis with no uniformity. This may lead to antitrust violations, with special customers receiving preferred treatment. It may also lead to a slowdown in receivables turnover without your knowledge of the reason for it. Special arrangements for credit are available only when published as a company policy. See Special Arrangements for Credit, page 102.

15. Large customers or distributors (not ultimate users) require special attention and separate credit procedures. These are set forth.

Helpful Hint: Credit limits for dealers, over a specified amount, and any increases thereon, should be approved by the treasurer. This will avoid a concentration of too much credit in one account, will backstop a line credit manager's decision, and, mostly, will avoid unexpected large bad debt losses.

16. Collection procedures are discussed in the next section.

COLLECTION PROCEDURES

We have observed that any good credit-granting system is combined with a good order-writing discipline. Equally important, it must be combined with a good collection system. The essence of a good collection system is a good, automated accounts receivable software system that provides for proper recording of billings, payments, credits, discounts, allowances, and transaction codes that facilitate collection work. Such systems are readily available for centralized large computers or for decentralized microcomputers. The accounts receivable function consists of getting the order, credit-approving it for shipment, and then collecting it.

It's not a sale until it's collected! Accordingly, the order writing and credit procedures described in Exhibit 3-1 include a collection procedure in pages 8 and 9 of the procedure.

Page 8 relates to a "field" procedure for collections. In the procedure illustrated, all collections are handled centrally, at the headquarters (home office) location. But headquarters personnel must have the cooperation and aid of field personnel. Hence, field people receive aged trial balances and issue credits necessary to keep accounts receivable clean. Commissions are charged back to sales representatives after 90 days delinquency, so the representatives are involved in rectifying the situation. Collection thus becomes a companywide function, involving sales as well as administrative personnel.

> CASE IN POINT: One company's top marketing management decided that sales representatives would not be involved in collection activities, that the sales representative's job was to sell and not take time away from selling effort to see that customers paid for previous sales. As a result, commissions were not charged back for uncollected

accounts. Within 90 days, there was a sharp increase in past due receivables that seriously affected the company's cash position. The president made an immediate decision to revert to the previous system. Within 30 days, receivables and cash position had improved. The key to the improvement was involvement of sales representatives in collections through the possibility of commission chargebacks.

Field collection procedures must be an integral part of a central collection effort. That central effort may be through division headquarters or at the corporate home office, but it is centralized. As a matter of simple internal control, the office that creates the sale should not be responsible for collecting for the sale or even for issuance of credits related to that sale (as a matter of convenience, the field may have limited authority to issue credits up to specific amounts, but never to negate the sale). This construction is not opposed to the responsibility accounting concept that those responsible for the profits in any profit center should control all activities of that profit center. Responsibility accounting is rife with examples of divided responsibility to achieve better internal control and corporate goals. For example, headquarters may control all cash and make all disbursements to achieve greater liquidity; payrolls may be accomplished centrally because of central computer capability; capital expenditures are a corporate decision-making responsibility in almost every company. So too, the sale is maintained inviolate by divorcing the collection function from the selling function.

A **centralized collection procedure** is shown in Exhibit 3-3. The key elements of this procedure are listed below, numbers conforming to those in the procedure:

1. Statements of account are prepared twice a month, in a timely manner. You can't collect without fast, accurate information.
2. Dunning is computer-automated. The first 75 days of dunning is on a form-letter basis.
3. The system provides for special terms, these varying by type of company or industry.
4. Legal collection action is a possibility that is pointed out to the customer after 60 days delinquency. This period may vary

(*text continues on page 99*)

Exhibit 3-3.   Collection procedures.

STANDARD OPERATING PROCEDURE		
Subject:	Number	
	HOP C-46	
	Page of	
COLLECTION PROCEDURES - HOME OFFICE	1 4	
	Effective	
	Date 5/5/	
Supersedes Cor. No. Page Dated	Related	
	S.O.P./H.O.P.	

PURPOSE: To provide a means for the timely processing and collection follow-up of customer statements of accounts and Dunning Notices.

METHOD: 1. Customer Statements of Account for each branch are prepared by Data Processing twice monthly—at the month end and mid-month. These aged customer statements are provided to collection correspondents; and copies mailed to Branch Administrators for order processing and collection follow-up in accordance with SOP C-25.

2. Dunning notices are prepared by Data Processing twice monthly for mailing to delinquent accounts. Each cycle provides the following requests for payment.
   a. Courtesy Notices - Accounts past due 15-30 days.
   b. D1 Form Letter - Accounts past due 31-45 days.
   c. D2 Form Letter - Accounts past due 46-60 days.
   d. D5 Form Letter - Accounts past due 61-75 days.
   e. Dun Master List - Accounts past due over 75 days.

3. Accounts with special terms (Activity Codes F-P-N-T) are excluded from the dunning cycle and appear on a dun master list when the invoice has been past due more than 60 days:
   a. If no payment has been made on Activity Codes P-N-T, a copy of the invoice is obtained and forwarded with D7 form with follow-ups as indicated in Step 6 below, with D8 form (Intent to Charge Back) sent to Branch.
   b. If no payment on Activity Code F (leases) refer problem to Leasing Desk as to reason for non-payment.

Date Prepared: 5/5/
HOP Correction No. 168

HOP C-46

STANDARD OPERATING PROCEDURE		
Subject:		**Number** HOP C-46
	COLLECTION PROCEDURE - HOME OFFICE	**Page** **of** 2 4
		Effective **Date** 5/5/
Supersedes Cor. No. Page	Dated	**Related** **S.O.P./H.O.P.**

4. After accounts have received a Courtesy Notice, D1 and D2 collection letter, the collection correspondents receive computerized copies of D5 forms for review before notifying customer of intent to place account for 3rd party collection. Earlier notices are mailed immediately without referral to the correspondents.

5. Correspondents check D5's for previous correspondence or referral to Branch for sales or service problem, etc.

6. If no prior problem, D5 is mailed and correspondent sends copy to Branch Administrator alerting him that account is in jeopardy of being litigated unless amount past due is paid within 20 days.

7. If no reply or payment within 20 days, the correspondent takes the following action:
   a. *Machine sale, Coupon book or balance over $300-*
      1. Telephones account to request payment or to determine reason for non-payment.
      2. If problem exists involving branch, follows Step (8a) below.
      3. If collection problem apparent and payment commitment cannot be obtained, customer is notified that account is being placed for collection.
      4. Submits commission charge back (S/C Branch Manager) copies of invoice, statement and collection folder to supervisor for review and placement with collection agency.
      5. Account is transferred to Doubtful trial balance.

   b. *Balances under $300-*Correspondent obtains copies of the following data and submits to supervisor for review and 3rd party collection placement.
      1. Customer invoices
      2. Customer statement
      3. D5 collection notice
      4. Commission charge back
      5. Account transferred to Doubtful trial balance.

   c. *Balances under $25.00-*Collection supervisor reviews accounts under $25.00 to determine whether to place for collection or to charge to Sales Allowance immediately.

8. Sales Disputes, Cancellations, Service Problems, *Pricing Disputes, Allowances, Lease Conversions, etc.*
   When problems of this nature arise, as a result of replies to dunning notices or telephone

Date Prepared: 5/5/
HOP Correction No. 168

HOP C-46

(continued)

Exhibit 3-3. *(continued)*

STANDARD OPERATING PROCEDURE			
Subject:			**Number**
			HOP C-46
			Page **of**
	COLLECTION PROCEDURES - HOME OFFICE		3 4
			Effective
			Date 5/5/
Supersedes Cor. No. **Page**		**Dated**	**Related**
			S.O.P./H.O.P.

discussions, the branch is notified immediately by memo from or by use of D8 form (Intent to Charge Back). The Branch Administrator or salesperson must correct the problem within 20 days and advise the correspondent in writing what action has been taken. In the event that no reply or payment is received within the 20 day period, the following steps are taken:

    a. Commission charge back initiated and forwarded to Branch Administrator and Branch Manager.

    b. Branch Manager notified of problem with request to investigate and notify correspondent within 10 days.

    c. If no reply or payment as indicated in Step B above, memo is sent to Zone Administrator with copies to either the District Manager or Zone General Manager for reply within 10 days.

    d. If no reply or payment, as indicated in Step C above, the problem and collection folder is submitted to the Collection Supervisor for further action.

    e. Manager Credit/Collections will be responsible for review of uncollected and unresolved sales problems with Vice President/Marketing.

Note: Copies of all credit adjustment correspondence will be forwarded to Branch Credit Department, if a return or billing adjustment is involved.

9.   After accounts have progressed through complete dunning cycle (C/N, D1, D2, D5) or have matured beyond 60 days past due on special term codes, the names, account numbers and balances are itemized on the dun master list. Copies are provided for correspondents and branch administrators.

Correspondents utilize the list in conjunction with their collection folders to:

    a. Check to make certain that each account has received collection activity.

    b. Follow-up on D5 and D8 forms to charge back commission and/or refer account for third party collection.

    c. Up-date collection activity on special terms (Activity Codes F-P-N-T) as detailed in Step 3 above.

10.   Branch Administrators use the dun list as a ready reference to accounts which are on credit hold.

11.   If details of the dun list balance require examination, the B/A should refer to copy of the customer's statement of account for clarification.

Date Prepared: 5/5/
HOP Correction No. 168

                                              HOP C-46

STANDARD OPERATING PROCEDURE		
Subject: COLLECTION PROCEDURE - HOME OFFICE	Number HOP C-46	
	Page of 4 4	
	Effective Date 5/5/	
Supersedes Cor. No. Page Dated	Related S.O.P./H.O.P	

12. Under the procedures as outlined above, all past due accounts should be referred to 3rd party collection and commissions charged back within 91 to 120 days past due. Sales problems and disputes should be referred by Manager Credit/Collection to Vice President/Marketing within 151 days past due.

13. *Area Collection*-Dunning cycles proceed as outlined above. Copies of D5's and dun master lists are mailed to Regional offices and collections proceed in the manner prescribed. Third party action and sales problems are referred to the Area Credit Manager for decision and further action.

INQUIRIES: Manager Credit/Collection Department
DISTRIBUTION: List 11.0 HOP Manual Holders

Date Prepared: 5/5/
HOP Correction No. 168

HOP C-46

(*text continued from page 95*)

with each company, but the important point is to adhere to a fast policy. *Do not permit accounts to be months old without legal action.* If your collection activity is slipshod, your accounts will work you to the end. You will, effectively, be financing them.

5. Delinquencies are not always a simple past due matter. Sometimes the company is at fault, and all sources must be researched to resolve any problems for which it is responsible. This requires field support.

6. The field office is alerted to the possibility of legal action. This means a salesperson's commission chargeback and a possible lost account.

7. At this time, telephone contact is made with the delinquent customer, commissions are charged back, and third-party collection action is commenced. The account is now considered "doubtful."

Exhibit 3-4.   Collections phone call activity.

CREDIT & COLLECTIONS DEPARTMENT

				5/16
NAME				WEEK ENDED

ACTION	INDIVIDUAL TOTAL			DEPARTMENT TOTAL
	D.P.	C.L.	D.C.	
Calls made	27	40	50	117
	4	33	21	58
Letter sent				
Orders — credit approved	_____	_____	_____	_____
	2 days	4 days	5 days	

Helpful Hint: Monitor the phone calling of your collection people. Exhibit 3-4 is a **weekly tally sheet showing the number of collection phone calls made and letters sent**. This can be compared to preset standards. Exhibit 3-5 is a **weekly tally sheet on disputes** (which usually are disclosed as a result of collection calls). Disputes result in uncollected accounts.

8. The field is involved in special problems as a result of the dunning procedure.
9. A dun master list is used to control all accounts that are now doubtful.
10. Field offices receive copies of the dun master list.
11. The field may cross-reference the dun master list to the detailed statement of account.
12. The entire cycle consumes about 120 days. Disputes are jointly resolved by a high marketing manager and the credit manager.

Exhibit 3-5.   Disputes activity.

TO: D.G., E.B., L.P.
FROM: Lauren B.

CUSTOMER SERVICE DEPARTMENT

Week Ended _____ 5/16 _____

Beginning number of open disputes	0
Plus new disputes received	75
Less disputes resolved	12
Ending number of open disputes	63
Number of credit memos issued	9

13. In some geographical areas, regional credit offices are established. This allows for closer contact with the field office and the customer. These area offices report to the home office credit manager, in keeping with the divided responsibility concept.

Collection Tip: Speed up collections using preauthorized debits. If amounts are small and tend to be the same each month, customers should readily approve withdrawals directly from their checking account.

See Chapter 18 for methods to improve cash flow through improved systems for receivables, in the section titled Accounts Receivable to Speed Collections and Cash Flow.

Special Arrangements for Credit

Any credit-granting procedure should possess the attribute of flexibility. There are always special types of accounts, special terms, special problems. Page 9 of Exhibit 3-1, order acceptance procedures, provides for this, in that larger orders receive special attention in paragraph 4. Similarly, paragraph 5 provides for exception control over special terms. Special arrangements for credit may be categorized as follows:

Dealer or Exception Accounts

These are accounts that are in a special category or above a specified credit limit. These are handled by exception. It is necessary to review every order against the credit limit and to know the status of the open account aging, instantly. Normally, computer processing does not permit this instant capability, because of the processing time and delaying editing routines. Moreover, most computer routines monitor and update billings, rather than open orders that may be in process. If your computer system does not possess instant review capability (usually available only with sophisticated online order-entry systems), here is a simple manual control monitoring system:

1. Process all orders and payments through a special accounts (SA) desk, where they are initialed before being passed on to normal order processing and cash application desks.
2. Special accounts desk receives a biweekly or semimonthly aged trial balance. Thus, if any checks or orders in 1 above bypass SA, they will appear on the next trial balance within two weeks.
3. SA desk pencil-posts each check and order to the aged trial balance (these are larger accounts, and there is usually only one check a month and one or two orders) and visually sights the adjusted balance, giving effect to unposted checks and unshipped orders. A credit decision may now be made.
4. On receipt of the biweekly aging, SA desk examines pencil nota-

tions on the old aging and carries forward any notations that have not yet been billed or posted.

5. Orders in excess of established credit limits are referred to the credit manager for review and, if more than a temporary increase in credit limit, to the treasurer for formal increase in the credit line.

Helpful Hint: Larger credit limits may be set, and increased sales obtained from special accounts, if these credit devices are considered:

- Financing statement filings (UCC-1s) covering liens on inventory and accounts receivable, and security agreements, to define conditions of default.
- Personal guarantees.
- Subordination agreements covering officer or stockholder loans.
- Signed statements of personal net worth (fraudulent statements may permit criminal action, if desired).
- Cross-corporate guarantees for parents of subsidiaries or corporations with interlocking directorates.
- Securities held in escrow with blank signed stock powers, to cover the corporation's stock or personally owned securities.
- Second mortgages on property. While these will not normally be foreclosed, in a bankruptcy you will be paid out of any remaining value in the property, instead of standing unsecured.
- Notes receivable to cover long past due items. This ensures automatic monthly payment without chasing the account. It also prevents claims against defective merchandise if collection ensues.
- Conditional sale instruments to keep title from passing until paid. Product may, thus, be repossessed, limiting your loss.

Leasing

As described in Chapter 2, page 57, this is a corporate borrowing technique. The corporation may also use it as a marketing or credit-granting device, with the same advantages accruing to the lessee. Independent leasing companies will carry the customer for periods ranging from 12 to 60 months, usually on full payout leases, for almost any kind of machinery, equipment, or product that is not immediately consumed. Your sales representative makes a normal sale and also obtains the customer's signature on the lease, and these advantages result:

1. You invoice the leasing company and take full accounting treatment for a sale.
2. The customer receives terms of payment, up to 60 months.
3. The cost of carrying the account over the extended time period is borne by the customer. This cost is expressed as an add-on interest rate. As a rule of thumb, simple interest rates are slightly less than double the add-on rate. For example, 6% add-on is less than 12% simple yield. Leasing yields for full payout leases generally run from 12% to 18% for 60-month leases. Shorter-term leases carry higher yields, as much as 30%, to cover the cost of processing the lease for a short period.
4. The monthly customer's payment is expressed as a specific dollar amount of rental. The customer does not usually consider the interest rate, only the dollar rental amount.
5. There may be a residual value or purchase option, say 10%, at the end of the lease. The customer would have to pay this 10% to take title. This residual value can belong to the corporation, rather than the leasing company, resulting in a hidden profit at the end of the lease. The amount of the residual depends on market conditions and the utility of the equipment, as well as its useful life.
6. The customer is not required to put up front money to purchase this asset. This makes for an easier sale.
7. The corporation can often receive a broker's commission from the leasing company for carrying its lease forms, again resulting in additional hidden profit for the company.
8. The leasing company is independent of the corporation, which makes collection easier. The company cannot also take the same tough posture in collection that the independent finance company takes.
9. Not all of your customers will request that the leasing company

pass through any available investment tax credit. Where this is not passed through, the leasing company obtains a tax benefit. You can negotiate a rebate on this—again more hidden profits.

10. The leasing company, being in the finance business, is better able to weather tight money times and may be able to "commit" itself to keeping a supply of leasing money available for your customers. Thus, if you were funding your own time-financing program, money availability might dry up more quickly than under a leasing company commitment.

Beware This Pitfall: Many states charge a use tax on the amount of monthly rentals, rather than a one-shot tax on the sale price of the equipment. Be sure you do not invoice and collect the sales tax from the leasing company in such states. Bill your equipment without such tax. The lessor will collect the use tax from the lessee and remit it to the taxing authority. Any national lessor can supply a list of the required states.

Revolving Inventory Plans

These are a form of floor-planning devices used to aid your customer, usually a dealer or distributor, in carrying your inventory. These plans may be administered through an independent leasing company, by a captive finance subsidiary (as described in Chapter 2, page 62), or directly by the company. The features of such a plan are:

1. The customer is permitted to pay over a period of months, usually 12 to 36 months.
2. The customer signs and a financing statement is filed (UCC-1) to protect the company's title to the equipment.
3. Rates paid by the customer are based on add-on rates and yields for the period financed.
4. A lease or conditional sale document is signed by the customer, further protecting your title.

5. Payments are made monthly until the equipment is sold. At the time of sale, the lease may be paid off and discontinued (nonrevolving plan), or a new piece of equipment may be shipped to the distributor, serial numbers substituted on the old lease, and monthly payments continued (revolving plan).

6. If the dealer sells the equipment under a lease to a consumer, the dealer merely sends in the lease and receives a check for the difference between the cost of the equipment and the price for which it was sold under the lease.

7. The customer should be audited two to three times per year to ascertain the location of the equipment. It should be in inventory. If it is not, the dealer is given 10 days to pay for it. Repeated inventory sales without payment should result in dropping the dealer from the program.

8. These are full payout purchases by your dealer, not subject to the return of equipment. Accordingly, the dealer is responsible for all local sales and use taxes, insurance, and the condition of the equipment.

Avoid This Pitfall: These are full payout leases, and the dealer should really capitalize these leases and treat them as balance-sheet assets and liabilities. In most cases, however, dealers use these as off-balance-sheet items. They do not appear. In analyzing a dealer's credit, remember to check on floor-planning commitments. Liabilities may be drastically understated.

Recourse and Buyback Commitments

These cover the gamut of selling and credit-granting plans in which the customer, again usually a dealer or distributor, has the right, or a limited right, to put back merchandise to you, the seller. These plans may include the following:

1. *Agency sales.* These are made to an individual who acts as your agent in reselling your product. They may not be accounted for as sales until the products are sold to the ultimate consumer.

2. *Consignment sales.* These are almost exactly the same as agency sales. They usually carry a memorandum invoice and are not booked as a sale until the consignee reports monthly that they have been sold.

3. *Buyback commitments.* These cover sales wherein the buyer is given an unadulterated right of return if a third-party sale does not result. Jewelry and seasonal products are usually sold to department stores this way. Variants on this device may prove useful as sales tools and may permit accounting treatment as a sale, provided a satisfactory estimate of returns can be made and a reserve established against such returns.

In one variation, the amount of the buyback commitment is drastically reduced after day one, and remains the same for six months. It then reduces straight-line to zero over months 7 through 18. This permits the company to take 1/3 (6/18) sale and income treatment immediately, and the balance over the last 12 months, under the most conservative treatment. Given a proper experience factor, the entire amount may be booked subject to a suitable reserve being established for returns. This type of variation on the **buyback commitment** is shown in Exhibit 3-6. Note that further protection is provided for the company in that equipment must be returned on a first-in, first-out basis.

The accounting for sales with recourse and buyback commitments is prescribed in FASB SFAS 48, Revenue Recognition When Right of Return Exists. This provides that where the sale has been completed, the buyer is obligated to pay, the payment obligation would not be mitigated by theft or destruction of the product, the buyer has economic substance, and the seller has no remaining significant obligations for future performance, revenue from the transaction is recognized as a sale at the time of sale. Any costs or losses that may be estimated as a result of the recourse arrangement will then be accounted for in accordance with SFAS 5, Accounting for Contingencies. (If the loss were probable and measurable, it would be charged to current earnings—i.e., a provision for bad debts and a credit to an allowance for doubtful accounts.)

Current Literature: The latest AICPA literature on this subject was released in 1999 in a publication entitled Audit Issues in Revenue Recognition.

Exhibit 3-6.   Buyback agreement.

BUYBACK AGREEMENT

AGREEMENT between Albert Corporation, a New York corporation ("ABC") and ("Dealer").

WHEREAS, Dealer is a dealer for the sale of   ABC's #900   Equipment ("Equipment") and is desirous of purchasing Equipment from time to time from ABC on the understanding that ABC is willing to repurchase Equipment from Dealer; and

WHEREAS, ABC is willing to repurchase Equipment from Dealer upon the terms and conditions hereinafter set forth,

THEREFORE, the parties hereto do hereby agree as follows:

1.   The terms and conditions of this Agreement shall relate only to units of Equipment purchased by Dealer from ABC at a cost of Two Thousand Five Hundred and Forty Five Dollars ($2,545) per unit of Equipment.

2.   Subject to the terms and conditions hereof, ABC shall repurchase units of Equipment from Dealer at the following prices during the following periods from the date of delivery of the Equipment to the Dealer:

Period	Amount	Period	Amount	Period	Amount
1 month	$1,636	7 months	$1,463	13 months	$ 665
2 months	1,628	8 months	1,330	14 months	532
3 months	1,620	9 months	1,197	15 months	399
4 months	1,612	10 months	1,064	16 months	266
5 months	1,604	11 months	931	17 months	133
6 months	1,596	12 months	798	18 months	- 0 -

In determining the number of months (a) fractional months shall be treated as whole months and (b) Equipment shall be repurchased on a "first-in, first-out" basis (i.e., the computation shall be made with respect to the oldest units of Equipment purchased by Dealer and not sold by Dealer, regardless of serial number). The computations shall be based upon the period commencing on the date the Equipment is received by Dealer and terminating on the date the Equipment is received by ABC. Units sold by Dealer shall be determined by serial number.

3.   (a) ABC's obligations to repurchase Equipment shall apply only if ninety (90) days have elapsed from the last order for Equipment placed by Dealer with ABC.

(b) If Dealer delivers the Equipment to ABC during the ninety (90) day period described in paragraph 3(a), ABC shall not be required to make such payment until the expiration of sixty (60) days from the date of the last delivery of Equipment from ABC to Dealer. If Dealer orders Equipment during such sixty (60) day period, ABC shall, at its election, deliver to Dealer either the unit of Equipment returned by Dealer or new Equipment, at no additional charge to Dealer.

(c) If Dealer orders Equipment from ABC within thirty (30) days from the date of ABC's payment to Dealer pursuant to paragraph 4(b), Dealer shall refund to ABC in full the amount paid by ABC hereunder, and ABC shall, at its election, deliver to Dealer either the unit of Equipment returned by Dealer or new Equipment, at no additional charge to Dealer.

(d) This Agreement shall not apply to any units of Equipment delivered to Dealer pursuant to Paragraphs 3(b) or 3(c), unless Dealer pays the full purchase price described in paragraph 1 with respect to such Equipment.

4.   (a) The provisions of this Agreement shall not apply unless Dealer has fully paid for each unit of Equipment which has been delivered by ABC to Dealer.

(b) If Dealer is in excess of 30 days past due in payment of other accounts to ABC, ABC may, at its election, apply the payments due to Dealer hereunder toward payment of such accounts, in which event Dealer shall pay the full purchase price with respect to units of Equipment ordered pursuant to paragraphs 3(b) and (c).

(c) If **ABC** receives Equipment from Dealer during a period when paragraph 4(a) is applicable, the Equipment shall, for purposes of paragraph 2, be deemed to have been received on the day next following receipt by **ABC** of payment of the amount owed by Dealer with respect to all Equipment received by Dealer.

5. **ABC** shall have no obligation to repurchase any Equipment which has been sold by Dealer. As used in this Agreement, a sale includes, but is not limited to, any sale on open account, conditional sale, installment sale, sale subject to a security agreement, or lease defined as a sale in accordance with Paragraph 4 of Opinion No. 27 of the Accounting Principles Board entitled "Accounting for Lease Transactions by Manufacturer or Dealer Lessors," a copy of which is attached hereto. Any questions concerning the applicability of these provisions should be directed to **ABC Corporation - Main Street - NYC, NY. Att, Vice President/Controller.**

6. Dealer hereby grants **ABC** the right to audit Dealer's records as to serial numbers, names of customers, location of machines and related information during normal business hours on at least 24 hours written notice.

7. **ABC** shall not be required to repurchase any Equipment which is not in the same condition in which it was delivered to Dealer, ordinary wear and tear excepted.

8. This Agreement may be terminated or the terms and conditions hereof, including, but not limited to, repurchase prices and periods, may be cancelled, modified or amended by **ABC** at any time, on notice to Dealer; provided, however, that no such termination or modification shall affect Dealer's rights hereunder with respect to Equipment purchased by Dealer.

IN WITNESS WHEREOF, the parties hereto have duly executed this Agreement.

Albert CORPORATION

Date:_____ By_____

Date:_____ By_____

(Z-2-56) 19-053-1M-1

(*text continued from page 107*)

The buyback commitment has these advantages:

✧ It is easier to convince the dealer to buy the product.

✧ The dealer can obtain bank financing more readily, as your buyback commitment is substituted for the dealer's credit.

✧ As a practical matter, if the arrangement is monitored properly, very few items are returned.

✧ The cost to the dealer of this plan is based on low bank rates, rather than the higher leasing company rates found in other time-payment plans.

4. *Recourse.* This is a device the company may use with leasing companies or financing institutions to encourage them to extend credit to the company's customers, usually dealers.

If the dealer does not pay, the company is on recourse and must pay. The lender, thus, has the protection of both you and your customer. As with buyback commitments, such transactions may not be booked as sales unless a reserve is established against potential returns. Experience may indicate that bad debts and returns under recourse arrangements are no worse than under normal sales without recourse. In this case, a full sale results, with a usual small charge to the bad debt provision and increase in the allowance for doubtful accounts.

The accounting for recording sales when receivables are transferred with recourse is based on FASB SFAS 77, Reporting by Transferors for Transfers of Receivables with Recourse. This provides that the transferor must give up control of all future economic benefits, must be able to reasonably estimate future collections, and may not be required to repurchase the receivables except pursuant to the recourse provisions (usually collectibility only). When all these conditions are met, the transfer of receivables with recourse shall be recognized as a sale. (See the discussion of off-balance-sheet financing.)

Captive Finance Subsidiary

This has been discussed in Chapter 2, page 62, as a borrowing technique, and should be reviewed in the context of a credit-granting device. Credit is, after all, totally dependent on the company's ability to borrow.

The captive finance subsidiary serves the same purpose as the independent leasing company described in the leasing section on page 103, above, with all the advantages set forth on page 62. However, with regard to the comparison between an independent leasing company and a subsidiary, the captive can offer these decided advantages:

1. The company is responsible for its own financial destiny and has the responsibility to supply its own funds to support a time-financing lease program. It is not subject to the outside pressures occasioned by an independent leasing company, which

may be unsuccessful in obtaining funds or may have other priority commitments.

2. The subsidiary can obtain better leverage on its debt-to-equity borrowing formula than the parent. This should result in a lower cost of money and either lower rates for the customer or more profit for the subsidiary.

3. The captive may utilize operating lease accounting for tax purposes, availing itself of depreciation benefits and obtaining cash flow benefits. These benefits accrue to the parent in a consolidated tax return, rather than to the independent leasing company.

4. The captive will use finance lease accounting for financial statement purposes, creating faster income in the earlier years, and producing more income for the parent when consolidating with the subsidiary.

5. The captive obtains the use of any available investment tax credit on purchases from the parent, albeit at the parent's cost, not the selling price. The ITC is lost on the sale to an independent lessor, unless a separate rebate is negotiated. Even then, the rebate becomes taxable, whereas the ITC is an "after-tax" item, a direct reduction in taxes. You would have to negotiate one and two-thirds the benefit, assuming a 40% tax rate, to obtain the same benefit as the ITC.

Special Terms of Sale

These may be granted to customers at no real cost to the company. They may sometimes be dressed as attractive marketing programs, giving the sales representative an opportunity to ease the customer into the sale. For example, a company that customarily sells on net 30-day terms may offer:

1. $\frac{1}{3}$ cash down, $\frac{1}{3}$ in 30 days, $\frac{1}{3}$ in 60 days
2. $\frac{1}{2}$ cash down, $\frac{1}{2}$ in 60 days
3. $\frac{1}{2}$ cash down, $\frac{1}{4}$ in 30 days, $\frac{1}{4}$ in 60 days

In the first two cases, you will average 30 days; in the third case, slightly better. The customer may very well view these as an improvement over net 30-day terms and certainly ought to have the option, at no cost to the company.

> *Be Careful of This:* If you customarily report agings on a 30-day basis, these accounts will flip over into past due columns, subject to routine dunning. There is nothing that aggravates a customer more than being dunned when the account isn't past due. Special activity codes are required to permit proper computer or manual aging for such terms. For example, if your system is a manual one, you could provide for the letter A to be posted to the customer's statement, signifying 60-day terms. When aging, any invoice marked A would be aged by a date plus 30.

Similarly, you may want to offer a discount for payment within 10 days (see page 20 for a discussion of the cost and disadvantages of cash discounts). Or you may have two different discount programs, say 2%/10 days and 1%/20 days. Further, your discount may apply only to certain products, not your entire line, and, in fact, your usual terms of sale may vary from product to product or line to line. All of these situations dictate the establishment of a special activity code, thereby flagging the special terms, and allowing the computer or manual system the opportunity to properly monitor the taking of improper discounts or any special aging requirements.

> *Word of Caution:* All special credit terms must conform to published policies and be processed through the special accounts desk as described on page 102.

INTERNAL CONTROL (FRAUD AND ASSET PROTECTION)

The essence of internal control in an accounts receivable operation is found in the following areas:

1. *Order entry.* A separate order department records the receipt of a properly credit-approved order. A fraudulent receivable (as might be used in a lapping fraud) cannot be created without a properly approved order.

2. *Billing.* A separate department (separate from credit or collection), which may be part of order entry, records the invoice. Each shipment must be assigned a sequential number by shipping personnel. This number becomes the bill of lading number as well as the invoice number. Each number must be accounted for monthly. Unaccounted-for numbers are carried forward as outstanding to next month.

The combination of order entry and sequential billing control avoids fraud by:

    a. Ensuring that every shipment is billed. No product goes out the back door without being billed.

    b. Avoiding the setting up of a fraudulent receivable. Strangely enough, if some companies are invoiced, they will pay those invoices. Checks can be received, pocketed, and later cashed, and then the fraudulent invoice can be credited out.

3. *Credit adjustment control.* The function of issuing credit to customers should be kept separate from the accounts receivable function. It may be part of the billing department, but it is entirely separate from the credit, collection, and cash application operations. Standards for the issuance of credits should be established to include:

    a. Authorized higher approvals are needed for allowances.

    b. Authenticated, sequentially controlled receiving reports support merchandise returns. These are issued only by receiving departments in warehouse locations.

    c. Limited write-off authority, say up to $100, may be given to the collection department, as an exception to the above rules. This will allow for minor, on-the-spot adjustments. It will create customer good will and provide for faster collection of receivables when minor disputes and problems exist.

These standards assure that billed items will be collected and will not be credited illegally. The system can be broken only through collusion on the part of two or more persons and two or more departments.

4. *Application of cash receipts.* The function of applying cash as a reduction to the customer's account receivable is a function normally handled within the accounting section. If it is handled as a part of the credit and collection department, there must be a division of responsibility from the collection section. A **basic cash application procedure** is set forth in Exhibit 3-7, the numbers below conforming to those in the procedure:

1. The mail room merely slits envelopes, without removing checks or contents. This is done to avoid unauthorized handling of checks and to avoid separation of checks from remittance advices.

2. In this procedure, with cash being applied in a separate accounts receivable department, the checks are initially taped in the accounting department to gain control of them.

3. Checks are then photocopied in the cash application section of the accounts receivable section. This is done to enable the actual checks to be deposited and postings to be made from the copies.

4. Checks are now machine-endorsed and meter-counted to tie in to the number of check copies made, the number of checks taped by the accounting department, and the number on the meter. This ensures that no checks are lost. Checks are hand delivered to the accounting department for deposit, and the checks are deposited before the close of bank on the same day.

5. Cash is now posted from check copies.

6. Special cash application procedures are delineated in this section, with particular attention being paid to on-account or un-applied cash, in a–c. Special transaction codes are used in d for analysis work (such as, is discount taken, is it paid in full, which product line is paid?). Sections e and f ensure that all payments will be identified promptly. Section g provides for on-the-spot minor adjustments for allowances, and section h provides for approvals for allowances of greater amounts. All totals are carefully controlled in i through m to tie in the amount of the checks and the adjustment to the accounts receivable records. A careful, daily filing system is established in n, for the purpose of rechecking on errors. Retention of these records can be

(text continues on page 117)

Exhibit 3-7. Application of cash receipts.

HOME OFFICE		
STANDARD OPERATING PROCEDURE		
Subject:		**Number** C-30
		Page of 1 3
APPLICATION OF CASH RECEIPTS		**Effective** **Date** 9/1/
Supersedes Cor. No. 6 Page C-30	Dated 1/3/	**Related** **S.O.P./H.O.P**

PURPOSE OF PROCEDURE: To establish and maintain accurate internal control over cash receipts and deposits; to deposit cash on same day as receipt.

METHOD:

1. *Mail Room*—will open envelopes:

   a) Do not remove contents
   b) Hand carry to Accounting Department

2. *Accounting Department*—will:

   a) Tape net cash receipts and count checks
   b) Staple all papers accompanying checks to the checks and discard envelopes
   c) Pass checks and attachments to Accounts Receivable Department

3. *Accounts Receivable Department*—will:

   a) Savicopy checks
   b) Document accompanying information
   c) Sort Savicopies by district

4. *Accounts Receivable Department*—will:

   a) Endorse checks
   b) Prove out the numerical count in the endorsing meter, the number of Savicopies and the original count by the Accounting Department
   c) Not withhold any check from the daily deposit unless it is legally imperfect
   d) Hand carry checks to the Accounting Department for immediate deposit

5. *Accounts Receivable Department*—will utilize Savicopies of checks and customer remittance advices to:

   a) Apply cash to the Accounts Receivable turnaround forms
   b) Key off the trial balance

6. *Accounts Receivable Clerks*—will adhere to the following standard procedures:

Correction 27
Page 1 of 3

C-30

(continued)

Exhibit 3-7. (continued)

HOME OFFICE		
STANDARD OPERATING PROCEDURE		
Subject: APPLICATION OF CASH RECEIPTS	**Number** C-30	
	Page of 2 3	
	Effective Date 9/1/	
Supersedes Cor. No. 6 Page C-30	**Dated 1/3/**	**Related S.O.P./H.O.P.**

a) A remittance advice is to be made for every check, recording full details of the application, and a copy of this remittance advice given to the Data Processing Department when applying an "on-account" or "unapplied" remittance.

b) "Unapplied payments" are to be credited against the oldest open aging column on the trial balance:

    1-A form letter should be sent to customer advising of application.

    2-Do not reduce original accounts receivable card. Instead, use the same invoice number, but apply as a credit, and show both original invoice and on-account payment on trial balance.

    3-Show date paid, not original invoice date, on remittance advice.

c) Computer transaction codes are to be used at all times.

d) All checks are to be qualified at once and any adjustments made immediately. Only where this is impossible will the check be placed in "suspense" account, each deposit therein to carry an individual account number.

e) The standard letter of "information and/or inquiry" is to be sent to the payor when there is any question as to correct application of the check.

f) The amount of the check (and any general ledger adjustment under $25) is to be entered in the space provided on the turnaround document.

g) Any journal entry of $25 or over must be approved by the Credit Department Manager and countersigned by the Assistant Controller and must be written up on a special journal entry form.

h) The net total of all checks is to be taped (by district) from Savicopies.

i) A net total of the credit to Accounts Receivable as reflected by turnaround forms is taped by district. The total net cash tape (i) must balance with the turnaround form credits to Accounts Receivable, less general ledger adjustments.

j) The final cumulative tape total of the net cash deposit (all districts) must reconcile with the original Accounting Department tape and with the Data Processing daily net cash run.

Correction 27
Page 2 of 3

HOME OFFICE		
STANDARD OPERATING PROCEDURE		
Subject: APPLICATION OF CASH RECEIPTS	**Number** C-30	
	Page　　**of** 3　　　3	
	Effective **Date**　9/1/	
Supersedes Cor. No. 6　　　Page C-30	Dated 1/3/	**Related** **S.O.P./H.O.P.**

l) The miscellaneous general ledger adjustment total is reflected on the IBM run in the general ledger column of the Daily Cash Receipts Report (See i and j).

m) Turnaround Forms, together with the appropriate remittance advices, are transmitted to the Data Processing Department, upon completion of each individual day's application.

n) All *customer remittance advices* are filed daily with the check Savicopies. The Accounts Receivable Department *remittance advice books* are maintained by district in chronological sequence.

Correction 17
Page 3 of 3
Date Prepared: 9/28/

C-30

(*text continued from page 114*)

established in accordance with each company's need, but two years is the normal retention period. Most collection actions have been completed or are well on the way by the end of two years.

Avoid the Following Pitfall: Files of check copies and remittance advices are very voluminous and the documents must be filed carefully, with plenty of room for retrieval and expansion. Avoid unauthorized entry into this file. If you don't, you'll attempt retrieval at a critical time and won't be able to locate the needed check copy. These files may be maintained in the cash application section, rather than the main file department.

Try This Helpful Procedure: Support the write-off of allowances in item 7 on page 125, below, and larger adjustments in item 8 on page 128, with rigid rules concerning when items should be written off, credited, or charged to the allowance for doubtful accounts. Minor allowances do not usually provide for reductions in gross product-line sales. Consequently, analyses of net sales can be fuzzed up by such allowances. Moreover, a separate procedure is needed to prevent the issuance of credits covering accounts in "doubtful," as these do not appear as bad-debt write-offs that are used to calculate the accounting provision for bad debts. The following write-off and credit memo policy could be adopted:

1. Write-offs up to $100 may be authorized by cash application personnel, without other approvals, as a charge to Sales Returns and Allowances.
2. Write-offs from $100 to $300 will require the approval of the assistant manager of the department (either credit and collection or accounting, depending on where the basic responsibility lies). Such write-offs will require separate product-line analysis by dollars and units, through credit memo issuance.
3. Write-offs of $300 and up need the appropriate department head's approval, and credit memos must be issued.
4. Write-offs of accounts in "doubtful" (that is, having been placed for collection with legal or third-party collection agencies) may not be handled through the issuance of a credit memo. These will be journal-entried as a charge to the allowance for doubtful accounts.
5. Annual write-offs of doubtful accounts should be made, as in (3) above, based on a review of collection activity. Such write-offs, if still alive as to collection, may be transferred to a suspense ledger where they may be controlled for continued collection, though completely written off. This annual write-off should be compared to the aggregate bad debt losses taken for tax purposes.

Tax Note: The use of an accounting Provision for Bad Debts and the offsetting Allowance for Doubtful Accounts is based on generally accepted accounting principles. For tax purposes, accounts are charged off in the year they become worthless. This is called the direct charge-off method, as opposed to the reserve method used by accountants. This will require setting up a deferred tax account for any differences between the two methods. Additional note: 75% of any book income in excess of tax income that results from using the reserve method will enter into the alternative minimum tax calculation. This is the adjusted current earnings (ACE) adjustment, for tax purposes.

ESSENTIAL REPORTS TO MONITOR PERFORMANCE

The treasurer's performance is measured by his or her success in collecting receivables—hence, turnover of receivables to sales and bad debt write-offs. The controller requires reports on total receivables to verify asset balances, and he or she reports operating results pertaining to amounts of receivables, collections, credits, past due accounts, and bad debt reserves. Essential reports prepared by the controller, for his or her own use and that of the treasurer and the credit and collection manager, are the following:

1. **Aged trial balance** (Exhibit 3-8). This is used by collection personnel as a collection aid, by credit personnel to approve credits on reorders, and by accounting personnel to prove out totals of sales, cash, and receivables and to estimate appropriate provisions for bad debts.

2. **Aged trial balance summary** (Exhibit 3-9). This is used by the treasurer and the credit and collection manager to monitor changes in the trends of past due receivables. These columns are easily adapted to graphs to present a visual picture of the trend lines. The detailed report in Exhibit 3-8 is summarized and posted to this report monthly, to present a continuing progress report on the changing ages of receivables.

3. **Sales to cash analysis** (Exhibit 3-10). This report is used by the treasurer and the collection manager as a summary report to show overall collections related to overall sales. This report is for a company with a normal 60-day collection period. Columns 2 and 3 show monthly sales and cash collections, respectively. Column 4 represents three

(*text continues on page 123*)

Exhibit 3-8. Aged trial balance.

DATE OF RUN 10/01/	A / R A G E D T R I A L B A L A N C E R E P O R T BILLING THRU 08/31/ PAYMENT THRU 08/31/					SUMMARY PAGE
	CURRENT	1 TO 30	31 TO 60	61 TO 90	91 OVER	T O T A L
REGULAR RETAIL	2723894.66 **	1267720.32 **	612947.91 **	283918.42 **	1016518.82 **	5905000.13 **
REGULAR DEALER	1061960.00 **	1098907.08 **	346667.05 **	222320.34 **	872215.47 **	3602069.94 **
DOUBTFUL RETAIL	34825.02 **	26927.87 **	15948.82 **	10732.23 **	695770.80 **	784204.74 **
DOUBTFUL DEALER	2125.59 **	429.20CR***	571.85 **	13848.91 **	148767.92 **	164885.07 **
REGULAR RETAIL	.00 **	.00 **	.00 **	.00 **	.00 **	.00 **
REGULAR DEALER	.00 **	.00 **	.00 **	.00 **	.00 **	.00 **
DOUBTFUL RETAIL	.00 **	.00 **	.00 **	.00 **	.00 **	.00 **
DOUBTFUL DEALER	.00 **	.00 **	.00 **	.00 **	.00 **	.00 **
T O T A L A / R	3822805.27 ***	2393126.07 ***	976135.63 ***	530819.90 ***	2733273.01 ***	10456159.88 ***

Exhibit 3-9. Aged trial balance summary.

A CORP.
AGED TRIAL BALANCE SUMMARY
($ 000's)

	Month	Current	1–30 days	31–60 days	61 days and over	Total
Retail	Jan 20	3013	2343	685	1425	7466
	Feb	2847	1922	1432	1535	7736
	Mar	2991	1668	1171	1982	7812
	Apr	3959	955	819	2068	7801
	May	3119	1672	460	2093	7344
	Jun	2459	1982	945	1926	7312
	Jul	3404	948	1210	1977	7539
	Aug	2444	2054	456	2117	7071
	Sep	2145	1664	1135	1983	6927
	Oct	2489	1241	818	2076	6624
	Nov	2089	1722	604	1905	6320
	Dec	1732	1471	923	1789	5915
Dealer & Foreign	Jan 20	1106	837	580	1041	3564
	Feb	1012	928	546	1132	3618
	Mar	1290	917	527	1182	3916
	Apr	971	1052	568	1148	3739
	May	1661	941	689	1059	4350
	Jun	1076	1602	694	1233	4605
	Jul	1251	939	1271	1427	4888
	Aug	1263	1067	1015	1807	5152
	Sep	1271	1140	756	1603	4770
	Oct	1802	1205	850	1369	5226
	Nov	1584	1536	908	1469	5497
	Dec	1467	1604	1129	1705	5905
Total	Jan 20	4119	3180	1265	2466	11030
	Feb	3859	2850	1978	2667	11354
	Mar	4281	2585	1698	3164	11728
	Apr	4930	2007	1387	3216	11540

Exhibit 3-10. Sales to cash analysis.

Sales To Cash Analysis
(In thousands of dollars)

HBJ 1/2   Revised 11/18

20	Sales $M	Cash $M	3 Month Composite Sales $M	Cash (60 day lag) $M	Difference $M (4-5)	Cumulative Cash Under (Over) Sales ÷3
Mar	3500					÷3
Apr	4100					
May	2886	3715	10486	10525	(39)	(13)
Jun	2771	3342	9757	10609	(852)	(297)
July	3581	3468	9238	10646	(1408)	(766)
Aug	3727	3799	10079	10917	(838)	(1045)
Sept	3165	2379	10473	10545	(72)	(1069)
Oct	3827	3739	10719	10442	277	(977)
Nov	3911	3427	10903	11199	(296)	(1076)
Dec	4590	3276	12328	11425	903	(775)
20 Jan	4037	4496	12538	11901	637	(563)
Feb	3770	3653	12397	11785	612	(359)
Mar	4440	3752	12247	12649	(402)	(493)
Apr	4290	4380	12500	12437	63	(472)
May	4390	4517	13120	11872	1248	(56)
Jun	3920	3540	12600	11209	1391	408
July	3937	3815	12247	11986	261	495
Aug	3626	3854	11483	12422	(939)	182
Sept	3130	4317	10693	12725	(2032)	(495)
Oct	4798	4251	11554	12093	(539)	(675)
Nov	3821	4157	11749			
Dec		3685				

months of sales, including the current month. Thus, the figure of $11,749 in column 4, line 21, is the sum of column 2, lines 19, 20, and 21, this being September, October, and November sales totals. Column 5 represents three months of cash collections, lagged 60 days. Thus, the figure of $12,093 in column 5, line 20, is the sum of column 3, lines 20, 21, and 22, this being October, November, and December collections.

In this report, the assumption is made that sales, say, in August, September, and October, totaling $11,554 (column 4, line 20), resulted in collections in October, November, and December (a 60-day lag) of $12,093 (column 5, line 20). The difference between these sales and lagged collections is an average in collections of $539 (column 6, line 20), and a cumulative *monthly* cash average collected of $675 (column 7, line 20). Note that the cumulative figures in column 7 are divided by three to obtain monthly figures. Thus, $539 ÷ 3 = $180, which is added to the previous cumulative total of $495 to give $675.

An average in three-month collections indicates that the 60-day turnover is being bettered. Further, at a glance, column 7 indicates whether we are collecting more than we are selling, an indication that our past due collection efforts are bearing fruit.

Try This Helpful Report: It's a one-liner that permits you to monitor performance at a glance, without getting lost in the welter of a mass of figures.

4. **Percentage of 61 plus days old to total A/R** (Exhibit 3-11). This report is used by the treasurer and the collection manager to follow the trend in various agings. The exhibit shows the 61 plus days old accounts. This means accounts that are 61 days past the due date or 91 days from date of invoice (assuming net 30-day terms). The same graph may be used to plot 91 plus days past due and 121 plus past due. The numbers are obtained from the appropriate column of the aged trial balance summary (Exhibit 3-9). High points on the graph may be marked to explain the effects of economic conditions, changes to more liberal credit terms, a systems failure, or ineffectual performance. Low points may indicate more rigid credit terms, introduction of discount terms, effective performance, an improvement in economic conditions, or a change to an improved system.

Exhibit 3-11.   Percentage of 61 plus days old to total A/R.

Percentage of 61 plus days old to total A/R

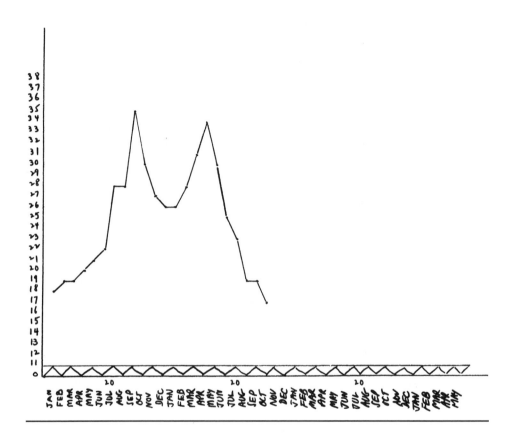

5. **Percentage of 61 plus days old collected** (Exhibit 3-12). Like the previous exhibit, this is used to spot the trends in collections related to accounts that are 61 days past due. Numbers are obtained from a cash receipts report (not illustrated here) showing the aging of cash collections, that is, relating the cash to the age of the invoice to which it applies.

If a computer run is not available to provide this report, it may be obtained using the following calculation and simply refering to the Aged Trial Balance Summary (Exhibit 3-9): Last month's 31 plus past due column would become this month's maximum 61 plus past due amount, if nothing were collected. Compare this result to the actual amount of the 61 plus past due shown in the summary, and the differ-

Exhibit 3-12.   Percentage of 61 plus days old collected retail.

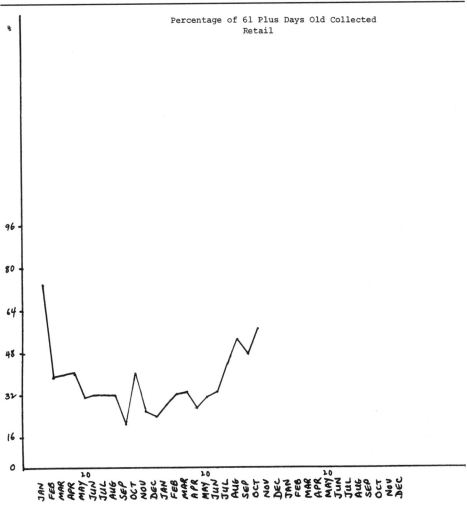

ence is added to or subtracted from last month's 31 plus column to obtain the total amount of 61 plus past dues that were collected.

6. **Monthly analysis of doubtfuls** (Exhibit 3-13). This report is used by the treasurer and the collection manager to monitor the status of doubtful accounts (those in the process of third-party collection action)—amounts collected, percent collected, amount of new doubtfuls, amounts written off to the bad debt reserve.

7. **Doubtful vs. bad debt reserve** (Exhibit 3-14). This report is used by the controller and the treasurer to constantly review and test

Exhibit 3-13. Monthly analysis of doubtfuls.

MONTHLY ANALYSIS DOUBTFULS
RETAIL (COLUMNS 1-6)
(3÷2)

						DEALER
1 MONTH ENDING	2 TOTAL DOUBTFUL	3 TOTAL $ COLLECTED	4 % OF TOTAL $ COLLECTED TO TOTAL DBTFL	5 ADDED TO DOUBTFULS	6 TOTAL DBTFL BAD DEBT WRITE-OFF	7 TOTAL DBTFL BAD DEBT WRITE-OFF
20						
JAN.	605326	14859	2	55229	58427	
FEB.	623669	16949	3	44846	10362	
MARCH	799186	21048	2	73296	39783	
APRIL	928322	40122	4	41165	60020	
MAY	870186	38520	4	62211	28005	-0-
JUNE	760559	84803	11	39223	22376	124377
JULY	787889	26574	3	86424	24251	-0-
AUG.	784205	32303	4	164027	24070	-0-
SEPT.	772707	34481	4	92977	45412	-0-
OCT.	891801	42415	5	72821	40540	-0-
NOV.	873395	35783	4	84222	18251	1791
DEC.	956864	32709	3	70294	36754	-0-
20						
JAN.	988299	41471	2	24930	23947	-0-
FEB.	1 208702	36755	3	87167	13676	2563
MARCH	1 233675	40010	3	99215	20750	-0-
APRIL	1 226240	51647	4	109696	32434	-0-
MAY	1 278912	42310	3	75083	39728	-0-
JUNE	1 256768	51682	4	112843	28400	-0-
JULY	1 335901	51158	4	109859	40046	-0-
AUG.	1 250818	46259	4	82149	55901	-0-
SEPT.	1 290570	37132	3	72322	24436	-0-
OCT.	1 363211	50850	4	157770	26728	-0-
NOV.	1 484200	34099	2	89571	34099	-0-
DEC.						

Exhibit 3-14. Doubtful vs. bad debt reserve.

	Initials	Date
Prepared By		
Approved By		

45-807 EYE-EASE
45-907 20/20 BUFF
NATIONAL Made in U.S.A.

DOUBTFUL VS. BAD DEBT RESERVE
MONTHLY ANALYSIS

Month END	DEALER Doubtful	Retail Doubtful	Total Doubtful		BAD DEBT RESERVE	
APRIL	446820	1005560	1 452380		1 753695	
MAY	454096	926234	1 380330		1 784086	
JUNE	433819	866776	1 300595		1 085093	
JULY	425775	845450	1 271225		1 795379	
AUGUST	421530	815730	1 237260		1 827417	
SEPT.	428486	734434	1 162920		1 819818	
OCTOBER	412900	700332	1 113232		1 821707	
NOVEMBER	404138	723307	1 127445			
DECEMBER						

the amount of the reserve (allowance for bad debts) against the total of receivables that may ultimately be charged to that reserve.

Avoid This Pitfall: The company's independent accountants may require an addition to the reserve to cover nondoubtful accounts, on the expectation, based on experience, that some of these accounts will become doubtful. The monthly bad debt provision should provide for this, if necessary.

8. **Schedule of bad debt reserve—annual** (Exhibit 3-15). This is used as an adjunct to the previous exhibit, showing the annual increase in the reserve (the provision in column 3), the decrease in the reserve due to write-offs, and the balance in the reserve (column 5). Column 6 shows the reserve as a percentage of the total balance sheet account receivable amount in column 7.

The total provision should be reasonably related to the actual write-offs for tax purposes, giving effect to that portion of the remaining doubtful accounts that may be expected to be written off. These numbers should be viewed on an aggregate basis, over the years.

The percent figure (column 6), studied together with the previous exhibit, will prove helpful in establishing a current monthly provision for bad debts to be used as an interim financial accrual.

9. **Receivable analysis—product line A** (Exhibit 3-16). This is used by the treasurer, the collection manager, and product line marketing managers. This report is also summarized for the entire company, all product lines. The same analysis may be done by territories, as desired. The report gives sales, turnover in days, total receivables, aging of receivables in two categories—current to 60 days past due, and 61 days plus past due, with percents of each to total receivables—and, in the last two columns, total collections, aged the same as the receivables, and with percents collected.

As a monthly running report, this permits ready monitoring of turnover and of past dues by percent of receivables and of cash collected. The trends are thus visually established in one report.

10. **Credit analysis codes** (Exhibit 3-17). These codes are used by operating managers, department heads, and product line managers

(*text continues on page 132*)

Exhibit 3-15.   Schedule of bad debt reserve — annual.

A. CORP.
Schedule of Bad Debts Reserve — Annual

			3 PROVISION	4 A/R WRITE-OFF	5 BALANCE	6 % Col.5 ÷ Col.7	7 Total A/R TRADE	
1	Balance	5-1-00			234410	5.1	4620000	1
2	FYE	4-30-01	11866	—	352276	4.9	7240000	2
3	FYE	4-30-02	26500	8638	53138	3.8	14060000	3
4	FYE	4-30-03	127114	5252	175000	8.4	2074000	4
5	FYE	4-30-04	159837	149837	185000	6.8	2716000	5
6	FYE	4-30-05	128467	14793	298674	7.2	4174000	6
7	FYE	4-30-06	371843	120517	550000	8.6	6390000	7
8	FYE	4-30-07	261600	251600	560000	7.5	7437000	8
9	FYE	4-30-08	288307	213191	635116	8.0	7913000	9
10	FYE	4-30-09	1100580	660696	1075000	10.0	10696000	10
11	FYE	4-30-10	1082998	832618	1325380	10.0	13240000	11
12	4 Mos ended	8-31-11	297871	223554	1399647	9.1	15404000	12

Exhibit 3-16.   Receivable analysis — product line A.

RECEIVABLE ANALYSIS

Product Line A

MONTH ENDED	SALES $M	#DAYS SLS/REC	TOTAL REC'S	AGING C-60 AMT.	%	P/D 61 + AMT.	%	COLLECTIONS TOTAL C-60 AMT.	%	P/D 61 + AMT.	%
20											
JANUARY	5 1 9	1 5 6	3454	1 346	39	1 444	42	679	22.7	544	73
FEBRUARY	6 22	1 8 2	3815	1 711	45	1 990	31	443	12.8	309	21
MARCH	7 84	1 5 5	3027	1 896	63	1 130	37	638	16.7	443	37
APRIL	8 74	1 2 4	2997	2 044	68	954	32	696	22.9	341	30
MAY	5 22	1 2 3	3046	1 946	64	1 100	36	646	21.5	417	44
JUNE	7 03	1 2 6	2906	1 857	64	1 049	36	694	22.7	388	35
JULY	6 33	1 4 4	2890	1 707	59	1 183	41	623	21.4	420	40
AUGUST	4 61	1 9 1	2676	1 499	56	1 178	44	675	23.3	358	30
SEPTEMBER	5 04	1 4 5	2327	1 494	64	833	36	652	24.3	468	40
OCTOBER	7 79	1 0 1	2533	1 576	62	957	38	548	23.5	294	35
NOVEMBER	5 35	1 2 3	2410	1 527	63	883	37	669	26.0	313	33
DECEMBER	7 52	1 0 4	2517	1 578	63	941	37	645	26.7	258	29
20											
JANUARY	7 42	1 1 0	2538	1 616	64	923	36	662	2.3	332	35
FEBRUARY	6 82	1 0 9	2630	1 826	69	804	31	538	21.1	293	32
MARCH	8 11	1 0 7	2793	1 890	68	903	32	645	24.5	335	42
APRIL	1 140	9 4	3418	2 400	70	1 018	30	358	13	394	44
MAY	3 14	28 8	2885	2 159	75	726	25	762	22.2	375	37
JUNE	3 66	20 6	2479	1 779	72	700	28	780	28.8	450	38
JULY	6 50	1 6 0	2874	1 896	66	978	34	787	24.7	560	80
AUGUST	9 41	1 0 1	3040	2 231	73	808	27	532	46	620	63
SEPTEMBER	8 44	1 2 0	3379	2 635	78	744	22	527	56	358	44
OCTOBER	1 083	9 3	3173	2 442	77	731	23	395	33	501	67
NOVEMBER	1 299	8 0	3470	2 668	77	802	23	220	24	554	75
DECEMBER	9 64	9 6	2979	2 115	71	864	29	353	49	411	51
20											
JANUARY	9 90	1 0 7	3326	2 344	70	982	30	601	55	386	44
FEBRUARY	9 76	1 0 1	3445	2 377	69	1 068	31	476	53	465	47
MARCH	1 067	1 0 6	3604	2 484	69	1 120	31	398	70	316	30

Exhibit 3-17. Credit analysis codes.

HOP/SOP MEMO

TO BE FILED WITHIN CORRESPONDING PROCEDURE

Memo To: Distribution   Subject: Credit Analysis (CRAN)

From: Eff. Date: 5/1/

HOP [ ] No.: _____   Title: Order Processing

SOP [x] No.: C-22

HOP [ ] Last Correction No.:_____   HOP [ ] New Correction No.: _____

SOP [ ] Last Correction No.:_____   SOP [x] New Correction No.: ___436___

Paragraph # Exhibit G   Page # 24   Affected

Use of the Credit Analysis Code is to be reinstated. The purpose of this code
is to identify and categorize all credits issued. This code is to appear in
the space just above the Credit Memo. No. as follows:

CODE	REASON FOR CREDIT
Ø	Defective Parts
1	Home Office Processing Error
2	Branch Processing Error
3	Valhalla Warehouse Error
4	Defective Paper
5	Machine Cancellation
6	Machine Replacement
7	Dealer Reimbursement - GSA
8	Dealer Reimbursement - Retail
9	Customer Error
A	Service Call Adjustment
B	Salesperson Error
C	Tax, Freight or Insurance Claim Adjustment Refund
D	Maintenance Agreement Cancellation

INQUIRIES: Manager, Order Billing

DISTRIBUTION: List 12.0 SOP Manual Holders
                    8.0 Branch Administrators

(*text continued from page 128*)

to analyze the reasons for the issuance of credits to customers. Each credit memo is coded with a reason for the credit, as listed in the exhibit. Credits are then sorted by dollar amount and by product line, and the report is run. Corrective action may be taken for excessive credit issuance as indicated by the code. The report may indicate the necessity for changes in the very system, itself. For example, excessive tax credits, code C, may indicate an improper procedure for obtaining and recording tax exemption certificates from users.

PRACTICAL POINTERS FOR SUCCESSFUL CREDIT GRANTING AND ACCOUNTS RECEIVABLE COLLECTIONS

Success in these areas requires an integrated system, starting with order-writing and credit-granting procedures, and continuing on to routinized collection procedures involving field personnel, with built-in features for internal security controls, and with timely reports designed to monitor performance by exception. A feature of the integrated system should be special credit arrangements for special types of customers and for special marketing programs.

4

Providing Insurance Coverage as Needed

The treasurer is responsible for providing insurance coverage for the company. This obligation is a defined treasurership function in the FEI official statement of responsibilities of the treasurer and controller, which may be found in "Treasurer's and Controller's Functions."

Insurance, by definition, is the indemnification of one by a third party against loss from a specified contingency or peril. The definition is key to an understanding of the treasurer's obligations in this area. The peril should be contingent, meaning unpredictable, and inherently infrequent. Frequent and predictable perils or losses should be self-insured on an accrual basis as a continuing operating expense.

Some perils, though infrequent, may be self-insured if they are predictable. Similarly, self-insurance is often a good idea for unpredictable losses that recur with some frequency, that is, on a spasmodic basis. Insurance, then, is the safeguard against the unknown, the unpredictable, the infrequent, the unanticipated, the unaccrued for or unprovided for expense.

This definition, however, does not encompass the overall insurance philosophy that the treasurer should bring to the company. If there is any conceivable type of peril that, if it struck, would impair the ability of the company to continue in existence, it should be provided for through insurance coverage. The type and amount of insurance will vary for every company, it being dependent on the individual nature of each company. Exhibit 4-1 is an actual **insurance record** for a typical

(*text continues on page 141*)

133

Exhibit 4-1. Insurance record.

INSURANCE RECORD AS OF November 30, 20____

INSURED _____

LOCATION _____

COMPANY	NO. OF POLICY	AMOUNT	TERM	EXPIRES MO.	EXPIRES DAY	EXPIRES YEAR	PREMIUM	COVERAGE
Federal	FMPO6900703	Various*	Cont.	Anniversary 5	1		$45,268.00	Commercial Property Policy
								*See separate summary of this policy. Annual premium adjustment.
Federal	FXL77742900	$ 10,000,000.–	1 Yr	7	15		$ 2,991.00	Umbrella Excess Liability Policy
								Retained Limit: $10,000.–
Federal	(74)11403043	Various	1 Yr	8	1		$ 5,072.00	Automobile Insurance
		$100,000/300,000–bodily injury						Mercedes Benz
		50,000–property damage						Mercedes Benz
		5,000–medical payments						Dodge Van
		uninsured motorists cov.						Citroen
		$ 50 deductible Comprehensive Fire/Theft						Cadillac
		$100 deductible Collision						Note: Oldsmobile eliminated 10/31/
		Towing coverage $25						
Federal	99990108	$ 2,450,000.–	1 Yr	5	9		$15,250.00	Contingent Business Interruption
								Fire, Ext. Cov., Vandalism, Earthquake Volcanic eruption.
								Loc:
								Atsugi City, Kanagawa Pref., Japan
Ins. Co. of North America	10HF2048	$ 2,450,000.–	3 Yrs	5	19		Annual $14,596.67	Contingent Business Interruption
								Fire, Ext. Cov., Vandalism, Earthquake.
								Loc:
								Atsugi City, Kanagawa Pref., Japan
Ins. Co. of North America	16142	$750,000.–under deck	Continuous				as per repts	Marine Open Cargo Policy
		50,000.–on deck						"All-risk" per policy terms/conditions
		50,000.–aircraft						Warehouse to warehouse coverage.

134

INSURED _____

LOCATION _____

COMPANY	NO. OF POLICY	AMOUNT	TERM	EXPIRES MO.	EXPIRES DAY	EXPIRES YEAR	PREMIUM	COVERAGE
Federal	(74)76322616	statutory	1 Yr	5	1		Deposit $49,080.00	**Workers' Compensation** All States except 'monopolistic' states Experience modification 1.21 (California 1.97) Audit 5/1 -5/1/ $46,237. addl prem. Total Earned Prem 5/1/ $70,573.00.
INA Life Ins Co of New York	NYD11948	statutory	Cont. Until Canc.				as per repts	New York State Disability
Lloyds London	to be assigned	various	1 Yr	10	15		to be determ. 'quoted prem $25,731.75	Aircraft Insurance Hansa Jet 320HFB Industrial Aid Use.

Hull

$575,000.—Hull "all-risk" coverage; agreed amount basis.
1% hull deductible applies in Flight, Taxying, and ingestion.
$500 hull deductible applies on ground.

Liability

$ 10,000,000.—Combined single limit Bodily Injury & Property Damage, Passenger Liability.
5,000.—Medical payments coverage any one person including crew.
100,000.—Admitted Liability coverage any one person including crew.
1,000,000.—Combined single limit Bodily Injury & Property Damage, Passenger Liability: NonOwned Aircraft Liability

Pilots

—Asst Pilot (Can act as Chief Pilot upon being type rated in aircraft)

Geographical Limits

Central America, South America, Caribbean, Bahamas, USA, Canada, Mexico.

Note: Pro rata, earned premium to follow as respects Argonaut Insurance Co. policy # H-5-682, covering policy period 8/24/ to 10/15/. (annual premium $7,957.00.) Lloyds London policy replaced Argonaut policy effective 10/15/

(continued)

135

Exhibit 4-1. *(continued)*

COMPANY	NO. OF POLICY	AMOUNT	TERM	MO.	DAY	YEAR	PREMIUM	COVERAGE
					EXPIRES			
Federal	80352291	various	Cont. Anniversary	9	14		Annual $ 8,050.00	Comprehensive Bond
	Limits							Deductibles
	$500,000.—Commercial Blanket Employee Dishonesty							$10,000.—Employee Dishonesty on Merchandise
	250,000.—Depositor's Forgery							2,500.—Employee Dishonesty excl. Merchandise
	25,000.—Credit Card coverage							2,500.—Depositor's Forgery
Peerless	805-37493	$500,000.—	1Yr	9	23		$ 380.00	General Term Bond for Entry of Merchandise Various Ports of Entry.
Aetna Cas.	72SB6381	$ 1,000.—	1Yr	3	10		$ 30.00	Continuous Bid & Perf. Bond Obligee: County of Los Angeles, Cal.
Aetna Cas.	72SB6669	$ 500.—	1Yr	5	19		$ 30.00	Franchise Tax Bond Obligee: State of Texas
Aetna Cas.	72SB25823	$ 5,000.—	1Yr	7	16		$ 100.00	Annual Bid & Perf. Bond Obligee: State of Kansas
Aetna Cas.	72SB25834	$ 5% Bid	1Yr	8	10		$ 25.00	Bid Bond Service Undertaking Obligee: City of Kansas City, Mo.
USF & G	2001-71	$5,595.06	1Yr	8	24		$ 212.00	Appeal Bond Obligee: XYZ (Kansas City, Mo.)
USF & G	1417-71	$5,000.	3Yrs	6	7		$ 287.00	Concessionaire Bond Obligee: University of Minnesota
USF & G	2704-70	$500.—	5Yrs	8	18		$ 50.00	Concessionaire Bond Obligee: NY State Dept of Soc Svcs
USF & G	1063-71	$100.—	5Yrs	4	29		$ 70.00	Concessionaire Bond Obligee: NY State Dept of Soc Svcs

COMPANY	NO. OF POLICY	AMOUNT	TERM	EXPIRES MO.	EXPIRES DAY	EXPIRES YEAR	PREMIUM	COVERAGE
Federal Ins Co	FMPO6900703	various	Cont. Anniversary	5	1		$65,268.00	COMMERCIAL PROPERTY POLICY

COMMERCIAL PROPERTY POLICY
"All-Risk" Coverage per policy terms/conditions.
$42,091.00 = Pers. Property Deposit
23,177.00 = All other premium portion
$65,268.00
Annual premium adjustment/repts of value.

Policy Deductible:
$1,000. deductible applies to all losses/damages.
$10,000. deductible applies to all Transit Losses.

Comprehensive General Liability $250 deductible
$1,000,000.–Personal Injury Liability
  250,000.–Property Damage Liability
1,000,000.–Aggregate Pers. Inj.–Products Liab.
  250,000.–Aggregate Prop. Dam.–Products Liab.
  500,000.–Bod. Inj.–Contractual Liab.
  250,000.–Prop. Dam.–Contractual Liab.
  500/1,000.–Bod. Inj. NonOwned Auto Liab.
1,000,000.–Prop. Dam. NonOwned Auto Liab.
Products Liability includes Broad Form Vendors

Additional Expense Coverage
$100,000.–limit @ NY Location
  25,000.–limit @ all other locations.

Additional Insured's coverage
Per location schedule as required by lease agreement.

Limits of Liability
$ 3,500,000.–Columbus Avenue,
  500,000.–Clairemont Avenue,
2,000,000.–1212 44th Ave.,
1,000,000.–43 Park Lane,
2,000,000.–13811 Artesia Blvd.,
1,500,000.–9710 W. Foster Ave.,
  500,000.–19433 E. Walnut Dr,
  450,000.–1465 NW 21st Terr.,
  750,000.–11742 W. 86th Terr,
  300,000.–14650 Southlawn Lane,
  500,000.–131 Beverly St.,
1,000,000.–136-140 Horton Ave.,
  250,000.–at any other location (un-named) within the territorial limits of policy.
  60,000.–while in Transit.

Named Locations

Building Coverage
$ 1,380,000.–
  115,000.–
  100,000.–
  32,500.–
  75,000.–

Fire Damage Legal Liability Coverage
$50,000.–limit; Blanket-All locations

(continued)

137

Exhibit 4-1. *(continued)*

INSURANCE RECORD AS OF _____ November 30, 20—

INSURED _____

LOCATION _____

Property Covered Under Policy.

1) Personal property of every kind and description (except as excluded) usual to the conduct of the assured's business, the property of the assured, or the property of others while in the actual or constructive custody of the assured and for which the assured is legally liable.

2) Improvements and Betterments to buildings occupied by, but not owned by the assured.

Property Not Covered on Policy

1) Animals, currency, money, notes, securities, stamps, deeds, letters of credit, tickets. . . .

2) Furs, jewels, precious metals

3) Aircraft, watercraft, vehicles licensed or designed for highway use.

4) Property sold under conditional sale, trust agreement, installments or other deferred payment plan.

5) Import/Export shipments.

Advertisers Liability Coverage
$100,000.–limit

Valuable Papers and Records Coverage
$250,000.–limit, NY location only

Earthquake & Flood Coverage
$ 50,000.–limit Deductible $1,000.–
Earthquake–California locations only
Flood–All locations

INSURANCE RECORD as of November 30, 20xx

Insured_____
Location_____

PREMIUM ANALYSIS: COMMERCIAL PROPERTY POLICY
                 Federal Insurance Company Policy #FMP06900703
                 Policy Period: May 1, 20xx to May 1, 20xx

Personal Property - Deposit portion of Premium....................$ 42,091.00
                 Named Locations $36,813.
                 Unnamed Locations   5,278.
                                   $42,091.

All Other Premium portion - not subject to adjustment.............$ 23,177.00
Buildings: Valhalla, NY............$ 1,617.
           Chicago, Ill............   521.
           Hartford, Conn..........   205.
           Indianapolis, Ind.......   117.
           City of Industry, Cal...   182.
                                   $ 2,642.

General Liability:
           Premises Liability......$ 3,553.
           Products Liability...... 8,457.
           Fire Legal Liability....   500.
           Auto Nonownership Liab..   506.
                                   $ 13,016.

Additional Expense Coverage......$ 350.

Valuable Papers & Records........$ 669.

Earthquake & Flood...............$ 1,000.

Transit Coverage.................$ 5,500.

                        Total Annual Premium including
                        Deposit premium portion = $ 65,268.00

Nov. 30, 20xx

(continued)

Exhibit 4-1. *(continued)*

INSURANCE RECORD AS of NOVEMBER 30, 20xx

Insured _____

Location _____

COMMERCIAL PROPERTY POLICY #FMPO 6900703   PREMIUM SUMMARY

POLICY PERIOD	May 1, 20xx	May 1, 20xx	May 1, 20xx	May 1, 20xx	May 1, 20xx
ACCOUNT RATE	.76	.65	.56	.336	.357
AVERAGE PERS. PROP. VALUES	$3,839,734.	$7,258,969.	$7,971,680.	$6,188,270.	5 mos. $7,705,177.
DEPOSIT PREMIUM	$ 27,880.	$ 45,444.	$ 77,301.	$ 51,019.	$ 42,091.
ALL OTHER PREMIUM	9,210.	18,071.	21,128.	20,300.	23,177.
ADJUSTMENT PREMIUM	13,875.	15,692.	3,991.	(6,000.)	to be det.
TOTAL	$ 50,965.	$ 79,207.	$ 102,420.	$ 65,319.	$ to be det.

Nov. 30, 20xx

(*text continued from page 133*)
company. It lists every policy, policy dates, and premium amount per year, and gives a summary of the coverage. To put this in perspective, this insurance record is typical for a company in the $50,000,000 to $200,000,000 annual revenues range, with 40 branch office locations and approximately 3000 employees. Each type of policy is discussed below, seriatim, as listed in the "coverage" column of the exhibit.

COMMERCIAL PROPERTY POLICY

This is discussed in a separate summary of the policy on pages 4 through 7 of the exhibit. Most business claims will be placed under this policy. It will, therefore, be discussed in a separate section.

UMBRELLA EXCESS LIABILITY POLICY

This is sometimes called a "blanket" policy, in that it insures against all risks that are not otherwise covered. Specific amounts of liability coverage are provided in the commercial property policy. For example, $1,000,000 is provided for personal injury liability. The umbrella provides coverage in excess of that, up to $10,000,000, at a small cost of only $2991 per year. This is true catastrophe insurance. It insures against the infrequent and absolutely unpredictable. Since it is an "excess coverage" policy, coming into play only after another policy has reached its limit, and then being subject to a $10,000 deductible, it carries a very small premium cost. This type of policy, the umbrella excess liability, is an absolute requirement for any complete insurance program. At one time, the illustrated company carried a $5,000,000 umbrella, which was adequate for its needs. The courts, however, began to grant personal injury awards in excess of $5,000,000. In keeping with the treasurer's philosophy of protecting the company against the utmost catastrophes, the coverage was increased to its present limits.

Automobile Insurance

This company has only a few owned vehicles for specific managers. Its other cars are leased, and the monthly rentals include insurance. This policy includes $100,000/300,000 bodily injury coverage, per person/occurrence, as a requirement of its umbrella excess liability policy. The latter policy must always be considered in establishing any other liability limits. Another feature of this policy is uninsured motorist coverage, to provide protection in the event of an accident with an uncovered driver.

Contingent Business Interruption

A basic ingredient of any catastrophe coverage is this type of business interruption insurance. In the present case, the company is covering manufacturing facilities in a foreign location against unpredictable, infrequent hazards, to include earthquakes, volcanoes, fire, and vandalism, any of which would cause an interruption or cessation in business. Such policies are sometimes called use and occupancy (U & O) insurance. They all indemnify for loss of net profits during the shutdown, for continuing fixed charges, for extra expenses to replace equipment, for overtime, and for having the product manufactured elsewhere. The insurance coverage may be obtained in connection with riots, civil commotion, fire, sprinkler leakage, flood, water damage, tornado, and boiler explosion. When one company depends on another for a continuous, uninterrupted supply of goods, it obtains "contingent" U & O insurance against the loss that it would sustain as a result of the supplier's inability to deliver. A form of business interruption insurance is often attached to an ordinary "all-risk" policy, like the commercial property policy, and provides additional expense or "extra expense" coverage to defray costs incurred as a result of the loss. In the insurance record illustrated, there are two contingent business interruption policies with two different companies. The reason is that the carrier prefers to spread the risk of loss and has requested the company to use two carriers, each carrying $2,450,000 of risk.

MARINE OPEN CARGO POLICY

The illustrated company imports some of its product and prefers to order it FOB shipping point. Since it assumes title on shipment, it must provide its own insurance coverage. Exporters will often provide FAS shipping terms, or CIF (freight alongside or cost, insurance, and freight), wherein the exporter provides the insurance coverage and includes its cost in the price. In this case, each shipment is covered separately. A report is supplied to the insurance company monthly, listing each shipment, and enclosing a check for the premium coverage, in arrears. The premium is based on the value attributed to each shipment. Coverage is to the recipient warehouse dock, at which point the commercial property policy picks up coverage.

WORKERS' COMPENSATION

These policies cover the employer for the entire liability under the various state laws, usually including occupational diseases among the covered hazards. The same policy often covers employer's liability insurance against common-law suits brought by employees to obtain damages for personal injuries. Premiums are based on payroll dollars, with a deposit being made using previous payroll periods as a basis. A subsequent audit determines the actual payroll. The audit is made by accountants for the insurance carrier. As a part of this audit, they classify the payroll by class of employee (that is, functions performed, as clerical, sales, manufacturing), and a separate premium rate is charged for each class of employee.

Try This Helpful Hint: Organize your payroll records by class of employee to conform to the workers' compensation policy requirements. You, rather than the insurance company auditors, will select the appropriate class, and you can often designate a lower rate class than the auditor would, at a significant premium saving. Moreover, at audit time, have your representative present to look over the classifications established by the auditor. Remember, the auditor may not understand the nuances of your operation and may misclassify payroll functions.

Avoid This Pitfall: Each state has different requirements for coverage. A blanket policy will not cover you in every state. Some states, in fact, require that coverage be carried with the state itself. Contact the state labor department in every state to determine requirements in this area.

Helpful Hint: Workers' compensation coverage is costly. Savings can often be achieved by joining a trade association that has arranged for carriers to cover its members at lower rates. Similarly, professional employer organizations (PEOs) lease employees to you and, because they have so many employees, are able to arrange for lower insurance rates on this type of coverage.

New York State Disability

Many states provide for mandatory insurance coverage for employees with regard to accidents and disabilities incurred off the job. This insurance, in combination with workers' compensation, which covers on-the-job accidents, provides complete coverage for all employees. The amount of the premium is set by law and is paid for by the employee through payroll deductions. The employer often elects to bear the full premium cost. The laws in each state must be checked carefully for coverage requirements. Private insurance is available in states without disability laws.

Aircraft Insurance

The illustrated company operates a corporate aircraft. In addition to normal property damage insurance, called hull, the company is covered for $10 million of liability insurance. This, together with its umbrella excess liability policy, gives the company $20 million of liability coverage, which is considered to be an adequate catastrophe amount, based on court awards for liability to injured parties in aircraft cases. The pilots are specifically named, they having previously been safety rated.

COMPREHENSIVE BOND

This is basic employee fidelity coverage, without the necessity for each employee to complete a fidelity bond application. Each employee is automatically covered, subject to the limits shown and the deductibles set forth. In this illustration, 2000 employees are covered for a premium of $6050 per year. Coverage includes protection against inventory thefts (subject to a high $10,000 deductible, since the product is bulky and not easily stolen, there are many locations, and the system of internal control is strong), cash defalcations up to $250,000, all other thefts up to $500,000 subject to a $2500 deductible, and blanket coverage for the loss of company-issued credit cards.

> *Helpful Hint:* The comprehensive bond is inexpensive catastrophe insurance, covering a variety of dishonesty risks at a low annual premium cost.

GENERAL TERM BOND FOR ENTRY OF MERCHANDISE

This special policy, together with the marine open cargo policy, provides complete coverage for all importations of product. The marine policy covers insurance in transit. The general term bond covers landed merchandise while it passes through customs and brokers' hands.

MISCELLANEOUS BID AND PERFORMANCE BONDS

These bonds may be required by municipal agencies that purchase products or services from the company. The bid bond is often in lieu of a certified check that must accompany government bids. The bond is inexpensive, may be continuous, and does not tie up cash while the bid is being negotiated or awarded. The performance bond, franchise tax bond, service undertaking bond, and concessionaire bond are all similar, meeting the specific requirements of various governments or agencies, insuring against the company's failure to perform under the specific contract. The appeal bond is a legal court requirement, which in this case insures against an appeal of $5595.06 for only $112, a cost of 2% per year. The appeal refers to an appeal from a previous legal verdict in a lawsuit.

COMMERCIAL PROPERTY POLICY

This is an "all-risk" policy covering inventory in warehouses and in transit, buildings and equipment, fire damage liability on rented premises, personal injuries, property damage, product liability claims, non-owned auto liability and property damage, personal property damage, advertisers' liability coverage, loss of valuable papers and records, and earthquake and flood damage. It excludes coverage of cash and securities, precious metals, aircraft, property sold under installments, and imports or exports, all of which are covered under previously described policies. To this extent, the policy is quite similar to the very familiar personal property floater that many individuals carry as part of their homeowner's policy. Everything you can think of is covered, except the specific excluded items.

This is the principal company policy, and most insurance claims will be placed under this all-risk policy. Losses in excess of the coverages set forth will be covered by the umbrella excess liability policy. Note that deductibles of $1000 to $10,000 for various parts of the policy serve to reduce the premium cost.

Helpful Hint: A claims analysis should be made each year, to determine the type and dollar amount of claims. It is possible that the deductible amounts under the policy can be raised, and the reduction in premium will more than offset the loss in insurance reimbursement of excluded claims. In the case of the illustrated company, this analysis caused the company to raise its deductibles to $2500.

The policy carries additional expense coverage, which pays for the extra costs involved as a direct result of a loss, as described under the contingent business interruption policy.

A premium analysis of the commercial property policy is attached, which indicates that approximately $22,000 of the premium is subject to monthly reports of values carried. The balance of $23,000 is fixed in amount, the major portions being attributable to premises liability, products liability, and transit coverage. This being the major discretionary policy, from a cost standpoint (workers' compensation cost is determined by the classifications of the various states), a premium summary follows the premium analysis sheet. The summary contains a breakdown of the premium over a five-year period and allows a rapid visual review of the components of the premium and the effect of the variable deposit premium on the total.

OTHER TYPES OF INSURANCE

✧ *Life insurance.* This is usually "key person" insurance, to provide funds to the company covering the loss of services of the key employee. This type of insurance may also provide cash for the purchase of the deceased's shares in a close corporation or to buy out her or his capital interest in a partnership.

Remember This: If the business is the beneficiary, the premiums are not deductible for tax purposes, nor are the proceeds on death included in income. Premiums are, however, deductible for financial accounting purposes.

There are some other accounting considerations involved with life insurance. Dividends may be applied as a reduction of premiums or may be left with the insurance company to increase the amount of insurance and, hence, the cash surrender and loan values. The loan value may be classified as a current asset unless a lending agreement or indenture requires it to be shown as an investment or other asset.

Split-dollar life insurance is a type of life coverage that provides some interesting benefits to the key employee. It generally provides that the premiums are split between the corporation and the covered employee. In the early years, say the first five years, the company pays about 80% of the premium, and bonuses out the 20% balance to the employee, taxable as wages to the employee and deductible (at a higher rate than the individual rate) to the company. The policy increases in cash value each year until the fifth year, when the cash value equals the aggregate premium payments made by the company. The company receives an assignment of insurance proceeds in an amount equal to its aggregate premium payments. As a result, the corporation is not required to charge earnings with its share of the premium payments in the early years. Rather, it records an asset account at cash value. Also, after five years, the cash value accruing to the individual will equal the aggregate after-tax cost of his or her bonused premium payments. In years after the fifth, the individual's premium payments increase and the corporation's decrease, both in amounts equal to the annual increase in their respective cash values. The employee may borrow his or her cash value at any time. The interest charge is low, usually between 6% and 9%. Moreover, the interest is never paid. Instead, it is merely added to the total loan due to the insurance company. At death, any open loan amount is deducted from the loan proceeds, resulting in the employee's having had the tax-free use of the cash value during his or her life. After seven to ten years, the policy becomes paid up and results in a lower overall cost than term insurance.

Word of Caution: In split-dollar policies where the company pays 100% of the premium, the employee is required to report as income the value of the one-year term insurance protection made available by the company (Rev. Rule 64–328, 1964–2 CB 11).

✧ *Extended coverage.* This is one of the risks insured against in contingent business interruption or use and occupancy policies. This provides for coverage from damages due to windstorm, hail, smoke, aircraft, vehicle, explosion, and riot, whether originating on your premises or elsewhere. It does not cover war, loss caused by foreign military forces, damage done at the direction of civil or governmental authorities, or explosions or fires caused by boilers, which are separately coverable.

✧ *Sprinkler leakage.* This covers loss due to such leakage, but not loss to the sprinkler system itself. Moreover, separate coverage is required for valuable papers and cash and securities, of the type provided under the commercial property policy.

✧ *Boiler explosion.* This covers losses to the property insured and to others caused by the explosion. It does not cover explosions caused by fire, or fire from any cause. Once again, the commercial property policy covers that type of loss.

✧ *Plate glass.* This policy covers not only the glass, but attached signs, lettering, and ornaments. Not covered is damage due to fire, earthquake, or workers involved in repairs or construction, all of which must be separately covered.

✧ *Selling price or profit insurance.* This may be included as part of the business interruption policy, or to cover inventory loss under the commercial property policy. Normal coverage pays for the actual cash value of the merchandise destroyed. For an additional premium, the profit that would have been made in a normal sale is also covered.

COINSURANCE

Many policies contain a coinsurance clause. The purpose of such a clause, from the insurance company's standpoint, is to offset the tendency of insureds to insure for only a small part of the total value of the property. This is often done because most losses are only partial losses. In the coinsurance clause, the insured agrees to carry insurance in an amount equal to a specific percentage of the value. The most common is an 80% coinsurance clause. If, under an 80% coinsurance policy, the insured carries insurance equal to only 70% of the property's value, he or she becomes a coinsurer for 10%. The insured thus bears ⅛ of any loss, and the insurance company bears ⅞—but in no case is the insurance company liable for more than the face amount of the policy. These principles are demonstrated in this:

Helpful Formula—for computation of claim against insurance company:

Claim Against Insurance Co.

$$= \frac{\text{Face of Policy}}{80\% \text{ of Value of Property at Time of Loss}} \times \text{Loss}$$

The formula applies if the policy is less than 80% of the value of the property—if the policy is 80% or greater of the value of the property, the formula does not apply and is not needed.

Remember these limitations to the claim:

1. The face of the policy
2. The actual loss

Example: Value of property is $100,000
Policy is for $70,000.
Property is completely destroyed in fire—loss is $100,000.

$$\text{Claim} = \frac{\$70,000}{80\% \times \$100,000} \times \$100,000 = \$87,500$$

Claim is limited to face value, or $70,000.

Under the same assumptions, had the property been 50% destroyed, or a loss of $50,000, the formula would result in:

$$\text{Claim} = \frac{\$70,000}{80\% \times \$100,000} \times \$50,000 = \$43,750$$

Claim is limited to computed amount.
Actual loss exceeds the computed amount.

Coinsurance, then, of 80% means that on *partial* losses, you recover only partially if you are covered for less than 80% of the actual value of the property.

> *Avoid This Pitfall:* Value of the property at the time of the loss is its "cash value" or "sound value," which generally means what the property would have been worth on the open market, had you offered it for sale. This can be a costly trap during inflationary times. A $50,000 store, 80% insured for $40,000, could have doubled in value to $100,000 by the time of the fire. By formula, the policy would pay only its face, a total of $40,000, despite the store's having a cost to replace it of $100,000. Your insurance coverage must be constantly reviewed in times of inflation to ascertain that coverage equals 80% of current cash value.

FREIGHT CLAIMS

Claims for loss or damage in transit may arise from shipments via common carrier, UPS, parcel post, or special delivery services. These claims require special handling, as they are generally small in dollar amount and frequent in occurrence, involving a great many different carriers. Consider self-insurance for this type of frequent risk.

> *Avoid This Pitfall:* UPS and other parcel delivery services have rules requiring that claims for undelivered merchandise be made within one year (six months for some companies). Often, the lack of delivery is not revealed until collection phone calls

are made, after about a 60-day period. Many times, the customer will ignore statements and collection calls, saying that
the amount simply isn't owed. Your collection calls must be
timely, in accordance with your procedures (see Chapter 3), in
order to discover the nondelivery in time to place a claim.

Thorough procedure dictates that these types of claims be logged
in, as a prelude to handling. The log should carry notations for:

- Date of claim
- Carrier
- Pro number (if any)
- Bill of lading number
- Our invoice number
- Date of loss
- Type of loss (fire, missing, damage, etc.)
- Date of second follow-up
- Date of third follow-up
- Date placed with our broker
- Date paid

The log is a handy device to permit:

- Accrual of dollar amount of claims for accounting entries (inventory, cost of sales, and insurance claims receivable)
- Follow-up on receipt of payments from carrier or broker

The log is supported by an alphabetical file of backup documents,
filed in order by name of carrier. The file in itself, without the log, is
not sufficient to permit accurate handling of claims. Documents can be
misplaced or misfiled, and it is inconvenient to have to pull and read
each file for follow-up purposes.

The log may be referred to, at a glance, to determine whether the
date paid has been completed on each line, or whether the second or
third follow-up notice has been mailed. If not, the detailed file may
then be pulled for action.

Exhibit 4-2. Freight claims procedure.

STANDARD OPERATING PROCEDURE	
Subject: FREIGHT CLAIMS	**Number** B-6a
	Page of 1 1
	Effective **Date** 2/9/
Supersedes S.O.P. No. Page Dated	**Related** **S.O.P.**

Purpose: To have branches initiate paper work for processing of freight claims through the home office.

Method: Freight claims for short deliveries, damaged merchandise, merchandise lost in transit or freight claims of any other nature are to be handled through the home office in the following manner:

Branch Office Secretary-

1. Obtain proof of shortage or damage in the form of bill of lading indicating the problem.

2. Write a covering letter to home office Purchasing Department requesting that claim be placed and enclosing proof in 1 above.

Home Office Purchasing Department-

1. Place claim

2. Advise branch office of disposition of damaged merchandise.

3. Will replace merchandise if lost in branch transfer.

For parcel post claims see procedure titled "Parcel Post Insurance" page B-21.

Inquiries: For inquiries contact the home office Purchasing Department.

DISTRIBUTION: Branch office secretaries/home office Purchasing Department

DLG:2/9/

The procedure in Exhibit 4-2, **freight claims**, details the method to be used by branch offices for placing claims. Insurance being a headquarters function, all such claims are placed with the home office. The home office purchasing department, in Step 2, provides the branch office with written notice that the claim has been placed. The branch may then discontinue its follow-up. The **claims procedures** in Exhibit 4-3 detail the steps taken by the home office purchasing department in placing these claims. These claims are considered a purchasing responsibility, as the loss or damage usually requires the initiation of a replacement purchase order.

Point of Information: The claims log and follow-up procedures are readily handled by $\frac{1}{5}$ of a person, less than two hours a

Exhibit 4-3.   Claims procedure.

CLAIMS' PROCEDURES

A. NONDELIVERY, SHORTAGE (CARRIER)

    1. Form letter to carrier requesting proof of delivery.

        a. Second request if no answer in fifteen days.

    2. Letter to consignee requesting copy of freight bill
        or affidavit.

    3. Claim filed after thirty days if no answer or notification
        of loss from carrier.

        a. Form letter to carrier of intention to file
            claim with:

            1. Certified Copy of Original Invoice
            2. Original Bill of Lading
            3. Original Freight Bill
            4. Consignee's Copy of Freight Bill
            5. Other Supporting Documentation

            Plus standard form attached!

        b. Form letter to Insurance Broker with attachment

            Copies of the above: a) 1, 2, 3, 4, 5 plus copy of
            letter to carrier.

B. DAMAGE (CARRIER)

    1. Form letter to carrier noting shipment was received damaged,
        of intention to file claim, and request for an inspection
        report (notify consignee, unless otherwise directed, to hold
        shipment pending inspection).

    2. Second request if no answer in fifteen days.

    3. Upon receipt of inspection report, or after thirty days,
        attach copy to form letter to our Insurance Broker with copies
        of all items listed under A3a above. (If inspection report is
        not returned, attach form letter noting unanswered second request.)

C. NONDELIVERY, SHORTAGE, DAMAGE (MAIL, PARCEL POST)

1. Proof of loss form, cover form letter to consignee.
   (Second request, two weeks.)

2. Post Office Form No. 1510 to Post Office with form letter.
   (Second request, two weeks; third request, one month.)

3. Upon receipt of above, attach with Certified Copy of Original
   Invoice to form letter to Insurance Broker. (If forms are not
   returned from Post Office, allow final two weeks and send form
   letter noting unanswered third request.) Form No. 1510
   applicable only on insured mail.

NOTES:

Emergency Tracing Procedure:

Phone Tracing Department, or Customer Service Department at
terminal of pick-up carrier. Supply shipper's name and location,
consignee's name and location, date of shipment, number of cartons,
commodity, weight, and freight bill number.

Certification to read:

"I hereby certify that this is a true copy of the_____
dated_____."

Signed_____
　　　　　　　　　　　　Customer Service Manager

Damage claims are to be reported within 72 hours. Loss and damage
claims must be filed within nine months.

Our Insurance Broker should pay all claims in from four to six
weeks and advise consignee as to disposition of damaged merchandise.

(*text continued from page 153*)

day, in a company making 20,000 shipments per month. Claims historically run at 1/4 of 1% per month of the total number of shipments and take up to six months to settle. There can, therefore, be as many as 300 outstanding claims for follow-up.

Second Point of Information: You will observe that the claims procedures allow the shipper two chances to collect. The initial claim is placed with the common carrier. If unpaid for any reason, the claim is formally placed with the company's insurance broker for payment under its commercial property policy, subject, of course, to its usual deductibles.

MEDICAL INSURANCE

Employee medical insurance programs generally are the responsibility of the personnel section. In some companies, particularly where these employee benefits are noncontributory (the company pays 100% of the premium charges), the administration of this function falls within the purview of the treasurer, as he or she is responsible for all other types of insurance. In such event, the treasurer should, as a minimum, provide for catastrophe coverage for employees, in the form of a major medical policy (usually paying 75 to 80% of hospital charges above a high deductible or on top of employee-paid Blue Cross/Shield coverage) or, perhaps, through a comprehensive medical policy. The comprehensive policy combines major medical coverage with basic hospital/medical coverage.

For example, the comprehensive policy may provide for a $250 deductible for doctors' bills and drugs and then pay 75% of all remaining charges up to $50,000. Such a policy may be expected to protect the employee and his or her dependents in the most extreme cases and so qualifies as a catastrophe policy. Variants allow for the first $2000 in charges to be paid in full, without coinsurance, for an increased premium, which the employee may be asked to bear—making a portion of the policy contributory. As another variant, the employee may be required to carry his or her own Blue Cross/Shield policy, whereas the company will supply the excess coverage on top of that. Should the employee not carry his or her own insurance, there would then be a $750 deductible before the major medical program came into play. This device effectively, then, has become a sharing of the risk of loss between three parties—the company, the employee, and the insurance company.

Managed health care plans or health maintenance organizations (HMOs) can generally provide the necessary medical coverage for employees at lower cost, as the employee must use the doctors enrolled in the health care plan. Some plans provide that the employee may select an outside doctor at an additional cost.

Cafeteria plans may be used to provide medical benefits. Cafeteria plans are employer-sponsored benefit packages that offer employees the choice of either taking cash or receiving qualified benefits like accident insurance, health insurance, group-term life insurance, or dependent care coverage. The employee does not include in his or her income any benefits received from the cafeteria plan. If the participant chooses cash, however, it is included in gross income as compensation (Code Sec. 125).

A typical cafeteria plan offers health insurance coverage and permits the employee to contribute toward a flexible spending account for reimbursement of uninsured medical expenses. The cost of the health insurance coverage provided by the employer, as well as the salary reduction contributions used to reimburse uninsured medical expenses, are excluded from employee gross income for federal income tax purposes and are excluded from wages for purposes of calculating income tax withholding and FICA taxes.

Absent a cafeteria plan, had the employee paid all or part of the cost of the health insurance coverage with after-tax compensation, that compensation would have been included in wages for income tax withholding and FICA taxes. The same would apply to the employee's payment of uninsured medical expenses. Further, neither the amounts paid for insurance coverage nor the amounts paid for uninsured medical expenses would have been deductible by the employee except to the extent that total medical expenses exceeded 7.5% of adjusted gross income.

Small businesses can take advantage of IRS Section 105 as a variant on the Section 125 cafeteria plans. Section 105 provides tax deductions for medical expenses. However, this is not insurance and does not replace existing coverage. Under this section, the employer can claim a 100% deduction for medical expenses, including premiums; uninsured medical, dental, and eye care expenses; term life insurance up to $50,000; and disability income premiums. This applies to sole proprietorships and small entities, including partnerships, C corporations, S corporations, and limited liability companies. The company employs a spouse under a family employment plan and qualifies for these benefits. Agreements and forms must be completed to meet the requirements of Section 105.

THE ANNUAL INSURANCE REVIEW

The company changes from year to year. It may grow, contract, or change products, locations, or methods of distribution. Each affects the type and amount of insurance coverage the company carries. The treasurer should conduct an annual review of the insurance record (Exhibit 4-1) with the insurance manager or the company's general agent, adding or reducing coverage as conditions require it. This would include a review and consideration of each policy, its limits and deductibles. Factors to be considered in this review would be:

- ✦ Retirement of fixed assets; additions to fixed assets
- ✦ Premises additions or reductions
- ✦ Inventory levels at various locations
- ✦ Cash valuation of all properties (inflation effect)
- ✦ Channels of product distribution
- ✦ Pertinent legal cases affecting insurance awards
- ✦ New contingent risks (new suppliers)
- ✦ New coverage requirements per checklist (boiler, glass, sprinkler)

This review will keep the insurance coverage current with the company's changing posture, avoiding uninsured catastrophe losses.

THE PERIODIC INSURANCE REVIEW

An overall insurance review should be conducted by an outside specialist once every five or six years. The specialist will take the work on a contingency basis, charging 30% of the first year's savings. Savings are readily attained, as the very presence of the specialist will cause the insurance broker to approach the carriers to demand lower rates. If these are not available from the existing carriers, the specialist will provide alternative sources. Further, the specialist will critique the scope and breadth of the insurance coverage to ensure that all risks are properly covered.

CLAIMS HANDLING

Freight claims are processed in the purchasing department, as described in detail, previously. All other claims should be processed by the accounting department under the aegis of the controller, subject to final review and approval of the treasurer. Most claims involve loss of or damage to inventory, fixed assets, or cash or securities. The controller maintains the records that provide the history of the acquisition, use, or disposition of these assets. Support and documentation for claims may be prepared by internal auditors or general accounting personnel. These records should be complete accounting workpapers, following all the tenets for the proper preparation of such papers. This means properly dated, reviewed, approved, indexed, and scheduled, with appropriate trails for the insurance company's reviewers.

Product liability claims, being non-asset-oriented claims, may be processed by the legal department or, if there is none, by a staff assistant to the treasurer. Where these involve loss of customers' property, the customer should be required to submit documented proof of loss, and depreciation should be applied to the customer's asset to obtain current sound value. These claims, if small in dollar amount, may be self-insured through the use of high deductibles on the commercial property policy.

Take This Precaution: Do not pay undocumented or unsupported claims. Establish a working procedure delineating the

Exhibit 4-4.   Insurance claims — liability on property damage.

HOP/SOP MEMO

TO BE FILED WITHIN CORRESPONDING PROCEDURE

Memo To: List 8.0, Branch Administrators   Subject: Insurance Claims—
                                                                Liability on Property Damage
From: Daniel L. Gotthilf, Controller   Eff. Date: March 2, 20__

HOP [ ] No.: _____   Title: INSURANCE CLAIMS – LIABILITY ON
                                                 PROPERTY DAMAGE
SOP [ ] No.:   B-7a

HOP [ ] Last Correction No.: _____   HOP [ ] New Correction No.: _____

SOP [ ] Last Correction No.: _____   SOP [ ] New Correction No.: ___365_____

Paragraph #   Page #   Affected

Insurance claims from customers, or others, for damage to property or persons, are handled by the controller's office. To substantiate a claim, we need:

1. A letter from the customer, or other claimant, giving a complete explanation of how the accident occurred, and date, time, place, witnesses.

2. A memo from our sales or service representative who witnessed the accident, explaining how and why it occurred, also giving date, time, and place.

3. If our sales or service representative was not present at time of accident, a service representative must make a service call to verify the damage and the machine problem, if any, and should prepare the memo in 2, above.

4. A copy of the service call report, if any, from 2 or 3, above.

Branch administrator should:

a. Investigate sales or service representative's claim.

b. Forward items 1, 2 or 3, and 4 to controller's office.

c. Advise customer that claim takes about three weeks to process for payment (if under $100).

d. Advise customer that we are not responsible for claims arising from his or her own error, carelessness, or negligence. In short, we are responsible only for damage caused by a defect in our machine (such as a leaky tank).

e. Send a cover memo with documents in b, recommending for or against payment of the claim, based on all the facts and an interrogation of sales or service representative, in a above.

INQUIRIES: Controller
DISTRIBUTION: List 12.0, SOP Manual Holders

support required before a claim will be paid. Such a procedure is shown in Exhibit 4-4, **insurance claims — liability on property damage**. This procedure avoids the payment of fraudulent claims.

Helpful Hint: See Strategic Risk Management in Chapter 19 for a discussion on additional insurance coverage for employee practices liability and business practices liability.

PRACTICAL APPROACH TO INSURANCE COVERAGES

You should not insure against every possible loss. The best approach is to insure against potential catastrophes that could impair the ability of the enterprise to continue to operate. For lesser losses, an analysis of claims should be made and deductibles established at premium savings that just exceed the deductible losses. New companies would do best to carry higher deductibles until a track record of claims is established.

Procedures for the placing and pursuing of claims should be documented and implemented. An annual review of the company's needs in the insurance area should be conducted to avoid uninsured losses.

5

Forecasting Cash Requirements as a Basis for Maintaining Adequate Funds

The provision of capital is a job function of the treasurer, as defined by FEI. The treasurer provides for both the short- and long-term capital required by the business, and the methods to accomplish this have been examined in Chapters 1 and 2. The controller, however, is responsible for planning for control, and this responsibility embodies forecasting cash requirements.

Operations are controlled through budgets. This is described in Chapter 6. The following budgets must be prepared before cash is forecasted:

1. Operating budgets
2. Administrative/financial budgets
3. Capital expenditure budgets

Data from these budgets is then used to complete the cash forecast. We may use the term *budget* to imply the total control plan, be it an operating plan for profits, or a cash budget or plan to control the in and outflows of cash. The word *forecast* is less extensive, merely being a prediction of cash position at a certain point in time. The cash forecast, then, is the end result of the cash budget—the final cash position resulting from the carefully controlled plan. The budget spawns the forecast.

Purposes of the Cash Budget

1. The cash budget allows analysis of other budgets for feasibility before they are approved. Can we afford them?
2. The cash budget minimizes the element of surprise as to climbing inventories, accounts receivable, investment in fixed assets, or income taxes. The budget shows the source and uses of cash as it relates to these items.
3. Monthly comparisons of budget to actual allow for a monitoring of performance and constant corrections in the cash forecast.

Presentation of the Cash Budget

The presentation of reports under the complete operating control plan, as described in Chapter 6, will include the following statements:

- ✧ Income statements
- ✧ Balance sheet
- ✧ Statement of retained earnings
- ✧ Statement of cash flows
- ✧ Supplementary financial data

In short, it includes everything that would be included in a published annual report for stockholders, and in the same format. The **statement of cash flows** has formally replaced the statement of changes in financial position, which was at one time called the source and application of funds, with a slightly different format. It is merely a reclassification of a standard cash requirement statement, with regroupings to fit the accepted format. It is also a requirement of the statement of cash flows that specific information about noncash investing and financing transactions be provided separately. An example of it is shown in Exhibit 5-1.

The supplementary financial data could include the **projected cash requirements statement** (see Exhibit 5-2). In reviewing the exhibit, it is obvious that the report has been prepared from other budgets—operating (sales, cost of sales, expenses of operations), financial/administrative (interest expenses, R&D expenses, depreciation schedules, subsidiary operations), and capital expenditures.

Observe these helpful hints in preparing the report:

1. Start with receipts from operations.
2. Add other income.
3. Deduct all budgeted expenses.
4. Show noncash items separately (amortization and depreciation).
5. Come down to a final "cash required" balance and a cumulative figure.
6. Add a section at the bottom showing how you will meet your requirements (in this exhibit, through bank debt).

The supplementary financial data should also include one other report, which is closely related to the cash requirement statement. The report provides **projected ratios** (Exhibit 5-3) of profitability, turnovers to sales, and liquidity of position. Just as the cash budget determines whether the other budgets are feasible, so, too, does the projected ratios report. There may be sufficient cash to meet the company's operating objectives, but the ratio analysis may indicate that the company's financial position is impaired, or that percentage returns that would be acceptable to shareholders are not being provided.

BUDGETING STEPS

Having seen the final reports and format, how do we get there? The following are the required steps to prepare the cash budget:

(text continues on page 168)

Exhibit 5-1. Statement of cash flows.

```
                Projected Statement of Cash Flows
                     Fiscal Year 20xx & 20xx
                          $000 Omitted
            Increase (Decrease) in Cash and Cash Equivalents
```

	Period Ended 20xx	20xx
Cash flows from operating activities:		
Cash received from customers — domestic	$ 22,189	
Cash received from customers — Canada	1,910	
Cash received from royalties	1,492	
Cash paid to suppliers	(13,443)	
Cash paid for operating expenses	(10,219)	
Cash paid for interest	(1,120)	
Net cash provided by operating activities	807	
Cash flows from investing activities:		
Cash paid for research and development	(165)	
Cash received from subsidiary	50	
Cash paid for fixed assets	(1,600)	
Net cash used in investing activities	(1,720)	
Cash flows from financing activities:		
Cash received from lease financing	25	
Cash received from other financing	25	
Cash payments on notes payable	(100)	
Net cash used in financing activities	(50)	
Net (decrease) in cash and equivalents	(961)	
Cash and cash equivalents at start of year	5,318	
Cash and cash equivalents at end of year	$ 4,357	

```
Reconciliation of net income and cash provided by operating
activities:
    Net income                                      $     108
    Adjustments to reconcile net income to
      cash provided by operating activities:
    Depreciation expense                                  981
    Prepaid commissions                                  (730)
    Inventory decrease                                    450
                                                     ---------
      Net cash provided by operating activities $     859
                                                     =========


Supplemental disclosures of cash flow information:
      Interest paid                                        8
      Taxes paid                                          40

      There were no noncash investing and financing activities.
```

Exhibit 5-2. Projected cash requirements statement.

Projected Cash Requirements Statement
Fiscal Year 20__
(000)

	May	June	July	August	Sept.
Sources of Funds:					
Receipts from Operations:					
Sales & Rentals - Retail & Dealer - *(1)	$4,347	$4,420	$4,420	$4,474	$4,528
Sales - Canada & Foreign - *(2)	382	382	382	382	382
Royalty Income - *(3)	235	279	348	265	365
Lease Financing Income - *(2)	5	5	5	5	5
Misc. Income - *(2)	5	5	5	5	5
TOTAL REVENUE RECEIPTS	$4,974	$5,091	$5,160	$5,131	$5,285
Cost of Sales	$2,670	$2,679	$2,689	$2,698	$2,707
Operating & Reclassed Expenses	2,154	2,169	2,184	2,199	2,214
Interest Expenses	224	224	224	224	224
R & D Expenses	33	33	33	33	33
	$5,081	$5,105	$5,130	$5,154	$5,178
Noncash Items					
Prepaid Commissions — Amort. Effect	$ (146)	$ (146)	$ (146)	$ (146)	$ (146)
Depreciation (excepting rental mach.) and Amort.	28	28	28	28	28
Depreciation - Rent. Mach. A	26	26	27	27	27
Depreciation - Rent. Mach. B	35	39	43	47	51
Depreciation - Rent. Mach. C	40	40	41	41	41
Other Amortization - *(4)	58	58	58	58	58
TOTAL NONCASH ITEMS	$ 41	$ 45	$ 51	$ 55	$ 59
Cash from Operations	$ (66)	$ 31	$ 81	$ 32	$ 166
Equity in Subsidiary	10	10	10	10	10
TOTAL SOURCES OF FUNDS	$ (56)	$ 41	$ 91	$ 42	$ 176
Uses of Funds					
Inventory	$ (100)	$ (100)	$ (100)	$ (100)	$ (50)
Fixed Assets - A	25	25	25	25	25
Fixed Assets - B	259	259	259	259	259
Fixed Assets - B(a)	7	7	7	7	7
Fixed Assets - C	24	24	24	24	24
Capital Expenditures	6	6	6	6	6
Other Notes Payable	10	10	10	10	10
Other Taxes Payable	10	10	10	10	10
TOTAL USES OF FUNDS	$ 241	$ 241	$ 241	$ 241	$ 291
Cash Required (Excess)	$ 297	$ 200	$ 150	$ 199	$ 115
Cum. Cash Required	$ 297	$ 497	$ 647	$ 846	$ 961
Cash Requirements fulfilled by:					
Increase in Bank Borrowing to 17MM and Cash on Hand at start	$5,318	$5,318	$5,318	$5,318	$5,318
Cash Towards Bank Balances	5,021	4,821	4,671	4,472	4,357
Cash Balances Required	$3,400	3,400	3,400	3,400	3,400
Dec. Bank Debt or Reduction in Balances	$1,621	$1,421	$1,271	$1,072	$ 957

Exhibit 5-3. Projected ratios.

```
                          Projected Ratios
                          Fiscal 20__ & 20__
```

Profitability	20__	20__
Sales growth	0.228	0.081
Gross profit margin	0.436	0.466
Operating expenses/sales	0.449	0.425
Pretax margin	0.099	0.059
After-tax margin	0.397	0.148
Return on average net worth	0.346	0.194
Return on total assets	0.105	0.054
Earnings before interest & taxes/total assets	0.175	0.122

Turnovers (to sales)		
Receivables	2.964	3.378
Inventory	4.691	5.270
Accounts payable	9.502	10.468
Working capital	3.734	3,835
Fixed assets	6.079	4.676
Net worth	3.229	3.012

Liquidity		
Quick ratio	1.018	0.996
Current ratio	1.686	1.706

(text continued from page 165)

1. Estimate account and note receivable collections.
   a. Consider the effect of seasonal or cyclical variations.
   b. Develop a collection pattern and lag relationships.
      (1) Age accounts receivable
      (2) Age cash collections
      (3) Develop the lag between sales and collections, for example:

<u>Days' sales in net receivables</u>

	Collected in month	Balance at end of month
Month of sale	4 days	24 days
Month after sale	12 days	12 days
Second month after sale		
Third month after sale	9 days	3 days
	3 days	0 days
	30 days	

      (4) Provide for the allowance for uncollectible items against sales.

      (5) Analyze receipts by class of goods and customers' geographical areas.

      (6) Consider cash discounts and returns and allowances as a percent of sales each month.

   c. Prepare a schedule showing **projected collections of accounts receivable** (see Exhibit 5-4) and ending cash.

2. Estimate cash payments for cost of sales. Either use a percentage estimate, based on historic gross profit ratios, or prepare a detailed purchase budget to include:

   a. Estimate of materials to be purchased.

   b. Purchase discounts to be taken.

   c. Seasonal or cyclical factors that will affect purchases.

   d. Consider vendor payment requirements. Prepare **projected payments for material purchases** as in Exhibit 5-5.

3. Prepare a schedule of **projected payments for operating expenses** (Exhibit 5-6). This schedule may or may not include interest, research and development, and financial management expenses, depending on the company's reporting format. Consider the following factors in preparing this schedule:

   a. Various payroll periods, such as biweekly for managers, weekly for office personnel, monthly for salespeople.

   b. Noncash charges included in expenses, such as depreciation and accrued expenses for taxes, insurance, or legal and professional fees.

4. Prepare a schedule of **miscellaneous cash requirements** (as in Exhibit 5-7). This is to include nonoperating payments of the following type:

   a. Note payments.

   b. Taxes.

   c. Loan repayments.

   d. Various nonoperating coded expenditures, such as:

      (1) Dividends.

      (2) Capital expenditures.

The capital expenditures estimate is often prepared as a separate budget. For this purpose, the **authorization for capital**

(text continues on page 174)

Exhibit 5-4. Projected collections of accounts receivable.

PROJECTED COLLECTIONS OF ACCOUNTS RECEIVABLE

(000's Omitted)

	Sales	Allowance for Un-Collectible Accounts	Estimated Collectible Balance	January	February	March	1st Quarter	2nd Quarter	3rd Quarter	4th Quarter	Balance Dec. 31 of Next Year
ACCOUNTS RECEIVABLE AND ALLOWANCE FOR UN-COLLECTIBLE ACCOUNTS AT DECEMBER 31 OF THE CURRENT YEAR:											
Prior to 4th Quarter	$ 596	$ 62	$ 534	$ 125	$ 124	$ 165	$ 414	$ 40	$ 40	$ 40	
4th Quarter	3,259	15	3,244	1,996	998	250	3,244	-	-	-	
Total	$3,855	$ 77	$3,778	$2,121	$1,122	$ 415	$3,658	$ 40	$ 40	$ 40	
PROJECTED SALES:											
January	$1,155	$ 2	$1,153	$ 231	$ 461	$ 346	$1,038	$ 115	$ -	$ -	
February	1,330	3	1,327	-	265	531	796	531	-	-	
March	1,915	4	1,911	-	-	382	382	1,529	-	-	
1st quarter	$4,400	$ 9	$4,391	$ 231	$ 726	$1,259	$2,216	$2,175	$ -	$ -	
2nd quarter	6,555	13	6,542					3,707	2,835	-	
3rd quarter	7,460	15	7,445						4,219	3,226	
4th quarter	8,185	16	8,169							4,629	$ 3,540
Total	$26,600	$ 53	$26,547	$ 231	$ 726	$1,259	$2,216	$5,882	$7,054	$7,855	$ 3,540
GRAND TOTAL	$30,455	$ 130	$30,325	$ 2,352	$1,848	$1,674	$5,874	$5,922	$7,094	$7,895	$ 3,540

Exhibit 5-5. Projected payments for material purchases.

PROJECTED PAYMENTS FOR MATERIAL PURCHASES

(000's Omitted)

	Purchases	Discount on Purchases	Estimated Balance	Payments							Balance Dec. 31 of Next Year
				Jan.	Feb.	March	1st Quarter	2nd Quarter	3rd Quarter	4th Quarter	
PAYABLES BALANCE JANUARY 1 OF NEXT YEAR	$ 320	$ 3	$ 317	$ 274	$ 43	$ -	$ 317	$ -	$ -	$ -	$ -
ESTIMATED PURCHASES:											
January	$ 461	$ 5	$ 456	$ 218	$ 201	$ 37	$ 456	$ -	$ -	$ -	$ -
February	544	6	538	-	257	237	495	44	-	-	-
March	412	4	408	-	-	195	195	213	-	-	-
1st quarter	$ 1,417	$ 15	$ 1,402	$ 218	$ 458	$ 469	$ 1,145	$ 257	$ -	$ -	$ -
2nd quarter	1,469	15	1,454				-	1,162	292	-	-
3rd quarter	1,927	20	1,907				-	-	1,524	383	
4th quarter	1,790	19	1,771				-	-	-	1,419	
Total	$ 6,603	$ 69	$ 6,534	$ 218	$ 458	$ 469	$ 1,145	$1,419	$ 1,816	$ 1,802	
GRAND TOTAL	$ 6,923	$ 72	$ 6,851	$ 492	$ 501	$ 469	$ 1,462	$1,419	$ 1,816	$ 1,802	$ 352

Unearned discount $ 2

$ 354

171

Exhibit 5-6. Projected payments for operating expenses.

PROJECTED PAYMENTS FOR OPERATING EXPENSES

(000's Omitted)

Department	Annual Budget	Jan.	Feb.	March	1st Quarter	2nd Quarter	3rd Quarter	4th Quarter
MOLDING								
Total expenses	$ 3,118	$ 216	$ 216	$ 262	$ 694	$ 606	$ 909	$ 909
Less Non-cash charges								
Supplies	$ 719	$ 51	$ 51	$ 60	$ 162	$ 143	$ 207	$ 207
Depreciation	220	18	18	19	55	55	55	55
Insurance	60	4	4	5	13	11	18	18
Taxes	32	2	2	2	6	6	10	10
Vacation pay	57	4	4	4	12	11	17	17
Total	$ 1,088	$ 79	$ 79	$ 90	$ 248	$ 226	$ 307	$ 307
Cash outflow	$ 2,030	$ 137	$ 137	$ 172	$ 446	$ 380	$ 602	$ 602
FABRICATION								
Total expenses	$ 1,168	$ 89	$ 89	$ 104	$ 282	$ 244	$ 333	$ 309
Less Non-cash charges								
Supplies	$ 136	$ 11	$ 11	$ 12	$ 34	$ 30	$ 37	$ 35
Depreciation	175	15	14	15	44	44	43	44
Insurance	6	1	-	-	1	2	2	1
Taxes	3	-	1	-	1	-	1	1
Vacation pay	38	3	3	3	9	7	11	11
Total	$ 358	$ 30	$ 29	$ 30	$ 89	$ 83	$ 94	$ 92
Cash outflow	$ 810	$ 59	$ 60	$ 74	$ 193	$ 161	$ 239	$ 217
ASSEMBLY								
Total expenses	$ 1,077	$ 74	$ 74	$ 92	$ 240	$ 204	$ 323	$ 310
Less Non-cash charges								
Supplies	$ 44	$ 3	$ 3	$ 4	$ 10	$ 9	$ 13	$ 12
Depreciation	15	1	1	1	3	4	4	4
Insurance	12	1	1	1	3	2	4	3
Taxes	6	-	1	-	1	1	2	2
Vacation pay	115	8	8	9	25	22	35	33
Total	$ 192	$ 13	$ 14	$ 15	$ 42	$ 38	$ 58	$ 54
Cash outflow	$ 885	$ 61	$ 60	$ 77	$ 198	$ 166	$ 265	$ 256
REPAIRS AND MAINTENANCE								
Total expenses	$ 600	$ 42	$ 42	$ 51	$ 135	$ 118	$ 175	$ 172
Less Non-cash charges								
Supplies	$ 95	$ 6	$ 7	$ 8	$ 21	$ 18	$ 28	$ 28
Depreciation	12	1	1	1	3	3	3	3
Insurance	2	-	1	-	1	-	1	-
Taxes	2	-	-	-	-	1	-	1
Vacation pay	13	1	1	1	3	3	4	3
Total	$ 124	$ 8	$ 10	$ 10	$ 28	$ 25	$ 36	$ 35
Cash outflow	$ 476	$ 34	$ 32	$ 41	$ 107	$ 93	$ 139	$ 137

PROJECTED PAYMENTS FOR OPERATING EXPENSES

Department	Annual Budget	Jan.	Feb.	March	1st Quarter	2nd Quarter	3rd Quarter	4th Quarter
PURCHASING								
Total expenses	$ 91	$ 7	$ 7	$ 8	$ 22	$ 21	$ 24	$ 24
Less Non-cash charges								
Supplies	$ 5	$ -	$ -	$ 1	$ 1	$ 1	$ 1	$ 2
Depreciation	2	-	-	-	-	1	-	1
Insurance	1	-	-	-	-	-	1	-
Vacation pay	2	-	-	-	-	1	-	1
Total	$ 10	$ -	$ -	$ 1	$ 1	$ 3	$ 2	$ 4
Cash outflow	$ 81	$ 7	$ 7	$ 7	$ 21	$ 18	$ 22	$ 20
GENERAL FACTORY								
Total expenses	$2,643	$ 201	$ 201	224	$ 626	$ 575	$ 729	$ 713
Less Non-cash charges								
Supplies	$ 144	$ 10	$ 10	$ 12	$ 32	$ 27	$ 43	$ 42
Depreciation	248	21	20	21	62	62	62	62
Insurance	28	2	3	2	7	7	7	7
Taxes	55	5	4	5	14	14	14	13
Vacation pay	45	4	3	4	11	11	12	11
Total	$ 520	$ 42	$ 40	$ 44	$ 126	$ 121	$ 138	$ 135
Cash outflow	$2,123	$ 159	$ 161	$ 180	$ 500	$ 454	$ 591	$ 578
SELLING & SHIPPING								
Total expenses	$4,267	$ 444	$ 381	$ 368	$ 1,193	$ 868	$ 1,247	$ 959
Less Non-cash charges								
Supplies	$ 2	$ -	$ -	$ -	$ -	$ -	$ 1	$ 1
Depreciation	9	1	-	1	2	2	3	2
Insurance	9	1	1	-	2	2	3	2
Taxes	30	2	2	3	7	8	7	8
Vacation pay	31	2	3	2	7	8	8	8
Professional fees	53	2	3	4	9	13	15	16
Bad debts	34	3	3	3	9	8	9	8
Total	$ 168	$ 11	$ 12	$ 13	$ 36	$ 41	$ 46	$ 45
Cash outflow	$4,099	$ 433	$ 369	$ 355	$ 1,157	$ 827	$ 1,201	$ 914
GENERAL AND ADMINISTRATIVE								
Total expenses	$1,392	$ 228	$ 108	$ 107	$ 443	$ 326	$ 312	$ 311
Less Non-cash charges								
Depreciation	$ 25	$ 2	$ 3	$ 2	$ 7	$ 6	$ 6	$ 6
Insurance	25	2	2	2	6	6	7	6
Taxes	11	1	1	1	3	3	2	3
Vacation pay	26	2	2	2	6	7	7	6
Professional fees	123	10	10	10	30	31	31	31
Total	$ 210	$ 17	$ 18	$ 17	$ 52	$ 53	$ 53	$ 52
Cash outflow	$1,182	$ 211	$ 90	$ 90	$ 391	$ 273	$ 259	$ 259

(continued)

Exhibit 5-6. *(continued)*

PROJECTED PAYMENTS FOR OPERATING EXPENSES

Department	Annual Budget	January	February	March	1st Quarter	2nd Quarter	3rd Quarter	4th Quarter
OTHER EXPENSES								
Total expenses	$__107	$_____9	$_____9	$___9	$____27	$____27_	$____27_	$____26
Less Non-cash charges - interest	$__107	$_____9	$_____9	$___9	$____27	$____27_	$____27_	$____26
Cash outflow	$___-__	$_____-_	$_____-_	$___-_	$_____-	$_____-	$_____-	$_____-
SUMMARY — ALL DEPARTMENTS								
Total expenses	$14,463	$1,310	$__1,127	$1,225	$_3,662	$_2,989	$_4,079	$_3,733_
Less Non-cash charges								
Supplies	$1,145	$ 81	$ 82	$ 97	$ 260	$ 228	$ 330	$ 327
Depreciation	706	59	57	60	176	177	176	177
Insurance	143	11	12	10	33	30	43	37
Taxes	139	10	11	11	32	33	36	38
Vacation pay	327	24	24	25	73	70	94	90
Professional fees	157	13	13	13	39	39	40	39
Bad debts	53	2	3	4	9	13	15	16
Interest expense	__107	_____9	_____9	____9	_____27	_____27	_____27	_____26
Total	$2,777	$ 209	$ 211	$ 229	$ 649	$ 617	$ 761	$ 750
Cash outflow	$11,686	$1,101	$____916	$__996	$_3,013	$_2,372	$_3,318	$_2,983_
DIRECT LABOR								
All departments	$4,769	$__327	$____327	$__410	$_1,064	$___892	$_1,434	$_1,379_
TOTAL CASH OUTFLOW FOR OPERATING EXPENSES	$16,455	$1,428	$__1,243	$1,406	$_4,077	$_3,264	$_4,752	$_4,362_

(text continued from page 169)

expenditure (Exhibit 5-8), discussed further in this chapter, provides the basic support.

5. Prepare the **cash budget** (shown in Exhibit 5-9). This is a simpler format than the cash requirements statement seen in Exhibit 5-2. It is merely a summary of the various schedules supporting the cash budget, and its purpose is to have a preliminary look at the ending cash balances, as well as:

a. The balance sheet

b. Projected ratios (Exhibit 5-3)

Both of these may now be prepared.

If a review of the ending cash, financial position, and ratios indicates that more cash is required, adjustments can be made to factor in additional cash (through short-term bank debt, for example), or to defer payments on trade accounts payable to a later period.

(text continues on page 178)

Exhibit 5-7. Miscellaneous cash requirements.

MISCELLANEOUS CASH REQUIREMENTS

(000's Omitted)

	Next Year's Payments (1)	January	February	March	1st Quarter	2nd Quarter	3rd Quarter	4th Quarter	Balance Debit (Credit) Dec. 31 of the Current Year	Total (1)+(2)	Next Year's Expirations and Accruals	Balance Dec. 31 of Next Year
Professional and other service fees payable	$ 200	$ 100	$ -	$ -	$ 100	$ 100	$ -	$ -	$ (200)	$ -	$ (157)	$ (157)
Notes Payable	500	500	-	-	500	-	-	-	(1,500)	(1,000)	-	(1,000)
Payroll Payable	300	300	-	-	300	-	-	-	(300)	-	-	-
Taxes — other than Federal income tax	141	-	-	-	-	-	-	141	(141)	-	(139)	(139)
Vacation pay reserve	300	-	-	-	-	300	-	-	(150)	150	(327)	(177)
Miscellaneous expenses accrued	250	250	-	-	250	-	-	-	(250)	-	-	-
Other assets:												
Prepaid interest	-	-	-	-	-	-	-	-	100	100	(50)	50
Prepaid insurance	146	146	-	-	146	-	-	-	47	193	(143)	50
Supplies inventory	1,245	311	-	-	311	311	311	312	100	1,345	(1,145)	200
Federal income tax	1,264	-	-	419	419	419	213	213	(838)	426	(951)	(525)
Loans—banks	350	-	-	-	-	-	-	350	(350)	-	-	-
Accrued interest payable	57	-	-	-	-	28	-	29	-	57	(57)	-
Total	$4,753	$1,607	$ -	$419	$2,026	$1,158	$524	$1,045	($3,482)	$1,271	($2,969)	($1,698)

Exhibit 5-8. Authorization for capital expenditure.

AUTHORIZATION FOR CAPITAL EXPENDITURE
(SEE SOP A8)

AUTHORIZATION NO.	DATE	FIELD SALES OFF. OR DEPT.	FOR HOME OFFICE USE ONLY TOTAL BUDGET FIELD SALES OFFICE	

CAPITAL EXPENDITURE BUDGET DATA	FIXED ASSETS	LEASEHOLD IMPROVEMTS.	FIXED ASSETS	LEASEHOLD IMPROVEMTS.
1. Total amount approved in the capital program for calendar year.				
2. Total authorizations previously approved–year to date.				
3. Total amount requested in this authorization.				
4. Balance remaining in approved capital expenditure budget.				

5. Reason(s) for Request

( ) Replacement   ( ) New or Changed Product   ( ) Hazard Elimination

( ) Reduction in Cost   ( ) Increased Facilities   ( ) Other - Explain Below

6. Does this Authorization involve a budget deviation? ( ) Yes ( ) No
If deviation, show total amount of excess: $
Explain necessity for budget deviation:

7. Description of Item:

Life in Years:
Cash Inflows (if any)
Yr. 1 $_____
2 _____
3 _____
4 _____
5 _____

8. Vendor's Quotation						H.O. INSTRUCTIONS
Item No.	$	Local Vendor	Item No.	$	H.O. Vendor	
						Requisition No. Purchase Order No.:

SIGNATURES	TITLE	DATE
ORIGINATOR		
RECOMMENDED	PURCHASING MANAGER	
RECOMMENDED	OTHER	
RECOMMENDED	PURCHASING MANAGER	
ENDORSED OR APPROVED	CONTROLLER	
ENDORSED OR APPROVED	OTHER	
ENDORSED OR APPROVED	OTHER	

Exhibit 5-9. Cash budget.

CASH BUDGET

	January	February	March	1st Quarter	2nd Quarter	3rd Quarter	4th Quarter
CASH BALANCE — Beginning	$1,664	$ 7	$ 59	$1,664	$ 97	$ 82	$ 158
RECEIPTS:							
Collections — trade account	2,352	1,848	1,674	5,874	5,922	7,094	7,895
Other income	8	8	8	24	24	24	24
Redemption of treasury bills	-	-	750	750	100	150	-
Loans from officers and stockholders	60	-	-	60	-	-	-
Total cash available	$4,084	$ 1,863	$2,491	$8,372	$ 6,143	$ 7,350	$ 8,077
PAYMENTS:							
Material purchase	$ 492	$ 501	$ 469	$1,462	$ 1,419	$ 1,816	$ 1,802
Operating expense	1,428	1,243	$1,406	$4,077	$ 3,264	$ 4,752	$ 4,362
Property additions	550	-	-	550	120	-	500
Dividends	-	-	100	100	100	100	100
Loans from officers and stockholders	-	60	-	60	-	-	200
Miscellaneous cash requirements	1,607	-	419	2,026	1,158	524	1,045
Total cash payments	$4,077	$ 1,804	$2,394	$8,275	$ 6,061	$ 7,192	$ 8,009
CASH BALANCE — Ending	$ 7	$ 59	$ 97	$ 97	$ 82	$ 158	$ 68

177

(text continued from page 174)

The cash budget is now "locked in" and transcribed to the cash requirements statement.

LONG-RANGE FORECASTS (SHORTCUT TECHNIQUE)

The long-range forecast for cash, considered to be anything over three months, is concerned with sales, profits, and balance sheet presentation. It therefore follows the five basic budgeting steps just described. There are some useful shortcuts, however, that may be used to generate the cash requirements statement. These are particularly good for the smaller company that does not budget on a formal basis. The basic budgeting steps are reexamined below, in this light.

1. Estimate accounts and notes receivable collections. Total sales will continue to be obtained from the projected income statement. Turnover on sales is now calculated, and receipts from sales are lagged into the cash requirements statement.

> *Avoid This Pitfall:* In calculating turnover, there may not be an even flow of sales or a uniformity of collectibility during the year. Uneven flows will distort the turnover figure. Resolve this by calculating turnover on a quarterly basis.

Turnover may be calculated simply:

Sales per quarter	$6,000 (a)
Receivables at end of quarter	$4,000 (b)
Percent of quarter's sales uncollected at end of quarter (b ÷ a)	66.67% (c)
Average number of days' sales uncollected (91* × c)	61
* Use actual number of days in the quarter.	

This could be further generalized, and it would be accurate enough for a long-range forecast, by assuming three months in the quarter. Then $3 \times c$ equals 2 months as the average number of months' sales uncollected. November sales may then be lagged into the January forecast as cash receipts, December as February receipts, and so on.

Assumptions using the lagging technique must be adjusted for the particular company. In the example just given, it was assumed that sales were equal in each month of the quarter, and relatively steady throughout each month. A further refinement, unnecessary under these assumptions, would be that November sales have an average date of November 15 and are collected by an average of January 15.

2. Estimate cash payments for cost of sales. Broad assumptions may be made as to the month in which the cash is expended, based on current paying habits:

    a. Payrolls are paid in the same month as the incurred expense.

    b. Vendors' invoices are paid in the following month.

Obviously, some adjustments will have to be made for major vendors who require payment in the current month or who extend terms into the second following month. But these are minor manual adjustments that do not affect the facility of the simplified calculation. Moreover, payrolls are always a separate and readily accessible figure from the total cost of sales, making the application of the assumptions uncomplicated.

Given these assumptions, the total cost of sales from the projected income statement may be divided between payrolls and vendor cost and applied to the proper month in the cash requirements statement.

3. Prepare a schedule of projected payments for operating expenses. The total should be adjusted downward for noncash items included in total operating expenses, such as depreciation, amortization, and accruals for taxes, insurance, and legal fees. This done, a further assumption must be made as to method of payment, based on current practice—usually current expenses being paid in the following month. The projected income statement's operating expenses may thus be lagged for one month.

4. Prepare a schedule of miscellaneous cash requirements. There are no shortcuts possible here. A review must be made of projected cash payments that are outside of operations as reflected in the projected

income statement. However, these are usually few and readily anticipated. Once again, they would include note payments, taxes, loan repayments, dividends, capital expenditures, and perhaps contingent payments from pending litigation.

The income projection will not reflect financial management policies to include efforts to:

a. Improve inventory turnover.
b. Improve accounts receivable collections.
c. Dispose of segments of a business.
d. Invest excess cash.

Therefore, the miscellaneous cash requirements schedule should be a net schedule, showing cash inflows and outflows for these purposes. Broad assumptions can be made as to the cash effect of these financial programs, based on management's goals—for example, a 10% reduction in the dollar value of parts inventories over the next 12 months, or a five-day improvement in days' sales uncollected, hence an 8% improvement (5/60).

5. Prepare the cash budget. This may be quickly prepared from the shortcut assumptions in the four previous steps. As before, the balance sheet and projected ratios must be reviewed to determine whether the results are acceptable.

> *Helpful Hint:* The entire shortcut budgeting process allows for several midstream budgeting changes to be made before the final cash requirements statement is prepared.

SHORT-RANGE FORECASTS

The short-range forecast is for three months or less. In most companies, it is prepared every month by the controller's department for the treasurer's review.

Using this forecast, each month of the year is forecast *three* times:

1. At the end of December, forecast January, February, and *March*.
2. At the end of January, forecast February, *March*, and April.
3. At the end of February, forecast *March*, April, and May.

This device enables us to compare plans three separate times and to determine why our plans change and the magnitude of changes from forecast to forecast.

In addition, three separate quarterly forecasts are made. The three quarterlies and the detailed three-month forecast are added together to give a one-year projection on cash. This is compared to the annual (long-range) forecast, and differences, if any, are explained.

This exercise focuses on aspects of cash flow that may have been missed in the broad annual forecast.

The techniques for short-range forecasts are:

1. The same as those for a long-range forecast, using the basic budgeting steps, if formal budgets are prepared, subject to near-term adjustments that are not always visible at the time long-range forecasts are made.
2. Estimate each line item on the cash requirements statement, if no previous budgets have been prepared, as follows:
    a. Estimate the average number of months' sales uncollected as done on page 178, and lag sales into collections for the next two or three months.
    b. Obtain marketing estimates of sales for nine or ten months forward, sufficient to permit you to estimate collections into the twelfth month of your projection. These estimates may consist of a sales projection for the next three quarters, without monthly detail.
    c. Estimate cost of sales from the sales projections in b. Lag payments based on current payment methods—for example, in the month following the expense. Payrolls can be separated out for payment in the current month, if staffing tables are available, or based on a percentage of current payrolls as related to the increase in budgeted sales.
    d. Estimate operating expenses as a percentage of current sales, based on the new marketing forecasts of sales. Assume these expenses are disbursed in the following month.

   e. Estimate miscellaneous cash requirements, using the technique on page 169. There are no shortcuts here. In the short run, all sources of cash receipts should also be taken into consideration. Usual sources of such receipts are:
- Accounts and notes receivable collections
- Cash sales
- Sales of fixed assets
- Sales of investments—stock or securities
- Sales of miscellaneous supply items
- Income from rent, royalties, services
- Dividend income
- Interest income from investments
- Recoveries from doubtful trade accounts
- Borrowings
- Insurance recoveries
- Lawsuit recoveries
- Return of advance payments or deposits
- Sale of capital stock or exercise of options

  3. Prepare the projected cash requirements statement as shown in Exhibit 5-2.

RAPID HANDLING OF CASH

It is evident from the previous discussion on both short- and long-range cash forecasts that mid-budget adjustments must be made. The technique illustrated provides for an interim look at the cash budget, Exhibit 5-9, to determine whether the pieces fit together—is there enough cash to implement the profit plan; does the balance sheet look all right in terms of the requirements of the owners, banks, the public; do the projected ratios meet the various requirements? If not, corrections must be made to the operating plan that generated the supporting budgets for the cash budget. As a minimum, this may require finding more cash (accelerating receipts or borrowing more) or deferring payables to the next period.

Deferring payments is, at best, a temporary measure and may adversely affect the company's credit rating; borrowing may not be possible or may be too costly; sales and operating expense budgets may already be strained to their maximums. The best response is to accelerate cash receipts into the bank by rapid handling at all phases of your system. This will require:

1. A knowledge of the entire operating system, available from:
   a. A systems study
   b. One strategically placed individual, say the controller, VP/administration, management information systems manager
   c. A committee of knowledgeable managers, say managers of billing, credit and collection, data processing, accounting, and field administration
2. Implementation of techniques for handling cash rapidly through the system. This could result in one or more of the following actions being utilized:
   a. Centralized handling and management of cash
   b. Little or no decentralization
   c. The use of fewer banks—fewer banks mean less balances
   d. Cash forecasts received from decentralized locations, if any
   e. Analysis of bank services being rendered and charges made
   f. Change of credit terms, discounts considered
   g. Reducing time and errors in billing
      (1) Examine time lag from decentralized shipping points to the billing office.
      (2) Consider decentralized billing, or systems changes to speed billing to centralized points:
         (a) Online data transmission devices
         (b) Terminals
         (c) Time-sharing devices to a central computer
         (d) Offline data transmission devices
   h. Analysis of customer needs in accounting procedures
   i. Recording sales net of discounts offered
      (1) Lapsed discounts are income and should be reported on separately.

       (2) Discounts offered may be deducted from balance sheet accounts receivable for proper tracking.

j. Lockbox handling of cash to avoid in-house clerical delays in posting and depositing cash (see page 9).

k. Decentralized collections and use of sales office support

l. Disposal of surplus equipment

m. Preparation of a laundry list of surplus supplies to be sold

n. Publishing close-out inventory lists or holding warehouse sales

o. Liquidating low-yield investments

p. Settling outstanding insurance or legal claims

q. Calling in security deposits and not placing new ones

r. Reexamining purchasing and manufacturing schedules to improve inventory turnover

s. Considering tax options:

       (1) Expense certain items for tax purposes that are deferred for books—software expenses, insurance, parts and supplies, fixed assets, tools.

       (2) Defer for tax purposes certain book income items—advance payments for goods or services.

       (3) Examine depreciation base and methods—tax and book need not be the same.

       (4) Lease and installment sales may be reported on an operating lease or installment sale basis for tax reporting.

       (5) Lease instead of buy.

t. Requisitions for funds by divisions or suppliers:

       (1) Telephone delays disbursement.

       (2) Examine use of sight drafts for sales people's expense reimbursements.

       (3) Consider sight drafts for vendors, such as frequent freight charges.

       (4) Record purchases net of discounts. Lost discounts are an expense.

       (5) Study "float" to carry minimum bank balances.

u. Studying and planning disbursements.

       (1) Don't pay early (see discussion on page 18).

       (2) Use sight drafts.

       (3) Use imprest and zero-balance bank accounts (see page 11).

Also see Improve Cash Flow Through Improved Systems for Receivables and Payables in Chapter 18 and On-Line Treasury Workstations in Chapter 19.

INTERNAL CONTROLS ON CASH RECEIPTS

The controller has the responsibility not only for planning and budgeting cash, an adjunct of which is the rapid handling of cash as just discussed, but also for the control of cash. This is control against losses through fraud, negligence, incompetence, or inept systems. No budget can be planned outside the framework of a rigid control system. Otherwise, there could be no assurance, with any degree of confidence, that the forecasted numbers would be attained.

> *Key Procedural Point:* As with any internal control system, cash control requires a separation of responsibilities for the actual handling of cash from the cash record keeping. When such a separation exists, fraud will require collusion, which, by definition, restricts the number of opportunities for such fraud.

Types of Cash Misappropriations

1. Outright theft without regard to controls or records
2. Lapping—misappropriating checks and reporting the cash received sometime later by misappropriating a check from another account
3. Overstating sales allowances or cash discounts allowed
4. Not reporting cash received from cash sales, unreported sales, accounts in the hands of third-party collection agencies, bad debt recoveries, refunds of deposits, down payments, collection of unrecorded items such as insurance claims, damage suits
5. Reporting part of the cash collected in 4 and holding back the balance
6. Undercharging accounts and holding back the difference when paid

7. Misposting records with amounts that disagree with the amounts collected, including falsifying totals
8. Falsifying records

It is apparent that these misappropriations will not continue unnoticed over a period of time unless collusion exists.

Checklist for Internal Control of Cash

1. Authorization for check writing should be separate from check signing authority.
2. Two check signers should be required.
3. Separate the responsibility for receiving cash and for depositing it, fixing the definite responsibilities.
4. Separate cash handling from record keeping.
5. Cross-check cash sales amounts from inventory records.
6. Divide responsibilities for receiving cash and paying cash, preferably in separate departments.
7. Cash receivers, appliers, or handlers should not have access to cash receipts books or records.
8. Bank reconciliations should be performed by personnel who have no other cash record-keeping responsibility.
9. Summary totals of monthly cash receipts and disbursements should be prepared by someone other than the daily posting clerks. Where there is a separate data processing function, batch totals of daily items should be prepared by the accounts receivable section for control overrun listings from data processing.
10. In a retail or cash sales business, use protective equipment—cash register, duplicate sales ticket. Read registers frequently, using separate personnel.
11. Mail receipts and checks should be tape controlled by accounting people, photocopies should be made of checks, and different accounting people should deposit the funds. Copies of checks should then be sent to accounts receivable application clerks for posting.
12. Store notes and post-dated checks separate from the accounts receivable posting function.

13. Deposit all cash and checks daily.
14. Company representatives selling for cash should be required to give receipts and retain a duplicate for future audit.
15. Internal audit should be conducted by an auditor reporting outside the accounting or collection departments. Audits should be made of all sources of receipts.
16. Personnel should be required to take annual vacations (rather than work through vacation periods), and shifts in jobs should be made frequently to prevent collusion.
17. Personnel handling cash and checks and cash records should be bonded through employee fidelity insurance (see Chapter 4).
18. In small companies, the division of internal control above is not possible because there are so few employees. Then, the owner or manager must maintain close supervision over the cash responsibilities and provide for frequent independent audits.

PRACTICAL CASH FORECASTING POINTERS

1. The cash budget proves the feasibility of the overall profit plan and all other budgets.
2. Short- and long-range cash forecasts need to be prepared and compared to actual results. This enables constant corrective action.
3. Procedures for rapid handling of cash may be established to provide for slack periods and to ensure meeting projections.
4. Internal cash control procedures are built around close supervision and a division of responsibility. Such procedures contribute to the validity of the cash forecasts.

6

Establishing the Plan for the Control of Operations

This is the first controllership function in the FEI definition: "To establish, coordinate and administer, as an integral part of management, an adequate plan for the control of operations. Such a plan would provide, to the extent required in the business, profit planning, programs for capital investing and for financing, sales forecasts, expense budgets and cost standards, together with the necessary procedures to effectuate the plan."

This, then, is called the profit plan, the budget, the operating control plan, the operating plan, or, simply, the plan.

TERMINOLOGY

We shall use the following definitions in establishing the plan for the control of operations:

budget The quantified plan of operations for given fiscal periods, expressed in the form of financial statements with sufficient supporting schedules to enable measurement of actual performance to budget.

forecast   A prediction of one aspect of the budget at a specific point or over a period of time, such as sales for the year or cash balance at the end. This is less extensive than the budget. As the term is used here, it does not refer to "financial forecasts," which may be the same as budgets, but usually refer to an objective, logical, supported statement of the most probable financial results. A financial forecast differs from a budget in that the latter involves motivational, control, and performance evaluation considerations as principal elements.

estimate or projection   An estimate based on assumptions that are not necessarily the most likely. A projection is often developed in answer to "What would happen if . . . ?" The assumptions of the budget result in estimated or projected financial statements.

Helpful Hint: The AICPA has published a Guide for Prospective Financial Statements, prepared by the financial forecasts and projections task force of the AICPA. This guide sets forth the professional standards for accountants regarding such engagements and also includes descriptions and recommendations regarding presentation and disclosure of prospective financial statements.

operating plan   The budget, as defined above.

profit plan   The initial profit target as expressed by the chief executive officer and as reflected in the bottom line of the budget. This, therefore, becomes the forecast of a number, stated either pretax or after tax.

THE BUDGETING CONCEPT

Even the small businessperson or retail store owner practices budgeting. The candy store owner estimates her sales every day—they depend on the weather—is it raining or too cold—and whether it is a school day—will the kids be in? She expects $200 in candy sales, knows her candy cost to be 20% or $40 and her daily operating costs to be $40 for rent, electric, heat, insurance, accounting, cleaning ($14,600 per year ÷ 365 days). She expects to net $120 for the day. In fact, she needs it. That's her minimum. She's got to clear $720 for six days' work to provide enough take-home cash to meet her own family needs. During the day, sales are slow. She doubts she'll exceed $180 for the full day. She immediately reacts and offers the next customers 2 for 1 specials (increasing her cost of sales to 40%). She completes the day and tallies up to $208 for the day. Her candy cost was $47.20, her operating expenses $40, and her net $120.80. She makes the day!

This example embodies all of the basic budgeting techniques:

1. The profit plan was established by the chief executive officer at $120 per day.
2. A budget, or operating plan, was established reflecting a 20% cost of sales, $40 in daily operating expenses, and a bottom line net of $120 a day as proposed by the CEO.
3. Communication was established with her family in determining that her daily home needs were $120.
4. Budget vs. actual (BVA) performance was measured during the budgeted period, during the day, to allow for corrective action to be taken, thereby assuring that the budget for the week or the year would be met.

The budgeting concept is embellished in the corporate world with some additional frills, mostly related to the extended span of control found in most larger companies, but the steps are the same. Let us examine them.

THE PROFIT PLAN

The profit plan for the enterprise is implicitly determined by the stock-holders and is reflected in the price/earnings ratio for the company's stock as determined by the marketplace.

These marketplace expectations are signaled to the board of directors and the president, who react to them, refine them, and examine them in light of their long-range goals. The profit objective is set and passed on to subordinates for implementation—to the VP/finance, the

VP/marketing, the controller, and responsible officers for manufacturing, research and development, and personnel and administration.

The profit objective is usually tied to sales growth and is quantified with one or more of the following yardsticks:

- ✦ Sales growth
- ✦ Gross profit margin
- ✦ Operating expenses to sales
- ✦ Pretax margin
- ✦ After-tax margin
- ✦ Return on average net worth
- ✦ Return on total assets
- ✦ Return before interest and taxes to total assets

The president may further specify certain minimum standards for liquidity and turnover of assets (see Exhibit 5-3 for projected ratios).

The controller is expected to interface with the other advised officers and translate these objectives into a formal budget.

THE BUDGET

The controller takes the following steps to "establish, coordinate and administer" the budget:

1. A budget committee is established to give final budget approval. This may be a committee of one, consisting of the president, but usually involves three to five corporate officers. It is preferrably chaired by the president or VP/finance, who can best interpret the financial goals established in the profit plan by the board or the president. Other members can be division heads and marketing and manufacturing officers. The rule to follow, as to membership, is that every arm of the organization must be represented, either by the directly responsible manager or by his or her superior. For example, if the president is on the committee, no one else must be on it, as the president has the ultimate responsibility

for all areas. If the president is not a member, then all officers reporting to the president should have membership.

The controller need not actually be a committee member. He or she will be at every budget meeting, anyway, to present, analyze, and interpret the budget for members of the committee.

2. A budget calendar is established and published, circulated to concerned managers, to establish the timetable and chronology of the budget. See Exhibit 6-1 for a **budget calendar**.

This particular calendar allows approximately 60 days for completion of the budget, from start to finish. It is important not to start the

Exhibit 6-1. Budget calendar.

BUDGET CALENDAR

1. Budget forms issued to field offices and home office
    departments. Goals are communicated.   6/30/

2. a. Branch budgets to district/zone offices for review
        and approval.   7/21/
    b. Home office budgets to superior for approval.   7/21/

3. Zone offices and home office departments send approved
    budgets to accounting department.   7/28/

4. Accounting department reviews budgets and sends them to
    data processing for data entry.   8/4/

Following dates are dependent on completion of step 4:

5. Data processing completes data entry and sends printout
    to accounting department.   6 days

6. Budget section edits printout and returns to data
    processing for correction.   4 days

7. Data processing corrects and prints out individual and
    consolidated budgets.   2 days

8. All budgets to budget committee for review and approval
    or adjustment.   5 days

9. Data processing adjusts budgets, if necessary, and sends
    approved budgets (6 copies) to accounting department.   2 days

10. Budget section issues approved budgets.   1 day

budget too far in advance, in order to obtain the latest inputs and changes that will affect the advance planning that goes into the budget.

> *Helpful Hint:* Stable companies, without seasonal aspects to their operation, may allow up to 120 days in their budget calendar. Volatile companies should focus on a 60- to 90-day advance period.

> *Another Helpful Hint:* In the illustrated calendar, certain dates are fixed (steps 5 through 10), and no variance in completion dates is permitted. These comprise the mechanical, accounting, and data processing steps that begin after the line departments submit their budget data.

The initial issuance of the budget forms to departments, in step 1 of Exhibit 6-1, includes the transmission of corporate goals as to sales and expenses. This transmission may be in a memo that accompanies the forms, or it may be on the forms themselves. This is discussed further in the next section, on communication.

3. Communication of the president's profit objectives is made, initially, to officers responsible for sales, manufacturing, administration, distribution, and finance. The profit plan, as described on page 191, is tied to sales growth and is expressed in the form of yardsticks, relating profits to a percentage of sales, net worth, or assets, as seen in Exhibit 5-3.

The question often arises as to whether budgets should first be submitted by the various departments or divisions who are responsible and then be compared to the profit plan, or whether the profit plan should be submitted to the departments with instructions to budget so as to achieve the profit plan. In other words, do we budget from the bottom up, or from the top down?

The answer is a little of both. Successful budgeting requires total involvement of the people who are expected to achieve the forecasted results. If a plan is submitted for these people, the operating personnel, and if their performance is to be measured against this plan, they should cooperate in setting the goals by which they will be measured.

This philosophy of employee involvement cannot be overdone.

A Word of Caution: Setting performance goals for employees without their concurrence in the attainment of these goals is certain to result in failure.

However, employees should not be permitted to set goals that are not consonant with corporate objectives.

In other words, enlightened management, sensitive to stockholders' needs, through the board of directors and the president, is in a position to determine the most likely attainable profit plan. This is imparted to officers, who distribute the plan to subordinates, sometimes explaining, exhorting, selling, demanding—some of each—as to the total soundness of the profit plan. The plan is then passed down to the lowest-level manager who has profit responsibility, with similar exhortations.

The communication process follows this chronology:

1. Explaining to all managers "why we budget."
2. Communicating the profit plan, distributing forms and the budget calendar, explaining corporate goals.
3. Reviewing submitted budgets in the budget committee and re-communicating the need for revisions to tie in to corporate goals.
4. Submitting an approved budget to all levels of "responsibility," with periodic progress reports to compare actual performance to budget and to explain variances.

The communication process is examined in detail below.

COMMUNICATION

Why Do We Budget?

This is the most common question. The budget, they say, takes a good deal of time to prepare, is only a guess, and probably is used as a yardstick to nail a manager with bad performance. Training classes and seminars are necessary to inculcate managers with the reasons and needs for budgeting. The following may serve as a checklist of points to be raised in the training session:

✧ The budget is an estimate of anticipated costs and expenses. A study of this helps us to understand our business better, to coordinate the efforts of all divisions, to provide top management with overall visibility of operations, and to avoid surprises.

✧ The budget is not restrictive. It allows for flexibility and improvement. It provides estimates of costs and expenses if goals are exceeded and, similarly, provides for reductions in expenses if goals cannot be met.

✧ The profit plan or objective is the sole important goal to be achieved. Failures to attain the stated goal are analyzed each period to determine the necessary corrective actions and to permit us to achieve the required goals in the future.

✧ Bad habits and poor management are eliminated. Errors are corrected at once.

✧ Every management decision is directed toward achievement of the profit plan as expressed by the budget.

✧ Forecasts of sales and expenses are based on past performance, plus planned changes and expected level of business activity. These forecasts recognize population trends, indicators of business activity, employment trends, and personal income levels. They are not guesses but intelligent estimates of future activity.

✧ The budget is a statement of policy, expressed in an overall profit objective. It is not a working guide or a tool for managing. Its objectives may be quantified into useful "rule-of-thumb" guides, such as the ratios in Exhibit 5-3.

✧ The budget is the tool that provides additional profits by using the processes of analysis and advance planning.

✧ Additional profits result because the key to successful operations lies only in the analysis and advance planning by all division managers before final budget approval.

✧ Large businesses have an attenuated span of control, and it is difficult to properly communicate corporate goals. The budget compresses the communication process into the quantified expression of a profit plan. Small businesses profit, equally, by an intensive study of past operations and future prospects.

✧ Day-to-day decisions are avoided, as decisions are preassessed through budgetary planning as to their effect on the entire business.

✧ Budgetary planning requires that plans be written and that the manager be held responsible for their execution. This instills the habit of analysis and advance planning.

✧ Participation by managers in the budgeting procedure creates thorough familiarity with the overall objectives of the enterprise, and thorough involvement. No one is left out or bypassed. Each manager can suggest and obtain the benefit of others' counsel. The final budget represents the combined judgment of all managers in the best ways to attain the profit plan.

✧ The budget not only coordinates efforts along the most profitable lines but helps in controlling operations through the issuance of periodic comparison reports of budget to actual performance.

✧ The budget uses "responsibility" accounting. It is as improper, however, to overbudget as it is to underbudget. For example, if each manager underbudgeted in order to look better in actual performance, the company would not have enough cash budgeted to meet its attainable goals.

✧ The budget uses the direct cost concept, with each manager being responsible only for those costs that he or she can control. There are no allocations or corporate pool charged in to any profit center.

Communicating the Profit Plan

This type of communication, including distributing forms and the budget calendar and explaining corporate goals, can become an easy task when managers have been pretrained as described above. This part of communication requires that each manager understand the "responsibility accounting" concept, which embodies the use of "direct costs" in the "profit center." The individual manager may then construct his or her own profit plan, which will become a part of the overall profit plan.

The distribution of the forms and the calendar and the imparting of the corporate objectives is best done in a general meeting with immediate subordinate managers, who, in turn, will hold similar meetings with their immediate subordinate managers. In this way, the importance of the budget—its timing and its goals—is given a personal touch with each immediate manager. It is not relegated to a written directive. These meetings will stress the concepts mentioned above.

1. *Responsibility accounting.* This requires the creation of profit centers at decentralized locations where costs may be controlled by a responsible manager. The local manager becomes responsible for the sales and administration at his office, as well as the generation of costs and profits. The manager is, therefore, "responsible" and he or she personally creates the operating plan for the office and is responsible for its results. The budget department merely supplies the manager with a printout of the budget, set up in a readable format, and then reports the results of actual operations to the manager, together with a statement of variances from the budget. The manager must explain and comment on these variances to her or his superior, who, in turn, is held accountable for the subordinate's performance. The system of responsibility, thus, channels up from the lowest level of managerial control to the highest.

2. *The profit center.* This is the lowest level on the **organization chart** at which the manager exercises control over revenues and expenses. Exhibit 6-2, Organization and Operations, is a chart for a marketing division. Each box on the chart represents a profit center, presided over by a manager who controls its expenses and is responsible for its revenues.

3. *Direct costs.* These are used in attributing expenses to the profit center. A direct cost is defined, for budget purposes, as "any cost that would be eliminated if the profit center itself were eliminated." This definition is necessary, as there often are costs endemic to the operation of the profit center that are not necessarily immediately controllable by the manager. They are, though, ultimately controllable.

Exhibit 6-2. Organization chart.

ORGANIZATION AND OPERATIONS

People depend on communication. Their progress hinges on their ability to communicate with others rapidly and conveniently. As technological progress makes the world smaller, the need for information grows greater. Whether people desire to copy directly, or to translate the language of computers and other electronic devices for others, they have a vital need for devices that make images. This is our field . . . and our future.

To carry out the far-reaching objectives Savin has set for itself requires:

1. A well-staffed organization, capable of functioning smoothly as our markets and products continue to expand.
2. Products that meet current and anticipate new market demands. This section describes our organization, how we operate, our products and their uses.

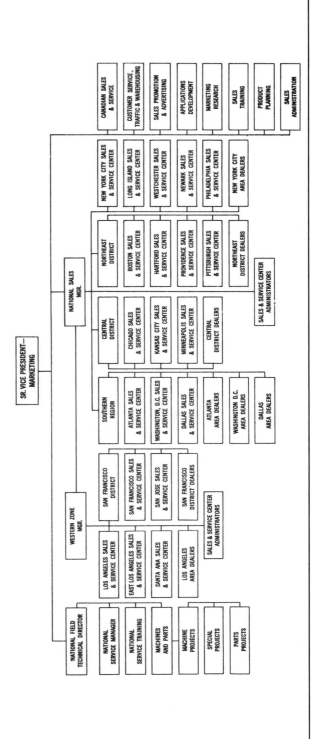

CASE IN POINT: Rent expense in a remote sales office, say with a five-year lease, may not appear to be under the control of the branch manager. It is, though, ultimately, as the office could be sublet, if necessary, and salespeople could travel from their homes.

The direct cost definition must be communicated to all managers to avoid arguments over what costs are charged to their profit center. This definition implies a degree of ultimate control that relates to the very existence of the profit center and is thus not an arguable concept as it relates to charging expenses into the cost center.

Stated another way, remove a box from the organizational chart and any costs that follow it are direct.

Helpful Hint: Avoid arguments. Do not allocate, apportion, or charge in to the profit center any costs that are not direct costs.

CASE IN POINT: In one company, a branch manager was charged for a portion of home office accounting services. He obtained a fee quotation from a local accounting firm to provide all tax and accounting services at half of the apportioned amount. It is difficult to assail his logic because of the artificial allocation of corporate charges.

4. *Intercompany transfer price.* This is the concept used to charge corporate pool and home office expenses to profit centers, without the necessity for allocations. Under this concept, the profit center is charged for merchandise purchases at lowest dealer price. This price includes a normal markup and element of profit for the home office, but is the same price at which an independent, non-company-owned dealer would purchase. The field manager cannot argue the logic of this charge, since if he or she cannot operate profitably on this basis, the company would be better off closing the field office (which is now a loss center, rather than a profit center) and franchising an independent dealer. All profit centers are compared on the same basis, using the published dealer price list, permitting gross profit margins to be compared against each other.

For corporate purposes, the artificial markup is easily eliminated to determine true gross profits.

Helpful Hint: If no published dealer price list exists, or if the company does not distribute through any secondary distribution level, a flat 40% discount from list price may be used to establish the transfer price. This is a wholesale concept that is equally understandable by departmental managers.

5. *The position description.* This document, described in Chapter 7 as a tool necessary in administering the plan for the control of operations, is shown in the "Treasurer's and Controller's Functions" for both the treasurer and the controller. Likewise, there is a position description for each box on the organization chart. Each manager of a profit center is so described.

This is an essential ingredient of communication in the budgeting process. Each manager must know where he or she fits in the organization and what his or her duties and responsibilities are, as they relate to profit objectives. These tools set the parameters for the job, avoid duplications by other managers, and fix responsibility for broad areas. I have often been asked why you can't merely tell a manager he or she is responsible for profits in his or her area, and that's it. Why do you need to go to the trouble and expense of the position description? The comment has merit. Profits are the goal, but where there is more than one responsible manager, more than one profit center, these corporate goals become interwoven, and each manager has functional responsibility to every other manager. Corporate policy in the form of social consciousness, antitrust adherence, corporate image, and overall corporate posture are ingredients in attaining overall profits. Each manager may achieve the profit goal, but the corporation may lose a damaging patent infringement suit that could destroy its profits. The position description approaches all these ends from a corporate, not an individual, standpoint.

6. *The chart of accounts.* This is the key accounting device used in fixing responsibility at the profit center level. An expandable **chart of accounts** is shown in Exhibit 6-3. It is vital that responsible managers understand that expenses and vendors' invoices must be properly coded

Exhibit 6-3.   Chart of accounts.

Chart of Accounts
FYE 4/30/

First Digit (High Order) — Position in Financial Statements

   1. Assets
   2. Liabilities
   3. Capital Stock and Surplus
   4. Sales and Operating Revenues
   5. Sales Returns and Allowances and Discounts
   6. Cost of Sales
   7. Operating Expenses
   8. Non-Operating and Royalty Income
   9. Non-Operating, Royalty, and R&D Expense

Second Digit— (Sub-Position in Financial Statements)

1	1. Current Assets
	2. Fixed Assets
	3. Deferred Assets
	4. Other Assets
2	1. Current Liabilities
	2. Long-Term Liabilities
	3. Other Liabilities
3	1. Capital Stock Issued
	2. Capital Surplus
	3. Retained Earnings
4,5,6	1. Electrostatic
	2. Xerograpic Products
	3. C Paper
	4. Diffusion Products
	5. Other Operating Revenues or Expenses
	6. Discounts
7	1. Selling Expenses
	2. Service Expenses
	3. Traffic and Warehouse Expenses
	4. General and Administrative Expenses
8,9	1. Royalties
	2. Interest
	3. Research and Development
	4. Miscellaneous

Third and Fourth Digits — (Major Descriptions)
Fifth and Sixth Digits — (Minor Descriptions or Branches)
Seventh Digit (Low Order) — (Reserve for Future Use)

to provide accurate information. Looking at the exhibit, you will observe that the simple numbering system used may be expanded on an almost unlimited basis, to permit a computer to generate the data required by cost centers (profit centers).

This chart of accounts allows you to "source code" each document, with a view to charging the cost involved into the originating cost center (using the direct cost concept set out in 3 above). As an example, advertising expense for direct mailing by a branch office would be coded 71XXXX. The first digit, 7, represents operating expenses; the second digit, 1, represents selling expenses; the third and fourth digits represents major descriptions of selling expenses, such as direct mailings, telephone canvassing, local advertising, etc. The fifth and sixth digits are encoded to identify each profit center or branch office. While this is a highly technical tool, and perhaps beyond the purview of the non-accounting manager, proper source coding is vital to generate accurate information.

In this regard, refer to the copy of the **accounts payable voucher** in Exhibit 6-4, which form is used to prepare every vendor's invoice for input to the data processing or accounting system.

Key Point: Note the box "Coding Approval, if $500 and Code 3." This indicates that an accounting officer must approve every expense item of $500 or more, so that the originating document is coded properly and results in an accurate report.

7. *Divided or functional responsibility.* This is the concept of "dotted-line" rather then direct responsibility. Communicating the profit plan and corporate goals requires an appreciation that *every* manager has dotted-line responsibility to every other manager. In a sense, each serves the other and reports to the other, both up and down and across the organizational ladder. The position description shows specific organizational relationships, but inherent in each manager's job are the unwritten relationships with all other managers. This is the concept of cooperation by which corporate goals are attained.

Helpful Hint: Organization charts should never show two direct lines upward for one manager. Each manager should have

Exhibit 6-4. Accounts payable voucher.

ACCOUNTS PAYABLE VOUCHER

TRANS A – B	VENDOR NAME					VENDOR NUMBER	A/P		– S –
							FREIGHT		– F –
							WEEKLY A/P		– W –
							(PLEASE CHECK ONLY ONE BOX)		

DUE DATE	CODING APPROVAL (If $500 & Code 3)		PURCHASE MONTH/YEAR	IBM Keypunch	
				By	Date

INVOICE DATE	LOC CODE	INVOICE NO.	QUAN.	PROD. CODE	INVOICE AMOUNT (BRACKETS=CREDIT AMT.)	CASH DISC.	GEN. LEDGER ACCT. NO.

TRANS CODES

A	B
1. Inventory Item	5. Vendor Invoice
2.	6. Vendor Credit Memo
3. Expense or Misc. Item	7. Charge Back to Vendor
4.	8. Credit Back to Vendor

GROSS INVOICE AMT.

DISCOUNT AMT.

Approved By

Accounting

NET AMT.

Instruction: A1. Inventory Control initiates form, records Vendor Name, our log no.
if applicable, inventory code, quantity, converted units.

only one superior. But every chart, likewise, should not skimp on showing dotted lines from field managers to home office staff managers. For example, the sales and service administrator in Exhibit 6-2 reports directly to the Western Zone manager. However, the home office national administrator, who reports to the controller (as seen in the position description in "Treasurer's and Controller's Functions"), carries a dotted line of authority to each sales and service administrator.

There is another important communications concept illustrated by this organization chart—that of divided responsibility. The basic responsibility accounting concept requires that a manager be responsible for all costs that are "direct" to his or her profit center. In Exhibit 6-2, however, the branch office manager (called the sales and service center administrator) does not report to the local branch manager, but rather reports directly to the zone manager. The shibboleth of "direct cost" control by the responsible manager is shattered. But every rule needs to be flexible to permit the organization to adapt to changing situations. In this situation, we find this:

CASE IN POINT: The illustrated company was in its first stages of direct distribution through sales offices. The local managers were primarily salespeople who had been promoted to branch managers. A concentrated branch manager training program had not yet been instituted. It was determined that each manager should concentrate on sales results and be provided with an office manager specialist to control expenses, until his or her training was completed. Since the achievement of high sales could be accomplished without the proper profit perspective, it was felt that the administration manager would more properly report to the zone manager. Branch manager training programs have now been completed, and sales managers are profit-oriented as well as sales-oriented. Organizational responsibilities have been changed, and administration managers now report directly to the branch manager. Through organizational flexibility and divided responsibility, the company was able to accomplish its profit plan during a period of change.

The point is, don't etch responsibility concepts in concrete. Change them to meet changing conditions, but keep the organization chart and position descriptions current!

Reviewing Submitted Budgets

Reviewing the submitted budgets and recommunicating the need for revisions is another vital part of the budgetary communicating process. The budget committee, as stated earlier, is composed of the president and/or key officers of the corporation. When individually submitted budgets are viewed in total perspective by the committee, they may not meet the stated corporate profit plan. It is no easy task to have to go back to managers who have labored over their budgets for weeks and convince them that revised estimates are required to meet the overall corporate goals. If, however, the communication process has carefully included the "Why Do We Budget?" checklist on page 196 as part of the training sessions, managers will understand the concept of overall profit objectivity. They can be readily convinced to make a revised contribution to the accomplishment of the profit plan. This may mean that one division manager may have to make a disproportionate effort, for which he or she obviously will expect to be rewarded.

> CASE IN POINT: A retail outlet in a major city, belonging to one of our largest retail chains, was a losing operation. A new manager was moved in and asked to budget a profit to permit the corporation to meet its stated return on invested assets objectives. The profits were earned, and the manager subsequently was promoted to president of the chain.

This art of recommunicating budgeted objectives is best accomplished by employing the following:

1. Management training—see checklist on page 548.
2. Management by objectives—setting performance goals; see discussion on page 535.
3. Personal negotiation—personal motivation by superiors with the promise of reward in the future, as in the Case in Point above.
4. Top management involvement—officers may hold splinter meetings with lower-level managers, personally imparting corporate goals. Higher management involvement lends a personal

touch to lower management involvement, boosts morale, and creates a team atmosphere.

Submitting an Approved Budget

Submitting the budget to all levels of responsibility, with periodic comparisons of actual performance to budget, is an essential ingredient of any formal budgeting system. This allows for midstream corrective action that ensures that the organization will reach its profit objective. This subject will be treated fully in Chapter 7, Administering the Plan for the Control of Operations. It deals with the budget review techniques to measure performance up to plan, describing how major variances are accounted for and controlled.

BUDGET VS. ACTUAL (BVA) PERFORMANCE

As indicated above, the reporting of actual performance as compared to budget is reserved for the next chapter. It is important, however, as basic to establishing the budget, that the finally approved budget be presented to the responsible managers in a readable format that will permit future comparisons to be done quickly and easily.

A **complete budget** is presented in Exhibit 6-5, including:

- ✧ Profit and loss (P&L) budget
- ✧ Sales budget
- ✧ Cost of sales budget
- ✧ Expense budget
- ✧ Employee forecast
- ✧ Standard branch P&L statement
- ✧ P&L explanations
- ✧ General budgeting instructions

The profit and loss budget is the lead schedule to which are posted
(*text continues on page 219*)

Exhibit 6-5. Complete budget.

Signature _____ Date

PPD BY _____

APPVD BY _____

Corporation

Profit & Loss Budget for Period Ended _____ Field Office _____

($000 Omitted — Hundreds in Decimals — Example 4.1 = $4,100)

Card Code [Z]

Ll. No.	Description		M O N T H S						Total 6 Months Budget (7)	Estimate for Next 6 Mos. in Total (8)	Total 12 Months (9)
			(1)	(2)	(3)	(4)	(5)	(6)			
	Sales										
01	– Machines	(Sch. I)									
02	– Paper	(Sch. I)									
03	– Other	(Sch. I)									
04	**Total Net Sales**										
05	**Less: Cost of Sales**	(Sch. II)									
06	**Gross Profit on Sales**										
07	Add: Dealer Handling Charges										
08	Less: Parts & Machine Destruction										
09	**Total Operating Income**										
	Less Branch Budgeted Expenses:										
10	Cleaning & Maintenance										
11	Personnel Recruitment										
12	Postage										
13	Salaries										
14	Sundry										
15	Telephone & Telegraph										
16	Travel & Entertainment										
17	Training										
18	**Total Branch Budgeted Exp.** (Sch. III)										
	Allocated Budgeted Area Exp.:										
19	Administrative	(Sch. III)									
20	Service	(Sch. III)									
21	Warehouse	(Sch. III)									
22	**Total Allocated Budgeted Area Expenses**										
23	**Total Budgeted Expenses**										
24	**Contribution to Non-Budgeted Expenses**										

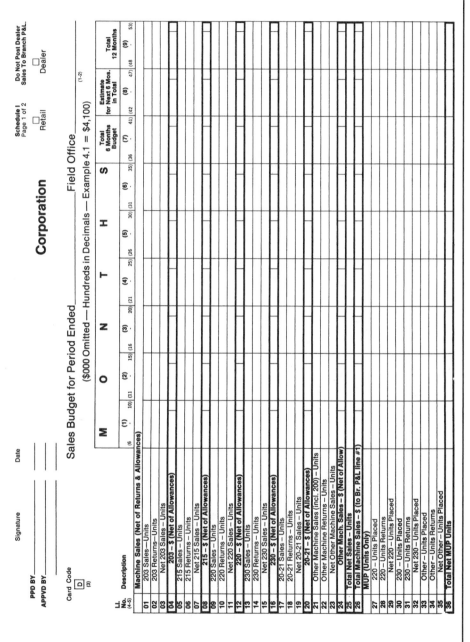

PPD BY

APPVD BY

Signature

Date

Card Code
D
(3)

Corporation _____ **Field Office** _____

Sales Budget for Period Ended _____

($000 Omitted — Hundreds in Decimals — Example 4.1 = $4,100)

Schedule I
Page 1 of 2

☐ Retail

Do Not Post Dealer
Sales To Branch P&L.

☐ Dealer

(1-2)

LL No. (4-5)	Description	M (1) (6	(10) (11	O (2) (15) (16	N (3) (20) (21	T (4) (25) (26	H (5) (30) (31	S (6) (35) (36	Total 6 Months Budget (7) (41) (42	Estimate for Next 6 Mos. in Total (8) (47) (48	Total 12 Months (9) (53)
	Machine Sales (Net of Returns & Allowances)										
01	203 Sales—Units										
02	203 Returns—Units										
03	Net 203 Sales – Units										
04	**203 – $ (Net of Allowances)**										
05	215 Sales – Units										
06	215 Returns – Units										
07	Net 215 Sales – Units										
08	**215 – $ (Net of Allowances)**										
09	220 Sales – Units										
10	220 Returns – Units										
11	Net 220 Sales – Units										
12	**220 – $ (Net of Allowances)**										
13	230 Sales – Units										
14	230 Returns – Units										
15	Net 230 Sales – Units										
16	**230 – $ (Net of Allowances)**										
17	20-21 Sales – Units										
18	20-21 Returns – Units										
19	Net 20-21 Sales – Units										
20	**20-21 – $ (Net of Allowances)**										
21	Other Machine Sales (incl. 200) – Units										
22	Other Machine Returns – Units										
23	Net Other Machine Sales – Units										
24	**Other Mach. Sales – $ (Net of Allow)**										
25	**Total Net Sales – Units**										
26	**Total Machine Sales – $ (to Br. P&L line #1)**										
	MUP (Units Only)										
27	220 – Units Placed										
28	220 – Units Returns										
29	Net 220 – Units Placed										
30	230 – Units Placed										
31	230 – Units Returns										
32	Net 230 – Units Placed										
33	Other – Units Placed										
34	Other – Units Returns										
35	Net Other – Units Placed										
36	**Total Net MUP Units**										

(continued)

209

Exhibit 6-5. *(continued)*

PPD BY _____ Signature _____ Date _____

APPVD BY _____

Schedule I
Page 2 of 2

Do Not Post Dealer Sales To Branch P&L.

☐ Retail   ☐ Dealer

Corporation

Sales Budget for Period Ended _____ Field Office _____

($000 Omitted — Hundreds in Decimals — Example 4.1 = $4,100)

Card Code [H] (3)

Li. No. (4-5)	Description	M (1) (6)	O (2) (11)	N (3) (16)	T (4) (21)	H (5) (26)	S (6) (31)	Total 6 Months Budget (7) (36)	Estimate for Next 6 Mos. in Total (8) (42)	Total 12 Months (9) (48)
	(10)	(15)	(20)	(25)	(30)	(35)	(41)	(47)	(53)
	Paper Sales (Net of Returns) 500 Copies Per Unit — Multiply 215 & 230 Units (1000 Copies) Times 2									
01	Regular Sales — Rolls									
02	Regular Sales Returns — Rolls									
03	Net Regular Sales — Rolls									
04	**Net Reg. Sales — $**									
05	MUP & Meter Rental Sales — Rolls									
06	MUP & Meter Sales Returns — Rolls									
07	Net MUP Sales — Rolls									
08	**Net MUP & Meter Rtl. Rev. Sales — $**									
09	CPN Sales — Rolls									
10	CPN Sales Returns — Rolls									
11	Net CPN Sales — Rolls									
12	Net CPN Sales — $ Value									
13	**Total Net Rolls**									
14	**Total — $ (to Br. P&L line #2)**									
	Other Sales — ($ Only)									
15	Service Contracts — Total $									
16	Service Call Billings — $ (incl. parts)									
17	E Mix Sales — $									
18	Carriers Sales — $									
19	Other Sales — $ (incl. mach. rental)									
20	**Total Other Sales — $ (to Br. P&L line #3)**									

(1-2)

210

Signature _____ Date _____

PPD BY _____

APPVD BY _____

Schedule II

Retail ☐   Dealer ☐

Do Not Post Dealer Costs To Branch P&L.

Corporation _____ Field Office _____

Cost of Sales for Period Ended _____

($000 Omitted — Hundreds in Decimals — Example 4.1 = $4,100) (1-2)

Card Code [L] (3)

LI. No. (4-5)	Description	M (1) (6 · 10	O (2) (11 · 15	N (3) (16 · 20	T (4) (21 · 25	H (5) (26 · 30	S (6) (31 · 35	Total 6 Months Budget (7) (36 · 41	Estimate for Next 6 Mos. in Total (8) (42 · 47	Total 12 Months (9) (48 · 53
	Machine Cost:									
01	203									
02	215									
03	220									
04	230									
05	20-21									
06	Other (incl. 200)									
07	**Total Machine Cost**									
	Paper Cost:									
08	Regular Sales									
09	MUP & Meter Rental Sales									
10	Coupon Sales									
11	**Total Paper Cost**									
12	**Other Sales Cost**									
13	**Total Cost of Sales** (to Br. P&L line #5)									

(continued)

Exhibit 6-5. *(continued)*

Corporation

Schedule III

PPD BY _____   Signature _____   Date _____

APPVD BY _____

Expense Budget for Period Ended _____ **Field Office** _____

($000 Omitted — Hundreds in Decimals — Example 4.1 = $4,100)

Card Code [P] (3)

Li. No. (4-5)	Description	M (1)	O (2)	N (3)	T (4)	H (5)	S (6)	Total 6 Months Budget (7)	Estimate for Next 6 Mos. in Total (8)	Total 12 Months (9)
01	**Cleaning & Maintenance**									
02	**Personnel Recruitment**									
03	**Postage**									
	Salaries:									
04	Managers									
05	Office Salaries									
06	Service Reps									
07	Warehouse									
08	Dealer Reps (Zone Only)									
09	Office Temps									
10	**Total Salaries**									
11	**Sundry**									
	Telephone & Telegraph:									
12	Telex & Cable									
13	Long Distance									
14	Base Charge									
15	Local Calls									
16	Other									
17	**Total Tel. & Tel.**									
	Travel & Entertainment:									
18	CR Reps									
19	Salespeople (incl. QMTM'S or MKTG. REPS) $100 Std. Trav. Allow									
20	Service Reps									
21	Managers									
22	Field Office — Administrative									
23	Dealer Reps (Zone Only)									
24	MTM's									
25	Other									
26	**Total Travel & Entertainment**									
27	**Training**									
28	**Total Branch Budgeted Expenses** (to Br. P&L line #18)									
	Allocated Budgeted Area Expenses:									
29	Administrative									
30	Service									
31	Warehouse									
32	**Total Allocated Budgeted Area Expenses**									
33	**Total Budgeted Expenses**									

212

Signature   Date

PPD BY _____
APPVD BY _____

Corporation

Employee Forecast (Head Count) for Period Ended _____ Field Office _____

Ll. No.	Description	M (1)	O (2)	N (3)	T (4)	H (5)	S (6)
	Sales:						
01	Zone Manger						
02	Assistant Zone Manager						
03	Regional and District Manager						
04	Branch Manager						
05	Dealer Manager						
06	Sales (incl. sales reps & trainees)						
07	Marketing Reps						
08	Senior Marketing Reps						
09	QMTM's						
10	MTM's						
11	CR Reps						
12	Dealer Reps						
13	National Accounts Sales Reps						
14	Telephone Solicitors						
15	Other (identify)						
16	**Total Sales Personnel**						
	Service:						
17	Zone Service Manager						
18	Dealer Service Manager						
19	Branch Service Manager						
20	Service Reps						
21	Other (identify)						
22	**Total Service Personnel**						
23	**Branch Warehouse Personnel**						
	Administrative:						
24	Zone Administrator						
25	Branch/Area Administrator						
26	Office Employees						
27	Office Temps						
28	Other (identify)						
29	**Total Administrative Personnel**						
30	**Total Field Personnel**						

(continued)

213

Exhibit 6-5.   *(continued)*

Standard Branch Profit & Loss Statement
(Expenses are Expressed as a Percentage of Sales and Not as Dollar Amounts)

Sales		100.00%
Cost of Sales		45.00
Gross Profit		55.00
Expenses:		
Advertising		.02
Amortization & Depreciation		1.45
Business Taxes		*
Car Rental Expense		1.44
Coin-Op Commissions		*
Cleaning & Maintenance		.32
Cost of Capital Invested — A/R		.55
Credit & Collection		.63
Dues & Subscriptions		*
Equipment Rental		*
Freight Out		1.10
Payroll Taxes		1.83
Personnel Rct Ads		.35
Postage		.44
Rent		1.30
Salaries & Commissions:		
Branch Office Salaries	4.12	
Sales Reps	16.42	
Service Reps	5.74	
Branch Warehouse	.89	
Total Salaries & Commissions:		27.17
Sales Incentives		.01
Sundry		.57
Supplies		.47
Training		**
Travel & Entertainment:		
Sales Reps	2.00	
Service Reps	1.20	
Other	.04	
Total Travel & Entertainment		3.24
Telephone & Telegraph		1.92
Utilities		.19
Total Expenses		43.00
Net Operating Profit Before Taxes		12.00
Less: Provision for Taxes		6.00
Net Operating Profit After Taxes		6.00%

 * The expense was either insignificant percentagewise or nonexistent for the
sample branches during the test period. However, these expenses will probably
occur sometime during the year for some or all branches.

** Training expense is incurred only at the zone level.

```
                    Standard Branch Profit & Loss Statement
      (Expenses are Expressed as a Percentage of Sales and Not as Dollar Amounts)


Sales                                                        100.00%
Cost of Sales                                                 45.00
    Gross Profit                                              55.00

Less Budgeted Expenses:
    Cleaning & Maintenance                    .32
    Personnel Recruitment                     .35
    Postage                                   .44
    Salaries                                13.35
    Sundry                                    .57
    Telephone & Telegraph                    1.92
    Travel & Entertainment                   3.24
    Training                                  **
Total Budgeted Expenses                                       20.19

Contribution to Non-Budgeted Expenses                         34.81

Less Non-Budgeted Expenses:
    Advertising                               .02
    Amortization & Depreciation              1.45
    Business Taxes                            *
    Car Rental Expense                       1.44
    Coin-Op Commissions                       *
    Cost of Capital Invested — A/R            .55
    Credit & Collection                       .63
    Dues & Subscriptions                      *
    Equipment Rental                          *
    Freight Out                              1.10
    Payroll Taxes                            1.83
    Rent                                     1.30
    Salaries & Commissions                  13.82
    Sales Incentives                          .01
    Supplies                                  .47
    Utilities                                 .19
Total Non-Budgeted Expenses                                   22.81
Net Profit Before Taxes                                       12.00
Less:  Provision for Taxes                                     6.00
Net Profit After Taxes                                         6.00%
```

  * The expense was either insignificant percentagewise or nonexistent for
    the sample branches during the test period. However, these expenses
    will probably occur sometime during the year for some or all branches.

 ** Training expense is incurred only at the zone level.

(continued)

Exhibit 6-5. *(continued)*

<u>P & L Explanations</u>

<u>PURPOSE</u>

This booklet has been compiled to provide a definition and interpretation
of all items that are used in the branch profit and loss statements (P&Ls)
and includes the following subjects:

1. Sales
2. Cost of sales
3. Adjustment to gross profit
4. Expense items
5. Allocation of expenses for area offices and some warehouse
6. Standard branch P&Ls

1. <u>Sales</u>

Branch P&Ls include all sales shown on the invoice register (branches)
and temporary PABST (zones) (PABST - product analysis by sales
territories), as well as coin-op sales, which are based on cash
receipts deposited into corporate bank accounts.

Usual trade-up allowances that are included in the invoice register and
temporary PABST as deductions are added back to sales for branch P&L
purposes. Non-comp. trade-ups are shown as deductions in the invoice
register, temporary PABST and branch P&Ls. See Cost of Sales section
for trade-up allowance adjustments.

2. <u>Cost of Sales</u>

Sales of all products are costed at lowest dealer price less 17% except
as follows:

A. Miscellaneous parts are costed at 60% of selling price. Labor and
   service contracts are considered to have no cost.
B. Docustat sales (receipts) are costed at 9%.
C. Coupon sales, regardless of size, are costed on the basis of 8 1/2"
   paper using lowest dealer price less 17%.
D. Freight out (charged to the shipping branch) on shipments from one
   branch to another.

Adjustments for trade-up allowances on Savin Equipment:

For trade-up on allowances <u>below</u> the lowest dealer cost less 17%, the
branch cost of sales (for the current sale on which the trade-in was
taken) is reduced (profit is increased) by the difference between the
allowance and the lowest dealer cost less 17%.

For trade-up allowances <u>above</u> the lowest dealer cost less 17%, the
branch cost of sales (for the current sale on which the trade-in was
taken) is increased (profit is reduced) by the difference between the
allowance and lowest dealer cost less 17%.

GENERAL BUDGET INSTRUCTIONS

What Is Budgeting?

The budget is a profit plan for the branch, district, zone, department, or division. Each of these is called a profit center. The budgets for all profit centers are combined into the profit plan for the corporation. Budgeting is the exercise involved in creating meaningful documents that will express the plans to achieve sales and the expenses associated with achieving those sales.

Your budget should be your best estimate of the sales that you can attain and of all expenses that you expect to incur to achieve those same sales. Your sales budget is not something that is unattainable; it is not a quota or a standard that you hope to reach. It is, instead, your most prudent estimate of those sales that you should attain, after giving consideration to all of the factors that might conceivably affect your achieving of these sales. Such factors are the general economy, sales representative turnover, the quality of your product, competiton in the area, your own managerial ability, and corporate support for your objectives. Underbudgeting sales does not mean that you have done a better job of selling. It generally means that you did not properly plan your activities.

Similarly, the budgeting of expenses is based on good judgment and best estimates of the various factors that might influence such expenses. Underbudgeting expenses is just as inaccurate as overbudgeting expenses and could have a deleterious effect on sales. For example, if you underbudgeted postage expense by not doing direct mailing, you would show a favorable variance on your postage expense, but you would probably show less sales than you should have for the period. The result would be less profit.

Budgets are required for a variety of purposes:

1. To estimate cash requirements to finance budgeted operations;
2. To enable sufficient inventories to be ordered to sustain the budgeted operations;
3. To permit staff departments to plan their service needs—for example, data processing to order the proper equipment to handle increased volume of data;
4. To plan staffing requirements;
5. To determine, in advance, that a profitable operation can be maintained.

Budgeting utilizes standard tools that help you to be a better ''budgeteer.'' These are listed on the following pages.

(continued)

Exhibit 6-5. *(continued)*

<u>GENERAL BUDGET INSTRUCTIONS</u>

<u>The Tools of Budgeting</u>

<u>The Budget Calendar</u>

The budget calendar presents a schedule of time in which forms and budgets should be prepared, approved, and formalized. Since every branch, district, zone, department, staff manager, and officer supplies budgets, it is important that these flow through the organization on a rigid time schedule. This will permit the results to be consolidated and formalized to attain the five objectives set forth in What Is Budgeting?

<u>Statement of Operations</u>

These are the ''actual'' results of operation, which are used for two purposes:

1. As a guide to preparing budgets for future operations.
2. For purposes of comparing actual operations to budgeted operations and explaining variances.

<u>Explanation of Variances</u>

In accordance with the budget calendar, actual figures are sent to all concerned, requesting an explanation of variances on the 22nd working day of the following month. Answers pertaining to these variances should be returned to the budget department on the 27th working day of the following month. Variance explanations are required for the following reasons:

1. To fix responsibility for budget changes.
2. To serve as a guide for the preparation of future budgets.

Incurring of Expenses Not Budgeted

Variance explanations will reveal expenses that have not been budgeted. If you have not budgeted an item, this does not mean that you cannot make the expenditure. The budget is merely a formal plan for anticipating and controlling profits, based on your forecast of what your expenditures will be. If you have not forecast an item correctly, you may still make the expenditure in accordance with existing procedures. However, the manager should plan carefully and economically. An operation that is not planned and does not conform to budget may disorganize the operation and probably result in an inefficient one. Moreover, underbudgeting is just as inefficient as overbudgeting. Plan carefully, make adjustments wherever necessary, and make each succeeding budget more accurate than the previous one.

<u>Forms of Budgeting</u>

1. Sales budget, form number (0-8-26) 1-08-9-321. Used for computing sales volume on machines, paper, and other supplies.

2. Expense Budget, Form number _____. Used to record estimated expenses to be incurred, from the alphabetical listing.

3. Capital Expenditures (Form number _____) and Leasehold Improvements (Form number _____). Used to budget expenditures over $100 for fixed assets and improvements to the premises (see page 00 for a complete description of these items).

<u>GENERAL BUDGET INSTRUCTIONS</u>

4. Forecast of Employees, Form number _____. Used to list the number of persons to be employed in each division (head counts, not dollars).

5. Sales and Expenses Budget Summary. Used to summarize the totals from item 1 (Sales Budget) and item 2 (Expense Budget).

6. Expense Comparison, Form number _____. Used by the budget department to compare your budget expenses with your actual expenses, and to show the variances. This also shows the results for last month. It is sent to you monthly with a request to explain major variances.

7. Operating Budget Comparison, Form number _____. Used by the budget department to summarize the figures from your sales and expense budget summary (No. 5, above). The budget department will also add cost of sales and will compute gross profit on sales and net operating income. Each month, your actual figures will be plotted against your budgeted figures and the overall variances will be shown.

(continued)

(text continued from page 207)

the results of the following sales budget, cost of sales budget, and expense budget.

Each budget has, in common, a format that shows six months in detail, and six months in total, to make up the year.

The P&L budget computes cost of sales at an intercompany transfer price as described on page 200, and only direct costs are included as expenses. Some expenses within the area are allocated (several branches sharing the same facilities or services), but no headquarters or home office corporate pool expenses are included.

The standard branch P&L statement is presented in two formats, one to conform to the same format used in the budget, the other, listing expenses in straight alphabetical order, for ease in comparison.

The P&L explanations are part of the communication and training process, explaining the nature of each item on the budget.

The general budgeting instructions are used to explain how each budget form is filled out. The instructions are complete and detailed to avoid error.

In total, these forms embody the previously discussed concepts of direct costing through responsibility accounting using profit centers. Planning operations, in addition, may require the expenditure of large sums of money for capital items that will benefit more than the budgeted period.

Exhibit 6-5.   *(continued)*

GENERAL BUDGET INSTRUCTIONS

PREPARATION OF PROFIT & LOSS BUDGET

General Instructions

All dollar amounts are to be rounded to the nearest hundred dollars, with
hundreds shown as decimals. Following are examples:

   4.1 = $4,050 through $4,149   4.2 = $4,150 through $4,249

Each column on the form has been numbered. For each line, enter the sum of columns
(1) through (6) in column (7). In column (8), enter your estimate (in total) for
the next six months for each of the budgeted items. In column (9), enter the sum
of columns (7) and (8).

Instructions by Line No.

1.	Enter amounts from line 26, schedule I, page 1.
2.	Enter amounts from line 14, schedule I, page 2.
3.	Enter amounts from line 20, schedule I, page 2.
4.	Enter the sum of lines 1, 2, and 3.
5.	Enter amounts from line 13, schedule II.
6.	Enter the difference between lines 4 and 5.
7.	Enter 10% of dealer shipments made from the branch. The branch does not get credit on dealer shipments made from Valhalla.
8.	Nonwarranty parts and machines destroyed must have a parts destruction request or machine disassembly request form completed as per SOP #B-16. These forms are costed at 20% of retail price and should be included in cost when forms are fully approved.
9.	Add line 7 to line 6 and deduct line 8. Enter the difference on this line.
10. - 18.	Enter amounts from lines 1, 2, 3, 10, 11, 17, 27, and 28, schedule III.
19. - 22.	Enter amounts from lines 29, 30, 31, and 32, schedule III.
23.	Enter the sum of lines 18 and 22.
24.	Enter the difference between line 9 and line 23.

Note: Nonbudgeted items will be shown in comparative reports, which will be sent
         to you after the end of each month.

Capital Budgeting

This chapter has been concerned with budgeting for profits, and previous chapters have dealt with obtaining short-range and long-range funds with which to operate. However, funds are needed only if they can be invested profitably, and profits are a measure of the return on assets. The company, therefore, must determine whether an investment is acceptable before making it. Four common methods of determining acceptability may be used:

1. *Payback.* Measures the net cash inflows against the initial cost to determine how many years of inflows are needed to obtain payback of the initial investment. This is usually expressed as a "two-year payback." The method has disadvantages in that it ignores cash inflows after the payback period, and it also ignores the decrease in the value of money due to inflation and the timing of its receipt, that is, its present value. Nevertheless, the method is simple and can be an acceptable yardstick.

2. *Return on investment.* Measures the percentage of the annual net cash inflows of the original investment. A $10,000 inflow per year requiring an original cash outlay of $50,000 results in a 20% ROI. This method does not work well if cash flows are unequal over the useful life, nor does it give consideration to the expected duration of the cash inflows. A 30% ROI for 10 years is obviously more desirable than a 30% ROI for a shorter period, but the simple percentage figure does not express that advantage.

3. *Present value.* Relates the cash inflows, for each year and for all years, adjusted for the time value of the money, to the original cash investment. The cash inflows are "discounted" back to the present. The method is difficult to compute manually, but any standard book of accounting tables contains present value tables that make the computation easy. Some electronic portable calculators, Hewlett-Packard or Texas Instruments, for two, contain preprogrammed systems to permit present value calculations at your desk. Spreadsheet preparers like Lotus and Excel provide present value formulas. All present value calculations require the use of the proper discount rate and a determination of the useful life of the project, both key to the calculations.

4. *Internal rate of return.* Similar to the present value or discounted cash flow method. However, it finds a discount rate for the expected cash inflows, using a trial-and-error method, which exactly equals the original investment. This rate of return is then compared to the company's standard or required rate of return to determine whether the project is acceptable.

Because of the sophistication required to reach a capital budget decision, field offices and divisions normally complete an authorization for capital expenditure (Exhibit 5-8) that describes the project, setting forth complete reasons for the expenditure. From this, the treasurer's office estimates the cash inflows and useful life with which to calculate acceptability.

Research and Development Budgeting

Many companies employ the capital budgeting techniques previously described for research and development (R&D) projects. They consider such projects to be in the nature of investments in fixed or wasting assets. Often they are. Other times, the projects result in formulae, processes, and know-how that may be either capitalized or charged to income as incurred.

New products are the lifeblood of an organization, particularly as life cycles shorten, and effective financial planning and control in this area is becoming increasingly important. The concepts of payback, return on investment, present value, and internal rate of return work well for R&D projects. The starting point to establish control is the authorization for capital expenditure (Exhibit 5-8). A variant on this is shown in Exhibit 6-6, the research project authorization request. The latter form provides more detail on the development steps, whether they are expense or capital in nature (which designation is subject to existing accounting policies), and the time periods required for development.

In addition to the above quantitative evaluation of R&D projects, a qualitative approach is useful as a planning tool.

(*text continues on page 224*)

Exhibit 6-6.   Research project authorization request.

<u>Product A B C</u>   Division

Date   <u>October 15, 20xx</u>
Requested By   <u>C.B.</u>

Auth. No.	Total Cost	Project Title	Approved
		Hi Speed XYZ Machine for	By P.H.
OK 193	$250,000	Product "A"	Date October 30, 20xx

PROJECT SCOPE AND OBJECTIVE
Design and build a new XYZ machine capable of operating at speeds up to 500 pieces per hour including an automatic ware take-out device and conveyor to the inspect and pack stations.

RELATION TO CORPORATE MARKETING AND/OR OPERATING OBJECTIVES
This equipment should enable us to maintain or exceed present quality standards, increase production capabilities and provide manufacturing cost reduction.

TIMETABLE OF INVESTMENT

Fiscal Year	20xx	20xx	20xx		Total
Time Period	6 Mos.	12 Mos.	4 Mos.		Project

EXPENSE

1. Development	35,000				35,000
2. Engineering		40,000	10,000		50,000
3. Market Development					
4. Pre-Operating			25,000		25,000
5. Other					
Total Expense	35,000	40,000	35,000		110,000

(continued)

Exhibit 6-6.   *(continued)*

CAPITAL					
6. Land					
7. Buildings					
8. Mfg. Equipment		75,000	65,000		140,000
9. Mobile Equipment					
10. Other					
Total Capital		75,000	65,000		140,000
Total Investment	35,000	115,000	100,000		250,000

Estimated Increase in Annual Net Sales $950,000

Estimated Date of Commercial Production   May 1, 20xx

Estimated Increase in Annual Net Profit $ 75,000

Cash Payback Period   3.2   Years

Discounted Cash Flow Profitability Rate   28.4   %

(text continued from page 222)
Qualitative Evaluation of R&D Projects

There are other types of research for which cost and profit calculations are not appropriate. Some examples are in the following list:

1. Research for the public good
2. Research on materials or processes to help the company survive special situations
3. Product improvement research of a continual and general nature
4. Certain fundamental research
5. Strategic research: essential projects with intangible financial benefit

The result of such research generally defies dollar evaluation. However, management should be able to judge these areas objectively

Exhibit 6-7.   R&D constraint analysis chart.

Industry Factors	Projects A	B	C	Company Factors	Projects A	B	C
Profit/Sales	—	—	—	Capital and debt	—	—	—
potential	—	—	—	Marketing strength	—	—	—
Growth rate/year	—	—	—	Manufacturing strength	—	—	—
Competition:	—	—	—				
Reaction	—	—	—	Know-how and patents	—	—	—
Patent protection	—	—	—				
Life cycle	—	—	—	Skills:			
Applications	—	—	—	Leadership	—	—	—
Market penetration	—	—	—	All other	—	—	—
Political/Social	—	—	—	Totals	=	=	=
Anti-trust	—	—	—				
Economic	—	—	—	Rate projects from 1 to 10			
Environmental	—	—	—	Discard projects below 70			
Social	—	—	—	Proceed if score is over 80			
				Use caution from 70 to 80			
Total	=	=	=				

enough to avoid losing effective control over the research operation. A good budget program can be of help here.

Pursuit of knowledge in a given field, without any regard for its eventual specific applications, presents evaluation problems. In certain cases, fundamental research could lend itself to direct dollar valuation. This would happen whenever a fundamental breakthrough opens the way to a series of exploitable new developments with predictable results and measurable markets.

Some of these subjective factors can be measured using constraint analyses that measure whether this would be a good business for anyone to be in, and, if so, whether it would be a good business for us to enter. Exhibit 6-7, the **R&D constraint analysis chart,** considers the various factors that affect each question.

Company Factors

1. Are capital and debt available, and how much is required? The lower the requirement, the less risk, and the possibility of more

competition. Hence, assign less points. If there is strong cash flow indicated with high capital and debt needs, score 10.

2. Score 10 for a good fit with existing marketing capabilities. Building from scratch is risky and costly.

3. Existing manufacturing facilities require less capital or debt and shorten the entry time to commercial introduction. Score 10 for this.

4. Know-how includes patents, design, engineering, manufacturing, marketing, and administrative skills.

5. Be certain that several suppliers of materials are available or that long-term supply contracts can be negotiated as an inflation hedge.

6. A project has the highest chance of success with a strong top manager, supported by middle management and skilled production workers.

Industry Factors

1. A rating of 10 should be based on the expectation of a 10% annual increase in sales, to be achieved in a reasonable time (say three to five years), and an ROI (see page 221) of 30% or more.

2. A top score should be based on 10% sales growth, after inflation, per year.

3. How will competition react, will patents keep competition out, and will the product have a long run or last just a few years?

4. Is there only one product or application from the research, or are there several, over which to spread the risk?

5. Can we penetrate the market with a breakthrough product, or is this merely state-of-the-art? Will we attain major market share?

6. Consider federal regulation constraints, pollution, social structures, and economic trends. If there are neither positives nor negatives in this category, assign it a 5.

There are 12 factors, 6 each for the industry and the company, with a rating on each factor from 0 to 10, for a maximum possible total of 120. Where there are subsets under major factors (competition, political/social, and skills), the sum of the scores under each subset should add to no more than 10. Projects will generally succeed with a score of 80 or more, unless extraneous influences, such as governmental constraints, are unexpectedly introduced. The chances for success deteriorate rapidly below 70. Additional factors can be substituted that may be more germane to certain industries or companies.

Also, see the discussion of off-balance-sheet financing, limited partnership, in Chapter 2 for a discussion of R&D funding.

BUDGETING POINTERS

Establishing the control plan for operations requires the formulation of a profit plan by the board and the president. This plan is translated into an operating program called a budget that results in projected financial statements and forecasts of sales, expenses, and capital requirements. The techniques for budgeting are communicated to all levels of management through careful training, and the operating plan is prepared, with each key manager being responsible for a profit center, exercising control over her or his direct costs of operation. This technique utilizes source coding of documents to enable proper charges to be made to cost centers, the preparation of plans or budgets for successive six-month periods, the comparison of budget to actual operations with reports of variances, and a series of reports in line with defined organization charts. This control program involves the broad management concept of planning corporate moves in advance, and then comparing performance to the plan. It is not concerned with the details of every transaction but only with the end result—profits. Budgeting is management accounting of the highest order, not based on the output of a green-eyeshaded Uriah Heep, but, rather, on the planned performance of the management group in setting goals and realizing them, utilizing the sophisticated planning tools of responsibility and budgetary accounting in achieving them.

7

Administering the Plan for the Control of Operations

In the previous chapter, we discussed the first controllership function, involved with establishing the plan for the control of operations. Inherent in planning for the control function is the "coordination and administration" of the previously established plan. You've got the plan. Now make it fly! This means you need an organizational framework to be sure people receive the plan, read it, understand it, are involved in it, and perform up to it. You'll want to establish budget review techniques to measure performance against the plan. This will involve the use of variance reports, which will be discussed in the next chapter. But, first you need the framework. The framework necessary to administer the plan for the control of operations requires the following:

- ✧ Organization charts
- ✧ Position descriptions
- ✧ Standard operating procedures
- ✧ Operating policies
- ✧ Personnel policies
- ✧ Publication control
- ✧ Exercise of authority

These devices are available to even the smallest company. They are quickly and easily constructed, and once completed, they attest to the internal control that is exerted by responsible management. They also make the plan work!

ORGANIZATION CHARTS

It is a business axiom that a company's success depends on having a sound organization plan. An organization chart serves to define:

- ✧ Responsibility
- ✧ Delegation of authority
- ✧ Span of control
- ✧ Job functions
- ✧ Reporting relationships
- ✧ Profit centers
- ✧ Cost centers
- ✧ Decentralized/centralized philosophy

This is a comprehensive list, yet every organization chart denotes these items, either specifically or inherently. The responsible positions are indicated. The lines leading from the top boxes indicate delegation of authority and span of control. The placement of the boxes, in relation to other boxes, implies the job function and reporting relationship. Each responsible box becomes a profit or cost center, and the flow of the lines will tell a good deal about the operating philosophy of the company.

Moreover, if a current organization chart is maintained with identifying names, a picture is painted for every employee that associates the individual with the job—and it is worth a thousand words.

One would suppose (as would your independent auditor) that the lack of even a simple and updated organization chart would indicate that there are unresolved questions of responsibility, authority, and reporting relationships—and if this be so, the organization, obviously, is unable to perform up to its promise.

In constructing an organization chart, the following principles should be considered:

1. Each person should report to only one superior.
2. Responsibility for performance of assigned duties must be accompanied by corresponding authority.
3. Each person's responsibilities should be clearly defined.
4. Charts must start at the lowest level that determines expenses and/or revenues.
5. Charts should top out with the recipients of profits, be they owners, stockholders, or trustees—not with the president.
6. Functional (dotted-line) relationships should be drawn.
7. Only a few subordinates (usually no more than six) should report to each superior (unless the subordinates all perform essentially the same job).
8. All essential functions should be charted.
9. Adequate checks and balances must be provided.
10. Committees should be identified and charted.
11. Names of individuals should be slotted and kept current.

These principles are evident in Exhibit 7-1, **organization manual**, which excerpts five pages from a manual, showing:

Page 1:   *Contents*—consisting of charts, titles and names, and committee profiles.

Page 2:   *Introduction*—giving a brief statement of purpose, and providing for update and change. (Note the "replaces" box at the bottom of the page.)

Page 3:   *Company chart*—the top chart, starting with the stockholders and board of directors.

Page 4:   *Controller's chart*—showing six persons reporting, and cross-reference at the bottom to titles and names.

Page 5:   *Titles and names*—the cross-reference from the controller's chart.

The responsibility for maintaining the organization manual in a current and updated position is that of the administrative planning department, which reports to the director of administrative operations (see page 4 of Exhibit 7-1) in the controller's area. This is the first step in the administration of the control plan.

(*text continues on page 236*)

Exhibit 7-1. Organization manual.

ORGANIZATION MANUAL

SECTION	Table of Contents
Section	Title
01	Organization Charts
02	Titles and Names
03	Committee Profiles
	Awards
	Banking
	Executive
	Options
	Product Development

Issued Date	Effective Date	REPLACES		Correction	
		Old Page Number	Dated (Effective)	Number	Page Number
2-1-	2-1-				

ORGANIZATION MANUAL

SECTION	Organization Charts

INTRODUCTION

The enclosed charts show organizational relationships and are in no way intended to reflect relative importance of positions.

The purpose of this section is to show the organizational structure of the Company. The charts included herein reflect the relationships of all management personnel and staffs. The manual will be revised from time to time as changes occur. Pertinent changes should be sent to the Administrative Planning Department.

Issued Date	Effective Date	REPLACES		Correction	Page No.
		Old Page No.	Dated (Effective)	No.	
2-1-	2-1-				01. 01. 01

(continued)

Exhibit 7-1. *(continued)*

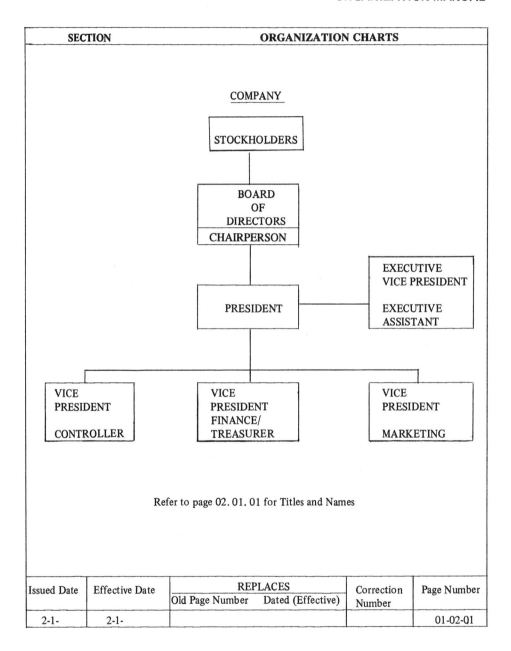

SECTION	ORGANIZATION CHARTS

COMPANY

STOCKHOLDERS

BOARD
OF
DIRECTORS
CHAIRPERSON

PRESIDENT

EXECUTIVE
VICE PRESIDENT

EXECUTIVE
ASSISTANT

VICE
PRESIDENT

CONTROLLER

VICE
PRESIDENT
FINANCE/
TREASURER

VICE
PRESIDENT

MARKETING

Refer to page 02. 01. 01 for Titles and Names

Issued Date	Effective Date	REPLACES		Correction Number	Page Number
		Old Page Number	Dated (Effective)		
2-1-	2-1-				01-02-01

ORGANIZATION MANUAL

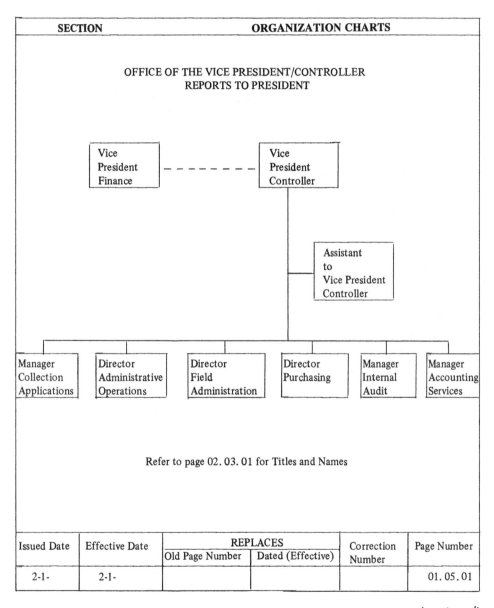

SECTION	ORGANIZATION CHARTS

OFFICE OF THE VICE PRESIDENT/CONTROLLER
REPORTS TO PRESIDENT

Vice President Finance — — — — — — Vice President Controller

Assistant to Vice President Controller

Manager Collection Applications | Director Administrative Operations | Director Field Administration | Director Purchasing | Manager Internal Audit | Manager Accounting Services

Refer to page 02.03.01 for Titles and Names

Issued Date	Effective Date	REPLACES		Correction Number	Page Number
		Old Page Number	Dated (Effective)		
2-1-	2-1-				01.05.01

(continued)

Exhibit 7-1. *(continued)*

SECTION	TITLES AND NAMES

CONTROLLER'S DIVISION

OFFICE OF VICE PRESIDENT/CONTROLLER . . . . NAME 1

DEPARTMENT	TITLE	NAME

ASSISTANT TO VICE PRESIDENT . . . . Name 2
MANAGER OF COLLECTION APPLICATIONS . . . . Name 3
DIRECTOR OF ADMINISTRATIVE OPERATIONS . . . . Name 4
DIRECTOR OF FIELD ADMINISTRATION . . . . Name 5
DIRECTOR OF PURCHASING . . . . Name 6
MANAGER OF INTERNAL AUDIT . . . . Name 7
MANAGER OF ACCOUNTING SERVICES . . . . Name 8

Issued Date	Effective Date	REPLACES		Correction Number	Page Number
		Old Page Number	Dated (Effective)		
2-1-	2-1-				02. 03. 01

POSITION DESCRIPTIONS

The position of each box on the organization chart is an indication of the character of the job, shows the reporting relationships, and, generally, summarizes the details that are found in the position or job description. Just as every procedural narrative has a flowchart to affirm its logic, so, too, does the organization chart affirm the logic of the position description. One does not exist without the other.

A **job description format** is shown in Exhibit 7-2, and a detailed position description for the treasurer and the controller may be found

(*text continues on page 238*)

Exhibit 7-2.   Job description format.

JOB DESCRIPTION FORMAT

Effective Date:

TITLE: DIVISION:
                                                                 DEPARTMENT:
REPORTS TO: SECTION:
                                                                 UNIT:

SUMMARY OF FUNCTION:

MAJOR DUTIES AND RESPONSIBILITIES:

ORGANIZATIONAL RELATIONSHIPS:

EDUCATIONAL REQUIREMENTS:

EXPERIENCE REQUIREMENTS:

Exhibit 7-3.   Guidelines for writing job descriptions.

```
To:  Distribution                    Subject:  Guidelines for Writing
                                               Job Descriptions
From:  Office Services
                                               5/12/
```

Below you will find Guidelines for Writing Job Descriptions. Please follow this procedure when writing job descriptions for those under your supervision.

<u>Procedure</u>

Drafts of job descriptions will be forwarded to the Personnel Department from the supervising manager of that position.

The Personnel Department will edit and prepare final drafts of the job description and submit it to the department head or executive for approval.

Job descriptions must receive final approval from the Personnel Department, which will then accept the responsibility for final typing, printing and distribution to holders of a Job Description Manual and the person or persons filling that job.

All job descriptions will follow the same outline as indicated below (see example attached):

<u>TITLE</u>: The title should be as simple and descriptive as possible; such as, "Supervisor — Customer Service."

<u>EFFECTIVE DATE</u>: This is the date of completion of the latest revision of the job description.

<u>DIVISION</u>: Indicate appropriate division; the major functional group headed by a policy-making executive reporting directly to the President.

<u>DEPARTMENT</u>: Indicate the primary functional subdivision of a division headed by an intermediate executive, usually but not necessarily supervising other managers.

<u>SECTION</u>: Indicate secondary functional subdivision of a division; primary functional subdivision of a department; a grouping of allied working units, headed by an intermediate manager who may occasionally supervise another manager.

<u>UNIT</u>: Indicate a group of closely related jobs within a section headed by working supervisors.

(*text continued from page 236*)

in the "Treasurer's and Controller's Functions." **Guidelines for writing job descriptions** are given in Exhibit 7-3.

It is necessary to distinguish between job descriptions as defined above, which are broad statements of duties and responsibilities, and the detailed job descriptions or work duties that should be prepared for each job in each department. Work duties spell out in specific detail just how a job should be performed. Each department head should maintain a work duties sheet for each job under his or her aegis, with a copy in the personnel department.

SUMMARY OF FUNCTIONS: This should be a one- or two-sentence statement encompassing the basic function and objectives of this job, and should enable anyone reasonably familiar with the organization to understand the primary purpose of the position.

REPORTS TO: The title of the person to whom this job reports should be entered here. This assumes the hiring and firing responsibilities.

MAJOR DUTIES AND RESPONSIBILITIES: This section should describe as briefly as possible the specific, basic and major duties and/or responsibilities of the individual filling the job. Whenever possible the descriptive terms used should be related to the objectives of a particular function rather than merely indicate what it is.

For example, the statement "supervises personnel processing customer orders for shipment and billing" would be better stated as follows, "supervises personnel in receiving phone and written communication from customers, and processes customer orders within 24 hours and ensures customer satisfaction through prompt and courteous handling of customer complaints."

ORGANIZATIONAL RELATIONSHIPS: This section briefly outlines the contact, coordination and reporting relationships between the individual filling this position and other key positions. The statement should include the types and frequency of reports generated by this position and to whom the reports are made. It should also include the source and types of reports and other information that should be furnished to the person filling this position. This statement should also include the requirements for coordination with other persons involved with administration, controls or the decision-making process related to this position.

EDUCATIONAL REQUIREMENTS: Indicate the minimum educational requirements necessary to be able to fill the job (such as, number of years and/or completion of college, technical or trade schools, advanced degrees, seminars, etc.).

EXPERIENCE REQUIREMENTS: Indicate the minimum number of months or years of experience in specific job categories necessary to perform this job.

(*text continued from page 238*)

Position descriptions should be:

1. Current.
2. Prepared for each box on the organization chart.
3. Reviewed by immediate superiors.
4. Filed in a position description manual for ready reference by all managers.
5. Prepared in a uniform manner using published guidelines.

The dotted line on the organization chart is supported in the job writing guidelines under the caption organizational relationships. While we have said previously that, in theory, each manager has a dotted-line relationship to every other manager, the specific relationships and interfacing of one department with another are set forth here.

Helpful Hint: Show the dotted line on organization charts and carefully consider these relationships in constructing the position description. This relates key managers to one another and is the cement in the organizational building blocks.

Standard Operating Procedures

We have seen that each employee within the department has a detailed work guide prepared for his or her job, and each employee's superior has a job description that broadly states his or her responsibilities. To effectuate the duties set out in work guides and job descriptions, the director of administrative operations, under the aegis of the controller, will prepare the standard operating procedures for the company.

The following guidelines should be followed in writing standard operating procedures:

- ✧ Codify all procedures in a manual.
- ✧ Use a simple numbering system for identification. For example, the first accounting procedure is A-1, the second is A-2. Purchasing is P-1, P-2, etc.
- ✧ Use a table of contents, divided in sections by major area, such as Accounting, Purchasing, Order/Billing, Data Processing, Office Services, Personnel.
- ✧ Index all procedures.
- ✧ Exhibit all forms as part of procedures, and prepare a forms index.
- ✧ Cross-reference "Procedures Applicable to Other Departments" with a contents listing that shows, for each department, those procedures that are not primary to it, but that involve the department. For example, an accounting procedure involving accounts payable is primary to the accounting department but secondary to purchasing, which must send a copy of a purchase order to the accounting department.
- ✧ If the manual becomes too bulky, divide it into separate binders

for ease in handling, using the categories in the basic numbering system.

✧ Always separate field procedures from home office procedures.
Use separate manuals.

✧ Require the controller to approve all procedures before publication and to obtain other necessary approvals where other
divisions are involved.

✧ Keep procedures current.

Helpful Hint: A change in a very detailed procedure may
mean a rewrite of the entire procedure. This takes time and
could delay the publication of the change. Speed this up by
using a special form entitled "Procedures Change Order"
(referred to as a PCO). This looks like a simple interoffice
memo but uses a special PCO masthead. The change is
described, and a printed legend on the bottom of the form
states that Procedure No. XXX will be updated soon.

✧ Use a special form for all procedures, to enable all personnel
to identify them, immediately, as procedures. Forms may be
color-coded, for emphasis, by category or department.

✧ Use the correction checklist (described below) to update the
procedures manual.

✧ Always start the procedure with a purpose, a general narrative,
and show its applicability. See this illustrated in a **branch office
procedure** in Exhibit 7-4.

Helpful Hint— Summarizing the purpose, narrative, and applicability makes it unnecessary for every employee to take
the time to read every procedure (some procedures run 10
to 20 pages). Only the first few paragraphs need be read
to ascertain whether one is involved.

✧ Give extensive and detailed instructions on how to complete forms properly, supporting these with an illustration,

(*text continues on page 244*)

Exhibit 7-4.   Branch office procedure.

Branch Office Procedure

Title COMMISSION AND SALES VOLUME ADJUSTMENTS CHARGEBACKS, REINSTATEMENTS, AND SPLITS	B.O.P Number: 4.02
	Page of 1 4
Vol. No. 4 Vol. Name: Financial Control	

PURPOSE:

To define the method and responsibilities for processing of adjustments, chargebacks, reinstatements, and splits on commissions and sales volume at the field level.

GENERAL NARRATIVE:

This procedure deals with the usage of the commission journal entry to effectively process entries involving commissions and sales volume.

APPLICABILITY:

Commission journal entries are only to be used if the amount involved is $10.00 or more. Adjustments under $10.00 for one employee can be processed on a commission journal entry provided that the aggregate total of the sums is $10.00 or more. Adjustments under $10.00 are covered on page 4 of this procedure.

PROCEDURE:

Branch Administration:

1) Completes a Commission Journal Entry Form (0-8-54) as follows: (Items are keyed to Exhibit A.)
   Item

A- Check applicable box. If "split" box is checked, insert selling branch code and shipping branch code.

B- Print (or type) account name and address.

C- Enter date journal entry is prepared.

D- J.E. number—leave blank

E- Branch code—Insert two-digit branch location code. If split is involved, enter the selling branch code on the first line and the shipping branch code on the second line.

F- Enter commission dollar amount to be charged or credited for first or only sales representative, field engineer, or customer representative involved, carried to two (2) decimal places.

G- J.E. date—Enter date from item C above

H- Salesperson number—Enter last two digits of employee (payroll) number for first or only sales representative, field engineer, or customer representative involved.

Supersedes		Orig. Code	Release No.	Effective
B.O.P. No.(s).	Page No.(s).	AP2	B.012	Date
				10/1/
Related Publications		Inquiries: Mgr. Administrative Control		

COMMISSION JOURNAL ENTRY

☐ CHARGE BACK ☐ REINSTATEMENT ☐ ADJUSTMENT ☐ SPLIT

"B" "A"

SELLING BR. _____
SHIPPING BR. _____

ACCOUNT NAME _____
ADDRESS _____

DATE PREPARED "C"
J.E. NO. "D"
(H.O. USE ONLY) 27-32

(1) C C	(2-3) BRANCH CODE	(5-11) COMMISSION X CHARGE (2 DECIMALS)	(5-11) NX CREDIT (2 DECIMALS)	(12-16) J.E. DATE	(19-20) SALESPERSON NO.	(21-26) INVOICE NO.	(33-40) ACCOUNT NO.
	"E"	"F"	"F"	"G"	"H"	"I"	"J"
4							
4							

(41-44) PRODUCT CODE	QUOTA POINTS X CHARGE (2 DECIMALS)	(45-48) NX CREDIT (2 DECIMALS)	SALES DOLLARS (49-56) X CHARGE (2 DECIMALS)	(49-56) NX CREDIT (2 DECIMALS)	(57-60) QUANTITY (2 DECIMALS)	(61) H.O. ONLY NON-PABST (N)	(80) TYPE
"K"	"L"	"L"	"M"	"M"	"N"	"O"	"P"

COMMENTS: "Q"

PREPARED BY "R"	TITLE "S"	APPROVED BY "T"	TITLE "U"
ORDER/BILLING DEPT.	DATE	ENTERED BY	DATE

ORDER/BILLING/DATA PROCESSING

243

(*text continued from page 241*)
cross-referenced to the detailed instructions. This is shown in Exhibit 7-4 page 2, which is a cross-referenced exhibit to the instructions on the previous page.

The **correction checklist**, seen in Exhibit 7-5, is used to make changes in any type of numbered manual. It may be used for the:

✧ Procedures manual
✧ Position descriptions
✧ Organization charts
✧ Policy manual
✧ Personnel manual
✧ Other manuals—price lists, service manuals, marketing memos, training memos, sales slants

Every manual is originally published with a correction checklist as the first page inside the front cover. Thereafter, every new procedure or correction to an original procedure is given a correction number, in sequence. This correction number appears on the procedure itself. The recipient merely crosses off the correction number on the Correction Checklist, ascertaining that it is in sequence. If it is not, an inquiry may be made of the systems and procedures department requesting a duplicate of the missing correction number procedure. To illustrate this, see Exhibit 11-6, which is a standard operating procedure form. At the bottom left, it will be seen that this is correction no. 253, and it will be seen to supersede correction no. 246 (found at the upper left of the form). Number 253 must be crossed off the appropriate correction checklist, and the procedure with no. 246 is simply thrown away, to be replaced by correction no. 253.

Internal auditors check correction checklist sequences on their periodic audits to determine that manuals are current and contain the latest changes. This is particularly important when there is a personnel change in a particular job. The old employee may be doing the job right, despite having an outdated manual. The new employee may very well pick up the obsolete procedure because the manual is not current.

Exhibit 7-5.   Correction checklist.

CORRECTION CHECKLIST

Upon receipt of a corrected page, circle or
cross out the appropriate number.

1	41	81
2	42	82
3	43	83
4	44	84
5	45	85
6	46	86
7	47	87
8	48	88
9	49	89
10	50	90
11	51	91
12	52	92
13	53	93
14	54	94
15	55	95
16	56	96
17	57	97
18	58	98
19	59	99
20	60	100
21	61	101
22	62	102
23	63	103
24	64	104
25	65	105
26	66	106
27	67	107
28	68	108
29	69	109
30	70	110
31	71	111
32	72	112
33	73	113
34	74	114
35	75	115
36	76	116
37	77	117
38	78	118
39	79	119
40	80	120

OPERATING POLICIES

Standard operating procedures are the blueprints that are behind the broad statement of duties set forth in the position descriptions. These procedures may be said to be the steps in the "how to" of the job. The company needs to augment these SOPs with a policy manual.

Each policy is not a "how to," but rather a statement of the prudence or wisdom that should be exercised in certain of the organization's affairs, consonant with the broad and overall philosophy of its management. This statement of management's material interest is expressed in the form of policies, which may run the gamut from antipolitical activities to zero defects in performance.

The **policy manual** is the highest authority for conduct in the corporation. It takes precedence over all other publications. An introduction to the policy manual is shown in Exhibit 7-6, page 1.

This manual is best arranged by subject matter to conform to the company's structure (sales, service, finance, administration), with subsets for broad categories, as seen in Exhibit 7-6, page 2.

Exhibit 7-6. Policy manual.

<u>POLICY MANUAL</u>

<u>INTRODUCTION</u>

The general purpose of the manual is to establish, clarify, and otherwise state for all corporate personnel those guidelines set forth as corporate policy.

If a conflict between SOP, HOP, the policy manual, or other related releases exists, the policy manual will take precedence.

Issuance and distribution of all policy manuals and subsequent policy releases throughout the organizational structure will be under the direction of the appropriate corporate officers.

Deviations from published policies will result in disciplinary review by a corporate officer.

<u>POLICY MANUAL</u>

<u>PURPOSE OF POLICY MANUAL</u>

<u>TABLE OF CONTENTS</u>

(continued)

Exhibit 7-6. *(continued)*

POLICY MANUAL		

Subject:
 	
Alcoholism - Drugs
	Number:
	    I 3
	Page of
	    1 1	

Effective **Date** **Date: 4/1/** **Prepared: 4/15/**	**Supersedes** **Cor. No.:**	**Inquiries:** Director of Personnel
Related Publications:	**Correction** **No:** 5	

It is considered that employees under the influence of alcohol or drugs
are not performing their job in the best interests of the company and, in
addition, may be endangering the health and welfare of fellow employees.

It is a company rule that an employee will be charged with misconduct if
he or she is in possession of, or is involved in the transportation or the
use of alcoholic beverages or narcotics in any form (unless prescribed by a
licensed physician) on the job. This also includes reporting to work when
under the influence of narcotics or hallucinogenic drugs, such as marijuana,
LSD, etc., or alcohol, or in possession of the above items on company
property. The parking lot and grounds are considered company property.

Employees involved in the use of any of the above will be subject to
immediate discharge.

Employees involved in giving, trading or selling any of the above items
will be reported to the appropriate authorities and subject to immediate
discharge.

A typical policy, this one on Alcoholism—Drugs, is at Exhibit
7-6, page 3.

Other subjects often covered in policies are:

AIDS
Antipolitical activities
Antitrust
Contributions
Credit terms
Employee stock options
Equal opportunity
  employment
Ethics
Exercise of authority
Extension of credit and
  pricing
Gifts

Gifts from suppliers
Labor charges
Lawsuits
Legal review of contracts
Machine service and sales of
  parts
Maintenance agreements
Meeting minutes
New products
Promotions
Public relations
Responsibility to auditors
Sexual harassment

Smoking	Technical opportunities
Stockholder and broker releases	Whistle-blowing
Substance abuse	Zero defects
Supplies noncompany	

Some of the above subjects, if employee-related, could be covered in the personnel manual (see Chapter 16). Examples are employee stock options, equal opportunity employment, and zero defects.

As indicated before, the statement of policy represents management's expression of the prudent way to conduct its affairs in the particular matter addressed in the policy. However, the saying and the doing are not always the same.

> CASE IN POINT: A company had a published policy directing its employees not to downgrade its competitors' products. The policy was intended to avoid antitrust actions. Unknown to the management, its salespeople persisted in stating that the use of a competitor's supplies in its equipment caused malfunctions—not borne out by the facts. The company was sued by the competitor, and lost on a treble-damage judgment with a cost running into the millions of dollars. To prevent this, training should have been conducted for field managers in the very good reasons for this policy to encourage continuing adherence.

PERSONNEL POLICIES

Some companies separate policy matters relating to their personnel from the standard policy manual and publish these policies in the form of a personnel policy manual or a personnel handbook.

This type of manual is to be distinguished from operating procedures involving personnel, which are printed in the SOP manual. Such a procedure might involve the steps and paperwork in giving an employee a raise—an operating procedure. However, the prudence or wisdom of giving overall raises would become a matter of personnel policy. This is sometimes expressed in a wage administration program that establishes wage levels for all classes of employees and determines when raises may be given. Other subjects that could be included in a personnel handbook would serve as orientation (for new employees), as well as to sketch prevalent policies.

PUBLICATION CONTROL

There are a variety of other manuals that a business may issue. These have the force of procedures or policy manuals, and so affect the administration of the operating plan. Consequently, the controller must exercise jursidiction over their publication—if only to ensure that they are kept current and that they are properly circulated to all concerned managers.

Typical of these manuals are:

Accounting manuals
Price lists
Sales programs
Service and parts manuals
Marketing directives

As with any policy manual, the basic decision regarding the issuance of the policy may not be the controller's, but the responsibility for publication and circulation is his or hers. More importantly, the lack of publication could be a serious omission that could adversely affect the successful administration of the operating plan.

The controller should require that, despite the source of authorship, the distribution and mechanics of publication of all manuals remain within his or her jurisdiction, possibly through the manager of office services or the systems and procedures department. This would enable controlled publication to those who need to know, and would verify that overall policies are considered and adhered to, that proper approvals have been obtained for new policies, and that circulation is conducted in a timely fashion.

Of the manuals listed above, only the accounting manual comes under the direct determination of the controller. It should therefore be reviewed as a controllership responsibility.

The Accounting Manual

Advantages

1. Ensures adherence to company policy where alternative coding situations exist.
2. Prevents variable practice regarding the coding of alternatives.
3. Helps train new employees.
4. Provides a basis for audit by both internal and independent auditors.
5. Identifies alternative situations, in advance, by the act of codifying all accounting situations in a manual.
6. Creates uniform systems for all personnel and all offices.
7. Provides documented advice to all manual users that these are policies of top corporate management.

Format

A page from an **accounting manual**, showing the Salaries and Wages account, is shown at Exhibit 7-7. This provides:

✧   A definition—of the account
✧   Inclusions—the nature of items to be included
✧   Exclusions—specific alternative situations to be avoided
✧   Classification—instructions for coding to the chart of accounts

There should, of course, be a table of contents and index to facilitate use by accounting personnel, as well as introductory instructions on how the material is arranged, whether by subject matter or chart of accounts, the former being preferable. In addition to the description of each account, as shown in Exhibit 7-7, the accounting manual may also have a section on policies (for example, what is the basis and life used for depreciation?) and procedures (such as, how to inventory fixed assets and what book entries are to be made).

Exhibit 7-7.   Accounting manual.

ACCOUNTING MANUAL

Major Account	Minor Account	Sub Account	Number
Salaries and Wages	Purchasing		114

DEFINITION:

Those personnel engaged in purchasing goods and services used in the manufacture or incidental to the manufacture of the company's products.

INCLUDING:

Personnel administering the purchasing function, negotiating with suppliers, determining economical purchase quantities from the cost standpoint, placing orders with suppliers, and following up on shipments and defective goods received.

EXCLUDING:

Those personnel who are preparing purchase requisitions for submission to purchasing will not be included in this category unless they are directly responsible to the purchasing function, as may or may not be the case with a material or inventory control section.

MAJOR EXPENSE CLASSIFICATION:

Purchasing salaries and wages will be included in Manufacturing Expense.

Issued By The Vice President and Controller	Date Issued	Supersedes Issue Date	Page 1 of 1

Be sure the manual:

✧ Is indexed and cross-indexed
✧ Is loose-leaf bound
✧ Has a correction checklist (Exhibit 7-5)
✧ Contains a section on:
    Forms (illustrating each)
    Policies (what to do and when to do it)
    Procedures (how to do it)
✧ Has tabs and subdividers for easy reference

Finally, the format of the accounting manual should be based on an outline presentation, showing main headings and subparagraphs, for easy reading. Use charts, graphs, and diagrams, where possible.

Avoid These Pitfalls:

1. Don't use individual names. Use titles. Otherwise you'll have to correct a page every time an employee turns over.
2. Do not squirrel the manual with the chief accountant. Distribute it to everyone who needs it and should use it.
   a. Keep a log of users for distribution of corrections.
   b. Number and log in each copy so that you can retrieve it on employee terminations.

EXERCISE OF AUTHORITY

Whether operations are conducted on a centralized or decentralized basis, decision-making authority must be vested in subordinates, to avoid higher managers having to examine every piece of paper. To this end, a standard operating procedure should be established that sets decision-making limits—limits of authority.

Helpful Hint: Psychologically, these limits are better received by employees if they are not titled limits of authority, but rather **exercise of authority**, to connote the employee's judicious use of his or her delegated authority.

These constraints should be observed in preparing the limits:

✧   Every possible expenditure should be listed.
✧   All decision makers should be included, in columnar form.
✧   Functional (dotted-line) authority should be shown as necessary approvers or endorsers.
✧   Use titles, not names, to avoid repeated corrections.
✧   Procedures and policies that relate to these expenditures should be cross-referenced as footnotes.
✧   Specifically prohibited authority should also be listed, such as pricing policies, credit terms, compensation plans.
✧   A catch-all category, with low limits, should be provided to catch forgotten or omitted authority. Title it Miscellaneous or Various.

A sample page from such a procedure is shown in Exhibit 7-8. This is one of nine pages of all possible authority for expenditure. The items to be included would vary based on the nature of each company.

The procedure includes several pages of footnotes referring to procedures and policies that govern these expenditures, as set forth in other publications. The procedure also includes an explanatory page that refers to the previously listed constraints, describes the use of the procedure in administering the plan for the control of operations, and further advises that each limit is a monthly amount per invoice, or series of invoices related to the same transaction.

Practical Pointers for Administering the Control Plan

Today's management accountant and financial executive operates in concepts, not details. These concepts are dynamic, in that they consist of

Exhibit 7-8. Exercise of authority.

EXERCISE OF AUTHORITY - FIELD SALES OFFICES
(BOP B-10)   Effective

ITEM (BOP & FOOTNOTES)	EVP & V.P. DLR. DIVISION	DIR. OF MKTG. DIR. F.O./ DLR. DIV.	AREA MGRS. & BR. GEN. MGRS. COMB. BRANCHES	BR. GEN. MGRS. W.M. ONLY BR.	OTHERS POSITION	LIMITS
Contributions: Misc. local contributions (C)	$ 50	$ 50	$ 50	$ 50		
Credit & Collection Fees & Serv.	2,500	1,000	500	500	Credit & Coll. Mgr.	Requirements
Credit memorandum approval & pymt. of accounts receivable balances related to adjustments for: a) Returned salable merchandise & correction of invoicing errors A-3,A-30,C-3,D-3	---To the extent of the original invoice or error being corrected---				Office-Cr. Mgr. or Supv.	250
b) Return & allowance for defective merchandise & the like A-3,A-30, C-3,D-3	5,000	2,000	500	500		
c) Refund or accounts receivable credit balances	---To the extent of the open balances ---				Credit & Collection Mgr. Approve:	
Credit Terms	---Per Published Corporate Procedures Only ---					
Delivery expense	1,000	750	500	500		
Employment agency fees	---To be paid by Employee through Payroll Deductions ---					
Entertainment (see Bus. Expense)						
Fees — Consulting	3,000	2,000	500	500	Division Officer	Requirement

the continuous productive activity necessary to implement the operating plan. The controller provides a framework for the operating structure of the enterprise. He or she provides organization charts, so that everyone knows where he or she belongs, and position descriptions, so that everyone knows what to do. Codified standard operating procedures provide the "how to," and operating policies are published to direct individual or group activities in line with higher management's overall philosophies. Ancillary publications such as price lists, accounting manuals, and marketing directives are used to augment standard operating procedures, and limits of authority are established to permit subordinates to exercise judgment in making expenditures. These devices enable the budget to be administered by the controller. They provide for the free flow of reports that enable us to monitor actual performance against the plan.

8

Systematic, Simplified Financial Reporting: Monitoring and Highlighting Results of Operations

Reporting and interpreting is the second controllership function listed in the FEI controller's definition, as exhibited in "Treasurer's and Controller's Functions." That function is "To compare performance with operating plans and standards, and to report and interpret the results of operations to all levels of management and to the owners of the business. This function includes the formulation of accounting policy, the coordination of systems and procedures, the preparation of operating data, and of special reports as required."

Acquitting this responsibility requires that the controller develop a reporting philosophy that will accommodate all users of reports (a part of which philosophy includes the definition of who shall be a user). We shall examine this further.

This chapter will be concerned with the presentation of reports on the budget (as defined at page 189) (otherwise known as the operating plan), and schedules or reports that support that budget. Various other special reports are covered in other chapters and are shown as exhibits to the related subjects—such as cash forecasts in Chapter 5, or insurance coverage in Chapter 4. Moreover, no attempt will be made to list or exhibit all the reports that might apply to every department of a typical business. Companies are so varied in their styles and operation that reports must be individually designed after a thorough study of each department's operations. For example, the credit and collection department would have some reports prepared within the department, others by the accounting department. The following information would be presented:

1. Aged trial balance
2. Analysis of bad debt losses by type of account, territory, size
3. Collections from bad or doubtful accounts
4. Credit held orders, by volume and prior period
5. Loss percentage to sales
6. Actual losses compared to reserve, by month and year
7. Collections compared to budget
8. Turnover of receivables, by month and quarter, by class
9. Collections as a percentage of sales, by age
10. Percentage of monthly collections, by age, to outstanding receivables, by age
11. Collection costs as a percentage of sales
12. Analysis of slow accounts by reason for slowness
13. Bad account write-offs, by quarter and year
14. Contacts made per collector
15. Collection cost, per collector, related to collections

Instead of presenting the detail of each such report—there could be thousands—we shall examine only those reports that demonstrate the theory and philosophy of effective management reporting.

A complete set of financial statements is the ultimate report that flows from any budgetary system. These statements are described in Chapter 5, in connection with cash budgeting, and include:

✧ Income statement
✧ Balance sheet
✧ Statement of retained earnings

✧ Statement of changes in financial position
✧ Supplementary financial data

Accordingly, our study will be concerned with:

1. A reporting philosophy
2. How to prepare reports
3. Budget vs. actual comparison (BVA)
4. Staff meetings
5. The monthly report
6. Operating reports
   a. Exception reports
   b. Trend reports
   c. Detailed reports
   d. Flash reports

A REPORTING PHILOSOPHY

The controller must design a complete accounting system to enable him or her to perform the controllership functions defined by the Financial Executives Institute and as delineated in the controller's position description (see "Treasurer's and Controller's Functions"). He or she has a responsibility to the owners, top management, industry associations, the SEC, stock exchanges, employees, and the public. The accounting system will result in the financial statements listed above. But he or she must design that system to permit the generation of reports that will serve the other users to whom he or she is responsible.

> FOR EXAMPLE: A cash receipts journal may be kept with a single total column and posted to the general ledger. This is certainly sufficient to generate a balance sheet but not to perform some of the credit and collection analyses listed above. Columns could be added for type of account, age of cash, product line, and territory, thereby enabling any of the previous analyses to be accomplished.

Essential to the proper system design is a study of the data structure of the company. Data inputs, processing, and reports are carefully examined as described in Chapter 14 under the section Organization Evaluation on page 526. After this study is completed, users of reports will be defined and their needs established. The reporting system may then be developed using the following caveats:

1. *Do not copy someone else's reports.* Reports must be tailor-made. They must meet the needs of your organization as developed by your own evaluation.
2. Financial reports will be required for publication and for top management. But most reports are nonfinancial and must meet the needs of operating managers. The accounting system must provide for the generation of *both types of reports.*
3. Operating reports should *compare performance to plan;* they should highlight deviations, suggest action, and relate current position to the ultimate goal.
4. The report format influences its usefulness. Hence, *show summary information* only, not details; determine whether last month or last year comparisons are the more meaningful; do not flood the user with masses of data or too many pages; show percentage relationships; show exceptions to plan as highlights.
5. *Use graphs and charts* frequently to add sauce to your presentation.
6. *Use acronyms* for report titles to create enthusiasm and facilitate familiarity by the user:

   FOR EXAMPLE: PABST = product analysis by sales territories
   SST = sales statistical tables

   See the section entitled A Management Acronym in Chapter 19 for a detailed description of other useable acronyms. The acronyms are familiar to every user. Calling for the report by acronym avoids receiving a wrong report with a similar title.
7. *Show the distribution* on all reports, so that each reader will know who else received it, without having to look it up. Don't waste the user's time.
8. *Show major assumptions* on the face, or attached to each report.

Avoid the reader's having to ask questions or research the underlying assumptions. Facts change with different assumptions.

9. *Publish only necessary and key reports.* Don't flood the company with unneeded reports. Don't distribute the report to anyone who doesn't need it.

10. *Reports must be issued on a timely basis* to be useful. Daily reports should be issued on the following day, weekly reports within three days, and monthly reports within ten days of the close.

11. Some *reports can create problems,* in addition to providing information:

    a. Reports are costly—to print, distribute, design forms, study systems, program, and prepare.

       Avoid This Pitfall: Because of the high cost of reports, design the report for broad distribution, not just for one or two individuals.

    b. Temporary reports often become permanent, at continued cost, and obsolete reports continue to be used.

       Helpful Hint: A frequent report study by the systems department will avoid the cost of obsolete reports as well as the issuance of misinformation.

    c. Effective use of reports requires teaching, explanation, and understanding by the recipient. This is costly but prevents the reports from degenerating into useless masses of data.

How to Prepare Reports

The following checklist has been used by a large public accounting firm in its consulting work, and it has general applicability to most internal financial and operating reports:

Reporting Level

1. Make results identifiable with the responsible executive.
2. Prepare for each executive a statement reflecting only results for which that executive is responsible.
3. Integrate individual statements in a pattern that clearly follows the organization chart—so that, for example, net profit can be "exploded" like a bill of materials.
4. Ignore subsidiary corporate entities for management reports when such corporate structure does not coincide with the management organization.
5. Design report structure so that statements for lower management levels can be added without altering existing statements.

Content

1. Present only one set of results. Avoid estimates that are subsequently connected to actual.
2. Compare results with expected performance.
3. Present results on an exception basis that emphasizes only good and bad performance.
4. Segregate controllable from noncontrollable expense.
5. Establish predetermined amounts for allocated expenses over which the charged department has no control.
6. Use standards for transferring costs that "flow" with production between departments.

Timing

1. Issue statements immediately after end of month, preferably within five working days.
   a. Use control totals. Do not wait for detail distributions.
   b. Accumulate "totals to date" as the month progresses.
   c. Do not cut off before end of month any item significantly affecting profits.
   d. Decrease monthly report load by issuing daily and weekly reports on items like sales, production, etc.

2. Stagger release of statements where necessary to ease digestion of contents.

Form

1. Present information in the same manner in which executives plan and think about their operations.
2. Let statements highlight results; do not try to present all the answers; leave exhausting details in the books to be used only for special statements and analyses when required.
3. Express results in one figure at the bottom of the statements; make the figure easily traceable to a single figure on the next "higher" statement.
4. Make statements easy to read.
   a. Use 8½" × 11" paper.
   b. Limit columns of figures to not more than three columns in a group.
   c. Leave plenty of white space on the page.
   d. Omit all cents; use thousands of dollars where possible.
   e. Segregate only significant expenses, group the remainder.
   f. Use operating terminology, but make items understandable to uninformed third parties.
   g. Clearly caption each statement and use informative headings.
   h. Show "year-to-date" figures to the left of account description.
5. Provide sufficient space on each statement for statistics and interpretive comments.

Helpful Hint: The maker should date and initial all reports. Date should show year, not just month and day. This permits intelligent review and later research, even though years have passed.

Another Hint: Provide binders for repetitive, important reports. This allows the user to retrieve the report more quickly, and assures you that all reports have been filed and are current (this may be audited periodically).

Budget vs. Actual Comparison

The crux of the budgetary system is the comparison of planned operations to actual results. These reports should follow the tenets previously described. They will then show results against plan, show percentage relationships, and highlight variances. In this manner, they fulfill the controllership function of interpretation. They are related to financial statements since the operating plan is presented in the format of a P&L statement. A Budget Report is prepared for each of the budgets shown in Exhibit 6-5. Only the P&L statement is exhibited below:

Exhibit 8-1 **Profit & loss budget vs. actual (BVA).** The report shows the current month in the left columns, with year-to-date on the right. Each line is numbered for easy reference. The percent column lists each line as a percentage of total net sales. Lines 10 through 18 represent budgeted expenses only, meaning controllable items. Lines 19 through 22 are allocated expenses, but not corporate allocations. They represent commonly shared expenses in an area, all of which are controllable. Line 24 shows the contribution to nonbudgeted expenses. Line 25 deducts nonbudgeted expenses, none of which are controlled by this profit center, but which are directly attributed to it. Cost of sales on line 5 is at an intercompany transfer price that precludes corporate allocations. Certain lines are cross-referenced to detailed schedules that follow.

The BVAs below, while not exhibited, follow the format of the budget at Exhibit 6-5.

❖ *Sales BVA.* This is Schedule 1 of the P&L BVA. The format is the same as the P&Ls. The report shows the sales of each significant product in units and dollars, net of returns and allowances. The final total of this report is carried forward to P&L BVA line 3.

❖ *Cost of Sales BVA.* This is Schedule II of the P&L BVA. It follows the same format. The cost is shown for the same sales items as in Schedule I. The final total is carried to P&L BVA line 5. Cost is at dealer list price.

❖ *Expense BVA.* This is Schedule III of the P&L BVA. Again, the same format is followed. Eight items of significant, controllable

Exhibit 8-1. Profit & loss budget vs. actual.

PROFIT & LOSS BUDGET
FOR PERIOD ENDING 04/30

Current Budget	Current Actual	— MONTH — Variance	%	Last Year Actual	Line Number		Current Budget	Current Actual	— YEAR TO DATE — Variance	%	Last Year Actual
					01	Machines (Sched I)					
					02	Paper (Sched I)					
					03	Other (Sched I)					
					04	Total Net Sales					
					05	Less:Cost of Sale(Sched II)					
					06	Gross Profit on Sales					
					07	Add:Dealer Handling Charges					
					08	Less:Parts & Mach.Destruction					
					09	Total Operating Income					
						Less: Branch Budgeting Expense					
					10	Cleaning & Maintenance					
					11	Personnel Recruitment					
					12	Postage					
					13	Salaries					
					14	Sundry					
					15	Telephone & Telegraph					
					16	Travel & Entertainment					
					17	Training					
					18	Tot Br Budgtd Exp(Sched III)					
						Allocated Budgeted Area Expense					
					19	Administrative (Sched III)					
					20	Service (Sched III)					
					21	Warehouse (Sched III)					
					22	Tot Allocat Budgtd Area Exp					
					23	Total Budgeted Expenses					
					24	Contribution to Non-Budgtd Exp					
					25	Less: Non-Budgeted Expenses					
					26	Net oper'g Prof./Loss Bef. Tax					

expenses are detailed. Some common area expenses are allocated on line 32 (not corporate allocations). The final total of budgeted expenses is carried forward to P&L BVA line 23.

✧ *Nonbudgeted Expenses BVA.* This is Schedule VI of the P&L BVA. These are expenses considered to be noncontrollable by the profit center's manager, even though they are direct costs of the operation. For example, rent is direct but is not readily controllable in the immediate budget period, since the lease runs for several years. The items, however, are listed, as they could become controllable at any time (the manager could elect to sublet the premises and seek less expensive quarters). These expenses, therefore, while significant in amount, are listed separately as requiring less scrutiny and control in any budgeted period. The total is carried to line 25 of the P&L BVA.

✧ *Employee Forecast BVA.* This Schedule IV is a head count of employees, actual to budget. It is simply an informative report and is not posted to any lead schedule.

> *Helpful Hint:* Reports are more valuable when reduced to units. A dollar amount payroll report would not be adjusted for payroll dollar increases. This unit head count report readily identifies every job category with an increased work count.

Variances of over 5% on sales and 10% on expenses are marked with an asterisk. The budget department obtains an explanation for such items for the budget committee.

> *Helpful Budget Hint:* The controller or treasurer, either of whom is present at most high-level staff meetings, should advise the budget manager of situations that will affect the budget and explain variances. This will speed up the process of communicating the final BVA figures, with explanations of variances, for the budget period.

> *Avoid This Pitfall:* The current budget columns should not be changed during the year. The budget as established (see Chapter 6) represents the operating plan for the year. Differences from plan will appear as variances. Managers, including top

management, should continue to observe these differences all during the budgeted period.

Exception: If a permanent change is made in the profit objective, as approved by the board, this may be reflected in a revised budget, which is, by definition, a bottom-line reflection of the profit plan.

Word of Caution: Budget vs. actual comparisons do not control operations. They only aid in control. Managers make decisions, not reports. Therefore, the BVA must be interpreted by the controller to managers, hence the explanation of variances, with suggestions for corrective action.

STAFF MEETINGS

Staff meetings belong under any discussion of reporting the results of operations. In this context, staff meetings mean any meetings involving managers concerned with attaining budgeted objectives. Thus, a line department, like a branch office, may have a staff meeting with the branch manager, office manager, and service manager, representing all of the concerned managers. Or, a headquarters staff manager, say a field administrative manager, may hold a staff meeting with line office managers for budget review purposes.

These meetings may be planning meetings (to work on submission of a new budget) or action meetings (to discuss budget vs. actual, BVA, results, to discuss variances, and to plan corrective action).

The budget reports previously exhibited should be discussed at a monthly staff meeting to be held immediately after their issuance. If the reports need interpretation (usually they are self-evident, particularly with an explanation of variances), a budget department representative, field accounting manager, or controller's representative should be invited to be present.

Helpful Hint: Staff meetings with subordinate managers serve to involve these managers in attaining the desired budget goal — make them feel a part of the team.

ACTUAL COMPANY EXAMPLE: One company was losing top department heads to other companies. The turnover seemed to be unrelated to any division or any particular senior manager. The controller instituted monthly or "sooner as needed" staff meetings, between managers of various departments, related to budgetary interpretations and corrective policies. Minutes were drawn and called to the president's attention. The president began to call his own monthly staff meetings to examine these minutes. This technique caused total involvement of middle managers in company policy, with the result that middle-manager turnover disappeared completely.

Try This: Minutes should be taken, typed, and circulated to any other concerned manager and to the immediate superior. This allows your superior to coordinate your midstream actions with those of other departments.

Avoid This Pitfall: Meetings should consist of three to five persons. Under three is not a meeting, it's a discussion between the manager and a subordinate and will not produce a free exchange of ideas. With more than five, the meeting can break down into a forum, with everyone trying to get a message in just to make points.

Use These Tools: Meetings are more effective if you use flip charts or an overhead projector to view transparencies. The act of preparing these tools in advance of the meeting leads to a well-thought-out agenda and a better meeting. Photocopies of the items on the chart or the projector should always be made for $8\frac{1}{2}'' \times 11''$ distribution to the attendees, in advance. This avoids wasting everyone's time copying key information.

Staff meetings should be chaired by the responsible manager of each box on the organization chart. Where organizational lines are crossed, there will still be a key profit center being discussed, and that manager should chair.

THE MONTHLY REPORT

To augment the BVA reports and staff meeting minutes previously described, as well as the standard reports and graphs to be outlined in the next section on operating reports, a monthly narrative reporting system should be used throughout the company. These fulfill the interpretive function.

Branch managers file a monthly report with their district manager; district managers report, monthly, to the zone manager; zone managers report, monthly, to the national sales manager; he or she reports, monthly, to the VP/marketing, who, in turn, reports, monthly, to the executive VP. Similarly, in the administrative area, branch administrators report monthly, to the zone manager (to whom they report directly, see page 199), with copies of all reports being sent to the controller to monitor the reporting system. Reports flow up the organization chart, are summarized by the immediate superior in a report to his or her superior, and so on to the president.

> *Useful Control:* Field operational audits are made during the month at various branch offices. These serve, in part, as the basis for the controller's own monthly report.
>
> *Helpful Hint:* The monthly narrative report should be not less than ½ page or more than two pages long. Less than ½ page is not informative enough. More than two pages tends to be verbose and full of excuses for poor performance.
>
> *Crux of Monthly Reports:* These monthly reports are broad summarizations of results of operations and plans for corrective actions for the various profit centers that are abridged further by top management, into broad company outlines. They are, thus, "exception reports" that permit management to make the necessary corporate decisions.

A variant on the monthly reports is quarterly earnings reports released to stockholders and regulatory agencies and the board of directors by the president. These generally contain a president's letter or comments that synthesize the monthly narrative reports, interpreting them for the users.

OPERATING REPORTS

Financial statements, budget vs. actual reports, and their supporting reports have been discussed in Chapter 5 and an earlier section of this chapter. Other chapters have exhibited reports that are pertinent to the subject matter of those chapters. This section will examine reports in general that are unique in form or style and present the message to management in a particularly effective way. They are the results of a reporting philosophy developed in the first section of this chapter and follow the dicta of report preparation set out in the next section.

Exception Reports

✧ Exhibit 8-2, **back order information report.** This report contains the interesting elements of which orders cannot be completed,

Exhibit 8-2. Back order information report.

BACK ORDER INFORMATION REPORT

INVENTORY CONTROL ONLY

DESCRIPTION	PART/ITEM NUMBER	QTY	NO. OF ORDERS	DATE OF OLDEST ORDER	COMMENTS	P/O DATE	ETA WHSE	EST QTY	COMMENTS
220 Console	4194 9597	56	26	11/19/		11/19___	12/23	140	
Carry Case Console	4940	4	3	11/19/		Will advise			
Offset E-Mix	7702	48	4	10/20/		10/21	12/5	96	
Cpn bk pad	0-2-8	62	6	9/15/		11/18	12/12	150 pads	
Bill Stuffers	z-2-580	4,000	6	9/9/		Shipping	12/9		
750 Price List	0-2-154	1,000	2	11/10/		11/10	12/5	5M	
750 Spec. Sheets	0-2-155	7,100	13	11/13/		12/5	12/23	50M	
750 Mailer	0-2-160	43,000	13	11/21/		Will advise			
750 Brochure	0-2-162	16,000	15	11/21/		Will advise			
215 Ser. Man.	0-12-57	5	2	11/26/		Will advise			
Label for Cass. Tape	0-13-29	1,200	2	11/14/		Will advise			
Coupon bk. env.	0-14-46	1,500	2	10/15/		Shipping	12/9		
App. for Emp.	0-16-6	50	1	11/18/		12/3	12/30	2M	
Letterhds.		7,000	2	11/10/		11/10	12/20	7M	

FROM PURCHASING: Branch Administrators
Customer Service Manager
Vice President/Administration
Controller
Inventory Control
Warehouse Manager
Director of Field Admin.
Dealer Managers list 7.0

RELEASE DATE FRIDAY

Report reflects status
through Thursday P.M.

_____
Inventory Control   Date

_____
Purchasing Dept.   Date

Exhibit 8-3. Shipping survey.

```
MEMO TO:  Executive Vice President      SUBJECT:  Shipping Survey

FROM:     Customer Service Manager      DATE:     March 26, 20__


A survey was conducted for the period February 17 through February 21
with the following results.

361 orders were processed as follows:

Shipped same day as received        28  -  8%
Shipped next day after received    127  - 35%
Shipped second day after received  160  - 44%
Shipped third day after received    46  - 13%

In addition to these orders, 33 others were processed outside of the
normal schedule as follows:

28 orders unable to ship as items were out of stock.
3 orders held for future delivery.
1 order held awaiting export documents.
1 order in customer repair.

Note:  Because of the Washington's Birthday holiday, we lost one full day
       of shipping due to the fact that none of our order pickers worked,
       nor did the vast majority of the common carriers.

We will continue to work toward maintaining this schedule and improving
wherever we can.


JK/GS



sc:  Warehouse Manager
     District Manager
     Controller
     Vice President/Marketing
```

gives estimated time of arrival of components to complete the orders (ETA), and presents pertinent comments. It is a weekly report, distributed to those concerned with filling parts orders.

✧ Exhibit 8-3, **shipping survey.** This is a narrative report to monitor shipping efficacy. It is short, clear, a summary, explains failures and suggests improvement.

Exhibit 8-4.   Credit analysis (CRAN).

DATE OF RUN 9/05

CRAN
ANALYSIS OF SOURCE OF CREDITS
FOR THE MONTH ENDED   7/31

TAB BY BRANCH WITHIN ANALYSIS CODE

BR	CODE	SOURCE OF CREDIT	AMOUNT
10	C	CUSTOMER ERROR	3,848.01
10	D	MAINTENANCE OR SERVICE ADJUSTMENT	413.40
10	F	SALESPERSON ERROR	280.90
10	G	TAX, FREIGHT OR INSUR. CLAIM ADJUSTMENT REFUND	272.96
10	H	UNSATISFACTORY OTHER THAN PAPER PARTS OR MACH.	206.70
10	1	ORDER DEPARTMENT PROCESSING ERROR	1,971.35
10	2	BRANCH PROCESSING ERROR	2,194.91
10	3	MAIN WAREHOUSE ERROR	764.00
10	6	MACHINE CANCELLATIONS	1,372.70
10	7	MACHINE REPLACEMENTS	1,619.50
		TOTAL	12,944.43*
12	A	DEALER REIMBURSEMENT-RETAIL	110.00
12	C	CUSTOMER ERROR	2,469.22
12	D	MAINTENANCE OR SERVICE ADJUSTMENT	1,550.88
12	E	RENTAL TERMINATION OR RENTAL ADJUSTMENT	65.71
12	G	TAX, FREIGHT OR INSUR. CLAIM ADJUSTMENT REFUND	10.10
12	H	UNSATISFACTORY OTHER THAN PAPER PARTS OR MACH.	5.75
12	2	BRANCH PROCESSING ERROR	3,809.99

❖ Exhibit 8-4, **credit analysis (CRAN).** This report, through prior coding of credit memos by reason for issuance, analyzes such reasons in summary form, by location of branch office that issued the credit, and in summary for the entire company.

❖ Exhibit 8-5, **call-back report (CABARE).** Using a familiar acronym for easy identification, this summarizes orders received from customers, by branch office location, and lists total customers who have not ordered a key product in three months or over, up to one year. Detailed names to support totals are sent to each location for follow-up action. Results for the previous five months are at the bottom of the form, thus giving a full six months look. If numbers in previous months decrease, from the bottom up, it means lost accounts are being regained. Looking at the eight months column, there were 555 accounts on 7/31 that were three months old; on 8/31, 423 of them still had not

Exhibit 8-5. Call-back report (CABARE).

CABARE – CALL-BACK REPORT

CUSTOMER BY BRANCH WITHOUT PAPER PURCHASES OVER 60 DAYS

BRANCH CODE	BRANCH NAME	3 MOS.	4 MOS.	5 MOS.	6 MOS.	7 MOS.	8 MOS.	9 MOS.	10 MOS.	11 MOS.	12 MOS.
10	MIDTOWN/N.Y.	53	28	19	20	9	16	6	10	9	54
12	BOSTON	79	28	19	15	14	27	12	8	9	51
13	NEWARK	36	23	5	8	9	14	10	8	6	49
15	PHILADELPHIA	29	17	15	9	7	14	3	8	3	28
18	WASHINGTON	27	20	18	12	16	7	2	7	4	58
20	CHICAGO	14	11	5	6	8	8	4	3	3	18
22	KANSAS CITY	26	8	10	13	9	4	3	3	1	9
30	ATLANTA	14	23	15	10	9	7	1	1	3	17
40	LOS ANGELES	38	31	20	45	27	19	15	20	7	60
41	E. LOS ANGELES	2	19	3	0	0	2	0	0	0	0
42	SAN FRANCISCO	43	31	29	16	10	10	11	4	0	42
43	SANTA ANA	5	13	5	3	2	8	7	7	0	3
48	SANTA CLARA	11	4	4	4	4	4	3	0	0	12
62	HARTFORD	2	6	5	2	3	5	1	0	2	3
72	PROVIDENCE	7	3	4	1	4	3	2	1	1	10
82	LONG ISLAND	16	9	10	12	10	37	6	6	0	29
83	WESTCHESTER/N.Y.	7	5	6	5	5	14	5	4	1	21
	GRAND TOTALS	409 *	279 *	192 *	181 *	146 *	199 *	91 *	90 *	49 *	464 *

DISTRIBUTION – D.L.G.
                G.S.C.
                R.K.L.
                A.M.

DATE	3 MOS.	4 MOS.	5 MOS.	6 MOS.	7 MOS.	8 MOS.	9 MOS.	10 MOS.	11 MOS.	12 MOS.
11/30		380	261	223	177	232	110	110	55	576
10/31			339	273	198	257	124	108	57	597
9/30				396	277	318	151	134	63	682
8/31					398	423	208	175	92	792
7/31						555	271	213	114	854

ordered and were now four months old, and so on up to the current month, 12/31, which indicated 199 of these accounts are now eight months without having ordered.

✦ Exhibit 8-6, **key volume report (KEVOL).** Here is an exception report for marketing that supplies the local sales office with the name of each "key" account that contributed more than 1% to total sales volume in the previous three months. The names, units of product, and percentage of volume are given. You know who your customers are! This report is prepared monthly with rolling quarters. Next month April will be dropped, May added, and the quarter will end July 31.

✦ Exhibit 8-7, **retail paper report (REPAP).** This illustrates the use of exception reporting against standards on a continuing basis. The standard is established in the fifth column from the right, representing three times the number of machines in the field each month. The quarters roll. Next month March will drop off the left side and this year's March will be added to the right side. The average number of rolls for each quarter on the page is computed and subtracted from the standard; if it is less than standard, an asterisk (*) is printed next to the result. The report shows an assumption under the heading caption that is important to an understanding of this report.

Trend Reports

Exhibit 8-8 is a graph summary of some of the data in Exhibit 8-9. This data is prepared by the national service department from an analysis of service call reports completed by field engineers after each service call. These exhibits are part of a total report for all products called the rainbow report. Data for each product is exhibited on a different color paper. This aids reader identification and makes for easier reading. The cover page supplies dates, assumptions, and distribution information.

✦ Exhibit 8-8, **travel and response time.** Here are two bar graphs, one representing the number of miles traveled to reach each call, and the second graph, the percentage of calls that took less than four hours to respond.

(*text continues on page 277*)

Exhibit 8-6. Key volume report (KEVOL).

RUN DATE 08/24/XX

KEVOL
KEY VOLUME REPORT
3 MONTHS ENDING JUNE 20XX
CUSTOMERS OVER 1.00%

BRANCH #	ACCOUNT #	CUSTOMER NAME	3 MONTHS TOTAL UNITS	%	BRANCH UNITS
22	000517	HALMARK CARD CO	508	10.39	4,890
	000962	CHURCHILL TRUCK LINES INC	80	1.64	
	000996	MEDCO JEWELRY	60	1.23	
	001432	IDEAL TRUCK LINES INC	60	1.23	
	204002	COMMERCE TRUST CO	90	1.84	
	601009	MILWAUKEE KANSAS CITY	310	6.34	
	603054	MISSION PHOTO	88	1.80	
	699953	PROCTER & GAMBLE	70	1.43	
	791131	SMITHVILLE COMMUNITY	60	1.23	
	901300	U S SAFETY SERVICE	146	2.99	
	941009	WHITAKER CABLE CORP	92	1.88	
22		* BRANCH TOTAL *	1,564	31.98	4,890

TYPE OF PAPER	U/M	# OF COPIES	KVOL U/M
200	1 ROLL	500	1 UNIT
215	1 BOX	1000	2 UNITS
220	1 ROLL	500	1 UNIT
230	1 ROLL	1000	2 UNITS

Exhibit 8-7. Retail paper report (REPAP).

REPAP DATE OF RUN MAR. 25, 20XX

RETAIL 200 PAPER SHIPMENTS FOR THE PERIOD BEGINNING MAR. 1, 20XX to FEB. 29, 20XX
INCLUDES COUPON SHIPMENTS BUT NOT COUPON SALES

BRANCH	MAR. 20XX	APR. 20XX	MAY 20XX	JUNE 20XX	JULY 20XX	AUG. 20XX	SEP. 20XX	OCT. 20XX	NOV. 20XX	DEC. 20XX	JAN. 20XX	FEB. 20XX	STD. 3 ROLLS PER MACH.	AVER. ROLLS FIRST QTR.	AVER. ROLLS 2ND QTR.	AVER. ROLLS THIRD QTR.	AVER. ROLLS 4TH QTR.
MACHINES IN THE FIELD																	
N.Y.C. PAPER SHIPPED																	
10 MACHINES IN THE FIELD																	
L.I. PAPER SHIPPED																	
82 MACHINES IN THE FIELD																	
WESTCH. PAPER SHIPPED																	
83 MACHINES IN THE FIELD																	
HOUSE PAPER SHIPPED																	
11 MACHINES IN THE FIELD																	
BOSTON PAPER SHIPPED																	

Exhibit 8-8. Travel and response time.

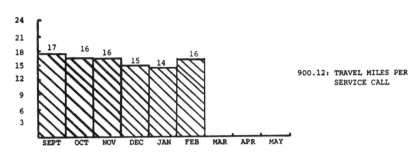

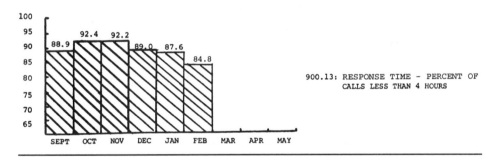

(*text continued from page 274*)

Thus, four hours is a standard against which the company is measured!

The bar graph allows for easy comparison!

❖ Exhibit 8-9, **service analysis for product A.** This is the summary data from which the graph in Exhibit 8-8 is prepared. It is not presented in graph or trend line format but is simply presented, in tabular form, to support the bar graphs.

Helpful Hint: In constructing bar graphs, note that each graph shows the required numerical information at the top of each column. Thus, the eye does not have to scan to the margin to identify the number related to the top of the bar.

In addition to the trend report type of graph, covering a period of months, many trend graphs cover years, showing performance year to year, or comparing one company against another.

Exhibit 8-9. Service analysis for Product A.

```
                      Service Analysis - Product A Data
                            February, 20xx


A. Product Performance Input:
   1.  Average monthly volume per machine . . . . . . . . . . . . . . 10220 lines
   2.  Lines between service calls . . . . . . . . . . . . . . . . . 14600 lines
   3.  Calls per machine per month . . . . . . . . . . . . . . . . . 0.70
   4.  Hours per machine per month . . . . . . . . . . . . . . . . . 1.30
   5.  Machine load per person . . . . . . . . . . . . . . . . . . .  31

B. Labor Expense Recapitulation:
   1.  Monthly labor cost* . . . . . . . . . . . . . . . . . . . . .$1100.00
   2.  Labor cost per machine  . . . . . . . . . . . . . . . . . . .   35.48
   3.  Labor cost per line . . . . . . . . . . . . . . . . . . . . .    0.003

C. Parts Expense Recapitulation:
   1.  Parts expense per machine . . . . . . . . . . . . . . . . . .$    9.20
   2.  Parts expense per line  . . . . . . . . . . . . . . . . . . .     0.0009

D. Product Expense Summary:
   1.  Total expense per machine . . . . . . . . . . . . . . . . . .$   44.68
   2.  Total expense per line  . . . . . . . . . . . . . . . . . . .     0.004

E. Contract Revenue:
   1.  Maintenance contract @ $25.00 per copy. . . . . . . . . . . .$   25.00

F. Profit (Loss) Machine/Month:
   1.  Profit (Loss) per machine per month . . . . . . . . . . . . .$  (19.68)


        *Includes management and fringe.
```

✧ Exhibit 8-10, **industry comparison graph (INCOM).** This graph compares our company against another company that releases data, as well as against an industry study that represents a standard. Sales are compared for each month of the year. Our company takes a look at three separate years. The inset graph on the upper left smooths out the months and presents quarters only for the current year, thus simplifying the graph. The inset at the right shows only the current year for our company, again simplifying the presentation. The use of industry data is part of the benchmarking process, which may lead to restructuring or reengineering key areas of the company.

✧ Exhibit 8-11, **revenue and income graph (RAIN).** Here is a summary of sales and income, for two years, by months. The trends are thus developed and seasonal or cyclical factors may be evaluated. The graph also indicates number of salespeople at the bottom, a significant determinant of the level of sales.

Exhibit 8-10. Industry comparison (INCOM).

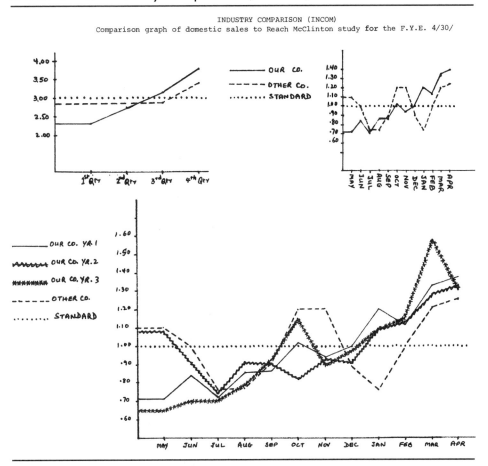

INDUSTRY COMPARISON (INCOM)
Comparison graph of domestic sales to Reach McClinton study for the F.Y.E. 4/30/

Word of Caution: In constructing graphs, be careful of the scale used. It must be such as to present meaningful information. For example, if you show sales at $50 million, and a 10% increase to $55 million, the graph will not show a sharp increase. If the same graph were used to compare the movement of expenses against sales, an increase from $500 to $1000 would be a 100% increase, which would appear disproportionate on the same sales scale. To avoid this disparity, use semilog paper to show expenses with a smaller slope to the line. If your purpose is to highlight and aggravate the expense increase, then, by all means, use standard graph paper.

Exhibit 8-11. Revenue and income (RAIN).

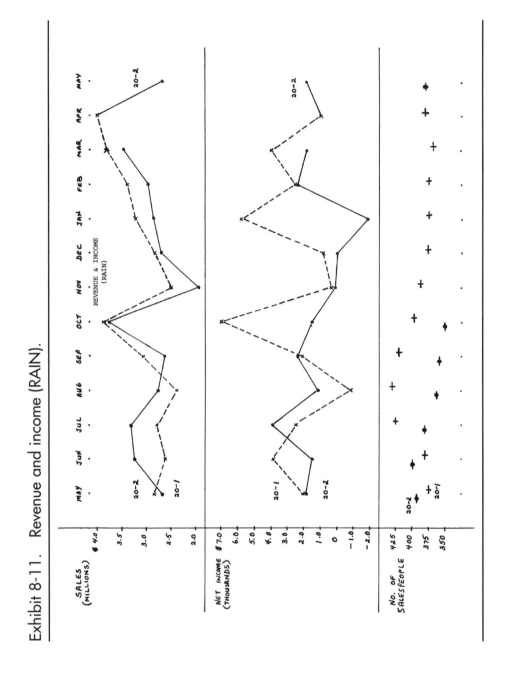

Exhibit 8-12.   Break-even analysis.

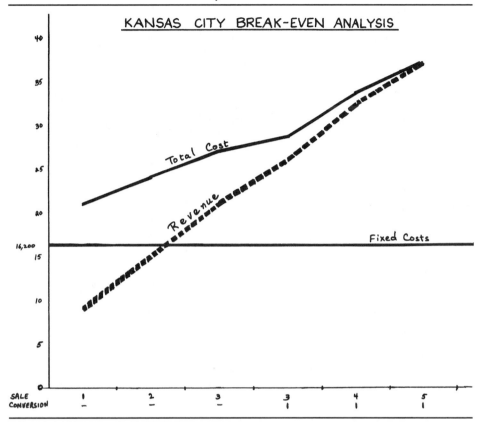

◇   Exhibit 8-12, **break-even analysis graph.** This graph uses normal direct costing techniques to construct the break-even graph. The graph, however, is not fuzzed up with masses of data that might confound the reader. The graph shows a $37,000 break-even volume, with fixed or period costs at the $16,200 level.

Helpful Hint: In constructing the graph, unit sales information is presented that serves as the underlying assumption for the $37,000 break-even volume. Units indicate that with 5 sales, 18 rentals, and 1 sale that is converted from a prior rental, the break-even volume is attained.

Assumption: The construction of this graph presupposes a definition of direct costs that is in line with that on page 198.

(*text continues on page 284*)

Exhibit 8-13. Box score.

BOX SCORE

BRANCH 22   KANSAS CITY

	MAY 20—	JUN 20—	JUL 20—	AUG 20	SEP 20—	OCT 20—
Sales $ (000's)	40	48	36	48	48	39
Net Income after taxes, $ (000's)	3	4	—	4	2	(1)
Machines in field	847	853	858	867	873	886
Machines sold	7	6	5	8	6	13
# of Sales People	5	5	6	7	9	8
Machines sold per person	1.4	1.2	.8	1.1	.7	1.6
Gross Profit $ (000's)	24	29	23	26	26	23
%	59.6	58.8	61.6	55.5	54.2	59.9
Operating Exps. $ (000's)	23	23	26	24	26	27
%	56.5	48.0	70.0	51.4	54.0	70.4
# of Rolls sold	1576	2200	1496	2342	2278	1698
Rolls sold per machine	1.9	2.6	1.7	2.7	2.6	1.9
# of Employees						
Salespeople	5	5	6	7	9	8
CRS	2	2	2	2	2	2
Service Reps.	5	5	5	5	5	5
Adm.	3	3	3	3	3	3
W/House	1	—	1	1	1	1
Machines in field, per service Reps.	169	171	172	173	175	177
# of Invoices	379	476	404	444	417	426
Invoices per Adm. personnel	176	159	135	148	139	142
Telephone soliciting Hrs	48	76	60	48	48	88
MUP-Machines:						
Cumulative	68	68	68	69	70	72
Current Month	—	—	—	1	1	2
MUP-Paper:						
Rolls sold last month	986	1018	503	970	931	764
" " per machine	14.5	15.0	7.4	14.1	13.3	10.6
Machines sold next month	6	5	9	6	13	17

BOX SCORE LEGEND

1. Sales: Per branch profit and loss statement.

2. Net Income After Taxes: Per branch profit and loss statement.

3. Machines in Field (Including MUP): Per REPAM Retail Machine Report, adjusted to agree with periodic physical inventories.

4. Machines Sold (Including MUP): Per branch cost of sales by product (COSBAB) MUP per REPAM Retail Machine Report.

5. Number of Salespeople (Including MTM): Per actual payroll records as at month-end.

6. Machines Sold per Person (Including MUP): A ratio computed by dividing the number of machines sold (including MUP) by the number of salespeople (including MTM).

7. Gross Profit on Sales: Per branch profit and loss statement, reflected before dealer handling credit.

8. Operating Expenses: Per branch profit and loss statement.

9. Rolls (in 500 sheets quantity) Sold (Including MUP): Per branch cost of sales by product (COSBAB).

10. Rolls (in 500 sheets quantity) Sold per Machine in Field: A ratio computed by dividing the number of rolls sold (including MUP) by the number of machines in field (including MUP).

11. Number of Salespeople (Including MTM): Per actual payroll records as at month-end.

12. Number of CR's: Per actual payroll records as at month-end.

13. Number of Service Representatives Including Managers: Per actual payroll records as at month-end.

14. Number of Administrative Personnel Including Branch Administrator: Per actual payroll records as as month-end.

15. Warehouse Personnel and Drivers: Per actual payroll records as at month-end.

16. Machines in Field per Service Representative: A ratio computed by dividing the number of machines in field (including MUP) by the number of service representatives.

17. Number of Invoices: Per data processing work counts report.

(*text continued from page 281*)

✧ Exhibit 8-13, **box score.** This is a trend report, in columnar form. Important operating data is listed in each row. Months are compared in the columns. It is an exception report to the extent that all key data has been extracted and summarized on this report.

> *Key Point:* A branch manager, or a traveling headquarters officer, armed with this report, and comparing it to other branches of similar size, can quickly identify adverse trends and trouble areas.

Page 2 of the report illustrates a legend that is used to identify the source from which each piece of data is extracted. The legend serves to avoid repetitive questions about the report's source data.

Detailed Reports

Not all reports need to be, nor should they be, exception reports, summaries, comparisons, or trend reports. Too much data suffocates, but, often, a good deal of data is needed on a timely basis to permit a quick look-in to facilitate making fast decisions. There is not always time to summarize each month's data, to compare it to prior months, or to chart it or graph it. The cost of doing this must be weighed against the need for such summaries.

The detailed reports, and the flash reports described in the next section, can fulfill the manager's immediate need for information. If the reports are carefully constructed, in line with the reporting philosophy described on page 259, the overall reporting cost can be reduced, with little or no reduction in the efficacy of these reports.

✧ Exhibit 8-14, **payroll distribution.** This is a payroll summary that lists key areas of the company, giving payroll dollars, head counts of employees, and a further head-count breakdown by each product line. While there is a good deal of information on each page, and no comparative information, the controller can use this report to quickly compare the broad summary totals to last week's report. If a head count has increased, he or she can identify it for immediate review or follow-up if there is a further increase next week. The reports are hole-punched

Exhibit 8-14. Payroll distribution.

PRO750 RUN DATE 12/29/　　　　PAYROLL DISTRIBUTION　　　　　　　　PAGE 47
S U M M A R Y　　　　　　　　　PAY PERIOD ENDING 12/31/
- - - - - -

T DISTRIBUTION CATEGORY	GROSS $	EMP. COUNT	P R O D U C T - L I N E C O U N T					
			0	1	2	3	4	5
CORPORATE OFFICE	90,671.17	164	159	4			1	1
OTHER OFFICE	35,341.16	128	126				2	
TOTAL OFFICE	130,012.33	292	285	4			3	
CORPORATE WAREHOUSE	2,761.54	5	9					
OTHER WAREHOUSE	6,489.00	20	20					
TOTAL WAREHOUSE	9,250.54	25	29					
CORPORATE SERVICE	9,513.82	20	14	2			3	1
OTHER SERVICE	111,862.74	289	15	136			73	65
TOTAL SERVICE	121,376.56	309	29	138			76	66
DEALERS	13,015.44	18	18					
BRANCH MANAGERS	38,821.70	41	18	8			15	
ZONE PRODUCT SALES MGRS	.00							
BRANCH SALES MANAGERS	.00							
QUOTA SALES MANAGERS	.00							
NATL ACCTS SALESREPRESENTATIVES	1,246.16	2	1	1				
SALESREPRESENTATIVES	67,614.93	194		54			100	
CUSTOMER REPRESENTATIVES	5,470.02	25		29				
S S R	13,222.40	35					39	
TELEPHONE SOLICITORS	705.50	4	4					
MISCELLANEOUS	2,833.45	8	8					
TOTAL PAYROLL	403,569.04	965	392	274			233	66

285

Exhibit 8-15. Sales support report.

SUPPORT SYSTEM

SALES SUPPORT REPORT
BY BRANCH
2 WEEKS ENDING 02/28/ and Y.T.D.

	# OF SALESPEOPLE	ACCOUNTS VISITED	AMT OF SUPPORT	BRANCH SUPPORT	DST/ZNE SUPPORT	NATIONAL SUPPORT	ACCOUNTS VISITED	TOTAL SUPPORT	BRANCH SUPPORT
			-------BI-WEEKLY-------				----YEAR TO DATE----		
Midtown	14	19	3	1	2	0	19	3	1
Elmsford	18	8	5	4	0	1	8	5	4
Wall Street	13	0	0	0	0	0	0	0	0
Lake Success	16	0	0	0	0	0	0	0	0
Cranford	8	19	4	3	1	0	19	4	3
Metro Region	69	46	12	8	3	1	46	12	8
Boston	9	46	15	5	10	0	46	15	5
Hartford	7	19	2	2	0	0	19	2	2
Providence	7	11	3	3	0	0	11	3	3
New England Region	23	76	20	10	10	0	76	20	10
Philadelphia	17	60	17	16	1	0	60	17	16
Wilmington	11	24	7	0	7	0	24	7	0
Baltimore	12	6	6	6	0	0	6	6	6
Mid-Atlantic District	40	90	30	22	8	0	90	30	22
Atlanta	8	0	0	0	0	0	0	0	0
Miami	0	0	0	0	0	0	0	0	0
Tampa	0	0	0	0	0	0	0	0	0
Jacksonville	0	0	0	0	0	0	0	0	0
Southeast District	0	0	0	0	0	0	0	0	0
Eastern Zone	140	212	62	40	21	1	212	62	40
Chicago O'Hare	8	6	3	0	3	0	6	3	0
Chicago Loop	10	0	0	0	0	0	0	0	0
Chicago District	18	6	3	0	3	0	6	3	0
Detroit	3	0	0	0	0	0	0	0	0
Ann Arbor	0	0	0	0	0	0	0	0	0
Detroit District	3	0	0	0	0	0	0	0	0
Pittsburgh	8	30	10	10	0	0	30	10	10
Minneapolis	9	5	5	1	4	0	5	5	1
Kansas City	7	14	8	2	6	0	14	8	2
Cincinnati	6	18	15	11	4	0	18	15	11
Central Zone	51	73	41	24	17	0	73	41	24
Los Angeles	18	47	16	16	0	0	47	16	16
East L.A.	6	33	17	17	0	0	33	17	17
Santa Ana	12	17	7	7	0	0	17	7	7
Long Beach	6	1	1	1	0	0	1	1	1
L.A. District	42	165	79	65	14	0	165	79	65
San Francisco	14	70	31	31	0	0	70	31	31
Oakland	6	22	9	9	0	0	22	9	9
San Jose	10	27	13	12	1	0	27	13	12
Denver	6	42	20	19	1	0	42	20	19
San Francisco Region	36	161	73	71	2	0	161	73	71
Dallas	14	0	0	0	0	0	0	0	0
Houston	6	4	1	0	0	0	4	1	0
Memphis	2	71	14	14	0	0	71	14	14
New Orleans	5	0	0	0	0	0	0	0	0

and filed in a loose-leaf book in order. He or she can flip back to last month or last year for instant comparative information. This would take days or weeks to accomplish through the computer every time he or she had a question. Even a time-sharing terminal or a PC would not supply the same speed as these visual, detailed comparisons.

✧ Exhibit 8-15, **sales support report.** This detailed report is provided to national sales managers with supporting detailed reports to

COPIES: President
         Executive Vice President
         Vice President/Marketing
         Director Field Operations
         Director Field Administration
         General Sales Manager

FROM: Manager, Systems & Programming, Headquarters
TO: DISTRIBUTION
DATE: 3/15/

SUBJECT: Field Support Reports: How to Analyze

Page 1 - Sales Support Report

  Taking Midtown as the example:

  1. Number of active salespeople in branch: 14
  2. Number of accounts visited by salespeople and support personnel: 19
  3. Number of salespeople supported during the period: 3
  4. Of the 3 people supported, 1 was by branch personnel (either branch
       manager, branch service manager, or an M.T.M.)
  5. Of the 3 people supported, 2 were supported by zone or district
       management (zone manager, A.Z.S.O., district manager, or zone
       service manager)
  6. There was no national support for Midtown salespeople (V.P.'s,
       national managers, or product managers)

Page 2 & 3 - Service reps and CR reps are analyzed as per Page 1

Page 4 & 5 - Type of call report

Taking Midtown as the example:

  1. Of the 27 accounts visited (19 salespeople, 8 CR reps, 0 service
  reps),

3 were presentations	1 was goodwill
4 were demo's	2 were new accounts (CR)
1 was a sale	4 were active accounts
6 were cold calls	(CR)
1 was a new coupon book account	2 were inactive accounts
3 were new major users	(CR)

Page 6 & 7 - Combined support report by individual

  Using National Sales Manager as an example:

  1. Number of accounts visited with salespeople: 6
  2. Number of salespeople supported: 2
  3. No service reps supported
  4. Number of accounts visited with CR reps: 8
  5. Total of CR reps supported: 1
  6. Total of accounts visited: 14
  7. Total people supported: 3

individual field managers. The report indicates the degree of national or headquarters support for field offices. Page 2 of the report gives a narrative explanation of the column headings. The report is exploded downward on subsequent pages (not exhibited), to show support for other than salespeople—that is, service technicians, customer relations representatives. Pages 4 and 5 analyze the types of calls made, and pages 6 and 7 provide details for each "supporter." There is a wealth of support information presented, but it is broken down into segments so that each manager can work with the detailed information that concerns only him or her. The entire report enforces management's philosophy of providing headquarter's assistance to its field managers and salespeople.

✧ Exhibit 8-16, **cumulative retail paper report.** This is a format for a report showing number of rolls of paper sold for each field office.

Exhibit 8-16.   Cumulative retail paper report.

DAILY   20xx

Date Prepared

CUMULATIVE RETAIL PAPER REPORT

		Mach In Field			2nd Prior Mo.			1st Prior Mo.			Current Month AT / AM PM			
BRANCH	People	200	210	220	200	210	220	200	210	220	200	210	220	BRANCH
ANA														ANA
ATL														ATL
BOST														BOST
CHI														CHI
DAL														DAL
HART														HART
K.C.														K.C.
L.A.														L.A.
L.I.														L.I.
NWK														NWK
NYC														NYC
PHIL														PHIL
PROV														PROV
S.F.														S.F.
SJO														SJO
WASH														WASH
WEST														WEST
TOTAL														

* Mach In Field is cumulative at start of current month.

INSTRUCTIONS:
    Figures shown are paper shipments - both regular and coupon:
        Shipping branches - From daily Telex or switchboard.
        Non-shipping branches - From order log before shipments.

DIST: EPC; RKL; GSC; DLG - Mon., Wed., Fri.
        Zone Mgrs.   - Friday PM (Their branches only)

The offices are listed on both the left- and right-hand edges so that the numbers can be traced more easily. The first four columns show number of salespeople and number of machines in the field (which determines the number of rolls of paper that might be consumed) by machine model number. Two prior months' and the current month's figures are then presented. The report is prepared daily. The source of the data is shown at the bottom of the report, as well as the distribution. A few key managers are, thus, able to track daily progress on supply sales, by branch, compared to prior months. Trends are quickly spotted, and the daily monitoring enables immediate corrective action to be taken.

✧ Exhibit 8-17, **cost/pricing product sheet.** This informational form is prepared for each product. The right-hand section shows all costs. The left-hand side shows prices for each level of distribution, percent of gross profit and mark-up, and percent and dollars of commission. A control product (standard pricing) is shown, and subsequent columns supply recommendations of accounting and marketing departments and then the final approved pricing column. At the bottom of the page, boxes are provided for all necessary pricing approvals, as well as for cost approvals on the right. These boxes ensure that no key manager has been bypassed in obtaining approvals.

> *Word of Advice:* Use detailed reports. If you depend only on exception reports, you'll lose much of the feel and flavor of the business, and you'll probably receive many reports too late for decision-making purposes.

Flash Reports

Any of the previously described reports may be a flash report. The flash report is supplied early in the reporting period, before complete or closed information is available. Often, therefore, the source data for the flash report is obtained off-line or outside the regular data system. For example, billings or shipments reports usually are generated from invoices. But final totals go through edit checks, proofreadings, bursting, mailing, corrections, sorting, computer input, and report preparation.

Exhibit 8-17.   Cost/pricing product sheet.

COST/PRICING PRODUCT SHEET

PRODUCT_____

( ) NEW PRODUCT   ( ) CHANGE   DATE:____/____/____ BY:_____   PRODUCT CODE_____

UNIT OF MEASURE

	UNIT OF MEASURE	CONTROL PROD. NO:	ACCOUNTING	MARKETING	APPROVED PRICING	DIRECT COSTS - EXCLUDING COMMISSIONS TO SALESPEOPLE			
RETAIL - SALES						**COST ELEMENT**	RETAIL	DEALER	OTHER
RECOMMENDED PRICE (S) .	———	$.				RAW COST (EFF DATE, VENDOR, FOB POINT,			
% GROSS PROFIT		. %				CURRENCY BASIS, UNIT)			
% MARK-UP ON COST		. %							
% COMMISSION		. %							
$ COMMISSION		$.							
RETAIL - RENTALS	UNIT OF MEASURE								
RECOMMENDED PRICE (S) .	———	$.							
% GROSS PROFIT		. %							
% MARK-UP ON COST		. %							
% COMMISSION		. %							
$ COMMISSION	UNIT OF MEASURE	$.				BROKERAGE			
						DUTY AT %			
DEALER						INSURANCE & HANDLING TO MAIN WAREHOUSE			
RECOMMENDED PRICE (S) .	———	$.				FREIGHT - IN TO MAIN WAREHOUSE			
% GROSS PROFIT		. %				ROYALTY: %or$; BASE: ; NAME:			
% MARK-UP ON COST		. %				ROYALTY: %or$; BASE: ; NAME:			
% COMMISSION		. %				ROYALTY: %or$; BASE: ; NAME:			
$ COMMISSION		$.							
MAJOR ACCOUNT	UNIT OF MEASURE								
RECOMMENDED PRICE (S) .	———	$.							
% GROSS PROFIT		. %							
% MARK-UP ON COST		. %							
% COMMISSION		. %							
$ COMMISSION		$.				FREIGHT - OUT - MAIN WAREHOUSE TO BRANCH			
GSA - SALES	UNIT OF MEASURE					FREIGHT - OUT - TO CUSTOMER			
						SPECIAL PACKING, HANDLING, OR RIGGING			
RECOMMENDED PRICE (S) .	———	$.				SALES OR OTHER TAX IF UNBILLED TO CUST.			
% GROSS PROFIT		. %							
% MARK-UP ON COST		. %							
% COMMISSION		. %							
$ COMMISSION		$.							
GSA - RENTALS	UNIT OF MEASURE								
RECOMMENDED PRICE (S) .	———	$.							
% GROSS PROFIT		. %							
% MARK-UP ON COST		. %							
% COMMISSION		. %							
$ COMMISSION		$.							
OTHER_____	UNIT OF MEASURE								
RECOMMENDED PRICE (S) .	———	$.							
% GROSS PROFIT		. %							
% MARK-UP ON COST		. %							
% COMMISSION		. %							
$ COMMISSION		$.				TOTAL COST			

GROSS PROFIT = PROFIT/PRICE   MARK-UP ON COST = PROFIT/COST
PRICE APPROVED   COST APPROVED

( )	( )	( )	( )	( )	( )	( )	( )		( )	( )	( )
V. P. MKTG.	EXEC. V. P.	PROD. MGR.	V. P./CONTR.	PRES.	DLR. MGR.				PURCH. MGR.	ACCTG. MGR.	V. P./CONTR.

O-8-76

This takes time and usually involves an end-of-the-month crunch with overtime for processing closing billing. The problem is simply handled by phoning, faxing results, or picking up totals from order logs, even before the invoice has been processed. See the instructions at the bottom of Exhibit 8-16, cumulative retail paper report. This detailed, daily report is, thus, a flash report.

The most common flash report is the quick P&L statement at month-end. It is prepared between one and seven days from the end of the month, usually using actual sales data and estimates of gross profits and expenses. As experience is gained in its preparation, the report can become quite accurate. At any rate, while the given month may present some problems, it is best presented on a cumulative basis, showing previous actual P&Ls, plus this one month's flash. The cumulative result, as the year draws closer to the end, is extremely accurate. If the assumptions used in the monthly flash are carefully worked out, the few inaccuracies in the report are more than offset by the speed with which it is delivered.

APPLICATION IN AN ACTUAL COMPANY: A large, public company continued to be late in its publication of monthly financial statements and quarterly releases of earnings. As it grew and acquired other companies, its reporting problems became further aggravated. Each quarter, its listed stock price declined as the public attributed the possibility of bad news to the delayed earnings. Utilization of flash P&L reporting was implemented, using standard journal entries to summarize the monthly close. Reports are now available on the seventh working day of each month. The result is more stable quarterly stock prices and added investor confidence in the management of the company.

✧ Exhibit 8-18, **flash cost change report,** is an example of a report prepared on the same day a vendor for the company notifies of a price increase. Rather than waiting for circulation of Exhibit 8-17, the cost/pricing product sheet, which shows markups, gross profits, commissions, and optimum pricing, this flash report is prepared at once to show the annual cost increase, it being $109,760, a 26.57% change. This is further broken down between the amount of increase by distribution channel, retail or dealer customer. In this case, the increase is equal

Exhibit 8-18.   Flash cost change report.

Purchasing Department   **1 /24/**   Dist:
                                                                                      Date   Purch
                                                                                                    Prod. Mgr.
                                        FLASH COST CHANGE REPORT   SM
                                                                                                    VP/Mkt.
                                                                                                    DP Mgr.
VENDOR(S) _____   B. Corp. _____   Cont.
                                                                                                    VP/Adm.
Effective Date of Change 2 / 1/   EVP

                                                                    Annual Cost Increase
Annual Purchase Quantity   4000   ea. $109,760.00
                              Quantity   Unit of Measure

Product	Present Cost	New Cost	$ Change	% Change
Roller A	103.28	130.72	27.44	26.57%

Product Code
439

Retail Profit Effect

Old Cost vs. New Cost

Present List Price	Mark-up Above Present Cost	Mark-up Above New Cost	Present Cost Markup Difference — New Cost Markup	
$180.00	$76.72 42.62%	$49.28 27.37%	$27.44 15.24%	X

				Annual Sales Qty Projected	Annual Profit Decrease
			Present Cost Mark-up	2000	$54,880.00

Present Block Price	Mark-up Above Present Cost	Mark-up Above New Cost	Present Cost Mark-up Difference — New Cost Mark-up	
$____	$ %	$ %	$ %	X

Dealer Profit Effect

Old Cost vs. New Cost

Present Highest Dealer Price	Mark-up Above Present Cost	Mark-up Above New Cost	Present Cost Mark-up Difference — New Cost Mark-up	
$144.00	$40.72 28.28%	$13.28 9.22%	$27.44 19.06%	X

				Annual Sales Qty Projected	Annual Profit Decrease
				2000	$54,880.00

Present Lowest Dealer Price	Mark-up Above Present Cost	Mark-up Above New Cost	Present Cost Mark-up Difference — New Cost Mark-up	
$____	$ %	$ %	$ %	X

for each class of customer. This flash report instantly identifies the effect on profits and permits management to react, today, if need be.

APPLICATION IN AN ACTUAL COMPANY: In a period of sharply rising, inflationary prices, one controller instituted the flash cost change report in anticipation of inflationary price rises. This enabled his company to react more quickly than competitors and to pass through immediate price rises to customers, as the necessity was indicated by the magnitude of the annual cost increase on the flash report. His company maintained its gross profit margins for the year, while competitors, because of their slower reaction time, suffered a decline in earnings.

Flash reports should be prepared using the features of other reports:

a. Present them so that they can be studied by exception, not too much detail. Show trends and percentages.
b. Summarize data and present only top-line information on the flash. Use narrative where necessary to make the point. The monthly narrative report described on page 268 is a flash report.
c. Circulate reports on a timely basis. Don't let the time of month throw you off. Flash reports may be prepared daily; Monday, Wednesday, and Friday; weekly; semimonthly; and even monthly.
d. Don't worry about 100% accuracy. If you explain your assumptions, the report will be close enough. Too many accounting reports show pennies, hundreds, and even thousands of dollars, when this amount of accuracy has no meaning.

Helpful Hint: With all these reports flowing in from all departments, how do you keep track of them? Use a calendar as in Exhibit 8-19, **departmental reports.** This shows each non-accounting-generated report, where it comes from, the due date, and the actual date received. A schedule of Accounting Department Reports is also shown at Exhibit 14-5, using the same format.

Another Reporting Hint: From time to time, prepare a report but hold back its distribution. If you don't get follow-up complaints, the report may not be being used. Perhaps it can be eliminated.

REPORTING CONCLUSIONS

The controller needs to develop a complete reporting philosophy to satisfy the needs of management, the owners, and government. This

Exhibit 8-19.   Departmental reports.

45-607 EYE-EASE
45-707 20/20 BUFF
NATIONAL   Made in U.S.A.

DEPARTMENTAL REPORTS
Non-Accounting Generated

	Responsible Department	Working Day Due	A C T U A L D A T E		
			January	February	March
Avg. No. Sales & MUP/ Salesperson	O/B	13	13	17	13
Advertising Budget	Purch	14	14	13	14
Word Processor Budget	Purch	14	14	14	14
Dacom Monthly Report	Rapifax	15	15	14	15
Delco Collections Summary	Credit	15	15	15	15
Branch A/R Summary	Credit	15	16	15	16
Doubtfuls to Reserve	Credit	15	15	15	16
Recourse Lease	Credit	15	15	15	16
GSA Leases	O/B	15	15	15	16
Paper Sales to Murritt	CSD	19	18	18	20
Position for Paper & Chemicals	Purch	20	20	19	20

means designing reports that suit your particular type of company, that compare performance to plan, that summarize and show trends through exception—reports that are key and necessary, are timely, contain distribution listings and major assumptions, and are zestfully formated. Budget reports should be presented and discussed at staff meetings, and a monthly report in narrative form is the ultimate flash report to apprise superiors of the results of operations. Specific reports should be presented in a variety of forms to maintain interest and to supply information—trend reports, graphs and charts, and timely flash reports. Detailed reports are not to be omitted, either. They may contain summary information, but, principally, they provide a storehouse of quickly accessed information, useful in making immediate decisions.

9

Implementing and Administering Tax Policies and Procedures

The fourth controllership function defined by the Financial Executives Institute, as listed in the "Treasurer's and Controller's Functions" and in the controller's position description, is "To establish and administer tax policies and procedures."

We may define a "policy" as "prudence or wisdom in the management of affairs" (a dictionary definition) or "a definite course or method of action selected from alternatives."

Once the alternatives are prudently selected, the "procedure" sets limits and controls on "how to do it."

This chapter will consider the following tax-related topics:

1. *Information on alternatives.* The source of tax information; where do you learn about it?
2. *The philosophy of responsibility.* Who selects the alternatives, and why?
3. *Alternatives.* What are the choices?
4. *Procedures.* The administration of selected alternatives.

Information on Alternatives

Not only are there tax alternatives in company management, but there are course alternatives in college accounting programs. Tax study is not a required course, but is a required foundation for any controller's job. If a study of federal taxes was one of many skipped electives in college, you can make it up with a night school course in a community college. Many CPA coach courses offer special Saturday tax classes, and local state CPA societies offer evening lectures. Seminars are held by the American Management Association (New York City–based, but with meetings held in major cities across the country) and by the continuing professional education department of the American Institute of Certified Public Accountants. Often, public accounting firms invite clients to in-house training courses for orientation to changes in the tax laws, and all of these offer tape cassettes for home study on particular areas of taxation. There are also legal associations and societies that offer tax lectures pointed toward lawyers, but these tend to be somewhat more technical than is required for the selection of alternative courses of action.

The best of these suggestions is the complete college night course, usually consisting of 45 class hours, and offered in either 8-week or 15-week programs. Time not permitting, a series of evening lectures in different areas of taxation, augmented by a home cassette general course, will provide the required basics.

> *Helpful Hint:* For those who commute to work by car, a tape cassette lesson can fill in unproductive time while driving.

Once the foundation is acquired in general federal taxation (state courses are unnecessary; the laws are too diverse and the dollar tax impact is usually not great; the computation of income mostly follows federal laws), all that is required, as in any good diet, is a modicum of lip service and some attention to the regimen—that is, an overview of tax law changes. This overview is available to the controller or tax manager from a variety of sources:

✧ Monthly reports are available from leading tax service publishers such as the Bureau of National Affairs, Research Institute of America, and Commerce Clearing House. A subscription to some level of tax service is required, with the monthly report provided as a free service. These reports highlight tax law changes and important tax court cases. In addition, the monthly bulletin published by your state CPA society usually has a tax section that addresses current changes. The AICPA has a tax division that publishes a monthly newsletter and a monthly magazine, *Tax Advisor*, a magazine of planning, trends, and techniques. Other professional groups, such as the National Society of Tax Professionals, also publish monthly newsletters containing similar information.

✧ Federal tax services are offered by the publishers above, in hard cover or CD-ROM. In either format, they offer a complete summary of federal tax laws, with plain language analysis of the code, annotated with pertinent references to the code. There are various price levels for these tax services, ranging from one-volume summaries to complete 30-volume libraries.

✧ *Journal of Accountancy,* published by the AICPA monthly, contains a tax practitioners' section and highlights significant tax areas that may be overviewed for pertinence.

✧ *Journal of Taxation* is a lawyers-oriented magazine that summarizes current tax cases. It, too, may be scanned for related cases and information.

✧ Independent accounting firms and corporate counsel usually publish releases for internal use (and often for dissemination to clients). Your lawyer or accounting firm will place you on the distribution list, on request. The larger firms publish monthly newsletters for clients that are often concerned with tax developments.

The controller may sample all or any of these sources, selecting for continued use one or more with which he or she is most comfortable. While two sources may supply repetitive information, one acting as a backstop for the other, I would recommend it. The second source is quickly scanned for only new information.

The Point Is: A solid tax background, obtained through a thorough federal tax course, is sharply honed by weekly or monthly reports that are quickly overviewed for areas that relate to your business.

THE PHILOSOPHY OF RESPONSIBILITY

Or, who selects the alternatives, and why.

The introduction to this chapter noted that the FEI has defined the tax responsibility as being within the controller's purview. But we can't all be experts in everything. And taxes really are such a specialized area that they really need the deft touch of the tax accountant or attorney. So let's leave this area of responsibility to the experts and stick to controlling operations.

Right? Wrong!

The nuances of taxation are no more esoteric than those of information technology, budgeting, auditing, or accounting—all of which are controllership functions. The controller is a generalist and needs to have a functioning knowledge of all these subjects. He or she need not be an expert in any of them.

The overall knowledge about the operations of the enterprise places the controller in a unique vantage point that the tax expert does not enjoy. The important tax decisions that affect the business do and should come from the controller, not the tax specialist.

Supported by a basic knowledge of taxation and kept current through monthly overviews of tax literature, the controller will spot tax law changes that affect the business. The lawyer, outside consultant, or tax accountant has many clients and is apt to miss the connection between a specific event and your business.

Once the controller has identified a feasible alternative, from his or her vantage point, the tax expert should be consulted for sophisticated advice as to whether the policy may be implemented.

Truism: The good tax ideas come from the controller who keeps current on tax developments, not from the tax experts.

Every company, of course, works to optimize cash flow and to pay the lowest taxes required by law, but not if the company objectives require a different result. A company with a high price/earnings ratio on its stock may be striving to build an earnings record to permit it to raise equity through common stock issuance. Taxes are then secondary. Depreciation methods would be selected that resulted in the most income and highest tax in the early years. Another company may have available operating loss carryforwards that would permit the sheltering of gain on a sale and leaseback transaction, the funds from which would be used to reduce short-term debt.

Truism: Tax policies attuned to defined corporate goals make these goals more readily attainable.

Don't abdicate this area of responsibility to the outside tax experts. They'll give you some good ideas and alternatives, but you'll miss a lot of others by not doing it yourself or within your department.

A proper approach to company taxation will be based on corporate goals, as expressed by the president through the budget (see Chapter 6) and reflected in the profit plan. This will be further depicted by the financial ratios shown in Exhibit 5-3. The company's tax posture will be devoted to the attainment of these quantified corporate objectives. The alternatives selected will be those that are consonant with the profit plan over the projected period.

ALTERNATIVES

What are the choices? Why are there choices?

Most of the alternatives arise because general accounting precepts, as promulgated by the Financial Accounting Standards Board and the American Institute of CPAs, differ from accounting as required by the Internal Revenue Code. In other cases, the code itself permits a variety of treatments. Listed below are the most common alternatives available to most businesses and a brief description of each. Details as to proper accounting treatment for reporting purposes may be found in APBs, SOPs, and ARBs (Opinions of the Accounting Principles Board, Statements of Position, and Accounting Research Bulletins of the AICPA), and in FASB statements and interpretations. For tax purposes, the Federal Tax Services and Regulations of the IRS should be reviewed.

> *Word of Caution:* Alternative minimum tax (AMT) rules have been adopted to ensure that corporate and high-income individual taxpayers who achieve tax savings by making use of certain deductions pay at least a minimum amount of income tax. The AMT is based on tax preference items resulting from deductions relating to depletion, intangible drilling costs, the excess of market value of incentive stock options over the price paid (for individuals only), certain excesses of bad debt reserves of financial institutions over actual bad debts, tax-exempt interest, the excess of a contribution's market value over cost, fast amortization and depreciation methods, certain long-term contract and installment method of accounting advantages, research and experimentation expenditures, 75% of the amount by which adjusted current earnings exceeds alternative minimum taxable income, and one-half of the excluded gain from the sale of qualified small business stock.

> *Helpful Hint:* The alternative minimum tax is 20% on amounts in excess of $40,000. However, the amount of the alternative minimum tax paid is allowed as a credit against the regular tax liability in future years. It is not lost. Therefore, the cost of using the alternatives will be the time value of money.

   1. *Advance revenues.* Examples are service contracts, for one year in advance, usually paid up front (for example, a television service contract), or coupon sales (used in the carbon paper industry to sell a one-year supply of carbon paper, paid in advance, future deliveries made against coupons, each of which provides for no charge delivery of a specific number of packages). For accounting purposes, these are generally unearned income items until shipped, at which time sales and income are recognized.

Prepayments received for services in one taxable year to be performed in the next may be included in gross income as earned by an accrual taxpayer. However, if the inclusion in income is deferred until the year succeeding the year of receipt and services are not performed by the end of the succeeding year, the income will be recognized in such succeeding year. This procedure is not applicable to amounts received under warranty or guarantee contracts, nor to prepaid rent or to prepaid interest. This requirement may cause a difference between accounting and tax treatment, as the accounting income is recognized when the service is performed, regardless of the tax year. (See Revenue Procedure 70-21 and Regulations Section 1.451-5.) There is a further requirement that the books of account (the booking rule) shall not reflect more income than the tax books (in other words, tax and accounting records must agree). Under some circumstances, the company could report this income when paid for, but only if it did the same for tax purposes.

Prepayments received for merchandise, such as the sale of coupons redeemable for carbon paper or other supplies, may be deferred for tax purposes until delivery is made. There is no booking requirement similar to that with prepayments for services. A company, thus, might recognize the gross profit on such sales, under certain conditions, while it deferred the tax until delivery is made.

2. *Bad debts.* Most accrual basis taxpayers record a provision for bad debts to a reserve for doubtful accounts, for financial accounting purposes.

The accounting provision, however, provides for more than just bad debts. It recognizes the reserve needed for billing adjustments and allowances and future merchandise returns that will be credited. It also recognizes the provision, based on an estimate, for accounts that will go bad in the future. For tax purposes, however, accounts must be written off when they become worthless. The two situations are quite different. The accounting reserve, generally, tends not to be large enough. The independent accountants will strive to see that the company maintains a conservative, or large, reserve. The tax people, on the other hand, will allow only worthless accounts to be charged off. The tax provision arises only from bad accounts, the accounting provisions from returns and allowances.

Helpful Hint: Always clean out and write off accounts against the reserve before the end of each tax year, to support the charge to the provision for bad debts. This should be done even though collection activity will continue to recover these accounts. These accounts receivable, if still being collected, should be recorded in a separate trial balance, for control purposes.

3. *Capital gains.* Financial accounting does not recognize the capital gains concept. However, for tax purposes, capital gains are distinguished from ordinary income. While they are taxed at the same rate, capital gains should be sought when there are capital loss carryforwards available to offset against the gains. Capital losses may be deducted against capital gains only. Moreover, contributions of appreciated property, if held for more than one year (the capital gains holding period), may be deducted at market value. In such cases, business transactions that result in income should be structured, where possible, to result in capital gains. These opportunities do not readily exist in the ordinary course of business but may be available in sale and leaseback transactions, sale of capital equipment, and royalty contracts. These are discussed in the paragraphs below.

4. *Captive finance subsidiaries.* The captive finance company is discussed on pages 62 and 110. From a tax viewpoint, the captive subsidiary offers the alternatives of using finance lease (sale treatment) or operating lease (recognition of rental income as received) accounting. The subsidiary may utilize accelerated depreciation benefits and retain any available investment tax credit. Consolidated tax returns may be filed with the parent. The result is usually losses for tax purposes and profits for accounting reporting. This provides immediate cash benefits, which, of themselves, produce profits.

> CASE IN POINT: One equipment manufacturer, earning about $1 million in profits a year, obtained cash flow benefits of $5 million over a three-year period, in addition to its regular earnings, through a captive finance subsidiary.

5. *Cash basis.* If average annual gross receipts are less than $5 million, the opportunity exists to report on an accrual basis for financial

accounting reporting and on a cash basis for tax reporting. This is a decided benefit when receivables are an important factor, as in the captive finance subsidiary. A similar advantage exists when purchases must be made on a cash basis from suppliers.

6. *Contingency reserves.* Generally accepted accounting principles (see SFAS 5, Accounting for Contingencies) properly indicate the establishing of contingency reserves if it is "probable" that an asset has been impaired or a liability incurred; an event is reasonably expected to occur to confirm the fact and amount of the loss; and the amount of the loss can be reasonably estimated. Thus, the financial statements may include an expense for a contingency reserve, which is not an acceptable tax deduction.

7. *Depreciation.* A choice of methods is permitted for accounting purposes. The method selected must be systematic and rational (Accounting Terminology Bulletin No. 1, paragraph 56). The declining-balance and sum-of-the-years'-digits methods meet these criteria, particularly where productivity or earnings are expected to be greater during the early years of the asset's life (ARB 44). Methods may be selected to accelerate or slow down deductions in early years. Proper depreciation planning will depend on the expectation of future profits. The fastest tax depreciation method is usually the 200% declining-balance method; it is generally faster than accounting methods.

Exhibit 9-1, **depreciation**, illustrates the differences in available deductions for depreciation under the straight-line, declining-balance, and sum-of-the-years'-digits methods.

Exhibit 9-2, **depreciation methods**, outlines the assorted types of depreciation that are available for accounting purposes. In item 2a of the exhibit, DD means double-declining method. Item 2c gives the formula for the sum-of-the-years'-digits as:

$$\frac{n \times (n + 1)}{2} = \text{sum-of-the-years'-digits}$$

For example, the sum-of-the-years'-digits for 5 years is 15 (5 + 4 + 3 + 2 + 1). By formula, where n = the number of years:

$$\frac{5 \times (5 + 1)}{2} = 15$$

Exhibit 9-1. Depreciation.

Year	STRAIGHT-LINE Annual Deduction	STRAIGHT-LINE Cumulative Cost Recovered	DECLINING-BALANCE Annual Deduction 150%	DECLINING-BALANCE Annual Deduction 200%	DECLINING-BALANCE Cumulative Cost Recovered 150%	DECLINING-BALANCE Cumulative Cost Recovered 200%	SUM-OF-THE-YEARS'-DIGITS Annual Deduction	SUM-OF-THE-YEARS'-DIGITS Cumulative Cost Recovered
1	$10	$10	$15	$20	$15	$20	$18	$18
2	10	20	13	16	28	36	16	34
3	10	30	11	13	39	49	15	49
4	10	40	9	10	48	59	13	62
5	10	50	8	8	56	67	11	73
6	10	60	6	7	62	74	9	82
7	10	70	6	5	68	79	7	89
8	10	80	5	4	73	83	5	94
9	10	90	4	3	77	86	4	98
10	10	100	3	3	80	89	2	100

As a general rule, *no matter what useful life is involved,* after half the useful life, you recovered only: $\frac{1}{2}$ the cost under the straight-line method; about $\frac{2}{3}$ under the double-declining-balance method; and close to $\frac{3}{4}$ under the sum of the year's-digits method.

≫ ANOTHER METHOD→ Consider decelerated depreciation. In your earlier low-income years you may wish to take less depreciation and save the lion's share for later higher-income years.

How decelerated depreciation works.—Essentially it can be the sum-of-the-year's-digits method in reverse. For instance, if in the sum of the year's digits method, equipment you just bought is going to last 5 years, you add up the digits for each year: 1 + 2 + 3 + 4 + 5 = 15. Then for the first year you deduct $\frac{5}{15}$ of your cost less salvage value; for the second you deduct $\frac{4}{15}$; for the third $\frac{3}{15}$; and so on. *Now to reverse the procedure:* If in the first year you deduct $\frac{1}{15}$ of your cost less salvage; in the second $\frac{2}{15}$; for the third $\frac{3}{15}$; for the fourth $\frac{4}{15}$ and for the fifth $\frac{5}{15}$, you come out with progressively higher deductions.

Depreciation alternatives present a marvelous opportunity for tax and accounting benefits.

Try This: If maximum deductions are desired in the early years, for tax purposes, use double-declining depreciation for the first three years of a five-year asset. Switch to straight-line for the last two years. Cumulative deductions, under this method, will exceed those under any other method.

Exhibit 9-2. Depreciation methods.

DEPRECIATION METHODS

1. Straight-line
   a. Time-related
   b. Output-related
      i. Service hours
      ii. Units of production

2. Decreasing charge
   a. Arbitrary assignment (first 2/3 life = DD)
   b. Fixed percentage of declining balance
   c. Sum-of-the-years'-digits $\left[\dfrac{n \times (n+1)}{2}\right]$
   d. Appraisal

3. Retirement and replacement

4. Interest
   a. Annuity
   b. Sinking fund

5. Appraisal (going-concern value)

For example: Assume a $100 asset, five-year life, and compare straight-line, double-declining, and double-declining for three years with straight-line for the last two years.

	Deductions	
S-L	D-D	D-D/S-L
$ 20	$40	$ 40
20	24	24
20	14	14
20	9	11 Switch to S-L
20	5	11
Totals $100	$92	$100

8. *Foreign currency translation.* Foreign currency transactions and foreign currency financial statements (those prepared in a currency other

than U.S. dollars and consolidated with or accounted for on the equity basis in the U.S. company's financial, statements) should be treated for accounting purposes by using the functional currency approach, in which assets, liabilities, and operations are translated at the current rate of the currency in which the foreign subsidiary operates, assuming that the currency has reasonable stability. (See FASB SFAS 52, Foreign Currency Translation.)

For tax purposes, no gain need be recognized if income is sheltered or deferred in a foreign subsidiary. See the next paragraph on ways to accomplish this.

9. *Foreign subsidiaries.* There are a great many **foreign subsidiary alternatives**, as delineated in Exhibit 9-3.

Before establishing a subsidiary or making a decision as to the form of the overseas organization, information should be obtained in the form of the tax treaty from the country being examined. Contact should also be made with the local embassy and trade offices to determine business and tax conditions. Accounting and legal firms may be helpful in obtaining such information. Many large public accounting firms publish accounting manuals and maintain offices in most foreign countries.

An accountant or attorney in the foreign country should be contacted to discuss local tax problems (in addition to the U.S. tax considerations) and to review any nontax factors that could affect a decision. For example, there may be an unstable political situation that would obviate the formation of a new company.

The form of organization would greatly depend on the income projections that have been made. If early losses are expected, a branch office will prove to be simple, with no tax problems, and will provide a complete tax deduction for these losses.

When profits result, the corporate form would be considered.

✧ A U.S. Possessions Corporation (USPC) must derive 80% of its gross income from a U.S. possession, including Guam, American Samoa, the Northern Mariana Islands, and the Virgin Islands. Seventy-five percent of gross income must be from an active business. Any tax due on income earned in the possession is offset by a special foreign tax credit. There is also a dividends-received deduction for dividends from a qualifying PC. There are special tax benefits offered by Puerto Rico. There is a capital gain on liquidation or sale of shares, and if the

Exhibit 9-3. Foreign subsidiary alternatives.

FOREIGN SUBSIDIARY ALTERNATIVES

I. INFORMATION
    a. Tax treaty
       1. Avoids double tax
       2. Lower W/T on dividends

    b. Embassies and trade offices

    c. Accounting firms—here and abroad
       1. Communication
       2. Local taxes
       3. Nontax considerations
       4. Forecast alternative income streams

II. FORM
    a. Branch—for early losses
       1. Avoids tax problems
       2. Avoids intercompany pricing problems
       3. Saves 1/2 the cost of starting up

    b. USPC
       1. 80% gross income from a possession
       2. 75% gross income from ''active'' business
       3. No tax until income is returned as dividends
       4. P/R tax benefits
       5. Individual shareholder avoids double tax
       6. Capital gain in liquidation or sale of shares

    c. CFC
       1. Over 50% stock or voting control
       2. High tax rate obviates deferral as tax credit eliminates U.S. tax
       3. Manufacture or other investment abroad
          (a) No tax
          (b) Second tier or sub-subs
          (c) De minimis exclusion of 5% of gross income or $1 million
          (d) 30% of gross income can be Subpart F type w/o being taxed as ''deemed paid''
       4. Buy U.S. components and finish
          (a) No U.S. tax until dividends paid
          (b) Foreign tax credits available on gross-up basis
          (c) Sec. 367 gains need ''clearance''
          (d) 30% of gross income can be Subpart F type w/o being taxed as ''deemed paid''
       5. Buy U.S. and sell abroad
          (a) Dividend is deemed paid
          (b) No tax benefit

    d. Interest charge DISC
       1. Defer income on $10 million of exports
       2. Interest is charged to the shareholder
       3. Liberal intercompany pricing rules
       4. Minimum capitalization of $2500

    e. FSC
       1. Foreign or USPC organization
       2. Substantial business outside U.S.
       3. 30% to 65% of export income exempt
       4. 100% dividends received deduction to parent
       5. Small FSC avoids foreign presence
       6. Small FSC excludes first $5 million of gross receipts

    f. ETC
       1. Not available to CFCs
       2. Tax reduction of 1-1/2 times export promotion expenses or 10% of export receipts, or
          increase in investment in export assets
       3. Phased out after 1971

shares are owned by an individual rather than a corporation, a double tax is avoided.

✧ The controlled foreign corporation (CFC) requires that the parent have over 50% stock or voting control. Any tax deferral advantages will be lost if the foreign country has a high tax rate, since the foreign tax paid will result in a foreign tax credit that may be greater than the U.S. tax. If manufacturing or other investment is done abroad, there will be no tax due. The CFC may establish its own subsidiaries, which will be tax free. The first $1,000,000 of gross income is excluded, and a maximum of 30% of the subsidiary's gross income may be subpart F type income without it being taxed. A CFC's subpart F income would include passive income such as dividends, rents, royalties (see Royalties, page 318), stock sales, income from services rendered outside the CFC's country to a related person, and income from the CFC's purchase and sale of goods to a related person where the goods are both produced and sold for use outside the CFC's country.

If the CFC buys U.S. components and finishes them abroad, as opposed to the complete manufacturing above, the CFC pays no U.S. tax until dividends are paid. However, if the CFC buys from the U.S. corporation and merely sells abroad, its income is deemed a paid dividend and there is no tax benefit.

> *Beware of This:* As a result of lower U.S. tax rates, many multinational companies will now generate foreign tax credits that they will never be able to use. These companies should repatriate U.S. income earned in foreign subsidiaries, shift taxable income from CFCs to the United States, increase the borrowings of CFCs to create interest deductions and reduce income abroad, increase intercompany transfer prices where possible, and increase management fees and charges for other services.

A foreign corporation (FC) not created in the United States and not doing business in the United States is taxed at 30% or the lower treaty rate on all U.S. source income. If the FC does business in the United States, it is taxed at the regular corporate rate.

There is a de minimis rule for CFCs that exempts from tax the lesser of 5% of gross income or $1 million of total foreign base company income. Moreover, current tax on dividends, interest, and investment gains in less-developed countries may be postponed until withdrawn.

✧ The Domestic International Sales Corp. (DISC) is a U.S. corporation that received a tax benefit by having the tax on 50% of its profits postponed for 10 years. Under current tax law, DISCs have been discontinued, except for the interest charge DISC, which continues to exist for small exporters. The interest charge DISC enables the small company to avoid having a foreign presence, as required under the FSC rules. Individual shareholders of the interest charge DISC may defer income attributable to $10 million or less of qualified exports, and corporate shareholders may defer $^{16}/_{17}$ of DISC income attributable to $10 million or less of qualified export receipts, subject to an interest charge on the DISC shareholders. The interest charge is based on the tax that would be due if the deferred income were distributed. The effect is to avoid the double tax on the corporation and the shareholder.

The DISC must have 95% of its gross receipts from exports, which could include sales to another DISC or to a broker for shipment abroad. It may not manufacture. Intercompany pricing rules are liberal. The minimum capitalization of the DISC is $2500.

✧ The foreign sales corporation (FSC) was created to give U.S. exporters a tax advantage to encourage competition with foreign export companies. It must be organized under the laws of a foreign country or U.S. possession, it must have a foreign presence and carry out substantial business outside the United States, it must have no more than 25 shareholders, and it must have a board of directors with at least one U.S. nonresident individual. The FSC rules replaced the DISC provisions after 1984. A transfer pricing method determines the percentage of foreign trade income exempt from U.S. tax. This may be from 32% to 65% for noncorporate shareholders and 30% to 65% for corporate shareholders. Generally, this will result in a 15% savings in income tax, based on a regular 34% corporate rate. The U.S. corporation is allowed a 100% dividends received deduction for FSC dividends. A portion of FSC income may be excluded from Subpart F income and eligible for tax deferral as not being from U.S. sources. There are special rules for a small FSC that may avoid the foreign presence rules. A small FSC excludes the first $5 million of gross receipts from taxable income. Also, see the interest charge DISC, which may defer tax on $10 million or less of qualified export receipts. Formation requirements and pricing rules for DISCs follow those of FSCs. Any U.S. company with a significant export business should consider utilizing the FSC as an income tax planning device.

Congress is currently considering repealing foreign sales corporations. The Senate Finance Committee has approved a bill to repeal the provisions of the tax code relating to FSCs. These provisions give U.S. exporters a tax advantage. However, opposition has recently been expressed by the European Commission, and the World Trade Organization has ruled that the FSC system violates WTO policies on export subsidies and must be dismantled. To comply with the WTO ruling and still prevent U.S. companies from suffering an operating disadvantage, the Foreign Sales Corporation Tax Act would dismantle the FSC system and change current tax rules to exclude certain extraterritorial income from gross income. The bill approved by the Senate Finance Committee would repeal the tax breaks, replacing them with an alternative system of benefits. Since extraterritorial income would be excluded for U.S. tax purposes, this is a means of avoiding double taxation, and no foreign tax credit would be allowed for income taxes paid on the excluded income. The extraterritorial income exclusion in the bill is parallel to the foreign source income excluded from tax under most territorial tax systems. The latest congressional action should be considered by existing FSCs and companies contemplating forming new ones.

✧ Foreign personal holding company (FPHC) rules have been established to discourage directing income to foreign corporations to avoid U.S. tax. Generally, these rules require U.S. shareholders of FPHCs to include in gross income their pro rata share of the FPHC's undistributed income. A FPHC is defined as having over 50% of its voting power or value in stock owned directly or indirectly by five or fewer individuals who are U.S. citizens or residents.

✧ Export trade corporations (ETC) were previously formed to encourage exports. ETCs were phased out after 1971 in favor of DISCs. However, those ETCs already qualified were allowed to continue in existence. The ETC is a form of CFC. The income of an ETC is excluded from Subpart F income, subject to limitations. While a foreign sales or service subsidiary may have Subpart F income because of transactions between it and its domestic parent, that income may also be excluded from tax. The ETC's tax is reduced by reducing its Subpart F income by the lesser of 1.5 times export promotion expenses, 10% of gross receipts from exports, or the increase in the investment in export trade assets.

10. *General purchasing power financial statements.* These represent financial reporting in units of general purchasing power. Many companies disclose supplemental accounting information restated for changes in the general purchasing power of the dollar, by applying the GNP Implicit Price Deflator. At present, there is no provision in the tax laws for recognition of any gains or losses that result from these restatements, and they do not offer a possibility for alternative tax planning.

11. *Imputed interest.* Financial accounting may impute interest to transactions that are essentially interest-free loans. The borrower may have taxable interest income, and the lender a tax deduction (see example on page 315, Leases).

12. *Interim financial statements.* Cumulative-effect type accounting changes made after the first quarter are included in restated net income of the first quarter and in any year-to-date financial reports that include the first interim period. Whenever financial information that includes those pre-change interim periods is presented, it is to be presented on a restated basis. Such accounting changes will create differences in taxable income and may require tax allocation. The tax effect of such changes may appear as a extraordinary item and should be considered as they relate to financial statement presentation.

13. *Inventory.* The opportunity for tax planning related to inventories is exceptional.

During times of increasing costs of materials, a change in the method of valuing inventories from FIFO to LIFO will result in reduced profits and increased cash flow from reduced taxes.

There are some disadvantages, however, to such a change, and the method should be carefully evaluated. Exhibit 9-4, **advantages and disadvantages of the LIFO method of inventory costing**, presents the advantages and disadvantages.

The SEC has placed restrictions on the references to and the type of disclosure made regarding the change.

In the state tax area, many states impose inventory taxes or personal

Exhibit 9-4.   Advantages and disadvantages of the LIFO method of inventory costing.

ADVANTAGES AND DISADVANTAGES OF

LIFO METHOD OF INVENTORY COSTING

Advantages of LIFO:

1. Improved cash flow from reduced taxes.

2. It serves to hedge a company's future earnings from

    future price declines.

Disadvantages of LIFO:

1. Impact on reported earnings and on a company's

    financial position.

2. Comparison of relative performance with other companies

    in the same industry that may not be on LIFO.

3. Possible adverse impact on the conventional application

    of a multiplier to earnings.

4. Need for modification or waiver of various restrictive

    covenants on loan indentures and other credit

    agreements restricting the amount of retained earnings

    available for cash dividends, reacquisition of stock,

    and borrowing formulas.

5. Impact on existing bonus and profit-sharing plans.

6. Inventories must be stated at cost; any market,

    obsolescence, or comparable reserves must be reinstated

    for federal income tax purposes, thereby generating

    income.

7. Some of the economic advantages of LIFO are lost in

    subsequent years if inventory quantities are reduced.

property taxes annually. Inventories may be planned to be in transit or at their lowest level on the imposition date.

> *Helpful Hint:* Review the state laws carefully. In many states, inventory of product in original cases is not taxable. It is presumed to be held for transshipment.

14. *Investment tax credits.* The company may recognize tax credits, if available, on investment in equipment over the life of the equipment, for accounting purposes. The credit may be flowed through, in the year of purchase, for tax reporting.

15. *Leases.* If capitalized, equipment under lease will be treated as fixed assets and depreciated over the useful life. This accounting treatment may result in a charge for depreciation that may be more or less than the deduction for taxes resulting from not capitalizing the lease and treating the rental payments as an operating expense.

Capitalization of leases should be determined on the basis of whether the lease is, in substance, an installment purchase. Generally, the lease should be capitalized if the lessee builds up material equity, or the lease term equals at least 75% of the useful life, or the lessee guarantees the lessor's debt, or the lessee assumes the risks and rewards of ownership, or the residual value at the end of the lease is nominal, or the lease provides the lessor with recovery of the investment plus a fair return.

The need for careful tax planning on leasing contracts has often been demonstrated through cases in which both parties have lost important tax benefits because the IRS has refused to recognize the agreements as leases for tax purposes. The IRS has treated these as sale contracts or as forms of financing. The IRS may take the position that a sale has transpired because ownership has in reality passed to the lessee. In sale and leaseback arrangements, the IRS has held this to be a form of financing, because ownership remains with the intended lessee—the reasoning being that the contract lessee did not sell the property, but simply mortgaged it to the contract lessor.

In these cases, if the contract is regarded by the IRS as a sale, there are these consequences: The monied party or contract lessor is taxed on any gain realized over an imputed sale price, which price would be the total present value of the required payments. The lessor would also lose the depreciation allowance and any investment tax credit. Moreover, the entire gain would be reportable in the year the contract becomes effective, unless the installment method were permitted. As to the contract lessee, or borrower, it would lose the deduction for periodic payments, except for the interest portion, and since the IRS deems the lessee to be the owner, it would take a deduction for depreciation and the ITC.

If the lease were considered by the IRS to be a financing arrangement, the imputed mortgage is arrived at as the totaling of the present value of the future payments. The lessee may deduct only the interest portion of the rental payments, which is the excess of the actual payment over the payment's discounted value in the year of the contract. The remainder of each payment, as well as the price of any purchase option, is treated as repayment of the loan.

The IRS considers certain guidelines, prepared from its rulings and policy statements, to arrive at a favorable presumption that a transaction is a lease:

✦ If there is a purchase option, the purchase price is not less than the fair market value of the property at the time the option is exercised.

✦ If there is a renewal option, the renewal charge will not be less than the fair rental value of the property at the time of renewal.

✦ If the lease term is 18 years or less, the residual value should be 15% or more. If the lease term is over 18 years, the residual value must be at least 5% of original cost if discounted at 6% to the year of the agreement.

✦ The estimated economic useful life of the property exceeds the original term by at least two-years or 10% of the original term, whichever is greater.

✦ The lessor's equity is 20% or more of the property's cost; that is, the lessee cannot finance more than 80% of the purchase price.

✦ If an involuntary conversion of the property results, the excess proceeds of the conversion belong to the contract lessor.

Helpful Hint: Independent appraisals that determine fair market value, residual value, fair rental value, and useful

life, if timely made, may prevent adverse decisions by the
IRS on audit.

The sale and leaseback of owned fixed assets is often used to raise
long-term funds (see discussion on page 61). When depreciable equipment is sold and leased back, if it is over one year old, it qualifies as a
Section 1231 asset, and a capital gain results on the sale for that portion
of the gain that exceeds the amount of depreciation taken in prior years.
Prior year's depreciation is recaptured at ordinary income rates.

Helpful Hint: A sale and leaseback may be accomplished by
selling at cost to a subsidiary on the cash basis for tax purposes
(a subsidiary may not be a cash basis taxpayer unless its net
revenues are not over $5 million per year and it does not carry
inventories). The subsidiary will then execute the sale and leaseback. The gain may then be recognized on the cost recovery
basis; that is, as cash is received (usually over a period of years
through payment of principal on notes), the first cash is applied
to a recovery of cost and the balance is recognized as gain.
This works to defer the gain to the later years. See SFAS 98,
Accounting for Leases.

16. *Marketable securities.* Persuasive evidence is needed to retain
the cost basis for securities classified as a current asset when the market
value is lower than cost. Generally, such evidence would be limited to
substantial recovery subsequent to the year-end. Failing this, the financial statements could reflect a charge to income that would not be allowed for tax purposes, no sale or exchange having taken place. The
financial accounting treatment of such securities is governed by SFAS
115, Accounting for Certain Investments in Debt and Equity Securities.
The accounting treatment is based on the classification of the securities
as being "held-to-maturity," "trading securities," or "available-for-
sale."

17. *Revenue recognition with right of return.* When the right of
return exists, the financial statements may not recognize the sale. For
taxes, in most cases, the sale would be recognized with no tax deferral.

For accounting purposes, the sale is analyzed to determine its economic substance (see SFAS 48, Revenue Recognition When Right of Return Exists). If the seller is exposed to risks of ownership through return of the property, the transaction should not be recorded as a sale—unless the price to the buyer is fixed; payment is not deferred until resale; the buyer's obligations would not be changed as a result of theft, destruction, or damage to the property; the buyer is not a straw party or conduit; the seller has no significant obligations for future performance to bring about resale of the property by the buyer; and future loss to the seller from future returns can be predicted. In such case, the recorded sale should be reduced by estimated returns to a net sales basis—again causing a revenue difference for tax accounting.

18. *Royalties.* The receipt of royalties from patent-licensing arrangements may, under carefully considered conditions, be capital gains income. In general, these requirements should be met:

⟡ Rights to patents should be transferred, in substantial measure.

⟡ Territorial limitations have been held not to invalidate the substantial transfer of rights. Licensing rights need not be worldwide to be considered sales for capital gains purposes.

⟡ Cancellation rights retained by the seller, if based on default or other reasonable grounds, should not affect the "sale" nature of an agreement.

⟡ Sublicensing restrictions have been repeatedly held by the courts not to be a substantial limitation with regard to a "sale" transaction.

⟡ Exclusivity of use need not necessarily be granted. As stated above, territorial divisions do not affect the substantiality of a sale of patent rights with regard to capital gains treatment. Moreover, the existence of a previously granted limited license would not obviate sale treatment. However, no consequential rights to use the patent for itself should be retained by the licensor. Courts have held, though, that the reservation of a license to itself by the grantor does not obviate the sale treatment.

⟡ When "know-how" is part of a bundle of rights transferred, consisting of patents and engineering information, the "know-how" takes on the nature of property for capital gains purposes and proceeds from "know-how" transfers should be taxable as capital gains.

> *Caution:* Structuring such contracts is not for amateurs or controllers. Suffice it for the controller to suggest the application of capital gains and to obtain professional tax and contract advice in structuring the agreement.

Royalty income of a controlled foreign subsidiary (CFC) must be derived from the active conduct of a business of the CFC in order not to be considered "effectively connected" to the parent and subject to inclusion of its profits as subpart F income in the U.S. parent. The CFC must conduct business in the foreign country through a fixed place of business, and the CFC must (1) be engaged in the development, creation, improvement, or production of and licensing of property (patents, etc.) that it has developed or substantially improved, or (2) must, through its own staff, be engaged in the business of marketing licenses of its property. The U.S. corporation must not (1) actively participate in soliciting or performing other activities required to arrange the license, or (2) perform significant services incident to such licenses.

> *Key Point:* Under these circumstances, then, patents could be sold to a CFC for improvement by it and the execution of licenses abroad, which would not be taxable subpart F U.S. income! (see IRC Sec. 864 (c) (4) (B), IRC Sec. 862 (a) (4), Sec. 882 of the Code (1966 Act), Regulations 1.954A-2(d) (i) and (iii), also S. Rep. No. 1707, 89th. Cong. 2nd. Sess. 20-21 and H-Rep. 1450, 89th. Cong. 2nd. Sess., 65).

19. *Special or extraordinary items.* The accounting concept of extraordinary item treatment (APB 30, Reporting the Results of Operations) is based on the infrequent and unusual nature of the item. The item may not meet the extraordinary concept but may still be considered for special item status because of its unusual nature or materiality. There is no similar concept in taxation. Financial statement planning will recognize this disparity.

20. *State taxes.* Because of the diverse nature of the state tax laws, state tax planning cannot be considered here, except as the broad planning moves would relate to the creating of a deductible state tax for federal purposes.

The most frequent state tax considerations are:

✧ *Whether or not to incorporate in a state.* Consider whether you have offices or assets, write orders or contracts, have sales representatives traveling, or need to collect money in the state. Most state tax services publish schedules or check lists showing whether these activities are considered doing business in the state. Incorporation requires the filing of an annual report or franchise tax return. An alternative is to file sales or use tax returns as a foreign corporation.

> *Helpful Hint:* Creating sales and accounts receivable in a state, together with the possibility of having to institute legal collection actions, does not always mean that you must incorporate and receive a license to do business in the state. Collection claims, in most states, may be assigned to collection attorneys who can bring actions in their own names, for the benefit of the assignor.

✧ *Which taxes to pay.* The state taxes to be paid will depend on whether or not you are franchised, in which case the annual report or franchise tax is due. If not, personal property or inventory taxes will, in any event, be payable in most states.

> *Interesting Sidelight:* Most states do not assess a penalty for failure of foreign corporations to file personal property tax returns. An assessor will file for the state on property that he or she can locate, at lower values than the company might file.

> *Helpful Sales Tax Hint:* When sales taxes are normally paid based on invoices billed to customers, do not neglect the opportunity to obtain a rebate of previously paid taxes when accounts receivable are written off as uncollectible against the reserve for bad debts. The same would apply to allowances and billing adjustments — tax-effect credits offered to customers.

PROCEDURES

How to control the payment of taxes and administration of tax policies:

1. Establish tax calendars, tax files, and ticklers.
2. Use Authorization for Payment and Narrative.
3. List payments on control sheet and calendar.
4. File documentation in tax file.
5. Reconcile taxes payable to general ledger, quarterly.
6. Procedure before the IRS.

Calendars, Tax Files, and Ticklers

Any tax service publishes federal and state tax calendars. The Prentice-Hall **Tax Calendar for fixed and recurring monthly dates** is shown in Exhibits 9-5 and 9-6. The fixed date calendar will change annually, as some taxes are due not on a specific date, but, for example, on a third Monday. The recurring monthly date calendar will change as state tax laws are revised.

Most large banks publish complete federal tax calendars. However, these are best prepared internally, based on the needs of each company. Other than payroll taxes and unemployment taxes (see the paragraph below), federal taxes include excise and corporate income taxes. Federal Agencies such as the Census Bureau and the Department of Labor also require the filing of informational reports.

Payroll taxes present a special problem and are not included in the regular state tax calendars. However, payroll guides are also published by most tax services. These guides explain the state payroll tax laws and will give due dates for state withholding tax, unemployment insurance tax, and disability tax. Exhibit 9-7 is a **timetable for the federal tax deposit** of payroll taxes.

As an alternative to use of the state tax guides, corporate representatives for legal service, such as Corporation Trust Co. or Prentice-Hall, supply weekly bulletins, tax reminders, and advices of tax law changes.

(*text continues on page 325*)

Exhibit 9-5.   State tax calendar — fixed dates.

PRENTICE-HALL
Tax Calendar of Fixed Dates

JANUARY, 20xx

CALENDAR OF ANNUAL, SEMI-ANNUAL AND QUARTERLY DATES FOR ALL STATES FOR JANUARY, 20xx

For acts to be performed or payments to be made monthly, see pages 1401 et seq.

In the items below if neither foreign nor domestic corporations are specifically mentioned, both are included, but the mention of domestic corporations is equivalent to the exclusion of foreign corporations, and vice versa. Dates below indicate last day for action. In the entries below, no cognizance is taken of Saturdays, Sundays or holidays, it being usually true that a return or payment due on such dates can be made on the following business day.

ALA.—Property taxes—Levy on personalty for nonpayment [¶ 31,685] .**Jan. 1**
Sleeping car cos.—Annual license tax to Dept. Rev. [¶ 49,500] .....**Jan. 1**
Electric, hydroelectric utilities license tax—Report, pay ¼ to Dept. Rev.
  [¶ 49,484.10] ....**Jan. 14**
Street, interurban RRs, water, gas, pipeline, heating companies license
  tax—Report, pay ¼ to Dept. Rev. [¶ 49,482] ....**Jan. 14**
Income tax—Individual's declaration and/or installment to Dept. Rev.
  [¶ 11,535] ....**Jan. 15**
Express companies—Exclusive intrastate businesses pay flat fee [¶ 49,-
  498] ....**Jan. 15**
Property taxes—Return on assessor's demand between Jan. 1 and this date;
  fee 50¢, thereafter penalty (3rd Mon.) [¶ 31,555; 31,580] ......**Jan. 21**
Tax on shares, domestic corp.--Report to Dept. Rev. and duplicate to local
  assessor (3rd Mon.) [¶ 31,920; 31,923] ....**Jan. 21**
Use tax—Quarterly return, pay Dept. Rev. [¶ 21,379] ....**Jan. 20**
Forest products severance tax—manufacturers and exporters, report and
  pay Dept. Rev. [¶ 45,712; 45,717] ....**Jan. 30**
Lodgings tax—Report to Dept. Rev. [¶ 21,167] ....**Jan. 30**
Income tax—Employer's withholding statement to employee; report, pay,
  quarterly withholding tax to Dept. Rev. [¶ 11,555] ....**Jan. 31**
Motor carrier's fuel use tax—Quarterly report, pay Dept. Rev. [¶ 45,284]
  ....**Jan. 31**

ALASKA—School tax—Due date [¶ 31,500] ....**Jan. 1**
Property tax—Assessment date [¶ 31,345] ....**Jan. 1**
Personal income tax—Pay 4th estimate installment to Comr. of Rev. [¶ 10,-
  317; 10,350] ....**Jan. 15**
Income tax—Report and pay to Comr. of Rev. tax withheld (plus school tax
  if any) during quarter ending Dec. 31 [¶ 10,360; 12,285.10; 31,500] **Jan. 31**
File annual withholding reconciliation [¶ 10,360; 10,634] ....**Jan. 31**
Business license tax—Renew license [¶ 21,227] ....**Jan. 31**
Income tax—Information return to Dept. Rev. by fish buyer and processor
  [¶ 10,335] ....**Jan. 31**
Property tax—Apply to Assr. for farm assessment [¶ 31,365] ....**Jan. 31**

ARIZ.—Property tax—Property assessed as of this date [¶ 31,540] ....**Jan. 1**
Telegraph, telephone companies—Personalty ownership inventory as of
  this date (report April 1) [¶ 49,422] ....**Jan. 1**
Property tax—Lien attaches (1st Mon.) [¶ 31,750] ....**Jan. 7**

Exhibit 9-6. State tax calendar — recurring dates.

10-22-

PRENTICE-HALL

Tax Calendar of Recurring Monthly Dates

All items in this calendar show acts to be performed or payments to be made at a definite date each month. For items that occur less frequently (annually, quarterly, etc.) than monthly, see pages preceding these.

In the items below if neither foreign nor domestic corporations are specifically mentioned, both are included, but the mention of domestic corporations is equivalent to the exclusion of foreign corporations, and vice-versa.

ALA.—Alcoholic beverage tax—Wholesalers and distributors report to Alcoholic Beverage Control Board [¶ 41,584] 10th
Tobacco use tax—Report, pay to Dept. Rev. [¶ 38,450] 10th
Gasoline and lubricating oil taxes—Carriers, warehouse and transfer companies report to Dept. Rev. [¶ 45,245; 45,250; 45,385; 45,390] 15th
Motor carriers tax—Report, pay to Dept. Rev. [¶ 49,264; 49,266] 15th
Oil and gas conservation and privilege taxes—Producers report pay Dept. Revenue [¶ 45,812; 45,817; 45,845; 45,850] 15th
Coal production tax—Report, pay Dept. Rev. [¶ 45,542] 20th
Gasoline inspection fee—Report, pay to Comr. of Agric. [¶ 45,450] 20th
Gasoline tax—Report, pay to Dept. Rev. [¶ 45,235; 45,260] 20th
Gasoline tax—Airport managers report to Dept. Rev. [¶ 45,235] 20th
Transient accommodations—Report, pay Dept. Rev. [¶ 21,167] 20th
Iron ore production tax—Report, pay Dept. Rev. [¶ 45,515; 45,525] 20th
Iron ore production tax—Transportation Co. report to Dept. Rev. [¶ 45,-515] 20th
Petroleum products inspection fee—Report and payment to Comr. Agric. [¶ 45,450] 20th
Lubricating oil tax—Report, pay to Dept. Rev. [¶ 45,380; 45,415] 20th
Motor fuel (non-gasoline)—Report, pay Dept. Rev. [¶ 45,320; 45,330] .20th
Sales tax—Report, pay to Dept. Rev. [¶ 21,379; 21,421] 20th
Leasing—Report, pay Dept. Rev. [¶ 21,221] 20th
Tobacco tax—Wholesalers, report-pay (also report purchases—applies to retailers) to Dept. Rev. [¶ 38,450] 20th

ALASKA—Alcoholic beverages-Report-pay [¶ 41,210; 41,215] ......Last day
Cigarette tax—Report, pay for previous month [¶ 38,300] ....Last day
Motor fuel tax—Report, pay Comr. Rev. [¶ 45,420; 45,425] .....Last day
Oil, gas production tax—Report, pay Comr. Rev. [¶ 45,507] ......Last day
Oil conservation tax—Report-pay Comr. Rev. [¶ 45,512] ....Last day

ARIZ.—Property tax (unsecured personalty)—Pay Co. Treas. [¶ 31,705] ....2nd Mon.
Alcoholic beverages wholesalers—Report, pay Dept. Rev. [¶ 38,518] ..10th
Use tax—Report, pay Dept. Rev. [¶ 21,379; 21,380] 15th
Sales tax—Report, pay Dept. Rev. [¶ 21,379; 21,380] 20th
Common, contract carrier—Report, pay MV Supt. [¶ 49,270] 25th
Private motor carriers—Report to MV Supt. [¶ 49,275] 25th
Gasoline—Distributors report, pay; carriers report to MV Supt. [¶ 45,-200] 25th
Motor fuel users—Report, pay MV Supt. [¶ 45,654; 45,655] 25th
Rental occupancy tax—Landlords report, pay Dept. Rev. (eff 12-31-74) [¶ 21,221] ....Last day

Exhibit 9-7. Federal Tax Deposit Chart.

20			20

This chart was prepared to **assist** employers in complying with Federal Tax Depository Regulations. It incorporates federal banking holidays.

Note: Check to ensure that the deposit due date for these liability periods is not affected by a non-banking date in your state.

FTD Due Dates for Employers following a **Semi-weekly** Deposit Schedule

JAN TO MARCH QUARTER		APRIL TO JUNE QUARTER	
PAYROLL DATE	*DUE DATE*	*PAYROLL DATE*	*DUE DATE*
1/1 to 1/4 (TUE)	1/7 FRI	4/1 (FRI)	4/6 WED
1/5 to 1/7 (FRI)	1/12 WED	4/2 to 4/5 (TUE)	4/8 FRI
1/8 to 1/11 (TUE)	1/14 FRI	4/6 to 4/8 (FRI)	4/13 WED
1/12 to 1/14 (FRI)	1/20 THU	4/9 to 4/12 (TUE)	4/15 FRI
1/15 to 1/18 (TUE)	1/21 FRI	4/13 to 4/15 (FRI)	4/20 WED
1/19 to 1/21 (FRI)	1/26 WED	4/16 to 4/19 (TUE)	4/22 FRI
1/22 to 1/25 (TUE)	1/28 FRI	4/20 to 4/22 (FRI)	4/27 WED
1/26 to 1/28 (FRI)	2/2 WED	4/23 to 4/26 (TUE)	4/29 FRI
1/29 to 2/1 (TUE)	2/4 FRI	4/27 to 4/29 (FRI)	5/4 WED
2/2 to 2/4 (FRI)	2/9 WED	4/30 to 5/3 (TUE)	5/6 FRI
2/5 to 2/8 (TUE)	2/11* **2/14 NY**	5/4 to 5/6 (FRI)	5/11 WED
2/9 to 2/11 (FRI)	2/16 WED	5/7 to 5/10 (TUE)	5/13 FRI
2/12 to 2/15 (TUE)	2/18 FRI	5/11 to 5/13 (FRI)	5/18 WED
2/16 to 2/18 (FRI)	2/24 THU	5/14 to 5/17 (TUE)	5/20 FRI
2/19 to 2/22 (TUE)	2/25 FRI	5/18 to 5/20 (FRI)	5/25 WED
2/23 to 2/25 (FRI)	3/2 WED	5/21 to 5/24 (TUE)	5/27 FRI
2/26 to 3/1 (TUE)	3/4 FRI	5/25 to 5/27 (FRI)	6/2 THU
3/2 to 3/4 (FRI)	3/9 WED	5/28 to 5/31 (TUE)	6/3 FRI
3/5 to 3/8 (TUE)	3/11 FRI	6/1 to 6/3 (FRI)	6/8 WED
3/9 to 3/11 (FRI)	3/16 WED	6/4 to 6/7 (TUE)	6/10 FRI
3/12 to 3/15 (TUE)	3/18 FRI	6/8 to 6/10 (FRI)	6/15 WED
3/16 to 3/18 (FRI)	3/23 WED	6/11 to 6/14 (TUE)	6/17 FRI
3/19 to 3/22 (TUE)	3/25 FRI	6/15 to 6/17 (FRI)	6/22 WED
3/23 to 3/25 (FRI)	3/30 WED	6/18 to 6/21 (TUE)	6/24 FRI
3/26 to 3/29 (TUE)	4/1# **4/4 CA**	6/22 to 6/24 (FRI)	6/29 WED
3/30 to 3/31 (THU)	4/6 WED	6/25 to 6/28 (TUE)	7/1 FRI
		6/29 to 6/30 (THU)	7/7 THU

FTD Due Dates for Employers following a **Monthly** Deposit Schedule

JAN TO MARCH QUARTER		APRIL TO JUNE QUARTER	
Monthly Dep JAN	2/15	Monthly Dep APR	5/16
Monthly Dep FEB	3/15	Monthly Dep MAY	6/15
Monthly Dep MAR	4/15	Monthly Dep JUN	7/15

IMPORTANT—Month used to determine safe harbor shortfall due date is the month in which the deposit due date (not payroll date) falls.

Safe-harbor SemiWk JAN	2/16 WED	Safe-harbor SemiWk APR	5/18 WED
Safe-harbor SemiWk FEB	3/16 WED	Safe-harbor SemiWk MAY	6/15 WED
Safe-harbor SemiWk MAR	4/15 FRI	Safe-harbor SemiWk JUN	7/15 FRI
Safe-harbor SemiWk APR	5/2 RDD†	Safe-harbor SemiWk JUL	8/1 RDD†
Safe-harbor Monthly **† Return Due Date**	5/2 RDD†	Safe-harbor Monthly	8/1 RDD†

NAR-BSC 18-3

(*text continued from page 321*)

If the company is represented in only a few states, the same information may be obtained directly from state agencies—labor department, income tax bureau, or secretary of state. Since this type of contact requires direct contact, and since the state agency does not provide mailing services for changes in the law, the use of tax guides and services is recommended if the company files in many states.

Having obtained the published tax calendars from the selected source, the company should establish its own calendar each month. A page from a **company tax calendar** is shown in Exhibit 9-8. The Date Due is obtained from the published tax calendar; the Date Submitted refers to the date the tax return was completed by the tax accountant and submitted for payment. The Date Mailed is subsequently entered to provide a record evidencing payment. It is easily scanned for open boxes.

Helpful Hint: If a penalty for late filing is assessed, the tax department would usually accept this calendar, showing date mailed, as satisfactory evidence that the tax was paid timely.

Exhibit 9-8. Company tax calendar.

The company tax calendar illustrated will have separate pages for:

✧ Sales tax
✧ Personal property tax
✧ Payroll tax
✧ Other taxes (occupancy, excise)

or for any other tax commonly imposed by most states due to the nature of the company's business. County or city taxes are listed within the appropriate state.

Having set up the calendars, which reflect due date:

1. A file is created for each tax.
2. The return to be filed is set up in a tickler file, approximately 15 days prior to the due date. The tickler file is merely a desk calendar.
3. On the tickled date, the return is removed from the tax file, completed, and submitted for payment, and the Date Submitted is completed on the Tax Calendar.

The Authorization for Payment and Narrative

When the tax return is submitted, an **authorization for payment** (Exhibit 9-9) is completed by the tax return preparer, who approves the authorization and draws the check (from a separate pegboard tax account). The authorization, return, and check are submitted for approval by the accounting service manager. After his or her approval on the authorization, the entire package is submitted to the check signatory.

If the payment is unusual in nature (a special assessment, a tax audit deficiency, interest or penalty, a new tax, over a prespecified limit for each kind of tax), a narrative explanation should be attached to the authorization. The narrative is a handwritten document explaining the reason for the unusual payment and relating the details of any audit deficiency.

Exhibit 9-9.   Authorization for payment.

AUTHORIZATION FOR PAYMENT

_7/19/_
(DATE)

Payee *Tax Collector — City of Hartford*

Amount *$597 46/xx*

Reason *1st Qtrly. Pymt. — Pers Prop. Tax - 20xx*

A/c Charged *74-05-62 0002*

Method of Repayment

Approved *pd*

Date Payment Completed *Chemical Bk Ck.# 2246*

(Use this form for all advances to salespeople, loans to employees, exchanges,
or payments without invoices.)

(0-8-56)

Key Point: Tax returns are detailed, complex, and routine. The
narrative becomes an exception report that saves you reading
every return. It provides you with an overview of the unusual
situation and allows you to form a judgment as to whether the
proper steps have been taken.

Helpful Hint: Run the "tax account" on an imprest basis — make
deposits only in the amount of the total of the daily checks you
write. This prevents fraud (your balance is just enough to cover
authorized checks written), saves on the cost of carrying idle
balances, and makes checkbook reconciliations unnecessary.
It may be operated on a zero-balance or minimum balance
basis.

List Payments on Control Sheet and Calendar

Signed checks are returned to the disbursing section (a separate person from the check drawer or return preparer) for mailing and entry on the company tax calendar in the Date Mailed column (see Exhibit 9-8). Concurrently, the dollar amount of the payment is entered on a **control sheet** for each class of tax—a separate sheet for payroll taxes, sales taxes, or personal property taxes. This sheet is illustrated in Exhibit 9-10. Line 37 of that sheet shows the entry of $597.46 of the Hartford, Conn., tax listed on the Authorization for Payment at Exhibit 9-9. This control sheet is used for the quarterly reconciliation.

File Documentation

After mailing by the disbursing section, the entire package (tax return, any invoice, authorization, narrative) is filed in the tax file (see page 321).

The file is best retained in the tax department, rather than the disbursements section, as the file is frequently consulted, certainly each month or quarter to file the next tax return.

Reconciliation

Quarterly, the general ledger is examined and each account to which tax payments are charged is traced back to the control sheet (Exhibit 9-10). Every item reflected on the general ledger as a tax payment must be accounted for on the control sheet. The internal audit section conducts this review.

Unlisted items are investigated for proper authorization for payment and backup documentation and are entered on the control sheet. Items listed on the control sheet but not found through the ledger are investigated for improper posting or coding errors.

Exhibit 9-10.   Control sheet.

CONTROL SHEET

PERSONAL PROPERTY TAX PAID
Y. E. 4/30/

PAGE 1 OF 4

	1	2	3	4	5	6	7	
1	ARIZONA							1
2	MARICOPA COUNTY			558829		6/7/74	10888	2
3					558829			3
4								4
5	CALIFORNIA							5
6	ALAMEDA COUNTY			174846		7/30/74	5629	6
7	CITY OF ALAMEDA			816		4/23/75	2682	7
8	" " "			816		4/8/74	2176	8
9	HUMBOLDT COUNTY			5598		8/1/74	2278	9
10	KERN COUNTY			2099		11/4/74	2281	10
11	LOS ANGELES COUNTY			2659568		3/6/75	5675	11
12	" " "			159568		8/1/74	10870	12
13	" " "			1413177		5/31/74	1927	13
14	MARIN COUNTY			2200		8/1/74	3169	14
15	ORANGE COUNTY			60514		4/16/74	2279	15
16	" " "			223072		4/12/74	10888	16
17	COUNTY OF SANTA CLARA			355636		4/12/74	10400	17
18	COUNTY OF SAN MATEO			455941		8/1/74	1027	18
19	COUNTY OF SAN LUIS OBISPO			1126		8/1/74	2272	19
20	SHASTA COUNTY			2969		8/1/74	2228	20
21	SONOMA COUNTY			1486		5/30/74	1028	21
22	VENTURA COUNTY			5262		5/6/74	2188	22
23					5588647			23
24								24
25	COLORADO							25
26	ALAMEDA COUNTY			10008		2/6/75	2589	26
27	COLORADO SPRINGS			8575		1/1/75	2456	27
28	CITY & COUNTY OF DENVER			205743		4/21/75	1502	28
29					224321			29
30								30
31	CONNECTICUT							31
32	SHELTON			4557		7/19/74	2248	32
33	STAMFORD			42528		7/19/74	2242	33
34	STONINGTON			23130		8/14/75	2581	34
35	WETHERSFIELD			6160		7/19/74	2248	35
36	HARTFORD			59743		3/20/74	2586	36
37	"			119486		12/21/74	6134	37
38	"			59746		7/19/74	2246	38
39	DANBURY					7/19/74	2271	39
40	EAST HARTFORD					7/19/74	2245	40

Procedure Before the IRS

What do you do when the tax collector comes to call? The steps are these:

1. Returns are checked for form and accuracy and classified for audit by the district or regional director's office. Mathematical errors are corrected, overpayments refunded, and demand made for additional tax.
2. A field audit on your premises is scheduled. You should have your tax attorney or accountant present.
3. Technical advice from the Washington National Office of the IRS may be requested by either the taxpayer or the district director, to resolve thorny procedural or technical questions.
4. After audit, adjustments are proposed to the taxpayer's liability. These may be agreed to, or contested by requesting a conference.
5. Each of the four IRS regions maintains an appeals office to hear taxpayer appeals. A request for an appeals conference should be addressed to the local district director, who will forward it to the appeals office. A conference will be arranged at a convenient time and place to discuss the disputed issues. You must submit a written protest setting forth facts, law, and arguments if the total amount exceeds $10,000 for any taxable period. If the amount is greater than $2,500, but less than $10,000, a brief written statement of disputed issues is all that is required. An oral request will suffice to obtain appeals office consideration for $2,500 or less issues and in all office interview or correspondence examinations.
6. District conferences are held by the conference staff without the examining officer. Matters under $2,500 can be settled by the conference staff chief. In matters over $2,500, the taxpayer is encouraged to bypass the district conference and go directly to the appellate division.
7. At the appellate conference, you may agree to any proposed decisions, and if you do not, you will receive a 90-day letter.
8. You may then pay the tax and apply for a refund or appeal to

the tax court, usually without paying in advance. If you fail to pay or appeal, the IRS will start any appropriate enforcement action.

9. After the case is docketed, you may call for a further conference with the appellate division to attempt to compromise or settle.

10. No appeal is permitted from tax court in cases handled under the Small Tax Case Procedure. Otherwise, appeal may be made to the court of appeals and then to the U.S. Supreme Court.

11. Previously, taxpayer ombudsman administered the IRS problem resolution program and could issue a taxpayer assistance order where the taxpayer might suffer significant hardship as a result of IRS actions. IRS Form 911 is used to apply for such assistance. The Tax Refund Act of 1996 created a new high-ranking IRS position of Taxpayer Advocate (TA) to replace the ombudsman program. The TA will supervise the problem resolution offices at the regional and local level.

Caution: Always appear at a conference, at any level, with your qualified agent or attorney. Don't do it yourself. The laws are too complex, and you may give evidence that can damage your position.

Further Caution: Always have your tax agent present when a field agent questions your employees or accounting personnel. Instruct your people to have no conversation with the agent without your tax professional being present, other than to produce books and records. Don't take a chance on wrong information being given to the field agent by an employee who is trying to show how smart he or she is.

TAX TIPS

The canny controller may have a limited foundation in taxes but maintains a stream of information on taxes to apprise him or her of alternative tax courses. The controller conceives the proper tax moves for the company, aided by, not led by, outside tax consultants. Proper tax planning is integrated with corporate goals as expressed by higher management. Often, the alternatives chosen will be treated differently from financial statements for tax purposes. Both effects need to be considered carefully. Administration of tax policies requires timely payments through the use of tax calendars, tickling due dates, and establishment of separate tax files. As with other responsibilities, control is achieved through division of responsibilities, exception reports (the narrative), and review of results through audit and reconciliation.

10

Organizing the Operational Audit

Auditing, financial or operational, is not a defined function of the controller or treasurer in the official EFI statement of responsibilities as exhibited in "Treasurer's and Controller's Functions." The controller, however, has the official duty for evaluating and consulting "as it relates to the attainment of objectives and the effectiveness of policies, organization structure, and procedures." Another defined duty is protection of assets "through internal control, internal auditing. . . . "

Inferentially, therefore, the FEI definition provides the authority for operational auditing—for the evaluation of the efficacy of the operating policies and procedures. It explicitly provides authority for the protection of assets, generally interpreted to mean through financial auditing and, again inferentially, through the operational audit of the system that spawns these assets.

The controller's position description in "Treasurer's and Controller's Functions," accordingly, provides under organizational relationships that auditors will report to him or her. The controller is responsible for the operating plan (see page 189) and should have the opportunity to review, check, edit, criticize, and validate the performance of that plan. There are those who will maintain that managers responsible for performance should not evaluate themselves, that this responsibility should be divided and undertaken by others as a performance check on any given manager. This is a valid argument as it relates to financial audits (concerned with preparation of financial statements), but it can-

not apply to operational audits (reviews of operating systems and procedures). There is a point beyond which responsibility should not be divided. The "buck" has to stop here. The controller has established
and implemented the operating plan and needs the tools to review its
efficiency—the internal audit of operations. The comparison of the actual results of operations to the budget is a "measure" of performance—a quantification of results. The operational audit is an "evaluation" of the plan—a statement of its effectiveness. Both are necessary!

This chapter will not consider financial audits, which are sometimes
the responsibility of the president, the treasurer, the controller, or even
the board of directors. The subject will be considered in Chapter 11,
Supervising Special Administrative Areas of Responsibility.

These pages will consider the operational audit as to:

- ✧ Purpose (why is it needed?)
- ✧ Nature (what should be audited?)
- ✧ Organization (how should it be audited?)
- ✧ Review (how and by whom should audit reports be reviewed?)

Purpose

The operational audit is an internal procedure, performed by company
personnel, that is philosophically oriented toward monitoring the possibility of attainment of the operating plan's bottom-line objective.

It does this, not through measuring and comparing actual results
to the budgeted figures, but through evaluating personnel, operations,
plans, policies, systems, procedures, and even the tools of management
(procedures manuals, organization charts, position descriptions, and the
multitude of other devices described in Chapter 7).

Operational audits are specific engagements by auditors to review
specific areas of the business. These audits are augmented by a system
of internal check and control, sometimes called automatic auditing, that
provides for a system of internal checking on each and every transaction
being processed regularly during the daily operations. Internal checking
is a controllership responsibility that, together with the outside audit

function, will be discussed more fully in the next chapter, Supervising Special Administrative Areas of Responsibility.

The *outside audit*, often called the external audit as opposed to the internal operational audit, is performed by independent public accountants. It is not oriented to the attainment of plan objectives but serves as the vehicle whereby the outside auditors express an opinion on the fairness, consistency, and conformity with accepted accounting principles of the company's published financial statements. Whatever the results of the operating plan, the outside audit reviews these results and expresses an opinion on them.

The differences between outside audits and operational, inside audits are:

1. Outside, independent audits are required by public agencies, financing institutions, stock exchanges and stockholders, contracting parties, creditors, directors, and top management. Inside audits are used by individual department heads and other management as a control tool to evaluate conformity to internal procedures.
2. The outside audit produces a formal report, supported by a body of accounting rules and dicta, that tells the recipients above whether the financial statements are fair, consistent, and in conformity with accounting principles. The inside audit report is less formal, and its format varies with the nature of the job being audited. It is designed for internal company use only.
3. Outside audits are performed by independent professionals, either management consultants, certified public accounting firms, or independent specialists in specific areas such as traffic, distribution, data processing, plant management, administration, or engineering, for a fee. Inside audits are done by company employees.
4. Outside audits review financial statements and the broader aspects of the internal control system. Inside audits may also review the internal control system but generally are concerned with individual segments of that system and a variety of reports, forms, and operating departments, rather than with the financial statements in themselves.
5. Outside audits are usually conducted at the end of fiscal quarters

or the year. Inside audits are performed on a continuing basis throughout the year.

6. Outside audits may be the responsibility of an officer other than the controller. Inside audits are the controller's responsibility in that they evaluate the soundness of the operating plan.

The *objectives* of internal operational audits may, thus, be said to be:

1. Evaluating actual operations (as opposed to budgeting, which measures results vs. a plan, and as opposed to outside auditing, which merely looks at the financial statements that result from these operations)
2. Controlling operations, through corrective action taken as a result of the audit evaluation
3. Integration with outside auditors in determining the validity of the system of internal check and control
4. Improving operations through the evaluation process, in that it identifies personnel, policies, and procedures that may be improved in the future, thereby permitting the more ready attainment of future profit plans
5. Providing for the protection of company assets
6. Preventing and uncovering defalcations or other fraud

The National Commission on Fraudulent Financial Reporting (the Treadway Commission) has studied the factors that tend to cause fraudulent financial reporting and has recommended possible steps to reduce its occurrence. Their report, titled Internal Control—Integrated Framework, was issued by the Committee of Sponsoring Organizations of the Treadway Commission and is referred to as the COSO report. The proposed recommendations apply to the public company, the independent public accountant, the SEC, and others to improve the regulatory and legal environment, and to the educational area. Although the report focuses on public companies, many of the recommendations would be helpful for private companies. The report is available from the Financial Executives Institute or the AICPA.

As a result, the AICPA has issued a new Statement on Auditing Standards (SAS), Consideration of Fraud in a Financial Statement Audit. This SAS 82 amends SAS 1, Codification of Auditing Standards and Procedures, and SAS 47, Audit Risk and Materiality in Conducting an Audit. In summary, the standard describes fraud and its characteristics and requires the auditor to specifically assess the risk of material misstatement due to fraud and how to respond to the results of the assessment. This document would be useful to treasurers and controllers in establishing a working environment that includes safeguards against fraud. The AICPA statement, described below, will facilitate the implementation of these changes.

The AICPA has, further, issued SAS 78, titled Amendments to Statements on Auditing Standards and Statements on Standards for Attestation Engagements to Incorporate the Internal Control—Integrated Framework Report (of COSO). This standard defines internal control in accordance with the COSO report and lists the five elements of the internal control structure:

1. *The control environment.* This sets the tone for the organization and the control consciousness of its people.
2. *Risk assessment.* The entity's identification and analysis of relevant risks to achieve its objectives, forming a basis for determining how the risks should be managed.
3. *Control activities.* The policies and procedures to help ensure that management directives are implemented.
4. *Information and communication.* Identifying, capturing, and exchanging information to enable people to carry out their responsibilities.
5. *Monitoring.* Assessing the quality of the internal control structure's performance over time.

NATURE

The operational audit, being concerned by definition with the evaluation of company operations, may evoke as its performance sphere any area or segment of the business. There should be no prohibitions on the divisions, segments, departments, committees, policies, procedures, personnel, or plans that the auditor may approach.

This authority should come down from the president in a stated policy manual release and be explicit in the position description for the auditor. Obviously, the one exception is the outside audit function, which would not be reviewed or audited by the inside audit group, it being performed by independent outside accountants on a fee-paid basis.

> *Avoid This Pitfall:* Don't conduct nit-picking audits. Since everything may be audited, a sense of proportion needs to be employed in determining what to audit. Nit-picking audits are divisive and contribute nothing to the overall achievement of company goals.

The following areas should be audited:

✧ Profit centers—areas that generate revenues and expenses, such as a branch office.
✧ Cost centers—areas that generate costs and expenses without revenue, such as a data processing department (assuming such charges are not allocated to users).
✧ Vertical systems—procedures that cause the generation of data to emanate from a profit or cost center and to cross departmental lines, such as a billing system that starts in a branch office and ends with a home office posting to an accounts receivable trial balance, or areas of an accounting department that generate reports for other departments.
✧ Internal check systems—areas of internal control and division of responsibility within one or many departments. This also includes overall policies.

Obviously, the audit of profit or cost centers will be for the purpose of improving profits or controlling costs through an evaluation of the operating systems being employed. The audit of a vertical system is merely a way to trace the practicability of a system across divisional lines, which would not otherwise be accomplished in the single audit of a profit or cost center. Audits or internal check systems will protect company assets and guard against fraud.

This list precludes the audit of:

✧ Personnel as a specific function. We do not set out to evaluate personnel. Our audit may reveal excellence or incompetence, and the audit report provides for such comment.

> *A Word of Caution:* Some chief executive officers require an audit of company personnel, with a view to evaluating an upgrading in weak areas. This is not an audit function, other than through audit report comment. Such an audit, if conducted, should be done by specially assigned people or the personnel department. An internal auditor cannot function or obtain the cooperation of employees if they believe he or she is constantly auditing them, rather than their departmental systems and procedures.

✧ Intradepartmental procedures, unless a question of internal control or security is involved. We do not need to review the detailed mechanics and work responsibilities within the department. This is the function of the department's manager. We review only those procedures that emanate from one department and affect another.

> For Example: The internal auditor does not review the methods employed by the switchboard operator to answer telephone calls. That is the function of the office service manager. The auditor does review the method employed by the operator in taking and transmitting messages for absent personnel, as these affect other departments.

✧ Repetitive functions such as bank reconciliations, vendor accounts payable statements, taking physical inventories, or accounts receivable confirmation. Such repetitive functions are operating responsibilities of department heads. The assumption of these duties by auditors tends to swell the auditing staff and turn it into an operating department, rather than a reviewing and evaluating section. The argument is made that the audit of these functions, by auditors, is a repetition of the work already being performed by the department, hence at greater cost. The argument is valid, but the conclusion is not. The purpose of the audit function is not to cut costs. Certainly that is an ultimate goal, but its purpose, as defined previously, is oriented toward the attainment of the operating plan's bottom-line objective. The cost of auditing, of this review function, is a budgeted cost. Any attempt to cut costs elsewhere, using the services of auditors, will impugn the stated objectives of this function.

To the extent that these functions affect other departments, and they all do, they should be the subject of internal audits on an occasional basis, but not on a continuing, operational basis.

ORGANIZATION

The "how do we audit operations?" facet of internal auditing includes:

1. *Overseeing the internal audit function.* Exhibit 10-1 is a **checklist for executives and directors** that embodies the principles of purpose and nature set forth in the pages above. This list was prepared by a large, independent accounting firm, Coopers & Lybrand (now PricewaterhouseCoopers), and circulated in a newsletter to all of its clients. It is a minimum checklist of internal audit procedures.

2. *A position description.* This should be prepared along the lines indicated in Chapter 7. It defines the functions and responsibilities of auditors. If separate auditors are used for the home office and field offices, a separate description should be prepared for each auditor. Exhibit 10-2 is a **position description for a field auditor**.

Helpful Hint: Note that the field auditor assists in interviewing, training, and maintaining field levels of administrative performance, in addition to straight auditing work. These are nonrepetitive functions related to the field auditing work, and they

Exhibit 10-1. Checklist for overseeing the internal audit function.

ACCOUNTING AND AUDITING

Overseeing the Internal Audit Function
A Checklist for Executives and Directors

The internal audit function is assuming ever-increasing importance as corporations expand and their accounting systems become more complex. Moreover, pressures on executives and boards of directors continue to mount, requiring them to maintain the utmost vigilance over all aspects of their companies' operations, including audit procedures. Equally important, a properly functioning internal audit system can help pinpoint areas of potential revenue improvement and cost reduction. As a basic guide, directors and executives may wish to use the following as a minimum checklist of internal audit procedures.

Organization

☐ The board of directors' audit committee should participate in approving the audit schedule, guiding the work of the internal audit staff in a broad sense, and overseeing the coordination of internal and external audit operations.

☐ The manager in charge of the internal audit function should report to an upper echelon executive who can ensure that deficiencies are considered promptly and that corrective action is monitored.

☐ The internal audit schedule should be established annually, in consultation with the company's external auditors.

Qualifications

☐ Appointments to the internal audit staff should be on the basis of capacity to advance to higher positions.

☐ Internal auditors, like their external counterparts, should engage in continuous training and self-improvement.

☐ Internal auditors should be in a position to maintain independence in matters they review.

Performance Guides

☐ Internal auditors should not be overly burdened with routine tasks.

☐ Internal auditors should have full access to all areas of the company that their work requires.

☐ The internal audit schedule should provide for coverage of all physical facilities within a reasonable time cycle.

☐ Internal auditors should submit periodic reports, which permit management to evaluate progress in terms of the established schedule.

☐ Internal auditors should observe generally accepted auditing standards as incorporated in the Statements on Auditing Procedure issued by the American Institute of CPAs.

☐ The team's work should be guided by written programs.

(continued)

Exhibit 10-1.   (continued)

Performance Guides *(continued)*

☐ Audit programs should be responsive to changing control conditions.

☐ The audit staff's work papers should include comprehensive documentation of all tests, stating what was examined, the procedure followed, and results.

☐ All audit programs should be signed off to indicate completion of steps.

☐ The results of each examination should be expressed in a written report oriented toward management and suitable for follow-up.

☐ The follow-up should include a mechanism to ensure that all control deficiencies signaled by the internal audit are corrected as soon as possible.

☐ The internal audit staff should review operational and administrative controls on a cyclical basis, with special attention to areas of potential revenue improvement and cost reduction.

Exhibit 10-2.   Position description — field auditor.

	POSITION DESCRIPTION
TITLE FIELD AUDITOR	DATE 7/24/
ORGANIZATIONAL UNIT Controller	JOB NUMBER

FUNCTION

Responsible to the controller for auditing the accounting and administrative control functions at field sales and service centers; for reporting the audit results in comparison with approved audit procedure; for providing recommendations for field procedural changes; for coordinating the initial interviewing and subsequent training of branch administrators.

RESPONSIBILITIES

1. *Interviewing.* Coordinate with the training manager (who interviews branch administrators for hire) in establishing definitive hiring criteria. Conduct preliminary interviews of branch administrators in the field, when requested by training manager, for new hires for replacement purposes. Recommend two to three interviewees to the zone manager for final interviewing and selection by the zone manager.

2. *Training.* Schedule training of new branch administrators for an initial two-week period, at a smoothly functioning branch. Upon completion of field training, spend three days in SOP manual training with new branch administrators, discussing concepts involved.

3. *Auditing.* Schedule unannounced audits on field sales and service centers at least once in every nine months. Conduct audits in accord with Internal Audit Questionnaire and Internal Audit Program. Complete audit report after each audit and supply the Summary Audit Appraisal to the controller each six months, covering all sales and service centers previously audited.

4. *Maintain field levels of performance.* Retrain branch administrators wherever necessary. Fill in for branch administrators in emergency cases.

5. *Procedures.* Recommend updating and changes in procedures, based on field audit work. Write recommended new procedures where applicable.

are consonant with the attainment of the corporate operating plan objectives.

3. *Internal audit programs.* These should be prepared for profit and cost centers, vertical systems, and internal check systems, as described in the section on the nature of audits. Exhibit 10-3, **field audit announcement**, is directed to field managers at profit centers that will be audited. It includes the auditor's position description, the actual audit programs, and a format of the reports that will follow.

Auditing Assist: Don't be afraid to circulate your audit program. The corporate goal is to achieve systems that work. If managers know what will be audited, the areas that you stress and consider important, you are more apt to obtain conformity to procedures.

Don't fear that disclosure of your programs will allow someone to construct a fraud, to circumvent the system. The audit program is designed to test for lack of internal control, lack of division of duties, fraud. The very publication of the audit program is a deterrent to fraud.

Absolute Auditing Requirement: The last paragraph of the field audit announcement exhibit provides for the submission by the field office of a memo on corrective action that must be taken within 30 days of the audit. The regional administrator will then comment on this in the monthly narrative report (page 268), which then flows up the management ladder in successive higher monthly reports, and the field auditor will review this deficiency at the next audit.

A **detailed internal audit program for a branch office** is shown in Exhibits 10-4, 10-5, and 10-6.

✧ 10-4—**audit procedures at the home office**. These procedures are performed at headquarters, prior to conducting the field audit, in preparation for the field visit. The procedure

Exhibit 10-3.   Field audit announcement.

MEMO TO: Distribution   SUBJECT: Field Audit Announcement
FROM: Controller   DATE: June 26, 20xx

Marketing Memo #148, dated June 12, provided that branch
administrators would report directly to branch managers.

In accord with this change, the controller's division has
established a field auditing procedure as follows:

   1. *Field Auditor's Position*. This describes the functions and
responsibilities of the field auditor.

   2. *Internal Audit Program at Home Office*. This indicates the
review work to be done by the field auditor, prior to the field
trip.

   3. *Internal Audit Program at Branch Office*. This indicates the
work to be done by the auditor in the field and is an extension of
the work done in the home office, No. 2, above.

   4. *Internal Audit Questionnaire*. These are questions that will
be asked by the field auditor, before beginning the audit in No. 3,
above.

   5. *Audit Report:*

       a. *Detailed Report*. Sent from auditor, with copies to
       controller, branch administrator, zone managers, and
       regional managers.

       b. *Summary Audit Report*. A summary based on a sent to
       executive vice president and vice president for marketing.

       c. *Audit Appraisals*. A summary each six months of all
       reports with A, B, C, or D ratings, addressed to executive
       vice president, with copies to vice president for
       marketing.

Field audits are conducted in each branch approximately once every
nine months, unannounced. Each audit will include all points noted
on the previous audit report.

Within 30 days of the audit, the report provided for in MM #148
should be submitted by the branch administrator to the regional
administrator, stating the corrective measures that have been taken
in response to the audit report.

Exhibit 10-4. Audit procedures at the home office.

```
INTERAL AUDIT PROGRAM FOR                        CORPORATION
_____

            BRANCH          OFFICES
            _____

       AUDIT PROCEDURES — AT HOME OFFICE

BRANCH OFFICE # _____LOCATION_____

          MONTH AND YEAR _____
```

A. **PETTY CASH**

     1.   Examine last two petty cash reconciliations.

         a.   Approve arithmetic.

         b.   Check petty cash fund balance to general ledger.

         c.   Examine propriety of signatures on petty cash vouchers.

         d.   Check names of all payees on expense report reimbursements against payroll records to verify employment as a service representative. Verify mileage on leased car.

         e.   Examine each petty cash voucher for propriety of expenditure.

     2.   Review accounting distribution of expense items.

     3.   List all items paid over the two months that are not in compliance with petty cash procedure SOP 24.

     4.   Number of times petty cash was reimbursed in last two months.

(continued)

takes about 2½ days. The auditor will generally preaudit two branches in this manner, preparatory to a two-week field trip to audit two branches.

✧ 10-5—**audit procedures at the branch office.** These procedures follow on and stem from the work previously done at the home office. Both financial and procedural areas are examined. This review consumes one week per branch.

✧ 10-6—**audit questionnaire for branch offices.** This is a "walk-through" review of the branch office. It is comprehensive,

(text continues on page 350)

Exhibit 10-4.   *(continued)*

B. __SALES__

1. Review Invoice Register for the Branch for
    the last month and do the following:

    a. Determine that bill only numbers are being
        used in sequence. Check with invoice control
        section to make sure that missing numbers are
        accounted for and carried as outstanding.

    b. List twenty-five machine transactions (go to
        the second prior month if necessary) indicating
        date, invoice number, model number, and sales
        amount. Allow room on work sheet for customer
        name, serial number, machine order, confirmation
        call, and delivery receipt. List must include two
        trade-ins.

    c. Examine posting copies of invoices for these
        transactions and slot in customer name and
        serial number of machine. Mark "L" for leased
        sales.

    d. Trace names into customer alphabetical file,
        record by checkmark (✓) machine order, con-
        firmation call, and delivery receipt columns.

2. List last ten coupon transactions (go to previous
    month if necessary), indicating date, invoice number,
    type paper, and unit price. Allow room on work sheet
    for customer name, coupon order form, terms of sale.

    a. Examine posting copies and list customer name,
        type paper, and unit price.

    b. Trace these into customer's alphabetical file
        and record (by checkmark) coupon order form and
        terms of sale (indicate terms not in accord with
        those on coupon order form).

3. Trace above ten coupon book numbers into coupon book report
    and log. Verify sequential redemption of coupons. List
    coupon book numbers and coupon numbers not
    redeemed in consecutive order. (Show name and original
    invoice number.)

4. Obtain numbering series of billings sent to branch.

5. Review terminology on twenty-five machine transactions
    (1.b., above) as to use of words "trade-in machine allowance,"
    or "demo allowance," in accord with SOP C-35.

6. Compare Monthly New Order Report to DEPAM.

C. <u>INVENTORY</u>

   1. Review Demo Materials Report from purchasing department. Note excessive use of paper and supplies per SOP C-6c. Review monthly purchase requisitions with the purchasing manager. Determine that merchandise is ordered for delivery in the following month, or three months hence, in accord with SOP E-6. Test methods of calculating quantities requisitioned for conformity to the procedure. Verify receipt of BTs by all branches.

D. <u>FIXED ASSETS</u>

   1. Review fixed assets schedule for branch and compare total per schedule to control accounts. Investigate difference.

   2. List five to ten items of major value from fixed assets schedule to physically verify presence and serial numbers at the branch office.

E. <u>PAYROLL</u>

   1. Obtain copies of weekly payroll time sheets for most recent period.

     a. Check to see if branch administrator has approved the record.

     b. Make copies and use at the branch offices as a verification of actual presence of employees.

   2. Review copies of last five Change of Status Notices sent in by Branch.

     a. Determine that all start-up papers are supplied in accordance with SOP B-2.

     b. Are the Change of Status Notices sent in on a timely basis, after date of hire?

     c. Are "Additional Comments" completed with reasons for hire?

(continued)

Exhibit 10-4.   *(continued)*

F. COUPON LIABILITY

    1. Obtain tabulation of unredeemed coupons rep-
         resenting coupon liability for field veri-
         fication of detailed support.

    2. List coupon books issued last year with no redemptions.

    3. List twenty accounts for field verification—
         ten shipments; ten new orders.

ACCOUNT NUMBER	ACCOUNT NAME	CPN. SALE DATE	INV. NO.	ORIG CPNS	CPNS REDEEMED

BAL. OF CPNS.	ORIG. AMT.	AMT. REDEEMED	BALANCE OF AMT.

(text continued from page 347)

covers all facets of the profit center's operations, is directed to determining conformity to company procedures and policies, does not require detailed work papers, and consumes one day out of the five required by Exhibit 10-5. This walk-through is usually performed after cash is counted upon arrival at the branch office.

Time-Saving Suggestion: If there are many branch offices and it is determined that 7½ days is too much to spend on each branch audit, an abbreviated 2½- to 3-day audit program may be conducted. This is shown in Exhibits 10-7, 10-8, and 10-9, which are **extracted highlights from the longer audit programs.**

(text continues on page 360)

G. <u>GENERAL LEDGER</u>

  1. Review general ledger accounts at end of most current month. Investigator will obtain the following information:

    a. Analyze balances with account numbers which are not listed on the chart of accounts and determine the adjustment required.

    b. Analyze debit accounts with credit balance and vice versa to determine reason for unusual balance.

    c. Analyze self balancing accounts to explain balances: i.e. exchanges, with copy, taxes payable.

    d. Analyze year to date balances that are contrary to what the account would normally contain. (Example: Credit balance in an asset account or debit balance on a liability account etc.) Determine the adjustment required.

    e. Review expense and income accounts - note and investigate unusual balances or abnormally high amounts.

H. <u>CREDITS</u>

  1. List credit number, names, and dates of last ten credits on a work sheet. Allow a column for date of return of merchandise.

I. <u>BILLING</u>

  1. Examine IBM billing correction log for the last month and record:

    a. Details of all errors made at the Branch during the preceding month, for later discussion at the field office.

  2. Examine five current days of billing packages from the field office. Test for conformity to billing procedure, SOP C-22, as to preparation of tapes, attachment of tapes to billing packages, use of customer labels, transmittal slip, account numbers of N/A, telephone number on new accounts, ''flags'' for coupon books, special instructions for commission adjustments when required, ''flag'' for leases.

J. <u>ACCOUNTS RECEIVABLE</u>

  1. Examine aging of accounts receivable at Branch for past six months, to determine trend in successful collections. Record these and discuss at field office. A bad aging may indicate failure to confirm calls (SOP C-4d), or improper confirmation calls, or improper follow-up of Credit Department correspondence and memos.

(continued)

Exhibit 10-4. (continued)

K. EXERCISE·OF·AUTHORITY

List last twenty disbursements and test whether approvals were proper within limits of Authority, SOP B-10. If last twenty items listed do not include items over $500 and over $1,000, locate two items over $500 and two items over $1,000 for similar test.

Vendor	Amount	SOP B-10 Page	Item	Proper Approval Yes	No

L. LEASED VEHICLES

List all leased vehicles in sales, service, warehouse, or administration. Complete last two columns at Branch:

Car No. or Serial No.	Driver Assigned	Examine Natl. Serv. Dept's Inspection Report On Hand (Yes) (No)	Describe Condition of Vehicle (A),(B), (C), or(D)	If (C) or (D) Remarks

Exhibit 10-5. Audit procedures at the branch office.

INTERNAL AUDIT PROGRAM FOR _____ CORPORATION
                      BRANCH OFFICES

          AUDIT PROCEDURES - AT BRANCH OFFICE

    BRANCH OFFICE # _____ LOCATION _____

          MONTH AND YEAR _____

A. **CASH**

    Count and list all cash on hand upon arrival:

    1. Petty Cash - Note any vouchers in excess of or contrary to limits
        established in SOP. Compare total to General Ledger account
        balance.

        a. Receipts from Cash Sales - Note by date of supporting in-
            voices of Bill Onlys if remittances are being made daily
            to Home Office; if not, determine reason.

        b. Review and run tape of current day's receipts to be deposited
            to Petty Cash. Obtain a copy of deposit receipt from bank.
            After Bill Only copies have been pulled from the file, trace
            deposit receipts to pull outs. Observe if Bill Only copy
            is noted with "Cash Sale."

    2. Review service representatives' expense reports paid through
        petty cash and verify the following:

        a. The reports are prepared complete with approval indicated.

        b. Rate of reimbursement agrees with current company plan and
            stated amounts.

        c. Deductions are made from expense reports for portal-to-portal
            mileage.

        d. Service representatives with company cars are traveling the
            minimum mileage stated by company policy as required for
            service representatives.

B. ACCOUNTS RECEIVABLE

    1. Examine current Aged Trial Balance. Determine that large amounts
        represent the detail in customer alphabetical file.

    2. Review file of cash sales and COD's. Note that they are being main-
        tained on a current basis. Determine adequacy of internal control.

    3. List and investigate current balances long outstanding and note volume
        and practices used to resolve them.

    4. Investigate unusual debits, credits and product codings.

    5. Review and list last 10 leased sales and determine that:

        a. Credit information is properly compiled and required reference
            and bank forms are completed.

(continued)

Exhibit 10-5.   *(continued)*

      b. Both the lease and the machine order form are signed.

      c. The lease form is properly completed as to taxes, trade-ins, allowances, and monthly payments.

      d. A proper down payment has been obtained and the monthly payment is properly calculated.

6. Review applicable credit and collection practices with procedural compliance. Select 10 representative accounts receivable to analyze:

      a. Determine whether a shipment was made while account was past due.

      b. Note if accounts receivable with outstanding balances over $500 are receiving special handling.

      c. Determine that Home Office Credit Department Correspondence is answered promptly.

      d. Establish that a collection tickler file or daily calendar follow-up file has been established for collection purposes.

7. Review last 10 shipments against coupon orders and determine:

      a. That coupons are being received with order or picked up on delivery.

      b. That first coupon shipments on new orders are properly noted on original for deletion from coupon book when issued by the Home Office.

8. Review last 10 coupon orders and determine:

      a. That all coupons in each book are issued in the same amount or value.

      b. That each coupon represents a minimum of 10% of the total quantity or value.

      c. That instructions on the original order for the deletion of the first coupon, if shipment has been made, are properly documented.

      d. That terms are in accordance with the printed order.

      e. That confirmation has been made as evidenced by Savicopy of checklist attached to Savicopy of order.

      f. That originals of orders and confirmation have been sent to the home office and copies maintained at the branch.

C.   **SALES**

1. On a test basis review internal control of shipping orders and invoices as follows:

      a. Review a selected group of the numbered copies of the invoices for missing numbers. List numbers missing. Trace and record status. Refer unlocated shipping invoice numbers to branch office personnel for further follow-up.

    b. Compare sequence of numbers with documented record of numbers sent from Home Office.

    c. Determine that Bill Onlys and/or invoices are secured and available only to authorized personnel.

2. On a test basis, review internal control of credit memorandums as follows:

    a. Review a selected group and record all missing numbers and locate them.

    b. See if reason for the credit is clearly stated.

    c. Verify that branch administrator approves BCA as indicated on the form.

    d. List a selected number of credit memorandums, or Bill Onlys, for trade-in allowances and verify the receipt or disposition of the equipment involved. Review method of internal control for trade-in machines. Examine perpetual care for trade-in machines. Follow up subsequent sale of trade-in machines and compare sale price to allowance. Determine that maximum allowance is in accordance with SOP.

3. List 10 customer invoice numbers and date of transaction for deliveries made only by branch office personnel. Include 5 machine invoices in the test. Trace the delivery receipts.

D.   <u>INVENTORY</u>

1. Conduct a tour of the warehouse and note the following:

    a. Restrictions as to entry of unauthorized employees.

    b. General condition and storage methods used for the merchandise.

    c. Review with warehouse supervisor or manager methods and records employed in the receiving and shipping of merchandise.

2. Review the following files representing equipment and supplies not on the premises and not billed:

    a. Shipments of merchandise to outside warehouses.

    b. Shipments returned to other branches or main warehouse on Branch Transfers - See if Branch Transfer file is maintained on a current basis and note unresolved transactions dating back for an unreasonable length of time.

    c. Equipment signed for by salespeople. Note dates, and reason for being outstanding for more than 60 days. Obtain serial number list from each salesperson and compare to salesperson's demo sheets. Examine overall method of controlling shipment and return of salesperson's demo machines. Verify to Mach. Activity List Cards.

(continued)

Exhibit 10-5.   *(continued)*

and 8½" x 14" cut sheet paper and all supplies. Review support for all reconciling items pertaining to inventory. Reconcile all physical inventory to perpetual inventory cards. Trace last 20 entries on each inventory card to shipping copy of invoice from which posted. Test 20 other entries at random for each card. Verify "PIENT" stamp on each.

4. Reconcile physical machine inventory to Mach. Activity List. Physically locate all equipment in the warehouses or determine its whereabouts.

5. Review the following reports relating to machines:

    a. Rental Billing Control - Compare to Mach. Activity List Rental Cards.

    b. Obtain at Home Office and compare to local demo and rental list.

E.   <u>FIXED ASSETS</u>

1. Verify the existence of vehicles listed at the Home Office. Complete schedule.

F.   <u>PAYROLL</u>

1. If checks arrive at the branch office during the audit, distribute them to employees; if not, verify by observation each employee listed on the time sheet from the home office.

2. Review employee time sheet for several pay periods and note the following:

    a. Agreement with stated company policy in regard to standard hours of work. See SOP and Personnel Handbook.

    b. Completeness of date, recording of hours, and approval indicated.

G.   <u>ACCOUNTS PAYABLE</u>

1. Examine all vendor invoices awaiting receiving reports, noting any amounts outstanding for any undue length of time.

2. Examine all receiving reports awaiting invoices, noting any amounts outstanding for any undue length of time.

H.   <u>SERVICE DEPARTMENT</u>

1. Review internal control for accounting of service call reports used as follows:

    a. Select a block of numbers and list all missing numbers.

    b. Investigate and attempt to locate missing numbers, review practices being followed to locate missing numbers.

    c. Review security provisions for unused Service Call Reports.

2. Examine Service Department Index Card Files for 70 day follow-up and one year follow-up on service contracts. Verify conformity to established procedures.

3. Trace 20 Service Call Reports into numerical machine files and into monthly Service Call Report File.

4. Test 20 Service Call Reports for proper entries in the Rental, Service Contract or Warranty boxes.

5. Test last 10 billable Service Call Reports to Bill Only File. Verify timeliness with which they were billed.

6. Test time required to dispatch 20 service calls at random. List all calls requiring more than six hours to complete.

7. Review parts log, as to entries; including receipt and disbursement of parts on service calls. Verify that there is a part received for every part distributed.

8. Review perpetual inventory cards to determine that entries are made on receipt of parts branch transferred and on disbursement of parts on Bill Onlys and on Service Call Reports. Determine that ''car stock'' of service representatives' parts is recorded. Review card entries for internally used parts.

9. Verify ''car stock'' of one service representative against entries on perpetual inventory record.

10. List serial and model numbers below of inoperable machines, length of time inoperable, and reason.

Model Number	Serial Number	Date Inoperable	Reason

11. Review work sheets for internal work in numerical machine file.

I. COUPON LIABILITY

1. Test last ten coupon deliveries to determine that shipment is not made without receipt of coupon.

2. List coupon books issued prior to the current year under review that show no redemption activity during the current year. Review with branch manager.

J. GENERAL

1. Examine permanent and working files to determine that they are neat, updated, and current (SOP A-45).

2. Determine that R.M.F.s and receiving reports are made out immediately on receipt of merchandise. Examine merchandise awaiting forms. Establish elapsed time from receipt to preparation of form.

(continued)

Exhibit 10-5.   *(continued)*

3. Examine R.M.F.'s awaiting issuance of B.C.A.'s. Is B.C.A. issued timely? Test last 10 B.C.A.'s to date of receipt of merchandise.

4. Open Bill Only File - Examine pink copies awaiting receipt of I.B.M. invoices. Are follow-ups made every 10 days? Are copies dated in upper-right hand corner indicating follow-up date?

5. Examine completed files to determine that completed Bill Onlys, Branch Transfers, Receiving Reports, and Bills of Lading are filed numerically.

6. Is Call Back Report filed with comments as to results?

7. Test last 10 shipments of machines to the Mach. Shipments Report. Ascertain that the report is prepared on a daily basis.

8. Examine end-of-month closing reports in SOP A-14 to determine that all closing is made in conformity with procedure on a timely basis.

9. Verify that daily billing, during audit periods, is sent to Home Office daily.

10. If audit covers a period over the fifteenth or last day of the month, ascertain that billing is sent to home office at the close of the day, by overnight mail, if required.

11. Examine all vendors' invoices ready for Headquarters payment. Trace them to petty cash to determine that payment has not been made by the branch. Examine statements and consignees' memos to be sure that there are no approvals on them. Verify that they are sent to the home office daily.

K.   ORDER PROCESSING

1. Examine 10 new accounts and 10 reorder accounts for the following:

   a. Telephone number on Bill Only on new accounts.

   b. Bill of lading attached to all accounts.

   c. Purchase order number must appear.

   d. Test old accounts against aged trial balance to determine delinquency and proper credit approval.

   e. D. & B. rating or bank and two credit references on new accounts.

   f. Is tax collected on new accounts or tax exemption certificate attached?

   g. If lease, is check made out to leasing company in proper amount?

   h. Are terms in accordance with company procedures?

   i. Examine branch administrator's approvals. Are these done daily rather than in groups?

   j. Is confirmation call report attached, if applicable?

   k. Is proper order form used; that is, machine order form, coupon order form, or sales representative's order form.

    l.   Is customer's signed order attached on new accounts?

    m.   Is equipment lease form accompanied by signed order form?

    n.   Is salesperson's order neat and legible; is Bill Only neat and legible;
        is master item terminology used? Test name and address of all
        accounts to master account list for proper entry.

    o.   Are all orders properly approved by branch administrator, initialed
        and dated?

    p.   Is commission properly computed on all accounts?

    q.   Is shipping date on Bill Only?

    r.   If rental, does per diem rate appear?

    s.   Is shipping date of Bill Only same as bill of lading date? Trace Bill Onlys to
        transmittal sheets to determine that date of transmittal sheet is same as Bill
        Only.

    t.   If Q.D.A., is copy of Q.D.A. attached? Check rate of annual usage to specs.

    u.   If conversion from rental, is rental allowance properly computed?

2. Examine advice to Home Office on termination of salesperson regarding list
   of rental accounts to be credited to new salesperson.

3. If no rentals were included in test in 1 above, examine last three rental
   orders for per diem dates and copies of rental agreements attached.

4. If no conversion from rental to sale was included in 1 above, examine
   last three conversions for proper computation of rental allowance.

5. Examine two trade-ins of equipment (one of which is a lease) for proper
   computation of trade-in allowance and commission compensation.

6. Examine one loan machine to a paper user for computation of commission
   adjustment.

7. Review date of receipt of last 10 machine orders at Branch and check date
   of delivery. Record delay in delivery dates more than one day after
   receipt of orders.

Invoice No.	Customer	Reason for Delay

(continued)

Exhibit 10-5. *(continued)*

L. BILLING

1. Check open transmittal slips to determine that they are kept current and that billing is completed and mailed to Home Office, within 24 hours of shipment.

2. Review file of tapes to determine that they are held for the time period, as required by SOP C-22. Are tapes headed up properly?

3. Determine that billing is split and mailed on the same day as typed.

4. Is customer label file properly updated?

5. Are master item list definitions used in typing line items?

6. Is fax from Home Office confirming price attached to the paperwork to cover all dealer shipments from the Branch?

7. Verify sequence of credit memos.

8. Verify sequence of invoices.

M. LEASED VEHICLES

Visually examine all vehicles listed on schedule prepared at Home Office. Rate cars A, B, C, or D, and if rated C or D, fill in reasons as to why. Note on schedule and investigate cars listed, not on hand, and vice versa.

Similar audit programs may be prepared for any profit or cost center. To construct such a program, the inside auditor should review:

1. The organization chart to determine reporting responsibilities.
2. Position description for the manager and work duties sheets for each employee in the department.
3. The data processing evaluation study, described on page 526, which lists all input and output reports and gives an overview of the entire system.
4. Work processing flow charts for the department, which, if not prepared in 3 above, would be prepared by the department manager. If not on hand, the auditor should prepare them. This should be augmented by 5.
5. A narrative summary of the general nature of the work prepared by this department. This gives the manager's version of what he or she thinks the work is.

Exhibit 10-6.   Audit questionnaire for branch offices.

INTERNAL AUDIT QUESTIONNAIRE FOR _____ _____ _____ INCORPORATED

BRANCH OFFICES

(Audit Procedures —— At Branch Offices)

BRANCH OFFICE:

LOCATION:

DATE OF AUDIT:

DATE OF PREVIOUS AUDIT:

OFFICE HOURS:

AUDITOR:

(continued)

6. Every input and output form used by this department.
7. Every report generated by this department.
8. Manuals and procedures used intradepartmentally.

> *Helpful Hint:* If a formal systems and procedure department exists, the audit need merely be a review of existing procedures as documented in the procedures manual.

FOR EXAMPLE: The systems group could establish the typical (usable by any company that ships product) **warehouse security and procedures** shown in Exhibit 10-10. The audit program is a review of each point, by observation and examination of records and files, to determine adherence to the procedure. The audit report is keyed to the procedure and reports on only those numbers that are not in conformity.

(text continues on page 370)

Exhibit 10-6. *(continued)*

I. <u>GENERAL</u>

   A. <u>EVALUATION OF INTERNAL CONTROL</u>   <u>Yes</u>   <u>No</u>   Comments

      1. Is fireproof and locked storage provided for:

         a. Personnel Files

         b. Customer Alphabetical Files

         c. Perpetual Inventory Records

         d. Service Department Numerical Machine File

         e. Customer Wheeldex or Kardex

         f. Bill of Lading Duplicate Warehouse copies

         g. Mach. Activity List Cards

         h. Employee Time Sheets

         i. Working Folders for Branch Administrator and Secretary

         j. Service Follow-up File

         k. One Year Service Contract File

         l. Service Call Report Nightly File

      2. Does the inventory and other Fixed Assets, including leaseheld improvements in the branch sales office, exceed $50,000 for each location?

      3. If so, is the excess reported to the Controller for additional insurance coverage?

      4. Is the record retention plan in A-29 being maintained?

      5. Do the files appear to be in good order?

      6. Does the work appear to be on a current basis?

      7. Names of Employees who have keys to the office and/or warehouse (Indicate o, w, or b for both with the name): and title.

         List Names:

		Yes	No	Comments
a.	Are monthly staff meetings held with the branch administrator, branch manager, service manager, and warehouse manager?			
b.	Does the service manager inspect all leased cars, those of sales and service representatives, quarterly?			
c.	Inspect two leased cars at random. Are they in a state of repair?			
d.	Inspect sales offices. Are lead cards filed away?			
e.	Inspect general offices. Are all papers and files removed from desks at night?			
f.	Inspect warehouse. Is stock neat and orderly on pallets?			
	Are shelves neat and orderly?			
	Are shipping supplies neatly arranged?			
	Are returned cartons carefully secured?			
g.	Inspect service area. Are tools secure?			
	Are unused machines crated or covered?			
	Are workbenches neat?			
	Are premises clean and orderly?			
8.	Names of employees who have keys to locks on file cabinets:			
9.	Does the branch administrator periodically review the work of his or her subordinates?			
10.	Who performs janitorial services? If outside agency, are outside personnel monitored? Is liability insurance carried by agency?			
11.	Is the lease for the premises available for inspection at the branch?			
12.	Are orderly files of Marketing Memos and Sales Slants maintained?			
13.	Is the SOP manual kept current? Is the Correction Checklist current?			
14.	Is the price book kept current? Is the price book correction checklist current?			

(continued)

Exhibit 10-6.   *(continued)*

	Yes	No	Comments
15. Are interim procedures (prior to formal SOP changes) noted in proper sections of the SOP manual?			
16. Are lead cards filed neatly by salespeople?			
17. Are numerical files maintained for Return Authorizations, Branch Transfers Out, Purchase Orders, Mach. Shipment Reports, Shipping Copy of Bill Only, Bills of Lading, machine folders in the Service Department, Returned Merchandise Forms?			
18. Is Call Back Report file being maintained?			

II. CASH

    A. EVALUATION OF INTERNAL CONTROL

1. Is a petty cash checkbook used?

2. Is actual cash on hand other than checks locked? Is the cash box secured? Names of persons having access to petty cash:

3. Are check receipts accompanied by a transmittal slip sent to the home office daily?

4. Are remittance advices mailed to the home office? If not, how often is check receipt examined for application advice? If not, is it prepared at branch for transmittal to home office?

5. Names of employees who:

    a. Open the mail

    b. File customer copy of invoice

    c. Transact cash sales

    d. Account for consecutive invoice numbers

    e. Approve service billings

6. Are any customer checks being withheld from remittance to the home office?

7. Have separate boxes been provided for cash sales and petty cash storage?

8. Is the practice of not making advances, loans, or I.O.U.'s, or cashing personal checks being followed?

	Yes	No	Comments

III. ACCOUNTS RECEIVABLE

    A. Evaluation of Internal Control

        1. Are aged trial balances held for at least three months?

        2. Is the A.T.B. examined before approving every order for credit?

        3. If not, how are customer orders approved for credit prior to processing?

        4. Are credit department memos answered promptly?

        5. Is the credit approval stamp being used for all orders where applicable? Are the bank and trade references checked on machine orders? Are credit department forms evidencing this attached to the order?

IV. INVOICES AND CREDITS

    A. EVALUATION OF INTERNAL CONTROL

        1. Do the customers sign purchase orders pertaining to sales of equipment?

        2. Is the Rental Billing Control Sheet used to ensure follow-up on monthly rental billing?

        3. Are the 70-day follow-up file and the one-year follow-up file for service contracts being used on a current and timely basis to ensure billing of service contracts?

        4. Are invoices checked for accuracy of prices and commission computations? How and by whom?

        5. Are all original documents attached to the order normally sent to the home office, with copies attached to the branch copy? Is master account list checked for proper name and address, account number, and tax code?

        6. If not, what check is made? Is master item list used to type proper description of items?

        7. If not, what is used?

(continued)

Exhibit 10-6. *(continued)*

	Yes	No	Comments

8. Are back orders held on unnumbered orders?

9. Are back orders cross-referenced on the preceding and following bill only?

10. Are the Machine Order Form and Coupon Order Form used where applicable?

11. Are confirmation calls made on all machine and coupon orders?

12. Are confirmation checklists completed for each call?

13. Are conditional orders held and not billed?

14. Are signed machine orders obtained even on leased sales?

15. Are rental accounts reviewed quarterly to test paper usage or possible additional shipment?

V. INVENTORY

   A. EVALUATION OF INTERNAL CONTROL

      1. Does a central shipping and receiving point exist for all incoming and outgoing merchandise?

      2. Is merchandise for resale stored behind partitions separating stock areas from passageways and all other parts of the building?

      3. Are the partitions from the floor to the ceiling?

      4. Is access limited to the branch manager, the branch administrator, and the warehouse manager only?

      5. Have unauthorized personnel been observed in the stockroom area?

      6. Is the stockroom area kept locked and separate from the office at all times?

      7. Is the person responsible for the merchandise always in the area?

      8. Which of the following are responsible for the repair parts inventory?

	Yes	No	Comments

a. Shipping supervisor
b. Warehouse manager
c. Appointed service rep
d. None of the above
e. Who?

9. Are Receiving Reports, Return Merchandise Forms, or Branch Transfer Receipts prepared for incoming merchandise? Are copies filed in numerical order in the Warehouse or office for the following:

   a. Merchandise returned from customer for credit

   b. Trade-in equipment

   c. Customer equipment in for repairs

   d. Equipment returned from demonstration (unless salesperson's demo machine)

   e. Inventory purchases

   f. Even exchanges

10. Are Return Authorizations completed to cover the return or pickup of merchandise as follows:

   a. Merchandise returned from customer for credit

   b. Trade-in equipment

   c. Customer equipment in for repairs

   d. Equipment returned from demonstration (unless salesperson's demo machine)

   e. Inventory purchases

   f. Even exchanges

11. Are Return Merchandise Forms marked NCI (No Credit Issued) for even exchanges? And all retail parts Returns?

12. Are Bill Only's marked with an 00 code in the shipping location column of even exchange shipments?
       w

13. Is movement of outgoing merchandise supported by standard pre-numbered Bill Only's?

(continued)

Exhibit 10-6.   *(continued)*

	Yes	No	Comments

14. Are materials and supplies removed for internal use or salespeople's demonstration use supported by unnumbered orders properly approved by branch administrator?

15. Are unnumbered orders in 14 above tallied and posted off Perpetual Inventory Cards monthly? Is Demo Materials Form completed monthly?

16. Are signed bills of lading received to cover the shipment of all machines from the warehouse?

17. Are signed delivery receipts kept on demos and turned in by the salesperson when a demonstrator is converted to a sale, and attached to original order?

18. Is issuance of repair parts to service reps covered by postings off Perpetual Inventory Cards? Are unnumbered orders used for this purpose filed by date, monthly?

19. Are machine movements posted to Mach. Shipments Report?

20. Are conversions from demo to sale posted on Mach. Shipments Report?

21. Are all machine movements or conversions posted to Mach. Activity List cards?

22. Is the monthly physical inventory of machines checked to Mach. Activity List card count?

23. Is master Machine Inventory Control Card checked to Physical Machine Inventory Count, monthly?

24. Are signed salesperson's demo sheets reconciled to Mach. Activity List Card counts?

25. Is Rental Billing Control List reconciled monthly to Mach. Activity List Rental Cards?

26. Is a monthly list of customer loan and demo machines prepared for the branch manager and reviewed by him or her?

27. How many loan machines have been out more than 60 days? Reason:

28. Is any customer-owned merchandise on premises clearly identified as customer-owned?

29. Are trade-in machines inventory cards kept current?

	Yes	No	Comments

30. Is oldest merchandise used first to fill orders?

31. Are 100-ft. rolls, only, used for 8-1/2″ and 11″ demonstration materials? If no, reason:

VI. FIXED ASSETS

   A. EVALUATION OF INTERNAL CONTROL

      1. Were any disposals made during the year? List:

      2. What, if any, vehicles are Company-leased, or Company-owned?

Vehicle	Year and Model	Use	Driven By	His or Her Position	Condition

VII. PAYROLL

   A. EVALUATION OF INTERNAL CONTROL

      1. Before distribution, does the branch administrator or branch manager review checks for reasonableness of pay and is he or she personally making distribution?

      2. Have all employees filled out insurance enrollment cards, W-4 forms, application, Wonderlic test, Blue Cross/ Blue Shield cards? Compare W-4 signature.

      3. Have all sales personnel read and signed Corporate Trust Policy and Restrictive Covenant? Is this counterinitialed by branch manager or branch administrator?

      4. Do sales and telephone sales personnel sign the employment letter when hired?

VIII. ACCOUNTS PAYABLE

   A. EVALUATION OF INTERNAL CONTROL

      1. Are vendor invoices sent to Home Office promptly for payment?

(continued)

Exhibit 10-6.   *(continued)*

	Yes	No	Comments
2. Are purchase orders for under $50 placed at the Branch Office by using a special purchase order containing this limitation?			
3. Are most items under $50 bought and paid for through petty cash?			
4. Are all items under $10 bought and paid for through petty cash?			
IX. PURCHASING			
A. EVALUATION OF INTERNAL CONTROL			
1. Test inventory levels of two major items (8½" and 11" paper) to required inventory level as per SOP E-6.			

(*text continued from page 361*)

4. *Training and conduct of inside auditors.* This is a necessary ingredient of a successful audit program. It is important that the auditor have accounting training, though a CPA certificate may not be necessary for anyone except the audit manager. While many audits are operational and not accounting-oriented, many others are. One-day field audits like those in Exhibits 10-7, 10-8, and 10-9 may be performed by non-accounting auditors, perhaps former field administrative people who have been successful in their positions and promoted.

Information on training is available from the Institute of Internal Auditors, and an excellent Course for Staff Auditors is offered regularly

Exhibit 10-7. One-day field audit program—home office.

ONE-DAY FIELD AUDIT PROGRAM

HOME OFFICE

A. PETTY CASH (A-24, B-10)

   1. Trace fund balance to general ledger. $_____$

   2. Review reasonableness of expenses and distribution thereof.

   3. Review field engineer expenses, as follows:

      a. Reports complete with approval.

      b. Rate of reimbursement agrees with current company plan, those with car insurance receiving 1¢/mile less.

      c. Test that deductions are made for portal-to-portal mileage.

      d. Verify employment.   Schedule _____

   4. Reimbursement of fund limited to once a month?

   5. Query petty cash clerk for any immediate problems requiring follow-up at branch. (Note below.)

B. SALES/ACCOUNTS RECEIVABLE/CREDIT (C-22, C-25)

   1. Review invoice register for consecutive numeric sequence of invoices. Copy home office accounting schedule of missing numbers for follow-up at branch.   Schedule _____

   2. Discuss any immediate problems with respective department heads:

      a. Retail sales with order/billing.

      b. Dealer sales with dealer service.

      c. Lease charge backs with credit's doubtful account collection desk.

   3. Copy current D5 letters held by credit correspondent for follow-up at branch. Indicate in margin of letter type of branch action being taken.

(continued)

Exhibit 10-7. *(continued)*

C. INVENTORY

    1. Review demo usage report (purchasing department).
        If excessive, copy for review at branch.   Schedule _____

    2. Copy most branch inventory projections and requests.
        Validate at branch, follow up consistent shortages, etc.

D. PAYROLL

    1. Copy most recent time sheet and verify against
        payroll records.   Schedule _____

    2. If present at branch on payday, arrange that
        paychecks be sent to auditor's attention. Have
        payees sign for checks. Retain and return for
        further review all undistributed checks.   Schedule _____

    3. Check out personnel ratios against ''box score''
        held by budget manager.

    4. Review sales personnel payroll records for proper
        employment letters.

    5. Review past sales personnel termination payroll drop
        sheets for disposition of demo machines. Trace into
        inventory records at branch. Sight, if necessary.   Schedule _____

by the American Management Association. Public accounting firms are not too helpful with literature for internal auditors, but business publishers like the American Management Association, Practitioners Publishing Company, and Prentice-Hall offer a variety of specialized books on the subject.

Auditors should be trained to:

1. Maintain objectivity during audits.
2. Refrain from establishing excessively close personal relationships with personnel in offices being audited, to assure continued objectivity on audits.

> CASE IN POINT: A traveling auditor consistently gave high marks to a field office that management, from observation from its vantage point, knew was not performing up to the auditor's reports. It was determined that the auditor, a bachelor, was

(text continues on page 383)

Exhibit 10-8. One-day field audit program — branch office.

ONE-DAY FIELD AUDIT PROGRAM

—————————— BRANCH OFFICE

A. PETTY CASH (A-24, B-10)

1. Perform a quick reconciliation, as follows:
Checkbook balance
Add: Prior period reimbursement (if in transit)
    Unreimbursed vouchers on hand
    Cash on hand (should be minimal)
    Sales representative advances (even if
    unauthorized)
Total (should equal general ledger balance)
If difference between total (above) and general
ledger balance is 2% or less, write off through
countersigning a voucher with the branch administrator for difference. Mark voucher ''cash short.'' If
difference is greater, complete remaining audit and,
if time permits, investigate.   Schedule _____|_____

B. ACCOUNTS RECEIVABLE/CREDIT (C-25)

  1. Spot-check ATB for long overdue balances. Note
     volume and explanations. Resolve.   _____|_____

                                                           Y   N

  2. Credit department approval obtained when doubtful
     accounts are shipped?   ☐   ☐

  3. Home office credit correspondence answered prompt-
     ly, with follow-up of D5 letter?   ☐   ☐

  4. Is ATB checked before each order is shipped?   ☐   ☐

C. BILLING (C-18b)

  1. Major user log.

     a. All pertinent information entered in log
       (name, address, customer #, machine #s, etc.)?

     b. Trace machine # to SAL.

     c. Is paper shipped automatically each month?
       Attach examples of noncompliance.   Schedule _____|_____

     d. If not, is it at customer request?

     e. At expiration of contract, is customer billed
       the difference in price per roll in the event of
       purchase of less than contracted amount?
       Attach examples of noncompliance.   Schedule _____|_____

     f. Trace last five shipments to invoice,
       then to perpetual inventory records. Is post-
       ing copy marked ''Pient''?   Schedule _____|_____

(continued)

Exhibit 10-8. *(continued)*

2. Coupon Books (CPN 5/18)

Y   N

   a. All pertinent information entered in log?   ☐   ☐

   b. All coupons issued in same amount for paper?   ☐   ☐

   c. Each coupon represents a minimum of 10% of total quantity purchased?   ☐   ☐

   d. Coupons redeemed sequentially?
     Attach example of noncompliance.

   e. Trace redemption of coupon to perpetual inventory records.

3. Billing/Order Processing (C-22, C-25)

   a. Are all orders billed and shipped within 24 hours? Verify.

   b. Follow up missing invoice numbers from invoice register in home office.   **Schedule** _____|_____

   c. Review daily invoicing (before bursting) for proper numeric sequence.   **Schedule** _____|_____

   d. Review credits (A-3, A-5).

     1. Trace most recent IMF to actual returned merchandise.

     2. Trace IMF to credit invoice and investigate any untimely delay.

     3. If machine, trace to SAL and perpetual inventory.

     4. Dealer returns should be supported by proper paperwork (RA, IMF, etc.).

   e. Bill of lading attached to invoice?   ☐   ☐

   f. Bank and two credit references appended to new account?   ☐   ☐

   g. Account number assigned? Trace to Rollex file.

   h. Confirmation call attached to machine and coupon book orders?   ☐   ☐

D. INVENTORY (A-16, A-21, A-32)

1. Determine that all merchandise is accounted for:

   a. Branch transfers in transit?

   b. Outside warehouses

       (1) Review executive permission.

       (2) Sight warehouse receipt/billing.

  c. Machines on loan (from SAL). Note length of time out.   Schedule _____|_____

  d. Machines on demo (C6c, C6d).

       (1) Compare SAL and sales representative demo sheets. Follow up discrepancies.   Schedule _____|_____

                                           Y   N

       (2) Demo sheet signed by sales representative and countersigned?   ☐   ☐

  e. Total machines in SAL should equal count plus all machines in field save sales and leases.

2. Spot-count 8-1/2″ 220 and 230 paper and reconcile with perpetual records.

3. Compare rental billing control with SAL. All rentals billed beginning of each month?   ☐   ☐

4. Trace recent interbranch and receiving IMFs to perpetual inventory records.

5. Count and reconcile some high-cost parts to perpetual inventory.

E. FIELD ENGINEERING (A-38, A-39, B-25c)

1. Select some service history cards at random.

  a. Trace machine number to service numeric file and satisfy that card data agrees with latest call report.

  b. Service contract expired? New one automatically billed?

  c. No contract, custom billed? Timely? Labor and parts billed at current retail price?

  d. Number of inoperative machines in service appear excessive? Explain.

F. PAYROLL

1. Compare head count of branch personnel against most recent time sheet.

2. If present on payday, follow procedures in home office payroll program re check-off.

Exhibit 10-9. One-day field audit program—evaluation of internal control.

ONE-DAY FIELD AUDIT PROGRAM

EVALUATION OF INTERNAL CONTROL

A. FILES AND GENERAL REVIEW   YES   NO

    1. Fireproof and locked storage provision

        a. Personnel files

        b. Customer alpha files

        c. Perpetual inventory records

        d. Service numerical machine file

        e. Customer Rolldex

        f. Warehouse duplicate bills of lading

        g. Savin activity list (SAL) cards

        h. Employee time sheet

        i. Service contract follow-up file

        j. Service contract file

        k. Major user control log

        l. Coupon book control log

        m. Salepeople's demo sheets

        n. Price books

    2. Files appear to be in good order?

    3. Paper work current?

    4. Orderly files of marketing memos, training memos, and new product fliers maintained?

    5. SOP manual and correction check list current?

    6. Price book and correction check list current?

    7. Are interim procedures (prior to formal SOP changes) noted in proper sections of SOP manual?

YES NO

8. Are numerical files maintained for:

    a. Return authorizations

    b. IMFS

    c. Purchase orders

    d. Shipping copy of invoice

    e. Bills of lading

    f. Machine folders in service area

9. Inspect sales and general offices.

    a. Sales lead card filed?

    b. All paper work and files cleared from desks at day's end?

B. WAREHOUSE

1. Inspect.

    a. Stock neatly stacked and palletized?

    b. Shelves neat and orderly?

    c. Packing and shipping supplies neat?

    d. Are returns kept separate and secure before replacement into inventory?

    e. Repacking of returns done?

2. Is salable merchandise partitioned off and separate from passageways and all other parts of building?

3. Are partitions floor to ceiling?

4. Is access to warehouse limited to branch manager, branch administrator, and warehouse personnel? Observe.

5. Any unauthorized personnel observed in stockroom area?

6. Is stockroom area kept locked and separate from sales and general offices at all times?

7. Is person responsible for merchandise and parts always in his or her area?

(continued)

Exhibit 10-9.   *(continued)*

	YES	NO
C. SERVICE		

   1. Inspect.

     a. Are tools secure?

     b. Unused machines crated and/or covered?

     c. Workbenches neat?

     d. Area swept clean? Orderly?

     e. Are parts locked away?

   2. Does service manager alone have access to parts inventory?

   3. Who, of the following, is responsible for repair parts inventory?

     a. Warehouse employee

     b. Service manager

     c. Appointed service representative

     d. Someone else? Who?

D. SECURITY

   1. Name and title of employees who have keys to office and warehouse.

   2. Name and title of employees who have keys to file cabinets.

   3. Conduct tour of branch. Check all outside windows and doors for proper locks and easy access. Note any areas requiring additional security.

Exhibit 10-10. Warehouse security and procedures.

WAREHOUSE SECURITY AND PROCEDURES
Effective Thursday, 11/12/

A. New Hours

8 A.M. — 4:30 P.M. No night work or overtime.

B. Our Trucks

1. **To be loaded in the morning at 8 A.M. and on the road by 8:30 A.M. They are to return by 4:45 P.M.**

2. All undelivered products to be taken off the truck, checked in by the plant supervisor, and rescheduled for the next day's load. After unloading, affix original bill of lading and order to the load. Order is to be re-initialed in lower right-hand corner with a two to the right of the initials, indicating that it was reloaded and rechecked a second time.

3. **There is to be no product on a truck overnight (this includes outside trailers).**

    a) If, in an emergency, the truck cannot be unloaded, then a seal, logged and identified, must be affixed by the supervisor in the evening. The following morning, the supervisor must verify that the seal was not broken, break the seal, and make an entry in the log. The log will show the truck number or description, seal number, date sealed, initials, date seal broken, initials.

4. Trucks are to be inspected weekly by warehouse supervisor to check all locks.

C. Doors

1. **All warehouse personnel are to use the regular employee entrance. The northeast door will be locked.**

2. **All bay doors are to be kept in a closed position unless a truck is in place, loading or unloading.**

3. **All emergency doors are to be kept closed.**

4. When closing in the evening, all doors are to be locked by the <u>supervisor</u>; these include bay doors, exit doors, warehouse office door. The following personnel will have keys to the above doors:

    > a. Warehouse manager
    > b. Warehouse supervisor
    > c. Director of personnel

    No other personnel will have keys, nor may they borrow keys, without the express written approval of the controller.

5. All files are to be locked within the office, with particular attention to four-drawer files storing invoices, copies of bills of lading, and orders.

(continued)

Exhibit 10-10. *(continued)*

6. Special files containing inventory control data on supplies and machines are to be locked and these separate keys are to be controlled by the inventory control group only. One key is to be held by the Accounting Services Manager, the other by the Inventory Control Manager. No other personnel will have keys, nor may they borrow keys without the express written approval of the Controller.

7. Main warehouse doors into the office area are to be locked, by the guard, when the lights are turned out, no later than 6 P.M. Supervisor assists guard when he or she leaves.

8. Keys and locks for doors are to be changed every six months.

D. <u>Internal</u>

1. All product is to be moved only with the proper paperwork attached as follows:

   Outgoing merchandise - Orders, Branch Transfers, with Bills of Lading
   Incoming merchandise - Receiving Reports, Branch Transfers, RMF's
   Internal transfers - Locator tickets

2. Clipboards are to be used, along with order picking trucks or fork lifts.

3. Reserve product or machines are to be released by inventory desk assigning specific location to pull product from.

4. Packing slips in self-adhesive envelopes are to be plainly visible on all shipments.

5. No bills of lading and orders are to remain in the office, but must be kept with pending orders to be released to office after shipment by common carriers or our own truck.

E. <u>Order Picking</u>

1. To be done by persons designated by plant supervisor.

2. All orders are to be initialed in the lower left-hand corner.

F. <u>Order Packing or Checking</u>

1. To be done by another and different person chosen by the supervisor.

2. Checker's initials are to be put on the bottom middle of the order or branch transfer.

G. <u>Shipping or Truck Loading</u>

1. To be finally done by a third party chosen by the supervisor (to include the manager, supervisor, assistant manager, or office designee).

2. His or her initials are to be put on the bottom right side.

   Summary: All orders are to have three sets of initials before they can be considered valid (including UPS shipments).

3. Our truck manifest should be signed by driver for unit count verification. Manifest is to be filed in date order and kept for one year.

4. Supervisor should personally check at least one load daily and supervise all other loading.

5. No outside trailers are to be loaded unless a cab is available for immediate shipment that day.

H. Receiving

1. All trucks and product received (including returned merchandise) are to be listed on a dock receiving log showing date, vendor, carrier, pro number, package count, and receiving report number or RMF or branch transfer number, which can be posted no later than 24 hours later.

2. The four-part detailed receiving report, RMF, or branch transfer is to be made out within 24 hours on all items received. There are three approved locations for creating receiving reports, RMFs, or branch transfers:

   a. Warehouse
   b. Parts Department
   c. Mailroom

   The 24-hour exception will apply to large parts shipments only. However, a blank receiving report or RMF must be made out showing the vendor or customer, marked ''Subject to detailed count.''

   Note: The supervisor or a responsible person must sign the receiving report, branch transfer, or RMF after completion.

I. Storage

We have a fluid reserve storage system.

1. Any product can be stored in any vacant bay.

2. Locator cards must be created, affixed, and turned into inventory control, showing item stored, count, location, date, and initials of warehouse employee who put away. Where machines are stored, only one ticket for the bay is necessary, but all serial numbers must be shown.

3. Locator tickets are to be matched with receiving reports, branch transfers, or RMFs and turned in together.

4. See supervisor for method of writing up serial numbers.

(continued)

Exhibit 10-10. *(continued)*

J. Inventory Usage

1. Inventory control is the only group allowed to assign product
    to be moved from reserve areas.

2. We are to use oldest product first, regardless of where stored.

K. Forward Storage Areas

Each product other than machines has been assigned a forward permanent
location from which orders are to be picked; when the forward bay runs
low or out, another unit from reserve must be put in place and straps
as well as corrugated material are to be removed. (Reserve unit can be
released only through inventory control.)

L. Returned Goods

1. Returned goods, prior to creating RMF, are to be in a fixed location,
    clearly marked. After the RMF is created, move to a second location,
    pending a decision as to whether the merchandise should be repacked
    or stored.

2. Supervisor is to review daily receipts to determine whether product is
    resalable and can be put into the forward location, or is to be repacked and
    sent to a repack station.

3. Repacking shall be kept current on a weekly basis.

M. Uniforms

All warehouse personnel, including drivers and helpers, will wear uniforms.

N. Short Record

Deliveries that are made to customers and that are short are to be recorded
in a log, with a page for each driver, showing date, customer, product,
quantity short, and driver's initials. Drivers will be required to initial
this log personally.

O. Loading or Unloading

The warehouse manager, warehouse supervisor, assistant manager, or office
designee is to be assigned to each ''open bay'' to cover all incoming or
outgoing trucks. An open bay with a truck or trailer in place, incoming or
outgoing, is never to be left unsupervised by one of these four persons.

P. Pickups

There is to be an RA number to cover all pickups.

DISTRIBUTION: Warehouse Manager; Audit Manager; Systems Manager; Controller.

(*text continued from page 372*)
squiring the office manager, an unmarried young woman. The manager rotated auditors and instituted rules of conduct that specifically limited this action.

3. Not establish policy or procedures.
4. Refrain from debating or arguing the propriety of extant policies or procedures.
5. Rotate between jobs, if staff permits, every two or three years.
6. Maintain a pleasant face and a helpful, constructive attitude during audits and report reviews.

5. *Whether to have a separate audit department.* This is a decision that varies by company. The question is not whether to conduct inside audits—these must be performed, even if by the owner in a small company, or a manager in a slightly larger company who divides his or her regular duties with an audit function. But should the company utilize one or more operational auditors, preparing formal position descriptions, internal audit programs, and training, as just discussed?

These factors should be considered in reaching a decision:

1. Are there many locations involved in operations?
2. Are there many employees, and in many locations?
3. Is the system of internal check incomplete?
4. Do the independent accountants comment unfavorably on the internal control systems?
5. Are there a variety of products and services?
6. Are inventories composed of many small items?
7. Are there a great many invoices to customers each month?
8. Can the independent accountant's work be reduced through internal audit?
9. Do competitors of similar size use operational auditors?
10. Have the outside auditors made major year-end accounting adjustments each year?
11. Are the profit plans being missed each budget period?

While the significance of an affirmative response to each question would vary with different companies, a positive answer to any one of the questions would indicate the propriety of establishing a separate operational audit function.

Review

The end result of the operational audit is the report. It may be presented orally in the small company but should be written when a separate audit function has been established. The report should be oriented toward all concerned levels of management and be suitable for follow-up.

Helpful Hint: Restudy How to Prepare Reports on page 261, as to reporting level, content, timing, and form. This all applies.

There are five basic reports generated by the audit department:

1. **Summary audit report**, Exhibit 10-11. This is a brief report, only a few lines, addressed (in this case) to the EVP, who is responsible for operations, and to the VP/marketing, who has overall responsibility, at the corporate level, for the branch being audited. Both officers report directly to the president. The report is prepared by the manager of the audit department (not the auditor, since he or she is addressing high corporate officers), and the controller (to whom the audit manager reports) is copied.

While the detailed report (see Exhibit 10-12) covers many items, this report extracts only those that are significant and should be called to top management's attention, to ensure that corrective action is taken. Thus, these officers are not burdened with excessive detail and may concentrate on the important areas. The summary, therefore, becomes an exception report. Further, copies of this summary are not sent to lower managers who receive the detailed report; the impression is thereby created that higher managers and officers also received the detailed report and that all items listed on it are significant and worthy of attention.

Note that the branch being audited is graded (see Exhibit 10-13).

2. **Audit report**, Exhibit 10-12. This is the detailed audit report that supports the previous summary audit report.

(text continues on page 388)

Exhibit 10-11.   Summary audit report.

(FORMAT OF ACTUAL REPORT)

<u>SUMMARY AUDIT REPORT</u>

May 22, 20__

To: Executive Vice President
     Vice President for Marketing

An internal audit was performed at   Corporation, Atlanta
Branch, on May 19, with the following results:

> 1. The plan of the warehouse does not permit restricted entry.
> 2. A shortage of one machine and 40 rolls of inventory was
>   observed.
> 3. Petty cash loans are made to employees, contrary to procedure.
> 4. Machine Order Forms are not being used.

Rating: The branch is rated (C).

John Smith, Audit Manager

sc: Controller

Exhibit 10-12. Audit report.

(FORMAT FOR AUDIT REPORT)

AUDIT REPORT

CORPORATION

_____ BRANCH

Date Submitted: May 20, 20__
Written by: Auditor or Supervisor
Submitted by: Auditor

Copies to: Controller
            Branch Administrator
            Branch Manager
            Zone Manager
            Regional Manager
            (Show names, not titles)

(FORMAT OF ACTUAL REPORT)

<u>AUDIT REPORT</u>

_____ CORPORATION

_____ BRANCH

May 20, 20__

To: Controller

An internal audit was performed at   Corporation, Atlanta Branch, on May 19, 20__, and, unless otherwise indicated, was concerned with assets and liabilities recorded as of April 30, 20__.

A. <u>Synopsis of Principal Items</u>

Not all items covered by the audit are included in this report. The following points are considered to be of significant interest to the readers:

1. Petty cash was not in balance, and personal loans are being made to employees (SOP 123).

2. Access to the warehouse area cannot be restricted (SOP 456).

3. 40% of machine orders tested were not written on Machine Order Form (SOP 789).

B. <u>Inventory</u>

1. Access to the warehouse, with the exception of repair parts, cannot be restricted, because of the present layout of the premises. This could contribute to an inventory loss (SOP 123).

2. 8-1/2" paper was 40 rolls short from perpetual inventory.

3. Sales representatives' demo sheets not countersigned by manager, administrator, or service manager. One machine could not be accounted for (SOP 456).

C. <u>Service Department</u>

1. Service reports are not filed on a timely basis in the numbered machine file (SOP 123).

D. <u>Rating</u>
Branch is rated (C).

We wish to express our appreciation for the courtesy and cooperation extended to us during the course of the audit.

John Smith, Branch Auditor

(text continued from page 384)

It is generally two or three pages, never longer, the first page being a cover page showing the subject of the audit and the distribution of the report. In this exhibit, a branch is being audited and the report is sent to the branch administrator (the office manager) and the branch manager (the general manager directly responsible). The branch manager's immediate superior is the regional manager, who reports, in turn, to a zone manager. In this company, there are 40 branches, 8 regions, and 3 zones. Thus, all of the directly concerned operating managers receive a copy of the detailed audit report. The controller is copied since he has direct responsibility for the audit department. The audit manager, if the department is large enough to have one other than the controller, is automatically copied but need not be shown on the distribution listing. Names, rather than titles, are copied, to ensure receipt.

The use of the cover page, with lots of white space and a precise delineation of names and date, sets the tone for the precision of the report to follow.

The second page of the report lists the principal items in A, gives more detail in B about one of the principal items (item A.2., warehouse security, indicated that inventory was not being controlled), and items C or more would list secondary items for comment. The branch rating is in item D.

The report format includes an opening paragraph showing the period covered and closes with a courteous expression.

The key items are briefly summarized and carried forward to the summary audit report.

Helpful Hint: Other than the cover page, there should be one or one and a half additional pages. More than that would be picayune and officious. We are seeking to report on major items, only, whose failure would affect the operating plan.

3. **Audit appraisals**, Exhibit 10-13. This is a semiannual summary of the grades on the detailed audit reports.

Each letter grade is simply defined, and the name of each office is listed under the appropriate column. Summary audit report copies are enclosed for ready reference, and the appraisal is directed to the officer directly responsible for operations under the president, in this case the

Exhibit 10-13. Audit appraisals.

To: Executive Vice President

Subject: Audit Appraisals - Office and Accounting Functions at Branch Offices

This report covers the appraisals of Branch offices audited during the first six months of 20___. The appraisals are classified as follows:

(A) Conditions were appraised as generally satisfactory.

(B) Conditions were appraised as generally satisfactory, with some areas being considered as less than satisfactory.

(C) Conditions were appraised as generally less than satisfactory, with some areas being considered as satisfactory.

(D) Conditions were appraised as generally less than satisfactory.

(A)	(B)	(C)	(D)
Name	Name	Name	Name

Indicate, in a footnote, any exceptions to the standard or the procedures which were not included for any particular Branch.

Copies of the summary audit reports are attached, for your referral.

Audit Manager

sc: Vice President for Marketing
Controller

EVP. Copies are sent to the VP/marketing, as he is responsible to the EVP for field operations, and to the controller, as the report emanates from one of his departments.

Some criticism of this type of report, using letter grades, will arise from the branches being judged. The report may be called schoolboyish and the assignment of grades, arbitrary, without due consideration to other factors such as attainment of sales objectives, motivation of personnel, or performance up to budget standards. This report, though, is a review of operating systems and procedures, only, and the assigned grade is concerned only with evaluating those procedures, and no other factors. The use of the grade provides a quick, incisive, recognizable standard for judging performance within operating areas, only.

Exhibit 10-14.   Individual systems report.

```
                    INDIVIDUAL SYSTEMS REPORT

                     FREIGHT PAYMENT PLAN
                        AUDIT REPORT




Period of audit:    Sept., Oct. & Nov. 20__
By:                 Field Auditor
To:                 Controller
                    Accounting Services Mgr.
Date submitted:     January 6, 20__



General

    A test check examination of the freight payment plan was performed on the
periods indicated. In an effort to further ensure accuracy, a roll-forward
method was utilized from August 20__.

    This report consists of two parts, as follows:

        Part I  - Itemized deficiencies
        Part II - Itemized corrective recommendations
```

Audit reports and appraisals are used by reviewers in evaluating managers for salary increases. Their primary purpose, of course, is to attain profit plan objectives.

4. **Individual systems report**, Exhibit 10-14. This report, called the ISR, is a detailed review of a specific system within an operating department. In this case, a freight prepayment plan procedure with the accounting department is being audited.

The familiar cover page sets forth the time period and type of audit, showing distribution. Since only one department is involved, the auditor reports to the department head, the manager of accounting services, and his or her superior, the controller. In this company, the audit department also reports to the controller, who would be copied were another department, not his or her responsibility, being reviewed.

This report shows deficiencies in performance and recommends corrections.

(*text continues on page 392*)

Freight Payment Plan   -2-   Jan. 6, 20__

Part I

DEFICIENCIES IN APPLICATION OF PLAN

1. Sight drafts are not being received from First National City Bank on a daily basis.

2. Imprest balance of $10,000 appears excessive, as illustrated by aggregate deposits vs. monthly ending book balance.

Sept. 20__	$2,680.37	$9,413.43
Oct. 20__	4,400.00	6,728.92
Nov. 20__	4,500.00	7,780.96

3. Freight bills are not audited as to rates.

4. Copies of drafts are not being presented to Data Processing for data entry disbursements journal.

5. Voucher proof program is used by Data Processing as disbursement journal.

6. Control log of issued drafts is not kept on current basis.

7. Duplicate copies of invoices are paid on a direct basis to freight companies under plan.

8. More than one vendor number is being issued to some vendors without justification.

9. There is inaccurate clerical recording of vendor invoice numbers.

10. Procedure does not define internal security requirements for unissued drafts.

Part II

RECOMMENDED CORRECTIVE ACTION

1. November 12, 20__, plan should be revised to agree with common business practice, of monthly statement being accompanied by cancelled drafts.

(continued)

Exhibit 10-14. *(continued)*

Freight Payment Plan	-3-	Jan. 6, 20__

2. Because of the limited period covered and additions being made under the plan, a conclusion cannot be rendered. However, it is suggested that a review be made in the future by Accounting to ascertain the most economical imprest amount.

3. ICC rates and rate changes should be maintained on a current basis, by accounts payable.

4. A detailed listing of vendor invoice numbers is necessary for internal control. Therefore, continuation of the existing run is justified.

5. Report should be reheaded as freight disbursement journal.

6. Procedure should be strictly adhered to.

7. Direct payments to all freight companies under the plan should be eliminated. Where duplicate payments were made, immediate follow-up is in order for reimbursement.

8. Accounting should conduct a review and eliminate duplicate numbers for vendors and report findings to Data Processing.

9. Detailed listing of disbursements furnished by Data Processing should be checked against original documents.

10. Unissued drafts should be kept in locked cabinet, with number control by authorized accounting personnel.

If the report is long or the system complex, the list of deficiencies could be keyed to the item number in the procedure and the procedure attached for easy reference.

5. **Audit program for a subsidiary,** Exhibit 10-15. This is not a report as such, but belongs in any listing of audit reports. This audit program is used by inside auditors for performing financial (not operational) audits of wholly owned subsidiaries. The reports that are generated (not exhibited here) are the usual financial statements—balance sheet, income statement, statement of retained earnings, statement of changes in financial position, statement of additional paid-in capital, and notes to financial statements. Included, too, would be an internal audit opinion as to scope, consistency, and conformity to generally ac-

Exhibit 10-15. Audit program for a subsidiary.

AUDIT PROGRAM

I. ACCOUNTS RECEIVABLE

   A. Obtain detailed aged trial balance, by customer, as of _____.
      If already reconciled* to general ledger, obtain a copy of the
      reconciliation and foot and agree all items to proper corresponding
      books and records. Report detail trial balance.

      1. Review reconciling items; obtain details and all supporting
         documents therefor. Verify the accuracy of each.

      2. Select 20% (stratified selection—large accounts only) of open
         accounts receivable for position confirmation as of _____.

      3. Set up control worksheet and numerical systems to control the A/R
         confirmations.

      4. Test-check 10% of smaller accounts (not selected for confirmation)
         against local telephone directory for name and address.

      5. Circularize receivables selected in step 2. Summarize results
         and follow up and note all exceptions.

      6. Age (or obtain an aging of) open receivables according to current
         (0–30 days), 30, 60, 90, and over 120 days.
         a. Confirm (positive) all accounts over 60 days $ _____.

      7. Obtain an analysis of the provision for doubtful accounts.
         a. Detail method of providing the bad debt write-off.
         b. Test the provision for adequacy against the results of previous
            tests.
         c. Review credit correspondence for further status of possible
            uncollectibles.
      8. Test-trace subsequent collections (receipts) subsequent to A/R cutoff
         date.

        * If not reconciled, reconcile!

(continued)

cepted accounting principles, quite similar to the opinion of an outside auditor.

This audit program is a good example of a complete financial audit program that may be used when independent public accountants are not retained to conduct the audit of the subsidiary.

While operational audits of the subsidiary may be performed, the financial audit is more usual. The subsidiary usually operates outside of the parent's normal systems and procedures, with its own profit plan. It generally supplies its own monthly financial statements, which are the ultimate measure of its effectiveness to plan.

Exhibit 10-15. *(continued)*

II. <u>FIXED ASSETS</u>

    A. Obtain detail of fixed assets inventory (listing). Obtain copy
        of invoice support for major items.

    B. Analyze the various fixed asset accounts for the current year and
        fully detail the method of capitalizing (standards, etc.).

    C. Analyze the various depreciation provision accounts. Fully detail
        the method of providing the depreciation reserve.

    D. Verify all additions and deletions from the fixed asset accounts.

    E. Examine the respective fixed assets recorded in the Automobile &
        Furniture & Fixtures account and any copy machines located in home office
        and included as a fixed asset.
        1. Reconcile this inventory in value to the account records.
           Note and follow up significant differences.
        2. Compare to detail records, and test-trace to purchase documents
           (vouchers) selected large items. Test pricing and cost.
        3. Note condition and age, and where possible estimate value (replacement).

    F. For rental and major user machines, obtain a complete listing as
        of _____ reflecting the following data:
        1. Customer Name
           Address
           Type of machine (description)
           Length of time in service (approximate)
           Machine serial number
           Monthly billing amount of rental
           Paper price
           Copy of contract (if any exists)
           Average paper usage last 3 months (asterisk if less than contract
           specifies)
        2. Accumulated depreciation on the equipment. Also, an explanation of
           depreciation method (life, method, etc.)

    G. See sales for additional tests of rental (billing).

III. <u>INVENTORY</u>

    A. Supplies
        1. If a detailed perpetual inventory record exists, obtain (or
           extract) a listing of all supplies on hand.
        2. If no perpetual inventory exists, physically verify (by count) the supplies
           inventory. Obtain clerical help if needed.
        3. Note the costing procedure and price out the supplies inventory
           on detailed worksheets. Test costing against invoices.

4. Check cutoff procedures by controlling receiving reports and shipping papers. (Close down shipping area while the physical inventory is in process.) Note all items in transit; follow up and document the validity of these. Obtain details of any consignments (or other inventory out on loan, demo, trial, etc.) and verify these. Obtain appropriate supporting documentation. Remove from inventory items picked/ordered prior to inventory date. Segregate these physically and do not count. Count all other items and list these, showing product description, code, number of pieces, etc.

5. Check condition of inventory items.
   (Items B to E apply to dealer acquisition only.)

B. <u>RIP</u>

1. If a detailed perpetual inventory record exists, obtain (or extract) a list of all machine inventory on hand (by serial number).

2. Verify that all inventory exists by taking a physical count and matching it to perpetual inventory; or list each machine by type, serial no., etc.

3. List RIP machines by location if off premises, and indicate type of placement, i.e., rental, demo, major user.

4. Verify that all machines ''sold'' have been replaced; note exceptions.

5. If foreign machine is included, cost a zero value.

6. Reconcile prices on inventory to general ledger.

C. For A and B above, review all transactions (interim) from last statement date to physical inventory date (on a broad basis to control activity); work back to reconcilable figures. Do the same to last RIP replacement date.

D. Verify that all foreign inventory has been either paid for or reflected as a liability.

E. Note whether foreign inventory is salable or nonsalable.

IV. <u>SALES/A.R./OTHER</u>

A. Sales cutoff/MUP & rentals—obtain copies of all contracts (MUP or rental if available).

1. Check billing on MUP and rentals (verify against fixed asset list).

2. Trace to A/R statement/Sales.

3. Test last ten invoices for cut-off date.

4. Note unusual billing procedures, amount, etc.

5. Select locations and confirm these (use discretion for selection; positive confirmation).

(continued)

Exhibit 10-15. *(continued)*

    B. SALES/OTHER

        1. Obtain a master listing of all customers (including name, address, type of machine, serial number, sale price, and any other pertinent marketing information if possible).

        2. Examine billing on a test basis and trace to data provided in A above. Also trace to A/R list; and verify A above against that list.

  V. <u>CASH</u>

    A. Determine amount and location of all cash funds, bank accounts, and other negotiable assets.

    B. Review and investigate internal control procedures. Evaluate such procedures by identification of selected transactions.

    C. Count all cash on hand.

    D. Check all bank reconciliations. If incomplete, these should be completed.

    E. Confirm bank balances.

  VI. <u>TAXES</u>

    A. Compare the net income per books with taxable income to be reported in the current year's tax returns.

    B. Summarize beginning and end-of-the-year balances of estimated liabilities and provisions not deductible for tax purposes.

    C. Review computation of federal income taxes.

    D. Review state and local taxes. Compare with last period.

    E. Review withholding procedures and test their functioning. Check accruals.

  VII. <u>CONTINGENT LIABILITIES</u>

    A. Establish the existence or absence of any contingent liabilities.

    B. Determine the effect of any existing or contemplated litigation.

    C. List long-term liabilities for leases.

    D. Any other.

  VIII. <u>ACCOUNTS PAYABLE</u>

    A. Check verification procedures and authorizations.

    B. Test monthly statements from vendors.

    C. Review unrecorded purchases of goods and services.

IX. <u>EXPENSES</u>

    A. Review and test internal accounting control and check.

    B. Review, analyze, and test operating accounts. Compare with last period and obtain satisfactory evidence to explain changes.

    C. Review travel expenses by tracing test transactions.

    D. Review commission payments.

X. <u>GENERAL</u>

    A. Note details on operation with regard to number of employees. If possible, detail salary, job responsibility, etc.

    B. List all service contracts by customer, effective date, expiration date (asterisk those over 1 year and those on foreign equipment), model no., and price, and note any special conditions in remarks column.

    C. Obtain a copy of all insurance policies covering inventory, fixed assets, autos.

XI. <u>SPECIAL PROCEDURES FOR SUBSIDIARIES</u>

    A. Check minutes of directors' and stockholders' meetings.

    B. Reconcile surplus accounts.

    C. Review intercompany profit eliminations.

    D. Review reconciliations of intercompany accounts.

AUDIT AFFIRMATIONS

The operational audit is a defined controllership responsibility, its purpose being the evaluation, control, and improvement of actual operations. It examines internal checks and controls and supports the examination by independent, outside auditors. It differs from outside audits by examining the details of individual systems, rather than the financial statements themselves. Operational audits are conducted of profit and cost centers, vertical systems and procedures, and internal check systems. Auditors utilize written audit programs and reports. Their reports keep all concerned managers advised of the effectiveness of operating procedures and provide a control tool to aid the manager in achieving his or her profit objectives. Every company, large or small, should utilize an audit capability, even if assigned individuals must perform it on a part-time basis.

11

Supervising Special Administrative Areas of Responsibility

The term *administrative* in the title refers to executive or management performance of duties. The FEI definition of controllership and treasurership functions in "Treasurer's and Controller's Functions" explains the broad areas of responsibility. The elements of these broad areas have been treated in other chapters of this book. However, inherent in these overall functions are specific management tasks that may be said to be subsets of the larger functions—hence, "special administrative areas of responsibility."

Moreover, in many companies, usually below the $50 million sales range, the controller or treasurer is asked to accept responsibility for areas that are not normally associated with her or his office. For example, customer relations is generally a marketing department, reporting to a general sales manager. In some companies, though, since the controller supervises the order/billing function, and since customer complaints are related to credits and billing adjustments arising out of the order/billing function, the controller's assumption of the customer relations responsibility is a natural process.

Furthermore, while the assignment of major functions to the treasurer or controller is clear, for a few functions, no clear-cut assignment is evident. There may be other financial or administrative officers who divide up functions. The National Conference Board, in a study on The

Duties of Financial Executives, reports that the following are Functions of Indefinite Responsibility:

✧ Cash budget preparation
✧ Formulation of disbursing procedures for pension plan payments and interest
✧ Accounts payable disbursement
✧ Annual report preparation for stockholders
✧ Contracts review for financial and tax provisions
✧ Confidential payroll handling

Many functions, too, **are frequently reassigned** from the treasurer to the controller and vice versa. Exhibit 11-1 lists some of these as reported in actual business practice by the Conference Board. It is important, therefore, that a clear, current organization chart exists (see Chapter 7) and that position descriptions are consulted for the exact determination of special areas of responsibilities in each company.

This chapter will examine each of these "special" areas, in alphabetical order, citing the authority for the responsibility by reference to the FEI definition or the position descriptions for the treasurer or controller in "Treasurer's and Controller's Functions."

ACCOUNTING CALENDAR

Various calendars have been exhibited elsewhere, as they relate to overall responsibilities—the budget calendar at Exhibit 6-1; the departmental reports calendar at Exhibit 8-19; various tax calendars at Exhibits 9-5 through 9-8, and data processing report and accounting department report calendars at Exhibit 14-4 and 14-5. In addition, the controller should personally maintain an **accounting calendar** as seen in Exhibit 11-2. The authority in the FEI definition is planning for control and reporting and interpreting. The tool to be sure that nothing slips through the cracks is the accounting calendar.

Exhibit 11-1. Functions most frequently reassigned from treasurer to controller.

Functions Most Frequently Reassigned from Treasurer to Controller

Financial Management
Maintenance of equity position and working capital ratio
Analysis and interpretation of economic conditions

Capital Expenditures
Analysis of need for appropriations
Control of payments

Budgets
Preparation of budgets
Administration of budget program

Inventories
Maintenance of inventory control records
Taking and costing inventories

Cash Management
Handling petty cash
Formulation of disbursement procedures for:

    Accounts payable
    Payrolls
    Pension plan payments
    Interest
Cash budgets

Taxes
Preparation and filing of tax returns
Appraisal of effect of taxes on company

Accounting
General and cost accounting
Plant and equipment accounting

Auditing
Internal auditing and checking
Arranging for outside credits

Financial Statements
Preparation, issuance and interpretation of financial statements
Preparation of SEC report (Form 10K)

Office Management and Methods

Government Orders and Regulations
Compliance with government orders and regulations

Statistics
Assembly, preparation and analysis of statistics

Payrolls
Preparation of wage, salary and confidential payrolls

Exhibit 11-2. Accounting calendar.

ACCOUNTING CALENDAR

1	2	3	4	5	6
Rent Checks Hand CD Summary	Payroll Summary	Depository Receipts	Blue Book (P/R sum.)	Cash Reg. for 10th	Overrides A/R.J.E.
7	**8**	**9**	**10**	**11**	**12**
C/R Summary	Life & Health Ins. Union Welfare Union Dues	Closing of Freight Plan	A/P Checks Closing of Purchases		
13	**14**	**15**	**16**	**17**	**18**
Bank Recs. G.S.A. report	Bank Recs. Special A/R Schedule	P/R Tax—State—City Summary and Reconciliation of Aged A/R		Flash P-L Report Gross Profit % Sch. Machines sold per salesperson Final PABST	Depository Receipts Sch. of MLP paper sales
19	**20**	**21**	**22**	**23**	**24**
Cash Req. for 25th. Auto Leasing Report Sales Tax Returns	Sales & Service Comm.	Docustat cust. comm.	Consolidated Financial Statements	Sch. of Expenses Financial Statements—Senox —SBMCL —Natl Photo	Financial Statements —EBM —Docustat —DE. Co
25	**26**	**27**	**28**	**29**	**30**
A/P Checks Sales Tax Returns Sch.—Loans to —Travel Advances —Deposits —Sales Sal. to Retail Sales	Cash Req. for 1st Missing Billing Control Sch. of Royalty Income Cafeteria P-L	EBM—Halifax P-L Sch.—Average price on coupon shipments	Update Stock Options F.A. Schedules Patent Sch. Deferred Prod. Dev. Sch.	Inventory Evaluation for Insurance Co. Def. Prof. Fees. Sch.	Sales Tax Ret. Overrides Notes Rec. Sch.

DAILY
Temp. PABST.
Cash Summary & Loan Schedule
Cost of Sales Control
Manual Checks
Taping and Depositing Cash Receipts

WEEKLY
Wed.—Car Maintenance Checks
Thurs.—Travel Exp. Checks
Fri.—Freight Checks
Fri.—Union Payroll Checks

BIWEEKLY
Reg. Payroll Checks
Private Payroll Checks
Blue Book—Payroll Summary

MONTHLY
Correction to COSAS
Status Report
Branch Petty Cash Reimbursements

QUARTERLY
Mr. Smith Interest
1/1, 3/1, 6/1, 9/1
Apr, July, Oct, Jan
—P/R Tax Return
—Royalty Exp. checks
—Financial Release
—Fed & State Est. Taxes (see tax calendar)
—Stock Purchase Plan
—Wage Continuation Insurance
—Correction to CASA
—Rolls Shipped per Machine
—Reconciliation of Rolls

SEMIANNUAL
Physical Inventory
CoSAS/CASA Reconciled

ANNUALLY
W2's, 1099, 1096, 3692, Fed'l Ins.
ABC Min. Royalty-Jan
Fed'l Tax Return
Certified Audit
Hertz–Mileage Credit

Helpful Hint: Prepare this on a monthly basis, as exhibited, rather than using a repetitive tickler file calendar. This saves you the trouble of retickling the same items each month. Instead, consult the accounting calendar daily.

Caution: Do not assign the perusal of this calendar to subordinates. They are not expected to have the same sense of responsibility that you have. They forget; there are terminations — *do it yourself!* It ensures that *all* major areas of responsibility will be handled on time.

ACTIVITY-BASED COSTING

The second controllership function in Appendix A, reporting and interpreting, provides the controller with authority for implementing cost accounting systems and reporting on their results.

Cost accounting is the branch of accounting that records and analyzes expenditures, and that interprets the data obtained, in the interest of providing management and direction to the organization. Cost accounting should include not only production activities, but selling, distribution, and financial activities. Cost accounting practice requires the design and installation of cost systems, the recording of transactions, preparation of reports and analyses for management, preparation of budgets, the reporting of actual results compared to budget, and the analysis and interpretation of these results.

Traditional cost accounting methods use direct costs of material and labor as the basis for allocating overhead to products. This arose in a manufacturing environment in which overhead was a small percentage of the direct labor expended. In today's manufacturing environment, however, direct labor has been greatly reduced through automation. As a result, indirect costs and overhead have become a larger percentage of total costs, and the use of direct labor as the basis on which to apportion costs can result in cost distortions and flawed pricing decisions. Simply put, the direct costs of material and labor no longer represent the majority of costs included in the product. Significant indirect costs in today's environment include the costs of engineering and field service support, which are unrelated to production, and other costs that are related to production orders rather than production quantity, such as order processing, purchasing, and setups. Further, traditional cost systems are not concerned with matters of quality and service, but these are important to the customer. The traditional system continues to be appropriate to measure inventory cost, but it does not enhance product profitability decisions.

Newer cost systems are required that are customer-oriented, measuring information about quality, service, delivery, and profitability. One such system is activity-based costing (ABC) and its companion, activity-based management (ABM). ABM utilizes the information developed by the ABC system to improve the decision-making process.

Activity accounting, instead of focusing on direct costs and overhead allocation, identifies the activities connected with a process that results in an output, and determines the cost per output, the time to execute the activity, and the quality of the output. ABC determines short- and long-term goals, which are measured against current results. The entire process of ABC provides managers with accurate product costs and information to keep operations competitive through continuous identification and elimination of inefficient and wasteful activities.

A good primer on implementing an ABC system is *Activity Accounting*, by James A. Brimson, published by John Wiley & Sons, Inc., in cooperation with the IMA. The suggested steps to implement an ABC system are:

1. Identify the activities that produce output, including production and support, to obtain cost and performance.
2. Determine the useful life or life cycle of the output to match costs to time periods, and to capitalize appropriate costs.
3. Trace costs to activities, including all resources needed to perform the activity—salaries, travel, machinery and equipment, and supplies. Express the cost of the activity based on a unit measure of output.
4. Identify performance measures, such as quality, cost, and time, all of which affect the ability of the activity to meet its goals.
5. Identify business processing costs, including plant, equipment, and data information systems, and assign them to output.
6. Aggregate the total cost of activities into a common function

and process, to enable focus on hidden costs arising from other departments, and to show the interrelationship of activities.

7. Determine the product cost by creating a bill of activities that summarizes the cost of all activities. Support costs become directly visible, rather than being lumped into overhead and apportioned to products.

ABC is worth a look if indirect costs are high in relation to materials and labor, and if products require more decision-oriented costing.

ANALYTICAL TOOLS

Various departments in the organization may use a variety of analytical tools to complete their missions. Some of these tools are:

operations analysis   The grouping together of various problems and problem-solving techniques, utilizing studies and surveys.

operations research   The application of quantified common sense, using the construction of models, either actual or simulated, and mathematical techniques to describe a process and predict the results of changes or innovations.

value analysis or **value engineering**   An organized and systematic approach to cost improvement, consisting of the repeated questioning of the value and contribution of functions and things.

quality control evaluation   The measurement of costs underlying quality-related activities, such as the cost of preventing product defects, cost of conforming products to specifications, and cost of failed products.

In practice, these tools will be used by the research, engineering, production, and quality control departments. The controller, however, as set forth in the treasurer's and controller's functions defined by the FEI, has the responsibility for reporting and interpreting, evaluating and consulting with all segments of management concerning any phase of the operation of the business. He or she should be familiar with these techniques.

Operations analyses and value analysis techniques tend to be non-numerical. As a result, the controller is not usually involved, other than on an advisory basis. Operations research and quality control evaluation, however, are mathematically oriented disciplines in which the controller is often a team player.

Operations Research

In many organizations, the responsibility for the utilization of the operations research technique (this being a mathematical process) will be placed directly on the controller's office. A good self-study course entitled Making Reliable Decisions with Linear Programming is available through the American Management Association. Complicated business problems may often be solved using experience, common sense, and the tools of operations analysis and value analysis. When there are many variables, however—when profit margins are close, when the best possible solution is required—the best tool to use is operations research. This, in turn, utilizes many mathematical tools to solve difficult problems and to offer many solutions. Some of these tools are:

- ✧ Dynamic programming
- ✧ Game theory
- ✧ Inventory modeling
- ✧ Linear programming
- ✧ Nonlinear programming
- ✧ Quadratic programming
- ✧ Queueing
- ✧ Simulation

Each of these techniques may be applied to specific types of business problems, but not to all problems. Linear programming, however, is generally the most useful technique for solving problems whose components can be objectively stated in numerical terms. As such, it can be readily understood and applied by the controller's office.

Linear programming may be further defined as a tool to:

✧ Solve problems that have so many components that interrelate in so many ways that one cannot easily evaluate the most economical alternative through the exercise of ordinary common sense. Linear programming develops a numerical statement of the alternatives to achieve a quantified common-sense solution to the problem.

✧ Analyze information to provide the best mathematical solution. This requires inputs in the form of requirements, objectives, and profit and cost data for each alternative. Mathematical formulas are then applied to determine the best solution.

✧ Formulate the problem in quantitative terms and apply the numerical solution to real-life problems. The solution, although mathematically correct, may not be applicable, however, unless all the variables of the real-life situation are included.

✧ Provide answers that are the best for the total problem, not just for the individual parts—e.g., how to ship product from three different locations to three different customers in the least costly way, or how to find the most economical way to blend, produce, and distribute products like food or petroleum.

✧ Apply the scientific method to the solution of business problems using steps to identify the problem area, specify relevant activities, gather data, establish the objective in numerical terms (generally using algebraic formulas), input data into a computer or apply a manual analysis, quantify the value of the result, report the results to appropriate management, and implement the changes.

Software applications may be purchased that incorporate operations research and linear programming techniques for inventory management: materials requirement planning (MRP) and just-in-time (JIT) inventory ordering and delivery. The controller must become proficient in or at least conversant with their use. Teamwork is important in order to use these techniques successfully, and the controller is a vital team member.

Quality Control Evaluation

The costs associated with quality-related activities are those for:

✧ Preventing product defects—job training programs, quality circles.
✧ Producing products that conform to specifications—inspection and testing.
✧ Product failures—rework, yield loss, warranty costs, return and allowance credits.

The reasons for evaluating quality control costs are:

✧ To budget properly
✧ For performance evaluation (management by objectives)
✧ To identify such costs with a view to decreasing them

As a result of the controller's involvement in reporting on budget results and performance evaluations, the controller is generally a member of the quality control evaluation team. Good background for this responsibility may be found in the Institute of Management Accountants (formerly the National Association of Accountants) research study entitled "Measuring, Planning, and Controlling Quality Costs," by Wayne J. Morse, Harold P. Roth, and Kay M. Poston.

Quality control cost systems have these features:

✧ Key measurements are made of factors that affect profitability—defect rates, rework cost, number of warranty claims.
✧ Quality cost data is used for internal, not external, purposes.
✧ The generators of quality costs are identified for management control purposes.
✧ Quality cost systems vary within each operating division, based on type of operation and need.
✧ Such systems cross organizational boundaries by following pro-

cesses from start to finish—design, purchase, manufacture, sales, administration.

✧ Quality costs are not stand-alone costs but are used together with other measures of quality and productivity—pricing levels, market, end use.

✧ Quality cost systems may require adjusting existing accounting information and developing new data suited to the desired objective.

The quality control cost system should not operate within the confines of the existing accounting system. Accounting systems are precise—to the penny. Quality cost systems require estimates. Such systems are consistent, however, allowing meaningful comparisons of costs in different time periods. The controller should understand the relationships between quality, productivity, and manufacturing, which a quality cost system will provide.

ANNUAL REPORT AND MEETING

The second FEI treasurership function is investor relations. This specifies the responsibility for liaison with investment bankers, financial analysts, and shareholders. The proxy statement, notice of annual meeting, and annual report are specific to the acquittal of that responsibility.

The treasurer, while directly in charge, may work with or through the company's advertising agency, legal staff, outside counsel, or internal advertising department in preparing the annual report, and with the office services department in arranging a well-planned annual meeting.

Helpful Hint: If time and economy in preparation are key, a financial printer will provide a better payoff than a commercial printer. They will do layout and advise on the legal requirements for size of type.

Annual Report Tip: The SEC's requirements for publication of reports and filing with the SEC are found in SEC Regulations 14a and 14c under the Securities Exchange Act of 1934.

AUDITS, EXTERNAL

The controller is the fulcrum between the independent auditors and the company. This responsibility is derived from the FEI-defined functions of planning for control and reporting and interpreting.

The differences between the inside or operational audit and the outside or external audit are explained in Chapter 10. Despite the differences, the controller is responsible for both audits. Many people, investors and the public, may believe that the independent auditor's certificate is a guarantee that the auditor has found the financial statements to be correct and reliable. Not so! The audit establishes fairness, consistency, and adherence to principles, not correctness. Moreover, management, through the controller's staff, is fully responsible for the company's financial statements, not the outside accountants.

> *Note This Difference:* The outside auditor will use care, diligence, and training in his or her audit. However, it is an audit of the controller's internally generated statements, reflecting the efficacy of the systems, procedures, internal auditing, and internal control established by the company controller.

In his relationship to the outside accountants, the controller should:

✧ Be friendly and cooperative.
✧ Provide complete access to all books, data, contracts, reports.
✧ Explain the system of internal check and control.
✧ Present an overview of operating systems and procedures.
✧ Establish a chain of communication between the auditors and his or her staff.
✧ Never question the reasons or motives for the auditor's review of any records.
✧ Maintain a cordial but aloof social relationship, to avoid impugning the auditor's independence.

Audits of public companies are required by stock exchanges, the

SEC, regulatory agencies, and banks and other creditors. Even where there is no legal need for an external audit, the company should have one. Try this. . . .

> *Helpful Hint:* Well-managed companies, no matter how small, would do well to have an annual, independent audit. This may prevent fraud, will verify the actual reported income, will confirm the values of the major assets such as inventory and receivables, and will give banks, lenders, major stockholders, and prospective buyers of the business (you may someday decide to sell out) confidence in the management and accuracy of the reported figures. The cost of the outside audit is small compared to the benefit of the confidence level obtained.

An adjunct to the external audit is the formation of an audit committee within the company. If possible, this should be composed of, or at least chaired by, outside directors. The controller should not be a part of the committee but will be invited to comment at most meetings (See The Audit Committee in Chapter 18.) The duties of the committee are:

1. Meet with independent CPAs before the annual audit to discuss the general scope of the audit and to firm up the audit engagement memorandum.
2. Meet with independent CPAs after the annual audit to review the certified financial statements and the management internal control letter.
3. Meet with independent CPAs at periodic intervals, to discuss interim quarterly reviews and FASB statements, interpretations, and proposals. Review the quality and depth of the company's accounting and financial departments.
4. Monitor the company's internal control systems through:
   a. Meetings with the internal audit manager to discuss audit programs and findings.
   b. Visiting branches or other locations to discuss accounting and internal controls.
   c. Meeting with the controller to discuss internal controls,

    recommendations of the independent CPAs in their management control letter, and alternative accounting policies.

5. Recommend the independent auditors for submission to voting approval by stockholders at the annual meeting.
6. Select among alternative accounting policies.
7. Review officers' expense account reimbursements.
8. Review and approve bank account signatories, or recommend such approvals to the banking committee.
9. Provide ready access to the board of directors for the company's independent CPAs and its internal auditors.
10. Report to the board of directors concerning the work of the committee and its findings.
11. Keep the size of the committee at three members to prevent it from becoming unwieldy, and rotate one member every two or three years to bring a fresh approach to the committee.

Benefit Programs

For a complete discussion, see Chapter 16, Developing and Administering Benefit Programs.

Customer Relations

This marketing function may be assigned to the controller when customer complaints and problems arise out of billing, issuance of credits, or processing of orders. The administration of the order/billing function is part of the FEI planning for control responsibility of the controller, and, in this case, the controller might well assume the customer relations responsibility. Similarly, the treasurer could assume it if the major associated customer-related problems arose from the credit and collection function.

Helpful Hint: Where there are a great many customer complaints, solve the problem by logging in phone calls and letters, log them out to various departments for corrective action, and log in the ultimate response to the customer. Establish a standard time for correction, say 48 hours, and follow up each logged entry for conformity to standard.

See Customer Relationship Management in Chapter 19.

ENVIRONMENTAL ASPECTS

The effect on the business of economic, governmental, and social forces—in short, the environment in which the company operates—should be appraised and interpreted by the controller as a major FEI responsibility. The treasurer, too, will find that these factors influence his or her performance with respect to provision of capital, investor relations, and short-term financing.

A subset of this major function is *compliance with federal regulations*, to include:

✧ Antidiscrimination
✧ Fair employment
✧ Consumer protection
✧ Federal aid
✧ Occupational safety and health
✧ Pollution control
✧ SEC disclosure
✧ Truth in lending
✧ Various state and federal laws on loans to officers and employees, directors' liability, and officers' responsibilities

Helpful Hint: Free literature covering most of these areas is available through the Department of Labor, the Equal Employment Opportunity Commission, or the National Labor Relations Board, all located in Washington, D.C. Request information on the Fair Labor Standards Act, the National Labor Relations Act, the federal Equal Employment Opportunity Act, the Civil Rights Act, and the Age Discrimination in Employment Act. You may also contact the respective state agencies in the area of civil rights and equal employment opportunity. The Bureau of National Affairs (BNA) publishes several works—the *Federal Labor and Employment Laws, Fair Employment Practices,* the *Law of the Workplace: Rights of Employers and Employees,* and *U.S. Labor and Employment Laws* by Ruth West. Callaghan & Co. publishes a looseleaf service titled *Labor and Employment Law:* Compliance and Litigation. Warren, Gorham & Lamont offers the *Personnel Directors Legal Guide* by Kahn, Brown, and Zepke. Prentice-Hall publishes three looseleaf services called *Labor Relations Guide,* the *Payroll Guide,* and *Personnel Management: Compensation.* The IRS offers the *Employer's Tax Guide* annually.

A question will often arise as to what extent compliance or reporting to governmental agencies is necessary when such reporting is for informational purposes only—in other words, the agency has no legal mandate requiring compliance. Typical are governmental studies on exports, imports, purchase order levels, manufacturing, capital expenditures, and debt financing. Obviously, the studies are conducted to enable the agency to garner useful statistical information that will assist private industry and government for planning purposes. Each company must evaluate the validity of these requests in terms of its own posture and the cost involved in generating such reports. As in many types of circularizations, once you respond, you're on the list and will be solicited continuously.

Helpful Hint: When responding to voluntary agency report requests, estimates are time saving and are, in fact, encouraged by the agencies. A broad, ball-park response, on time, is considered better than none at all.

A second subset of this major function is *social disclosure.* The SEC is considering the extent to which corporations should be required, in annual reports, to report on employment conditions, environmental impacts, and various other social consequences of their operations. Techniques for gathering and reporting information concerning the social impact of business on consumers, employees, and the general public should be encouraged by both the SEC and corporations. A special AICPA task force studying social impacts has recommended that such disclosures be permitted, but not required, in sections of reports not covered by an auditor's opinion.

> *Helpful Hint:* Stockholders can be advised that considerable information on some areas of business performance relating to pollution and employment practices already exists as a result of government requirements, without the necessity of characterizing this in published financial reports.

The task force's comments were directed at measurement areas, attestation and presentation, rather than at the broad implications of social policy. The AICPA's accounting standards division will supply copies of the task force study on request.

> *Accounting Requirements:* Accounting for Environmental Liabilities, Asbestos Treatment Costs, and Costs to Clean Up Environmental Contamination are discussed in Emerging Issues Task Force Abstracts EITF 93-5, 89-13, and 90-8, respectively. Under certain circumstances, costs may be capitalized. In addition, the AICPA has issued an exposure draft on a proposed statement of position entitled Environmental Remediation Liabilities that provides authoritative guidance on specific accounting issues concerning the recognition, measurement, display, and disclosure of environmental remediation liabilities. Moreover, the SEC staff issued Staff Accounting Bulletin SAB 92, which requires separate presentation of the gross liability and related claim recovery in the balance sheet. SAB 92 also sets forth other accounting and disclosure requirements relating to product and environmental liabilities.

Also see Strategic Risk Management in Chapter 19.

Hiring Your Replacement

Every manager, the treasurer and controller included, should have a potential replacement who is several years away from assuming that position. Obviously, this benefits the company, since it ensures that there will be no void in the organizational structure in the event of any unanticipated occurrence. However, managers are sometimes loathe to hire such a person, fearing that they will lose their jobs to the replacement. This never happens! If one's job is in jeopardy, it will not be saved simply because there is no understudy. Higher management will merely replace the weak manager with a new hire. On the other hand, there is a decided advantage to the manager in having a strong replacement on board. The manager can be promoted or make a career move without leaving chaos behind. The mark of a good manager is having good people in his or her department who perform well in their current jobs and, in turn, are capable of moving up within the organization.

Lower-level hires are normally screened by the personnel department, with final interviews by the hiring manager. However, your replacement—the heavy hitter, the one you will groom for succession—needs to be hired using different techniques. This takes time, but the cost of the time is considerably less than the cost of failure (see step 1, below). You won't have a failure in hiring a "key" manager if these steps are followed:

1. *Evaluate cost.* The cost of hiring or replacing a key employee has been estimated at $80,000 per hire. This includes recruitment fees, training cost, and opportunity cost. In hiring, you're making an $80,000 decision. Ergo, you should spend more time to hire the right person.

2. *Define the job requirements.* Know what the job requires. Then interview to find a person who meets those requirements. A longer interview allows you to break down the interviewee's behavior patterns to determine whether he or she meets your job requirements—i.e., can operate independently, desires to succeed, will travel extensively, will do the work without delegating, etc.

3. *Screening interview.* Give VIP treatment to the prospect—show

the candidate around, shut off your phone, create a bond between you. You ask the questions. The questioner controls the interview. If the candidate asks questions (how much does it pay?), respond with a question (what are your salary requirements?). Track the prospect's responses. Make sure the answers are fleshed out and complete. Make the candidate speak about himself or herself, not just about job qualifications, at this time. Have the prospect speak, first, for about 35 minutes. You then speak, and explain the job for 10 minutes. Every time you tell the prospect something new, qualify him or her by asking if that's the kind of job he or she wants (in other words, is he or she still a candidate for the job?). If your gut feeling about the candidate is not good, terminate the interview. Dance out of it politely; stand up, say thanks, and end it.

4. *Fill out forms.* Get a family financial requirement form that includes the prospect's budget, living costs, and required income. Ask for a character reference from someone in a similar position, not a superior (you can use the reference as a job prospect if the present candidate doesn't work out). The completion of this form is the start of the prospect's commitment.

5. *Do a selection interview.* This interview should last three to four hours. Start it at 3 to 4 P.M. (it is later in the interview process and will decrease the prospect's role playing). Ask the "high school question"—tell me about yourself, going back to high school. Let the interviewee talk about this for about an hour. Prod for information about friends, parents, dating, study habits, sports. The candidate is talking about himself or herself and will begin to feel comfortable, to unburden himself or herself, and to trust you. Keep prodding and asking questions to flush out the answers.

Do an in-depth probe of at least one area for about 45 minutes. Do this by layering your questions—if you hear the interviewee say she or he did something, say, "How did you do it?" Keep pushing. This shows whether he or she can handle it.

Then, do your company sell for about twenty minutes.

Next, ask if there are any areas of concern. You can now ask any personal questions, and you'll receive an answer, as you've established trust, and the prospect is not now role playing. At this point, verify that he or she is still a candidate. If not, terminate the interview. If yes, ask for a home interview.

6. *Home interview.* Take about 30 minutes at the prospect's home. Do it in a family room. See who is dominant. If the spouse is dominant and not supportive, you may not want to hire. Be sure you have a team player. If the prospect had any doubts about coming to work for your company, you've now overcome them. He or she will come to work for you, since you spent the four hours in interviewing and took the trouble to come to his or her home.

7. *Mutual commitment.* Ask if the candidate will commit to a specific work schedule and, given time constraints, to work related to the job requirements to be done within the next 60 days. Ask for a commitment to receive feedback, to agree to your objectives, and to supply the necessary reports. If you receive these commitments, you, in turn, commit to training, benefits, feedback, and pay level.

If, at this time, the candidate negotiates pay, get a further commitment as to work performance. (This is why you want his or her commitment first.)

Shake hands, and say, it's a deal. You've got your heavy hitter. You've spent about a half day on the process, but you've assured the prospect's success, and your own, at a big benefit to the organization.

HUMAN RESOURCE ACCOUNTING (HRA)

The most important assets in the organization for ensuring continued profits and growth are human assets. One way of assessing human asset performance is through the operating plan and the budget versus actual reports, as described in Chapters 6 and 8. Other performance reports are generated through the management by objectives program, Chapter 14, and through monitoring and reporting on personnel performance, discussed in this chapter. However, survival in our complex competitive business environment has created a need for formal measurement systems to evaluate our human resources. Traditional accounting systems are not useful for this purpose.

Human Resource Theory

HRA goes beyond the traditional quantitative accounting measurements. The American Accounting Association's Committee on Human Resource Accounting has defined it as "the process of identifying and measuring data about human resources and communicating the information to interested parties." Such a measurement process is the responsibility of the controller, as part of the FEI functions in Appendix A of planning for control and reporting and interpreting.

The good manager is aware of the importance of human factors in achieving the organization's goals. If the manager can quantify these factors, he or she reports on them, as in management by objectives or monitoring and reporting on personnel performance. If he or she cannot, the manager intuitively considers them in planning, budgeting, and interpreting his or her results. It is clear, however, that changes in productivity provide measuring opportunities in human resource accounting. Productivity problems arise because of human factors, such as competence and motivation.

Competence, for example, can be affected by training programs. The investment in training programs can increase profits. Therefore, a rate of return on the investment in training can be quantified.

In short, goals may be set to measure behavior under prescribed circumstances. Exhibit 11-3, **setting goals to measure the unmeasurable**, refers to goal setting based on perceptions and attitudes, as well as results. As item 9 of the exhibit points out, "If you can't count it, measure it, or describe it, you probably don't know what you want and often can forget it as a goal."

Application of the Theory

Assume that you were to measure the leadership capability of the corporation as a whole. This is certainly a measurable variable that could be quantified, as could the character of motivational forces, the quality of the communication process, and the ability to interact across organiza-

Exhibit 11-3. Setting goals to measure the unmeasurable.

1. It is often necessary to devise measurements of the present level in order to be able to estimate or calculate change from this level.
2. The most reliable measures are the real time or raw data in which the physical objects involved comprise the measures to be used (dollars of sales, tons of output, number of home runs hit).
3. When raw data can't be used, an index or ratio is the next most accurate measure. This is a batting average, a percentage, a fraction, or a ratio.
4. If neither of the above two can be used, a *scale* may be constructed. Such scales may be "rate from one to ten," a nominal rating against a checklist of adjectives such as "excellent, fair, poor," or one which describes "better than" or "worse than" some arbitrary scale. (These are useful but are far less precise than the above.)
5. Verbal scales are the least precise but can be extremely useful in identifying present levels and noting real change. *Verbs* such as "directs," "checks," and "reports" are indicative of actions to be taken.
6. General descriptions are the least useful, but still have value in establishing benchmarks for change. "A clear, cloudless fall day" is obviously not the same as a "cloudy, foggy, misty day," and the two descriptions could be used to state conditions as they exist and conditions as they should be.
7. The statements of measurement should be directed more toward *results* than toward *activity*. (Much activity may prove impossible to state in specific terms, whereas results of that activity can be stated.)
8. In stating results sought or in defining present levels, effort should be made to find indicative, tangible levels and convert verbal or general descriptions into such tangible scales, ratios, or raw measures where possible.
9. If you can't count it, measure it, or describe it, you probably don't know what you want and often can forget it as a goal.

Source: George S. Odiorne, *Management Decisions by Objectives,* Prentice-Hall, Inc., Englewood Cliffs, N.J., 1969, p. 27.

tional lines, to make decisions, to control operations, or to set performance goals.

A budget for the leadership function could be prepared. For example, the leadership function could be divided into subsets to include (1) the degree of trust superiors have in subordinates and (2) the extent to which superiors draw on subordinates' thoughts and ideas and use them constructively. Each subset could be rated on the following scale: (1) no confidence in subordinates, (2) condescending trust in subordinates, (3) substantial but not total confidence in subordinates, and (4) complete confidence and trust in subordinates in all matters. Then each of the subsets could be ranked from 0 to 100% and a total percentage obtained for the leadership function for the organization.

Once the budget was established, the leadership function could be reevaluated at target dates, say semiannually. At that time, the budgeted percentages, for each subset and in total, could be compared to the reevaluated results. The variances could then be explained in narrative form.

Uses of Human Resource Accounting

HRA may be used to:

1. *Reduce employee turnover costs.* The costs of training to retain employees on the payroll can be measured against the hiring and training costs.
2. *Evaluate management development progress.* The cost of hiring, training, continuing education, and improvement of new managers' development may be measured against the costs of hiring new managers.
3. *Budget capital projects and performance evaluation.* The cost of the investment in the hard assets, as well as the human training costs, may be evaluated and measured against expectations.

These uses may be measured by identifying the functions and subsets involved in each process. For example, the leadership function is evaluated in connection with all three uses above.

Learning Human Resource Accounting

The Institute of Management Accountants (IMA) has published an excellent primer on the subject, entitled, *Human Resource Accounting: Past, Present, and Future,* by Edwin H. Caplan and Stephen Landekich. Caplan is professor of accounting at the University of New Mexico, and Landekich is the research director of the IMA. The book will supply the background upon which each controller can build his or her own system to suit his or her own operating environment.

INTERNAL CONTROL

The controller, through the protection of assets FEI function, has the overall internal control responsibility, and the treasurer, through the banking and custody function, the responsibility for cash control.

Internal check and control, sometimes called automatic auditing, augments the internal, operational audit described in the previous chapter. The efficacy of the system of internal control is measured and reported on by the external auditors (see page 337).

The techniques of internal check and control are as varied as businesses are. The following steps, however, are inherent in most good internal control systems:

1. *Accounts receivable controls.* These include order entry, billing, credit adjustment, and application of cash receipts (see Chapter 3 for details).
2. *Division of responsibility.* This consists of subdividing work so that no single individual has complete control over the physical asset, recording, or summarizing of the account involved.
3. *Work flow verification.* One employee, usually in a different department or acting independently, carries forward the work of the previous employee and, in so doing, automatically verifies it, without duplicating it.

   FOR EXAMPLE: Individual cash receipts from customers are posted by one employee, all checks are totaled and deposited by a second employee, and a third verifies that the individual totals of all customers posted by the first equal the deposit of the second.

4. *Protection of work.* This means providing mechanical aids to deter fraud (a check writer to prevent check raising), as well as physical facilities (a locked computer room to prevent tampering with program controls).

CASE IN POINT: A company did not lock up its customer files each evening. An employee photocopied customer names and sold them to a former, disgruntled salesperson, who contacted each customer, cut prices, and succeeded in poaching most of the accounts. A simple locked file could have avoided a disaster.

5. *Supervision.* This is indigenous to good internal control. The best system of internal check will fail unless properly supervised.
6. *Work duty specification.* The written requirements and the "how-to" of each job should be prepared and kept current for each job. Internal control cautions should be a part of such specifications.
7. *Vacations and job rotation.* These should be required. Do not offer pay in lieu of vacation. Frauds are discovered during absences or job changes.

Helpful Hint: Job rotation also provides additional trained employees, to help out during sickness, strikes, or terminations—prevents shut-downs.

8. *Internal audit.* Described in Chapter 10, the operational audit verifies that the systems and procedures that make up the internal control system are working.
9. *Outside audit.* This serves as an independent appraisal of the efficacy of the system of internal control, helps to detect and prevent fraud, and is almost the only deterrent to fraud at higher level, by officers and executives.
10. *Bonding.* When all else fails, this provides protection against most business frauds, including theft, embezzlement, and loss of valuable records. Small losses need not be covered, but catastrophes can be averted (see page 145).

In addition to the specific steps to obtain internal control set forth above, an environment, a climate for fraud and negligence prevention must be established. Policies should be written to encompass: (1) the six AICPA questions regarding the company's activities in dealing with derivative financial instruments, as listed on page 73, and (2) the five elements of the internal control structure in the standard issued by the AICPA, listed on page 339. These policies should be published as standard operating procedures (see page 240) and policy manual procedures (see page 246), as appropriate.

INVENTORY TAKING AND CONTROL

Physical inventories are taken to:

- ✧ Prevent fraud.
- ✧ Verify the accuracy of perpetual inventories.
- ✧ Verify shrinkage percentages and computed gross profit margins.

The controller's authority for inventory taking is derived from the FEI functions of reporting and interpreting and the protection of assets.

Inventory taking is an element of internal control, and like systems of internal control, the methods for inventory taking vary with the type of business. The following characteristics are essential to good inventory taking:

1. Cycle count where possible, to avoid having to take one massive inventory at year-end.
2. Count twice, whether on cycle or periodically. Once a year is too long to wait to determine whether recorded profits are accurate, to ascertain that there is no fraud or inventory loss.
3. Announce 30 to 45 days in advance, to allow locations time to schedule and plan, arrange stock, and employ counters.
4. Send written instructions on the techniques to be used, with

the advance announcement, to provide for a uniform inventory taking. Include uniform forms and schedules.

5. Train and send observers to key locations. This will ensure that the proper techniques are used and an accurate inventory is taken.
6. Preprint items to be taken rather than leaving it up to each location to determine whether something is inventory.

> FOR EXAMPLE: Are tools inventory or assets; do we count shipping supplies?

7. Count twice or verify all high-value items.
8. Log in inventory schedules from all locations, to be sure none are missing, and log out all costed and extended completed schedules, for the same reason.
9. Establish verification edits to recheck specified quantities, costs, extensions, and footings.

Inventory control is further gained through inventory analysis, which, in the case of many items, requires a computerized assist. Reports should be prepared to:

❖ Analyze inventory investment through usage distribution reports.
❖ Identify imbalances in the inventory through inventory turnovers.
❖ Evaluate the levels of customer service at each inventory segment.
❖ Examine both direct and indirect inventory costs.

The technique to accomplish this control is as follows:

❖ Survey inventory records and determine the adequacy of available data and the probability of obtaining useful results.
❖ If adequate data does not exist, begin to create it and to accumulate meaningful information for future analysis.

✧ Take into effect abnormalities as to lead time, cyclical patterns of demand, unusual cost.
✧ Select random samples and gather data as follows:
   1. Classify by dollar value of usage and level carried.
   2. Obtain amount of investment in slow-moving stock and turn-over times.
   3. Evaluate inventory controls, ordering techniques, and areas of improvement.
   4. Obtain space requirements and how well they are utilized.

After analyzing the resultant reports, the following gains can be expected:

1. The size of the inventory investment can be reduced.
2. The balance of inventories can be improved.
3. Customers will receive better service.
4. Costs, both direct and indirect, can be reduced.
5. Better inventory control procedures will be established.

Legal Liaison

The responsibility for the interrelationships between the company and corporate counsel is not specific to the FEI financial definitions. Where house counsel does not exist, these relationships are often assigned to a specific officer, most usually the treasurer or the controller. The controller's authority derives from the evaluating and consulting function "concerning any phase of the operation of the business as it relates to the attainment of objectives." The treasurer's authority is related to his or her investor relations function, in that his or her maintainance of a market for the company's securities and "adequate liaison with invest-ment bankers, financial analysts, and shareholders," carries with it the need for legal liaison.

The corporate policy manual (see page 246) should specify the responsibility for legal liaison under the caption lawsuits or legal review. This should clearly indicate:

✧ Who initiates legal contacts.
✧ Who responds to summonses or legal letters.
✧ Who signs contracts (and contracts need to be defined).

Such a statement of policy is necessary to avoid unauthorized and continuing legal expenses. These legal actions sometimes take years to develop, and some legal firms bill only at the end of the case. More important, legal action results in counteractions, and the effect on the corporation can be significant. This should be controlled, therefore, at the higher management levels.

LOANS TO EMPLOYEES

Loans to officers and employees may be subject to state, federal, corporate charter, banking, SEC, and accounting rules and principles. They should not, therefore, be handled through normal disbursing channels as are travel advances or expense reimbursements. A travel advance not supported quickly by an expense report becomes, in effect, a loan to the employee that should become the treasurer's responsibility. The treasurer's authority is defined by the FEI under the banking and custody and credit and collections functions.

Each employee's loan should be supported by a demand note receivable and a **loan agreement letter**, shown as Exhibit 11-4. The terms of the agreement letter will be such to protect the company in terms of the various rules and principles cited above. The exhibited letter contains the following features:

✧ The loan is payable on demand.
✧ The purpose of the loan is personal and not for stock purchases.
✧ Stock owned or to be purchased will be held as collateral.
✧ A repayment schedule is specified, subject to call on demand by the company, at any time.
✧ A nonusurious interest rate is specified.
✧ Authorization for repayment through payroll deduction is given.

Exhibit 11-4.   Loan agreement letter.

LOAN AGREEMENT LETTER

FROM: Treasurer
  TO: Employee
DATE: 10/30/

SUBJECT: Loan - $2,100

Effective October 19, 20xx, we are making a $2,100 loan to you.
This loan will be evidenced by a demand note, in the amount of
$2,100, plus 6% per annum interest.

We understand that this loan is for personal purposes and that you
herewith authorize payroll deductions, over a 2 1/2 year period
(65 bi-weekly payroll deductions, to include principal plus interest).

If, at any time during the tenure of this loan, you exercise any of
your ABC stock options, you agree that ABC will hold this stock as
collateral for repayment of the loan. During this period, if you
sell shares of stock that we are holding as collateral, the
proceeds will be used to repay the loan and any balance will be
returned to you.

It is clearly understood that the purpose of this loan is not to
purchase option shares of ABC stock.

You further understand that this is a demand note that is callable
at any time, at ABC's option. It is not our present intention to
demand payment of this note, as evidenced by the 2 1/2 years of
payroll deductions that are being made above, but ABC retains the
right to discontinue these payroll deductions and to call for payment
of the remaining balance on the demand note, at any time, at its
option.

_____
Treasurer

                                    AGREED TO AND ACCEPTED

                                    _____

                                    Date:_____

MANAGING PEOPLE

Every manager, whatever his or her position with the company, has a
responsibility to the people he or she manages—to bring out the best
in them, to permit them to fulfill the requirements of their jobs with

maximum effectiveness, to recognize their potential for promotion—all with a view toward simplifying attainment of the corporate profit objectives.

Managing people requires structuring a proper operational framework, through the use of position descriptions, organization charts, standard operating procedures, policy manuals, and other administrative aids as described in Chapter 7. Everyone must know what the job is, to whom he or she reports, and what is expected.

Personnel management is discussed in some detail in Chapter 14 under Controlling the Data Processing Function. The principles set forth, a management philosophy, setting a management example, and management by objectives, are applicable, equally, to the treasurer's and controller's management of other departments and people reporting to them.

Management Philosophy

While the development of a management philosophy is an element of managing people, it is of concomitant importance in the controller's functions of planning for control and reporting and interpreting. The plan for control and the formulation of reporting policies should be shaped, in tone and style, by the controller's philosophy of management, which will be attuned to that of the corporate hegemony as it relates to her or his own field of control. There are three rudimentary requirements to developing a management philosophy:

1. *Artistry.* The controller must acquire, possess, and demonstrate a superb command of his or her craft. The controller will bring to the profession an educational background in accounting, finance, taxes, and management. This will be honed with continuing professional educational courses given by local chapters of the state CPA society, the Institute for Management Accountants, or the American Management Association. Proficiency will be maintained by extensive reading of:

a. *The Journal of Accountancy*—published by the AICPA and oriented to an overview of the profession.
b. *Management Accounting* and *Strategic Finance*—both published by the IMA, and pointed to specific technical accounting areas.
c. FASB releases—published by the Financial Accounting Standards Board, consisting of exposure drafts of discussion memoranda, interpretations, and pronouncements relating to accounting principles.

Helpful Hint: The FASB publishes a periodic status report, and the AICPA, *The CPA Letter,* a monthly news report for members of the AICPA. Each is in pamphlet form, approximately four pages, and deals with current and projected studies, SEC trends in accounting, auditing standards, management advisory service issues, and other current developments.

d. *The Accounting Review*—a quarterly publication of the American Accounting Association, consisting of academic treatments of theoretical problems in accounting—presenting a thorough analysis of current issues in the profession.
e. *The Financial Executive*—published by the Financial Executives Institute, dealing with current issues of interest to the financial manager, and augmented with position papers on SEC and accounting proposals by the profession or other regulatory agencies.
f. SEC releases—distributed to registered companies, directly by the SEC. These releases are proposals for changes and Accounting Series Releases (ASRs) initiating changes.
g. Monthly business magazines—Any one of several business monthlies will keep the controller abreast of current business developments and practices, and will demonstrate the applicability of the technical positions previously studied in a through f. Typical are *Forbes, Business Week, Dun's Review, U.S. News & World Report, Finance.*
h. Business dailies—*The Wall Street Journal* and *Journal of Commerce* provide on-the-spot information on current trends and developments.
i. CPA magazines—published by the various state societies for CPA members.

This would appear to be a massive amount of reading, but it is not. Each publication need only be scanned for special articles of interest, and those often can be scanned or sight-read for pertinent matter. See page 299 for tax literature sources.

This reading will be put to good use in thousands of ways—during the conduct of the year-end audit, in formulating interim accounting policies, in creating new operating techniques and evaluating old ones. They are the colors on the controller's palette with which he or she appoints the operating picture.

2. *Creativity.* The artistry of the controller must express itself, not in a me-too approach to management, but with originality. One cannot copy systems, procedures, forms, and operating techniques from other companies, even competitors. Every business is different, and every organization, composed of individuals, is different. The successful controller will use his or her artistry as a departure point from which to create a plan of operations that is unique and suitable to the company.

3. *Excitement.* The artistic and creative controller will almost certainly, without trying, engender in the company an enthusiasm and excitement that breeds success. The controller or treasurer, using the management accounting techniques described in these chapters, is surely as innovative and original in his or her planning and fruition of the corporate plan as any novelist, painter, or film-maker.

> *Helpful Hint:* Hold monthly staff meetings with your people to apprise them of plans and current developments, to keep them enthused and excited about the job everyone is doing. One-on-one meetings during the month aren't as good. They're usually too concerned with specific operating details and exigencies of the moment.

MONITORING AND REPORTING ON PERSONNEL PERFORMANCE

The reports previously defined in Chapter 8 concerned budget performance as it relates to the operating plan. Those reports are generally prepared in financial statement format.

In addition, the reports exhibited under the management by objectives section, in Chapter 14, measure the performance of all managers and personnel, in all departments, against stated objectives. These reports are quantified, but they are mostly nonfinancial.

Similarly, there are objective reports that may be designed for any department. Typical of these are reports that pertain to the performance of the personnel department and that constitute a measure of the efficacy with which personnel policies and procedures are practiced. These reports include:

1. **Employee turnover**, shown in Exhibit 11-5. The turnover total is sometimes shown as a percentage of total starting employment, and sometimes as a percentage of average employment over the period. Whichever method is used, it should be consistently applied from period to period. The advantage of calculating percentage turnover based on starting employment is to demonstrate performance in retaining employees for all days during the period studied based on an initial target. However, for long periods, such as an annual turnover report, average turnover gives a more meaningful statistic than turnover based on starting employment. In short periods, such as monthly or quarterly reports, the variation is small and may be ignored. Turnover percentage should be compared to prior periods and to industry statistics. Turnover reports should be prepared by department to identify high-cost areas. Excessive

Exhibit 11-5. Employee turnover calculation.

<table>
<tr><td colspan="3" align="center">ABC Corporation
Employee Turnover
For the Three Months Ended March 31, 20__</td></tr>
<tr><td></td><td>Last Yr.</td><td>This Yr.</td></tr>
<tr><td>1. Head count at 1/1</td><td>450</td><td>500</td></tr>
<tr><td>2. Hires 1/1–3/31</td><td>75</td><td>100</td></tr>
<tr><td>3.</td><td>525</td><td>600</td></tr>
<tr><td>4. Head count at 3/31</td><td>475</td><td>550</td></tr>
<tr><td>5. Turnover 1/1–3/31</td><td>50</td><td>50</td></tr>
<tr><td>6. Average head count [(1 + 4)/2]</td><td>463</td><td>525</td></tr>
<tr><td>7. Turnover percentage (5/6)</td><td>10.8%</td><td>9.5%</td></tr>
</table>

turnover is costly. Turnover is also a measure of hiring and personnel management techniques.

2. *Absenteeism and lateness.* These reports should be prepared by department to identify weak areas. They should show total work days in the period, number of days late or absent, and the percentage of such incidence.

3. *Tenure.* This report, again by department, will show tenure in years and months (3–11 would represent 3 years and 11 months). An average total should be shown for the department and the company. Prior period comparisons should be exhibited. Obviously, shortened tenure will show weakness in leadership and in benefit programs.

4. *Cross-training.* This report will list each department on one page and will show the number of employees who are cross-trained in one or more jobs, the percentage cross-trained, and the comparison to prior periods.

5. *Miscellaneous.* Other reports can be tailored to benefit programs, such as the number and percentage enrolled in educational assistance programs or in the savings and retirement program—always compared to prior periods.

PRODUCT PRICING CONTROL

The responsibility for pricing products is found in the FEI controllership functions definitions under the planning for control heading, "cost standards," and in the evaluating and consulting function, as costs relate to pricing policies.

Inherent in this responsibility are the interrelationships between accounting, marketing, and selling divisions. **Procedures must be designed to coordinate all these areas of the business**, to supply them with proper costing information, and to obtain the necessary approvals before publishing any prices.

One such procedure is shown at Exhibit 11-6. It is characterized

(*text continues on page 445*)

Exhibit 11-6.   Product pricing procedure.

STANDARD OPERATING PROCEDURE					
Subject:				Number	HOP M-550
				Page of	
	PRODUCT PRICING			1	8
				Effective Date 7/2/	
Supersedes Cor. No.	Page	Dated		Related	
246	1	3/10/		S.O.P./H.O.P.	

PURPOSE:	To establish a responsibility for the coordination of all phases of the introduction of a new product, and to provide a means for the establishment and approval and distribution of prices, price changes on all products, and assignment of product codes.
EXHIBITS:	1. Notification of Vendor Pricing, Exhibit A 2. Cost/Pricing Product Sheet, Exhibit B 3. Price Book Cover Sheet, Exhibit C 4. Price Book Pricing Sheet, Exhibit D
SUMMARY:	This procedure deals with the responsibility for the coordination of all phases of a new product, from the introduction, product codes assignment stages, to establishing new pricing and changes to existing item/product pricing, the preparation of the required forms and subsequent distribution of same, to expedite items/products introduction and established items/products pricing.

METHOD:

A. ROUTING OF NEW VENDOR PRICES AND ASSIGNMENT OF PRODUCT CODES

PURCHASING DEPT.:		1. Prepares a five (5) part Notification of Vendor Pricing Form (attached as Exhibit A), one form for each item/product involved, upon receipt of a Vendor invoice changing a price for an existing item/product, or when a new item/product is ordered.
	NOTE:	For each item/product, a separate Notification of Vendor Pricing Form is required. Multiple items/products *are* *not* to be transcribed to a single Notification of Vendor Pricing Form.

HOP Correction No: 253
Date Prepared: 6/19/

HOP M-550

STANDARD OPERATING PROCEDURE		
Subject: PRODUCT PRICING	Number HOP M-550	
	Page of 2 8	
	Effective Date 7/2/	
Supersedes Cor. No. Page Dated 246 2 4/2/	Related S.O.P./H.O.P.	

PURCHASING DEPT.: *CON'T*	2. If a new item/product is involved, pulls the Purchasing Follow-up File copy (last) of the Notification of Vendor Pricing Form and forwards the balance of the set to Order/Billing for assignment of the appropriate Product Code.
	3. Files the Purchasing Follow-up File copy (last) of the Notification of Vendor Pricing Form, in the Follow-up File, *two (2) working days* from the date of issuance.
	4. If a change in price, holds for step 9, below.
ORDER/BILLING DEPT.:	5. Assigns Product Code and updates the Master List.
	6. Issues memo to List 5.0 (Execs., Staff, & Dept. Heads) announcing Product Code assignment.
	7. Dates and initials Purchasing/Data Processing Department copy (original) of Notification of Vendor Pricing Form in the space provided, signifying the Product Code assignment and:
	a. Posts the newly assigned Product Code to Order/ Billing Departments Product Master File.
	b. Forwards balance of Notification of Vendor Pricing Forms to the Purchasing Department.
PURCHASING DEPT.:	8. Removes the Purchasing Follow-up File copy (last) of the Notification of Vendor Pricing Form from Follow-up File, and posts the newly assigned Product Code to same, and refiles in the Follow-up File.
	9. Affixes all applicable back-up vendor documentation to verify and support changes in item/product price(s), to the balance of the Notification of Vendor Pricing Forms and forwards complete package to the Accounting Department.

HOP Correction No: 253
Date Prepared: 6/19/

HOP M-550

(continued)

Exhibit 11-6. *(continued)*

STANDARD OPERATING PROCEDURE		
Subject: PRODUCT PRICING	Number HOP M-550	
	Page of 3 8	
	Effective Date 7/2/	
Supersedes Cor. No. Page Dated 246 3 4/2/	Related S.O.P./H.O.P.	

ACCOUNTING DEPT.:	10. Reviews Notification of Vendor Pricing Forms and verifies costs submitted from the Purchasing Department by examining all applicable back-up documentation.
	11. Obtains Savicopy of quotations.
	12. Requests back-up support when memos are submitted concerning costs.
	13. Prepares a new Cost/Pricing Product Sheet (attached as Exhibit B) for: **a. New Items/Products** **b. Items/Products having a sufficient change in cost to affect profitability.**
	14. Calculates appropriate duty and freight.
	15. Establishes retail, dealer, and Murritt prices using standard margins and markups.
	16. Submits completed new Cost/Pricing Product Sheet to the appropriate Product Manager, for approval.
	17. Retains balance of Notification of Vendor Pricing Forms and attached applicable back-up Vendor documentation.
B. ESTABLISHMENT OF NEW PRICES AND PRICE CHANGES	
PRODUCT MANAGER:	18. Reviews submitted prices on Cost/Pricing Product Sheet and either approves or recommends changes to prices, indicating same on the Cost/Pricing Product Sheet.
	19. Submits the Cost/Pricing Product Sheet to the Executive Vice President for approval.
EXECUTIVE VICE PRESIDENT:	20. Reviews existing prices, recommended changes thereto, and new prices on the basis of:

HOP Correction No: 253
Date Prepared: 6/19/

HOP M-550

STANDARD OPERATING PROCEDURE		
Subject: PRODUCT PRICING	Number HOP M-550	
	Page of 4 8	
	Effective Date 7/2/	
Supersedes Cor. No. 246	Page 4	Dated 4/2/	Related S.O.P./H.O.P.

EXECUTIVE VICE PRESIDENT: *CON'T*	a. Increase or decrease in costs. b. Increase or decrease in Sales volume. c. Unsolicited comments from Customers. d. Competitive Prices. e. Current economic conditions. 21. Confers with the Sales and Marketing Divisions to determine approval of recommended pricing. 22. Approves or changes submitted prices, indicating same on the Cost/Pricing Product Sheet. 23. Advises the President if recommended pricing is in accordance with established margins or higher than the established margins. 24. Confers with the Accounting and Marketing Divisions if price recommendations submitted by Accounting differ from Marketing's. 25. Reviews recommended price changes for approval. 26. Submits recommended price changes with applicable backup papers to the President for approval.
PRESIDENT:	27. Reviews submitted price changes for approval. 28. Returns approved or changed prices with Cost/Pricing Product Sheet to the Executive Vice President.
EXECUTIVE VICE PRESIDENT:	29. Reviews approved or changed prices. 30. Returns approved or changed prices to the Accounting Department. 31. Notifies the Customer Service Department, applicable Product Managers, and Director of Advertising of new and/or changes to prices.
ACCOUNTING DEPT.:	32. Upon receipt of approved or recommended price changes to the Cost/Pricing Product Sheet from the Executive Vice President, retrieves balance of the Noti-

HOP Correction No: 253
Date Prepared: 6/19/

HOP M-550

(continued)

Exhibit 11-6   *(continued)*

STANDARD OPERATING PROCEDURE		
Subject: PRODUCT PRICING	Number HOP M–550	
	Page of **5** **8**	
	Effective Date 7/2/	

Supersedes Cor. No.
          246
	Page
	          5
		Dated
		          4/2/

(continued row: Related S.O.P./H.O.P.)

ACCOUNTING DEPT.:
Con't.

fication of Vendor Pricing Forms, dates and initials Purchasing/Data Processing Department copy (original) of Notification of Vendor Pricing Form/package and affixes all backup Vendor Price/Change documentation and Cost/Pricing Product Sheet to Notification of Vendor Pricing Forms.

33. Forwards the complete Notification of Vendor Pricing Forms package and attached backup documentation (Cost/Pricing Product Sheet & Vendor Price/Change documentation) to the Vice President/Controller for approval.

VICE PRESIDENT/
CONTROLLER:

34. Reviews Notification of Vendor Pricing package (Cost/Pricing Product Sheet and Vendor Price/Change Pricing documentation) and either approves or disapproves recommended pricing.

35. *If the Notification of Vendor Pricing package is disapproved:* confers with the Executive Vice President to resolve pricing.

36. *If the Notification of Vendor Pricing package is approved:* indicates same in the appropriate space provided, and forwards complete package to the Accounting Department.

ACCOUNTING DEPT.:

37. Enters the established (approved) Retail and Lowest Dealer Prices to the Purchasing/Data Processing Department copy (original) of the Notification of Vendor Pricing Form and dates and initials in the appropriate space provided.

38. Pulls and retains for Accounting files the Accounting Department copy of the Notification of Vendor Pricing Form, and the Cost/Pricing Form, and forwards to the Order/Billing Department for reference and file.

HOP Correction NO: 253
Date Prepared: 6/19/

HOP M-550

STANDARD OPERATING PROCEDURE		
Subject:	Number	HOP M-550
PRODUCT PRICING	Page of	6 8
	Effective Date	7/2/

Supersedes Cor. No.	Page	Dated	Related
246	6	4/2/	S.O.P./H.O.P.

ACCOUNTING DEPT.:
Con't.

39. Removes the Order/Billing Department copy of the Notification of Vendor Pricing Form, and forwards to the Order/Billing Department, for reference and. file.

C. DISTRIBUTION OF PRICE CHANGES

ACCOUNTING DEPT.:

40. Distributes specifications, costs, applicable Vendor Price/Change backup documentation, and prices to the Purchasing Department, for costs keeping and further/ future pricing.
41. Forwards the balance of the Notification of Vendor Pricing Forms to the Data Processing Department, for completion of master items list/cards containing costs and product codes from Order/Billing Department.

DATA PROCESSING DEPT.:

42. Enters applicable information (Cost, Lowest Dealer Price, List Price, Product Code, and item/product description) from the Notification of Vendor Pricing Form, and updates Product Files.

43. Initials and dates Notification of Vendor Pricing Form, bursts form, and returns the Purchasing/Data Processing Department copy (original) to the Purchasing Department.
44. Retains the Data Processing Department copy (2nd) of the Notification of Vendor Pricing Form for Data Processing Files.

PURCHASING DEPT.:

45. Clears follow-up file, and files Purchasing/Data Processing Department copy (original) of Notification of Vendor Pricing Form in permanent Files.

CUSTOMER SERVICE DEPT.:

46. Prepares a new pricebook release or a correction to the pricebook announcing the new prices.

HOP Correction No: 253
Date Prepared: 6/19/

HOP M-550

(continued)

Exhibit 11-6 *(continued)*

STANDARD OPERATING PROCEDURE		
Subject: PRODUCT PRICING	Number HOP M-550	
	Page of 7 8	
	Effective Date 7/2/	
Supersedes Cor. No. 246	Page 7	Dated 4/2/	Related S.O.P./H.O.P.

CUSTOMER SERVICE DEPT.:	47. Distributes new Price Book Pricing Sheet (Exhibit D) with Price Book Cover Sheet (attached as Exhibit C) to the Executive Vice President, Vice President/Marketing, Vice President/Controller, Accounting Services Manager, appropriate Product Manager, and President, for approval initials on the Price Sheet.
	48. Distributes initialed pricebook additions as follows:
	  a. Dealer Prices:
	    List 5.0-Execs., Staff, & Department Heads
	    List 7.1-Dealers
	    List 8.1-Br. Admins & Br. Managers
	    List 10.1-Overseas Affiliates
	  b. Retail Prices:
	    List 5.0-Execs., Staff, & Department Heads
	    List 8.1-Br. Admins. & Br. Managers
	    List 9.1-Service Managers

PRODUCT MANAGER/ DIRECTOR OF ADVER-TISING	49. Coordinates with the Executive Vice President on preparing Marketing Memos, Production Specification Sheets, and Advertising requirements.
	50. Prepares Marketing Memos, Product Specification Sheets, and Advertising releases as required.
	51. Distributes Marketing Memos and Product Specification Sheets as follows:
	  a. List 6.0-Field Sales Personnel
	  b. List 9.0-Field Service Personnel

CREDIT DEPT., CUSTOMER SERVICE DEPT., ORDER/ BILLING DEPT., PARTS DEPT. OF WAREHOUSE, AND BRANCHES:	52. Screens all orders held, such as Standing Orders, Quarterly Orders, Advance Orders, Credit Hold Orders, Back Orders, and adjusts price as follows:

STANDARD OPERATING PROCEDURE		
Subject: PRODUCT PRICING	Number HOP M-550	
	Page of **8** **8**	
	Effective Date 7/2/	

Supersedes Cor. No.
    246
	Page Dated
	  8 4/2/
		Related
		S.O.P./H.O.P.

CREDIT DEPT., CUSTOMER SERVICE DEPT., ORDER/ BILLING DEPT., PARTS DEPT. OF WAREHOUSE, AND BRANCHES:
    Con't.

52. a. *Price Increase.* No adjustment necessary if order date prior to effective date of the increase.
    b. *Prior Decrease.* Adjust prices in customer's favor.

D. SPECIAL PRICES-RETAIL

BRANCH MANAGER:

53. May authorize deviations from published prices within the guidelines set by the applicable zone General Manager, or set forth in SOP.

E. SPECIAL PRICES-DEALER

DISTRICT MANAGER: (DEALER REPRESENTA- TIVE)

54. Prepares Dealer Change of Status Form requesting Special Prices.
55. Forwards Dealer Change of Status Form in accordance with SOP C-6e.

EXECUTIVE VICE PRESI- DENT: MANAGER, NATIONAL DEALER MAN- AGER:

56. Reviews Dealer Price Book every six (6) months and continues or discontinues Special Pricing in effect.

F. NATIONAL ACCOUNTS

BRANCH MANAGER:

57. Forwards request for National Account Pricing upon request of Customer or sales representative to the National Accounts Manager.

NATIONAL ACCOUNTS MANAGER:

58. Approves National Account pricing and prepares a National Account Memo and distributes it to Lists 5.0, 7.1, and 8.1.

INQUIRIES:

Executive Vice President, Vice President/Controller, and Director of Purchasing, Manager—Accounting Services.

DISTRIBUTION:

List 11.0 HOP Manual Holders

(*continued*)

Exhibit 11-6. *(continued)*

NOTIFICATION OF VENDOR PRICING

FROM: _____   DATE: __/__/_____

☐ NEW ITEM   ☐ PRICE CHANGE

⑥   _____ⓐ_____   _____ⓑ_____   _____ⓒ_____   _____ⓓ_____
        PRODUCT TYPE   VENDOR NAME   INVOICE NUMBER   INVOICE DATE

ACCOUNTING DEPARTMENT
ONLY

NEW RETAIL   NEW (LOWEST) DEALER

☐☐☐☐☐☐ _____ⓕ_____   ☐☐☐☐☐☐ _____ⓗ_____
13   18 EXISTING RETAIL   19   24 OLD (LOWEST) DEALER
   ⓔ   ⓖ

        PRODUCT CODE   ITEM/PRODUCT DESCRIPTION
   ⓘ ☐☐☐☐   ☐☐☐☐☐☐☐☐☐☐☐☐☐☐ ⓙ
      9   12   31   45

        NEW COST
   ⓚ ☐☐☐☐☐☐   _____ⓛ_____
      25   30   OLD COST

ON HAND INVENTORY LEVEL: _____

ORDER/BILLING DEPT.:   DATE PRODUCT CODE ASSIGNED: __/__/ BY _____
ACCOUNTING DEPT.:   DATE PRICING APPROVED: __/__/ BY _____
VICE PRESIDENT/CONTROLLER: DATE APPROVED: __/__/ BY _____
DATA PROCESSING DEPT.:   DATE KEYPUNCHED: __/__/ BY _____

INSTRUCTIONS

NEW ITEMS:
Purchasing Dept. prepares one form for each item involved and completes items a through d and j and k, above.
Order/Billing Dept. completes item i, above.
Accounting Dept. completes items e and g, above.
Data Processing Dept. enters items e, g, and i through k, above.

PRICE CHANGES:
Purchasing Dept. prepares one form for each item involved and completes items a through d and i through l, above.
Accounting Dept. completes items e through h, above.
Data Processing Dept. enters items e, g, and i through k, above.

DISTRIBUTION: 1) Purchasing/Data Processing Dept. 2) Data Processing Dept. 3) Accounting Dept.
                4) Order/billing Dept. 5) Purchasing Follow-Up File

(0-5-3)   HOP M-550

COST/PRICING PRODUCT SHEET

Product _____

( ) New Product   ( ) Change   Date: __/__/__   By: _____   Product Code _____

Unit of Measure _____

Retail Sales	Unit of Measure	Control Prod. No:	Accounting	Marketing	Approved Pricing	Direct Costs Excluding Commissions to Salesmen			
						Cost Element	Retail	Dealer	Other
Recommended Price (S)	_____	$.				Raw Cost (Eff Date, Vendor, FOB Point, Currency Basis, Unit)			
% Gross Profit		. %							
% Mark-Up on Cost . .		. %							
% Commission		. %							
$ Commission		$.							
Retail - Rentals	Unit of Measure								
Recommended Price (S)	_____	$.							
% Gross Profit		. %							
% Mark-Up on Cost . .		. %							
%Commission		. %							
$ Commission	Unit of Measure	$.				Brokerage			
						Duty at %			
Dealer						Insurance & Handling to Main Warehouse			
Recommended Price (S)	_____	$.				Freight - in to Main Warehouse			
% Gross Profit		. %				Royalty: % or $; Base: ; Name:			
% Mark-Up on Cost . .		. %				Royalty: % or $; Base: ; Name:			
% Commission		. %				Royalty: % or $; Base: ; Name:			
$ Commission		$.							
Major Account	Unit of Measure								
Recommended Price (S)	_____	$.							
% Gross Profit		. %							
% Mark-Up on Cost . .		. %							
% Commission		. %							
$ Commission		$.							
SA - Sales	Unit of Measure					Freight - out - Main Warehouse to Branch			
						Freight - out - to Customer			
						Special Packing, Handling, or Rigging			
Recommended Price (S)	_____	$.				Sales or Other Tax if Unbilled to Cust.			
% Gross Profit		. %							
% Mark-Up on Cost . .		. %							
% Commission		. %							
$ Commission		$.							
SA - Sales	Unit of Measure								
Recommended Price (S)	_____	$.							
% Gross Profit		. %							
% Mark-Up on Cost . .		. %							
% Commission		. %							
$ Commission		$.							
Other _____	Unit of Measure								
Recommended Price (S)	_____	$.							
% Gross Profit		. %							
% Mark-Up on Cost . .		. %							
% Commission		. %							
$ Commission		$.				Total Cost			

Gross Profit - Profit/Price   Mark-Up Cost - Profit/Cost

Price Approved   Cost Approved

( )	( )	( )	( )	( )	( )	( )	( )	( )	( )	( )	( )
V.P. Mktg.	Exec. V.P.	Prod. Mgr.	V.P./Contr.	Pres.	Dir. Mgr.			Purch. Mgr.	Acctg. Mgr	V.P./Contr	

(continued)

Exhibit 11-6. *(continued)*

PRICE BOOK COVER SHEET
FOR
PRODUCT PRICING PROCEDURE
HOP M–550

_____
PRODUCT NO.

DATE _/_ _/_____

_____( ) NEW PRODUCT _____ ( ) CHANGE _____

_____ _ _/_ _/_____

EXECUTIVE VICE PRESIDENT   DATE   ( ) APPROVED   ( ) CHANGED

COMMENTS:_____
_____
_____

_____ _ _/_ _/_____

VICE PRESIDENT MARKETING   DATE   ( ) APPROVED   ( ) CHANGED

COMMENTS: _____ _____
_____
_____

_____ _ _/_ _/_____

VICE PRESIDENT/CONTROLLER   DATE   ( ) APPROVED   ( ) CHANGED

COMMENTS: _____
_____
_____

_____ _ _/_ _/_____

ACCOUNTING SERVICES MGR.   DATE   ( ) APPROVED   ( ) CHANGED

COMMENTS:_____
_____
_____

( ) W.P.   ( ) FAX   ( ) COPIERS

_____ _ _/_ _/_____

PRODUCT MANAGER   DATE   ( ) APPROVED   ( ) CHANGED

COMMENTS:_____
_____
_____

_____ _ _/_ _/_____

PRESIDENT   DATE   ( ) APPROVED   ( ) CHANGED

COMMENTS:_____
_____
_____

FORWARD TO
( ) CUSTOMER SERVICE MANAGER

PRICE BOOK							
Subject:						Page of	
						Effective Date	
Supersedes Cor. No.		Page		Dated		Date Prepared	
Approved By:	Pres.	Exec. V.P. V.P./Mktg.	V.P./Contr.	Acctg./Svc.	Prod. Mg.	Correction Number	

Appropriate Product Manager's initials signifying approval of Product Pricing release.

(*text continued from page 433*)
by a smooth flow of information from the purchasing department, which initiates the cost change, to the order/billing department, which codes the product for data processing purposes, to the accounting department, which establishes pricing at standard markups, to marketing product managers who review and recommend prices, to appropriate officers who review the recommendations of marketing and accounting in light of corporate objectives, back to accounting for distribution of approved prices to all departments, to the data processing department to revise related DP files, to the customer service department for price book issuance, to product managers for marketing circularization, and to customers.

Product pricing control is the "top line" in generating profits. A coordinated procedure, administered by the controller, is essential to assuring that these top-line profits are brought home.

PROFIT IMPROVEMENT PROGRAMS

Sometimes called PIP, cost reduction, cost control, or plain cost cutting, these programs are continuous with some companies, explosions with others. The determination as to whether they are ongoing or sporadic will depend on the company and its officers' philosophy of management.

The best program is probably a compromise between the two methods. Cost controls need to be maintained on a continuing basis. But there is slippage in every system, and a periodic tightening of controls will always produce savings.

The origination, implementation, control, and reporting of these profit improvement programs is usually assigned to the controller and should, in fact, be initiated by him or her independently. Most of the FEI defined functions serve as the authority for the controller's role in PIP—planning for control (procedures to effectuate the plan), reporting and interpreting (the coordination of systems and procedures), evaluating and consulting (the attainment of objectives and the effectiveness of policies), and the protection of assets (through internal control, internal auditing).

The following areas should be reviewed in cost control programs:

1. *Advertising and promotion.* May be discontinued with no deleterious effects for brief periods of time. Promotional work in the securities and investor relations area may also be curtailed.

2. *Branch offices or decentralized independent operations.* May be discontinued if they are direct loss operations. These are sometimes maintained for marketing purposes, to hold a national posture or provide a network of offices, which may be unnecessary in a short-run period.

3. *Cafeteria operations.* Are usually provided for employees at a loss. These can be closed and sandwich machines substituted, or the operation of the cafeteria may be contracted out to an independent service on a fixed-fee basis, thereby eliminating the loss. Problems such as food shortages and employee turnover are eliminated.

4. *Centralized purchasing.* May be employed where the company has many locations. A low limit, say $100, could be established and only items under that limit may be purchased in the local office. This procedure submits the over $100 purchase order to closer centralized (and less involved) scrutiny. Quantities and even need can be independently evaluated. There may be a personnel savings—a central office can do the same job with fewer people than many independent offices.

5. *Collections of accounts receivable.* May usually be decentralized without adding people. Most such work is done on the phone, and there

can be a significant saving in the telephone cost if it is done through the local office. Collection staff need not be added, since regular order takers may be trained to check credit lists or aged trial balances, and to obtain collections on the same phone call in which the order is taken.

6. *Commissions for salespeople.* May be restructured, raising them and eliminating base salary or guaranteed draw. This will tend to shake out the unproductive salespeople more quickly and to compensate the big producers more highly. Unit selling cost per salesperson will be reduced.

7. *Compensation policy.* Should be reviewed with regard to having quotas or bonus programs for salespeople and their managers. These programs work better in an expanding economy, but then, so do any programs. Quotas and bonuses can be eliminated at all levels and, instead, profit sharing can be substituted to give salespeople and managers a share in profits that equals last year's bonus (if the same level of profits is at least achieved), and also gives them 50% of the increase in net income (or any desired percentage), before such profit sharing. This type of program, if properly structured, should eliminate bonuses and extra commissions during periods when the company's profits are declining, due to disparities in product mix sales.

8. *Contests for salespeople or classes of customers.* May be eliminated with no short-run effect. Or, national contests (at high cost) may be eliminated in favor of less expensive local contests.

9. *Demonstration materials and free give-aways used by salespeople.* May be eliminated, or more carefully doled out by supervisors. Total amounts should be budgeted at lower levels.

10. *District offices and zone or outlying staff offices.* May be closed and operated out of other local sales offices. Some managers try to become empire builders, creating their own sphere of control—separate staff and offices that often duplicate other corporate functions.

11. *Forms.* May be produced by using computer software, eliminating the cost of buying blank form stock. Simply scan in your preclassifying forms and have them available on screen.

12. *Freight charges.* May be raised to more than offset the increase in freight costs. In many cases, freight and delivery charges are intended to be borne by the customer, but they are not, because of creeping increases in freight costs that are accepted at lower levels and not called

to management's attention. Freight companies do not send out formal notices of rate increases—they just happen.

Helpful Hint: Freight charges should be reviewed periodically by an outside freight specialist, who will check the rates charged by carriers. This type of review is done on a contingency basis, with the specialist receiving 30% of the first year's savings. This is an arrangement similar to the periodic insurance review.

13. *Inventory controls.* Are a continuous and ongoing program, as discussed on page 424. Costs are controlled and profits improved by good inventory taking and good inventory management. However, some immediate steps can be taken if there are inventory losses. A guard can be hired for sensitive areas during working hours and alarm systems connected to detective services installed for night hours. One guard can watch a vast inventory area using in-house television monitoring. If necessary, undercover agents can be used to staff working crews to protect against mysterious disappearances of inventory. An immediate warehouse security system should be installed—see Exhibit 10-10—to prevent mysterious disappearance. Establish an immediate perpetual inventory control, a manual procedure, wherein the inventory clerk reports not to the warehouse manager, but to the accounting manager. He or she should control the location and picking of each order and spot-check and cycle-count inventories.

14. *Legal costs.* May be reduced by negotiating issues instead of litigating them. Settle, don't sue, in the short run to keep costs down. Hold off new issues until a later time—patent infringement suits and antitrust issues. Institute a legal liaison procedure and policy as described at page 426.

15. *Study the size of the product line.* Reduce it by eliminating loss items and leaders, which may not be necessary in the near term.

16. *Mail and messenger service.* May be curtailed with no loss in revenues. Mail once a day instead of picking up several times in the morning and afternoon. Eliminate messengers, limousines, and special delivery services.

17. *Office machines.* Should be examined for effective utilization.

PCs with word processing software can save 25% of a secretary's time. Dictating machines, even inexpensive portable tape recorders, can save the substantial time spent by an author and secretary in personal dictation.

18. *Office temporaries.* Should not be authorized and should be eliminated in interim periods of cost reduction. Regular staff will handle the work if it needs to be done.

19. *Order handling.* Can be streamlined to eliminate main office edits and reviews. Just give the order a cursory check and process it. Put teeth in this by penalizing salespeople for errors they make on the order. This can save personnel.

20. *Office services.* May be curtailed in central locations. Eliminate private secretaries in favor of a secretarial and typing pool. Add voice mail and automated telephone systems to reduce human intervention.

> *Helpful Hint:* This saves having to hire a new secretary every time a new managerial job is created. You simply don't have secretaries, using the pool instead.

Failing this extreme, double-up or quadruple-up on the use of secretaries, several managers sharing. Share by location of office, rather than division or type of work.

Other office service areas—clean and maintain premises twice weekly, instead of daily; have individual department heads do their own interviewing for new hires, bypassing personnel; examine dial 9 or centrex telephone systems to save on phone operators.

21. *Payroll costs.* May be reduced by simplifying payroll systems (see Zero-Balance Accounts and Imprest and Color-coded Accounts in Chapter 1). Reduce payroll taxes by outsourcing functions to independent contractors who may be former employees. Also, determine that portion of a salesperson's pay and earnings that is attributable to travel expenses, and therefore not subject to withholding or payroll taxes as wages. Consider your cost of handling payroll check writing and record keeping. Perhaps an outside payroll service will be more economical. This should be reviewed periodically, as the cost effectiveness will change with the type and amount of payrolls and number of people.

Other payroll-saving steps: Freeze wages over a limit, say $25,000 per year; grant wage increases under that limit only once each year, whether from merit, annual, or promotion, and then subject to a percentage limit, say a range of 5% to 10%; reduce salaries of key managers and officers by 10% to 20% if over $45,000 per year.

> *Helpful Hint:* Partially offset payroll reductions with company-paid insurance benefits. Under Sec. 79 of the IRC, company-paid term insurance in excess or discriminatory amounts is taxable to the employee, but only on the small excess amounts. This may be tied to split-dollar insurance with a cash surrender value that will exceed the employee's income tax. The company, thus, will obtain a tax-deductible expense, in full, and the employee will pay less tax. This makes it possible to reduce salary and offset it, partially, with an insurance benefit increase.

> *Helpful Hint:* Avoid personnel recruitment costs on hiring new or replacement employees by advancing agency fees and then recovering this from the employee over a six-month period, through payroll reductions. Caution: Some states do not permit such deductions unless they are an employee loan being repaid. Exhibit 11-7, **authorization for repayment of employee loans**, will satisfy this requirement in most states.

Freeze new hires; require two approvals on any replacements: review each individual job with the superior and determine the necessity for that job (there is probably 10% to 20% inefficiency built into every organization that does not practice continuing cost control); eliminate all overtime.

22. *Petty cash.* May be reduced in outlying offices by scheduling prompt central payments. The reduced fund results in reduced expenditures.

23. *Postage.* Can be budgeted at 80% of the previous run rate. Discontinue the use of priority mail, express mail, and overnight deliveries by companies such as Federal Express. Batch mail to repetitive locations; mail only once a day; defer direct mail programs.

24. *Price increases.* Should be effected, selectively, to pass on appropriate cost increases to customers. This requires good product

Exhibit 11-7. Authorization for repayment of employee loans.

AUTHORIZATION FOR REPAYMENT OF EMPLOYEE LOANS

I herewith acknowledge that I am accepting my position
with   Corporation ("   ") on
a "No Fee Paid By Company" basis, and that the payment
of my employment agency fee is my sole responsibility.

I have requested, and herewith acknowledge receipt of,
a loan of $_____ to pay this fee. I authorize
the employment agency listed below to record said amount
as a loan made to me.

I further authorize   to deduct twelve (12) equal
payments of $_____ each from my biweekly pay for
repayment of the above loan. Deductions shall commence
starting with my first full pay period.

Should my employment with   terminate for any
reason, prior to repayment in full of the above loan,
I agree to authorize deductions of any balance from my
accrued vacation or severence pay, if any. If, after
these deductions, there is any remaining balance, I
agree to pay it forthwith.

NAME OF AGENCY:_____

ADDRESS:_____

By:_____
   (Employee's Signature)

Date:_____

   _____
   (Location/Department)

pricing control as evidenced by the procedure at Exhibit 11-6, to avoid cost increases creeping through without pricing actions.

25. *Relocations of company personnel from one location to another.* Should be avoided. Relocation policy includes personnel benefits such as air fare to search for a home, home closing costs, fixing-up costs, costs and losses of moving from the old home, and interim hotel expenses. These far exceed the cost of hiring someone new in the immediate location. The benefit of the experienced employee in the relocated job is a short-lived one (in six months the new employee is experienced) and may be considerably offset by hiring someone experienced in the same industry.

26. *Reports.* That no one wants are often generated. See the report study evaluation discussed on page 526 and detailed on page 259. With such a study, many reports may be eliminated.

> *Reporting Hint:* Discontinue distribution of some reports that you suspect are not needed. See whether you get any complaints after two successive periods of nondistribution. If not, write the recipients and "tell them" you have discontinued the report because of lack of need. Always give an alternative source of the information, perhaps in another format.

27. *Second source.* Should be considered from suppliers. This may result in lower prices or reduced quantity ordering requirements. If quantities are large enough, purchases can be made from two sources, with the original vendor reducing the price to meet the second source. Alternatively, single sourcing may result in savings when two sources are being used to divide up insufficient quantities.

28. *Service support functions.* May be discontinued. This may include goodwill ambassadors, institutional showrooms, public relations personnel and services, or customer relations people who follow up on the salespeople. All will result in short-run savings, but the cost of discontinuing these services and then restarting them may obviate their discontinuance.

29. *Severance policy.* Should be defined, in writing, for terminated employees, particularly at times of layoffs. Superiors tend to soften the blow with extra severance pay.

Helpful Hint: Many companies pay one week of severance for each year of service, with a minimum of one week and a maximum of two months. Severance is a company option, not an employee right, and its grant should depend on the employee's cooperation and attitude.

30. *Shipping and distribution costs.* Should be studied by qualified in-house people or outside professionals every several years or when the company changes its distribution methods. Outside consulting firms will perform the initial analysis and teach future analyses to company personnel so that distribution costs may be monitored internally. Methods of shipping, routing, and warehousing are studied, together with effective space utilization for various types of inventories. In short, the "logistics" of shipping and distribution are studied. The result may be a shifting of inventories, storage in different locations, shipping in carload lots or containers, drop-shipping from vendors to customers, storage in bonded warehouses, shifting to consignment sales—but whatever the change, it will be cost-effective.

31. *Staff functions.* Much like service support functions, may be reviewed and reduced or eliminated. These would include levels of administrative or marketing management that are not direct to the operation. For example, four salespeople may have a team leader; four team leaders may report to a sales manager; two sales managers may report to a general manager. All levels between salesperson and general manager could be eliminated for limited periods without reducing sales effectiveness. Many headquarters employees, such as staff assistants, liaison managers, administrative assistants, secretaries, assistant supervisors, product managers, assistants to, are performing functions that could be reduced or discontinued without affecting the profit objective in the near term, and many of them are probably doing work that their superiors should be doing, or could be doing in tight times.

32. *Sundry expenses.* Are a catch-all category in any business used to record those expenses that cannot be classified in the chart of accounts as it presently exists. Sundry expenses are hard to analyze and control when they are improperly recorded this way. Eliminate the caption. When an item arises that does not fit the chart of accounts, add a caption to the chart that does fit. Provide for numbering expansion in the chart of accounts as shown in Exhibit 6-3 and discussed on page 201.

33. *Telephone expenses.* Are one of the most fruitful areas for cost control. Telephone calls may be eliminated by using facsimile devices or magnetic tape transmission over dial-up phone lines to central switching terminals. The efficacy of these systems depends on the volume of transmissions and the need for speed and accuracy.

Magnetic tape and diskette transmissions off word-processing equipment, through modems, may offer side benefits of being able to store correspondence on tape or disk, rather than in traditional files, as described in Chapter 13 on records retention.

Special self-dial systems may be used in place of operator-assisted telephone service. These are dial 7 or 9 systems, and Centrex systems, which completely bypass the operator. Long-distance calls are blocked out on these systems. Using a central in-house operator, only, for long distance keeps better control. Use a long-distance log and have the employee's supervisor initial every call; budget long-distance calls at 80% of prior levels; charge department heads 25¢ on each dollar in excess of the budgeted levels (do it as a contest to get cooperation, with the winner getting all contributions from the losers); eliminate interbranch phone calls; when calls must be made, direct dial to save 30% of the cost of the call if operator-assisted; require messages to be written, not phoned, to outlying offices; use the FAX in lieu of the phone; remove instruments from every desk—keep only one or two in a department; eliminate private wires and telephone numbers unless they fit into the phone system being used. Managers and executives abuse private numbers more than anyone; make long-distance calls after 6 P.M. to obtain lower rates; require supervisors to personally sign every FAX message before it is sent; consider digital, computer-driven phone software for high volume long-distance and international calls. The phone company is a rate oligopoly. It makes a guaranteed profit. You don't!

34. *Training expenses.* May be curtailed or eliminated for brief periods, in both the selling and administrative areas. As a substitute, use on-the-job training. Have new salespeople trail experienced ones. Have administrative, technical, and service personnel instructed in one step at a time, on-line, before proceeding to the next. Eliminate the costly travel and hotel expenses of central training courses; substitute

cassette tape training programs augmented with on-location in-house television or film projectors; design programmed learning courses, consisting of successive question and answer steps.

> *Helpful Hint:* Develop a competent salary level and benefits program to eliminate most employee turnover. This will keep training costs down for new employees and permit them to be trained on-the-job.

35. *Travel expenses.* Require special control. Employees often like to travel, create trips, and end up visiting friends and family and, as a side benefit, making a profit on their per-diem expenses.

> *Try These Steps:* Budget travel at 80% of previous levels; require a **travel authorization** (Exhibit 11-8) from all employees who do not customarily travel as a part of their jobs; require two levels of approval on employees who do customarily travel, one of which must be the division manager; do not permit approvers to delegate approving authority to secretaries or subordinates; discontinue all credit cards; do not pay meal expenses unless the travel is overnight; specify by title only those who are permitted to entertain; do not authorize or reimburse company employees who entertain other company employees — thus, eliminate working lunches or dinners; use a uniform **Statement of Reimbursable Expenses** form (Exhibit 11-9), which sets out some of the rules and limitations, and back these up with a written travel procedure.

36. *Typing of reports, interoffice memos, and schedules.* Can be reduced substantially, to take the load off the typing pool. Require: interoffice memos to be produced by the authors on PCs using word processing software or handwritten; reports are not typed unless for external or Board submission; all schedules are to be handwritten. Save the time to prepare, type, and proofread, when a single preparation will achieve the same result.

Answer correspondence by replying directly on the same letter,

Exhibit 11-8.   Travel authorization and travel advance request.

TRAVEL AUTHORIZATION AND TRAVEL ADVANCE REQUEST

EMPLOYEE NAME_____POSITION_____LOCATION_____

PRODUCT LINE_____

DIVISION   _____DEALER SALES   _____RETAIL SALES _____SERVICE

_____ADMIN.   _____WHSE.   _____OTHER
                                                              (Specify)

PURPOSE OF TRAVEL_____

_____

DEPARTURE DATE:_____ TRAVELING TO: _____

IS AIR TRAVEL INVOLVED?   _____

    YES _____   _____

    NO_____   _____

                                                   _____

NUMBER OF NIGHTS EXPECTED TO BE AWAY FROM HOME_____

TRANSPORTATION $_____

HOTEL, MEALS, ETC. $_____   PER AUTHORIZED EXPENSE LIST
                                               BOP 4.06.
OTHER (Explain) $_____

TOTAL ESTIMATED EXPENSES $_____

    TRAVEL ADVANCE REQUESTED?

    NO
                                               ADVANCE MAY NOT EXCEED TOTAL
    YES   AMOUNT REQUESTED $_____   ESTIMATED EXPENSES BY MORE THAN 10%

IF YES, IS AMOUNT TO BE ADVANCED BY HOME OFFICE_____PETTY CASH_____

TRAVEL AUTHORIZED BY_____TITLE_____

AIR TRAVEL AUTHORIZED BY_____TITLE_____

ATTACH COPY OF APPROVAL TELEX IF APPLICABLE.

photocopying it, and returning the original, or use snap-out carbon type speed memos. The degree of clarity and formality obtained on typewritten letters, for unimportant purposes, is unnecessary and costly.

Additional Profit Improvement Programs

There are additional major longer-range programs whose goal is to increase corporate profits, other than by eliminating or reducing line-by-line expenses. These include the following:

Exhibit 11-9. Statement of reimbursable expenses.

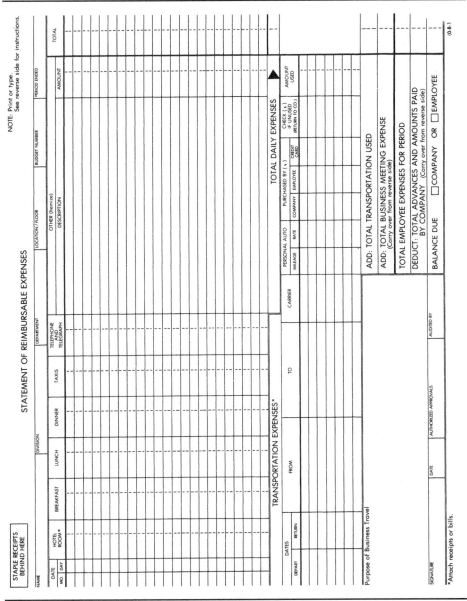

(continued)

Exhibit 11-9.   *(continued)*

DETAIL OF BUSINESS MEETINGS EXPENSE

These expenses are to be shown in total in the space provided on the front side of this form. Each payment must be listed separately. All gratuities for porter, etc. are to be summarized on a daily basis. Tips in connection with an underlying expense, such as meals and taxis, are to be included with that expense. In order to comply with tax laws, the occupation of each person and the business purpose of the business discussion are to be described in sufficient detail so as to clearly establish the business relationship between the Company and the persons present at the business meeting. If related meetings take place with reference to a particular expenditure, state on succeeding lines the date, hours and place of the related meetings.

DATE	MEETING PLACE AND CITY	NAME, FIRM AND OCCUPATION OF PERSONS PRESENT	BUSINESS PURPOSE	DESCRIPTION OF EXPENSE	AMOUNT

TOTAL (Carry forward to front side of this Form.)

ADVANCES AND AMOUNTS PAID BY COMPANY (Include Transportation)

DATE	DESCRIPTION	AMOUNT
PREVIOUS BALANCE DUE COMPANY		

TOTAL (Carry forward to front side of this form.)

INSTRUCTIONS FOR THE USE OF THIS FORM

1. USE OF THIS FORM - This form is to be used to account for all authorized business expense reimbursements, including the use of credit cards, cash advances, and any direct payments which are to be made by the Company in behalf of the employee. If an independent contractor accounts to the Company for such expenses, this form must be used.

2. RECEIPTS - A receipt for each item of hotel expense, transportation expense, and each other expense item is to be attached to this report. Each payment is ordinarily considered to be a separate item. Tips should be included with the underlying expense. Cancelled checks, check stubs, and non-itemized credit card billings are not deemed to constitute receipts for this purpose.

1. *Benchmarking.* A tool to help productivity management and business process reengineering. It enables a company to evaluate competitors' processes and utilize them to achieve best practices to improve performance, lower costs, and become more competitive. Data on competitors is obtained from product litera-

ture, annual reports, industry publications, benchmarking visits, security analysts, library databases, and former employees. This is often accompanied by total quality management studies.

2. *Downsizing, reengineering, and restructuring.* Studying all phases of operations; selling off, combining, or eliminating segments of the business; outsourcing services to independent contractors; and generally reducing total employment and total costs.

3. *Financial electronic data interchange (EDI).* Working with customers and suppliers, called "trading partners," to receive payments, make payments, and update receivables and/or payables electronically, without paperwork, thereby increasing accuracy, efficiency, and timeliness and reducing cost.

4. *Just-in-time inventory management.* The process of involving vendors in production scheduling to enable delivery of inventories precisely at the beginning of production, resulting in the reduction of inventories and inventory carrying costs.

5. *Total quality management.* Evaluating all facets of the organization, with a view to restructuring corporate institutions to meet customer expectations and requirements and lower costs.

6. *Value engineering.* A scientific approach to obtaining equal or better performance from a product at lower cost. This is accomplished by a detailed test and scrutiny of each part and every operation in the manufacturing of the product.

7. *Shared services centers.* Sharing staff support services (see Chapter 18).

PUBLIC RELATIONS

The treasurership function of investor relations, as listed in the FEI definition in Appendix A, involves liaison with investment bankers, financial analysts, and shareholders, with a view to establishing and maintaining an adequate market for the company's securities (see Security Analysts and Stockholders in the following section). The public relations function is oriented toward maintaining and improving the company's image in the eyes of the public. A good image not only helps the marketing people sell the product, but can increase profits and enhance the marketability of the company's securities. The investor relations and public relations functions are mutually dependent.

Public image–improving activities include the following:

- ✦ Product articles
- ✦ Financial articles
- ✦ Organizational changes and promotions releases
- ✦ Interviews with key personnel
- ✦ TV, radio, and panel appearances of key managers
- ✦ Sponsoring sporting events
- ✦ Lecturing at associations and trade shows
- ✦ Charitable contributions
- ✦ Sponsoring community events
- ✦ Key manager participation in fund-raising for charities

Professional PR firms may be retained to perform the function, or an in-house desk can be established to coordinate the release of company information to the media. In either case, the company should:

1. Identify the reason a PR program is wanted—who is the audience, and what message do we want to promote?
2. What are the best media sources—who are our contacts, and what standards do they use in running an article?
3. Establish liaison with all operating departments to ensure that the PR coordinator is in the loop for all of the PR activities listed above.
4. Capitalize on your PR successes—send worthwhile releases to certain classes of customers, to designated security analysts, to employees, stockholders, and lenders. Maintain contact with media sources to assure repeat successes.

A good PR program can increase sales and profits at low cost. The financial officer can make a major contribution in this direction.

SECURITY ANALYSTS AND STOCKHOLDERS

The treasurer, through his or her FEI function of investor relations, has the responsibility to maintain an adequate market in his company's securities. Contacts with analysts and shareholders, however, are subject to disclosure rules and inside information rules as set forth by the SEC. In general, projections of sales and profits should not be released to anyone unless they are released to everyone. Analysts, however—and this may include bankers, investors, or shareholders—may require detailed information about the company's operations before making substantial investments in its stock. Specific information may be given as to production and selling levels in units, but no total volume or profit projections should be made unless you are prepared to disseminate these to the entire financial community (and face the embarrassment and possible consequences of not meeting these projections). For your protection, keep a written record of everything you say to an analyst and file it as a permanent record. The record may be maintained simply on the **Security Analyst Report** shown at Exhibit 11-10.

UNREASONABLE ACCUMULATION OF EARNINGS

The IRS imposes an accumulated earnings tax, really a heavy penalty, on a corporation, with high cost to its key people, for allowing earnings to accumulate beyond the "reasonable needs" of the business. This is a punitive tax of up to 39.6% on the corporation, with additional penalties to its officer and director shareholders. The penalty is often imposed and most often accepted by the corporation, without litigation. Most corporations do not have a defense and prefer to keep minority shareholders from suing officers and directors to reimburse the corporation out of their own funds for these penalties. There is no immunity for any corporation, but smaller and close-held ones are particularly exposed, these being the ones that try to avoid paying out dividends to save the principal shareholders income taxes.

The controller is responsible for tax administration as a major FEI

Exhibit 11-10. Security analyst report.

<u>SECURITY ANALYST REPORT</u>

DATE_____   PERSONAL INTERVIEW_____

                                       TELEPHONE INTERVIEW_____

NAME_____COMPANY_____

ADDRESS_____

CITY_____STATE_____ZIP_____

TELEPHONE_____
          Area Code   Ext.

PARTICIPANTS IN INTERVIEW:_____

                          _____

                          _____

                          _____

                          _____

GENERAL NATURE OF INTERVIEW:_____

_____

_____

_____

_____

_____

_____

_____

_____

_____

_____

function. This includes establishing tax policy and thus, legitimate avoidance of paying undue taxes. He or she has the additional responsibility of protection of assets, which would be dissipated through this penalty tax. The treasurer, on his or her part, has the investment responsibility to invest the company's funds as required. It is surely a requirement to invest funds in a manner to avoid this punitive result.

The IRS has further ruled that the penalty tax is a Subtitle A tax on which the 5% negligence penalty can be imposed. More woe! But whether there is negligence will depend on the facts of each case.

In general, if you do not distribute retained earnings, you should have a written plan for their utilization, a backup plan, written evidence why plans were not implemented (board meeting minutes are good), and information that you tried to execute the plan, that retention was required by competition or banking money requirements, and that tax avoidance was not the principal consideration in retention.

The "Bardahl" business cycle formula defense has been effective for businesses with inventories. This formula has, similarly, been used to determine the operating capital needs during one business cycle of a service industry, in the motor freight business, without inventories. Exhibit 11-11 demonstrates the operating capital determination using the **"Bardahl" formula defense** against the penalty tax. Average receivables were used in the formula, rather than peak receivables, since it took no longer to collect larger receivables. Amounts due from officers, employees, and shareholders can be included in the receivables if they are a legitimate business activity. Time allowance for payment of accounts payable must be taken into account.

The statute does not contain a comprehensive definition of reasonable business needs. However, a number of acceptable and unacceptable grounds for accumulating income are listed in the regulations (Sec. 1.537-2). Acceptable grounds listed are business expansion and plant replacement, acquisition of a business, debt retirement, working capital, investments or loans to suppliers, and self-insurance of product liability. Unacceptable grounds listed are loans to shareholders and expenditures for their personal benefit, loans to relatives or friends who are not connected to the business, loans to a commonly controlled corporation, investments not related to the business, and accumulations to provide against unrealistic hazards.

Exhibit 11-11.   "Bardahl" formula defense (accumulated earnings).

"Bardahl" Formula Defense

(accumulated earnings)

1. Yearly revenues	$3,937,894
2. Average accounts receivable	$354,767
3. Turnover rate of average accounts receivable (line 1 ÷ line 2)	11.10
4. Days in accounts receivable cycle (365 ÷ line 3)	33
5. Accounts receivable cycle as a percent of year (line 4 ÷ 365)	9.04%
6. Yearly expenses	$3,572,050
7. Expenses for one accounts receivable cycle (line 6 × line 5)	$322,913
8. Average accounts payable	$175,807
9. Turnover rate of average accounts payable (line 6 ÷ line 8)	20.32%
10. Days in accounts payable cycle (365 ÷ line 9)	18
11. Difference in accounts receivable cycle and accounts payable cycle (line 4 - line 10)	15
12. Non-deferred expenses for one accounts receivable cycle as a percent (line 11 ÷ line 4)	45.45%
13. Operating capital needed for one business cycle (line 7 × line 12)	$146,764

One of the conditions that must exist before the tax is imposed is an intent to avoid the income tax on the company's shareholders. The unreasonable accumulation creates a presumption of intent to avoid the tax on the shareholders. This presumption can be overcome by showing that tax avoidance was not one of the purposes of the accumulation.

BOTTOM-LINE BOOSTERS

The treasurer, and mostly the controller, are responsible for overseeing special administrative areas that are not specific to their defined functions. Juxtaposed to these specific duties are inherent responsibilities for the proper management of timed events through the use of the accounting calendar, the annual report and annual meeting, the coordination of external audits, the origination and administration of benefit programs, the possible assumption of even the customer relations function, and the evaluation of environmental, economic, and social forces on the business.

The treasurer must provide for automatic auditing through internal check and control and must protect the bottom line through proper periodic inventory taking and control procedures. His or her contribution to corporate profits is expressed through control of legal matters and loans to employees, and, mostly, through management of people and development of a management philosophy that will set the tone for operations, directly reflecting her or his artistry, creativity, and excitement.

The controller will establish product pricing control to prevent cost increases from slipping through the cracks, and he or she will examine the 36 ways and seven additional longer-range programs to assure profit improvement through expense reduction programs. The treasurer will deal with security analysts and stockholders to provide a ready market for the company's securities, without making inadequate disclosures, and both financial officers will protect the corporation against penalties for unreasonable accumulations of earnings through the use of written plans for earnings utilization, supported by proper documentary evidence as to their implementation and augmented by a formula calculation of the operating capital needed in the company.

Thus, the controller and treasurer will look beyond their specified tasks to determine the intrinsic responsibilities of their jobs. They will grasp those implied responsibilities with fervor and devotion, thereby assuring that even the less apparent facets of the business are under control and contribute to profits.

12

The Art of Handling Mergers and Acquisitions

The position description of the treasurer in "Treasurer's and Controller's Functions" provides under organizational relationships that the treasurer "analyzes and is primarily responsible for negotiating the acquisition of companies brought to the corporation's attention by the executive vice president." The definition of the controller's and treasurer's functions published by the FEI includes as a treasurer's function the provision of capital and investments, both of which embrace the act of making acquisitions.

Handling mergers and acquisitions is a special area of responsibility that would be properly included under that caption in the previous chapter. Because of its significance, the amount of dollars involved, and the potential impact on future earnings, however, it is best treated as a separate subject. Every company, at some time in its history, either acquires or sells a company. Any evaluation of acquisitions relates, equally, to your company being the acquirer or acquiree. When an acquisition or divestiture does occur, the responsibility for its artful handling falls to the treasurer or the controller.

TAX CONSIDERATIONS

Rule of Thumb: Never make an acquisition solely for tax reasons. There must always be a good business purpose. But always consider the tax effects to obtain the lowest present and future cost. Adverse tax implications need not negate a deal if the business purpose is met.

Seller's Rule of Thumb: No deal can be made without a careful evaluation of tax considerations in determining net profit on the sale.

Inherent in these rules are opposite goals for the buyer and seller. What is tax-deductible to the buyer is usually taxable to the seller and vice versa. Since the buyer is usually the dominant party, larger than the seller, it must bring to the negotiations a delicate understanding of the seller's tax problems.

As discussed in Chapter 9 under the Philosophy of Responsibility as it relates to taxes, the controller needs to have an overview of the entire tax situation and to spawn the good tax ideas. The experts can then structure the contract to achieve the desired tax result.

Avoid This Pitfall: Do not structure the contract without expert tax advice. The controller's tax knowledge is expected to be general, not specific in these areas. Tax laws require that T's be crossed and I's dotted. An inept contract can have horrendous tax consequences.

Exhibit 12-1, **Provisions of the Tax Law**, lists those sections of the Code that relate to acquisitions and mergers. Each of these sections is discussed in the Research Institute of America (RIA) Federal Tax Service. The total reading consists of 70 pages for the 27 sections. A good course in home study would be to read a section a night, perhaps 2 to 3 pages. In 10 or 15 minutes a night, all pertinent areas of the Internal Revenue Code relating to acquisitions could be reviewed in a month.

REASONS FOR ACQUISITIONS

Companies acquire other companies for as many reasons as there are companies. A few of the most common reasons and a brief discussion of each follow:

Exhibit 12-1. Provisions of the tax law.

Provisions of the Tax Law

Section 46	Amount of Investment Tax Credit
Section 47	Recapture of Investment Tax Credit
Section 172	Net Operating Loss Deduction
Section 269	Acquisitions Made to Evade or Avoid Income Tax
Section 302	Effect on Recipients of Distributions in Redemption of Stock
Section 306	Effect on Recipients of Dispositions of Certain Stock
Section 317	Definitions
Section 331	Gain or Loss to Shareholders in Corporate Liquidations
Section 332	Effect on Shareholders in a Complete Liquidation of a Subsidiary
Section 333	Effect on Shareholders in a One-Month Liquidation
Section 334	Basis to Shareholders of Property Received in Liquidations
Section 336	General Rule for Recognition of Gain or Loss to a Corporation in Liquidation
Section 337	Effect on a Corporation of Sales or Exchanges in Connection with a Twelve-Month Liquidation
Section 341	Collapsible Corporations
Section 354	Recognition of Gain or Loss to Shareholders in a Reorganization
Section 356	Receipt of Additional Consideration by Shareholders in a Reorganization
Section 358	Basis to Shareholders in a Reorganization or Tax-Free Incorporation
Section 361	Nonrecognition of Gain or Loss to a Corporation in a Reorganization
Section 362	Basis of Property to Corporations
Section 368	Definitions Relating to Corporate Reorganizations
Section 381	Carryovers in Certain Corporate Acquisitions
Section 382	Special Limitations on Net Operating Loss Carryovers
Section 453	Installment Method
Section 483	Interest on Certain Deferred Payments
Section 1245	Gain from Dispositions of Certain Depreciable Property
Section 1250	Gain from Dispositions of Certain Depreciable Realty
Sections 1371-1378	The Electing Small Business Corporation (Subchapter S)

1. *New products.* Instead of developing your own new products through research and development, a company can be bought that has already developed the desired product.

2. *Vertical or horizontal integration.* Vertical integration is the purchase of companies from whom you buy or sell, thereby saving the profit that others normally make on your company. Horizontal integration involves companies making a different product but selling it within your industry, usually to the same customers. Cost savings are explicit in horizontal integration.

3. *Personnel.* A company may seek to buy a marketing force, a research capability, manufacturing expertise, or top management through an acquisition.

4. *Profits.* Acquisitions are often made of companies that have a good earnings track record or the potential for good earnings. The trick here, obviously, is to discount those earnings at a yield that makes the acquisition feasible. You mustn't overpay for future earnings.

5. *Tax benefits.* Under some circumstances, companies can be

acquired that have net operating loss carryforwards that can be utilized by the acquirer. This cannot be done if the primary purpose is the utilization of the tax losses, but given other benefits, the tax considerations could sweeten the purchase price and make for an easier acquisition. Exhibit 12-2 lists the **conditions in which tax losses may be utilized**.

6. *The seller must sell.* The death of an owner, with improper tax planning, may force the sale by the deceased's estate. There are, often, time considerations that impel the estate to make a quick sale. The buyer may be getting a bargain purchase.

7. *Realization of goals.* The buyer may simply be in a position to acquire a company in a field in which it has always wanted to be. This may be nothing more than the realization of early dreams.

8. *Fixed assets.* As with personnel, a company may seek to buy the assets, physical plant, or manufacturing facilities of the acquiree. This may be done because the assets cannot be built or purchased elsewhere for the equivalent cost, or because assets of this excellence cannot otherwise be obtained. This would pertain to the acquisition of a retail store with a preferred location, or a factory in a highly skilled labor area.

9. *Listed stock.* A private company may desire to go public. One of the routes is acquisition of a smaller company, already listed. Similarly, "going private" may be accomplished through merger.

10. *Diversification.* While this may be accomplished to a limited degree through integration, the company may desire to protect future earnings by diversification of markets, product lines, and technology.

11. *Future benefit.* Long-range planning may indicate a change in marketing effort to an industry that will grow at a greater rate than ours.

12. *Balance sheet advantages.* The seller may have a strong current ratio that, when consolidated with ours, would improve our position. Similarly, it may have a debt-to-equity ratio that, in consolidation, would improve ours.

13. *Liquidity.* Related to the balance sheet advantages, the seller may have cash, high receivables, and inventory, a segment of

Exhibit 12-2. Utilization of tax loss carryforwards by acquirers.

1. WE ACQUIRE
   a. Use "A," "C," "D," "F," or "G" reorganization.
   b. Loss limitation applies (see 5, below).
   c. Section 269 applies—principal purpose cannot be to secure the benefit of the loss.
   d. In "D" or "G" reorganizations, substantially all the assets must be acquired.
   e. Carrybacks permitted only for "F" reorganizations.
2. OUR SUBSIDIARY ACQUIRES
   a. Use "A" or "C" reorganization.
   b. Loss limitation applies (see 5, below).
   c. Section 269 applies—principal purpose cannot be to secure the benefit of the loss.
3. CONTINUE OLD BUSINESS
   a. (1) We acquire them in "B" reorganization in nontaxable purchase.
      (2) They continue to operate as a subsidiary.
      (3) Section 269 applies—principal purpose test.
      (4) Lisbon Shops applies—their losses cannot offset our profits.
   b. (1) We acquire in an "A" or "C" reorganization.
      (2) Loss limitation applies (see 5, below).
      (3) Section 269 applies—principal purpose test, if we get more than 50% control.
      (4) Lisbon Shops applies—their losses cannot offset our profits.
4. LOSS CORPORATION IS THE ACQUIRER
   a. Preacquisition losses may not offset built-in gains of an acquired corporation, over the next five years, if more than 50% control passes.
   b. Gains on postacquisition assets may be sheltered.
5. LOSS LIMITATION RULES
   a. After a substantial ownership change (more than a 50% change in ownership of a 5% or more shareholder within a three-year period), the taxable income of the loss corporation available for offset by prechange NOLs is limited to the fair market value of the loss corporation immediately before the ownership change, multiplied by the long-term tax-exempt rate published by the IRS. Any excess limitation may be carried forward to the next year's limitation.
   b. The old business must be continued for two years (Sec. 382).
   c. The annual income limitation is reduced by built-in losses (the excess of asset basis over fair market value on the date of the ownership change) and increased by built-in gains.
   d. Limitation may be reduced in bankruptcy by certain interest payments to creditors and debt discharge.

the business that could be sold off—all of which he will sell to us for stock. This liquidity may be obtained at less cost than through the issuance of new stock or debt.

14. *Source of supply maintenance.* Related to integration, but usually done because of a supplier's weak financial condition. The company may acquire a supplier in distress. Or, a supplier may be acquired to prevent a competitor from obtaining it.

15. *Market protection.* A distributor or dealer may decide to sell out. The new buyer might not buy our product, and an acquisition might be indicated.

Word of Caution: Consider antitrust regulations and restraint of trade. Obtain legal advice in these areas before acquiring any company. For companies with annual sales or assets of at least $10 million, there may be legal requirements to notify the Federal Trade Commission and the Justice Department of acquisition plans, even before any stock purchases are initiated.

EVALUATION OF ACQUISITIONS

The acquisition-minded company should, first, evaluate the above-enumerated reasons and reduce to writing its acquisition goals. Through this technique, time will not be wasted on reviewing candidates that do not meet the corporate criteria.

The acquisition goals will vary for every company, but once established, they provide a quick checklist for evaluating a potential acquiree. If these broad goals are met, the acquisition evaluation may proceed. Exhibit 12-3, **Acquisition Goals**, is an example of a broad corporate statement in this area.

Having met the acquisitions goals requirement, a preliminary financial evaluation may then be prepared. This is a **schedule of merger analyses** shown in Exhibit 12-4. The data is filled in based on an expectation of the type of agreement that would be reached. The schedule permits a quick determination of book value, earnings, working capital,

Exhibit 12-3. Acquisition goals.

MEMO TO: Executive Vice President SUBJECT: Acquisition Goals
     Treasurer
     Controller   DATE: November 5, 20__

FROM: President

1. Produce increased earnings per share during the year of the acquisition.

2. Improve the market diversification of net income.

3. Develop and maintain a working environment that will enable us to attract and retain high-talent employees at all levels.

4. Seek profitable markets in which new technologies are needed.

5. Our technological and/or marketing resources must make a significant contribution to the other company, and its to ours.

6. Provide good, skilled, experienced, loyal management that will remain with the company.

7. An industry that will be in the ascendency during the first part of the twenty-first century.

8. A company that has grown faster than GNP for past three years.

9. Growth rate must be equal to industry rate.

10. For other than our own distributors, minimum sales will be $3 million and minimum earnings after taxes will be $150,000.

11. Minimum of 50% gross profit and 5% net after taxes. Minimum return on investment will be 15-20%. Minimum of three consecutive years of earnings.

12. Our net worth capital shall not be adversely affected and acquisition must have a favorable effect on the company's cash flow.

Exhibit 12-4. Schedule of merger analyses.

SCHEDULE OF MERGER ANALYSES

	000 omitted	
	Qty	%
Per cent of dominance		
Seller received_____ our shares for_____ of its shares		
Our shares to be held by seller after merger		
Our shares held by us before merger	1,240	
Total our shares after merger		

	Qty	%
Distribution of our shares to seller		
To principal stockholders		
To all other directors and management		
To minority group		
To minority group		
Total		100

	$ Amt.	Per Common Share
Book Value (Equity)		
Seller's before merger		
Ours before merger	6,197	5
Merged company's		

	$ Amt.	Per Common Share
Earnings (after tax)		
Seller's before merger		
Ours before merger	2,034	1.64
Merged company's		

	X book value	X Earnings	Per Common Share
Price			
Seller's			
Ours	12	37	60

	$ Amt.	Per Common Share
Book value traded		
Seller's book value received in merger		
Our book value traded away		

	$ Amt.	Per Common Share
Earnings (after tax) traded		
Seller's earnings received in merger		
Our earnings traded away		

	$ Amt.	Per Unit
Interest compared to dividends		
Seller's annual dividend before merger		
Seller to receive interest from bonds to be issued in merger		

	$ Amt.	Per Common Share
Increase in market value to seller		
Market value of seller before merger		
Market value of us before merger	74,400	60
Combined market value before merger		
Per cent of shares to be held by seller (item 2) _____ %		
Market value of seller after merger		
Market value of seller's option stock before merger		
Market value of seller's option stock after merger		

		Ratio
Working capital		
Seller's before merger		
Ours before merger	6,509	4.9 to 1
Merged company's		

		%
Return on investment		
Seller's before merger		
Ours before merger		33

return on investment, and market value increase after the merger. If the analysis indicates continuing dominance and increases in the other components, the evaluation may continue. During the course of negotiations, this schedule will again be completed, each time a new acquisition price is proposed during the course of the negotiations.

The conformity to acquisition goals and the schedule of merger analyses may be completed without any contact with the seller. If these preliminary tests are passed, initial contact may then be made with the seller and the **acquisition evaluation checklist** in Exhibit 12-5 should be completed. This will present, on four brief pages, a summary of the acquisition for higher management review. It, together with the financial review in the schedule of merger analyses, will enable top management to quickly determine whether to proceed with negotiations.

If the acquisition is to be pursued, a financial-operations review should be initiated. A complete audit is performed by our independent accountants (sometimes our internal auditors). An operations review is performed by company personnel. Company personnel may be a corporate development department, an internal auditor, the treasurer, the controller, or the manager of each of the departments being reviewed. All such reviews are evaluated by the treasurer and controller, and the previously estimated purchase price is firmed up and presented to the seller.

DETERMINATION OF THE PRICE

A business is bought for future profits! All of the reasons for acquisitions propounded on page 468 have at their core the ultimate goal of increased profits.

Therefore, an attempt must be made to project future earnings and the rate of growth of these future earnings before a purchase price is determined.

Helpful Hint: Since the purchase price depends on future earnings, and since the business is usually "new" to the purchaser,

(*text continues on page 480*)

Exhibit 12-5.   Acquisition evaluation checklist.

ACQUISITION EVALUATION CHECKLIST

A. Vital Statistics

1. Company_____Phone_____

2. Address_____Zip Code_____

3. Type of Business_____

4. Annual Sales $_____ Net Income $ _____

5. Number of Employees_____Number of Plants_____

6. Location of Plants_____

    _____

7. Backlog $ _____Inventory_____

8. State of Incorporation_____

9. Reason for Sale_____

10. Terms_____

11. Finder_____Phone_____

12. Terms_____

B. Key Management Executives

1. Name_____8. Appraisal of Current Effectiveness

2. Age_____   _____

3. Title_____9. Growth Potential

4. Time with Company_____   _____

5. Contract_____yes_____no   10. Approves of Merger____yes_____no

6. Terms_____   11. Willing to Continue With New Company

7. Shares Beneficially Owned_____   _____yes_____no

12. Percentage Total Stock Outstanding Owned by Officers, Key

    Executives_____%

C. Capitalization

	Par Value	Shares Authorized	Shares Outstanding	Equity
1. Shareholders' Equity				
Preferred	____	_____	_____	____
Common	____	_____	_____	____

2. Long-Term Debt　　　　　　Amount　Due Date　＿＿＿＿Terms＿＿＿＿＿＿

　　Issue　　　　　　　　　　＿＿＿　＿＿＿＿　＿＿＿＿＿＿＿＿＿＿＿

　　Issue　　　　　　　　　　＿＿＿　＿＿＿＿　＿＿＿＿＿＿＿＿＿＿＿

3. Potential Dilution (number of shares)

　　Convertibles ＿＿＿＿＿＿　Options ＿＿＿＿＿＿＿　Warrants ＿＿＿＿＿＿

4. Securities Traded　New York Stock Exchange ＿＿＿＿　American Stock Exchange ＿＿＿

　　　　　　　　　　Over the Counter　　＿＿＿＿　Regional Exchanges　　＿＿＿

D. **Financial Data**

1. Balance Sheet　Net Worth $＿＿＿＿＿　Current Ratio ＿＿＿＿＿＿＿＿

　　　　　　　　Fixed Assets $＿＿＿＿　Depreciation $ ＿＿＿＿＿＿＿＿

2. Profit and Loss　Sales (current) $＿＿＿＿　Sales (last year) $＿＿＿＿＿

　　　　　　　　Earnings (current) $＿＿＿　Earnings (last year) $＿＿＿

　　　　　　　　Per Share (current) $＿＿＿　Per Share (last year) $＿＿＿

E. **Plant & Equipment**

1. Facilities　　Average Age ＿＿＿＿years　Obsolescence ＿＿＿＿years

2. Annual Investment in New Plant and Equipment per Employee $＿＿＿＿

3. Annual Investment in New Plant and Equipment per $ Sales　$＿＿＿＿

F. **Marketing**

1. Principal Products	Markets	% of Market	Name of Competitors
＿＿＿＿＿＿＿	＿＿＿＿	＿＿＿	＿＿＿＿＿＿＿
＿＿＿＿＿＿＿	＿＿＿＿	＿＿＿	＿＿＿＿＿＿＿
＿＿＿＿＿＿＿	＿＿＿＿	＿＿＿	＿＿＿＿＿＿＿
＿＿＿＿＿＿＿	＿＿＿＿	＿＿＿	＿＿＿＿＿＿＿

2. Growth Potential	Market	Current	Next 12 Months	Next 5 Years
＿＿＿＿＿＿	＿＿＿	＿＿＿	＿＿＿	＿＿＿
＿＿＿＿＿＿	＿＿＿	＿＿＿	＿＿＿	＿＿＿
＿＿＿＿＿＿	＿＿＿	＿＿＿	＿＿＿	＿＿＿
＿＿＿＿＿＿	＿＿＿	＿＿＿	＿＿＿	＿＿＿

G. **Sales**

1. Number of Sales Personnel ＿＿＿＿＿＿　Method of Compensation ＿＿＿＿＿

2. Principal Customers ＿＿＿＿＿＿＿＿＿＿＿＿＿＿＿＿＿＿＿＿＿＿＿＿＿＿＿＿＿

3. Pricing Method ＿＿＿＿＿＿＿＿　Industry Pricing Method ＿＿＿＿＿＿＿＿

(continued)

Exhibit 12-5.   *(continued)*

  4. Percent of Selling Price for: Direct Labor _____ % Raw Materials _____ %

                                       Overhead   _____ % Selling Expenses ____ %

                                       Profit   _____ %

  5. Product Mix   Number of Items _____ % Catalog _____   % Other _____

  6. Sales Support Services: Advertising _____   Promotion _____

                                 Brochures   _____   Other   _____

H. Industrial Relations

  1. Compensation Review: 6 months _____   One Year _____ Other _____

  2. Wage and Salary Structure: Above Industry ____ Below Industry _____

                                           Average _____

  3. Motivation Techniques   Yes   No

        Incentive and/or Bonus   ___   ___
        Profit Sharing   ___   ___
        Stock Purchase   ___   ___
        Stock Options   ___   ___
        Hospitalization Benefits   ___   ___
        Other   ___   ___

  4. Management Development Program   Yes _____ No _____

  5. Labor Conditions in Industry   Superior _____ Average _____ Poor _____

  6. Relationship with Union   Superior _____ Average _____ Poor _____

I. Business and Legal Aspects

  1. Accounting

      Name of Auditor _____ Phone _____

      Address _____ Zip Code _____

      Contact _____

  2. Legal

      Name of Counsel _____ Phone _____

      Address _____ Zip Code _____

      Contact _____

J. Miscellaneous   (Checklist of available printed materials)

Annual Report	_____	Proxy Statement	
Prospectus	_____	Interim Financial Reports	_____
Organization Chart	_____	Company Brochures	_____
List of Customers	_____	List of Distributors	_____
Licensing Agreements	_____	Union Agreements	_____
Leases	_____	Insurance Policies	_____
Salary & Wage Structure	_____	Benefit Plans	_____
Sales Catalogs	_____	Data Sheets	_____

Internal Communication Media (house organ, etc.) _____

K. Acquisition Assessment

1. Evauation of Business

	Yes	No
Technical Superiority	___	___
Patent Protection	___	___
Market Strength	___	___
Industry Vitality	___	___

2. Reason for Acquisition _____

_____

3. Major Competitors

Company	Share of Market
_____	_____
_____	_____
_____	_____
_____	_____

4. Alternative Acquisitions

Company	Share of Market
_____	_____
_____	_____
_____	_____
_____	_____

5. Evaluation of Management

	Yes	No
Management Ability	___	___
Leadership	___	___
Creativity	___	___
Stability	___	___
Integrity	___	___
Growth Potential	___	___

6. Management Motivation and Goals

Cash	____	Income	_____	Financing	_____
Capital Gains	____	Retirement	_____	Succession	_____

(*text continued from page 475*)

you should require the old owners to continue to manage the business for several years. Their continued management will minimize the risk of low earnings. The lower your risk, the more you can pay for the purchase.

CASE IN POINT: The owner of one business rejected a cash offer of $1 million in favor of receiving a payment of 5 times his annual profits, above a base, for 3 years. The former owner continued to manage the company during this "earn-out" period and ultimately received $2 million for the company via the earnings route.

The rationale for purchases based on an earn-out formula is an acceptable concept to most sellers. They can obtain a higher selling price for their company as a result of minimizing the buyer's risk and deferring a portion of the payment until earnings have been attained, earnings that they are in a position to control through their continued management of the operation.

Future earnings may be determined by:

1. Forecasting—using standard techniques to project earnings out for several years to be covered by the earn-out.
2. Projecting out prior years—this being a study of past earnings, with adjustments being made for known changes. In short, it assumes that future earnings will be the same as average past earnings. It is less accurate than the first method, which takes into consideration future plans, the economy, new products, and the changing business environment.

Helpful Hint: The AICPA has published a Guide for Prospective Financial Statements. It defines the differences between projections (for a specific purpose) and forecasts (expected financial position) and tells how to construct, examine, and report on prospective financial statements. The guide also includes SEC Guides for Disclosure of Projections and IRS Regulations Regarding Tax Shelter Opinions. A summary of the **guidelines for preparation of financial forecasts** is shown in Ex-

Exhibit 12-6. AICPA Guidelines for Preparing Financial Forecasts.

The following is a summary of the guidelines for preparation of financial forecasts.

Financial forecasts should be prepared in good faith.

Financial forecasts should be prepared with appropriate care by qualified personnel.

Financial forecasts should be prepared using appropriate accounting principles.

The process used to develop financial forecasts should provide for seeking out the best information that is reasonably available at the time.

The information used in preparing financial forecasts should be consistent with the plans of the entity.

Key factors should be identified as a basis for assumptions.

Assumptions used in preparing financial forecasts should be appropriate.

The process used to develop financial forecasts should provide the means to determine the relative effect of variations in the major underlying assumptions.

The process used to develop financial forecasts should provide adequate documentation of both the financial forecasts and the process used to develop them.

The process used to develop financial forecasts should include, where appropriate, the regular comparison of the financial forecasts with attained results.

The process used to prepare financial forecasts should include adequate review and approval by the responsible party at the appropriate levels of authority.

hibit 12-6. (See also Chapter 19, the section entitled The Business Plan.)

Once the forecasted or projected future profits are determined, **six methods of determining the purchase price** are available. These are shown in Exhibit 12-7. Methods 4 and 6 of the exhibit are the same, showing five years of average profits, less a deduction for a normal return on the investment in net assets, assumed here to be 12½%. The remaining amount is the excess profits of the business over the normal return required on the investment in net assets. These excess profits are capitalized at three years and four years, respectively, in the examples. The purchase price would, therefore, be the $100,000 for the net assets, plus the goodwill, as determined in the examples.

Method 3 is a variant on 4 and 6, producing essentially the same result but averaging only the last three years of profits, instead of the last five. In actual practice, the seller is often able to negotiate the use

Exhibit 12-7.   Six methods of determining the purchase price.

SIX METHODS OF DETERMINING THE PURCHASE PRICE

Data: Net Assets $100,000
Profits of last 5 years: $19,000, $19,500, $19,000, $21,500, $21,000
Total $100,000
Average $20,000

(1) "Years' purchase of past annual profits."
Profits of second preceding year ....$ 21,500
Profits of first preceding year 21,000
Total, and price to be paid for goodwill ....$ 42,500

(2) "Years' purchase of average past profits."
Average profits of last 5 years (as stated above) .... $ 20,000
Multiply by number of years of purchase   2
Goodwill .... $ 40,000

(3) "Years' purchase of excess profits."

		12 1/2% of	
Year Preceding Sale	Profits	Net Assets	Excess
Third	$19,000	$12,500	$ 6,500
Second	21,500	12,500	9,000
First	21,000	12,500	8,500
	Total payment for goodwill		$24,000

(4) "Years' purchase of average excess profits."
Average profits of past 5 years ....$ 20,000
Deduct 12 1/2% of $100,000 12,500
Excess ....$ 7,500
Multiply by number of years of purchase   3
Goodwill ....$ 22,500

(5) "Capitalized profits, minus net assets."
Capitalized value of average net profits, or total
value of business $20,000 ÷ 12 1/2% $160,000
Deduct agreed value of net assets other than goodwill ... 100,000
Goodwill .... $ 60,000

(6) "Excess profits capitalized."
Average profits of past 5 years .... $ 20,000
Deduct profits regarded as applicable to net assets
acquired — 12 1/2% of $100,000   12,500
Remaining profits, regarded as indicative of goodwill .. $ 7,500

Goodwill - $7,500 ÷ 25% (or 4 years) .... $ 30,000 of only the most recent year of earnings, which, during a period of an inflationary economy, would be most apt to be the highest of the last five years.

Methods 1 and 2 are commonly used to calculate the goodwill of a company, but they suffer the disadvantage of providing for no return on the $100,000 of invested assets. As a result, the computation produces a higher goodwill amount.

Helpful Hint: The use of a higher goodwill amount may produce a desired psychological result when breaking down the purchase price between hard assets and goodwill for future earnings. The seller will see this as getting more on futures. An offset can be made by reducing net assets for an obsolescence factor, thereby resulting in the same purchase price offer as using methods 4 or 6.

Method 5 capitalizes average profits 8 times (100% ÷ 12½%) and then deducts the average net assets. This results in a higher goodwill figure by assuming that profits should be capitalized at the same normal rate of return, 12½%, used for the investment in net assets. Actually, profits are more tenuous than assets, and the payback should be over a much shorter period, using capitalization rates of 33⅓% or 50%.

Helpful Hint: A public company with a quoted price/earnings ratio of, say, 20 times (earnings at $1 per share, stock selling at $20) may use a capitalization rate based on anything up to 20 years and may pay for the acquisition in stock without suffering dilution of earnings. *Caution:* Discount the 20 to some lesser number based on the expectation of lower market-generated p/e ratios, or the possibility of a downturn in the economy that could depress stock prices. Your acquisition would then turn dilutive if the rate were not discounted.

DETERMINING THE METHOD OF PAYMENT

Having determined the price, the method of payment will depend on:

1. The tax consequences to the seller
2. The buyer's financial position

3. The liquidity and P/E ratio of the buyer's stock
4. The earn-out contract

Tax Consequences to the Seller

The seller may be seeking a tax-free sale or may desire to receive, in exchange for the business, stock that can be held for appreciation and subsequent disposal at capital gains rates. In this event, the various provisions of the tax law in Exhibit 12-1 would come into play. The goal is to structure a *tax-free reorganization*. The seller exchanges his shares for ours, and we pick up his assets at his tax basis. Convertible securities, if given, must not be converted for five years, to retain the tax-free status.

The IRS Code allows for a tax-free statutory merger or consolidation. In a merger, A is merged into B and B survives. In a consolidation, A and B combine to create a new C, which is the consolidated company. There are three types of tax-free reorganizations:

- ✧ Type A—Cash. The shareholder gets cash, up to 50%, and stock. The cash received is taxable as a capital gain.
- ✧ Type B—Stock swap or tender offer. The buyer must issue only voting stock and receive an 80% minimum of the acquired company, and a parent-subsidiary relationship is then established. You cannot buy shares for cash even shortly before the tender offer. You cannot give a guaranty as to the future value of your stock, and you may not pay the finder's fees of the selling company or the nontaxability of the reorganization will be destroyed.
- ✧ Type C—Acquisition of assets. The buyer must acquire substantially all of the assets of the seller corporation and must give only voting stock. Some or all of the liabilities may be assumed, but you must obtain at least 90% of the net assets (assets minus liabilities). Thus, the selling company may retain only 10% of net assets to pay off any dissenting stockholders.

The issuance of *contingent stock* (not all shares being issued immediately) may destroy the tax-free reorganization, as the seller is receiving something other than voting stock. This would defeat a stock swap, Type B, or acquisition of assets, Type C. But the IRS will allow contingent shares to be issued if:

    a. The maximum number of shares to be issued is predetermined.
    b. At least 50% of the maximum shares are issued at closing.
    c. The contingent share payout does not exceed five years.
    d. There is a contract (not a certificate or warrant).
    e. There is a good business reason for the contingent issuance, such as not being able to determine the value of the purchase and needing future earnings as a guide.

When contingent shares are issued, the unstated interest rules on deferred payments may come into play. Section 483 imputes a higher interest rate, giving the seller an interest deduction, but:

Beware This Pitfall: It causes taxable interest income to you, the buyer.

Avoid This Pitfall by: (1) Specifying an 8% interest charge, if over $3000 and more than one year; use 110% more for sale and leasebacks. Unstated interest is calculated based on the excess of the sum of payments due in more than six months over the sum of the present values of the payments. Present value is based on the applicable federal rate—the short-term rate if less than three years, the mid-term rate for three to nine years, and the long-term rate for over nine years. The 8% rate will usually avoid unstated interest under this formula, but it should be checked. IRS Code Sec. 1274(d) controls. (2) Issuing the shares into escrow, pending their possible return if the future earnings level is not met, thus completely avoiding the interest income imputation. While in escrow, the seller must have voting rights to the shares, and dividend rights.

A *spin-off* may be accomplished prior to the tax-free merger or acquisition. This is the disposal of unwanted assets or a segment of the business. Usually, if the business is over five years old and there is a business purpose for disposal, a spin-off will be tax-free.

> *But Use Caution:* If the merger follows too closely on the spin-off, it may be taxable. It would be best to go for an IRS ruling, prior to spin-off.

A variety of types of security may be given to effect the merger, as long as they are voting securities. Warrants are not stock, however, and if given with voting stock, they must be valued and would be dividend income to the seller, not capital gain.

Voting preferred stock is also acceptable. Class A preferred, paying a cash dividend, or Class B preferred, paying a stock dividend, may be used, and the dividends would be taxable dividend income to the holder. A convertible preferred is sometimes used, convertible into common in increasing amounts, say 4% each year, in lieu of the cash dividends. The increments of 4% would be a taxable dividend to the holder. There are advantages and disadvantages to convertible preferred, which are discussed below.

The Buyer's Financial Position

The buyer's financial position may be such that immediate cash is needed, even more than the 50% in a Type A merger. In this event, a *taxable acquisition* may need to be structured. The buyer may acquire stock or any of the assets, but instead of giving voting stock, you give more than 50% in cash or other securities, with the following tax considerations:

a. The seller has capital gain but may use the installment sale method (as long as the shares are not publicly traded) and spread out the tax over the payout period. No contingent payout is permitted on the installment method.

> *Word of Caution:* Effective for sales and other dispositions occurring after December 17, 1999, the installment method may not be used to report income from an installment sale if that income normally would be reported under an accrual

method of accounting, unless certain farm property, timeshare rights, or residential property is involved; see Code Section 453(a)(2).

Helpful Hint: Use a convertible debenture. This is taxable to the seller, but it carries a lower interest rate to the buyer and does not dilute earnings until conversion. If the buyer puts certain restrictions on the bonds, such as making them non-negotiable for a period of time, they may not be taxable until the restrictions lapse. The gain to the seller is locked in until conversion.

Another Pitfall: The conversion feature on bonds creates a contingent aspect, as the value of the bond fluctuates based on its conversion feature. As a consequence, the installment sale method may not be used.

b. If the seller sells assets, the seller will effectively lose the capital gain treatment on that portion of the assets that have depreciated. Thus, the seller must recapture depreciation as ordinary taxable income. Similarly, the seller would have a recapture of any investment credit, which would have to be paid, whether or not the seller had any taxable income.

c. A calendar year reorganization (Section 332 and former Section 337) may be undertaken by the seller, with usually no tax to the seller's corporation. Inventory or assets may be sold with no gain being recognized, except for the ordinary income, taxed at the corporate level, as a result of recapture of depreciation, described above.

d. If the seller is willing to be taxed on the sale, and the buyer wants a higher, or stepped-up tax basis, you must buy assets, rather than capital stock.

e. Finder's fees and SEC registration costs are deductible to the acquiring corporation, and the IRS has ruled that they are not taxable to the selling corporation.

Avoid This Pitfall: Nontaxability applies only to finder's fees and registration costs, nothing else. If you pay the seller's accounting or legal fees, it can make the entire sale taxable in an otherwise tax-free reorganization.

The *cash tender offer*, fully taxed to the seller, is often used where there are numerous stockholders, or where the buyer is not negotiating directly with management but approaches the stockholders. It has these advantages:

✧ Sections 13 and 14 of the Securities Exchange Act of 1934 cover tender offers and regulate certain acquisitions of stock that is publicly traded. In addition, various state laws regulate tender offers and require certain disclosures. These specify the form and content of such offers and management's recommendations and provide a broad antifraud provision. Such disclosure requirements apply to acquisitions of more than 5% of a class of equity securities. Filing with the SEC must be made as early as practicable on the date the bidder disseminates the tender offer, with a copy delivered to the target company after notification by telephone and mailing of copies to the target's national securities exchange. However, this disclosure is less burdensome than the disclosure on a merger or stock swap, which may need stockholder approvals and 20 days advance notice on exchange. This needs disclosure, but only at the time of the tender, and the SEC usually will not examine the offer until you exercise the tender.

✧ The disclosure does not need independent public accounting audits and certifications of financial statements.

✧ The disclosure does not need extensive information as to the nature of your business. You are, thus, less vulnerable to attack or resistance by a recalcitrant management group.

✧ Your total investment can be much less than in a merger. You do not need to acquire "all" of the stock, or even the 80% minimum for a stock swap.

✧ You may withdraw within 7 to 60 days for any reason.

✧ You need not name the exact source of your funds, such as the bank that makes the loan for purposes of the tender.

✧ You need not disclose your "ideas" to manage the newly acquired company nor tell of the "minor" changes you plan.

It has these disadvantages:

✧ Under SEC 16, a 10% holder must file with the SEC in ten days, just as if you had taken the company over in a tender. You must give ten years of information, the source of your funds, the amount of shares held, and the name of your partners or group or syndicate. The ten days begin on the date of your option, contract, or commitment, not on actual receipt of the stock.

✧ You must accept, pro-rata, during the first ten days when you get more stock than you desire. This gives management more time to fight the tender—up to ten days.

✧ If a complete disclosure is not made, the SEC or management may sue. This obviates the blind tender offer.

✧ The disclosure must relate your plans to sell, merge, liquidate, or change the corporate structure. If you do not so disclose and you later do a merger, even though you did not intend to do so at the time of the cash tender offer, you expose yourself to litigation.

✧ The offer is subject to the 1967 "corporate takeover bill" and to the SEC rules that followed that bill.

These management defenses are available:

a. The buy-in. The tenderee can use its own funds to buy in its own stock on the open market. The courts will allow this if management shows that the tenderer will hurt the company. Management normally cannot buy in after notice of the tender, unless it files the number of shares it will buy and its source of funds, in a notice to all shareholders and the SEC.

b. Management may advertise, say the price offered is too low, tell its plans, make promises. The SEC will look at the offer to be sure it is not false or misleading. The SEC may, in fact, sue the tenderer, which will prejudice the stockholders.

c. The tax consequences may be adverse to stockholders, who may not be prepared to be taxed on their gain.

d. Management may quickly merge with another company.

e. Management may alert the Justice Department, which has been taking a more active advance role in acquisitions.

f. Alert management is sensitive to the possibility of a takeover and may even have boilerplate press releases prepared, mailings to shareholders, and signed and sealed documents (undated, already in Washington), to be completed for quick SEC filing, charging antitrust violations by the tenderer.

g. Stock held by employees in Employee Stock Option Plans, the Employee Stock Ownership Trust, the hands of management, can be marshalled for a solid block. Loans may be made to employees to exercise large blocks of key employee stock options, or stock may be given away, free to employees, in amounts based on seniority. These all provide excellent employee benefits, in return for which management is assured of employee support in the takeover fight.

h. Large blocks of stock may be held by friendly institutions, known to the alert company. The company may have held many meetings, over the years, with these institutions.

i. The company may enlist the aid of its national union to resist the tender. If labor resists, on a national basis, the tenderer may withdraw.

j. Management, with shareholder approval, can raise the percentage of votes required to approve a merger, to call a special stockholders' meeting, or to remove a director from the usual 51% to 70% or 75%.

k. Long-term employment contracts with top executives will present the tenderer with the problem of managing the company, as it will be bound by the contracts.

l. The company may stagger the board of directors—for example, with three out of nine directors due up for election in any year. Using this device, the acquirer would need at least two years to gain control of the board.

m. The certificate of incorporation may be amended to require five to eight directors for a quorum, with the chairperson having the tie-breaking vote.

n. Standby directors can be named in advance, and voted on at the annual meeting, who would fill any vacancy, automatically, in prescribed order.

o. The company may reorganize itself in a different state, like Delaware, that makes corporate takeovers more difficult. In fact, ten states have anti-takeover statutes that, in general, provide that the target company may call for a state securities hearing on the fairness of the proposal, providing for an automatic 30-day delay. The states are Virginia, Idaho, Indiana, Ohio, South Dakota, Kansas, Minnesota, Nevada, Wisconsin, and Hawaii.

p. Litigation on antitrust arguments, securities regulations, or other regulatory agencies is a common defense. Even if ineffective, the suit allows time to counteract the offer.

q. Dilution of outstanding shares may be effected (the poison pill defense). Preferred stock could be issued at a high dividend rate, say 11% (the high cash dividend discourages takeover), convertible into a large block of common voting shares, say 15% to 20% of the outstanding (which would make it more difficult to obtain control). A variation on this technique is the grant of rights to existing stockholders, excluding any acquirer, to purchase new common shares at 50% of market value.

r. A white knight, or a friendly acquirer, could be solicited. This could result in an equal purchase price, but on terms more favorable to management.

s. The Pac-Man defense could be employed. The target becomes the acquirer and makes an offer to acquire or gobble up the suitor.

t. Golden parachute awards, or high severance compensation arrangements, can be offered to management, to be effective on the completion of any hostile takeover. This can make it too costly for the acquirer to complete the takeover.

Caution: Under the Tax Reform Act of 1984, excess golden parachute payments will be income to the individual and not deductible to the corporation.

u. A leveraged buyout (LBO) can be initiated by management. Funds are borrowed from banks or financial institutions in the amount of undervalued assets, and management buys the company.

v. A recapitalization is initiated. As in the LBO, funds are borrowed against the undervalued assets. The cash is then used to change the objective and direction of the company, or to issue a cash dividend to stockholders. This provides the stockholders with the value not recognized by the stock market. At the same time, it creates a massive debt load that is unattractive to the acquirer.

Caution: In both an LBO and a recapitalization, there must be sufficient predictable cash flow to provide for the debt service on the new debt. The company should have a strong enough market share to ensure protection against unexpected product pricing changes that could reduce its cash flow.

Convertible preferred stock, if voting, may be used in a tax-free reorganization, and if nonvoting, in a taxable purchase. In general, like convertible bonds, it carries a low equivalent interest rate (dividend) but may be more attractive than bonds. It has these advantages:

✧ You postpone dilution of earnings.
✧ The conversion price may be above the common based on the fact of the preferred dividend.
✧ The seller receives income, via the dividend, over a period of years (which may be a strong psychological point in making the purchase), without the necessity of giving income to all common stockholders.
✧ The seller is protected against the volatility of the buyer's stock. The preferred dividend gives downside protection.
✧ Earnings per share should be increased. You will earn more on the preferred (on the seller's business that you bought for your preferred) than you pay out to the seller in preferred dividends. The leverage should increase EPS and the market value of the buyer's stock.

It has these disadvantages:

✧ Pro forma earnings per share, giving effect to conversion, must be shown in the Form 10-K and in the annual report, if the conversion price is below market value.

✧ If a major portion of the value of the preferred is attributed to the common stock, the preferred may be considered a residual security, not a senior security. Moreover, since the common stock may fluctuate, the value of the conversion feature may fluctuate, and the preferred may be considered as a residual security one year and not the next. If considered as a residual security, earnings would be reduced by the amount attributable to the residual security, further reducing pro forma EPS.

✧ The convertible preferred, if not registered, has no market and provides no downside protection. Registration is expensive.

✧ It may be hard to buy back convertible preferred later, especially if you divest yourself of the acquisition.

✧ The risk is greater, as you are committed to an after-tax dividend, which you cannot convert to debt. Some preference stock may circumvent this risk by (1) paying no cash dividends, (2) setting a convertible feature that compounds annually at over 3% (meaning you get 3% more common, compounded, each year), (3) setting a conversion price that compounds at a rate equal to that above, thus, 1:1 in year 1, then 1.03:1, in year 2, etc., or (4) redeeming up to 3% of the total issue each year at par. The IRS has ruled that the yield to the seller is ordinary income, but this is no worse than any dividend the seller might receive. On the other hand, the buyer does not reduce EPS (as the redemption is not an expense but a capital transaction).

✧ If the dividend is too low, and less than 75% of its value is in the preferred stock itself, its issuance may not be attractive to the seller.

Liquidity and P/E Ratio of the Buyer's Stock

The liquidity of the buyer (or lack of it), coupled with a high price/earnings ratio on the buyer's own stock, may dictate that a common stock, or convertible into common, purchase be made. By completing the worksheet at Exhibit 12-4, the buyer may determine that it is possible to offer far more than a competitive bidder, and still not dilute earnings or book value per share.

In this case, the determined purchase price could be paid through a pooling of interests, rather than a purchase. The pooling would be tax-free or taxable, based on the same considerations as any purchase.

Pooling and purchase accounting is governed by the Accounting Principles Board Opinion No. 16, Business Combinations, and Opinion No. 17, Intangibles (referring to the goodwill element in the purchase). These two opinions, in general, limit the use of poolings; in purchases, provide rules and guidelines for allocating fair value to the assets and liabilities purchased; provide for amortization of goodwill (the excess of fair value of the purchase price over the fair value of the assets and liabilities) over the period to be benefited, but not more than 40 years. Prior to this opinion, goodwill need not have been written off at all. For tax purposes, goodwill is a Sec. 197 intangible and must be amortized over 15 years.

The pooling method accounts for a business combination as a joining of companies that exchange their equity securities. It is not considered an acquisition or purchase, since the union takes place without anything being disbursed. The former ownership interests must continue, the old bases of accounting are kept, each carries forward its assets and liabilities to the combined company at their recorded amounts, and new goodwill does not arise. The combined company's income is that of the constituents for the entire fiscal period in which the union occurred. This means that a pooling in the last month of your fiscal year is effective back to the start of the year. Previously reported income of both companies for prior years is combined and restated as income of the pooled company.

> *Word of Caution:* For years the FASB has had an ongoing project on business combinations. The project focuses on goodwill and whether the pooling method of accounting is needed. The pooling method is not generally used outside the United States, and the FASB is tentatively recommending its discontinuance. There is substantial opposition, however, to discontinuing its use. An exposure draft of the FASB's conclusions is not expected until mid-2001. There will be comments and revisions thereafter. Keep posted on these developments.

The purchase method, previously described, accounts for the business combination as an acquisition of one company by the other. The buyer records, at cost, assets acquired and liabilities assumed. Goodwill is recorded for any difference between the cost (purchase price paid) and the sum of the fair values of the tangible and identifiable intangible assets minus liabilities. The goodwill must be amortized as charges to earnings, not exceeding 40 years, and the future income of the buyer includes the seller's income, only after the date of acquisition, based on the cost to the acquirer.

> *Word of Caution:* It is obvious that the determination of fair values of assets and liabilities requires careful study and detailed consideration, as these will be recorded on the books to affect future earnings, through amortization of goodwill that will arise, depreciation of assets, or interest charges arising from the present value of future liabilities.

Warrants may be used in lieu of stock. The warrants may trade at 25% of the price of the common stock. Their issuance thus creates value. Warrants are not considered an underlying security, since they are not stock, and therefore do not dilute EPS. Warrants may also be used together with debentures. This creates fixed interest charges and makes the company more vulnerable to cyclical downturns.

> *Helpful Hint:* The high fixed interest charges could be offset by acquiring a company with large cash flow, say an insurance company, despite its low earnings. It might be bought for below book value (if you offer a good growth stock in exchange). In this case, purchase, don't pool. This creates negative goodwill that can be written up to book value over the years, thereby creating income.
>
> *Another Hint:* Having served the above purpose, the low-income, high-cash-flow company may then be spun off, tax-free. It is probably worth more as a separate entity than in consolidation. The price for which it is sold is then plowed back into new, future earnings.

Don't neglect cash. In times of a depressed stock market and low P/E ratios, stocks lose appeal and the seller may prefer cash. Many buyers with high liquidity make the most advantageous acquisitions in depressed markets.

When liquidity problems do not permit the luxury of cash acquisitions, a good technique is to buy assets for preferred stock, and earnings (minus the preferred dividend) for common stock.

Helpful Hint: Exhibit 12-8 illustrates the **method of allotting the purchase price to preferred stock and common**

Exhibit 12-8.   Stock allotment to the acquisition price.

STOCK ALLOTMENT TO THE ACQUISITION PRICE

Assumptions

1. Assume the preferred stock to be issued at 6%.
2. Assume the capitalization of goodwill to be on the basis of 20%.

Determination of Net Assets — Preferred Stock

	A	B	C	Total
Assets as valued	$100,000	$60,000	$150,000	$310,000
Liabilities	30,000	20,000	50,000	100,000
Net assets for which preferred stock should be issued	$ 70,000	$40,000	$100,000	$210,000

Capitalization   of Excess Profits — Common Stock

	A	B	C	Total
Average annual net profits	$ 10,000	$15,000	$ 8,000	$ 33,000
Preferred dividends - 6%	4,200	2,400	6,000	12,600
Excess remainder	$ 5,800	$12,600	$ 2,000	$ 20,400
Capitalization of remainder at 20%..	$ 29,000	$63,000	$ 10,000	$102,000

Summary of Stock Allotment

	A	B	C	Total
Preferred stock	$ 70,000	$40,000	$100,000	$210,000
Common stock	29,000	63,000	10,000	102,000
Total	$ 99,000	$103,000	$110,000	$312,000

stock, respectively. The method is to issue preferred for the net assets and to issue common for the earnings, after deduction of the preferred dividend, based on a reasonable capitalization rate. The preferred dividends, obviously, may not exceed the earnings of either company.

A study of Exhibit 12-8 indicates that a 6% dividend on preferred and 20% on the common provides the same income after dividends, whichever is computed first. Once the preferred dividends of 6% have been deducted, it does not matter what capitalization rate is used for the remaining average income, since the two remain in the same proportion.

The Earn-Out Contract

The earn-out contract, being a key motivator for the seller, in arriving at a higher price than he or she would otherwise receive, also determines the method of payment.

The earn-out contract, as well as all the negotiated details, needs to be set out in a memorandum that will memorialize the agreement, prior to going to actual legal contracts. The memorandum should be in letter form, should tell the details of the purchase, and, in fact, should have a brief reference to every clause that will ultimately be in the contract—down to the minutiae of assignability of the contract, which state law will prevail, and whom the old owner will report to.

Helpful Hint: The guideline for preparing the memorandum should be an actual contract. If none is available from a prior acquisition, make one up for this purchase, but don't allow the seller to see it until after the memorandum is prepared and agreed to. Changes to the memorandum may be quickly incorporated into the actual contract, and you are much more likely to get quick approval on the contract when the seller later tells his or her lawyer that he or she has already agreed to a specific point.

A **sample letter memorandum** is seen at Exhibit 12-9. Attached to it is a detailed schedule showing earn-out examples under many different performance levels. The seller can see exactly how many shares will be received under differing circumstances.

If there is any misconception on either the acquirer's or the acquiree's part, this will surface in the memorandum. Sometimes, in fact, the seller may seem to have been very amenable and anxious to sell, during the verbal negotiations. But when the memorandum arrives, shock sets in! The seller suddenly realizes that he or she is selling the business, a life's work. He or she may have second thoughts or even try to strike a better deal. Better to face these now than have the seller walk out of the closing. Therefore, the memorandum should be direct and to the point, covering all points, but not so severe and rigid (as in a contract) that it will scare the seller off.

> *Important Point:* Observe that the earn-out formula sets a base for earnings. This is what we are capitalizing and paying 5 times for. The seller gets paid more only for increases over the base.

> *Avoid This Pitfall:* Insist that the seller use an attorney for his or her own protection, not only in reviewing the contract, but in assuring that he or she conforms to SEC regulations on the sale of the securities. This will also avoid the seller's claiming that he or she was bilked by you or your attorneys. If the seller refuses, have him or her sign a waiver of damages.

ACQUISITION RULES OF THUMB

The acquisition goals of the organization are worked out as seen at Exhibit 12-3. These goals vary from company to company. Listed below
(text continues on page 502)

Exhibit 12-9.   Memorandum of agreement (acquisitions).

OUR CORPORATION
ADDRESS

May 31, 20———

Mr. Jack Smith
ABC Company
Address

Dear Jack:

Confirming our discussion of May 8th, we are interested in purchasing your business on the following basis:

1. <u>Purchase Price</u> - The initial purchase price will be five times pretax earnings, for the last one-year calendar period ended December 31, 20xx. These pretax earnings will be adjusted upward for profit sharing, cash bonus, and profit-sharing retirement expenses (approximately $13,000), and for personal expenses that need not be a charge against the new business operation (approximately $5,000 to $10,000). For example, if pretax earnings for the year ended December 31, 20xx, were $27,000, add to this profit-sharing bonuses and expenses of $13,000 and nonrecurring personal expenses of $10,000, to arrive at adjusted pretax earnings of $50,000. Five times this equals $250,000, which would be the initial payment.

We would then offer a two-year earn-out period, with a required maintenance of earnings in the third year. We would pay seven times pretax earnings in excess of base year earnings for each of the two years. In the above example, the $50,000 of base year earnings would be adjusted to our accounting basis. These adjustments would include the deferral of service contract income and amortization over a 12-month period (you state that this will have very little effect, as you sold the same number of service contracts last year as this year). You are taking coupon books into income when sold. We would adjust these to reflect income when shipped or paid. Presumably, there should be very little effect if the amount of coupon books that you have sold this year is approximately the same as last year. Depreciation would be changed to our basis instead of your own three-year basis, which would result in an increase in earnings.

Having arrived at adjusted pretax earnings, the base for first-year earn-out would be these pretax profits recast onto our accounting basis, for the year ended December 31, 20xx. The earn-out will be seven times the excess over that base for the year ending December 31, 20xx, with a 40% escrow holdback. The base will then be increased for the second-year earn-out, and you will be paid seven times the excess pretax earnings over the second-year base, again using our accounting basis. There will again be a 40% escrow holdback, but there will be adjustments if your earnings drop below the earn-out base and you must maintain earnings in the third year. Attached is a schedule of examples indicating how the earn-out will work.

(continued)

Exhibit 12-9.   *(continued)*

Mr. Jack Smith
May 31, 20xx
Page Two

For example, if your adjusted base for earn-out in the first
year remains at $50,000 and if you were to increase earnings by
$20,000 in each of the next two years, you would receive seven
times $20,000 for each of these years, or $140,000 for each of the
two years, a total earn-out of $280,000. Adding this to the
initial payment of $250,000 would result in a total payment of
$530,000 for the purchase. If your earnings only exceeded the
$50,000 base by $10,000 each year—that is, $60,000 in the first
year of the earn-out and $70,000 in the second year of the earn-
out—you would then earn $70,000 for each of the two years, a
total of $140,000, which, added to the initial payment of
$250,000, would result in a total purchase price of $390,000.

As a final example, if you exceeded your base by $30,000 each
year and showed earnings of $80,000 in the first year and $110,000
in the second year, your total earn-out for the two-year period
would become $420,000, which, added to the $250,000 initial
payment, would make a total purchase price of $670,000.

Prices for our merchandise that will be charged to you during
the period of earn-out will be lowest dealer published prices.

ABC will operate as a subsidiary of our corporation. As soon
as practicable, our corporation will be prominently displayed on
all signs, letterheads, etc., and the ABC identification will be
displayed in successively lesser prominence.

You would operate basically along the principles of our
corporation's branch offices throughout the United States. If our
corporation assumes responsibility for accounting functions that
ABC is now doing, we will charge you at the cost to our
corporation, but no higher than ABC is now paying.

Legal and accounting expenses of the sale are the
responsibility of the selling stockholders and will not be
considered as expenses to be charged against ABC.

During the earn-out period, if you earn 20% below the earn-out
base in any one year, our corporation, at its option, may take
direct control of operating its subsidiary.

You will be responsible for marketing our corporation's
products in your present territory.

Your board of directors will be asked to resign in favor of
our corporation's nominees. You will, of course, continue to be
respesented on the board during the earn-out period.

2. Piggyback Rights - Our corporation will give you one piggyback
right for registration of your shares.

3. Accounting - You agree to utilize the services of accountants
of our corporation's choice, after the purchase, which we have
indicated at this time to be Coopers & Lybrand. Such accounting
charges during the earn-out period will be charged against ABC's
operations, but will not exceed accounting charges incurred by ABC
prior to acquisition.

Mr. Jack Smith
May 31, 20xx
Page Three

4. <u>Operations</u> - You agree not to pay any sums to your employees
except regular salaries, commissions, bonuses, and reimbursement
for reasonable expenses. You will keep present insurance in effect
and will not diminish it. You will use your best efforts to
preserve your business intact and to keep your employees and to
preserve your relationships to suppliers, customers, and
employees. You will not make any charitable contributions. You
will not mortgage, lien, or encumber any of your assets, or sell,
assign, or transfer your assets, except inventory in the normal
course of business. You will not become liable for legal,
accounting, or other fees, except as approved by our corporation.
You will establish banking relations as you deem desirable,
provided that, except for payroll checks and checks payable to our
corporation, no check in excess of $5,000 shall be drawn by ABC
unless countersigned by our president or vice president/
controller. Salaries will continue to be drawn as at present.

You will continue to devote your full time, skill, and
attention exclusively to your work at ABC, during normal business
hours. All developments, inventions, trade secrets, improvements,
and discoveries, by ABC or you, will belong to our corporation.
You will not enter into any commitment of capital expenditures in
excess of $3,000 without prior permission from our corporation,
except purchases from our corporation and inventory items.

You agree to maintain secrecy concerning our corporation's
affairs and have all the other obligations of an executive
employee - to devote full time and efforts to the business. For a
period of five years after termination of employment, for any
reason, you agree not to enter into competition with us, nor
engage in, as principal, agent, employer, stockholder, officer, or
otherwise, any such business.

This agreement is binding upon you and your successors and
assigns.

Your employment may be terminated for a period of three
consecutive months, or five months, even though not consecutive,
if you become mentally or physically unfit, or otherwise unable to
perform your duties.

Our corporation may, at its election, take out and maintain
life insurance on you, as we deem necessary, and our corporation
shall be named the beneficiary, and you agree to cooperate in the
procurement of application for such life insurance.

5. <u>Stock Price</u> - The price of the stock will be the average of the
closing price of our corporation as traded on the New York Stock
Exchange for the 30 days prior to signing the contracts. The stock
price for earn-out purposes, each year, will be the average of the
closing prices for the month of December of each year,
respectively, 20xx and 20xx. There will be no upper or lower limit
upon the calculation of the price of the stock.

(continued)

Exhibit 12-9. *(continued)*

```
Mr. Jack Smith
May 31, 20xx
Page Four



6.  New Products - ABC will be granted distribution rights on all
of our corporation's new products, to the extent that these
products are distributed through dealers in the normal course of
our corporation's business.

I trust this summarizes the discussions that we have had and our
understanding. This is not an offer, but is subject to approval by
the president and our board of directors, but I believe that it is
a viable arrangement that they will, in my opinion, approve. If
you have any questions concerning any portion of this, please feel
free to call me.



Kindest personal regards.

Very truly yours,




_____

Vice President/Treasurer

copies:  President
         Executive Vice President
```

(text continued from page 498)

are some of the rules of thumb used by companies in evaluating acquisition candidates:

- ✧ Don't acquire companies unless you are a growth company, that is, (a) you have successive increases in earnings at a rate greater than the GNP, (b) you use conservative accounting techniques, and (c) you already have high quality of management.
- ✧ Always use an earn-out formula.
- ✧ Your return on investment should be at least 15%.
- ✧ Pay not more than $1\frac{1}{2}$ times net worth.
- ✧ The seller should have a 50% gross profit margin on sales.
- ✧ The seller's pretax profits should be 10% or more.
- ✧ The seller must have had required earnings for the past three years.

45-608 EYE-EASE
45-708, 20/20 BUFF
NATIONAL

Earn - out Examples

	Pre-Tax Earnings	Initial Payment of Our Corp. Stock	Value of Stock Earned	Stock Issued	Stock in or (out) of Escrow	
I						
Base Period Earnings	50000	250000				
Year 1 Earnings	70000		100000	60000	40000	
Year 2 Earnings	90000		100000	60000	40000	Base is 70M
Year 3 Earnings	90000		—		80000 ←〈80000〉	
or						
Year 3 Earnings	80000 *		—		20000 ←〈80000〉	60M to our Corp.
or						
Year 3 Earnings	74000 *		—		〈80000〉	80M to our Corp.

* 5 Times Amount below 90,000 base is returned to Our Corporation, but not more than is in escrow.

	Pre-Tax Earnings	Initial Payment of Our Corp. Stock	Value of Stock Earned	Stock Issued	Stock in or (out) of Escrow	
II						
Base Period Earnings	50000	250000				
Year 1 Earnings	40000		—			
Year 2 Earnings	60000		—		Average for first 2 yrs is equal to or under base — Earn out ENDS	

	Pre-Tax Earnings	Initial Payment of Our Corp. Stock	Value of Stock Earned	Stock Issued	Stock in or (out) of Escrow	
III						
Base Period Earnings	50000	250000				
Year 1 Earnings	60000		50000	30000	20000	
Year 2 Earnings	56000		—		〈20000〉	To our Corp. Earn-out ENDS

	Pre-Tax Earnings	Initial Payment of Our Corp. Stock	Value of Stock Earned	Stock Issued	Stock in or (out) of Escrow	
IV						
Base Period Earnings	50000	250000				
Year 1 Earnings	70000		100000	6000	40000	
Year 2 Earnings	65000				〈25000〉	To our Corp.
Year 3 Earnings	65000 *			15000 ←〈15000〉		

* Third Yr. Base is 65,000 for full earn-out

	Pre-Tax Earnings	Initial Payment of Our Corp. Stock	Value of Stock Earned	Stock Issued	Stock in or (out) of Escrow	
V						
Base Period Earnings	50000	250000				
Year 1 Earnings	40000 *		—	—		
Year 2 Earnings	70000 **		50000	30000	20000	Base is 60M
Year 3 Earnings	55000			20000 ←〈20000〉		

* Must earn over 60,000 in 2nd year for any chance of additional Stock.
** Third year minimum is 55,000 (Average of years 1 and 2)
or

	Pre-Tax Earnings	Initial Payment of Our Corp. Stock	Value of Stock Earned	Stock Issued	Stock in or (out) of Escrow	
Year 3 Earnings $	52000			50000 ←20000→	15M to our Corp.	

   ✧ Pay no more than 8 times the earnings average.

   ✧ Don't try to make a "bargain" purchase.

   ✧ You must "sell" the prospective seller on your company.

   ✧ If no earn-out, give the previous owner other incentives.

   ✧ The seller must have competent management.

   ✧ Don't expect miracle future earnings from the seller.

   ✧ The buyer's EPS must increase in the year of acquisition.

   ✧ There must be synergy—a real business fit or purpose.

ARTFUL ACQUISITIONS

The mergers and acquisitions responsibility rests with the treasurer. Tax considerations, while inherent in the acquisitions process, are never a reason for making an acquisition. There are, on the contrary, a variety of good and solid business reasons for making acquisitions. Goals must be carefully set in approaching target companies, and the price should be determined by projecting out prior years' profits or forecasting future earnings using formal forecasting techniques. The method of payment may be artfully constructed, depending on whether the seller has a tax-free reorganization or a taxable exchange. A variety of securities may be given by the buyer—even cash may be used! The combination of the business interests may be treated, for accounting purposes, as a purchase or as a pooling of interests, depending on the method of payment and type of agreement. A memorandum agreement is used to reduce the agreements to writing, before contract, and this should always include an earn-out formula. Pinpoint acquisitions—develop rules of thumb in considering candidates. Be an artful acquisitor.

13

Establishing and Administering a Records Retention Program

The controller's functions of planning, reporting, consulting, and protection of assets encompass the records retention responsibility. Records need to be filed, sorted, stored, and retrieved for a variety of reasons—for historical reviews, tax audits, litigation, vendor and employee claims. This function logically falls under the aegis of the principal operational manager, the controller.

What Is It?

The name *records retention program* is universally used to define a program that has a great many more aspects than mere retention of records. A complete records program embraces the following features:

1. *A current filing system* concerned with day-to-day operations, and located close to the user departments.
2. *A long-range filing system* in a permanent storage facility, off-premises, properly arranged for quick retrieval.

3. *A definition of which records to retain* and, therefore, which records to destroy.
4. *A systematic records destruction procedure* to allow for retention of the records defined in No. 3.
5. *A security system* to protect the integrity of both current and long-range records.

WHAT ARE THE NEEDS AND BENEFITS?

The needs and benefits of a records retention program vary with the record to be retrieved and the need to retrieve that record. Assume, for example, that our company signs a manufacturing agreement with another company, licensing that company to use our patents and know-how to manufacture a product for us and others, with an annual ten-year licensing fee paid to us, which we take into income on a capital gains basis. That contract needs to be filed in a safe place for three years after the filing of the last tax return at the end of the tenth year. The last tax return is filed in April of the eleventh year (assuming there is no extension of the time to file), and the record may not be destroyed until the fourteenth year. During this extended period of retention, in addition to the IRS, others may want to examine the contract: our independent accountants, to review the basis for accrual of income and capital gains treatment; the Federal Trade Commission, to determine that we are not in restraint of trade or, perhaps, in connection with an industrywide antitrust review; the SEC, in the event the contract is material and requires public disclosure (through the filing of a Form 8K or as an exhibit to a registration statement); various department heads, to check on cost formulas, termination clauses, purchase order requirements, and payment terms; and, of course, corporate officers, with regard to contract disputes arising with the licensee. The need to retrieve in this particular circumstance, and the benefits, by definition, arise out of the solution to the need. Obviously, the cost and impediment to a successful solution can be severe if the contract, or a key document related to it, cannot be located.

Perhaps the most frequent example of the frustrations involved in not being able to locate a record is found at income tax audit time. The revenue agents are voracious in their need for documents and to "show me." Your argument is half lost if you cannot turn up that four-year-old canceled check or March 5, years ago, petty cash voucher. But even more important than a casual record, you may need every book of original entry for any specific year.

In summary, the needs are as varied as the records being sought, and the benefits are as many and varied as the needs giving rise to them. Business is built around the written word, and proper control requires that the related document be made available on command.

How Is the Program Established?

A records retention program is established by the controller identifying and defining the five features set out beginning on page 505. This requires setting up rules or a procedure to handle each feature. The method of codifying these procedures is set forth in Chapter 7, describing the procedures manual. An outline of the components of each of the five features follows:

A Current Filing System

1. Locate it close to the user departments to save steps.
2. Do not allow entry into the file department by anyone except the file department manager and his or her people. This is necessary solely to prevent disruption of the basic filing system.
3. Establish written rules on where to file each type of document. The way you file is not important, only that you are consistent, your method is written down, and the record can be retrieved based on a knowledge of your filing system. A few helpful filing hints are:
   a. Never file by person's name (senders or receivers leave the company, and people can't recall who wrote what).
   b. File by broadest possible category. For example, memos to salespeople may be filed under "sales memos," broken

down into subsets for training memos, pricing memos, competitors' equipment, sales slants, procedures, sales contests, performance reports, and so on.

4. Do not permit individual managers to maintain their own desk files or departmental files, unless these are used in daily operations. Next year, move even daily files out of the department and into the central file department.

5. Files, whether central or working departmental, should be retained only by the sender, never the receiver (to cut down on duplicate and unnecessary file retention).

6. Individual files maintained by corporate officers should be summarized by broad category (step 3b), and a listing of these broad categories must be sent to central files for available reference by key managers and other officers.

7. Department heads should require a quarterly desk inspection by all employees (every drawer and file is opened and reviewed) to determine that no key records are being squirreled.

8. Managers should personally inspect the desk of every terminated employee to determine that an orderly transition of work is made to the replacement employee and that pertinent records are sent to central files.

9. Organizationally, the central file manager should report directly to, or on a line to, the corporate controller.

10. Central files must be revolved yearly, with transfers being made to permanent files, to allow room for this year's current filing. Working files should usually include 16 months of records; that is, December's files are not transferred to the permanent file room until the end of April.

11. Originals should not leave the files unless legally required. In such a case, a photocopy is made, dated, and marked with the name of the recipient, to be removed and destroyed when the original is returned.

A Long-Range Filing System

1. A permanent, locked storage facility is required. This presupposes adequate space in a secure area, sprinklered for fire protection. Files may be cardboard transfiles.

2. The storage area should be reasonably close to the main facility, even if facsimile transmission of documents is used. This allows for ready access without each request requiring a major expenditure in time, effort and dollars.

3. Entry into the secure area must be limited to the area manager or the central file manager.

4. Written rules on filing are required and may be the same as those used for the current filing system.

5. The area file manager should report to the central file manager in the controller's division.

6. Every file or transfile must be numbered within an area location.

7. The general contents of each file must be labeled on the front of each carton.

8. A listing is made of each carton number and its contents, such listing organized by subject matter (see step 3 of the previous section).

9. A cross-reference locater listing is maintained by carton number, showing the location by subject matter.

10. Originals should not leave the files unless legally required. In such a case, a photocopy is made, dated, and marked with the name of the recipient, to be removed and destroyed when the original is returned.

A Definition of Which Records to Retain

This subject is covered in considerable detail in a publication by The American Society of Corporate Secretaries, Inc., entitled *Survey on Records Retention Practices*. It is available from the society, which is located in New York City, for $90. Their telephone number is (212) 681-2000.

This publication lists the gamut of corporate and business records, the legal and business reasons for holding them for certain periods of time, and the authority for these decisions. There are generally minimum holding periods that may be adapted or lengthened for each particular company, depending on its own requirements.

The **list of records to be reviewed for holding period** is complete and concerned with every phase of the operation of the enterprise. An example of the detail provided is shown on a typical page exhibited in Exhibit 13-1. The list below is not intended as a substitute for a thorough review of the cited publications. It lists, however, the most common business records that take up the most space and gives the minimum retention period:

Document*	Holding Period in Years
Accounts payable (vouchers and invoices)	6
Bank statements and reconciliations	6
Canceled voucher checks	6
Cash receipts books	Permanent
Claim files—against us	6
Claim files—by us	3
Employee travel expense reports	6
Financial statements—internal	5
General books—all journals	Permanent
Physical inventory records	6
Payroll registers	6
Payments and reports to government agencies	6
Cancelled stock certificates	Permanent
Contracts, agreements, and leases	Permanent
Basic scientific records	Permanent
Correspondence with vendors	2
Orders filled	2
Sales correspondence	2
Sales invoices	6
General correspondence	Permanent

*The document may be a paper document, computer tapes, diskettes, or CD-ROMs.

A Systematic Records Destruction Procedure

1. The records retention listing above should be published and made available to all managers of departments.
2. A standard operating procedure should be circulated giving the times of records destruction and the authority and the responsi-

Exhibit 13-1.   Records retention periods.

Employees' applications (after termination)
Employees' tax withholding statements
Express receipts
Freight bills
Freight claims (after expiration)
Freight drafts
Labor contracts (after expiration)
Manifests
Remittance statements
Receiving reports
Sales slips
Salespeople's expense accounts
Service reports
Shipping tickets

5 to 6 years

Correspondence, license
Correspondence, purchase
Correspondence, traffic
Complaint reports
Credit memos
Employees' daily time reports
Equipment inventory records
Insurance, fire inspection reports
Internal audit reports
Monthly trial balances
Payroll, overtime
Photographs of installations, etc.
Price exceptions and adjustments
Safety reports
War contracts and all papers pertaining thereto

6 to 7 years

Bond registers
Bonds, cancelled
Claims, closed, against company
Contracts and agreements (expired)
Correspondence, war bonds
Credit files
Employee record (terminated)
Expense reports
Federal income tax returns
Insurance, group disability
Inventory, recaps
Invoices, copy of order
Invoices, paid
Patent assignments

6 to 7 years

Payroll, bonus
Payroll, general
Payroll, part time
Payroll, temporary
Price and policy bulletins (superseded)
Real estate records (after disposal of land and buildings)
Stock dividends checks, cancelled
Stockholder lists

7 to 8 years

Checks, payroll
Commission statements
Correspondence, production
Cost statements
Employees' earning record
Employees' salary & wage rate change
Insurance, pensions (after expiration)
Purchase orders for capital expenditure
Sales sheets
Specification sheets

8 to 9 years

Accident reports (after settlement)
Agreements, leases (after expiration)
Checks, dividend
Checks, general
Checks, petty cash
Compensation cases (after closing)
Engineering problems (killed)
Vouchers, cash
Vouchers, numeric copy

9 to 10 years

Vouchers, A-Z copy
Voucher register

10 years

Insurance claims after settlement
Payroll, Series E Bonds (life of bond)
Vouchers, capital expenditure

17 years

Agreements, licenses

Permanent

Agreements, deeds
Applications filed with regulatory agencies
Engineering and research project records
Ledgers and journals, cash
Ledgers and journals, customer

bility (central files manager) for such destruction. The destruction date, each year, should be the day following the filing of the tax return for the appropriate year. Extensions in filing should be taken into consideration. For example, a company on an April 30 fiscal year normally files its tax return on July 15. Thus, a record dated December 1, 2002, on 3-year retention, is scheduled for destruction after July 15, 2006. If an annual destruction date of the first Tuesday of each February is established, this record would be slated for destruction in February 2007.

3. A listing of cartons and records to be destroyed should be circulated to all key managers, 30 days before destruction, with *positive* confirmation required that no listed records need be retained.

4. Notations of destroyed cartons should be made on the listing in step 8 of the long-range storage procedure, with the date of destruction. This, itself, is retained as a permanent record, to prove destruction in any future litigation on proceedings.

5. Prior to each destruction, the listing of records to be destroyed is approved by the controller, after the receipt of all positive confirmations from key managers. The controller retains this listing in a working file as a backup for the central file original listing.

6. The retention period, as adjusted from the Prentice-Hall or Corporate Secretaries listing, should be reviewed for changes every second year. These changes should relate to updates in the general listing as provided by the appropriate publication, based on changes in the existing law, and changes required in the adjusted dates used by the company, based on changes within the company's own procedures.

A Security System

1. A **file retrieval procedure** is necessary to ensure control over the transmittal, storage, and retrieval of all current and historical

filed documents. This procedure is detailed at Exhibit 13-2, together with supporting forms to administer the procedure.

2. Records destruction should be accomplished either by sale to a responsible scrap dealer (who will promptly shred and bale the material) or by burning under observation by a responsible company representative.

   a. Records should not be left, untended, at a municipal dump to be destroyed at some later date.

   b. Purchasing and operating a paper shredder or baler is costly and not recommended unless there is considerable volume, in which case it may be cost-justified.

   c. Destruction may be integrated with a trash or garbage disposal system utilizing a compacter and baler.

3. No personnel should be permitted in the records room except file department personnel. This includes other department heads, officers, and auditors.

   a. As an exception, file units may be assigned to specific departments, and personnel from such departments may have free access to such records.

   b. The balance of the records room should be fenced off from the free access area.

4. The records room should be clean, dry, and well lighted.

   a. Avoid dampness and excessive dryness.

   b. Do not use sprinkler protection because water damages more records than actual fire. Tightly packed records in metal files will usually not be damaged irreparably by fire.

   c. Metal, interlocking files are better than cardboard, as they are more fire resistant.

5. File papers away when not in use, and clear all office desks at night.

6. Use special, fireproof metal files for irreplaceable, important records.

7. Provide for duplicate copies of important records, computer tapes, or diskettes, and store them in a separate location, away from your place of business. This would include all data necessary to reconstruct accounts receivable records and a trial balance:

Exhibit 13-2. File retrieval procedure.

STANDARD OPERATING PROCEDURE		
Subject:	Number	HOP M-550
FILE RETRIEVAL	Page of	1 2
	Effective Date	4/1/
Supersedes Cor. No. Page Dated	Related S.O.P./H.O.P.	

PURPOSE: To ensure appropriate controls for the transmittal, storage, and retrieval of all filed documents, present and historical.

METHOD:

DEPARTMENT HEAD: 1. Completes requisition for filed documents as follows:

      a. Checks block "Other" and indicates "File"

      b. Date—current date

      c. Attention—to file clerk

      d. Date needed

      e. Requested by— department name

      f. Approved by—department head's signature

      g. Description of document—title, date

      h. Special instructions

  2. Forwards requisition to file clerk.

FILE CLERK: 3. Enters document in File Retrieval Log (see Exhibit A).

  4. Pulls requested document from files.

  5. Files requisition in place of original document to serve as "out card."

  6. Prepares a letter of transmittal (see Exhibit B), attaches document(s), and forwards to department head.

DEPARTMENT HEAD: 7. Returns File Retrieval Log upon return of the document.

  8. Pulls requisition from file, and refiles original document.

  9. Destroys requisition.

  10. Reviews File Retrieval Log daily for documents not returned within the 48-hour period, and prepares a Document Return Request (see Exhibit C).

  11. Adjusts File Retrieval Log to reflect 24-hour extension date in Date to be Returned column.

Date Prepared: 6/13/
Correction No. 88

STANDARD OPERATING PROCEDURE		
Subject:	Number	
		HOP G-220
	Page of	
FILE RETRIEVAL	2	2
	Effective	
	Date	4/1/
Supersedes Cor. No. Page Dated	Related	
	S.O.P./H.O.P.	

DEPARTMENT HEAD: 12. Returns document to file clerk upon receipt of Document Return
                                Request.
FILE CLERK: 13. Processes per steps 8–10 above.

INQUIRIES: Office Manager
DISTRIBUTION: List 11.0-HOP Manual Holders
Date Prepared: 6/13/
Correction No. 88

(continued)

(text continued from page 513)

  a. Last month's aged trial balance.

  b. Copies of daily billings to customers.

  c. Last month's cash disbursements journal.

  d. Capital asset records.

  e. Copies of current month's journal entries.

  f. Copies of important contracts.

  g. Summary individual earnings payroll records, quarterly.

  h. Last month's data processing tapes.

  i. Microfilm copies of important computer programs.

Storage and Retrieval Systems

Storage of records is the phrase used for inactive records. Retrieval most often applies to current, working records. Most inactive records are retained for a period of years, or permanently, in accord with the established records retention program. Many permanent or long-retention-period documents need to be retrieved frequently. Examples would be installment contracts payable over a period of years, standing customer

Exhibit 13-2. *(continued)*

FILE RETRIEVAL LOG

Date Out	Date to Be Returned	Return Date	Document Title and Number	Document Date	Department For

LETTER OF TRANSMITTAL

This is the document you requested. Please return to file department within 48 hours.

Document Date	Document Title	Document #

(continued)

orders, working contracts, cost records, and tax returns. Inactive records simply need be filed in the records room under the records retention procedures described previously. Active records require a current filing system as described on page 507. There are degrees of sophistication to both the active and inactive filing systems contemplated. Filing systems can include the manual systems previously described, or:

1. Computer media storage
2. Word processing storage

Exhibit 13-2. *(continued)*

DOCUMENT RETURN REQUEST

DATE: _____

DEPARTMENT: _____

SIGNED OUT DATE: _____

DATE TO BE RETURNED _____

DOCUMENT TITLE _____

DOCUMENT NO. _____

DOCUMENT DATE _____

ADDITIONAL COMMENTS _____

_____

_____

_____

(*text continued from page 517*)

3. Microfilm storage
4. Microcomputer disk storage

The overall features of each concept are discussed below.

COMPUTER MEDIA STORAGE

Words, numbers, statistics, and data may be computer inputted and stored on computer disks or tape. Since the computer reads tape sequentially, this is best for chronological storage. A variant may include the use of disk storage devices for random access retrieval.

The limitation of such a system is that most file copies need to be put into computer-readable form. This means preparation of computer tape through a keyboard input device or remote terminal. In some cases, when paper tape or magnetic tape is prepared as a byproduct of another operation, these tapes can be "pooled" (run through a black box that converts them into computer-readable tape).

As a consequence of the input difficulties, computer tape storage is used in limited applications. Where the application is suitable, however, computer tape storage is fast, economical, and desirable.

An example of an application using computer tape storage of an office document is to be found in an automated billing system. The invoice is typed for mailing to the customer. A byproduct of this typing is a computer diskette or a magnetic tape cassette. The byproduct is then mailed or passed through a terminal, then over telephone lines, into the computer. It is processed by the computer's central processing unit and outputted onto tape or disk for storage and future retrieval.

Obviously, the cost of setting up such a system, utilizing a computer, terminals, and input devices would be prohibitive, except for the largest systems. Nevertheless, the computers and terminals are often on hand for typical data processing operations. These may be easily interfaced with word processing equipment to create a billing system of the type above, at very little cost. Storage and retrieval, in such a case, become available at practically no cost as a by-product of the system itself. In network systems, file servers store data for downloading to other PCs, providing instant availability of stored data.

WORD PROCESSING STORAGE

As used here, word processing is intended to mean typewritten words that can be edited, corrected, deleted, added, manipulated, and stored (see Microcomputer Storage on page 522).

The stored data can be transmitted via modem over ordinary telephone lines. Typical applications involve processing orders and transmitting them to a warehouse for picking and delivery; doing billing at remote office locations and transmitting the data to a central office computer for further data processing; or simply storing letters on disk for retrieval as needed.

One office equipment manufacturer, Canon, markets a filing system priced in the $5,000 range, consisting of a microcomputer and software that stores a document, say a letter, in an electronic folder in an electronic file drawer. The letter can be retrieved by date, name, or key word. It is retrieved to a screen and then printed out, all in the same amount of time it would take to open a file drawer and find and withdraw the letter. Electronic filing has the added advantage of never misplacing a document. When you retrieve it and print it out, it's still on file.

Another manufacturer, Micro-intelligent Systems, markets a laptop-size storage device and viewer that holds 25,000 documents, scans in new ones at 12 pages a minute, and prints out at 4 pages a minute; it is priced in the $5,000 to $7,000 range.

Similar equipment is available from Xerox and other manufacturers.

MICROFILM STORAGE

Other than manual systems, perhaps the best-known storage and retrieval systems are microfilm. As a rule of thumb, however, microfilm systems are not the most economical for straight storage purposes. Manual systems are usually less costly and safer. When tied to a timely retrieval system, though, microfilm can offer many advantages. Some advantages are:

1. 98% of needed storage space can be saved by reducing hard copy to microfilm.
2. Microfilm copies are acceptable to federal and state agencies.
3. Records can be retrieved more quickly.
4. Records may be copied, automatically, at the time of retrieval, for delivery to the user.
5. Refiling of the microfilm is automatic and less time-consuming than refiling a manual record.
6. Microfilm records need to be indexed to be retrieved, whereas manual file records are usually not indexed, thereby providing greater knowledge and control of the contents of the record room.
7. Large documents or voluminous files that require absolute protection and permanent storage are better handled through microfilm.

Microfilm systems, despite some advantages, are not the end-all of storage and retrieval systems. On the contrary, there may be some disadvantages:

1. The cost may be prohibitive. Some elements of cost to set up a microfilm system are:
    a. Labor is required to prepare files for filming; this involves proofreading, indexing, unstapling copies, reviewing developed film, and reshooting where necessary.
    b. Camera cost to buy ($1,800 to $2,500) or rent ($3.50 to $5.00 per day).
    c. Film cost and developing cost (approximately $3.50 per thousand documents).
    d. Floor space for camera, file cabinet, and copier.
2. The run rate may be too time-consuming. Approximately 2,000 documents a day can be processed. It may take too long to get into the system.
3. Files must be rearranged for filming, including unbinding and unfastening and unstapling.
4. Some colors and carbon copies do not copy well. Where credit balances or losses are in red, they will not show up differently on film and may need to be circled.
5. Only one person can use the reader at a time.
6. It may take longer to retrieve a microfilm copy than a hard copy, depending on the type of indexing system used.
7. Loss of film through accident or theft is not readily detectable and is more likely to happen than to a large file of hard copy records.
8. Internal Revenue Service may require transcription of photographic copies to hard copy.

One of the best uses of microfilm is to interface it with a manual system, instead of making a complete conversion to microfilm. This will allow a company to avail itself of most of the advantages, while at the same time avoiding the obvious disadvantages of microfilm. The following items could be microfilmed within the manual system:

1. Customer invoice copies, which are voluminous, sequential, and usually permanent as to retention, may be filmed without much initial preparation and with no indexing.
2. Large, permanent documents, such as books of original entry, may be filmed and kept safe in locked, fireproof files.

The above two categories encompass all of the large, bulky, permanent files that are not actively used. Microfilming in these categories should begin after the completion of the federal tax audit or six years, whichever is later. There is no point in microfilming these records during their active periods, unless the entire filing system is set up on microfilm. Under the type of system proposed, microfilm is used primarily for storage purposes, not retrieval.

Such a system requires the rental of a camera, once a year, and an inexpensive reader and photocopier. The cost would be between $3,000 to $5,000 and is the type of equipment that the manufacturers finance on three-to five-year full payout leases, with monthly costs running about $100 on a five-year lease.

MICROCOMPUTER STORAGE

Microcomputers (PCs) can store information on diskettes or tape drives. Both are used for backup and retrieval purposes. Each double-sided, high-density diskette holds about 1,300 kilobytes of information, or about 510 typewritten pages, assuming 250 double-spaced words per typewritten page.

A hard disk drive is an auxiliary storage device. It is a sealed unit that is not removed from the computer. One 100-MB (megabyte) hard disk can store about eighty times as much as a single diskette. This is the equivalent of over 40,000 typewritten pages. Computers normally have additional drives to accommodate diskettes, providing enormous storage capacity.

Additional resources are available to meet the unique needs of individual departments. The accounting department, for example, needs to retrieve financial statements, accounting standards, and tax forms and regulations. These items can be stored on a departmental intranet at low cost (try Microsoft Internet Server) to serve all personnel in the department.

An accounting application available from OutlookSoft's Everest is not only budgeting software but also an Internet-based management portal that provides analytic information, performance reports, and competitive analysis to managers. It utilizes the power of the Internet, Excel, and centralized database technologies to provide web-based analytic capabilities.

Traditional document storage vendors like Canon can supply document recorders in the form of a compact desktop system that records documents onto CDs or your network. The system provides optical character recognition and reads bar codes. Then it instantly stores the information as searchable fields. To access your images, merely place a CD into any PC using a recent Windows version, or retrieve them over your network. As a result, documents no longer need to be warehoused but are placed in ministorage.

Electronic filing systems are available in single desktop units that scan, store, retrieve, fax, and print documents. Backup files are read to 3.5″ optical disks that store up to 14,000 pages, about the same as a four-drawer letter-size filing cabinet. Such systems are available from Canon, DocSTAR, and Xerox. These systems eliminate file cabinets, save space, provide security, allow document sharing, permit instant retrieval, and prepare secure backups.

SUMMARY

The records retention program is the responsibility of the corporate controller. Such a program envisages a controlled current filing system, a long-range filing system, a well-defined list of which records to retain for how long, a systematic records destruction program, and an overall security system to protect these files. There are a variety of programs available to the user, including manual systems, computer storage, word processing, and microfilm storage. These can be integrated into manual systems, in part, depending on the size of the system and the amount of data.

14

Controlling the Data Processing Function

The controllership function of reporting and interpreting and that of evaluating and consulting, as set forth in the FEI definition, include the coordination of systems and procedures, the preparation of operating data and reports, and the evaluation of organization structures and procedures. This is, logically, a controller's responsibility, since the generation of financial statements and supporting reports is a byproduct of the flow of data through the organization. Management of this function requires:

1. Organization—a proper organizational structure within the centralized data processing department, and proper interfacing with other departments, including decentralized PC users.
2. Personnel management—establishing standards of work performance, monitoring performance, cross-training, educational advancement, and integration into the entire organization.
3. Control—control and monitoring of the work flow, systems and procedures work, and operations input and output.
4. Security—development of suitable security procedures for hardware, forms, and software.

ORGANIZATION

Three organizational problems exist in the data processing area: the organizational structure of the department itself, the location of the department within the overall corporate organization, and the integration of microcomputers into the corporate data structure. A proper evaluation of the data structure is required before the organization chart can be implemented.

Evaluation

This is the process wherein the entire company is examined as to the data inputs, processing, and output or reports. This is an overview of the enterprise and leads to a decision as to whether or not to automate, the type of equipment to use, and to whom the department will report. A decision must also be made as to whether the responsibility for data processing control will be centralized or decentralized. The results of this study will be different for every company, and the scope and amount of detail in the study will often depend on the size of the company and its data processing expertise. This study includes:

1. A listing of all output reports and data contained in them
2. A cross-listing of reports containing duplicate output data
3. A similar listing of input data
4. Interviews with top management to obtain their impressions of the present reporting system and what they really want
5. Work counts associated with all listings, such as number of vendors, checks written, invoices to customers, statements mailed, credits issued, employees, commission checks written, journal entries, total number of customers per period, items of inventory, and frequency of shipments

While the results of this study vary by company, the study itself creates a better understanding of the company, shatters some myths about volumes of work, and permits the controller to determine the data processing needs of the company.

A typical result of such a study might reveal that the present system is providing voluminous information in tremendous detail—too much, and too late. Top management might prefer more timely flash reports with fewer numbers, to give a fast status report on overall operations. This could mean a requirement for faster automation of initial input (for example, grocery stores now routinely scan bar codes on most of the items they have for sale). Or, it could mean a requirement to completely bypass machine handling of data (for example, branch managers fax to headquarters, daily, with orders and written information).

This study will be quite useful, as we shall see in the control section, in establishing edit control to provide more correct output (for example, the highest commission on any product is $600 and the computer may be programmed to identify for review any higher amount). The volume of data will also identify the proper type of equipment to use in the data processing department, or whether to use any at all. A daily newspaper, for example, must meet a daily publication deadline, or it will soon be out of business. This requires daily processing of data to its culmination, and so the computer must be used. A trading stamp company, on the other hand, processes a great many books of stamps, but the urgency of meeting a deadline is not present, and most trading stamp companies rely on manual work, rather than the computer, to handle the requirements of the business.

In evaluating the need for a machine system, advantages and disadvantages of automation may readily be set forth, but the advantages are manifest and the disadvantages easily resolved:

1. Machines are not sick and absent from work. When they break down, the manufacturers maintain 24-hour repair staffing.
2. Typewritten or written data may be machine-oriented free, as a byproduct of the typing or writing. This results from storage on diskette or file servers in a network environment.
3. The same data is used for many types of reports, and the computer can process and reprocess it without further repetitive writing.
4. The machine will not make transcription errors, under proper control, nor will it make arithmetic errors.

5. Security with machines is better. They don't quit and go to work for competitors.
6. The computer can perform processing and arithmetic functions far more quickly than persons, and in more depth.
7. Machine output reports are more readable than handwritten.
8. Storage of information and security are better by machine.

The most commonly mentioned disadvantages, and their solutions, are:

1. The cost of hardware and software is enormous. (The system must be cost-justified in terms of the results achieved.)
2. The staffing for the data processing organization is a problem; personnel are difficult to find and high-salaried, and there is high turnover to competitors. (Data processing personnel must be properly motivated within the company, as must any employee, and their salaries are consistent with those of any corporate high-technology people.)
3. The responsibility for processing functions, like payrolls and monthly financial statements, rests with a few, key, difficult to control people. (The responsibility rests with the controller and the data processing manager, who, it is hoped, are no more difficult to control than any other managers. Adequate cross-training and backup personnel are available on every job.)
4. The time required to hire the right people and to implement the programs, systems, and procedures is prohibitive. (Time is a major consideration, but the results to be achieved must justify the advance planning and expenditures. See No. 1, above. As with any capital expenditure, cost justification is required.)

Having evaluated the data processing system, a decision to implement a data processing department may now be made. Even in a situation that specifies decentralized PCs, it is common to clear data through the centralized data processing department. Central control is necessary to protect the integrity of corporate database files and to establish a security system to protect against unauthorized entry into databases.

Centralized and decentralized computer control can be compared as follows:

Centralized Control

◇ Unauthorized access to computer hardware and sensitive data is properly restricted.
◇ Software applications are developed by trained professionals.
◇ New software programs and changes to existing ones are thoroughly tested, debugged, and documented.
◇ Purchasing costs of hardware and software are lower.
◇ The development of new applications takes longer.
◇ Large mainframe computer systems cost more than PCs.

Decentralized Control

◇ The development of new applications is quicker.
◇ PCs and related software are less costly than large mainframe systems and centrally developed applications.
◇ Purchases of PCs can be managed through decentralized department budgets.
◇ Individual user purchases of PCs lead to a lack of compatibility among various users.
◇ Overall cost of decentralized purchasing of PCs is increased by failure to properly negotiate pricing or to obtain purchase discounts for timely payment or volume purchases.
◇ Both the effort in purchasing hardware and the hardware itself are often duplicated by various users.
◇ Applications developed by PC users are limited in use to the user-developer, are relatively inefficient and difficult to use and maintain, lack audit trails, and do not ensure the integrity of their data.
◇ Equipment may not be maintained properly because of lack of maintenance standards or procedures.
◇ Decentralized systems may be improperly installed from a working standpoint and may impose safety hazards.
◇ The software is generally not compatible with other software used within the company.
◇ Susceptibility to viruses is increased by the use of untested application software.

Word of Caution: The advantages offered by PCs may dictate their use, but standard policies should be developed regarding the purchase and installation of hardware and software. Policy statements should be a part of the appropriate policy manuals. This is essential in the case of PCs that produce critical output.

Helpful Hint: Examine client-server networks, which have many of the features of both centralized and decentralized systems. All of the features of centralized control are present, at low cost.

Implementation

This requires, as a first step, identifying, hiring, and training the data processing staff. Staff may be obtained from:

1. Company personnel files
2. Personnel agencies specializing in DP personnel
3. Management advisory staffs of independent accounting firms
4. Recommendations from peers, banks, consultants, and associates
5. Advertising in national papers, local area papers, and DP magazines

For the company new to data processing, interviewing and identification of the right personnel may be done by the company's outside consultants or accounting firm, although this should not be necessary. The same techniques should be brought to interviewing and hiring the DP manager as are used with any other management people. You may not have the ability to judge a candidate's technical competence, but you can evaluate him or her for management ability, and proper reference checks can verify the former. Once you have identified, hired, and trained the new DP manager in the standard corporate training program, which may simply involve time spent with other managers, he or she is ready to take a place in the organization and to establish the structure of his or her own department:

1. *Corporate organization.* The data processing manager may report directly to the controller, or through an operations manager, administrative control manager, management information systems manager, or director of administration and then to the controller. Regardless of the type and size of company, the data processing control function is a controllership responsibility.

2. *Departmental organization.* An average **organization chart for a data processing department** is shown in Exhibit 14-1. This includes systems and programming and operations (computer and data entry).

In this chart, data entry operations reports to the operations manager, as do the actual computer room and the input/output staff, which is a control function, responsible for balancing all reports.

Systems analysts and programmers report to the systems and programming manager, and both he or she and the operations manager report to the head of the department, who, in turn, reports to the controller.

There are no dotted lines of interface on this chart, showing the functional relationships of one department head to another. In the company illustrated, the data processing manager has full department head status, and as shown on page 707 of the controller's position description in the "Treasurer's and Controller's Functions," he or she interfaces with the auditors, the manager of the accounting services department, the national administrator (responsible for branch office administrative operations), and the order/billing manager. These key managers, together, are responsible for the administrative operations of the company. All report to the vice president/controller.

PERSONNEL MANAGEMENT

The need to manage personnel is a key ingredient of every manager's job, including that of the treasurer or controller. There seems to be

Exhibit 14-1. Organization chart—data processing.

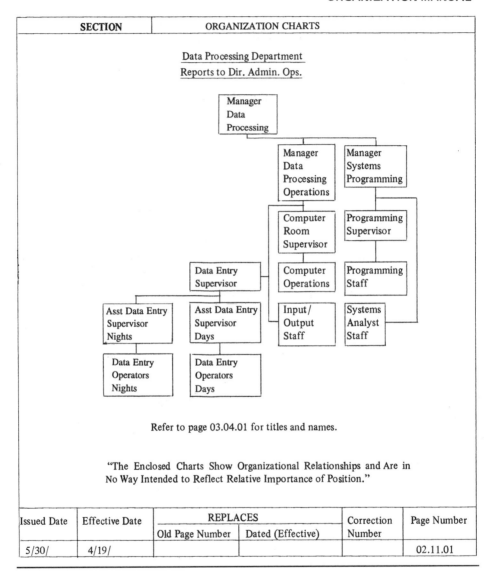

ORGANIZATION MANUAL

SECTION	ORGANIZATION CHARTS

Data Processing Department
Reports to Dir. Admin. Ops.

Manager
Data
Processing

Manager Data Processing Operations — Manager Systems Programming

Computer Room Supervisor — Programming Supervisor

Data Entry Supervisor — Computer Operations — Programming Staff

Asst Data Entry Supervisor Nights — Asst Data Entry Supervisor Days — Input/Output Staff — Systems Analyst Staff

Data Entry Operators Nights — Data Entry Operators Days

Refer to page 03.04.01 for titles and names.

"The Enclosed Charts Show Organizational Relationships and Are in
No Way Intended to Reflect Relative Importance of Position."

Issued Date	Effective Date	REPLACES		Correction Number	Page Number
		Old Page Number	Dated (Effective)		
5/30/	4/19/				02.11.01

a certain mystique, however, surrounding data processing personnel, perhaps because the discipline of data processing (as it relates to the computer) is only 40 years old, which fills the manager with trepidation.

Standard personnel management techniques apply, no less, to data processing people. These include:

A Management Philosophy

This is first and foremost and relates to the manager's own attitude and approach to people. It means proper training of the manager (in this case the controller) and the manager's immediate subordinates (the operations manager or data processing manager), leading to identification with corporate goals. This may be done formally, through management training courses within or without the company, or informally, through conversations with higher management or by a project of personal education in management by the controller. The vital point is that the controller be aware and proceed to develop a corporate philosophy that is imparted to personnel as a continuing and ongoing part of their jobs.

A Management Example

Once the corporate philosophy has been adopted, as described above, the controller proceeds to implement this by setting an example of a manager in action. This requires the adoption of traits that must be expressed on the job, even though they are not characteristic of the controller's nature. Through attention and effort, they become second nature. Only the rare manager is endowed with all these appearances. The rest of us must develop them and can be equally successful.

These traits are leadership, integrity, and sensitivity. There are others, but these are the ones needed to succeed.

✧ *Leadership* encompasses the marks of management with which personnel will identify. It may simply mean the proper appearance in front of subordinates (from not too many drinks at the Christmas party to leaving your tie knotted on a hot summer day) (although the standard needs to apply to the particular circumstance—no tie may be appropriate for the manufacturer of sport shirts). Or it may mean taking the lead in cutting his or her own departmental budget, selling this to and obtaining the support of his or her people.

Case in Point: One company had a desperate need to reduce corporate payrolls by 5%. The controller took the lead by instructing the payroll department to reduce his salary by 10%. The manager of the data processing department immediately volunteered to take a 5% pay cut. The section managers — the data processing operations manager and the systems and programming manager — agreed to reassign work tasks, to absorb some of the tasks themselves, and not to replace attrited employees for the next 60 days. As a result, within two months, the data processing department had fully achieved the 5% payroll cut and set the tone for the entire company. The two managers who took pay cuts more than made these back on the next round of payroll increases.

✧   *Integrity* is the adoption of a standard of moral value that is seen by subordinates as an indicator of a sense of conscience and respect for duty. The manager's expression of this morality is seen and sensed by his or her subordinates, who will respond in kind. To this extent, it is another form of leadership.

Another Case in Point: A DP manager had evaluated and cost-justified a new, more powerful computer. The project received higher management approval and, on the strength of this, five programmers and analysts were hired to take the company into the new machine. The company, in a cost reduction move, subsequently raised its return on investment objectives and re-evaluated the ROI on the new computer. The DP manager responded by selling the changed decision to the new personnel and offered them two alternatives — to find room in the training budget to give them advanced educational training in the new machine in anticipation of eventually being able to cost-justify it under the newer ROI standards, or to use best efforts to relocate them to another company that was currently using the new machine. One accepted the latter alternative and was immediately relocated, at the same salary, using a data processing personnel agency that had, in the past, worked closely with the DP manager. The other four employees, seeing the sincerity of the proposal, elected to remain with the company and eventually were rewarded by seeing the company reselect the larger computer. The DP manager's integrity in either training people in the new machine or actually transferring them to a company using it, in the face of a corporate decision to abandon the computer, was a commitment to the conditions of their hire. This action won the respect of the employees and maintained a cadre of trained people, prepared to take the company into the next higher phase of its computer operations when conditions permitted it.

✦   *Sensitivity* is the ability to be receptive to and respond to the feelings of employees, to enable the manager to exercise the traits of leadership and integrity that command the respect and cooperation of those employees.

This management attribute connotes a perception of the employee as an individual. It means observation of his or her performance and questioning the reasons for lack of it or, equally important, determining how to maintain consistently high performance.

The manager who is sensitive to the feelings of employees, enabling them to act in the company's best interest, sets a management example that encourages all employees to attain the overall corporate goals. But the manager should:

> *Avoid This Pitfall:* Do not set up a climate that encourages invalid complaints. That's like "sick call" in the army. Any malingerer can use it to avoid responsibility. Repetitive invalid complaints will identify the exaggerator, who should be firmly upbraided.

Management by Objectives

Having developed a philosophy and proceeded to set an example of management using leadership, integrity, and sensitivity, the manager sets objectives for personnel and measures their performance against these objectives.

In some companies, management by objectives is a corporate program, administered by the personnel manager, utilizing specialized

Exhibit 14-2.   Management by objectives form.

Performance Planning and Evaluation
for
Management by Objectives

CONFIDENTIAL

Employee Name (Last, First and Initial)		Serial Number	Date Employed	
Position Title	Position Code—4 digit (Optional)		Date Assigned Present Position	
Date Assigned to This Appraiser	Date of Performance Plan		Date of Performance Evaluation	
Location		Office or Dept. Number		Division

forms designed for this purpose. Exhibit 14-2 depicts a **management by objectives form** that is part of a formal program.

A formal management by objectives program starts with top management's (the board of directors and/or president) goal or objective for the coming year, usually expressed as X dollars of sales and earnings. This may be quantified by product line or class of sale, such as wholesale or retail, but does not usually go beyond that degree. This objective is passed down to those reporting directly to the president. They set their broad objectives, consonant with the president's goals. The treasurer, for example, may establish a goal of improving accounts receivable turn-

(*text continues on page 539*)

PERFORMANCE PLANNING

PERFORMANCE EVALUATION

RESPONSIBILITIES (Key words to describe the major elements of this employee's job.)	PERFORMANCE FACTORS AND/OR RESULTS TO BE ACHIEVED (A more specific statement of the employee's key responsibilities and/or goals he or she can reasonably be expected to achieve in the coming period.)	RELATIVE IMPORTANCE	ACTUAL ACHIEVEMENTS	LEVEL OF ACHIEVEMENT — FAR EXCEEDED	CONSISTENTLY EXCEEDED	EXCEEDED AT TIMES	MET	UNSATISFACTORY

CHANGES IN PERFORMANCE PLAN (May be recorded anytime during the appraisal period.)

OPTIONAL ADDITIONAL PLANS (Where considered appropriate by manager and employee.)

ADDITIONAL SIGNIFICANT ACCOMPLISHMENTS

CONTINUING RESPONSIBILITIES (Responsibilities, not covered at left, to be considered only when they have had a significant positive or negative effect on the overall performance.)

RELATIONSHIPS WITH OTHERS (JOB RELATED) (Significant positive or negative influence this employee has had on the performance of other employees.)

OVERALL RATING (Considering all factors, check the definition that best describes this employee's overall performance during the past period.)

Satisfactory
- ☐ Results achieved far exceeded the requirements of the job in all key areas.
- ☐ Results achieved consistently exceeded the requirements of the job.
- ☐ Results achieved exceeded the requirements of the job at times.
- ☐ Results achieved met the requirements of the job.

Unsatisfactory
- ☐ Marginal performance. Must improve to satisfactory.
- ☐ Inadequate performance. On Notice.

(continued)

Exhibit 14-2.   *(continued)*

COUNSELING SUMMARY

Employee Strengths   **Suggested Improvements**

1. _____   1. _____
2. _____   2. _____
3. _____   3. _____

SIGNIFICANT INTERVIEW COMMENTS

(Record here only those additional significant items brought up during the discussion by either you or the employee that are not recorded elsewhere in this document.)

_____

_____

_____

_____

_____

_____

_____

_____

_____

_____   _____   _____
Manager's Signature   Print Name   Date of Interview

EMPLOYEE REVIEW

Optional Comments: If the employee wishes to do so, any comments concerning the performance plan or evaluation (for example, agreement or disagreement) may be indicated in the space provided below.

_____

_____

_____

I have reviewed this document and discussed the contents with my manager. My signature means that I have been advised of my performance status and does not necessarily imply that I agree with this evaluation.

_____   _____
Employee's Signature   Date

MANAGEMENT REVIEW

Optional Comments _____

_____

_____

_____

_____   _____   _____
Reviewer's Signature   Print Name   Date

(text continued from page 536)

over by five days, thereby increasing cash flow and decreasing interest costs on short-term borrowings by X dollars. These goals, in turn, are passed down to the next level. Second-level managers then set their objectives within the framework of their superiors'; the credit and collection manager, for example, to support the treasurer's goal, may set his or her objective as reducing 90-day past due accounts receivable by 20% or X dollars. Each manager also identifies trouble areas in her or his department that affect overall performance. An example: to reduce departmental turnover by X%, thereby saving X dollars in personnel recruitment costs. The department manager imparts these goals to his or her employees, receives back their suggestions, and creates final objectives that have the input and support of his or her people. The entire company is thus involved in the attainment of the corporate objectives. Bimonthly or quarterly reviews of progress are a part of the program, to monitor progress and allow for midstream correction. Annual evaluations give consideration to the success in meeting objectives.

> *An Obvious Pitfall:* Avoid permitting managers to set objectives that are too easily attained, thereby restricting corporate growth.

An informal management by objectives program may be implemented quite simply, using the same techniques as above but dispensing with the use of special forms, with each manager being responsible for those in his or her department attaining their objectives. There is no formal measurement process by the personnel department.

> *The Key Point Is:* Given the dignity of a formal procedure, each manager should set objectives for personnel reporting to him or her and measure their performance against these objectives.

> *Helpful Hint:* A prerequisite to any management by objectives system is the definition of the basic responsibilities of each employee. There must be a position description (see Chapter 7) for each job. Standards of performance should be established, to augment the functions described in the position description. Exhibit 14-3 is the first page of a 21-point list of **typical standards for programmers**. Addended to it is an 8-point standard for programming trainees.

Exhibit 14-3. Standards of performance for programmers.

PROGRAMMING STANDARDS

PURPOSE: This standard specifies the procedures and techniques to be
used by SAVIN programmers. The use of these standards will optimize
program efficiency and improve communication in the Data Processing
group. Program maintenance is greatly simplified if programs are
adequately annotated and uniform techniques are used.

RESPONSIBILITY: It will be the responsibility of the Programming
Manager and the Documentation Administrator to enforce these standards.

STANDARDS:

1. No program assignment or program change is to be accepted without
    Standard Program Specifications acceptable to the Programming
    Manager.

2. These standards will be adhered to in all programs, unless specific
    authorization has been given by the Programming Manager.

3. All programs will be written in COBOL, unless otherwise specified
    by the Programming Manager.

4. Where a source statement book is available for a file, record,
    or processing description, it must be used. Further, the programmer
    should use the actual book data names and not an independent data
    description.

5. The program name assigned by the (Analyst) must be used for the
    PROGRAM-ID and for the source statement library entry. Program
    segments will use the program name, followed by a two-digit segment
    number (01 through 99). Each program change will be assigned a
    version number. The PROGRAM-ID must be held in a six-character
    data item immediately following the WORKING-STORAGE SECTION entry.

    e.g. WORKING-STORAGE SECTION.
          77   W-PROGRAM-ID   PIC X(6) VALUE 'APS101'

    EACH TIME A NEW PROGRAM VERSION IS COMMENCED, THIS DATA ITEM
    MUST BE CHANGED, AS WELL AS THE PROGRAM-ID. A REMARKS LINE SHOULD
    BE ADDED TO DESCRIBE EACH CHANGE.

```
               PROGRAMMING STANDARDS
               (As applied to Trainees)



1)   Keep your Project Leader informed daily as to the status
     of all incomplete programs assigned to you.

2)   Ask your Project Leader for help in setting up job(s) for
     testing.  (Do not submit any program for testing without
     notification.)

3)   After two hours of trying to debug a program, make certain
     that you get help.  (Do not use 'TRACE' or 'EXHIBIT' state-
     ments unless asked to do so.)

4)   Make ALL corrections to your source deck before resubmitting
     for another compilation/test; then resubmit as soon as possible.

5)   Code all corrections to your program(s) if more than 10 lines.

6)   Always inform your Project Leader of any problems encountered
     in obtaining compilations, tests, etc.

7)   When coding, use the general programming standards as set
     up by the department head.

8)   Unless otherwise authorized, a flowchart must be drawn and
     the logic accepted by the Programming Manager before coding
     commences.
```

Whether or not there is a formal Management by Objectives program, following are guidelines to be used in setting objectives:

When setting objectives for any individual's job, it is important to remember that the objective should not simply be a restatement of all the aspects of the individual's job description. The purpose of setting objectives is to pick five to seven key goals or results to achieve within a specified time.

The objectives or goals or results desired should be stated as precisely as possible. The best way of achieving precise descriptions is to quantify the objectives. For example, the objective to "lower production costs" should be defined as "lower the cost of producing model 250 by 7% by September 1." Unless the goal or objective is specifically defined, it will be difficult to determine to what degree it has been reached at the end of the specified period. Nonspecific goals also result in a failure to properly appraise the magnitude of the job necessary to meet that goal.

For example, in discussing decreasing costs, it is obvious that if you are producing three different items, you should be talking about three separate cost reduction goals rather than one. Additionally, when goals or objectives are nonspecific, the managers who have to do the job to achieve those goals do not investigate all the variables related to achieving them. For example, in one company a computer operations manager set a goal "to reduce the total time for processing customer statements by 10%." Not only did the manager fail to meet this goal, but she was barely able to hold the time down to the previous level. The fact that had been overlooked was the sales manager's goal. He had reached his goal of increasing volume with many new accounts, and so the billing had increased. If more effort were devoted to identifying the specific objective, it would have been related to "average time per statement" rather than the general way in which it was described. This is a very common error.

Results or objectives may be stated in dates for completion when no other measurement seems appropriate. For example, "complete a study of alternate life insurance programs by August 1 and recommend a new program to the president by November 1." This could even be restated as "recommend to the president by November 1 a new program that will provide benefits to match or exceed those offered in this area, but with no increase in cost for employees or the company." The more precise statement not only provides guidelines for evaluating the adequacy of the program, but provides considerable guidance to the person who has to accomplish the work.

Below are some criteria that will help you to analyze your objectives to determine whether or not they are specific:

"Good" commitments are:

1. Stated in terms of end results.
2. Achievable in a definite time period.
3. Definite as to the form of accomplishment.
4. Related to management of the business.
5. Important to the success of the business.

6. Precisely stated in terms of quantities, where possible.
7. Each limited to one important commitment to a statement.
8. Those that require stretch to improve results or personal effectiveness.

"Poor" commitments are:

1. Stated in terms of processes or activities.
2. Never fully achievable; there is no specific target date.
3. Ambiguous in defining what is expected.
4. Theoretical or "idealistic."
5. Not of real consequence.
6. Either too brief, indefinite, long, or complex.
7. Compound, covering two or more commitments to a statement.
8. Lacking requirement for improvement. Following established routines and procedures will assure the commitment.

Although the objectives you list should not cover your entire job, they should cover those important or critical areas that will probably require your major efforts during the specified period. Do not list routine duties that are normal functions, and that do not require major efforts to bring about changes or upgrading. If your statement of objectives ends up describing the maintenance of normal performance in your area of responsibility, do not bother writing it.

Below are possible objectives that may be written for a plant superintendent:

1. Reduce plant operating costs to $0.94 per M units produced, by January 1.
2. Speed increase in #53 grade in the range of 100 fpm or more, by June 30.
3. Set up central planning office where orders will be accumulated, by April 1.
4. Late orders not to exceed 10% of all orders shipped, by June 30.
5. Reduce budget $450.00 per month (3.5%), by January 1.

6. Analyze, develop drawings, and submit recommendations to determine feasibility of relocating printing and cutting sections, by December 1.

7. Reduce exempt and nonexempt factory payroll $1,500.00 per month, by October 1.

8. All first-level supervisors attend in-plant training program stressing leadership techniques and communication, by June 30.

9. Obtain closer cooperation and communication between departmental supervisors, by December 31.

10. Plan and carry out specified reading program in area of production management, by October 15.

11. Attend AMA Workshop Seminars on production and inventory control, by March 31.

Giving due consideration to these guides, the following pages present a formal outline for implementing the objectives program, showing, step by step, how the objectives are communicated to all company employees:

OUTLINE FOR
COMMUNICATING COMPANY OBJECTIVES

1. The president communicates his or her objectives to managers answering to him or her.

2. These managers draft specific objectives relating to the performance of the unit under their responsibility.

3. These managers meet with the president separately to discuss and mutually agree upon that manager's objectives for the current fiscal year.

4. Each of these managers will then take the agreed-upon objectives and expose them in a group discussion with the next level managers

reporting to them. The purpose of the meeting will be twofold, as follows:

   a. To explain our interest in the steps we will be taking to increase our communication regarding objectives.
   b. To fully explain the objectives of that division and to involve the lower-level department heads in an open discussion covering ways in which they may develop objectives in their own areas of responsibility to meet the greater team objectives of that division. Each of these department heads will then be required to return within five working days with a draft of her or his specific objectives and will meet separately with the division head to discuss and mutually establish objectives for that department.

5. Each department head will then meet with a group of managers answering directly to him or her to carry on the same type of meeting as was conducted by the division head. (The director of personnel may meet with department heads either as a group or individually to provide guidance in wording or identifying objectives as well as to provide guidance in conducting the face-to-face meetings between the department head and subordinate managers.)

6. Attached is a form for recording objectives and recording due dates or anticipated review dates. Expected completion dates should be either the date on which a project must be completed or the end of the period, such as the end of the fiscal year. The form also includes a section for review notes concerning the progress on each of the objectives, but there is no "evaluation" section per se. Results can be written in at the follow-up sessions between a manager and his or her superior. Our aim in this program is to achieve management participation without introducing a concept of a new or different evaluation procedure, or another way to pressure a manager.

The personnel department will, in addition, develop a "performance evaluation guide" to be used by managers in reviewing and evaluating their subordinate managers, no less frequently than annually. (There is no formalized program at present.)

OBJECTIVES PLANNING

Job Title _____ Name _____ Date _____

Priority	Objectives	Expected Comple- tion Date	Results
1.			
2.			
3.			
4.			
5.			
6.			
7.			

7. It is understood that the establishing of certain objectives for one particular department or division may require the cooperation and a similar objective on the part of another division or department. For example, should the marketing division desire to establish a program of collection and analysis of certain sales data, it may be necessary for discussion and a mutual agreement between marketing and data processing to establish due dates when such a program would be available from the computer. Data processing would also have as one of their objectives the related due dates for the revision or creation of necessary programs to provide the data needed by marketing.

Follow-up

1. The president would maintain a file of the objectives as stated by the managers reporting to him or her.

2. These managers would, in turn, maintain a complete file of objectives for all of the managers or supervisors under their responsibility.

3. The president and each manager will meet individually with his or her subordinate managers for the purpose of reviewing objectives, no less than quarterly. However, when an objective of any manager involves a completion date that is not consistent with a quarterly review, that specific objective may be reviewed by the two appropriate managers on a frequency as desired by the senior manager.

4. In the event that because of either conditions beyond the corporation's control or decisions made by the corporation, it is necessary to revise or eliminate objectives within a division, the changes may be accomplished only with the approval of the president. Changes in objectives at any level within a division would require the approval of the head of that division prior to the change.

5. Within 90 days of the date of introduction of the program, the president will meet with managers answering to him or her to evaluate the program's progress.

In summary, management of the personnel of the data processing department is no mystery. It involves the same techniques that the good manager brings to managing people in any department.

THE KEY IS:

Employees are individuals, and different things motivate each one. How can we reach each person when everyone is so different? Does a common denominator exist? It does—it is *involvement*. All people are more productive when they experience *pride* and a *sense of accomplishment* in their work. People need to be *recognized* for their efforts, not only financially, but with *praise*, *status*, and even constructive criticism.

Involvement is the key to productivity. When you involve an individual, you are actually telling him or her, "I feel you have something to offer; you are a responsible individual who has an important role in our company. I recognize your ability and seek your help with this project."

The steps to take are these:

1. Fully communicate goals and objectives of both your job and their own, the role of the department, general targets of the company, etc.
2. Through discussion, get them to spell out specific job duties and responsibilities.
3. Let each employee set objectives to be reached for each responsibility in terms of time, dollars, number of pieces produced, etc.
4. Help each employee write an operating plan as to *how* the objectives will be reached.
5. Measure the progress and discuss problem areas along the way.
6. Help each employee develop strengths and correct any limitations blocking his or her effectiveness.
7. Reset goals and objectives for the next time period.

Through this technique, not only do we have a highly motivated, responsive work cadre, but we also have developed independent, capable workers whose personal desires more nearly align themselves with the desires of the company.

CONTROL

The third aspect of the management of the data processing function, preceded by organization and personnel management, is control. This ensures that the DP manager will not become the tool of the department, the machine, or the system; that he or she will not need to accept excuses that the machine is down, the program doesn't work, the key punch operator didn't show up to work, the input hasn't come in from another department . . . and on and on. Control involves direction, regulation, verification, and planning. In short—no surprises.

CASE IN POINT: The Equity Funding insurance scandal, perhaps the biggest insurance fraud in history, was based on the recording, by the computer, of nonexistent insurance policies. With proper input/ output controls in the DP department, and the tieing out of report totals, one to the other, the scheme could not have succeeded. It would have had to involve too many lower-echelon personnel. It succeeded with the involvement of only a few key people, simply because quality controls were omitted in the DP department.

The fulcrum for this control system is the input/output staff (see Exhibit 14-1 for organization chart position), sometimes called the quality control staff, reporting directly to the manager of data processing operations. It is set apart from data entry as well as from systems and programming. It cannot, thus, be manipulated by other sections of the department but is concerned only with proper, quality-controlled operations.

Let us see how control works.

It starts with the formal implementation of a systems and procedures department. This may consist of one person and, at first, is not concerned only with computer documentation, but rather with the flow of data, paperwork, and reports that are manually generated. The work study used in the evaluation process, described on page 526, is the first task of the new systems and procedures department. Not only is this fundamental to the decision on whether and how to automate, but it is equally fundamental to the management of the company that functions under manual control. These are the steps taken by the systems group:

1. Evaluate the reporting system (see page 526).
2. Establish major business categories that will require system control, such as accounting, order/billing, purchasing, data processing, office services, personnel, production, sales, research. Use the organization chart to help in this.
3. Establish position descriptions for each job (Chapter 7) in a management capacity, and work standards (Exhibit 14-3) for each employee reporting to a manager.
4. Write down the operating procedures for each department if they involve the transmission of data outside the department—that is, the procedures are interdepartmental.
5. Record these procedures in a procedures manual, organized by major business categories, containing an index, and with provi-

sion for update and correction through a correction checklist (Chapter 7).

6. Require, through one of the interdepartmental procedures in the procedures manual, that all intradepartmental procedures and work rules be written down, kept current, expanded to fit new jobs, and kept under the control of the department head.

The duties and responsibilities of every employee have now been written down and circulated, the flow of paperwork has been delineated in the procedures, interdepartmental relationships have been established, and the framework for a control system is in place.

The performance within this framework must now be measured and monitored. Monitoring measures progress, avoids surprises, allows corrective action, and provides that deadlines will be met. The entire system is monitored through the **data processing report schedule** shown in Exhibit 14-4. This records and tracks each machine-generated report, comparing delivery dates to due dates and input delivery dates to input due dates. Tracking of input data provides an early warning that output reports may be late. This schedule is updated and recirculated for every new date or change listed therein. Each department head examines the schedule for those items that affect his or her area, taking corrective action necessary to meet the due dates.

Similarly, various departments receive reports from data processing that are used as a basis for generating various manual reports. Most of these are accounting-department-generated. Others come from the purchasing or production department. A **report schedule, for monitoring purposes**, is shown at Exhibit 14-5. This shows each manually generated accounting department report, the due date, and the actually delivered date for each of three months. The accounting manager uses this to monitor the production of his or her own department, and other recipient managers use it to plan reports and work that they, in turn, generate off these reports.

We have just examined how finished report production is monitored. This involves circulation of status reports interdepartmentally. However, the work in progress also needs to be monitored within each department. Such reports are mainly for the department head's use but may be circulated to other department managers who have an interest in the work. A **systems and programming department status report**

Exhibit 14-4. Data processing report schedule.

A/R Cash Good Thru: 10/16
Billing Updated Thru: 10/15

Data Processing Report Schedule
For Month of _____

Control Code	Report Name	Input Due Date	Input Rec'd	Proof Due Date	Proof Rec'd	Report Due	Run Date	Rerun #1	Rerun #2	Date Mailed	Date Rec'd	Distribution	Comments
SAR85	A/R Dunning Letters					10/16	10/11			10/15			
SAR21	A/R Cash Update F.O.M.					10/16	10/12			10/14			
SAR31	A/R Reg. Cash Only E.O.M.					10/16	10/14			10/14			
SCA15	A/R Mthly Cash Receipts					10/16	10/15			10/15			
SCA20	A/R Mthly Cash by G/L					10/16	10/15			10/15			
SCA25	J/E by G/L					10/16	10/15			10/15			
SCA40	J/E Single Entry					10/16	10/15			10/15			
SCA50	A/R Mthly Cash Aging					10/16	10/15			10/15			
PRO200	P/R Master Updates 9/18 Union	10/15	10/15	10/16	10/16	10/16	10/15			10/16			
PRO300	P/R Adjustments 9/18 Union	10/15	10/15	10/16	10/16	10/16	10/16			10/16			
PRO600	P/R Checks 9/18 Union			10/16	10/16	10/16	10/16			10/16			
PRO700	P/R Register 9/18 Union					10/16	10/16			10/16			
GLS042	Freight Purchases by Dis. Code												
GLS042	Purchases by Dis. Code												
DBS810	Invoice Reg						10/16						
AP1096	A/P Bank Rec Proof						10/16			10/17			
	Master Billing Register					10/17				10/17			
	Master Billing Invoices					10/17							
COMO30	Commission J/E Proof					10/17	10/17			10/17			
AP0004	A/P Vendor Master Updates 9/28	10/16	10 16			10/17	10/17			10/17			
AP0019	A/P Details-Proof 9/28	10/16	10 16			10/17	10/17			10/17			
AP0023	A/P Cash Req. 9/28					10/18							
AP0022	A/P Checks 9/18					10/18							
AP015B	A/P Check Register 9/18					10/18							
COMO70	Commission Master Update					10/18							
	Br. Billing Close												

551

Exhibit 14-5.   Accounting department report schedule.

ACCOUNTING DEPARTMENT REPORTS

Based on Other Departmental Input

#	Report	Working Day Due	January	February	March
1	Flash - Income Statement	5	1-8	2-7	3-7
2	Balance Sheet and Operating Statement	10	1-15	2-14	3-14
3	PABST Reconciliation	10	1-15	2-14	3-14
4	Diversified Balance Sheet & Operating Stmt.	11	1-16	2-15	3-15
5	Monthly Expenses by Budget Code	11	1-16	2-15	3-15
6	Monthly Expenses - Summary	11	1-16	2-15	3-15
7	Comparison of Operations to Budget	12	1-17	2-18	3-18
8	Schedule of Gross Profits	12	1-17	2-18	3-18
9	Temp. PABST	3	1-6	2-5	3-5
10	Travel Advances	13	1-20	2-19	3-19
11	Loans to Employees	13	1-20	2-19	3-19
12	Sundry Receivables	13	1-20	2-19	3-19
13	Royalty Income	13	1-20	2-19	3-19
14	Bad Debt Resume	14	1-21	2-20	3-20
15	GSA Sales	14	1-21	2-20	3-20
16	Cafeteria P & L	14	1-21	2-20	3-20
17	Avg. No. of Retail Sales per Salesperson	14	1-21	2-20	3-20
18	Telephone Expense - by Zone & Branch	14	1-21	2-20	3-20
19	Postage Expense - by Zone & Branch	14	1-21	2-20	3-20
20	Personnel Recruitment Exp. - by Zone & Br.	14	1-21	2-20	3-20
21	Rapifax Billing	15	1-22	2-21	3-21
22	Comparison of Selling Salaries to				
23	Retail Sales	15	1-22	2-21	3-21
24	Bank Letter - Financials	16	1-23	2-24	3-24
25	President - Report Book	17	1-24	2-25	3-25
26	Avg. No. of Rolls Shipped per machine	17	1-24	2-25	3-25
27	Demo Materials Summary	18	1-27	2-26	3-26
28	MAL	18	1-27	2-26	3-26
29	PABST - Final	19	1-28	2-27	3-27
30	RVA	20	1-29	2-28	3-28
31	A/R Summary	20	1-29	2-28	3-28
32	Savinair	20	1-29	2-28	3-28
33	Restan	20+	1-30	2-28	3-31
34	Rosia	20+	1-30	2-28	3-31
35	Leased Cars	20+	1-30	2-28	3-31

is shown in Exhibit 14-6. This lists open projects and compares actual to budgeted hours, dates, people, and worker-days, showing the percent complete and any comments.

> *Note of Caution:* This is not an exception report, but rather contains a great deal of detail about each job. Each line must be scrutinized carefully to get the full benefit of the report. If this report is simply scanned or only one column is monitored, important warning signals may be missed, such as the actual start date.

In addition to monitoring the overall activities of the department, that is, all its tasks, in Exhibit 14-6 through the department status report, each specific project is tracked, in detail, by the project manager. Exhibits 14-7 through 14-13 are a series of forms to meet this need:

- ✧ Exhibit 14-7, **new project request**, or Exhibit 14-8, **program change request**, to define the job.
- ✧ Exhibit 14-9, **project status notice**, to the user department head, to keep him or her informed of project progress.
- ✧ Exhibit 14-10, **implementation schedule**, prepared by the project manager for assignment of tasks to her or his people.
- ✧ Exhibit 14-11, **program assignment form**, to define the specific program and assign it to a specific programmer.
- ✧ Exhibit 14-12, **trouble scan request**, to identify programming problems and correct them.
- ✧ Exhibit 14-13, **Gantt chart**, to establish scheduling.

The skillful utilization of these monitoring tools will provide all the controls necessary to have a smoothly functioning data processing department. The final aspect of control to be considered is that of security.

SECURITY

Data processing security involves not only safeguards to prevent theft, fire, power failure, or negligence, but also provision for the proper and accurate generation of data.

(*text continues on page 562*)

Exhibit 14-6. Systems and programming department status report.

**SYSTEMS AND PROGRAMMING
DEPARTMENT STATUS**

As of Date 9/6/

Proj. Leader: BAM

STAFF STATUS

	Systems				Programming			
	Budgeted	Actual	On Termination	Open	Budgeted	Actual	On Termination	Open
	6	6			12	10		

PROJECT STATUS

Project Name	Scheduled Dates		Current Dates		Current Weeks Staffing Allocation				Total Worker-Days		% Complete To Date	Est. Act Final Total	Comments
					Systems		Programming						
	Start	Completion	Actual Start	Current Completion	People	Worker-Days	People	Worker-Days	Budgeted	Expended			
PR2070-P/R Master Update PGM.	8/16	9/6	8/19	9/6			1	1	14	7	100	—	Program is now Undergoing Extensive System Testing in 'Operations'
PR1200-State 941 Forms	8/19	9/13	8/19	9/20			1	0	15	5	70	15	
PR1300-Print Federal 941 Forms	8/19	9/13	8/19	9/20			1	0	15	3	30	15	
SAR110-A/R File Reload (New SAR91)	8/14	9/13	8/30	9/13			1	2	10	3	25	10	
Branch Number Processing Changes	8/20	9/20	8/20	9/20			2	5	20				
Docustat Program Maintenance	9/4	9/13	9/4	9/13			1	3	8	3	40	8	

Exhibit 14-7. New project request.

NEW PROJECT REQUEST

DATA PROCESSING
SYSTEMS & PROGRAMMING

REQUESTOR'S NAME	REQUESTING DEPT.	DEPT. MANAGER'S SIGNATURE

DATE REQUESTED	PRIORITY	TARGET DATE
/ /		/ /

GENERAL DESCRIPTION OF REQUEST

Attach sheet if space is insufficient

PROBLEMS OR DEFICIENCIES TO BE OVERCOME BY PROJECT

Attach sheet if space is insufficient

FOR SYSTEMS DEPARTMENT USE

PROJECT ASSIGNED TO	DATE ASSIGNED	ESTIMATE
		WORKER-HOURS COST
	/ /	

SUMMARY OF FINDINGS - PROJECT RECOMMENDATIONS

Attach sheet if space is insufficient

Exhibit 14-8.   Program change request.

PROGRAM CHANGE REQUEST

REQUEST DATE
/   /

REQUESTOR'S NAME

DEPT HEAD'S SIGNATURE

REQUESTING DEPT

PROGRAM NO.

PROGRAM NAME

DESCRIPTION OF CHANGE

REASON FOR CHANGE

DATE REQUIRED
/   /

DOES THIS CHANGE AFFECT ANY OTHER DEPT?   yes ○   no ○

IF YES, HAVE THEY BEEN INFORMED?   ○   ○

DATE RECEIVED
/   /

DATE ASSIGNED
/   /

ASSIGNED TO

ESTIMATE
WORKER- HRS COST

DATE COMPLETED
/   /

PRODUCTION DATE
/   /

ACTUAL
WORKER- HRS COST

COMMENTS, IF ANY

Exhibit 14-9. Project status notice.

PROJECT STATUS NOTICE

Systems & Programs

TO   :   P S N no. _____

SUBJECT: _____   ISSUED BY: _____

                                              DATE: _____

```
┌─────────────────────────┐
│ BASED ON MEMORANDUM     │
│   FROM      DATED        │
│                          │
└─────────────────────────┘
```

ACTIVITY	DATE	REMARKS
1. Scheduled start		
2. Original estimated completion		
3. Revised estimated completion		
4. Completed as of		

Reason for revision (if applicable):

Remarks:

If you have any questions, please contact our Systems & Programs Dept. and refer to JOB NUMBER _____ and PSN no. shown above.

Exhibit 14-10.   Implementation schedule.

DATA PROCESSING
SYSTEMS & PROGRAMMING

IMPLEMENTATION SCHEDULE			
		DATE PREPARED / /	
F U N C T I O N S	ASSIGNED TO	SECTION	PRIORITY

Exhibit 14-11. Program assignment form.

	NEW
PROGRAM ASSIGNMENT FORM	CHANGE
	ONE-TIME

SYSTEM IDENTIFICATION:	DATE PREPARED / /
PROGRAM IDENTIFICATION:	PROGRAM NUMBER:
REQUESTED BY:	DATE REQUESTED / /
SYSTEMS ANALYST:	PROGRAMMER ASSIGNED:
DATE ASSIGNED / /	DATE REQUIRED: / / ESTIMATED WORKER-DAYS:

COMPLETION DATES

PROGRAM ANALYSIS:	FLOWCHART:	CODING:
DATA ENTRY:	COMPILED:	FIRST TEST:
TESTING COMPLETED:	PROGRAM ACCEPTED:	

INPUT: OUTPUT:

PROGRAM SPECIFICATIONS:

Exhibit 14-12.   Trouble scan request.

TROUBLE SCAN REQUEST

OPERATIONS REPRESENTED BY_____

REQUESTED (DATE)_____

EFFORTS BY OPERATION

TROUBLE DOCUMENTED WITH

○ tape dump
○ disk file dump
○ run listings
○ spo messages
○ authorization forms

○ others _____

TROUBLE DESCRIPTION

SYSTEMS & PROGRAMMING FINDINGS and COMMENTS

Exhibit 14-13. Gantt chart.

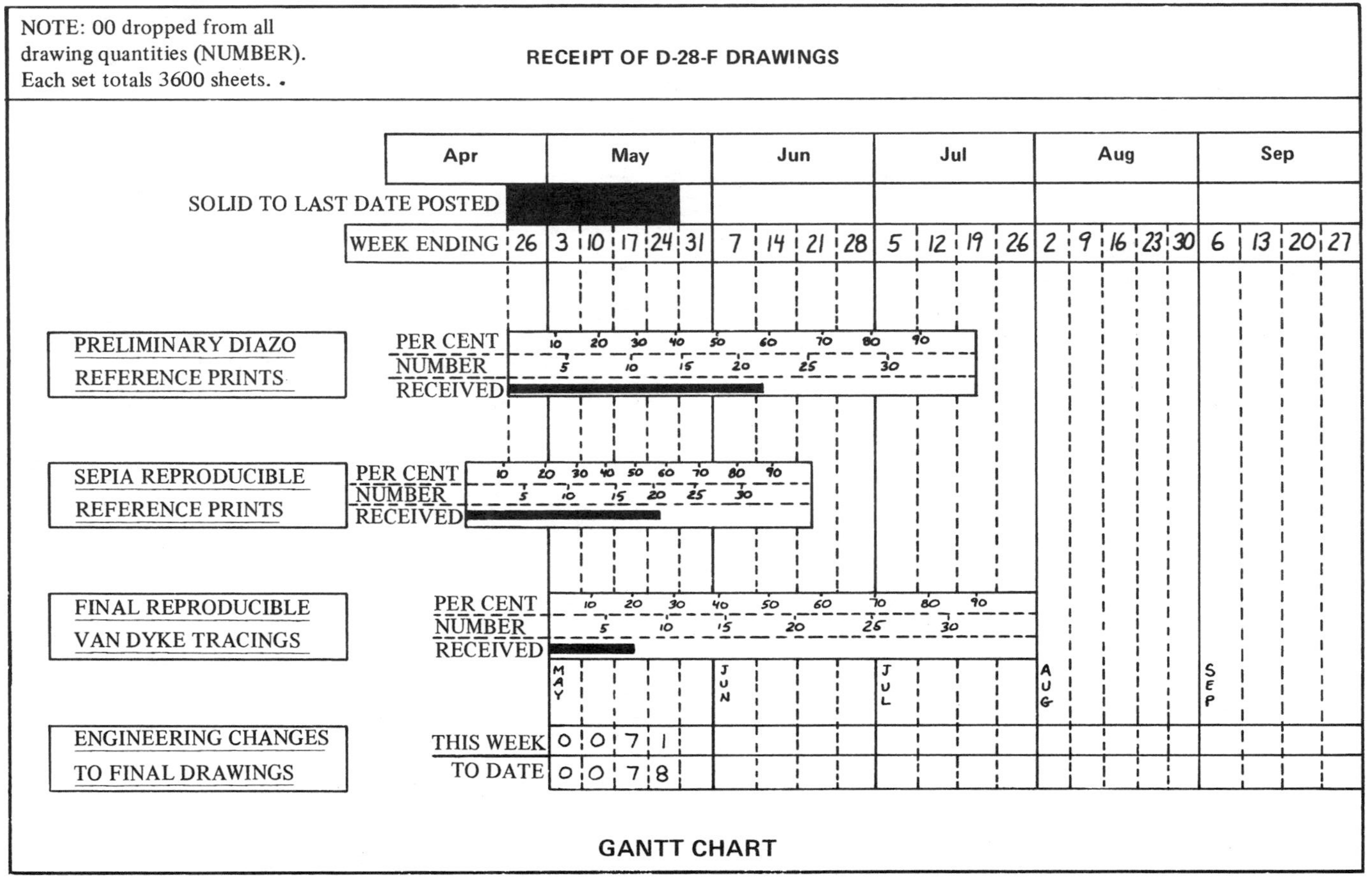

RECEIPT OF D-28-F DRAWINGS

GANTT CHART

NOTE: 00 dropped from all drawing quantities (NUMBER).
Each set totals 3600 sheets. •

561

(*text continued from page 553*)

The input/output staff, described on page 549, has the responsibility to tie-out and sign off on all reports before they are released. Where control totals are not a part of the program, this staff strikes manual totals to verify the program result. All related reports are cross-checked and tied-out. Batch totals and counts are verified. The end result provides assurance that:

1. All input data has been processed.
2. The correct program and report has been run.
3. The data has been processed without error.
4. Proof totals have been checked, and the report is not at variance with any other report.
5. The totals of this report are/will be carried forward to other appropriate reports.

For example, all customers' invoices are batch-totaled, with hash totals by invoice number and totals of dollar amounts. Invoices are run through the invoice register program. The totals are carried forward to the sales program, accounts receivable program, sales taxes payable program, freight billable program, product line sales program, average pricing program, credit analysis program, and product line analysis by sales territories program. The output of the invoice register program is the input for each of the other listed programs. There is no possibility for undetected fraud or error.

The detailed work performance standards for the input/output staff clearly delineate the cross-checking controls to be effected for each program. These, of course, will vary with each particular company, but it is essential that proper planning and effort be put into this part of the control system. In this regard, the systems department plays a vital role in designing, analyzing, programming, and "running" the system. It uses a **documentation checklist**, shown in Exhibit 14-14, to be sure that every aspect of the system is controlled. This begins with the assignment of the job and ends with the **run book standards**, shown in Exhibit 14-15. The operation run book contains complete instructions to run each program within each system. It ensures that the program will be run in the proper sequence, proper edits will be performed, and proper control routines will be utilized.

Exhibit 14-14. Documentation checklist.

| | | | SYSTEMS AND PROGRAMMING | | ○New |
| | | | DOCUMENTATION CHECKLIST | | ○ Revised |

JOB NO. _____ SYS. & PROG. CLEARING _____
DATE _____ OPERATIONS CLEARING _____

	S & P	OPER'S
○ ASSIGNMENT FORM		✕
○ SYSTEM FLOW		✕
RECORD LAYOUT		
○ CARD		✕
○ TAPE		✕
○ DISK		✕
○ PRINTER LAYOUTS		✕
○ CARRIAGE TAPE (PRINTER)	✕	
○ COBOL LISTING WITH XREF.		✕
○ TEST RESULTS (CHECKED BY PROJECT LEADER)		✕
○ PROGRAM NARRATIVE		✕
○ DATA ENTRY INSTRUCTIONS	✕	
○ INPUT-OUTPUT CONTROL		✕
○ EXECUTE SETS	✕	
○ CATALOGED EXHIBITS		✕
○ SOURCE DECK		✕
○ RUN BOOK INSTRUCTIONS	✕	
○ OTHERS (TABLES, ETC.)		

Exhibit 14-15.   Operations run book standards.

SYSTEM/PROGRAMMING STANDARDS

OPERATIONS RUN BOOK

PURPOSE: This is an outline of the information that will be required
for the Operations Run Book before a system is accepted for production.
This is a preliminary draft; a more comprehensive description will
be provided later.

GENERAL OUTLINE

Each data processing system will be maintained in a separate Run Book.
The Run Book will be divided into sections, with a separate section
for each subsystem or jobstream (Daily Processing, etc.).

Each section will contain the following:

 1. Jobstream flowchart.
 2. File retention schedule.
 3. Listing of any pertinent system codes.
 4. File backup procedures for every file.
 5. Run instructions for each program.
 6. Program restart procedures.
 7. Report distribution (not in Run Book).
 8. System failure instructions.
 9. File and record description, including location of key data (physi-
     cal, not data).
10. Run controls (balancing procedures, error action).

Each book will contain a Table of Contents.

PROGRAM RUN INSTRUCTIONS:

The run instructions for each program will include the following:

1. Run sheet. This will contain an input/output diagram showing
    all files used and the physical devices assigned. If forms are
    printed, the form number and the corresponding carriage control
    tape must be identified. Indicates whether a control or date
    card is used. A brief (one- or two-sentence) description of the pro-
    gram function is required. Note any special conditions (copy of first
    page of program narrative).

2. Control or date data entry instructions.

3. List of all console error messages. Must indicate the reason
    for the message and the action to be taken (e.g., cancel). On
    the new systems, these are not permitted (other than ''JOB TERMINATED
    ABNORMALLY'').

4. Sample printer output with alignment instructions.

The Run Book must contain an 80-80 listing of the jobstream JCL cards for
each job. Indicate where data cards are placed in the JCL. Sort control
cards must be listed with the JCL.

Try These Other Helpful Security Hints

- ✦ Lock up money-oriented forms—checks, invoices, credit memos, accounts receivable statements—to avoid stealing and substitution of a falsified document.
- ✦ Divide responsibilities—programmers have no access to the computer; computer personnel have no access to programs; operations personnel have no access to money-oriented forms; other departments have no access to the computer room, to programming records, to forms; decollation and distribution of reports is performed by another department; accounts receivable and collection functions are separate; the authority to issue credits to customers is part of the collection function, not that of accounts receivable.

In addition to the security against incorrect reports and fraud, steps must be taken to provide for the basic protection against catastrophe—fire, theft, bombing, earthquake, flood. No amount of insurance can compensate you for the difficulties involved in re-creating your files and records. Security against catastrophe basically involves storing duplicate records, computer tapes, or diskettes off-premises and replacing them with updates each month. In that way, only the current month's transactions must be restructured in the event of a disaster. Storage can be done in a vault at a local bank, or in a safe on other company-owned premises.

The following vital files should be duplicated and maintained off-premises:

- ✦ Daily billing
- ✦ Monthly accounts receivable
- ✦ Customer name/address master file
- ✦ Year-to-date payroll

The billing file should be updated daily to include daily billing. The accounts receivable file should be updated to include the daily transaction register of cash and journal entries.

This daily updating means that files must be run and delivered to the vault daily. Time-intensive, and a bother, but well worth the effort in the event of a fire. These files are the only ones necessary to enable the company to continue operating without sustaining any losses. It will not be necessary to so control accounts payable, as these can be reconstructed from bank records.

The systems department should further review the paperwork flow of the business to determine what additional security is needed in this particular company. For example, orders in the process of being shipped are pre-data entry, but they should be controlled off premises to avoid much customer dissatisfaction.

Try This Helpful Security Device for Orders

Copies of all orders written by the order/billing department or computer backup disks are mailed on a daily basis to one of two post office boxes rented at the local post office. The boxes are used alternately, month to month. On the first of each month, one box is emptied, and that empty box is the one to which orders are then sent for the current month. The contents of the emptied box are put through a shredder under the supervision of the order/billing department manager. In the event of a fire, pertinent batches of orders are easily retrieved, since they are still in their original postmarked envelopes.

This system will allow the company to fill all orders, collect all accounts receivable, continue to pay and account for all employee payrolls, and, effectively, generate financial statements from the end of the preceding month. The only remaining requirement is to safeguard the data processing programs themselves.

Accomplish the Security of Data This Way

- ✧ Duplicate and store off-premises all source decks.
- ✧ Duplicate program documentation and store off-premises.
- ✧ Run cumulative files onto tape and store off-premises.
- ✧ Microfilm the run book and store off-premises.

✧ Microfilm unaudited tax year general ledgers and store off-premises.

✧ Microfilm posting copies of invoices for permanent off-premises storage.

CASE IN POINT: A distribution company sustained a $2 million warehouse fire—a total loss. The cumulative perpetual inventory file had been duplicated and retained off-premises, at the end of each month. Current month's usage was easily re-created from the daily billing update file, also retained off the premises. Receipts were built up from proofs of delivery supplied by vendors and common carriers. Within a month the entire perpetual inventory at the time of the loss was reconstructed and submitted to the insurance company for full payment.

These additional security devices can be provided for hardware. The computer manufacturer will lend assistance and advice in each area:

1. Sprinkler protection (in specific areas)
2. Fireproof and explosion-proof window guards
3. Humidity control
4. Bypass electrical generator

PRACTICAL POINTERS FOR CONTROLLING THE DATA PROCESSING FUNCTION

The data processing function, whether manual or automated, is vital to the success of every operation. It must have proper organization within the corporate structure; its personnel should set objectives, consonant with corporate goals; all phases of the input and output of the department should be monitored and controlled; and positive security procedures should be instituted against fraud or other disasters.

15

Administering Stock Option and Incentive Plans

Stock option and incentive plans, regardless of the verbiage with which they are varnished, are nothing more than profit-sharing plans, and, as such, they represent the best way to motivate and retain employees, from the lowest ranks to the most key. Current income tax treatment is a determinant of the amount of after-tax benefits to be retained. Tax treatment notwithstanding, these profit-sharing devices work in any tax climate to perform their basic function, that of increasing the profits of the enterprise through employee motivation. These plans are variously known as qualified stock option plans (incentive stock options or ISO) and nonqualified stock option plans (nonstatutory stock options). The features of each, means of administering and controlling them, and their accounting and tax aspects are discussed in this chapter.

QUALIFIED OR STATUTORY STOCK OPTIONS

Features

Qualified or statutory stock options are options granted to individual employees to buy stock in their employer corporation. There is usually no income realized by the employee on receipt of the grant nor on exercise of the option, though the exercise may cause alternative minimum taxable income (AMTI) to be increased by the excess of the fair market value of the stock, when the option holder's rights to the stock are freely transferable or not subject to substantial risk of forfeiture [IRS Code Sec. 58(a)], over the price actually paid for the stock under the terms of the ISO. The option price may not be lower than the fair market value of the stock at the time of grant of the option, and the option is nontransferable, except by death. ISOs are not available to owners of more than 10% of the stock of the corporation, except under special rules. Further, the employee must remain an employee until three months before the option is exercised. After exercise, the stock may not be sold within the later of two years from the date of grant or one year from the date of exercise.

The gain on the eventual sale of the stock, if it is held for the time period described above, is a long-term capital gain. If the stock is sold before the time period set forth, the gain on the sale is taxed as compensation, and hence ordinary income, and the corporation receives a tax deduction for the same amount. The obvious advantage to the employee is one of leverage. The optionee receives the right to buy the stock at today's price for years to come, with no cash outlay required. In effect, he or she has a "call" on the corporation's stock, without having had to pay for it. The right to exercise is generally spread out over a period of years. Thus, if the company's stock appreciates, the employee is induced to remain with the company until the exercise of all available options has been completed. In order to be "qualified" and enjoy this favored tax treatment, an incentive stock option plan must meet all of the following requirements:

1. The option must be granted within 12 months before or after adoption of the plan approved by shareholders. The plan may not run for over ten years, and must state total shares available for option and the classes or employees covered by the plan.

2. The option may not be exercised later than ten years after grant; only the employee may exercise it during the employee's lifetime, and there are restrictions on transfer at death.

3. The option price at the time of grant may not be less than the fair market value of the stock (usually the average of the high

and low traded prices for an exchange-traded company, or the average of the high bid and low asked prices for over-the-counter stocks). For private companies, a good-faith attempt to value the stock accurately must be made.

4. If options are granted to employees owning more than 10% of voting power, the grant price of the option must be at least 110% of fair market value, and the term of the option may not exceed five years.

5. The aggregate fair market value of qualifying incentive options exercised by any one employee under all plans of the employer group may not exceed a limit of $100,000 per calendar year.

Tax Treatment and Accounting

Tax Accounting

The difference between the exercise price (the grant price) and the fair market value of the stock at the time there is no risk of forfeiture or restrictions on transfer is an increase to AMTI and may subject the optionee to alternative minimum tax, subject to the $33,750 exemption for single individuals and $45,000 for married persons. With proper planning of stock sales and a gift-giving program over a period of years, the alternative minimum tax can generally be avoided.

Financial Accounting

SFAS 123, Accounting for Stock-Based Compensation, sets forth the accounting rules for recording and disclosing the treatment of stock options. Under the standard, companies are required to recognize an expense for all stock-based compensation awards, including stock options, granted after December 31, 1996. The expense is measured as the fair value of the option at the grant date and is recognized over the vesting period of the option. However, the standard allows a company to continue to measure compensation cost in accordance with APB 25, called the intrinsic-value-based method, which generally results in no income at the time of grant. Should a company elect to continue to account under APB 25, it must make pro forma disclosures of net income and earnings per share as if the fair-value-based method of accounting had been used.

> *Helpful Hint:* The Tax Reform Act of 1986 changed the rules so as to permit the exercise of options in any order, regardless of the date of grant. Therefore, if the stock price falls below the grant price, the company can issue the executive a second ISO with a lower exercise price.

The incentive stock option plan, like all other option plans, is a profit-sharing device, to the extent that the optionee, once he or she purchases the shares, participates in the profits of the corporation like any other shareholder, receiving dividends and presumably, if there are profits, a higher stock price as reflected in the fair market value of the shares as determined with reference to the company's price/earnings ratio.

An incentive plan, like any of the other plans discussed in this chapter, is applicable to both public and private companies. Because most option plans have a market value feature, they are generally thought to be useful only to the public company with a readily ascertainable market for its shares. All that is needed, however, is a relatively simple formula to determine stock price, consistently applied from year to year, and a stock option program may become a viable profit-sharing device for the privately owned company.

> *Helpful Hint:* Valuation of closely held stock, aside from arriving at an option grant price, should be a continuing thing. Tremendous tax payments may depend on the outcome of IRS disputes over the stock's value. Even the continuity of the business may be at stake if a liquidation at sacrifice price is necessary to pay estate taxes. Particularly in a declining market, an owner may find an excellent tax planning opportunity, since the value of a closely held company is related to the value of equivalent publicly traded companies.

The plan will meet the requirement of the Code even if the employee must first offer the stock to the corporation before selling it, and the corporation may pay the employee to cancel the option. This makes it possible for the closely held corporation to offer options to its employees as an "incentifying" device, without actually losing control of any of its shares. Payments received by the employee for cancellation of the option are taxed to him or her as ordinary income and are likewise tax-deductible by the corporation. If stock acquired under an option is not held the required time (two years after grant or one year after exercise), any gain on disposition is ordinary income, and the corporation can also deduct the same amount as compensation paid to the employee. No deduction is given the corporation when it transfers the stock on exercise of an option.

For financial accounting purposes, then, there is no charge against current earnings when the option is granted or exercised, or when the stock is disposed of, whether it be an early or a normal disposition. Earnings will be charged if payment is made to cancel the option. If the corporation repurchases stock from the employee at a higher than grant price, earnings are not charged. The corporation is merely buying treasury stock, and any gain or loss is deferred until eventual disposition of the treasury stock. As previously stated, however, the corporation is allowed a tax deduction, but not a financial accounting deduction, for an early (under two years after grant or one year after exercise) disposition. This becomes a Schedule M-1 item on the corporation's Form 1120 tax return, to reconcile book income with taxable income. It is reflected on the company's books through a direct reduction in the current tax liability and an increase in paid-in capital, in accordance with APB Opinion No. 15. This handsome aspect of the qualified plan is generally overlooked—it can actually decrease taxable income with no effect on financial reported income, or, said another way, it can increase total net worth by the tax effect of the allowable deduction. The simplest way to monitor the availability of this benefit is to send a questionnaire, annually, to each optionee, requiring a report as to sales of option stocks, the date acquired, option price, date sold, and sale price. This is most easily accomplished on January 31 of each year, at which time Form 3921 must be sent to each employee who exercised stock options during the year. **Form 3921** (see Exhibit 15-1) must be filed at an Internal Revenue Service Center by February 28, with a covering summary Form

Exhibit 15-1. IRS Form 3921, information return for qualified stock options.

Form **3921** (Rev. Sept. 1971) Department of the Treasury Internal Revenue Service	**Exercise of a Qualified or Restricted Stock Option** (U.S. information return under section 6039(a)(1) of the Internal Revenue Code)	For calendar year 20_ _ _	**Copy A** For Internal Revenue Service
1. Corporation Transferring Stock	a. Name and address (including ZIP code)	2. Name of corporation whose stock is transferred (if different from corporation transferring stock)	
	b. Employer identification number ▲	4. Date option granted	5. Date of transfer
3. Person to Whom Stock is Transferred	a. Name and address (including ZIP code)	6. Option price	
		7. Fair market value of stock at time option exercised	
		8. Place an "X" in the appropriate box to indicate whether the option exercised is: a. A qualified stock option under section 422(b) . . . ☐ b. A restricted stock option under section 424(b) . . . ☐	
	b. Identifying number ▲	9. No. of shares transferred ▲	

574

4067. The Internal Revenue Code section covering qualified stock options is Section 422. Incentive stock options are covered by Section 421.

Noncorporate and Nonpublic Use of Options

A typical method for finding the market value of options granted in the stock of a nonpublic company is to use the price/earnings ratio of similar or competitive public companies. If this is not available, a P/E ratio may be "attributed" to the company based on offers it may have had to buy the company or that the company, itself, may have made to buy others. Failing such offers, the company may analyze its own financial position, history of earnings, and future prospects to arrive at a value for the corporation that it would consider a reasonable selling price should a buyer materialize. The option price is now discernible:

Number of shares outstanding	50,000
Net income, last fiscal year	$100,000
Price at which the company would sell	$500,000
Price/earnings ratio	5 to 1
Fair market value per share (option price)	$10

It is possible that the price at which the company would sell is more or less than the P/E ratio, in which case one or the other figure must be used. The P/E ratio, if readily evident, is usually more accurate, since, by definition, it encompasses a fair market value price for the company that discounts all factors affecting earnings. No adjustments, therefore, need be made to the P/E ratio calculation. If the price at which the company would sell is used, then a myriad of adjustments could be made to increase the sophistication of the calculation. Is the price payable in installments; is investment letter stock used to buy the company, subject to the usual selling restrictions; what is the interest rate on the time payout; how is property paid in lieu of cash to be valued? All of these factors should be discounted or present valued to arrive at a reduced selling price in terms of cash today.

Helpful Hint: Statutory options, while applicable only to corporations, can be an equally effective incentive device for employees of individual proprietorships, partnerships, or noncorporate joint ventures. While the plan will not be considered "qualified" for IRS purposes, all of the features may be adopted by the enterprise to achieve the motivational aspects of the plan. The employee receives a call on the stock for up to ten years at a fixed price. If the option is structured so that it may be exercised only to the extent of 25% each year after the first year, the employee is effectively wedded to the company for at least this five-year period, particularly in a period of increasing earnings and P/E ratios, which is exactly the time when you want and need that employee. Such a plan reduces key personnel turnover, increases employee morale, and induces each optionee to be profit-motivated.

A Typical Statutory Plan

A fully qualified **incentive stock option plan** for key employees, containing this 25% per year exercisable feature, is shown in Exhibit 15-2. The incentive stock option contract, between the company and the employee, specifies the number of shares granted, the price, the expiration date for exercise, the 25% exercise limitation, the employee's requirement for continued employment, and certain IRS rules that allow exercise while there are prior outstanding options. The **notice of grant of incentive stock option** is shown inn Exhibit 15-3.

Beware This Pitfall: The Code requires an incentive stock option plan to be approved by the stockholders of the employer corporation. Treasury regulations amplify this, requiring consent of a majority of the voting stock. This means an absolute majority of the outstanding stock. Thus, if stockholders holding 40% of the voting stock voted and approved the plan by 80% of the votes cast, this would be only 32% (80% × 40%) of the outstanding stock and would not constitute majority approval.

(*text continues on page 581*)

Exhibit 15-2.   Incentive stock option plan.

_____

_____, INC.
INCENTIVE STOCK OPTION PLAN

1. *Purpose of the Plan*
   The purpose of the Incentive Stock Option Plan of   , Inc. is
to promote the interests of the Company and its shareholders by strengthening the
Company's ability to attract, motivate and retain employees of training, experience,
and ability, and to provide a means to encourage stock ownership and proprietary
interest in the Company to officers and valued employees of the Company upon whose
judgment, initiative, and efforts the continued financial success and growth of the business of the Company largely depend.

2. *Definitions*
   (a) "Board" means the Board of Directors of the Company.
   (b) "Committee" means the Incentive Stock Option Committee of the Board, unless
the Board appoints another committtee to administer the Plan.
   (c) "Common Stock" means the no par value Common Stock of the Company.
   (d) "Company" means   , Inc.
   (e) "Eligible Person" means an employee eligible to receive an incentive Stock
Option.
   (f) "Employee" means any full-time employee of the Company, or of any of its
present or future parent or subsidiary corporations.
   (g) "Fair Market Value" means the book value of a share of Common Stock
computed as of the last completed quarter of the Company nearest to the date as of
which fair market value is to be determined.
   (h) "Participant" means any Eligible Person selected to participate in the Incentive
Stock Option Plan pursuant to Section 5.
   (i) "Plan" means the Incentive Stock Option Plan as set forth here, which may be
amended from time to time.

3. *Shares of Common Stock Subject to the Plan*
   (a) Subject to the provisions of Section 9 of the Plan, the aggregate number of
shares of Common Stock that may be issued or transferred or exercised pursuant to
Incentive Stock Option under the Plan will not exceed 10% of the number of all shares
of Common Stock then outstanding. Of that number, the maximum aggregate number
of shares of Common Stock for which Incentive Stock Options may be granted under
the Plan will not exceed 1,000.
   (b) The shares of Common Stock to be delivered under the Plan will be made
available, at the discretion of the Board of Directors or the Committee, either from
authorized but unissued shares of Common Stock or from previously issued shares of
Common Stock reacquired by the Company.

4. *Administration of the Plan*
   (a) The Plan will be administered by the Committee, which will consist of two or
more persons (i) who are not eligible to receive Incentive Stock Options under
(continued)

Exhibit 15-2. *(continued)*

the Plan, (ii) who have not been eligible at any time within one year before appointment to the Committee for selection as persons to whom Incentive Stock Options may be granted pursuant to the Plan.

(b) The Committee has and may exercise such powers and authority of the Board as may be necessary or appropriate for the Committee to carry out its functions as described in the Plan. The Committee has authority in its discretion to determine the Eligible Persons to whom, and the time or times at which, Incentive Stock Options may be granted and the number of shares subject to each Incentive Stock Option award. The Committee also has authority to interpret the Plan, and to determine the terms and provisions of the Incentive Stock Option agreements and to make all other determinations necessary or advisable for Plan administration. The Committee has authority to prescribe, amend, and rescind rules and regulations relating to the Plan. All interpretations, determinations, and actions by the Committee will be final, conclusive, and binding upon all parties.

(c) No member of the Board or the Committee will be liable for any action or determination made in good faith by the Board or the Committee with respect to the Plan.

5. *Eligibility*

(a) All full-time salaried Employees who have been determined by the Committee to be key employees are eligible to receive Incentive Stock Options under the Plan. The Committee has authority, in its sole discretion, to determine and designate from time to time those Eligible Persons who are to be granted Incentive Stock Options. Each Incentive Stock Option will be evidenced by a written instrument and may include any other terms and conditions consistent with the Plan, as the Committee may determine.

(b) No person will be eligible for the grant of an Incentive Stock Option who owns or would own immediately before the grant of such Incentive Stock Option, directly or indirectly, stock possessing more than 10% of the total combined voting power of all classes of stock of the Company or of any parent or subsidiary corporation. This does not apply if, at the time such Incentive Stock Option is granted, the Incentive Stock Option price is at least 110% of the Fair Market Value. In this event, the Incentive Stock Option by its terms is not exercisable after the expiration of five years from the date of grant.

6. *Terms and Conditions of Incentive Stock Options*

(a) The purchase price of Common Stock under an Incentive Stock Option will be at least equal to the Fair Market Value of the Common Stock on the date of grant. A Certificate of Fair Market Value shall be prepared and delivered by the Company to the Participant.

(b) Incentive Stock Options may be exercised as determined by the Committee but in no event after 10 years from the date of grant.

(c) Upon the exercise of an Incentive Stock Option, the purchase price will be payable in full in cash or, in the discretion of the Committee, by the assignment and delivery to the Company of shares of Common Stock owned by the Optionee. Any shares so assigned and delivered to the Company in payment or partial payment of the purchase price will be valued at their Fair Market Value on the exercise date.

(d) The Fair Market Value of the shares of Common Stock for which any Employee may exercise Incentive Stock Options under the Plan in any calendar year will not exceed $100,000 plus any unused limit carryover to such year as determined under Section 422A(c)(4) of the Internal Revenue Code.

(e) An Incentive Stock Option may be exercised while there is "outstanding" within the meaning of Section 422A(c)(7) of the Internal Revenue Code any Incentive Stock Option granted before the granting of such Incentive Stock Option to purchase stock in the Company or in a corporation that is a parent or subsidiary corporation, or in a predecessor corporation of any such corporation.

(f) No fractional shares will be issued pursuant to the exercise of an Incentive Stock Option nor will any cash payment be made in lieu of fractional shares.

7. Adjustment Provisions

(a) If the outstanding shares of Common Stock of the Company are increased, decreased, or exchanged for a different number or kind of shares or other securities, or if additional shares or new or different shares or other securities are distributed with respect to such shares of Common Stock or other securities, through merger, consolidation, sale of all or substantially all the property of the Company, reorganization, recapitalization, reclassification, stock dividend, stock split, reverse stock split or other distribution with respect to such shares of Common Stock, or other securities, an appropriate and proportionate adjustment may be made in the maximum number and kind of shares provided in Section 3.

(b) Adjustments under Section 7(a) will be made by the Committee, whose determination as to what adjustments will be made and the extent thereof will be final, binding, and conclusive. No fractional interest will be issued under the Plan on account of any such adjustments.

8. General Provisions

(a) Nothing in the Plan or in any instrument executed pursuant to the Plan will confer upon any Participant any right to continue in the employ of the Company or any of its subsidiaries or affect the right of the Company to terminate the employment of any Participant at any time with or without cause.

(b) No shares of Common Stock will be issued or transferred pursuant to an Incentive Stock Option unless and until all then applicable requirements imposed by Federal and state securities and other laws, rules, and regulations, and by any regulatory agencies having jurisdiction, and by any stock exchanges upon which the Common Stock may be listed, have been fully met. As a condition precedent to the issuance of shares pursuant to the grant or exercise of an Incentive Stock Option, the Company may require the participant to take any reasonable action to meet such requirements.

(c) No Participant and no beneficiary or other person claiming under or through such Participant will have any right, title or interest in or to any shares of common stock allocated or reserved under the Plan except as to such shares of Common Stock, if any, that have been issued or transferred to such Participant.

(d) The Company may make a loan to a Participant in connection with the exercise of an Incentive Stock Option in an amount not to exceed the aggregate exercise price of the Incentive Stock Option being exercised and the gross amount of any

(continued)

Exhibit 15-2.   *(continued)*

Federal and state taxes payable in connection with such exercise for the purpose of assisting such Optionee to exercise such Option. Any such loan may be secured by shares of Common Stock or other collateral deemed adequate by the Committee and will comply in all respects with all applicable laws and regulations. The Committee may adopt policies regarding eligibility for such loans, the maximum amounts thereof and any terms and conditions not specified in the Plan upon which such loans will be made. In no event will the interest rate be less than the mimimum rate established by the Internal Revenue Service for the purpose of the purchase and sale of property pursuant to Code Section 483.

9. *Amendment and Termination*
    (a) The Committee will have the power, in its discretion, to amend, suspend, or terminate the Plan at any time. No such amendment will, without approval of the shareholders of the Company, except as provided in Section 9 of the Plan:

   (i) change the class of persons eligible to receive Incentive Stock Options under the Plan;

   (ii) materially increase the benefits accruing to Eligible Persons under the Plan;

   (iii) increase the number of shares of Common Stock subject to the Plan; or

   (iv) transfer the administration of the Plan to any person who is not a Disinterested Person under the Securities Exchange Act of 1934.

    (b) No amendment, suspension or termination of the Plan will, without the consent of the Participant, alter, terminate, impair or adversely affect any right or obligation under any Incentive Stock Option previously granted under the Plan.
    (c) An Incentive Stock Option held by a person who was an Employee at the time such Incentive Stock Option was granted will expire immediately if and when the Participant ceases to be an Employee, except as follows:

   (i) If the employment of an Employee is terminated by the Company other than for cause, for which the Company will be the sole judge, then the Incentive Stock Options will expire three months thereafter unless by their terms they expire sooner. During said period, the Incentive Stock Options may be exercised in accordance with their terms, but only to the extent exercisable on the date of termination of employment.

   (ii) If the Employee retires at normal retirement age or retires with the consent of the Company at an earlier date, the Incentive Stock Options of the Employee will expire three years thereafter unless by their terms they expire sooner. During said period, the Incentive Stock Options may be exercised in accordance with their terms, but only to the extent exercisable on the date of retirement.

   (iii) If an Employee dies or becomes permanently and totally disabled while employed by the Company, the Options of the Employee will expire three years after the date of death or permanent and total disability unless by their terms they expire sooner. If the Employee dies or becomes permanently and totally disabled within the three months referred to in subparagraph (i) above, the Incentive Stock Options will expire one year after the date of death or permanent and total disability, unless by their terms they expire sooner. If the Employee dies or becomes permanently and totally disabled within the three-year period referred to in subparagraph (ii) above, the Incentive Stock Options will expire upon the later of three years after retirement or one year after the date of death or permanent and total disability, unless by their terms they expire sooner.

10. *Buy-Sell Option*
   At any time upon ninety (90) days' written notice to the Company, the Participant (or his estate or legal representative, as the case may be) will have the right to sell to the Company, and the Company will be obligated to buy, all or any of the Common Stock owned by the Participant at the Fair Market Value. At any time upon thirty (30) days' written notice to the Participant (or his estate or legal representative, as the case may be), the Company will have the right to purchase from the Participant (or his estate or legal representative, as the case may be), who shall be obligated to sell, all or any of the Common Stock at Fair Market Value. The Fair Market Value for all or any of the Common Stock will be equal to the Fair Market Value as evidenced by a certificate prepared and delivered by the Company at the time the buy or sell option is exercised pursuant to this paragraph 10.

11. *Effective Date of Plan and Duration of Plan*
   This Plan will become effective upon adoption by the Board subject to approval by the holders of a majority of the shares which are represented in person or by proxy and entitled to vote on the subject at a special Meeting of Shareholders of the Company. Unless previously terminated, the Plan will terminate on October 31, 20xx.

(*text continued from page 576*)
Administration of Option Plans

The administration of any type of stock option plan requires control over the number of shares granted and exercised and provision for determination of shares available for grant and calculation of unexercised shares at any given point in time. This information is required for presentation in the notes to financial statements in the capital stock footnote to the annual report. It may also be required if form S-8 is filed with the Securities and Exchange Commission in the event that the option plan is registered for public trading. A typical **annual report footnote to the financial statements** that illustrates the type and amount of disclosure required with regard to stock option plans of

Exhibit 15-3. Notice of grant of incentive stock option.

Dear   :

At the direction of the Board of Directors of   , Inc., you are hereby notified that the Board or the Stock Option Committee has granted to you on   an incentive stock option, pursuant to its Incentive Stock Option Plan.

The option granted to you is to purchase   shares of the no par Common Stock of the Company at the price of   per share. It is the determination of the Board of Directors that on the date of the grant of this option the fair market value of the Company's no par Common Stock was   per share.

I enclose a copy of the Incentive Stock Option Plan governing the option granted to you, and your attention is invited to all the provisions of the Plan.

Your stock option is in all respects subject to the terms and conditions as provided for in the Incentive Stock Option Plan, including, but not limited to, the following:

a. Your option may not be exercised more than ten years after the date it is granted to you;

b. Your option may be exercised by you, but only by you, during your lifetime prior to three months following the termination of your employment unless your employment is terminated for cause or without the consent of the Company. If your employment is terminated for cause or without the consent of the Company, your option (to the extent not previously exercised) shall terminate immediately;

c. Your option shall become exercisable, cumulatively, as to the following percentages of the shares subject to this option on the following anniversaries of the date the option was granted to you:

Percent	Anniversary Date
25%	First
25%	Second
25%	Third
25%	Fourth

d. In the event of your death while you are an employee, or within three months from the date of termination of your employment unless your employment was terminated for cause or without the consent of the Company, your option may be exercised by your estate, or by the person to whom such right devolves from you by reason of your death at any time prior to six months after the date of your death or ten years after the date of this option, whichever date first arrives;

e. Your option is nontransferable otherwise than as may be occasioned by your death, and then only to your estate or according to the terms of your Will or the provision of applicable laws of descent and distribution;

f. Your option, which is an incentive stock option as defined in Section 422A of the Internal Revenue Code of 1954, as amended, is exercisable while there is outstanding (within the meaning of such Code) any other incentive stock option granted to you at an earlier time;

g. In the event that the right to exercise your option is passed to your estate, or to a person to whom such right devolves by reason of your death, then your option shall be nontransferable in the hands of your executor or administrator or of such person, except that your option may be distributed by your executor or administrator to the distributees of your estate as a part of your estate.

At the time or times when you wish to exercise this option, in whole or in part, please refer to the provisions of the Incentive Stock Option Plan dealing with methods and formalities of exercise of your option.

_____

Chair

_____

President

any type is presented in Exhibit 15-4. The grant and exercise of options may be recorded in a **stock option ledger**, a page of which is reproduced at Exhibit 15-5. This is used to accumulate, on one page, all the historical information that will ever be needed with reference to any option—the date of grant, number of shares, price at time of grant, date and amount of shares exercised, market value at date of exercise, number of shares terminating, and the balance of shares that may be exercised at the present time or in the future. Information can be pulled from these ledger pages to present total option information in any required format. Exhibit 15-6 presents an **employee stock option summary sheet** that is used by the employee's supervisor as a basis to recommend the grant of additional options. It summarizes all previous grants and exercises, keying off each exercise against the original grant, to enable the reviewer to ascertain readily how many shares remain unexercised attributable to each grant and showing the cumulative unexercised shares from all grants. This record is posted concurrently with the stock option ledger page to provide an instantly retrievable summary for management review.

Exhibit 15-4.   Notes to financial statements — stock options.

Notes to Financial Statements

Stock option activity for the year ended April 30, 20 __	NUMBER OF SHARES	OPTION PRICES
Outstanding at April 30, 20 __	190,971	$11.88 to $63.38
Changes during the year:		
Granted	142,575	3.75 to 10.00
Exercised	—0—	— —
Terminated	85,322	7.75 to 55.00
Outstanding at April 30, 20 __		
(exercisable, 55,452 shares)	248,224	3.75 to 63.38

At April 30, 20 __,   had received notices of election to convert options for 25,100 shares to nonqualified stock options and options for 7,000 shares were eligible for conversion to non-qualified stock options.

There were 19,482 shares reserved for future grants. On July 9, 20 __, the Board of Directors authorized, subject to approval of the stockholders, the granting of options for an additional 50,000 shares.

Under   amended Employee's Stock Purchase Plan eligible employees may purchase up to 75,000 shares of   stock at the lesser of 85 percent of the market value on the offering date or at the end of the subscription period. At April 30, 20 __, 267 employees of   had subscribed to purchase 21,448 shares under the plan and 5,529 shares had been purchased.

During fiscal 20 __,   : a) entered into an agreement with   Company, Ltd. to 1) sell 20,000 shares of common stock at $4.875; 2) sell an additional 80,000 shares of common stock at $4.875 prior to December 17, 20 __; and 3) issue warrants for the purchase of 150,000 shares of common stock at $7.70 per share

expiring at the rate of 37,500 quarterly, commencing March 15, 20 __; b) issued 5,529 shares of common stock purchased under the Employee's Stock Purchase Plan.

Statutory (ISO) Summary

In summary, then, incentive stock option plans offer certain favorable tax benefits to the corporation and the employee if the preset conditions under the Code are met. These benefits generally do not tax the employee at the time of grant or exercise and offer long-term capital gain treatment if the stock is held for two years after grant or one year after exercise. Subsequent grants at lower prices may be exercised before prior grants at higher prices. This condition makes incentive options desirable even in times of a declining stock market.

Exhibit 15-5. Stock option ledger.

STOCK OPTION LEDGER
J. SMITH

GRANT CODE C

OPTION PRICE	DATE OF GRANT	NUMBER OF SHARES	# SHARES EXERCISED	# SHARES TERMINATED	DATE	BALANCE EXERCISABLE FUTURE	NOW
$ 17 00	6-23-03	1000			6.23-03	1000	
					6.23-04	750	250
	SPLIT	500			9-11-04		
$ 11 33		1500			9-11-04	1125	375
	SPLIT	1500			1-31-05		
567		3000			1-31-05	2250	750
					5-1-05	2250	750
					6-23-05	1500	1500
			1500		11-17-05	1500	—
					5-1-06	1500	—
					6-23-06	750	750
			750		4-01-07	750	—
					6-23-07	—	750
			750		8-02-07	—	—

Exhibit 15-6.   Employee stock option summary sheet.

EMPLOYEE STOCK OPTION SUMMARY
QUALIFIED STOCK OPTION PLAN

NAME: _J. Smith_   DEPARTMENT: _V.P._   LOCATION: _01_

REPORTS TO: _H. Jones_

GRANTS

Grant Code	# of Shares This Grant	Cumul.	Option Price This Grant	Date Granted
A	6,000	6,000	$ 2.92	7-21-01
B	6,000	12,000	8.50	6-23-02
C	3,000	15,000	5.67	6-23-03
D	1,000	16,000	39.1875	3-22-06
E	* 2,000	18,000	27.6875	8-02-07
F	2,000	20,000	11.875	3-20-09
G	* ⟨2,000⟩	18,000	—	10-10-09
H	10,000	28,000	6.75	10-10-09
I	3,000	31,000	3.00	6-11-10
J				
K				
L				
M				
N				
O				
P				

*Transferred to Non-qualified

EXERCISES

Grant Code	# of Shares This Time	Cumul.	$ Amount This Time	Date Exercised $	Cumul. Amounts	Cumul. Shares Unexercised
A	3,000	3,000	8,760	PRIOR 4/30/04	8,760	12,000
A	1,500	4,500	4,380	7-21-04	13,140	10,500
Ⓐ	1,500	6,000	4,380	11-17-05	17,520	9,000
B	4,500	10,500	38,250	11-17-05	55,500	4,500
C	1,500	12,000	4,380	11-17-05	59,880	3,000
Ⓑ	1,500	13,500	12,750	4-02-07	72,630	2,500
C	750	14,250	2,190	4-02-07	74,820	1,750
E						3,750
Ⓒ	750	15,000	4,252	8-02-07	79,077	3,000
Ⓔ	2,000	TRANSFERRED TO	NON-QUALIFIED			1,000
						3,000
						13,000
						16,000

1. Insert grant code for option exercised.
2. Circle grant code when option is completely exercised.

Nonqualified or Nonstatutory Stock Options

Features

A nonqualified stock option plan is any plan that is not qualified and, therefore, not the recipient of the favorable tax treatment that accrues to qualified plans. Nonqualified plans are diverse in their terms and conditions, each containing a somewhat different wrinkle, limited only by the imaginations of the plan designers. Their commonality is their purpose, the same as in qualified plans, of motivating employees through profit-sharing incentive. Options in such plans are usually granted at market value or below, although in some cases, they are granted at prices above market value. The Code provides that a nonqualified option is taxed when granted if the option has a readily ascertainable fair market value. If the option is not traded on an established market, it has a readily ascertainable value only if it is transferable, it is exercisable immediately and in full, there are no restrictions or conditions that could affect its fair value, and the fair market value is readily ascertainable. These conditions are seldom met, and therefore most nonqualified options that are not publicly traded are not taxed on grant. The option would then be taxed on exercise, but only if the grant price were less than the fair market value. In such case, the income would be taxed as compensation, at ordinary income tax rates, and would be deductible by the corporation. When compensation results, the company is required to report the appropriate payroll taxes.

If the nonqualified option is traded on an active market or has a readily ascertainable fair market value, the employee has ordinary income in the amount of the fair market value in the year of the grant, less any amount paid for the option. There is no tax due on exercise. When the stock is later sold, there is a capital gain or loss on the sale. The basis of the stock sold is the fair market value of the option on which a tax was paid, plus the amount paid for the stock.

If there are restrictions or conditions, such as vesting requirements, an employee may elect, under Code Sec. 83(b), to be taxed on the spread between the exercise price and the fair market value at the date of exercise, rather than waiting until the stock is sold. The election must be made within 30 days of the date of the grant, and any future appreciation on sale is taxed at capital gains rates. This would be a good strategy to avoid paying tax at higher ordinary income rates in the future, based on the expectation of higher stock prices.

This means that the employee may have a tax to pay at the time of grant, if the stock is traded on an active market, or on exercise, if an 83(b) election is made. On the other hand, the holding period for capital gains is less than that for ISOs. Moreover, with emerging and growing companies that are not yet publicly traded, the use of nonqualified options enables key employees to receive bargain grants at low prices that are not subject to tax at the date of grant. Further, nonqualified options can be used as an incentive for one or a few key employees, without the need or cost to set up a formal ISO plan.

A corporation may use both qualified and nonqualified plans at the same time.

Tax Treatment and Accounting

Nonqualified options, further, have become more attractive in recent years as the gap between ordinary income tax rates and capital gains rates has narrowed. Tax rates, then, combined with climbing stock market prices, have made the nonqualified stock option a most attractive incentive strategy. By properly structuring their terms, such as requiring the ability to exercise at the rate of 25% each year, the same inducement for continuous employment can be provided as with ISOs. From the employee's standpoint, moreover, the holding period for whatever long-term capital gains benefit there may be is one year, compared to up to two years with an ISO. As an added advantage, the nonqualified option may be granted to holders of more than 10% of the company's stock.

From a tax standpoint, any option that does not meet all the requirements of a qualified option is defined as a nonqualified option. As such, when the nonstatutory option is granted at fair market value, there is generally no tax due at the time of grant, depending on whether the option has a readily ascertainable fair market value (see the Features section). If the option is granted at below market value, the spread is generally taxable to the employee as compensation at the time of exercise. If the option has no ascertainable fair market value, which is almost always the case for nonpublic companies, there is no income realized on the grant of the option. If the option has a readily ascertainable fair market value, usually by being traded on an active market, ordinary income will result in the year of the grant in the amount of the fair market value, less the amount paid for the option. See the Features section for more details. The company receives a tax deduction in the same amount as the employee has taxable income, and, for financial accounting purposes, paid-in capital is increased, as with qualified options (page 573). Within this framework, a variety of nonqualified plans may be structured to meet the requirements of the company.

Helpful Hint: Officers and directors of companies registered with the SEC who are considered to be "insiders" are subject to the recapture of profits rule under Sec. 16(b) of the 1934 Securities Exchange Act. If the stock is acquired, held less than six months, and then sold, the profits may be recovered by the company or by a stockholder acting on the company's behalf. However, optionees may count the period following the option grant as part of the six-month holding period. This works to permit immediate resale of stock acquired through exercise of an option granted at least six months earlier without bringing the insider trading rule into effect. This has effectively eliminated the need to use stock appreciation rights (SARs), which provided executives with cash equal to the appreciation in the value of the stock without having to buy the stock and resell it, since the resale is not subject to the insider profit recapture.

At the time of exercise of the option, if the stock is not vested, ordinary compensation income will result in the year in which it becomes substantially vested. It is substantially vested when it is transferable or when there are no longer substantial risks of forfeiture. Ordinary compensation will be the unrestricted value of the stock less the amount paid for it. When the stock is finally sold, the employee's basis is increased by any ordinary income reported on exercise or when the stock became substantially vested, and the gain on sale is capital gain.

Helpful Hint: Under the Code, an employee may make a Section 83(b) election to be taxed on the value of the stock at the time of exercise, even though it would not be normally taxable until it became substantially vested. The taxable income would then be the unrestricted value of the stock less the amount paid for it. If the value of the stock were zero or very low, there would be little or no tax due at the time of exercise. The benefit is that once the 83(b) election has been made, any future gain on sale is taxed as capital gain. As a general rule, for nonpublic-company stock, it pays to make this election on exercise. The election must be made within 30 days after receipt of the stock by filing with the IRS center, with a copy to the company.

A Typical Nonqualified Plan

The most common nonqualified plan is one that offers almost all of the features of the standard qualified plan, except that one of its features is changed to make it nonqualified. For example, the option may be exercised up to 11 years after grant, rather than 10 years. If tied in with an exercise privilege of 25% per year, it provides for continuity of employment on the part of each grantee. Even more simply, the standard option plan may provide for the grant of qualified or nonqualified options, as long as they are not issued in "tandem." The mere designation of the grant as nonqualified by the company makes it so, even though the terms and conditions are similar to those of the qualified grant. The actual contract and all supporting documentation would have to bear the words "nonqualified" in their title and terms.

A Nonqualified Plan With Option Repurchase Feature

An attractive nonqualified plan may commonly be structured to take advantage of the tax to the employee on the difference between the fair market value of the stock purchased and the purchase (grant) price, which is taxed as earned income in the year the option is exercised.

Because this tax treatment may require a substantial cash outlay by the optionee at the time the option is exercised, the plan could permit the optionee to exercise less than all of his or her options, while the issuing company would purchase back the remaining options for the difference between the fair market value and the exercise price. To give an example, suppose company A grants employee B a nonqualified option to purchase 2,000 shares of stock at $15 per share, which is the market value. The stock price then rises to $30 per share. B will then exercise her option for 1,000 shares, which will require a cash payment of $15,000. In addition, B will be taxed on the difference between the fair market value of the stock and the exercise price, say at an earned income rate of 50% (say, an incremental federal rate of 39% and state tax of 11%), bringing the total cash outlay involved to $22,500. Now, suppose at the same time A purchases B's remaining option of 1,000 shares for $15,000, on which B will be taxed in the amount of $7,500. The effect of this is to bring B's total cash outlay to $30,000, of which $15,000 has been provided by A, which, in turn, will receive a tax deduction for $30,000 (B's taxable income of $15,000 on the grant/market value at purchase spread, plus the $15,000 cost of buying B's remaining option). B has paid $15,000 for stock worth $30,000 and, effectively, pays no tax on the difference. This type of arrangement may be artfully combined with an option feature like a decrease in the exercise price in proportion to an increase in the stock price, providing even more beneficial results to A and B. Such a feature is called a "variable-price" option.

A Nonqualified Plan With Variable-Price Feature

The variable-price nonqualified option is primarily directed at solving the employee's tax problem when exercising the option (the difference between the price paid for the option, or the grant price, and the market value at the time of exercise will be taxed at the highest bracket that applies—say, an incremental federal rate of 39% and state tax of 11%). In some cases, this type of option can net the optionee even more after-tax money than the usual qualified option. In a variable-price plan, assume a market price at the time of grant of $100 and a market value at exercise time of $160. This $60 increase in the stock price is deducted, dollar for dollar, from the $100 grant price, resulting in a new exercise price of $40 per share. The optionee has ordinary income of the difference between the market price at the time of exercise and the exercise price, or $120 ($160 minus $40). This $120 is earned income subject to the 50% maximum, and the tax would therefore be $60 per share. The company, similarly, has a tax deduction of $120 and an increase in paid-in capital of the tax effect, or $60. Adding the employee's tax of $60 to the purchase price of $40 gives a cost of $100 per share. This will equate to the same cost as if a qualified option had been granted at the $100 market value at the time of the grant. However, the optionee has received a more favored tax position using the variable-price option. The tax basis is now $160 per share ($40 purchase price plus ordinary income of $120), whereas the qualified basis would be $100. If the holder now sells one year after exercise at, say, $200, the long-term capital gain would be only $40. Taxed at 28%, there would be a tax of $11 per share, netting $189 after tax. With an original cost of $100 ($40 purchase price plus $60 tax paid on exercise), net after-tax income would be $89 per share. Contrasting this with the qualified option, there would be no long-term capital gain treatment unless the stock had been held for two years from the date of grant. There would, thus, be ordinary income of $100 a share ($200 sale price minus $100 exercise price), a 50% tax of $50, and net after-tax income of $50 per share, compared to $89 for the variable-price shares. If the holder had waited the full two years to obtain the 28% long-term capital gains rate, the tax of $25 would net $75, still less than the $89 under the variable-price plan. There is a further advantage over the qualified option. With a qualified option, an AMTI Adjustment exists for the difference between the grant price (which is the exercise price) and the market value at the time of exercise (see page 571). This amount is subject to a 26 to 28% tax.

From an after-tax dollar standpoint, the company is in about the same position on either the variable-price or the qualified option. It would have collected $100 from the employee in the qualified plan, with no tax deduction. In the variable-price plan, it collects $40 and receives a tax deduction as employee compensation paid of $120, worth $60 to the company, resulting in a net of $100—about the same under either plan. From a financial accounting standpoint, neither the qualified nor the nonqualified plan illustrated has any effect on net income reported, since they were both granted at market value, with no discount. Paid-in capital, and hence net worth, are increased by the tax effect of any disposition made under the qualified plan in less than two years from the grant date, or $50 in this example. There would also be a corresponding reduction in the current tax liability account. In the case of the variable-price plan, the corporation would have an ordinary tax deduction for compensation paid of $120 on exercise, and the tax effect of $60 would increase paid-in capital and decrease the current tax liability.

A Nonqualified Plan Based on Junior Stock

Most stock option plans provide employee incentives, in the form of stock, based on overall corporate performance—the incentive is based on stock appreciation, which is related to bottom-line earnings, P/E ratio, and the company's stock price. However, companies that are strapped for cash can attract and hold strong people by offering "junior stock." At the same time, the incentive to the executive will be tied to specific individual performance goals, rather than company performance.

The company gives the executive the right to buy junior stock at a low price, say one-fifth the value of the common. This junior stock will also carry one-fifth the voting rights and one-fifth the dividend of the common. Upon the executive's attainment of his or her individual performance objectives, the junior stock will convert automatically into common shares, worth five times as much as the junior shares. (The common shares have probably also appreciated in value during the intervening performance period.)

If the individual does not meet the performance goals, the company buys back the junior stock at the original price paid—the employee gets his or her money back, albeit without interest. If the goals are met and the common stock is issued upon conversion, the gain is ordinary income to the executive. There is no tax effect to the corporation upon conversion, as the exchange of junior stock for common stock is internal to the company. From a financial accounting standpoint, however, the company must recognize the dilution of equity on its balance sheet, this being the difference between the amount paid for the junior stock and the market value of the common at the time of conversion. This is a charge to paid-in capital. The transaction would also cause a dilution in calculating primary earnings per share, because of the additional common shares outstanding.

> *Helpful Hint:* If the individual needs long-term capital gains to offset existing capital losses, instead of ordinary income on conversion, he or she must notify the IRS under Section 83(b) of the Code, within 30 days of the purchase of the junior stock, of his or her election to be taxed at the time of purchase. Even though there is no tax due on purchase (assuming that the junior stock is issued at fair market value, which is purported to be one-fifth of the value of the common), the election must be made to ensure capital gains treatment at the time of conversion. Absent this election, the gain at conversion will be ordinary income.

Standards of performance are up to the company. They may include, for example, sales targets, departmental profit goals, or unit productivity goals. The standards should be fairly difficult to meet to justify the low price for the junior stock. It may be desirable for public companies to obtain an outside valuation of the junior stock from an investment banker to prevent a challenge by stockholders or the IRS. The plan will require stockholder approval because of the potential for dilution of stockholder's equity.

This plan has an advantage over ISOs in that there is no $100,000 maximum value that an executive can exercise in any one year. Moreover, unlike the case with ISOs, the grantee gets his or her money back if results are bad. No common stock ends up being issued if individual goals are not met. On the other hand, this plan requires the executive to commit up-front cash, whereas ISOs typically give him or her up to five years, and may give up to ten years, to make that cash commitment (but financing can be arranged by the company for the amount of the commitment, with the junior stock being pledged to secure the loan). Another disadvantage to the employee is that junior stock is behind common stock in the event of a bankruptcy or liquidation of the company.

Junior stock would seem to be appropriate for new ventures, new projects, and growth companies, where earnings are expected to surge. There is less chance for sharp appreciation, and therefore less motivation, in larger, more stable companies.

FINANCING OPTIONS

Qualified options generally do not require any formal company financial assistance. One of their principal features is to permit the grantee to receive and hold the option for up to ten years, subject to no tax. This permits the optionee to observe the market and not exercise the option until the market price is significantly higher than the grant price. In this enviable position, the optionee is usually able to obtain financing from friends, relatives, or even banks. Bank loans to purchase stock are subject to Federal Reserve Board requirements, which are similar to the margin requirements established by brokerage houses. The margin rates fluctuate, tied to the money supply, but generally range from 65% to 80%, as a percentage of market value that a bank may lend. This type of loan has the disadvantage that a drop in market value will occasion a margin call by the bank that the employee may not be able to meet. Banks do not count fractions of a point in stock value, so that a $\frac{1}{4}$-point drop could require 1 point in margin. As an example, a bank lends 80% of market value when 5,000 shares of stock are selling at $4 per share—a $16,000 loan. The market value declines to 3\frac{3}{4}$ a share. The bank will value the stock at the nearest lower whole point, or $3 a share. Their maximum loan of 80% on $15,000 can be $12,000. The margin call is, thus, $4,000 on a $\frac{1}{4}$-point drop with a total market value drop of only $1,250 on the 5,000 shares. A better strategy for the employee could be personal loans over a 36-month period. This requires a uniform pay-down at standard interest rates over the loan term, at the end of which the stock would be owned outright. At some point, say after a year, a small portion of the stock could be sold to meet future loan payments. The balance of the stock would then be held to obtain the expected appreciation. As another alternative, some companies may make a loan to the employee for a six-month or one-year period, to provide bridge financing until the first sale of stock is made. This does not require a formal loan program, but the corporation should require that the stock be held as collateral for repayment of the loan. The features of this type of loan are discussed in Chapter 11.

Nonqualified options present some special problems with regard to financing. The cash needs are usually more stringent, as an immediate tax must be paid on exercise on the difference between the exercise price and the market value on the date of exercise. Of course, if this spread is large, the employee will exercise and sell the same day, going for the assured profit, despite the ordinary tax rate that attaches to that profit. In this case, no financing is needed, at least not for more than a few days. However, if he or she elects to go for the long-term gain after one year, then he or she may require financing to purchase the stock, and, perhaps, to pay the tax on exercise, should the tax payment date fall prior to sale of the stock. In the case of a straight wage-earner, subject to wage withholding taxes and filing no estimated tax returns because he or she has no other income, a sudden surge of income through the exercise of nonqualified options could throw him or her into a position where estimated income tax returns would have to be filed at the next quarterly due date. This makes the need for cash urgent and imminent. The employee's company may provide financing through a formal plan, available to all key option holders. State laws must be researched first, however, as some states prohibit corporations from lending money to employees to finance stock purchases. A notable example of this is New York State. If state laws prohibit such loans by the parent corporation, a subsidiary corporation in another state without such prohibition may be used. Delaware, a common home for many corporations, has no such restrictions. This notwithstanding, Regulation G of the Federal Reserve Board established a limitation of 35% of the market value, at any time, as the maximum amount of such a loan by a corporation. This may be a benefit, as the corporation can lend more money to the employee after exercise, should the market value rise. A **financing plan for either qualified or nonqualified options** is illustrated in Exhibit 15-7. Under this program, 30% of market value is loaned to the employee to provide a 5% cushion under the 35% FRB maximum loan requirement. This avoids having to call the optionee for margin as a result of slight fluctuations in the market value. The loan is secured by the stock and a nonrecourse note. The nonrecourse note

Exhibit 15-7. Financing plan for stock options.

<u>Description of Financing under the ''Special'' Qualified Stock Options</u>

''Special'' Qualified Stock Options or Nonqualified Stock Options arising from the rescinding of the former (as described in Paragraph 2 of the Explanation of 20xx''Special'' Qualified Stock Option Plan) will be available for ''special'' financing by the Company, on request. This financing will have the following features:

1. Senox Limited, our wholly owned subsidiary, <u>will lend you 30% of the market value</u> of the stock on the day you exercise your option. An example of the loan and the funds that you, yourself, would have to provide is set forth below:

a.	Date of grant	August 2,20xx
b.	Option price at date of grant	$25 per share
c.	No. of shares granted	500 shares
d.	Percent eligible for exercise after each year	25%
e.	Value of grant (500 shares × $25)	$12,500
f.	Amount eligible for exercise after each year ($12,500 × 25%)	$ 3,125
g.	Assumed market value on August 2,20xx	$ 30 per share
h.	Total market value on August 2,20xx of exercisable shares (125 shares at $30)	$ 3,750
i.	Maximum Senox loan ($3,750 × 30%)	$ 1,125
j.	Funds you must supply (line 6 minus 9)	$ 2,000 20xx

2. In accordance with regulations of the Federal Reserve Board, your total loan from the Company <u>may not exceed 35% of the market value</u> at any time. Note that in the example above we have made a loan of 30% of the market value. This would permit the price to drop as much as 15% before the Company must require that you place additional collateral with us, in the form of more stock or additional cash in sufficient amounts to keep your loan below the legally permitted 35% of market value. An example of a call for additional collateral is set forth below:

a.	Assumed market value 6 months after exercise on February 2,20xx	$ 24 per share
b.	Total market value of shares previously exercised (125 sh. × $24)	$ 3,000
c.	Maximum legal loan ($3,000 × 35%)	$ 1,050
d.	Additional collateral required (line 9 minus 13)	$ 75*

   * This may be supplied to Senox in cash or stock. If in stock, it must have a market value of $75; for example, 3.1 shares of Savin at $24 = $75.

3. On the other hand, if the market value of the stock rises by the time you exercise additional shares, Senox would lend you 30% of the value of all of the shares you would hold after your additional exercise. An example of this is given below. Note in this example that Senox would lend you $1,875

(continued)

Exhibit 15-7. *(continued)*

Description of Financing . . . . . (cont'd)
Page -2-

    (line 20) as compared to the loan on the first exercise of $1,125 (line
9). This is the result of the increase in the market value of the shares
to $40, in the example:

a.	Market value on date of second exercise (8/2/)	$40
b.	Shares to be exercised on August 2, 20xx	125 shares
c.	Total shares to be owned after August 2,20xx	250 shares
d.	Market value of shares to be owned (250 × $40)	$10,000
e.	Maximum Senox loan ($10,000 × 30%)	$ 3,000
f.	Additional Senox loan to be made August 2,20xx (line 19 minus 9)	$ 1,875
g.	Funds you must supply (line 6 minus 20)	$ 1,250

4. <u>Security</u> will be required for each loan made by Seno Limited in the form of
a nonrecourse note that you will be required to sign in favor of Senox. In
addition, Senox will hold your stock as security for payment of the note.
In short, this means that if you do not repay your loan to Senox, Senox
may look only to the stock it holds for payment on the loan and will have
no other recourse to you nor any of your assets.

5. <u>Your holding period for capital gains</u> begins on the date you exercise your
stock options, despite the fact that Senox is holding these securities for
repayment of your loans. You may sell stock at any time, concurrently with
the payment of the loan to Senox, and you will receive any excess proceeds
from Senox.

6. <u>Additional financing assistance</u> may not be supplied by Savin or Senox in
exercising these options. However, Savin will recommend to major banking
facilities that additional loans be made available to you to assist you
in financing 70% of the option price, which is your obligation. However,
you will be unable to place this stock as security with the banks, and the
purpose of these bank loans cannot be attributed specifically to acquiring
the stock, but rather, must be attributed to your overall financial needs.
There is no assurance that our banks will make these loans available to
you. These loans will be contingent on the bank's usual credit review—including
your own personal credit situation, your existing loans, the individual
bank's lending requirements, and the general money and economic situation.

7. <u>Your request for financial assistance</u> in the exercise of your options
should be made to the treasurer's office, setting forth the date of the
original grant, the number of shares originally granted, the price of the
grant, the amount of shares you desire to exercise, and the date on which
you desire to exercise your shares.

means that the corporation may look only to the stock for repayment
of the loan, not to any other assets the borrower may have.

The company may further assist the option holder with financing
by providing introductions to banks with which it deals and making
specific recommendations to bank officers for key employees. Bank accommodations for these recommendations are usually a matter of customer goodwill and are done without any corporate guarantees for the
employee.

OPTING FOR OPTIONS

It is possible to effectively reach and motivate the myriads of individuals involved in any company's growth. The best technique to use is some sort of profit-sharing plan. The best of these is probably the stock option plan. It is glamorous, smacking of ownership in the enterprise, simple to understand, and easy to administer. It may be adapted to any form of organizational structure and provides interesting tax benefits to both the company and the recipient. Stock option plans may be tied in to individual performance by varying the amount of shares granted or by issuing junior stock, but they mainly stress overall company performance and goals, since their ultimate value over the years comes down to bottom-line performance, earnings per share after taxes. As the company is successful in its environment, so, too, may the key manager share in that success through the proper incentive option plan. The stock option plan will work in any tax climate and under any market conditions.

16

Developing and Administering Benefit Programs

The treasurer's and controller's functions defined by the Financial Executives Institute are listed in Appendix A. The sixth treasury function, investments, indicates that the treasurer will "establish and coordinate policies for investment in pension and other similar trusts." Exhibit 11-1, a study of the Conference Board, points out, under cash management, that the function of pension plan payments is often reassigned from the treasurer to the controller.

The lines of responsibility in this area often cross, but the development and administration of benefit programs generally fall to the treasurer or controller in most companies. In smaller companies, the treasurer or controller will have direct responsibility for benefit programs. In middle-sized companies, a personnel manager or benefit specialist, reporting to the treasurer or controller, may assume this function. In large companies, we often find an officer with a title related to personnel or human services, reporting directly to the president. When such is the case, the controller, through the first controllership function in the FEI definition, planning for control, is required "to establish, coordinate and administer . . . the necessary procedures to effectuate the plan [for the control of operations]." This includes all pertinent personnel policies and procedures. These personnel responsibilities are part of the "framework" necessary to administer the plan for the control of operations, as described in Chapter 7.

The controller also has a further evaluating and consulting function described in Appendix A, to interface with the personnel or human services manager. This is demonstrated in the controller's position description, in Appendix A, under Organizational Relationships, showing that the controller "advises, consults with, coordinates with, and provides administrative support . . . [to the] Director of personnel and office services."

The treasurer, when assigned this responsibility, derives authority for this function from the broad insurance function in the FEI definition, although that responsibility for insurance coverage is usually identified with corporate assets or casualty protection. The controller, likewise, has an insurance responsibility under the protection of assets function. The employees are certainly the company's most valuable asset. The treasurer has further involvement through his or her investment function, when funds from pension or other trusts are invested.

Types of Plans

The usual types of employee benefit programs are:

1. *Employee stock ownership trusts.* The trust borrows funds from a bank to invest in company stock. The company makes contributions to the trust, which are used to repay the bank loans. The company's contributions are tax-deductible and are not taxed to the trust. Up to 15% of payrolls may be contributed. Some companies use this device to refinance existing bank loans, thereby obtaining a tax deduction for the loan repayment. It is a good device where the company has no objection to earnings dilution through stock giveaways.

2. *Employee stock purchase plans.* The employee subscribes to company stock up to, say, 10% of wages to a limit of $25,000 in stock value per year, payable through payroll deductions over a maximum of 27 months. The price the employee pays may be as low as 85% of the

market value on the date he or she subscribes or at the end of the payroll deduction period. There is no tax effect to the company or the employee on the up to 15% spread. The employee may withdraw from the plan at any time and receive the return of the payroll deductions, with interest. This type of plan is usually one with high employee participation, since it is practically risk-free. It provides a built-in profit or a certain return on savings. The plans are qualified under the Internal Revenue Code.

Employee stock purchase plan options are very similar to ISOs; both are statutory options entitled to preferential tax treatment. ISOs, however, are subject to different eligibility requirements. Employers may elect to provide ISOs to key employees only, while providing options to all employees under an employee stock purchase plan.

3. *Executive compensation.* This includes nonsalaried benefits to high-tax-bracket executives. The benefits include educational trusts, company cars, medical programs, investment and financial advisory services and liberal expense accounts, deferred compensation programs, and life insurance. (The value of the discriminatory excess of life insurance under Sec. 79 of the Code is the cost of such group term life insurance provided by the employer, to the extent that such cost exceeds the sum of the cost of $50,000 of such insurance and the amount, if any, paid by the employee toward that insurance. Cost, as defined, refers not to the actual premium paid for the coverage, but to the cost determined by a uniform premium table in the IRS regulations, called Table I cost. The Table I cost for the amount of the insurance provided is compared to the Table I cost for $50,000, and the difference is ordinary income, included in the employee's income for the tax year within which the plan year ends. This excess amount also constitutes "wages" for Social Security purposes. Note that this employer-provided benefit often includes salary reduction.)

4. *Options.* Both qualified and nonqualified options are discussed in Chapter 15.

5. *Payroll deduction plans.* These include noncontributory plans (no company participation) for employee credit unions (employees save, lend money to themselves at interest, and pay dividends to shareholders, all under federal and state regulation), Treasury bonds purchase, or savings bank deposit. The company may contribute on a *pari passu* or some lesser basis.

6. *Profit-sharing plans.* These plans represent one of the oldest types of benefit programs. They may include key managers or all employees. Payments may be in cash, stock, or deferred compensation after retirement. Pension plan contributions by the company may be geared to profits.

7. *Qualified pension and retirement plans.* These plans include defined-benefit and defined-contribution plans, IRAs, SEPs, SIMPLE plans, Keogh plans, 401(k) cash or deferred arrangement plans, profit-sharing plans, and money-purchase plans. Generally, all these provide a tax deduction to the company for the contribution but are not taxable to the participant until the funds are withdrawn at retirement.

The most common of these are discussed below.

401(k) Plans

These plans provide for the deferral of compensation through cash or deferred arrangements under Sec. 401(k) of the Internal Revenue Code. Such a plan is a profit-sharing or stock bonus plan containing a qualified cash or deferral feature. The cash or deferred amount is often an annual employer contribution or bonus that the employee may defer or take out at once in cash. The plan may also be a salary reduction plan, under which the employee defers some regular salary and has it contributed to the plan by the employer. The employer is not required to contribute its own funds, though it may. The plan is qualified, meaning that the amount of compensation deferred is not currently taxable to the employee, but the employer is allowed a deduction for this same amount. 401(k) plans may be in addition to other qualified plans, as well as IRAs. This is, therefore, an opportunity for any employee, including highly compensated employees, to invest in retirement funds on a pretax basis; that is, federal withholding tax and the withholding taxes of most states are based on salary *minus* the 401(k) contribution. The maximum contribution for 2000 is $10,000.

These plans provide for more favorable tax treatment on distribution than an IRA. Lump-sum distributions from 401(k)s are eligible for five-year income averaging or, in certain cases, capital gains treatment, unlike distributions from IRAs, which are subject to ordinary income tax.

Strict rules governing withdrawal of funds are a serious drawback to these programs. As a rule, withdrawals from 401(k) plans are not allowed before age 59½, except in the case of retirement, death, job change, becoming disabled, or financial hardship. IRS Reg. 1.401(k)-1(d) (2) of 1988 explains when hardship withdrawals are permitted. The employee must show an "immediate and heavy" financial need without other available resources. Safe harbor financial needs that qualify are medical expenses, purchase of a principal residence, college tuition, and payment to prevent eviction from or foreclosure on a principal residence. Beginning with 1989 plan years, only elective deferrals may be withdrawn for hardship. Even if the employee is qualified for a hardship withdrawal, any withdrawals taken before age 59½ are subject to income tax plus a 10% penalty.

As an alternative to hardship withdrawals, the 401(k) plan may allow employees to borrow. These payouts are considered loans, not distributions subject to income tax. The plan may allow employees to borrow up to half their account to a maximum of $50,000 at an interest rate slightly higher than prime, say prime plus ¼%. Unless the amount borrowed is used to buy a home, the plan may require repayment within five years, although no repayment is required in the event the employee leaves the company. If he or she is still employed, in the event of a default on the loan repayment, the 10% penalty tax for early withdrawal will apply, as well as income tax.

Sec. 501(c)(9) Trust

A Sec. 501(c)(9) trust, known as a voluntary employees benefit association, or VEBA, is a tax-exempt trust formed to pay life, health, and disability benefits to employees. Under such a program, the benefits are not insured with commercial insurance companies. Therefore, benefits may be custom-designed, at lower cost, as the usual 8 percent annual retention charge by the insurance company is avoided. There is also no state premium tax, which is levied on insurance carriers and averages about 2%. Moreover, the liability may be funded by the employer at a slower pace, rather than setting aside full reserves for each disability. Income on the trust assets accrues tax-free. On the other hand, administration is complex, and an insurance company is usually needed to service the claims, at a cost of about 2% to 4% of claims.

Employees may be required to contribute to the plan, but they may not be required to enroll in the plan as a condition of employment. Often, the employer will pay the premiums for employee medical coverage, and the employees will elect to pay for medical coverage for their dependents. Employer contributions are tax-deductible and are not income to the employee. Employee contributions may be deductible to the extent that they are paid for insurance that constitutes medical care. For contributions to be deductible as medical expenses, the employee must itemize nonbusiness deductions, and the amount deductible is limited to the excess of expenses over 7.5% of adjusted gross income. In addition, federal income taxes are not paid on the investment of funds held in the trust between time of premium payment and the paying of benefits.

> *Beware of This:* Some states — Connecticut, for example — have a special tax on noninsured employee welfare benefit plans.

Deferred (Nonqualified) Compensation Plans

These are nonqualified plans that can be tailored to meet the requirements of any company. Such a plan may be integrated into any existing performance bonus or nonqualified profit-sharing plan without changing the features of those plans. A particular **deferred compensation plan** that meets IRS requirements to keep the compensation from being taxable to the employee (and hence deductible to the company) in the current year is set forth in Exhibit 16-1 (see the section in the exhibit on taxability).

> *Beware of This:* You may not intend to defer compensation, but under Code Sec. 461, there is a potential trap in the case of

Exhibit 16-1. Deferred compensation plan for officers.

GENERAL

Officers may elect, prior to 5/1 of each year, to defer Officers' Profit-Sharing Bonus, or up to 20% of regular salary, to be earned in the ensuing year, starting 5/1 and ending 4/30 of the following calendar year. Example: The election must be made prior to 5/1/XX for the fiscal year 5/1/XX–4/30/XX.

DEFERRAL

All or any part (percentage) to be earned may be deferred (1) until the following year's distribution, or (2) until the third following year's distribution, or (3) until the fifth following year's distribution, or (4) until retirement or termination of service. Once elected, the election may not be changed.

PAYMENTS

Payment, at the end of the deferral period, may be in (1) a lump sum, or (2) installments over a five-year period, or (3) installments over a ten-year period. The election for the type of payment must be made at the same time as the deferral election and, once made, may not be changed.

ERISA

This is an unfunded arrangement maintained primarily for the purpose of providing deferred compensation for a select group of highly compensated management. The Plan is exempt from the participation, vesting, benefit accrual, funding, and fiduciary provisions of ERISA. Only a single, identifying statement need be filed with the Department of Labor.

DEATH BENEFITS

The employee may designate a beneficiary for any unpaid payments. The designation is revocable.

FORFEITURE

The right to receive deferred compensation is forfeitable based on the employee's agreement (1) to work for the Company (or its subsidiaries) for the number of years of the deferral (but not the payment); (2) to refrain from disclosing trade secrets or other information valuable to the Company's business; (3) to refrain from engaging in a competitive business as owner, employee, or otherwise; (4) to not commit a crime involving moral turpitude; or (5) to fail to render consulting service on request.

FUNDING

The Plan is unfunded and not trusteed. The Company may use the funds for any purpose whatsoever. Any employee claims for compensation payment will be those of an unsecured general creditor.

(*continued*)

Exhibit 16-1. *(continued)*

INVESTMENT INCOME

The employee will earn income, to be credited to his or her deferred account, and to be paid at the time the deferred compensation is paid, at a rate equal to the 180-day Certificate of Deposit interest rate of Chase Bank.

TRANSFERABILITY

The rights herein are not transferable or assignable by the employee.

COMMITTEE

The Plan will be administered by an independent administrative committee, consisting of three outside independent directors of the Corporation, with discretion to change the manner of payment of deferred compensation in the event of disability or hardship.

TAXABILITY

It is intended that the Company not take a deduction, and the employee not report income, until the year when the deferred compensation is paid.

ACCOUNTING

Since payments are contingent and forfeitable, no charge will be made to earnings currently until payments are actually made, although footnote disclosure may be required if a material contingency exists.

(text continued from page 606)

a deferred bonus to a controlling stockholder. This may have been accrued as a payroll expense in the current year, but unless payment is actually made within 2½ months of the end of the tax year, the deduction is barred, and you have, in effect, created a deferred compensation program for that controlling stockholder.

Defined-Benefit Plans

These are qualified corporate retirement plans (QCRP) under the Internal Revenue Code. Such a plan is a form of pension plan. It allows the employee to retire with a predetermined benefit, determined as a percentage of preretirement income. The employer's contributions reflect a defined or assumed benefit for the employee, but they must not be computed based on corporate profits. Benefits may be based on length of service, salary, or any nondiscriminatory method. The plan may be integrated with Social Security benefits. Like all qualified plans, a defined-benefit plan must be in writing, legally binding, and for the exclusive benefit of the employees and their beneficiaries, and it must benefit a broad class of employees without discriminating in favor of owners, officers, or highly paid employees. Payments are tax-deductible to the company, and income on the trust funds compounds tax-free. There is a $170,000 limit on individual benefits for 2000 (tied to Social Security retirement age), subject to increases based on cost of living adjustments. From an accounting standpoint, costs are distributed over the periods of funding the liabilities.

Defined-benefit plans differ from defined-contribution plans, described below, in two ways:

1. The employer's annual contribution is not predetermined, but rather is the amount needed to provide the predetermined benefits.
2. No individual accounts are established for employees. Instead, the entire plan fund is available to pay all benefit obligations as they arise.

Defined-Contribution Plans

A defined-contribution plan is a QCRP that is a form of pension plan, based on profit sharing. These plans are most often used by small and medium-size companies, as they encourage increased production and contributions may be passed in years of low profits without disqualifying the plan. Contributions are made to an employee trust based on a percentage of profits, or a percentage of profits above a minimum level, or contributions that increase as profits increase, or a combination of any of these. The employee may also contribute. The dollar limit on annual individual additions is the lesser of $30,000 or 25% of compensation. There will be no cost of living adjustments to the defined-contribution limit until the defined-benefit limit reaches $170,000.

A variant is the money-purchase pension plan, in which the defined amount must be set aside annually and may not be passed in times of low earnings. There is a 10% excise tax for underfunding. Usually, the company contribution is a flat percentage of payroll. The advantage is known costs, for budgeting purposes. Since benefits are directly related to tenure, the younger employees will receive greater benefits and the older executives or owners will do less well.

The contribution to these plans may be up to 25% of compensation. As a result, money-purchase plans are often used in tandem with profit-sharing plans (say 10% contribution for the money-purchase plan and 15% for profit-sharing). This avoids the requirement to make a 25% contribution that would exist if the money-purchase plan were used alone.

Another variant is the target benefit plan. This combines the features of a defined-benefit plan and a money-purchase pension plan, in that the benefit is defined, as in the former, but it may fluctuate, as with a defined-contribution plan, based on changing fund earnings or cost of living index changes.

Simplified Employee Pension (SEP) Plan

This is another QCRP, but less complicated than other pension plans. The employer may contribute up to 15% of compensation, up to a maximum of $30,000, directly to the employee's IRA. The employee may make a deductible contribution, in addition, of an amount equal to the lesser of $2,000 or 100% of compensation. These plans have simple legal requirements and no red tape, and benefit owners, executives, and highly paid employees as well.

> *Word of Caution:* Participants must include employees earning over $450 a year for 2000, even if part time; anyone who worked during three out of the last five years; and employees at least 21 years old. Nonresident aliens and union employees may be excluded.

SIMPLE Retirement Plans

These plans are oriented to certain small employers. One type of SIMPLE plan is in the form of a SIMPLE 401(k) plan (see above). A more common form is the SIMPLE IRA. The employer may not use this if any other tax-favored plan is maintained, with the exception that it may be adopted for nonunion employees if the employer maintains a qualified plan for employees covered by collective bargaining. The elective contribution of the employee is not included in gross income. The employer receives a deduction for its matching contribution.

Eligible employees include those receiving at least $5,000 in compensation for each of the past two years. A self-employed individual is considered an employee and is eligible if her or his earned income is at least $5,000. Nonresident aliens and union employees may be excluded from participation. An employee may terminate participation at any time during the year but may not reenter until the following year.

The employee may elect to receive payments in cash or as a contribution to the SIMPLE IRA account. The employee may elect to contribute up to $6,000 per year for 2000, adjusted for inflation, and this may be matched by the employer, allowing for a maximum deferral of $12,000. A self-employed individual may also make a matching contribution and it will not be treated as an elective contribution made by the individual. The employer must match an employee's elective contribution not exceeding 3% of the employee's compensation but may elect to limit its match to a minimum of 1%.

> *Helpful Hint.* The top-heavy rules (see below) do not apply to SIMPLE plans.

Vesting

Qualified plans provide for two types of *vesting*, or entitlement to benefits, even in the event of job change, as follows:

1. *Five-year cliff vesting.* No benefits are vested until after five years, at which time 100% is vested.
2. *Seven-year graduated vesting.* Twenty percent is vested after three years, and this amount increases 20% each year thereafter, until 100% is vested after seven years.

Top-Heavy Rules

Top-heavy plans, which mostly benefit officers, stockholders, and highly paid employees ("key employees"), are subject to special rules. A key employee is defined as an officer, one of the ten largest owners, a 5% owner, or a 1% owner earning $150,000 or more. If more than 60% of the account balances under a defined-contribution plan or more than 60% of the present value of the accrued benefits under a defined-benefit plan belong to key employees, the plan is considered to be top-heavy. In such a case, in order for the plan to continue to be qualified, compensation in excess of $200,000 (inflation-adjusted with 1989 as the base year) may not be taken into account for any employee; special vesting rules would apply, providing for three-year vesting or six-year graded vesting (20% vested in less than three years, increasing by 20% per year starting in year three, until 100% is vested after six years); and a minimum contribution of 3% of pay must be made for non-key employees for defined-contribution plans for each top-heavy year, and a minimum benefit accrual of 2% of compensation multiplied by the number of years of service, but not over 20%, for defined-benefit plans. The latter is limited by the percentage contributed on behalf of the key employee with the highest percentage. These limitations may not make the additional contributions so onerous that the top-heavy feature needs to be eliminated.

Employee Convertible Debenture (ECD) Plan

This is an example of a deferred compensation plan that is not qualified. Some nonqualified plans merely provide for cash payments in the future, which may be vested or may be subject to forfeiture when certain restrictions lapse. Other plans provide a future award of stock to the employee, or the grant of an option to buy stock at a favored price. The ECD plan is a combination of both of the foregoing. It may be tailored to meet individual company needs. An IRS ruling could be requested to confirm the tax aspects.

Selected employees are granted the right to buy a specified amount of ten-year subordinated convertible debentures, paying interest at floating quarterly prime rate, at 90% of fair market value (fair value may be based on a multiple of book value or a price/earnings ratio for privately held companies). The ten-year bonds are convertible into common stock at the face value of the bond divided by 120% of the fair market value of a common share of the company's stock on the date of the grant. There is a five-year waiting period for exercise in the event of termination of employment. The difference between fair market value and the cost of the debentures is taxable to the employee and deductible to the company in the year of grant. The conversion of the bonds into stock at a later date is a nontaxable event. Gain on the sale of the stock is a capital gain.

> As an example, a $1,000 bond is purchased at $900 when the common stock has a fair market value of $25. The $100 difference is deductible by the company as compensation paid, and is taxable to the employee as compensation earned. The tax basis of the bond to the employee is $1,000, including the $100 of reported taxable income. The debenture is converted into $33\frac{1}{3}$ shares of common ($1,000/$25 × 120%) having the same tax basis as the bond, $1,000. The acquisition date of the bond is carried over to the common stock for purpose of determining long-term gain. If the stock is sold for $2,500 one year after the acquisition date of the bond, the long-term capital gain is $1,500. In effect, this $1,500 gain is contingent deferred compensation that has been transformed into a taxable long-term capital gain for the employee. However, that $1,500 gain is not tax-deductible to the company.

FRINGE BENEFIT PROGRAMS

Exhibit 16-2 is a **listing of most available benefits and their tax consequences.** Administration of benefit programs requires that formal pro-

Exhibit 16-2.   Tax treatment of fringe benefits.

Tax Treatment of Fringe Benefits

Some fringe benefits are always taxable, others are always tax-free, and still others are taxable for highly paid people (but not for other employees) if provided for under a discriminatory plan. The table below covers most cases.

Virtually all fringe benefits are deductible by the company except for incentive stock options and compensation that exceeds what is "reasonable." In certain cases, the company cannot take the deduction until the officer or employee reports the income — for example, nonqualified stock options, grants of restricted stock or stock or equity appreciation rights, and contributions to nonqualified retirement plans.

Perquisites of the job are deductible if they are "ordinary and necessary" business expenses and not excessively lavish, except that business meals and entertainment are only 50% deductible.

Tax-Free to Officer (Unless Total Compensation Package Is Unreasonable)	*Tax-Free to Officer if Provided to Most Employees Under Nondiscriminatory Plan*	*Taxable to Officer*
Accident and health plans*	Accident and health plans*	Bonuses
Business meals and entertainment	Adoption benefits plans	Car for commuting and other personal use
Death benefit to family up to $5,000	Cash-or-deferred [401(k)] plans	Financial counseling services; may be partly deductible
De minimis fringe benefits	Child care or dependent care	Golden parachutes
Disability insurance	Discounts on company products	Life insurance coverage over $50,000
Gym or other health or exercise facility (but cost not deductible by company if provided under discriminatory plan)	Educational expenses, whether or not job-related	Moving expenses; partly deductible
Incentive stock options	Legal expenses	Restricted stock, normally taxable when restrictions expire
Interest-free loans to $10,000	Life insurance coverage up to $50,000*	Sick pay
Meals and lodging on company premises, but only if furnished for convenience of employer*	Meals provided at cost	Stock appreciation rights, when exercised
Nonqualified retirement plans, benefits taxable and deductible when received	Medical reimbursement plans*	Stock purchase plan (discriminatory): value of discount or matching contribution by company
	No-additional-cost services (such as hotel rooms otherwise unused)	Travel (personal) on company plane, with limited exceptions
	Retirement plan contributions; nontaxable until withdrawn	

Tax-Free to Officer (Unless Total Compensation Package Is Unreasonable)	Tax-Free to Officer if Provided to Most Employees Under Nondiscriminatory Plan	Taxable to Officer
Parking, free or discounted Travel, first class, on business Travel on company plane for business and very limited personal travel Working condition fringe benefits such as business use of company car	Stock purchase plan discount	Vacation pay * * * * * * Other fringe benefits as negotiated by individuals

* Taxable to partners and 2%-or-more stockholders of S corporations, and to self-employed.

cedural documentation and publication of the various benefit programs be completed (see Operating Policies and Personnel Policies in Chapter 7). Typical policies and procedures for the policy or personnel manual are:

❖ *Cafeteria plans.* These provide employees with a choice of taking cash or receiving qualified benefits such as accident and health coverage, group term life insurance, or dependent care coverage. Benefits provided are not included in income, unless cash is taken.

❖ *Choice plans.* These plans offer a way to buy other benefits in exchange for choosing not to be covered by health insurance or for unused vacation time. The benefits an employee elects not to receive may be traded for other benefits, such as life insurance, medical benefits, or long-term care plans. The employee has a choice.

❖ *Disability insurance supplement.*

❖ **Educational assistance program** (Exhibit 16-3). These benefits are deductible by the employer and may not be excluded from gross income by the employee. They are also subject to tax withholding.

❖ *Financial planning services.*

(*text continues on page 619*)

Exhibit 16-3.   Educational assistance program.

Personnel Policy and Procedure	Policy/Procedure No. ___EB - 110___ Effective Date _____12/1/_____ Page No. ____1____ of ____3____
Title: EDUCATIONAL ASSISTANCE PROGRAM	

POLICY

The Company provides financial assistance for educational courses that will help employees acquire job-related knowledge or skills. Employees may take advantage of the program to improve their current job performance or to improve their potential for internal advancement.

RESPONSIBILITY

The Facility Personnel Representative is responsible for the administration of this program. However, the immediate supervisor or manager should provide assistance to employees who are interested in establishing an educational program.

ELIGIBILITY

All regular full-time employees with a minimum of six months of Company service prior to course enrollment are eligible for reimbursement for *job-related courses*.

All regular full-time employees with one year of Company service prior to course enrollment are eligible for reimbursement for courses required for a *job-related degree*.

GENERAL

1. Courses need not be those required for a degree, but must be directly related to the employee's present position or to a reasonably predictable future assignment.
2. Courses must be offered by an accredited educational, vocational, or technical institution and must be taken outside of normal working hours.
3. Courses for covered undergraduate, vocational, or technical study may be reimbursed up to a maximum of $1,000 in any fiscal year (May 1 to April 30).
4. Graduate-level courses will be reimbursed up to a maximum of $2,000 in any fiscal year (May 1 to April 30).
5. Veterans eligible for government tuition assistance have the option of using either veterans' benefits or the Educational Assistance Program. Employees cannot receive Educational Assistance payments *and* veterans' benefits for the same course.

PROCEDURE

1. *Educational Planning*
   An employee should first discuss the proposed course of study and the institution with his or her immediate supervisor to determine whether the course meets the guidelines of the Educational Assistance Program.

2. *Application for Approval of Reimbursement*
    a. Employee responsibilities
        (1) The employee prepares the Educational Assistance Request (Exhibit A), which may be obtained from the employee's immediate supervisor or from the facility personnel representative.
        (2) An Educational Assistance Request must be submitted prior to enrollment in the course. If the employee wishes to know before paying for courses whether the reimbursement will be approved, the request form should be submitted six weeks prior to registering for courses.
        (3) After completion of the Educational Assistance Request, attach a copy of the course description and forward to immediate supervisor.
    b. Management responsibilities
        (1) In branch locations, supervisor and/or department manager approves and forwards to facility personnel representative. Facility personnel representative then forwards to appropriate director or vice president.
        (2) In home office, supervisor or manager forwards directly to appropriate director or department head.
        (3) Director, department head, or vice president approves or disapproves application. If it is approved, he or she then forwards it to Home Office Personnel Department. If it is disapproved, it is returned with a written explanation to facility personnel representative in branch locations or appropriate manager in home office location.
        (4) Home Office Personnel Department returns "Final Approval" copy via appropriate facility personnel representative to immediate supervisor/manager.
        (5) Immediate supervisor/manager is responsible for notifying employee of outcome and retaining copy of approved Educational Assistance form.
3. *Reimbursement*
    a. After successfully completing the course, employee gives immediate supervisor/manager a copy of the tuition receipt and final grade.
    b. Immediate supervisor/manager should attach these to the "Final Approval/Course Completion" copy and forward to Home Office Personnel Department for payment. Managers in home office locations forward directly to Home Office Personnel Department.
    c. After final approval by Director of Personnel, Educational Assistance Request is forwarded to Accounts Payable for payment.
    d. Termination
        (1) If an employee leaves the Company for any reason before completing the course, no reimbursement will be made.
        (2) If an employee leaves the Company for any reason after completing a course approved for reimbursement, payment will be mailed to employee.

(continued)

Exhibit 16-3. *(continued)*

Corporation

Educational Assistance Request

ELIGIBILITY:
1. After six (6) months' full-time employment, request job-related courses only.
2. After one (1) year's full-time employment, request job-related or job-related degree courses.

INSTRUCTIONS:
1. Prior to enrolling for course, complete this section of Educational Assistance Request and present to your Supervisor.
2. Upon notification of approval, enroll, pay fees, and keep your payment receipt.
3. Upon course completion with a grade of "C" or better, give payment receipt and final grades to your supervisor, who will initiate reimbursement.

E M P L O Y E E

Name		Soc. Sec. No.	Employment Date / /
Location ☐ Home Office ☐ Branch _____ ☐ Dealer Division		Department	Position Title
Accredited Institution: Name	Street Address	City	State	Zip

Present Education Level: College
(Check highest completed) ☐ High School ☐ 1 ☐ 2 ☐ 3 ☐ 4 ☐ 5 ☐ 6 | No. of hours remaining to earn your degree _____

COURSE TITLE	COURSE DESCRIPTION	BEGINS	ENDS	CREDIT HRS.	TUITION COST
1.		/ /	/ /		
2.		/ /	/ /		
3.		/ /	/ /		

COURSE(S) ARE: ☐ JOB-RELATED ☐ FOR A JOB-RELATED DEGREE	SUB TOTAL	
Type Degree: _____	Registration Fee	
STATE REASON FOR TAKING COURSE(S):	Laboratory Fee	
EMPLOYEE SIGNATURE:	TOTAL COST	

A P P R O V A L S

▶ **FIRST LEVEL** (Supervisor and/or Department, Area, or Branch Manager)
1. Review request for Educational Assistance with employee to be sure he or she is eligible for reimbursement and understands procedures for approval and reimbursement.
2. Register approval or disapproval. Detach and maintain "Initiating Department Copy" for follow-up. Send remaining copies to Division Director or Vice President for Final Approval.
3. After receiving notice of approval from Personnel, inform employee. Maintain "Final Approval/Course Completion" copy to process reimbursement when course(s) completed.

REQUEST IS: ☐ APPROVED ☐ DISAPPROVED SIGNATURE: _____ DATE ___/___/___

▶ **FINAL** (Division Director or Vice President)
1. Register approval or disapproval. Send completed form to Personnel Department, H.O.

REQUEST IS: ☐ APPROVED ☐ DISAPPROVED SIGNATURE _____ DATE ___/___/___

▶ **PERSONNEL**
1. (a) If approved forward FINAL APPROVAL/COURSE COMPLETION copy to employee's Supervisor/Manager.
   (b) If disapproved, forward all copies to employee's Supervisor/Manager.
2. Retain remainder of copies in follow-up files.

R E I M B U R S E M E N T

1. SUPERVISOR obtain tuition receipt and final grade from employee and enter final grade on form. Attach copies to "Final Approval/Course Completion" copy and send to Personnel Department.

FINAL GRADE(S) EARNED: 1) ___ 2) ___ 3) ___ MGR: _____ DATE ___/___/___
2. PERSONNEL DEPARTMENT enter required information on form and submit form with a check request to Accounts Payable.
3. ACCOUNTS PAYABLE enter required information on form, prepare check and foward to employee's Supervisor with "Employee" copy of form. Send "Personnel" file copy to Payroll Department.

PERSONNEL DEPARTMENT	ACCOUNTS PAYABLE
Evidence of successful course completion, school invoices, bills, and receipts have been reviewed. Reimbursement is due as follows:	
Course Tuition Amount $_____ Balance Available $_____	
Tuition Payment This FY $_____ Total Amt. Reimburse $_____	
AUTHORIZED SIGNATURE DATE	

(*text continued from page 615*)

❖ *Group automobile insurance.*
❖ **Holidays** (Exhibit 16-4).
❖ *Homeowner's insurance.*
❖ *Long-term care insurance.*

Helpful Hint: Your local Chamber of Commerce will probably publish **information on practices of other companies concerning holidays and personal days.** A typical such survey is shown in Exhibit 16-5.

• **Personal days** (Exhibit 16-6).
• **Sick time** and attendance record (Exhibit 16-7).
• **Summary of employee benefit programs** (Exhibit 16-8). This is a summary of documented plans, procedures, and policies that is published in the personnel and policy manuals. It is a handy, in one place, guide that usually is part of the start-up package for new employees.

Helpful Hint: Blow your own horn. Tell employees the value of the benefits the company is supplying. Exhibit 16-9 shows the **tangible value of weekly benefits for an employee earning $24,000 a year**. This could be added to the summary of employee benefit programs or simply be used as a handout with the new employee start-up package. Update this annually for changes in insurance, Social Security, and workers' compensation rates.

ADDITIONAL PERKS FOR EXECUTIVES

Rank has its privileges. In addition to the perks listed in Exhibit 16-1 and the fringe benefits set forth above, the following are typical of additional

(*text continues on page 624*)

Exhibit 16-4.   Personnel policy for holidays.

Personnel Policy and Procedure	Policy/Procedure No. __EB - 130__
	Effective Date _____12/1/_____
	Page No. ___1___ of ___1___
Title: HOLIDAYS	

POLICY

The Company provides nine paid holidays each year.

SCHEDULE

The holidays to be observed are the following:
1. New Year's Day
*2. Washington's Birthday
*3. Memorial Day
4. Independence Day
*5. Labor Day
6. Thanksgiving Day
7. Day after Thanksgiving
8. Christmas Day
9. "Floater" Day (to be announced each year by Corporate Personnel Department)

* These holidays are always celebrated on a Monday, allowing for a three-day weekend.

If a holiday falls on Saturday, the holiday is celebrated on Friday; if on Sunday, the holiday is celebrated on Monday.

GENERAL

1. Facilities with responsibility for customer service must arrange for sufficient coverage when customers in their area are working on an xyz holiday.
2. If for any reason an employee is required to work on a holiday, the employee will receive overtime pay in addition to holiday pay.
3. On the day preceding a holiday, the normal working hours will remain in effect.
4. Employees will not be paid for a holiday if they have an unexcused absence the day before or the day after a holiday.

Exhibit 16-5.   Holiday schedule survey.

WESTCHESTER PERSONNEL COUNCIL	FROM _____
1111 Massachusetts Ave. White Plains, New York 11111 Tel. 111-111-1111	TO _____
An affiliate of THE COUNTY CHAMBER OF COMMERCE, INC.	_____
Westchester County National Chamber ACCREDITED business organization	_____

20   HOLIDAY SCHEDULE SURVEY

TOTAL NUMBER EMPLOYERS RESPONDING TO SURVEY - 147

HOLIDAY	DAY	DATE	FULL DAY	HALF DAY	SKELETON	UNDECIDED
New Year's Day	Thursday	Jan. 1	142		6	
Day After New Year's Day	Friday	Jan. 2	58	2	8	1
Martin Luther King's Birthday Observed	Monday	Jan. 19	36		3	
Lincoln's Birthday	Thursday	Feb. 12	15		3	
Washington's Birthday Observed	Monday	Feb. 16	97		7	1
Good Friday	Friday	April 17	37	5	4	
Memorial Day Observed	Monday	May 25	137	1	6	
Independence Day Observed	Friday	July 3	121	1	6	2
Independence Day	Saturday	July 4	2			
Labor Day	Monday	Sept. 7	136	1	5	1
Columbus Day	Monday	Oct. 12	61		7	1
Election Day	Tuesday	Nov. 3	13	2	3	1
Veteran's Day	Wednesday	Nov. 11	29	1	4	1
Thanksgiving Day	Thursday	Nov. 26	141		6	1
Day After Thanksgiving	Friday	Nov. 27	90	2	11	1
Christmas Eve	Thursday	Dec. 24	20	2		
Christmas Day	Friday	Dec. 25	140		7	1
New Year's Eve	Thursday	Dec. 31	6	1		

(continued)

Exhibit 16-5. *(continued)*

NUMBER OF PERSONAL DAYS	TOTAL NUMBER OF RESPONDENTS	NUMBER OF FLOATING HOLIDAYS	TOTAL NUMBER OF RESPONDENTS
1	5	1	23
2	21	2	15
3	19	3	5
4	6	4	1
5	10	5	5
6	2	6	1
9	1		
10	1		
12	2		
As Needed	1		

Also . . .

Twelve firms give employees their birthday as a holiday. Two firms give employees a day and six give ½ day for Christmas shopping. One firm gives the date of employment as a holiday, while another has a special "company" holiday. One company offers Easter Monday as a holiday, and another offers Rosh Hashanah and Yom Kippur. One firm gives employees the Friday before Labor Day as a Holiday. One gives ½ day on the Friday before Memorial Day and Labor Day. One firm gives employees five Fridays in May as holidays, and another gives employees six ½ day Fridays during the summer. Two companies give a full week at Christmas, and one gives two weeks.

TOTAL NUMBER OF HOLIDAYS AND PERSONAL DAYS PER YEAR	TOTAL NUMBER OF RESPONDENTS	TOTAL NUMBER OF HOLIDAYS AND PERSONAL DAYS PER YEAR	TOTAL NUMBER OF RESPONDENTS
2	1	13	17
3	1	13½	1
5	2	14	10
6	1	14½	2
7	5	15	7
7½	1	15½	2
8	6	16	2
9	10	16½	1
9½	1	17	7
10	13	17½	1
10½	1	19	1
11	28	21	1
12	24	22	1

Exhibit 16-6. Personnel policy for personal days.

Personnel Policy and Procedure	Policy/Procedure No. ___EB - 140___
	Effective Date _____12/1/_____
	Page No. ____2____ of ____2____
Title: PERSONAL DAYS	

POLICY

The Company provides personal days that employees may use for religious observance, personal business, or other personal needs.

GENERAL

1. *Entitlement*

   All regular full-time employees become eligible for three (3) personal days as of January 1. These personal days may be used between January 1 and December 31 of the same calendar year. They may not be carried over from one year to the next.

2. *New Hires*

   During the first year of employment, personal days are prorated based on the following hire dates:

Date of Hire	Personal Days
January through April	3
May through August	2
September through November	1

   Employees hired in December do not receive a personal day for that calendar year. Employees are considered probationary for the first 30 calendar days of employment and therefore are not eligible for benefits.

3. *Intended Uses*

   Personal days may be scheduled for religious observance or personal business or used as additional sick days or to cover emergency needs. Personal days may also be scheduled to extend approved vacation time if business operations permit.

   If an employee has exhausted his or her Personal Days and requests time off for religious observance, excused time without pay may be permitted. The Company will make every effort to provide reasonable accommodations and still maintain normal business operations.

4. *Termination*

   Personal days are a benefit for active employees. Unused days will not be paid upon termination.

(continued)

Exhibit 16-6.   *(continued)*

PROCEDURE

1. *Approval*
   Employees must obtain approval in advance for personal days. The only exceptions
   to this will be when personal days are used for sick days or emergency situations.
2. *Recording*
   Personal days may be approved in one-half-day increments, but not in other fractional parts of a day.
   Personal days will be recorded on time sheets using the code "P."

---

benefits made available to officers, executives, and some management
levels:

❖ *Medical catastrophe.* Most insured medical programs provide
   benefits to executives in excess of the standard coverage and
   deductibles.

❖ *Use of company cars and drivers.* Cars and drivers are often
   made available for the executive and/or his or her family for
   personal use.

❖ *Executive dining facilities.* This can include a special dining
   area for executives only, or providing free meals for certain
   classes of employees in the company dining room.

❖ *Club memberships.* Membership may be in a private luncheon
   club or a country club. The Revenue Reconciliation Act of
   1993, known as RAR 93, eliminates this as a tax deduction to
   the employer. The benefit is taxable to the recipient.

❖ *Financial counseling.* This fringe benefit is most often reserved
   for the manager level and above. It may include the free use
   of an outside financial consultant, or no-charge access to in-
   house financial and tax personnel. It may occasionally include
   access to an investment banker for advice on tax-sheltered investments.

❖ *Periodic physical examinations.* These are usually annual or
   biannual medical examinations that are not covered under the
   standard medical insurance program. They may be provided
   by a company physician or a designated outside physician who
   bills the company directly.

❖ *Use of company facilities.* Depending on the business of the
   company, it could make its product or service available to the
   (text continues on page 629)

Exhibit 16-7. Personnel policy for sick time.

Personnel Policy and Procedure	Policy/Procedure No. ___EB - 150___
	Effective Date _____12/1/_____
	Page No. ___1___ of ___2___
Title: SICK TIME	

POLICY

Paid sick days are provided so that employees do not experience a complete loss of earnings during brief periods of illness or disability.

ELIGIBILITY

Eligible employees are employees whose regular work schedule is 30 hours or more per week.

After completion of an initial 30-day probationary period, employees are eligible to receive sick pay for time lost due to illness.

GENERAL

1. Sick days are to be used for illness or disability only.
2. Employees are credited with five sick days each year on the anniversary date of their employment.
3. On each anniversary of employment, an employee may "bank" any unused sick days. Banking means carrying unused sick days over from year to year to provide income protection in case of future illness or disability. A maximum of 45 sick days can be banked.
4. Sick pay may not be used for absence due to illness of other persons in the family or for personal business.
5. Sick days may not be scheduled in advance unless medical evidence is submitted in advance indicating a required hospital stay.
6. Terminating employees will not be paid for unused sick days.
7. Employees who have used all of their sick days, including those that were "banked," cannot use any of the next year's sick days until the anniversary date is reached.
8. Sick pay will be calculated at the employee's equivalent daily or hourly rate of pay.
9. Employees authorized to leave work because of illness before the completion of a full work day will generally receive full pay for that day without deductions from their authorized sick days. Sick pay will begin with the first full day of absence. Management discretion must be used to avoid abuse of this practice by an employee who may report to work for very short periods of time when he or she is too ill to work.
10. The employee's manager should request a doctor's certificate when:
    a. An employee is returning to work following three consecutive days of absence.
    b. The employee has had excessive absences.
    c. The manager believes the employee may be misusing sick days.

(continued)

Exhibit 16-7.   *(continued)*

11. Paid sick days will be used as hours worked in a week for the purpose of calculating overtime. Unpaid sick days will not be counted as hours worked for any purpose.
12. When employees are hospitalized because of accident or illness during vacation, they may ask that the number of hospitalized days be charged against sick leave rather than vacation time if the doctor furnishes a statement.
13. Employees may not use sick days to extend vacation.
14. Employees who are ill and unable to report to work must notify their supervisor no later than the beginning of the work day. Employees who are absent must notify their supervisor each day unless other arrangements are specifically made with the supervisor.

PROCEDURE

1. *Department Manager*
   a. Records full or partial days of absence of all employees on Employee Yearly Attendance Record (Exhibit A).
   b. Notes time absent due to illness on standard weekly time sheet. (See P/P C - 20.)
   c. Forwards weekly time sheet to the Payroll Department, Home Office.
2. *Payroll Department*
   a. Checks payroll records for number of sick days, if any, previously paid to the employee.
   b. If sick days are available, pays employee for days lost because of illness.
   c. If sick days are unavailable, Payroll notifies the department manager.

EMPLOYEE YEARLY ATTENDANCE RECORD

Key

V — Vacation	S — Sick
EP — Excused Paid	EU — Excused Unpaid
U — Unexcused	F — Funeral
JD — Jury Duty	L — Late
H — Holiday	

Name _____

Date of Hire _____

	1	2	3	4	5	6	7	8	9	10	11	12	13	14	15	16	17	18	19	20	21	22	23	24	25	26	27	28	29	30	31

Exhibit 16-8. Summary of employee benefit programs.

SUMMARY OF EMPLOYEE BENEFIT PROGRAMS
AS OF 1/1/

This is a summary. See individual plans, procedures, and insurance policies for complete details.

I.   Coverage. All full-time active employees. Spouses and unmarried children from 15 days up to 19 years of age are eligible for benefits under appropriate medical and dental plans. Unmarried students are eligible, if dependent, to age 23. Coverage starts on the first day of employment, with no waiting period.
II. Dental insurance. Provides coverage based on a schedule of dental procedures, with no deductible and no co-insurance. Member dentists will usually work based on the schedule, resulting in maximum coverage.
        Excludes orthodontics and periodontics. Place claims directly with American Medical Insurance Company.
III. Lead incentive plan. Pays $75 for a machine sold at list price, $50 for sale of a new machine below list price, $35 for sale of a refurbished machine, and $25 for leads to a rental. A referral form must be completed in advance, and the sale or rental must take place within 90 days. Managers are not eligible for referral awards.
IV. Life insurance and accidental death or dismemberment. One times annual compensation to $75,000. Place claims with   .
V.   Long-term disability. Coverage starts after three months of total disability to age 65. Coverage is 60% of annual compensation to a maximum of $3,000/month. Benefits are integrated with Social Security payments. Place claims with
VI. Medical care. Standard 120-day Blue Cross Plan. This covers doctor bills and hospital room. Place claims directly with doctors and Blue Cross.
VII. Savings and retirement plan. Employees may save from 1% to 6% of their total compensation per year. The company will match this with a contribution of 25%, 40%, 50%, 75%, or 100%, for employees who have been employed with the company or an acquired subsidiary for up to 4, 9, 14, 20, and over 20 years, respectively. You may also save up to an additional 5%, which the company will not match. However, all income earned on your total savings is tax-free, as is the company's matching contribution, until you withdraw them from the plan.
        The proceeds are invested in common stocks, government securities, or short-term money funds by the trustees. Interest and dividends earned are not taxable to the employee.
        Employees must have worked 6 months before being eligible to participate.
        Company contributions vest (belong to the employee) after 3 years.
        Savings may be withdrawn only for certain hardship reasons.
        Employment tenure is based on original date of employment with the company or any acquired subsidiary.

(continued)

Exhibit 16-8. *(continued)*

VIII. Short-term disability. Disability up to 3 months, if not job-connected, is covered under the New York State Plan, for New York State employees, and by   , at coverage roughly comparable to New York State, for Connecticut employees.

IX. Sick days, holidays, personal days, and vacations.

Sick days: 5 days per year are available. Proof of illness or doctor visit is required. Sick days may be carried over to a maximum of 45 days.

Holidays: 9 per year, including Washington's Birthday, Memorial Day, Labor Day, Thanksgiving, day after Thanksgiving, Christmas Day, New Year's Day, and one floater (to be announced), usually following a regular holiday to provide a 4-day weekend.

Personal days: 3 per year, after one year, for religious observance, personal business, or other personal needs.

Vacations: If employed		
	Under one year	Prorated
	1–5 years	10 days
	5–15 years	15 days
	Over 15 years	20 days

Vacations must be taken and, if not taken, are lost. No pay may be taken in lieu of vacation. Vacations are not available to employees terminated for any reason.

X. Surgical and major medical care. Covers 90% of charges up to $10,000, and no co-insurance for $10,000 to $1,000,000, after a $100 to $300 deductible for individual or family, respectively. Coverage is based on a schedule of surgical procedures. Coverage is included for:

Surgery	Anesthesia
X-ray and laboratory	Radiotherapy
Doctor attendance in hospital	Home health care
Maternity	

This policy may be converted to an individual policy within 31 days after termination for any reason, without a medical examination. Conversion includes coverage under IV and V.

Mental Illness is covered up to 80% of charges, to a maximum of $1,000 per year.

Coverage excludes eyeglasses, hearing aids, periodontics, drugs, cosmetic surgery, and pre-existing conditions within the previous 90 days.

Place claims with Connecticut General's local claims office.

XI. Tuition payment plan. An Educational Assistance Program pays for tuition for job-related educational courses, for employees with six months of tenure. One-year employees may receive reimbursement for courses required for a job-related degree. An Educational Assistance Request form must be completed.

XII. Unemployment benefits and Social Security. The company supplies standard coverage under the federal and state unemployment and Social Security regulations.

XIII. Workers' compensation: The company supplies standard workers' compensation coverage, as required by law, for all employees. This provides coverage for on-the-job accidents.

Exhibit 16-9. Tangible value of weekly benefits.

TANGIBLE VALUE OF WEEKLY BENEFITS FOR AN EMPLOYEE EARNING $24,000 A YEAR	
INSURANCE (Life, Family Comprehensive Medical, Travel)	$ 65.84
SOCIAL SECURITY	35.30
PAID VACATIONS	17.68
PAID HOLIDAYS	17.68
• UNEMPLOYMENT COMPENSATION	7.42
PAID SICK DAYS	10.60
SUGGESTION PROGRAM	1.90
LONG-TERM DISABILITY	3.84
DENTAL INSURANCE (Family Coverage)	6.54
• EMPLOYEE EDUCATION	0.58
• JURY DUTY	1.90
FUNERAL LEAVE	5.30
F. E. CAR INSURANCE	15.38
STOCK PURCHASE PLAN	6.92
LEAD INCENTIVE PROGRAM	7.68
• WORKERS' COMPENSATION	7.16
TOTAL WEEKLY	211.72
TOTAL MONTHLY	917.45
TOTAL YEARLY	11,009.44

executive. For example, a software developer could make financial software available to the executive for his or her personal computer; a copier manufacturer could supply personal copiers for home use.

✧ *Family members on business trips.* Such trips would be fully paid or reimbursable to the executive by the company. If properly structured, they may meet IRS requirements for deductibility. If not, they are taxable income to the executive.

Word of Caution: Under RRA 93, reimbursed meals and entertainment expenses are only 50% tax-deductible to the corporation.

Additional Caution: An employee is generally required to include in income the amount by which the fair market value of the fringe benefit exceeds the amount paid for the benefit, if any.

✧ *Deferred compensation.* This benefit enables the manager to defer compensation, pending the completion of certain milestones. The funds are allocated to the manager, but tax is not paid until the funds are received. See a typical plan in Exhibit 16-1.

POSTEMPLOYMENT BENEFITS

The cost of most postemployment benefits is charged to current income in accordance with the rules of SFAS 112, Employers Accounting for Postemployment Benefits. This covers benefits provided to former or inactive employees after employment, but before retirement. Such benefits include salary, supplemental unemployment benefits, severance, disability-related benefits, job training, counseling, health care, and life insurance. Generally, employers must recognize the obligation to provide postemployment benefits in accordance with SFAS 43, Accounting for Compensated Absences, if the obligation is attributable to past services, the employees' rights accumulate or vest, payment of the benefits is probable, and the amount to be paid can be reasonably estimated. If these four conditions are not met, the employer accounts for postemployment benefits in accordance with SFAS 5, Accounting for Contingencies, when the liability is probable and the amount can be reasonably estimated. If the obligation is not accrued in accordance with SFAS 5 or 43 only because the amount cannot be reasonably estimated, the financial statements must disclose that fact.

KEEP SCORE

Good benefit programs reduce employee turnover. Exhibit 11-5 illustrates an employee turnover calculation.

17

Economic Appraisal

In private accounting, the functions of the corporate controller have been defined and published by the Financial Executives Institute, as exhibited in Appendix A. This lists economic appraisal as the last of the defined controllership functions. This function is "to continuously appraise economic and social forces and government influences, and to interpret their effect upon the business." The management accountant must undertake this responsibility in order to perform his or her job effectively.

WHY DO WE USE ECONOMIC APPRAISAL?

The principal values to consider in managing a business are the net income and return on investment to its stockholders. But management has other responsibilities: to the community and to the company's employees, vendors, and customers. These seemingly disparate interests work together to create a business environment in which all are mutually interdependent. Fulfilling these interlocking responsibilities requires that management operate in a reasoned and professional manner to develop the financial strength, through earnings and clever balance sheet management, to survive the vicissitudes of economic downturns and other business adversity. This will require investments in research to benefit the future, in new products and technology, and in productivity improvements. Meeting these responsibilities is made possible through the implementation of a structured business plan and the necessary administration of a plan for the control of operations. Economic appraisal is another management tool to ensure that the financial officers make the correct decisions to achieve their goals. Making correct decisions is clearly not based on intuition alone. It requires utilizing all the available tools, and perhaps some intuition, and then springing into action. The Air Force, in studying the success of certain fighter pilots who consistently won dogfights in combat, determined that winners complete a loop faster than losers; the loop includes observation, orientation, decision, and action. The analogy in business is obvious: Observation means getting the facts; orientation is assessing them and their effect on the current business situation; and making the decision and taking action means doing it fast! Fast-response companies go directly to the end user for sales information, bypassing the wholesaler's shelves. These are companies that have internal controls that assure a fast reporting system allowing for quick response. These are companies that assess world and local economic conditions to provide better observation tools to start the loop.

It is significant, however, that the most sophisticated observation and orientation are tools on which management bases its decision, often with intuition, and often wrongly.

> *Case in Point:* Detroit kept giving us big cars when the economics of the times indicated that we wanted economical cars with responsive features and a ride with more "feel." Detroit thus left the market for such cars to the Japanese. Even worse, as the yen appreciated, instead of picking up market share as a result of the price differential, Detroit raised car prices, seeking more immediate short-term profits, but again giving the market to the Japanese by keeping the price differential the same.

Economic appraisal, therefore, is grist for the manager's decision-making mill. You can't grind out profits without it!

Why Do We Use Economic Indicators?

Economic indicators, sometimes called *aggregates* or *macroeconomic variables*, are measures of economic activity that big corporations and government use as observation tools in making operating decisions. Small businesses that follow these aggregates can use the same information, with perhaps faster response because of their small size and flexibility, in the decision loop.

In every business, large or small, the principal business functions of marketing, operations, and financial management are affected by the current level and any movement in these economic indicators.

> *Word of Caution:* Different businesses may be affected differently from others as the indicators move. An increase in dollar exchange rates has opposite effects on the importer and the exporter. An increase in interest rates means different things to the bank (the lender) and the borrower.

These variables are:

- ✧ Gross national product (GNP)
- ✧ Unemployment
- ✧ Interest rates
- ✧ Inflation
- ✧ Foreign exchange rates

A subset of economic indicators is the familiar leading indicators. The leading indicators are available on a more timely basis than the macroeconomic variables, they are more measurable, and the direction of their movement is more discernible. They are therefore considered to "lead" the aggregates in forecasting the direction of economic movement, and they ultimately affect the level of the five aggregates themselves. It is generally believed that three consecutive declines in the leading indicator average presage a downturn in the economy. The U.S. Department of Commerce publishes 12 leading indicators monthly. They are:

1. Number of hours in the average workweek. Hours change first, then a change in the number of employed persons is expected to follow.
2. Number of initial claims for unemployment insurance. Trends in initial claims by newly unemployed persons may be projected out to future unemployment expectations.
3. Volume of manufacturers' new orders. Such orders make it possible to estimate later sales to the end-user consumer.
4. Vendor performance. A slowdown in deliveries of raw materials to manufacturers by vendors may indicate greater demand by the manufacturers and subsequent increased finished goods sales.
5. Net business formation. New businesses today indicate new production in the near future.
6. Volume of contracts and orders for plant and equipment. These indicate the committed future dollars to be expended on capital investment.
7. New building permits. As permits are issued, housing starts will begin.
8. Volume of inventories on hand and on order. Companies increase inventories when they anticipate future sales increases.
9. Change in sensitive materials prices. Increases in materials prices indicate greater demand for materials and a probable coming increase in production of finished goods.
10. Stock market prices. The market reflects expectations about the health of the economy.
11. Money supply. Monetary fluctuations generally occur before economic fluctuations, because of the lag effect in monetary policy.
12. Change in credit outstanding. Increases in credit outstanding may foretell production increases as a result of the financing required to initiate production.

Word of Caution: As with any economic indicator, the meaning of changes in the leading indicators is subject to interpretation and judgment, and changes may affect different businesses in opposite ways.

Economic variables and leading indicators are published on a regional and local level, as well as nationally. Local indicators behave separately from national indicators, just as local industries, markets, and suppliers do. National trends and data should always be compared to the local information as part of the observation process, before decisions and judgments are made. For example, several years ago, Houston was in the throes of a recession because of softness in the oil sector, while New York City was enjoying a financial boom as a result of strength in the stock market. Westchester County, a suburb of New York, benefited from the city's fallout, with increases in housing starts and full employment. If your business is confined to a regional or local area, use the appropriate data. At the same time, monitor national trends for their possible effect on the local situation.

When analyzing your economic data, always remember that economists disagree among themselves as to the meaning of some of the movements in the indicators, as well as in their forecasts of the effect on the economy. For example, are higher interest rates good or bad? As inflation increases, interest rates will rise, since borrowers tend to borrow more (creating more demand for funds), believing that they will be able to repay the loans in the future with cheaper dollars. At the same time, lenders tend to raise interest rates to increase their return from cheaper dollars. This effect should not be characterized as good or bad, but rather as an economic effect to be measured and used in making business decisions. For example, as interest rates start to rise, the astute treasurer may want to lock in long-term rates on debt to be repaid in the future with cheaper dollars. However, consider that as inflation causes higher prices relative to foreign products, the dollar's value will decline, as foreign exchange will be more in demand to buy the cheaper foreign merchandise. But will this really happen? Rising inflation will cause higher interest rates, as stated above. Foreign investors will purchase more U.S. investments for their higher yields, thus strengthening the dollar. Both effects are possible, and either may occur—and each has, at different times. You should hone your analysis by determining which is the tail and which the dog. Is inflation the cause or the effect of high interest rates? Are these interest rates expected to be short- or long-term movements? Are these major movements on the economic scene, or just ripples? What is the trend of the data? Trend is more important than any other factor in analyzing the data. As another example, in the following discussion on GNP, it is pointed out that increases in GNP are positive, meaning more production and sales. But the numbers themselves, and the trend in the numbers, cannot be analyzed in a vacuum. The indicators interact. If the leading indicator for inventories, item 8 on the leading indicator list, shows a marked increase at the same time as an increase in GNP, it should be inferred that the main reason for the GNP increase was the heavy inventory buildup. This probably occurred because consumer spending slowed, and it would be reasonable to expect that production will also slow soon, as manufacturers work off excess inventory. This could presage an economic slowdown. On the other hand, if it is determined that the inventory increases are in imported goods, such a buildup in unsold foreign merchandise could lead to slower imports in the following quarter, thus contributing to growth by helping the trade balance.

> *The Rationale for It:* Economic effects are neither good nor bad, and the science is not exact. Economists do disagree. However, the indicators identify movements and trends that are signals of economic activity. If that activity is properly monitored, decisions can be made that will redound to the benefit of the enterprise.

WHAT ARE THE SOURCES OF ECONOMIC INDICATORS?

Economic information and data are available from an enormous variety of sources. Many of these are listed below.

✧ Newspapers (Sunday *New York Times* business section, *The Wall Street Journal, Crains, Barrons*); an example is given in Exhibit 17-1

- ✧ Banks (money-center banks publish local, regional, and national economic data and analyses)
- ✧ Libraries
- ✧ University economics departments
- ✧ Professional economic forecasting services
- ✧ Business magazines (*Business Week, Forbes, U.S. News & World Report, Fortune, Time, Newsweek, Money, The Economist*, various industry magazines)
- ✧ Radio and TV (particularly public broadcasting business shows)
- ✧ Federal government agencies (e.g., U.S. Bureau of Labor Statistics for unemployment data and forecasts)
- ✧ Board of Governors of the Federal Reserve System
- ✧ Federal reserve banks (regional banks in Atlanta, Boston, Chicago, Kansas City, Minneapolis, New York City, Philadelphia, Richmond, St. Louis, and San Francisco, for the *Federal Reserve Bulletin*)
- ✧ U.S. Department of Commerce—*U.S. Industrial Outlook*
- ✧ U.S. Government Printing Office—Superintendent of Documents, Washington, DC 20402
- ✧ *Economic Report of the President* (available annually in February from the U.S. Government Printing Office, above)
- ✧ Trade associations
- ✧ Chambers of commerce (both national and local)
- ✧ Economic development corporations (in local communities, devoted to attracting businesses to the area)
- ✧ Power utilities (these usually have development departments)
- ✧ Names, addresses, and phone numbers of **additional useful sources** listed in the AICPA's Accountants Business Manual; see also Exhibit 17-2

Helpful Hint: If a small business does not have an appropriate department to collect this data, suggest appointing one person (not a full-time job) to accumulate suitable newspaper data for the analysis.

(*text continues on page 640*)

Exhibit 17-1.   Economic data.

November 15, 20

THE ECONOMY

Gross National Product Annual rate, 1982 dollars, in billions	**III Q'87** $3,831.2	**II Q'87** $3,795.3	**Year Ago** $3,683.3
Real G.N.P. Growth Annual rate, 1982 dollars, in percent	3.8	2.5	2.4
Corporate After-Tax Profits In billions, annual rate	**II Q'87** $134.5	**I Q'87** $136.6	**Year Ago** $138.0
Industrial Production Index Percent change, monthly and year to year	**Sept.** 0.2	**August** 0.3	**Year Ago** −0.1
Housing Starts Thousands of units, annual rate	**Sept.** 1,669	**August** 1,596	**Year Ago** 1,680
New Orders for Durable Goods By manufacturers, in billions	**Sept.** $107.80	**August** $106.62	**Year Ago** $108.98
Plant and Equipment Spending In billions, annual rate	**III Q'87** $398.04	**II Q'87** $377.65	**Year Ago** $387.42
Mfg. Inventory-Shipments Ratio Current dollars	**Sept.** 1.59	**August** 1.62	**Year Ago** 1.41
Sales at Retail Outlets In billions	**Oct.** $127.4	**Sept.** $128.8	**Year Ago** $121.6
Index of Leading Indicators Percent change, monthly and year to year	**Sept.** −0.1	**August** 0.6	**Year Ago** −0.4
Employment In thousands	**Sept.** 114,515	**August** 114,817	**Year Ago** 111,989
Unemployment In thousands	7,089	7,221	8,329
Unemployment Rate In percent	5.8	5.9	6.9
Merchandise Exports In billions	**Sept.** $21.0	**August** $20.2	**Year Ago** $17.5
Merchandise Imports In billions	$35.1	$35.9	$30.1
Current Account Surplus/Deficit Goods and services, in billions	**II Q'87** $−41.1	**I Q'87** $−36.8	**Year Ago** $−34.7

PRICES

G.N.P. Price Deflator	III Q'87	II Q'87	Year Ago
Annual rate, in percent	2.4	3.5	3.6

Consumer Price Index	Sept.	August	Year Ago
1967 = 100	344.4	342.7	330.2

C.P.I. Annual Rate	Sept.	3 Mos.	12 Mos.
In percent	2.1	3.6	4.3

Producer Price Index	Sept.	3 Mos.	12 Mos.
Finished goods, annual rate in percent	2.9	0.3	2.6

Cash Wheat Price	Last Week	Prior Week	Year Ago
No. 1 K.C., per bushel	$2.84	$2.81	$2.73

Crude Oil, W. Texas Intermediate	Last Week	Prior Week	Year Ago
Friday spot price, per barrel	$18.93	$18.80	$15.65

Dow Jones Industrial Average	Last Week	Prior Week	Year Ago
Friday close	1,935.01	1,959.05	1,873.59

PRODUCTION

Steel	Last Week	Prior Week	Year Ago
Thousands of net tons	1,866	1,875	1,329

Autos			
In units	N.A.	183,001	177,192

Domestic Crude Oil	Oct.	Sept.	Year Ago
Thousands of bbls./day	8,233	8,084	8,419

Oil Imports (Crude and Products)	Last Week	Prior Week	Year Ago
Thousands of bbls./day	8,019	7,592	6,449

Electric Power			
Millions of kilowatt hours	46,441	46,974	44,978

Coal (Bituminous)			
Thousands of net tons	N.A.	19,863	N.A.

Paperboard			
Thousands of tons	688.9	702.2	675.2

Freight Car Loadings			
Billions of ton-miles	19.5	19.6	18.2

Lumber	August	July	Year Ago
Millions of board feet	3,643	3,695	3,557

(continued)

Exhibit 17-1. *(continued)*

FINANCE			
Federal Funds Rate	**Last Week**	**Prior Week**	**Year Ago**
Average, in percent	6.68	6.43	5.98
Prime Rate			
Most major banks, in percent	8.75	8.75	7.50
1-Month Commercial Paper			
In percent	6.65	6.63	5.83
Corporate AA Industrial Bonds			
Yield in percent	10.00	10.00	9.00
30-Year Treasury Bonds			
Yield in percent	8.87	8.78	7.59
Gold			
Friday P.M. London fix, per ounce	$464.95	$460.00	$408.25
Money Supply Growth	**3 Mos.**	**6 Mos.**	**12 Mos.**
M-1, annual percent change	7.0	2.8	8.5

Industry studies and comparative interpretations are an aspect of economic effects on the business. Publications of business services companies are helpful in this area. Dun & Bradstreet offers a series of weekly, monthly, and some quarterly publications on the following trends and outlooks:

✧ Business failures—comment and analysis.

✧ Wholesale commodity prices—noting changes in 30 basic commodities.

✧ Wholesale food prices—comment on costs of 31 primary foods.

✧ Bank clearings—volume changes in 26 major cities.

✧ Trade review—interpreting retail, wholesale, manufacturing developments.

✧ New business incorporations—comparative, by states.

✧ Building permit values—totals from major cities.

✧ Businesspeople's expectations—summary of nationwide interviews.

Exhibit 17-2. Sources of business/economic statistics.

BUSINESS/ECONOMIC STATISTICS

Governmental

Bureau of Economic Analysis
Commerce Dept.
Main Commerce Bldg.
Washington, D.C. 20230
(202) 523-0777

Bureau of Labor Statistics
Wages and Industrial
  Relations
Labor Department
441 G Street, N.W.
Washington, D.C. 20212
(202) 523-1382

Census Bureau
Governments Div.
Commerce Dept.
Washington, D.C. 20233
(301) 763-4040

Council of Economic
  Advisers
Executive Office
Statistical Office
Old Executive Office Bldg.
Washington, D.C. 20500
(202) 395-5084

Federal Reserve System
Research and Statistics
20th and C Sts., N.W.
Washington, D.C. 20551
(202) 452-3301

General Services
  Administration (GSA)
18th and F Sts., N.W.
Washington, D.C. 20405
(202) 708-5082

International Trade
  Administration
Trade Information and
  Analysis
Commerce Dept.
Main Commerce Bldg.
Washington, D.C. 20230
(202) 377-3808

Office of Management and
  Budget
Executive Office Bldg.
Washington, D.C. 20503
(202) 395-3080

Nongovernmental

American Economics Association
2014 Broadway
Nashville, TN 37203
(615) 322-2595

American Enterprise Institute for
  Public Policy Research
Economic Policy Studies
1150 17th St., N.W.
Washington, D.C. 20036
(202) 862-5800

American Institute for Economic
  Research
Great Barrington, MA 01230
(413) 528-1216

Brookings Institution
1775 Massachusetts Ave., N.W.
Washington, D.C. 20036
(202) 797-6000

The Conference Board
845 Third Ave.
New York, NY 10022
(212) 759-0900

Economic Policy Institute
1730 Rhode Island Ave., N.W.,
  Suite 812
Washington, D.C. 20036
(202) 775-8810

Institute for Contemporary
  Studies
243 Kearny St.
San Francisco, CA 94108
(415) 981-5353

International Economic Policy
  Association
5428 MacArthur Blvd., N.W.,
  Suite B1
Washington, D.C. 20016
(202) 686-2020

International Society of
  Statistical Science in
  Economics
536 Oasis Dr.
Santa Rosa, CA 95407
(707) 575-3529

National Association of
  Business Economists
28790 Chagrin Blvd., Suite
  300
Cleveland, OH 44122
(216) 464-7986

National Bureau of Economic
  Research
1050 Massachusetts Ave.
Cambridge, MA 02138
(617) 868-3900

National Chamber
  Foundation
1615 H St., N.W.
Washington, D.C. 20062
(202) 463-5552

National Planning Association
1424 16 St., N.W., Suite
  700
Washington, D.C. 20036
(202) 265-7685

U.S. Chamber of Commerce
1615 H St., N.W.
Washington, D.C. 20062
(202) 463-5552

These, augmented by industrywide studies, can provide the CPA and controller with a sufficient base for economic interpretation. Industry statistics are available from the following sources:

- Prentice-Hall—*Almanac of Business and Industrial Financial Ratios,* by Leo Troy.
- Dun & Bradstreet—Key Business Ratios (from 125 lines of retailing, wholesaling, manufacturing, and construction).
- Financial Research Associates—Financial Studies of the Small Business, Orlando, FL.
- Robert Morris Associates—RMA Annual Statement Studies, Philadelphia, PA.

In addition, many banks supply comparative ratio studies on specific industries. The Bank of New York, for example, has available an excellent study on sales finance companies, giving pertinent ratios for that industry, particularly related to percentages of receivables and outstandings. The more general industry studies offer percentages on:

- Cost of goods sold
- Gross margin
- Compensation of officers
- Rent paid on business property
- Repairs
- Bad debts
- Interest paid
- Taxes paid
- Amortization, depletion, and depreciation
- Advertising
- Pension and other employee benefit plans

Carrying industry aspects one step further, the CPA and controller should study the macroeconomic effect of current situations on the business. A knowledge of the following variables can be related to the specific industry and business to aid in effective short- and long-range planning.

✧ The level of economic activity
✧ Consumption versus savings
✧ Level of investment
✧ The supply of money
✧ Federal monetary control
✧ Fiscal and budgetary policies
✧ Economic fluctuations and growth
✧ Effects of overseas trade
✧ Economic forecasting
✧ Forecasting product demand

The AICPA has published a 20- to 24-hour self-study course called Macroeconomics and Company Planning to help one understand these factors and thus to improve financial planning.

How Does Economic Appraisal Affect the Operating Plan?

Each of the five macroeconomic variables will be examined for its effect on the company's operating plan.

GNP

The gross national product is defined as the value of all goods produced and services sold during a stated period of time.

Increases in GNP mean more production and sales, and hence more personal income and consumption and more demand for the company's product. As personal income increases, it is theoretically possible that these increases could find their way into increased personal savings, rather than consumption. However, even if this were to happen, banking institutions would reinvest those savings in the economy in the form of mortgages and business loans, with the same end result: increased production, product demand, and consumption.

In these circumstances, the observant operations manager will consider space requirements, ready production facilities, and stock of inventories and will prepare to buy materials that are in short supply or to arrange forward contracts for their purchase. The marketing manager will understand that big increases in GNP are good for luxury items, and small increases will benefit the necessities like food, clothing, and shelter. Financial managers will arrange capital availability for the expected production increases and will plan to invest surplus cash at the best rates and least risk.

Unemployment

As the rate of unemployment increases, disposable income decreases, and the possibility of reduced sales looms. Luxury items are hit first, and marketing people will need to search out the proper incentives in order to sell them. The production manager will understand that more workers with good skills will be available at lower rates, although they will need training (were the rate to decrease, he or she would have to utilize less skilled workers, at higher rates). Financial planners will be prepared for lower sales and less income. They know that the government will be receiving less income from business taxes and paying more out in unemployment benefits. As a result, both corporate and individual taxes may be expected to increase. Government deficits will increase, and this deficit financing will drive up interest rates. There will be opportunities for the observant financial manager to arrange his or her loans early, at the best rates, in anticipation of this gloomy scenario.

Interest Rates

Interest-rate management is the area of most concern to the controller and financial managers.

As with other indicators, the reasons for the rise or fall in rates is not always evident, and economists are often at odds as to the future direction of the rates. Interest-rate movements are the variable economists predict most commonly, and their predictions can have devastating effects on stock market prices. Where they fail, why should we try? Because we don't need to forecast accurately, only to follow trends and to take short-run, and sometimes long-run, actions. We can change these actions at any time—reverse course—if we see the trends turning around.

Interest rates are defined as the "prices in financial markets." A formula for interest rate is:

Interest rate = real interest rate + expected inflation
$$+ \text{ risk premium of borrower} + \text{random elements}$$

The real rate of interest is based on the time value of money. It is the value, absent inflation and risk, that one would place on forgoing consumption today and making a productive investment for the future. It is thus the rate of exchange between "present" goods and services and "future" goods and services. This rate has historically been relatively stable in the 3 to 4% range and is not expected to change in the future.

Expected inflation is a component of the interest-rate formula. The interest rate suggested by the rate of exchange between present and future money is called the *nominal rate of interest*. The nominal rate reacts to the expected change in prices of goods and services (inflation), as it represents the exchange between money now and in the future. A formula for the nominal rate of interest is:

$$(1 + \text{nominal rate}) = (1 + \text{real rate}) \times (1 + \text{inflation rate})$$

For example, if the annual real rate without inflation is 4%, and inflation is expected at a 6% rate, the nominal rate is 1.1024 (1.04 × 1.06), or 10.24% (1.1024 − 1).

The risk element in the equation is based on the inability to predict the inflation component accurately and on the worsening of credit quality of issuers of debt in times of recession. The random element in the equation represents those factors that either increase or decrease interest rates but are unrelated to inflation or credit quality.

In analyzing interest rates, the financial manager must always be aware of the effect of the inflation rate on the real rate of interest.

There is an aphorism that "capital markets are efficient." The capital market determines interest rates and stock prices. In a truly efficient capital market, the market is all-wise and has all pertinent information available to it, all the time, in order to reflect fair interest rates and stock prices. In this case, investors cannot obtain returns on investment that exceed the opportunity costs of the investment. There is, therefore, a zero net present value to all investments. Economists tend to believe in the theory of efficient capital markets. Businesspeople usually do not, and properly so, as they are dealing in unique, local environments that may behave differently from the capital markets. Within their local sphere, though, they assume that their competitors have all the information they have, and that the local capital market is generally efficient. Nevertheless, businesspeople always strive for a positive present value on investment in the short run, and this can mean long-run positive net present values.

To assume that the theory is wrong all the time is corporate derring-do that cannot be justified: Don't sell equity now, as our stock is undervalued; don't borrow long-term, as rates are bound to come down; don't invest in plant and equipment, as rates are too high. To repeat: The financial manager's job is not to predict rates or foretell the future, and certainly not to take actions based on fortune telling. Rather, he or she analyzes trends as a basis for making decisions and taking action. This action is based on the best available observations and decisions he or she can make.

> *The Crux of Interest Management:* Interest-rate risk needs to be managed in times of high rates and low rates. Do not sit on the sidelines and wait for rates to change. Instead, study the economic indicators, catch the trend, try to anticipate peaks and lows in interest rates — then, take action.
>
> *Develop an Interest-Rate-Risk Strategy:* When you anticipate, through study of the indicators, that rates are near their lows, recommend lengthening the term of liabilities and shortening asset maturities. Take on more fixed-rate debt and less floating. As rates turn upward, the company will be properly positioned. When rates climb to near their top, reverse the strategy.

Integral to a proper strategy is anticipatory identification of those tools that can enable one to achieve strategic goals, such as interest-rate futures, options, swaps and hedges, setting up proper bank credit lines, issuing debt, and retiring or converting debt. A tool not to be forgotten is to ensure that guidelines, systems and procedures, internal controls, and authority are in place to permit fast response when action time comes.

Interest-rate-risk management will reduce the cost of debt, increase net income, improve earnings per share, and improve the quality of the balance sheet. It's worth practicing it.

Marketing managers understand that high interest rates mean fewer installment credit sales and fewer sales finance–type leases. Therefore, production will be lower, and capital spending on plant and equipment will be less. Inventories will turn more slowly because of lower demand, resulting in higher carrying costs and employee layoffs. Prices of product will have to rise to cover the higher costs, and this, in turn, will mean still lower sales and a continuation of the downward spiral. Consumers, meanwhile, will be saving more, because of the higher interest rates on their savings, and they will be spending less. This increased saving will mean more investment by the banking system in production facilities, more goods produced, and lower interest rates. Lower interest rates whet the consumer's appetite for spending, as opposed to saving, and demand increases. Operating managers increase inventories and place orders for short-supply materials, employment increases, and we're moving again—a new cycle has started.

Inflation

Inflation is defined as an increase in the volume of money and credit relative to available goods, resulting in a substantial and continuing rise in the general price level. More simply, it is an increase in prices, and the rate of inflation is the percentage rise in such prices. The opposite condition, deflation, is a decrease in prices. The term *disinflation* refers to a slowing in the rate of inflation.

Increases in the rate of inflation mean a decrease in the demand for marginal and nonessential products and services, because essential services cost more and must be bought anyway. Personal incomes, at least in the short run, are relatively fixed. As a result, when prices rise without proportionate increases in fixed income, the available purchasing power is skewed more heavily to essential services than to marginal products. This situation is further aggravated when inflation-fighting steps are initiated—usually wage controls without equivalent price controls—or when Social Security payments or food stamps are not indexed to cost of living increases.

However, when wages and prices increase at the same rate, there is no inflationary effect. Moreover, inflation affects different industries and different areas of the country in different ways. Some industries will have rising prices at the same time as others decrease prices, and labor and purchasing costs will vary by industry. Each company must evaluate its own relative position and vulnerability to the general level of inflation.

An increase in the inflation rate could mean:

✧ Decrease in purchases of nonessential products
✧ Lower production
✧ Higher unemployment
✧ Higher credit or installment sales
✧ Higher interest rates (to give lenders higher yields to compensate for the cheaper dollars they'll receive when loans are repaid)
✧ Higher prices (to offset lower profits)
✧ More short-term debt issued by corporations
✧ Lower prices (to increase sales volume and profits, to offset the inflated dollars received, and to increase production, thereby reversing the cycle)

Inflation can also have effects somewhat opposite to those above, because of the interaction of other economic variables:

✧ Personal income could increase across the country.
✧ Employment could remain stable as a result of the increase in income.
✧ GNP could increase, resulting in higher employment.

✧ Wages could rise.
✧ Prices could rise.
✧ The rate of inflation could increase as prices rise faster than wages.

Other inflation scenarios are also possible. The observant manager will orient the business to the industry and the nation, will observe the phenomena, and will make a decision as to the effect of the economic conditions on the business. He or she will then respond quickly by taking decisive action as to production, wages, pricing, and marketing programs.

A decrease in the inflation rate could mean the following:

✧ Prices begin to fall.
✧ Interest rates decline (as loans will be repaid with higher-value dollars).
✧ Consumers increase purchases despite fixed incomes.
✧ Production increases to accommodate increased demand.
✧ Materials cost less, increasing profits.
✧ Employment increases.
✧ Wages increase.
✧ Some prices start rising to offset the lower dollars received.
✧ Personal incomes begin to rise to keep pace with prices.
✧ The cycle begins to reverse.

The observant manager orients himself or herself to recognize the phase through which the business cycle is passing. He or she watches trends and is able to decide when to increase production and prices. He or she is not captive to inflation or deflation, but is merely an observer who adjusts operations, marketing, and financial programs to achieve the best result, given the extant economic conditions.

Foreign Exchange Rates

Foreign exchange rates affect all domestic companies, not just those whose products are exported to foreign markets.

As the dollar increases in value relative to a foreign currency, the cost of U.S. products in terms of that currency will climb. As a result, export sales to that country will decrease, and finished goods inventories will increase. Importantly, domestic sales in the United States will decrease, as the dollar price of the foreign-made product will be lower. Companies that sell similar products, even those that are not exporters, will be placed at a competitive disadvantage to the lower-priced foreign-made product. Operating and financial managers will have to consider whether to relocate production facilities to the foreign country to take advantage of the lower production costs.

In time, the foreign competitor will increase production to meet the increased sales demand. This foreign competitor will sustain increased employment and wages, and probably will pay more for raw materials because of the increased demand. The cost of the foreign product will increase, and the U.S. company will begin to enjoy a competitive advantage as the cycle changes.

While the dollar remains strong relative to a foreign currency, capital from that country will flow into U.S. investments, mainly because of the lower risk and higher interest rate. This foreign capital increases the funds available for investment in U.S. capital projects, and the increased supply of funds will probably result in lower interest rates. As interest rates decline, foreign investment will decrease, and the cycle will reverse, until eventually, because of the lack of available investment funds, interest rates will again rise.

Under present world systems, foreign currencies fluctuate widely and frequently against each other, despite the efforts of the central bank of each country to maintain a stable purchasing power. Under the post-World War II Bretton Woods Agreement, nations agreed to stabilize exchange rates internationally. These efforts are sometimes more illusory than real, as each government pursues its own goals with respect to what it regards as the proper value for its currency in world markets. In effect, rates have fluctuated widely, akin to a free-floating system.

The former gold standard was a rigid monetary system that depended on international gold movements to signify increases and decreases in national money supplies. Political or economic events in gold-producing countries such as Russia or South Africa could affect U.S. monetary policy without regard to basic economic policy in the United States. This was an unsatisfactory system, but it had the advantage of being more stable than the present, pseudo-stabilized free-floating system.

An alternative being espoused by many U.S. politicians is to peg the dollar's value to a basket of major traded commodities, including gold, based on their relative weight and importance in the world economy. If the price of the international basket of commodities were to rise, monetary policy could be tightened by raising interest rates. However, if there were no inflation in the home market, and commodity prices at home were stable, no tightening would be indicated.

Regardless of which system is in use to influence the movement of foreign exchange, observation of the trends in movements should trigger appropriate action on the part of operating managers, as indicated above.

What Do We Do With It All?

If the economic indicators above indicate anything, it is that the signals are often mixed. Indicators interact, producing different results, and the movement of a variable in one direction usually produces a change in effects, causing a reversal of the direction of movement. The cycles reverse!

However, tracking the movement of the indicators does produce meaningful information that can assist the operating, marketing, and financial managers in making decisions for the well-being of the enterprise. For example, the indicators usually react as follows:

1. Higher GNP signals.
2. More employment required to increase production.
3. Higher wages to attract the employees, and higher prices for goods, because of the higher cost of wages and raw materials (although, in time, increased production will exceed demand and result in lower prices and a reversal of the cycle).
4. Higher interest rates, to afford higher returns to the lenders, in the face of expected repayment with cheaper or inflated dollars.

5. Lower export and domestic sales, because of the inflated (seemingly stronger) dollar relative to certain foreign currencies.
6. Higher deficit balance of payments because of lower exports.
7. Higher sales in the United States by foreign countries.
8. Higher investment in the United States by foreign investors because of the high interest rates and low risk.
9. Higher taxes on individuals and corporations to fund the deficit.
10. Less spendable income as a result of the higher taxes.
11. Lower sales, production, employment, and prices because of less consumer spending and corporate capital spending, and more funds available for capital spending from foreign investment.
12. The cycle reverses.

On a global level, world GNP is slowing down—the result of the development of major welfare programs in many industrialized states. Further, these states have regulated industries and increased taxes to pay for these programs. These programs have reduced corporate profits and resulted in less incentive for investment, thereby further slowing productive growth. Less GNP has led to higher prices, inflation, and higher taxes to offset the reduced revenues. There is nothing on the global horizon to indicate that this cycle will reverse, as interest rates are high worldwide, meaning that investments will not seek higher interest levels in different countries. These perceptions may not offer managers sufficient incentives to diversify operations and make capital investments abroad.

There is a perceived interaction and trend among this welter of information. There is an opportunity to determine which is cause and which is effect: Are the trends of short- or long-run duration, are the movements strong or weak? For the section above on each macroeconomic indicator, there is an opportunity to take operating actions as discussed: to increase employment and production, to adjust pricing and wages, and to manage the interest-rate risk through adjustment of the maturity of assets and liabilities and the utilization of hedging strategies.

An example of grasping the opportunity was seen in the utilization of high-yield or "junk" bonds by savings and loan institutions and many commercial banks. These institutions were facing losses because of the advent of high interest rates—competition with money market instruments issued by investment bankers for consumer deposits, and the need to pay high rates to attract deposits. They countered by offering to supply takeover funds to corporate acquisitors through investment in high-yield bonds. They were in the unique position of having any potential losses guaranteed by the Federal Saving and Loan Insurance Corporation, whereas any gains would be kept to pay for the higher cost of deposits. This strategy, in itself, was an excellent example of decisive action to increase profits given a set of economic conditions. Unfortunately, the institutional funds were used to take over companies at uneconomic prices, with 20 to 25 times price/earnings ratios. In many cases, the interest cost on the new debt exceeded expected earnings.

Case in Point: At Supermarkets General, earnings were less than $150 million to pay more than $200 million of interest expense. At Allied Stores, the earnings were $300 million to pay $450 million of interest cost.

These takeovers are generally considered to be one of the contributors to the market collapse on Black Monday, October 19, 1987. The cost of the eventual bailout of the savings and thrift institutions is estimated at tens of billions of dollars.

An Economic Lesson: There was no saving and investment involved in these takeovers that would result in long-run productivity. Funds were used to purchase existing production at inflated multiples. As a result of these two factors, there was no possibility of future return on investment. In looking at the interest-rate formula on page 645, there was no possibility of a "real" return, as there was no productive investment. There could be no "nominal" return, as the risks were prohibitive, in most cases, because of the high interest costs and limited earnings to cover those charges.

THE INDICATORS OF PROFITS

The principal economic indicators—GNP, unemployment, interest, inflation, and foreign exchange—and the more timely leading indicators are measures of economic activity that business managers can use to their advantage. The direction and the severity of movements are of no importance to the manager—only the trends. This data can serve as an observable base for decision making, leading to actions that could increase production and sales, control wages and purchasing costs, limit the company's exposure to interest-rate risks, and ensure that the company profit plan is achieved. The management accountant can assist in the performance of this analysis as an important contribution to the success of the organization.

18

Today's Treasurer and Controller

Evaluating and consulting is the third controllership function in the FEI definition: "To consult with all segments of management responsible for policy or action concerning any phase of the operation of the business as it relates to the attainment of objectives and the effectiveness of policies, organization structure, and procedures." This provides the definition and authority for the controller in today's information economy.

TYPES OF CONTROLLERS AND TREASURERS

Controllers come in all shapes and sizes, depending on whether the company is centralized or decentralized and on its volume and profits. We can classify them as follows:

✧ *Small-company controllers* are defined as controllers in companies with under 100 employees and, usually, under $20 million in revenues. They may have the title of general manager or chief operating officer as well as controller. These controllers are generalists. They do everything in all areas. They often do purchasing, personnel management, office management, and all treasury and accounting functions. The information technology or data processing function is generally part of the accounting responsibility. These individuals are key decision makers and are part of top management. They have the greatest responsibility of any individual in the organization. They earn between $50,000 and $80,000 a year, depending on the size and profitability of the company.

✧ *Medium-size-company controllers* are defined as controllers in companies with 100 to 500 employees and revenues of $20 to $100 million (most banks consider companies with under $100 million in revenues as small to middle-market companies). These companies may have both a treasurer and a controller and separate managers for the purchasing, personnel, office management, and information technology functions, most of whom report to the controller. Because of their broad areas of responsibility, these controllers have great financial impact on the organization. They earn between $80,000 and $150,000 a year, depending on the size and profitability of the company.

✧ *Large-company controllers* are defined as controllers in companies with over 500 employees and revenues above $100 million. These companies generally have separate people to handle the treasury and operating functions, and the controller tends to concentrate mostly on accounting functions. These controllers' salaries are generally $100,000 or more. In some companies, the controller is the CFO (chief financial officer), with responsibility for accounting and treasury functions.

ATTRIBUTES OF THE TREASURER AND CONTROLLER

Communication

The position descriptions of the treasurer and controller in Appendix A set forth the major duties, responsibilities, and organizational relationships of any of the above types of controllers or treasurers. Generally, these involve serving management, stockholders, lenders, customers, governmental authorities, and society. Most of this involves making financial statements available, but the responsibility to society involves nonfinancial considerations including the community and the environment.

The position description for the vice president finance and treasurer states, "Continuously appraises economic and social forces and government influences, and interprets their effect upon the business." Therefore, while there may be social and ethical constraints on the way the company operates, the first responsibility of the controller is to the success of the company.

To serve the diverse interests of the named users, the treasurer or controller requires, of course, an accounting education. Beyond that, however, the successful financial officer must possess extensive communication skills, a creative bent, and a versatile approach to understanding the information technology (IT) aspects of the organization.

Communication presupposes the ability to motivate people to attain their desired goals. The good communicator has the ability to speak and write clearly and concisely, to formulate ideas that are easily understood. This skill may be innate, but it also can be honed and learned through proper study. Colleges offer after-hours courses in grammar and speech, both of which are essential to developing good communication skills. The *Gregg Reference Manual* is a good library addition that presents both the basic rules and finer points of writing, including new expanded Internet topics.

Further, the good communicator requires knowledge about a variety of subjects. Some of the key words in the FEI definition in Appendix A are *profit planning, capital investing, budgeting, procurement of capital, systems and procedures, accounting, banking arrangements, credit and collection, evaluating and consulting, tax administration, investments, insurance coverage, governmental reporting,* and *economic appraisal.* The position descriptions in Appendix A continue with financial objectives, cash flow, securities, and data processing or information technology. How can one person have a command of all this knowledge? How can there be time to do all this technical learning and, also, to keep up with current events in the world around us? Through education and reading. Continuing education courses in these subjects are available for CPAs through state CPA societies and for both CPAs and non-CPAs through the American Management Association and the Institute for Management Accountants. Courses are available in half-day or full-day seminars or through self-study. To augment this basic education, continuous reading of current literature is required. This includes accounting, business, financial, tax, and management magazines, newspapers, and newsletters. How can one person read so much with so little time available? Specialized courses in speed reading are available for home study. The Evelyn Wood book *Reading Dynamics* teaches a method of absorbing entire pages, permitting a magazine to be read and understood in 10 minutes. (See Chapter 11, Supervising Special Areas of Responsibility under the section entitled Management Philosophy for a suggested list of reading materials and a reference to the creativity that the controller must possess.) For outside interests and general knowledge, listen to National Public Radio while driving to work. It's fun, exciting, and educational. To improve technology literacy, a monthly audiocassette is available from the Gartner Group that discusses IT issues and the use of IT to achieve business goals.

Creativity

At age 76, Galileo, the father of physics and a noted philosopher, bemoaned the fact that he no longer thought with the vigor of his youth and could not understand discoveries and truths he had developed at age 24.

Einstein developed the theory of relativity at age 18. He conceived of it philosophically, and it was not until years later that he proved it arithmetically.

The treasurer and controller must not only possess her or his own creativity, as described in Chapter 11 under Management Philosophy, but encourage it in others.

Creativity is frequently the province of youth, as illustrated by the above examples. That is not to say that older experts cannot be creative, but their creative successes are less frequent and are more often looked upon as astounding. Grandma Moses' creative artistic success in her sixties was so considered. And Galileo, who was creative until his death at age 78, thought of his later ideas as less fruitful than those of his youth.

Use creative people to advance ideas. Do not be afraid to give young people an opportunity to astound you with their original ideas and input.

Motivate and reward creativity in others. The best reward is recognition. Recognition need not be public. It is enough to show people that you value their intelligence, their contribution, and their ingenuity. Show them that you like them. Become a friend. There's truth to the saying, a friend is anyone who likes me. Friends are loyal and supportive and recognize each other's strengths.

Beware of This: If your best people are not permitted to innovate and create, they will leave for jobs where they can. The new generations of employees have confidence in themselves and they will not stay with a company that does not recognize their talents.

Versatility

Traditionally, the basic functions of the treasurer and controller have been grounded in finance and accounting. Today, however, these financial officers are more versatile, being more concerned with value-added functions that improve cash flow, such as risk management, interdepartmental consulting, strategic planning, enterprise resource planning, and computer systems. The time-honored functions of budgeting, financial reporting, and tax compliance can be handled quite well by subordinates using proven software on a repetitive basis. The result is that IT has merged into finance and accounting, meaning that operating executives have to be knowledgeable in finance, accounting, and information technology.

Be a manager—of any department, regardless of your special technical skills. Be incisive. Communicate, create, be versatile, and encourage the people around you to innovate, present new ideas, and be creative.

CASH FLOW AND THE CONTROLLER/TREASURER

The first paragraph of this chapter describes the third controllership function, evaluating and consulting for the purpose of attaining the objectives of the organization. The objective of any commercial company is to attain a high level of profits and commensurate positive cash flow.

However, profits may be reported for financial accounting purposes without adequate cash flow. An investment in capital expenditures or prepaid advertising will not reduce current profits and may be required to assure future profitable operations, but it will reduce current cash flow. Over the long term, profits and cash flow will generally move together. There are, nevertheless, measures that can improve cash flow without having a negative effect on current or future profits—in fact, they may actually lower costs and increase profits. See the index under cash flow for methods of improving cash flow in specific areas. Other methods follow.

Capacity Cost Management

A system for fully utilizing the organization's resources to achieve a continuing flow of productive processes with minimum disruption is a capacity cost management (CCM) system. A CCM system identifies the constraints that result in disruptions to the continuous flow of processes and reduce output and increase costs. Finance and accounting managers are usually responsible for the design, implementation, performance, and reporting of the system. This requires conjoining the financial and operational information databases to result in a current reporting and analysis tool that is always on. This may be a stand-alone system or part of an enterprise resource planning system, described in Chapter 19.

Electronic Commerce

Electronic Data Interchange

Vendors and purchasers may use electronic data interchange (EDI) to conduct their business. Unique software and direct connections enable the computers of the involved companies to communicate with each other. The purchaser may review the vendor's inventory, prices, and availability for shipment; place electronic orders; and pay for the purchase through EDI, either directly or through an intermediary bank. This results in faster payments and increased cash flow for the vendor, as well as lower costs of processing and shipping orders. From the purchaser's standpoint, payments are usually faster, but this is offset by lower costs of placing orders and so will result in higher profits and cash flows. A disadvantage of EDI is that to interface the user companies, technical support by a software specialist is required. This can be costly and time-consuming.

The Internet

The Internet can perform the EDI functions described above without the need for technical software support. Internet communication is available to all companies, without the need for customized software to enable communication. E-mail is common to all, and standardized software, such as Microsoft Access, can permit database information to be shared.

Beware This Pitfall: Internet transactions are not presently subject to sales taxes, but they may be subject to state use taxes.

E-Procurement Systems

Internet shoppers and consumers were the precursors to e-procurement systems. These are mostly used for purchasing products that are not directly used in production, such as office supplies, job supplies, small tools, and repair items. Direct links are established to specific supplier web pages. The vendor's web site provides detailed specifications, prices, photos, and descriptions. Electronic requisitions and purchase orders are processed, and vendor invoices are paid on receipt. The cash flow benefits of EDI are available, with none of the support problems.

Web Site Development Accounting

The costs of developing web sites are generally governed by Statement of Position (SOP) 98-1 of the AICPA, Accounting for the Costs of Computer Software Developed or Obtained for Internal Use.

Rules for capitalizing or expensing follow:

⟡ Preliminary development costs, including exploratory and feasibility costs, are expensed as incurred.

⟡ Application development stage costs, including internal and external costs incurred to develop internal-use software during this stage, should be capitalized. Training costs during this stage should be expensed.

⟡ Data conversion costs, from old to new systems, should be expensed, even if incurred during the application development stage.

⟡ Postimplementation/operation stage costs, including internal and external training costs and maintenance costs, should be expensed as incurred.

⟡ Upgrade and enhancement costs, defined as modifications to existing internal-use software that result in additional functionality, should be expensed as incurred, except for external costs in the application development stage.

Capitalization of costs may not begin until the preliminary project stage is completed, management has authorized the project and committed to funding it, and it is probable that the project will be completed and the software will be used to perform the intended function. If, after capitalization has begun, it becomes no longer probable that the project will be completed and placed in service, no further costs should be capitalized and adjustments for impairment should be considered in accordance with the provision of SFAS No. 121, Accounting for the Impairment of Long-Lived Assets and for Long-Lived Assets to Be Disposed Of.

Shared Services Centers

Cash flow may be improved through an examination of staff support services activities with a view to determining whether cost savings can be obtained through innovative handling of such activities. Shared services centers (SSCs) may decrease costs, simplify activities, and improve core staff services like accounting, corporate affairs, facilities, finance, human resources, information technology, and legal services. SSCs present an alternative to in-house services through outsourcing and restructuring of core staff support services.

With an SSC, a single provider offers common services like accounts receivable collection to two or more users. The SSC is an independent business, with its own resources, specializing in the offered service. A contract is signed with each user specifying the type, details, and cost of the service. The SSC takes full responsibility for the performance, cost, timeliness, and overall quality of the offered service. From the user's standpoint, the SSC can leverage resources to create value, achieve cost savings on nonessential costs, and improve the quality of the support work. The Institute of Management Accountants has published Statement on Management Accounting No. 5G, entitled Implementing Shared Services Centers. This provides details on this unique method for solving the complex business problems posed by staff support activities.

Improved Systems for Receivables and Payables

Accounts Receivable: Speed Collections and Cash Flow

1. Consider discounts for prompt payment (see Special Arrangements for Credit in Chapter 3).
2. Use trained in-house collectors or outsource collections.
3. Do repetitive billing through credit card companies. This is outsourcing of billing, resulting in instant payments.
4. Accept credit card payments.
5. Have the customer approve the use of preauthorized debits

of the customer's account for repetitive monthly billings and authorized clearinghouse (ACH) debits for variable amounts.

6. Do centralized billing and collections to assure timely work and a uniform level of performance in these activities.
7. Establish letter of credit payment for large and repetitive shipments.
8. Use lockbox systems (see Increasing Cash Flow Through Banking Arrangements in Chapter 1).
9. Speed up billing to start the collection clock running sooner. Require billing on the same day as shipment.
10. Mail bills at a post office to avoid missed mailbox pickups.
11. Send selected invoices (over a specified dollar amount) by priority mail.

Accounts Payable: Slow Payments and/or Reduce Costs

1. Take discounts on a controlled basis (see Financial Arrangements With Vendors and Payments Controls in Chapter 1).
2. Use professional outsource payers to save costs.
3. Pay vendors using a bank account in a remote city to obtain additional float on uncleared funds.
4. Order and pay through EDI, the Internet, or an e-procurement system (see above) to reduce costs.
5. Pay with a credit card, ACH debit, or electronic check to reduce payables costs.
6. Reimburse expenses through payroll checks to save on check preparation costs.
7. Issue company credit cards to employees to eliminate individual check reimbursements.
8. Centralize bill paying to avoid early payments by outlying offices and to obtain maximum discounts.
9. Establish one vendor for similar items to avoid duplicate processing.
10. Consider the use of purchasing cards to reduce costs.
11. Avoid duplicate payments by utilizing written checklists for processing invoices.

MATERIALITY

All of the functions and job responsibilities set forth in Appendix A—planning, reporting, evaluating, protecting assets, providing capital, communicating, the entire gamut—have one goal: to achieve the corporate profit plan as described in Chapter 6. The treasurer and controller must be creative in their management of people, as described above, and in designing the architecture of the reporting system, but they cannot be creative in managing earnings. There is no place for managed earnings in either public or private companies. The integrity of the reporting system is a direct reflection of the integrity of the chief financial officer and the entire company. A proper consideration of the recording and disclosure of material items will assure the integrity of the reporting system.

The Securities and Exchange Commission has taken the lead in identifying reporting practices that result in the misuse of materiality concepts to explain departures from generally accepted accounting principles, for the purpose of managing earnings of public companies. SEC Staff Accounting Bulletin No. 99 (SAB 99), Materiality, presents a number of examples of what is acceptable practice and what is not. It makes the point that a company cannot justify intentional misstatements by stating that they are not material. An article in the September 2000 issue of the AICPA's *Journal of Accountancy,* Earnings Management and the Abuse of Materiality, examines SAB 99 with a view to evaluating materiality in the preparation of financial statements. These comments apply to private companies as well, since the accounting principles are the same for public and private companies.

Companies manage earnings to support stock prices; obtain loans; conform to lending covenants, contractual agreements, and regulatory provisions; meet performance bonus goals; hire key personnel; acquire other companies; and meet market expectations. The pressure to meet these objectives can be enormous. Making earnings decisions based on materiality is the principal method used to manage earnings.

In 1980, the Financial Accounting Standards Board issued Statement of Financial Accounting Concepts No. 2, Qualitative Characteristics of Accounting Information. FASB Concepts No. 2 defined materiality in its glossary of terms as "the magnitude of an omission or misstatement of accounting information that, in the light of surrounding circumstances, makes it probable that the judgment of a reasonable person relying on the information would have been changed or influenced by the omission or misstatement." FASB concluded that materiality relates to the "qualitative characteristics," especially relevance and reliability, that make a difference to a decision maker. "A decision not to disclose certain information may be made, say, because investors have no need for that kind of information (it is not relevant) or because the amounts involved are too small to make a difference (they are not material)." Magnitude or dollar amount, by itself, "will not generally be a sufficient basis for a materiality judgment." For example, $10,000 may not be material to a company with $1,000,000 of pretax earnings (1%), but it certainly is to a company with $100,000 of pretax earnings (10%). Moreover, when considering restrictive covenants attached to debt agreements, there is no concept of materiality. A violation of the covenant exists based on the legal wording of the agreement, regardless of amount. As another example, users of financial statements frequently analyze trends in revenues, costs, and profitability. Misstatements of small amounts that reverse these trends may be considered material.

The needs of various types of users of financial statements may determine the materiality of different items. Using a multiple of, say, 10 times earnings in the determination of the purchase price of a business in a buy-sell agreement will have the effect of blowing up a small adjustment by 10 times, making it a large adjustment. Similarly, a securities analyst determines a target stock price based on a multiple of earnings, say 20 times. A minor adjustment can expand the stock price by a material amount.

Financial statements include the use of estimates, typically in determining contingent liabilities, fair values, useful life, allowances for doubtful accounts, amortization periods, losses on uncompleted contracts, and impairment of assets. Such estimates are considered soft, or subjective, assessments, with higher quantitative levels of materiality than for hard, or objective, assessments, which deal with assets like cash or inventories, where smaller differences may be material. The practice of netting hard and soft differences can also create a problem. In the examples given above, a hard difference of a shortage in cash of $10,000 is a certain difference. It has, in fact, been realized and should not be netted against the soft, uncertain difference of a gain of $10,000 arising from a revision to an estimate of collections on accounts receivable, which has not yet been realized and may never be. Differences should be evaluated separately and in the aggregate. Changes in the trends of differences, particularly when they serve to increase earnings, may be an indication of fraud in the preparation of the financial statements.

Other factors that affect the determination of materiality are whether the item is recurring (a lower dollar threshold) or nonrecurring (a higher dollar threshold), whether the effect on current earnings is small but future earnings will be affected (a lower dollar threshold), and whether segment information is affected significantly in terms of profits and trends (a lower dollar threshold).

Managing earnings by fabricating reported financial statement results probably does nothing to increase a company's stock price. Over the long term, the market is unerring in its evaluation of trends, which determine a price/earnings ratio. The integrity of the reported financial statements does more to gain the confidence of the user and investor than managed earnings.

THE AUDIT COMMITTEE

The first paragraph of this chapter deals with the third controllership function in the FEI definition, evaluating and consulting. The controller is thus empowered to recommend to top management the benefits of having an effective audit committee to enable the company to attain its objectives.

The SEC and the AICPA's Auditing Standards Board have adopted rules that require independent auditors to discuss with audit committees the auditors' judgment about the quality, and not just the acceptability under generally accepted accounting principles, of the company's accounting principles as applied in its financial reporting. Further, the New York Stock Exchange, the American Stock Exchange, and the National Association of Securities Dealers have adopted rules that define independence more rigorously for audit committee members, require audit committees to include at least three members and be composed solely of independent directors who are financially literate, require companies to adopt written charters for their audit committees, and require at least one member of the audit committee to have accounting or financial management expertise. The SEC requires companies to provide in their proxy statements a report from the audit committee that discloses whether the audit committee has reviewed and discussed certain matters with management and the auditors and whether anything came to the attention of audit committee members that caused them to believe that the audited financial statements contain any materially misleading statements or omit any material information; that companies disclose in their proxy statements whether the audit committee has a written charter and file a copy of their charter every three years; and that companies whose securities are listed on the NYSE or AMEX or are quoted on Nasdaq disclose certain information about any audit committee member who is not independent.

These rules have equal application for nonpublic companies, subject to modification based on the size of the company. In small companies with as few as three directors, one director with financial expertise can fulfill the audit committee function. In even smaller companies, where there are only one or two related-party directors, the chairman of the board should perform the functions of the audit committee. Even the smallest company would be well advised to have one independent director with financial or accounting expertise to perform this function. This will assure that material differences and accounting principles are properly applied and that the financial statements are presented with integrity.

See Audits, External, in Chapter 11 for details on the duties of the audit committee.

The Public Oversight Board (POB) is an independent, private-sector body that monitors and reports on the self-regulatory programs and activities of the SEC Practice Section of the Division for CPA Firms of the AICPA. The POB, which is funded by the AICPA, has published a report that urges the audit committee to consider a dialog with internal and external auditors regarding the following issues:

- ✦ Accounting implications of new, significant transactions
- ✦ Changes in or continued use of elective accounting principles
- ✦ Application of such principles and aggressiveness or conservatism

✧ Use of reserves and accruals

✧ Significant estimates and judgments used in the financial statements

✧ Auditors' methods for risk assessments and their results

✧ Changes in scope of the audit resulting from such risk assessments

✧ Emergence or elimination of high-risk areas

✧ Effect of environmental factors on financial statements and the audit

✧ Other questions that may influence the quality of the financial statements

Helpful Hint: Assistance in this area is available from a report by Arthur Andersen called New Responsibilities and Requirements for Audit Committees. This may be downloaded from Andersen's web site at *www.andersen.com*. Another large accounting firm offering assistance is the KPMG Audit Committee Institute at *www.us.kpmg.com/auditcommittee*. KPMG offers a report, which may be downloaded, called Shaping the Audit Committee Agenda.

PRACTICAL POINTERS FOR SUCCESS FOR TODAY'S FINANCIAL EXECUTIVES

Today's successful financial manager excels in communication, which presupposes the ability to motivate people to attain the desired profit goals. Advances in information technology provide the resources to obtain continuing education and to augment communications skills. Further, e-commerce, electronic data interchange, e-procurement systems, and advanced receivables and payables systems can reduce costs and improve the cash flow of the enterprise. The treasurer and controller will lead in embracing a change to electronic systems and realizing increased profits and growth for the enterprise. The chief financial officer will understand the qualitative concept of materiality as it relates to the reported financial statement numbers and will take the lead in establishing an independent and financially knowledgeable audit committee. These steps will assure the integrity of the financial reporting process and will set the tone that is essential for an ethical and responsible enterprise.

19

Today's Management Tools

While the definition of the jobs of the controller and treasurer and the related position descriptions found in Appendix A have not changed, the means (tools) to accomplish the stated objectives do change with advances in technology.

◈ Personal computers are available to individual employees, at low cost.
◈ Global communication is provided at little or no cost through e-mail and digital telecommunications.
◈ Infinite knowledge and instant access to it is in the province of every employee through the Internet.
◈ Access to unlimited company information is provided through intranet applications.
◈ The synthesis of all this available and instant information into usable knowledge allows the treasurer and controller to add value to their performance.

Given the basic educational background required to fulfill the positions of treasurer and controller, and assuming continuing professional education to retain currency of technical skills, the following additional tools should be considered.

E-Business

There is much ado about the differences between new-economy and old-economy companies. The differences are only those of newness, time in business. New-economy companies are striving to attain the attributes of old-economy companies—to establish market leadership, a global brand and presence, and best practices performance; to acquire assets; and to be profitable. The goals are the same. Only the tools for attaining success are different. The new-economy companies are being innovative in the delivery and communication of information. Some of these tools are discussed in the following sections.

Customer Relationship Management

The Internet era and the expansion of global commerce have made competition more prevalent and insidious. Customers have more knowledge and are more mobile and demanding. Getting and retaining customers is a battle, and the war will be won by companies that put resources into the fight.

Customer relationship management (CRM) is an e-business model that integrates the sales effort with the company reporting system. A shared companywide database captures all pertinent customer information needed for marketing and billing. An application service provider delivers an outsourced data center and client server on a secure basis. The functions of outside sales, inside sales, customer service, customer support, order processing, and financial reporting are seamlessly integrated.

CRM gives sales representatives access to the system, which will record all past orders; customers can place orders or request information online; sales leads are directed to sales representatives; customer e-mail can be managed; and new products and services are disseminated to customers.

The controller should lead in exploring, understanding, and recommending this business model. Once it is approved, the controller will be a principal team member in guiding the installation of the model to a successful conclusion. Outside consultants experienced in CRM should be retained to assist in the design and implementation.

See Customer Relations in Chapter 11 for a discussion on the responsibilities of the controller in this area.

E-COMMERCE

An e-commerce solution to business management offers a high-performance, scalable approach that will allow the company to start simply and grow quickly. It provides a web presentation of the company's goods and services, online order processing and invoicing, automated customer service inquiries, and online payment and transaction processing. Alternatively, it can offer an application service provider (ASP) solution, rather than a web site. Either approach enables the development of a dynamic, online, database-driven Internet presence. The web site is integrated with an existing order entry system that accepts electronic payments and creates complete online shopping and bill payment. This can improve margins by providing a low-cost, online sales channel; streamlined, automated, efficient paperless processes; and faster, more responsive customer service. A typical e-commerce solution is available from Information Technologies Corp. in Danbury, Connecticut.

The ASP approach will usually take longer and cost more than the web site alternative, but it can be customized and provides more capability. Both approaches may look the same, in that hardware and software are not owned by the user. The ASP owns, maintains, and supports the technology for the application, like e-purchasing, often partnering with other vendors who can support different parts of the total information technology package. The hardware vendor may partner with an accounting software vendor and a purchasing software vendor to arrive at an integrated system. The ASP offers no or lower software costs and administrative costs, online software upgrades, module expansion as the business requires it, no requirement for in-house IT specialists, global information access, and expanded customer services. This all means no investment on your part in hardware or software, no software licenses or technical support agreements, and no in-house network administrators. Supply chain management is enhanced, since salespeople, vendors, and customers can access your accounting system from anywhere at any time. Your independent accountant can also access the system, making journal entries and preparing financial statements. In short, the ASP is a sole vendor that allows you to eliminate hardware and software vendors and in-house personnel to service them.

The disadvantages are that the system may be risky, possibly unreliable, possibly not secure, or not properly customized to do the required job, and that the ASP vendor may not be financially sound. In the event of a failure, dispute, or break-up with the ASP, it may be difficult to obtain the accounting software that you have configured and the ASP may not release important data that it holds. If a smooth transition away from the ASP is required, the ASP may not cooperate or provide service during the transition period, creating a billing crisis. These contingencies should be anticipated at the start of the ASP arrangement by entering into a termination agreement that delineates the responsibilities of both parties in the event of separation.

Alternatively, the web site application offers a faster way to get into e-commerce, as the vendor usually owns the hardware, software, and databases, and custom applications are generally not available. A complex web system could have extensive database accessibility for authorized employees, general ledger and financial statement capability, e-purchasing, vendor payments, expense reporting components, billing, and customer interface.

To lead the development or to take part in the evaluation of e-commerce systems, the controller should understand ASP, database structure, web site design, e-purchasing, and customer relationship management.

E-PURCHASING

Manual purchasing systems require larger inventories and more personnel to fill expected individual requisitions. Typical requisitions are for office supplies, calling cards, and maintenance and repair items. Payment for purchases requires more personnel to process paper and make timely payments. Employees often circumvent official purchasing policy by buying from unapproved sources. An e-purchasing system may be implemented to overcome these disadvantages of manual systems. Such a system may be part of an e-business solution or an electronic data interchange (EDI) solution, or a stand-alone system may be installed at a lower cost. A web-based system can be employed to illustrate a catalog of products, enabling immediate deliveries and automatic payment.

The essence of an e-purchasing system is that individual employees are able to place their own orders for items that have been budgeted for with vendors approved in advance. The system tracks the complete history of the transaction, from purchase requisition through delivery and payment. Further, prepackaged orders can be made available for specific events, such as ordering supplies and business cards for a new employee. Employees from remote locations may enter the system directly and receive prompt deliveries. E-purchasing results in substantial savings to the corporation.

ENTERPRISE RESOURCE PLANNING

Enterprise resource planning (ERP) systems provide more, better, and more timely information to assist managers to make more, better, and more timely decisions, thereby lowering costs and increasing profitability. ERP systems integrate and automate the various business activities (excellent for activity-based costing systems) and share this information through the enterprise in real time. The ERP system follows production by employee, job, location, and activity. This detailed process improves quality, especially for companies in low-price, high-volume areas such as mass merchandising, as opposed to those companies with a specific market niche.

ERP software enables companies to exchange information throughout the organization, using modules for auditing, payroll, purchasing, order processing, billing, manufacturing, inventory, and costing. Instead of having a separate system for each department, a single, seamless, enterprisewide system is used. This information exchange speeds up order processing and delivery to the customer, at no additional cost, reduces inventory levels, speeds the billing process, and measures the performance results on a continuing basis.

Software for any size company is available from vendors, either directly through the software vendor or through a value-added reseller (VAR). VARs typically sell versions of the software that have been modified for specific industries. Vendors and VARs can be found on the Internet. Typical vendors are Baan, J. D. Edwards, Great Plains, Infoflo, Ingram, Macola Software, Micro, Oracle, Navision, PeopleSoft, QAD, Ross Systems Renaissance, SAP, and Solomon. Be aware that the design of vendor software varies and that a particular vendor's software may not suit every company. Similarly, VARs are not totally independent, as they tend to specialize in one vendor's products. A consultant with accounting and software experience can help bridge these gaps, particularly if the consultant has experience in your industry.

> *Word of Caution:* Determine whether the consultant receives a commission, referral fee, or advertising subsidy from the vendor. These are not unusual, but they should be disclosed so that you, the user, can evaluate whether you are getting the best system.

For the smaller company, it is most important to identify a system that is proven and can be scaled to the company's needs, yet allows room to upgrade as the business grows. The smaller company does not have the resources or information technology (IT) staff to devote to such a project and would do well to identify a proven system.

Systems that are industry-oriented can accommodate large-company manufacturing concepts like materials requirements planning (MRP), manufacturing resource planning (MRP), and supply chain management (SCM). Figure the time for implementation at 8 to 18 months. This is after the initial feasibility exploration and selection of the consultant, vendor, or VAR and depends on the company's commitment to a fast and successful implementation. The smallest workable system may cost about $50,000 and take a year to complete. Larger systems can cost $2,000,000 and take four years to complete. Employees with some IT experience earn about $90,000 per year, and a project manager, $100,000 to $200,000. ERP consultants get $200 per hour. Companies may implement ERP using either outside consultants or in-house company leaders. Consultants will get the system up and working more quickly, but at substantially higher cost.

To assist in this endeavor, an analytical solution called enterprise performance management (EPM) may be used. One such solution available from Gentia Software provides the ability to measure, analyze, and optimize business results, thereby allowing the company to align strategy and objectives with the overall performance of the business.

PERFORMANCE VIEW

Performance View is a nonfinancial examination of the organization with the goal of directing company efforts to the most profitable future. The critical factors for success are identified and measured in the future, enabling these measures to be used to assess progress in achieving specific targets linked to an entity's vision and performance. Instead of tracking only past performance, this method provides insights for the future. It is a new tool to augment historical reporting.

Performance View consulting is a service available from CPAs who have been trained by the AICPA in techniques for performing this service. Training is also available to nonmembers of the AICPA and includes the following:

- ✧ How to identify critical success factors and performance indicators
- ✧ How to develop a hierarchy of measures, including benchmarking
- ✧ How to scale the service to suit any size company
- ✧ How to apply this approach to any industry
- ✧ How to diagnose all issues and develop a strategic plan
- ✧ How to implement the service
- ✧ How to report and drive performance
- ✧ How to set up performance-based compensation programs

The AICPA offers software called CPA Views that aids in understanding, measuring, and communicating the operational performance of the company in the context of its strategic objectives.

SysTrust

The AICPA has created a comprehensive assurance service called SysTrust that attests to a business system's availability, security, integrity, and maintainability. It evaluates information protection, security testing, and systems reliability. The web system of the company includes hardware, software, people, procedures, and data to produce information. This service results in a WebTrust seal that builds trust and confidence among consumers and businesses purchasing goods and services on the Internet. The WebTrust seal assists online businesses and their customers to assess, and then reduce, the risks of doing business electronically.

Training in these assurance techniques is available to members and nonmembers of the AICPA at a cost of $645 and $745, respectively.

Strategic Risk Management

The treasurer and/or controller should be aware of business risks that can reduce profits or even destroy the company. Some of these are insurable, or partly insurable. Others are not. Identifying the risks and taking preventive measures requires education and training. Some of these risks are:

❖ *Employment practices liability.* Companies face legal actions for age, race, and gender discrimination; sexual harassment; failure to accommodate disabled persons; unsafe working conditions; hostile or unhealthy working environments; invasions of personal privacy; and wrongful terminations.

❖ *Business practices liability.* Legal actions may result from unfair labor practices, product liability, professional performance liability, retirement plan and pension funding liability, directors' and officers' liability, foreign operations, and currency risk.

Some of these risks may be insurable (see Chapter 4). Typical of the insurance polices available is employment practices liability insurance, which not only covers the monetary losses sustained but will provide attorneys and experts to help in the company's legal defense. Insurance, however, never covers all the losses and may be subject to high deductibles, and often the loss is difficult to prove. The best way to manage these uninsured risks is to identify the risk, quantify the potential for loss, and establish procedures to avert the loss.

Case in Point: An employee sued the company for a bad back injury that he claimed was caused by workstations that were not ergonomically designed to avoid such injuries. The controller had read about a similar case and had previously received an expert opinion that the company's workstations were properly designed to avoid back injuries. Case closed.

Recognition of the potential for loss falls under the province of the controller because of the possible loss of corporate assets, covered by the protection of assets function described in Appendix A, "To assure protection for the assets of the business through internal control, internal auditing, and assuring proper insurance coverage." The tools of internal control are set forth in Chapter 7; of particular importance in avoiding these uninsured risks is the policy manual, discussed in the section Operating Policies. The prudent controller will take the lead in establishing policies for inclusion in the policy manual to avoid the enumerated risks. Thereafter, the controller should exercise the internal audit function as part of the function of protection of assets. The objectives of internal operational audits are described in Chapter 10 and include evaluation of personnel policies and providing for the protection of company assets.

THE BUSINESS PLAN

Every organization must have a business plan—for its lenders and investors, for estate valuation, to attract key employees, for sale of the business, for purchase of a business (see Exhibit 12-6, AICPA Guidelines for Preparing Financial Forecasts, as it relates to mergers and acquisitions), for an offering statement of an entity's debt or equity interests, to plan the future. It's simply good business to plan ahead.

A business plan is related to a budget, but it is not a budget. A budget is prepared for internal use as part of establishing the plan for the control of operations (see Chapter 6). It contains considerably more detail than a business plan and does not address the nonfinancial aspects of the business. Further, the business plan is oriented to a specific purpose—obtaining bank credit, acquiring a company, obtaining investment funds, selling stock, growing the business. A business plan also contains a substantial narrative that includes topics in addition to the financial statements, as follows:

- ✧ Summary of the proposal
- ✧ Description of the project
- ✧ Description of the products and services
- ✧ Markets and marketing
- ✧ Competition
- ✧ Risk factors and solutions
- ✧ Use of proceeds
- ✧ The company
  - ✧ Background
  - ✧ Objectives
  - ✧ Description of common stock
  - ✧ Principal stockholders
  - ✧ Management
- ✧ Financial exhibits
  - ✧ Summary of projections
  - ✧ Report of independent CPA
  - ✧ Projected financial statements—three years

✦ Balance sheets
✦ Income statements
✦ Income statements—percentages
✦ Cash flow statements
✦ Financial ratios
✦ Return on assets
✦ Significant accounting policies and significant assumptions

Example: Wal-Mart, the world's largest retailer, with revenues of $134 billion, recently stated that it expected a slowdown in business momentum in the last half of the year. It saw no signs of this, but it could not prepare its business plan based on the notion that the present momentum would continue. Thus, it prepared a forecast and assumptions (a business plan) that started with budgets that flow up into the final plan. There was less detail in the business plan than in the budget.

Prospective financial statements that are part of the business plan may be either forecasts or projections. The AICPA Audit and Accounting Guide for Prospective Financial Information provides professional standards for CPAs to use in preparing such statements. If prospective financial statements are prepared internally, they should follow the standards set forth in the guide. Users of the statements will have more confidence in them if the standards are met.

Financial forecasts are defined in the guide as prospective financial statements that present, to the best of the responsible party's knowledge and belief, an entity's expected financial position, results of operations, and cash flows. A financial forecast is based on the responsible party's assumptions regarding the conditions it expects to exist and the course of action it expects to take. Each monetary amount in a financial forecast may be expressed as a single-point estimate of forecasted results or as a range within which the responsible party reasonably expects, to the best of its knowledge and belief, the item or items subject to selected key assumptions to fall. If a forecast contains a range, the range must not be selected in a biased or misleading manner (for example, a range in which one end is significantly less likely than the other). Minimum presentation guidelines for a financial forecast are presented in the guide and should be reviewed. When the prospective financial statement is for general use (to be used by parties who are unable to ask the responsible party about the presentation), a forecast should be used.

Financial projections are defined in the guide as prospective financial statements that present, to the best of the responsible party's knowledge and belief, given one or more hypothetical assumptions, an entity's expected financial position, results of operations, and cash flows. A financial projection is sometimes prepared to present one or more hypothetical courses of action for evaluation, as in response to a question that begins, "What would happen if. . .?" A financial projection is based on the responsible party's assumptions reflecting the conditions it expects would exist and the course of action it expects would be taken, given one or more hypothetical assumptions. A projection, like a forecast, may contain a range. Minimum presentation guidelines for financial projections are presented in the guide and should be reviewed. When the prospective financial statement is for limited use (to be used by the responsible party alone or by the responsible party and third parties with whom the responsible party is negotiating directly—for example, in negotiations for a bank loan), either a forecast or a projection may be used (since the third party can ask questions of the responsible party and negotiate terms). However, because the financial projection is not appropriate for general use, it should not be distributed to those who will not be negotiating directly with the responsible party (for example, in an entity's offering statement for equity or debt).

Some Words of Caution: The business plan should not:

- ❖ *Be too thick or heavy.* If it is more than 15 to 18 pages, it won't be read.
- ❖ *Be spiral bound.* Use a flat binder so that it can be filed easily.
- ❖ *Contain illustrations.* It's a financial document, not a brochure.
- ❖ *Use small print.* The reader must not have to strain to read it.
- ❖ *Use color.* It's a financial document, not a brochure.
- ❖ *Have small margins.* Use plenty of white space to make reading easier.
- ❖ *Have a hand-out.* The document should be self-contained.

- ❖ *Be without a table of contents.* This allows the reader to navigate the document.
- ❖ *Be without captions on each page.* Use large headings.
- ❖ *Use legal size paper.* Keep it at 8½" x 11".

The narrative content should not:

- ❖ *Be too technical.* Define technical terms for the reader.
- ❖ *Be disorganized.* Follow a clear path.
- ❖ *Use the first person.* Use the Company and Management, not we.
- ❖ *Expand the biographies.* Keep it short and simple.
- ❖ *Use too much history.* This is a future look.
- ❖ *Omit any topics.* Use the items in the table of contents.

A Management Acronym

Create an acronym to serve as a management model. It should be catchy, concise, and capable of being used in any area of the business as a management tool. A common acronym, widely used, that could be applied to the controller's area is as follows:

The GOSPEL

Goal	To have the best accounting department in our industry
Objective	To complete monthly financial closings on the third day of the month following
Strategy	To train our personnel in the techniques of rapid closings
Plan	To conduct in-house training seminars on the techniques of rapid closings
Evaluation	To measure the results versus the three-day standard
Linkage	To measure the improvement in the performance of

other departments as a result of the accounting
department's having achieved its goal

Another example is:

COORS

Coordination   To work with other departments to speed the flow
                 of data to accounting
Objective   To complete monthly financial closings on the third
                 day of the month following
Opportunity   To improve the flow of financial information on a
                 more timely basis to investors and lenders
Reward   To gain the confidence of lenders and investors in
                 the professionalism of the company
Stock   To see an increase in the price of the company's
                 stock as a result of the increased confidence of
                 financial statement users

Still another example is:

FATSO

Fraud   Consider the possibility of fraud and unreported
                 income.
Analysis   Conduct an analysis of key financial factors such as
                 gross profits, credits issued, and sales by quarter, and
                 consider non-business-related factors.
Trust   Focus on employees in positions of trust who can
                 affect financial results, costs, and revenues.
Significance   Examine significant factors like the standard of
                 living, net worth, and credit ratings of key
                 individuals.
Ongoing   Establish quarterly or semiannual updates of the
                 analysis.

COMPUTER PRINTING

Computer output, including word processing documents, tax returns, spreadsheets, and other reports, is usually laser printed and then copied and collated for distribution. The cost and time of using copiers should be compared to the cost and time of printing directly from the computer's laser printer. The cost of direct copying includes the cost of paper, service, toner, and capital. The cost of direct laser printing includes only the cost of paper and toner. The cost of capital for the laser printer is an indirect cost and need not be considered. The significant cost factors are speed, number of copies, and cost of the toner cartridge (usually lower for a laser cartridge).

PUBLIC AND PRIVATE OFFERINGS

Private offerings that are exempt from the 1933 SEC Act include:

- ❖ *Private placements or venture capital.* Venture capitalists are private investors who rely on a company-prepared business plan, require a minimum of 20% equity, and have a perceived exit strategy consisting of the company's buying back stock, being acquired, or going public. Private placements generally involve the sale of high-quality stocks or bonds to institutional investors such as banks, trust funds, or insurance companies. The offering must be nonpublic, or private. Whether an offering is public or private will depend on a number of factors, such as the number of investors (a private placement must have less than 25 accredited investors, or perhaps more if they are sophisticated) and the number of securities offered and their dollar value (a private placement must not be so large as to appear to be a public offering), and the securities must be bought for investment by the purchaser (the shares will be marked "unregistered").
- ❖ *Regulation A*–Regulation A (Reg. A) of the Securities and

Exchange Commission (SEC) permits up to $5 million to be raised in any 12-month period, including up to $1.5 million offered by all selling shareholders. There is a "test the waters" provision of Regulation A that permits preoffering solicitations of indications of interest subject to SEC oversight. A written document or scripted radio or TV broadcasts may be used to determine whether there is any interest in a contemplated securities offering. Reg. A requires an offering statement, not a registration statement (the financial statements may be unaudited and may be a compilation or a review). The SEC prefers to see reviewed financial statements. If the company does prepare audited financial statements, they must conform to Article 2 of Regulation S-X. There are no limits on the number or type of investors.

✦ *Regulation D.* Regulation D (Reg. D) of the SEC permits up to $1 million per year to be raised under SEC Rule 504. There are no SEC disclosure requirements, although the state may have its own disclosure requirements. Under SEC Rule 505, up to $5 million may be raised during a 12-month period without advertising or solicitation. This type of offering may be made only to accredited investors (those with a minimum of $1 million net worth, $200,000 of individual income, or $300,000 of joint income with a spouse) or no more than 35 nonaccredited investors. The purchasers of securities acquire restricted securities (they may not be sold for one year).

✦ *Rule 506.* This permits an unlimited dollar amount to be raised from up to 35 nonaccredited investors and an unlimited number of accredited investors.

The Initial Public Offering (IPO)

Long-term debt techniques are discussed in Chapter 2, and equity is described as the ultimate and longest-term debt. The treasurer's primary function in the FEI's definition is "provision of the capital required by the business." The cost of equity is not the only consideration in deciding to take the company public. There are subjective advantages and disadvantages to going public.

Pros	Cons
Raise expansion capital at low cost	Fishbowl oversight by the SEC and stockholders.
Provide for a future capital market	Issue tax-advantaged stock options to key employees
Complete disclosures are required	High legal and accounting costs (9% to 14% of the offering)
Allow the owners to cash out	Continuing quarterly reporting
Value the owners' interest for estate planning	Liability to SEC and third parties
Provide competitive advantage	Possibility of a failed offering
Provide the ultimate recognition of success	Annual stockholders' meetings
Facilitate acquisitions	Continuous interface with analysts
Achieve customer recognition	Perceived need for short-term profits
Provide liquidity for stock holdings	Interim and annual audit costs
	High fee to initial underwriters

Helpful Hint: An alternative to doing an IPO is to acquire a public shell (an inactive company that previously went public but now has no assets or liabilities, only stockholders) in a reverse acquisition. The old stockholders will usually retain 5% to 10% of the public company. After the reverse acquisition, additional shares may be sold to the public in a secondary offering or one of the private offerings described above may be used.

Offerings of up to $10 million may be done by small business issuers (SBI) under Regulation S-B using Form SB-1. An SBI must have annual revenues of under $25 million and a public share float of less than $25 million. Form SB-2 may be used with no limit on the amount of the total offering. SB-2 offerings require more disclosures concerning securities sales than SB-1 offerings.

The financial statements required under Regulation S-B are GAAP financial statements. They must be audited and consist of a balance sheet for one year and statements of income and cash flows for two years. Audited statements must be less than 10 months old. Any required interim statements must be less than 134 days old. The accountant's report must be a clean opinion, except for a going concern qualification. Newer companies are allowed to supply fewer financial statements.

> *Be Aware of This:* While an audited balance sheet is required for only one year, the company must have had three audited balance sheets in order to comply with the requirement for two years of statements of income (since opening inventory at the beginning of the one year is derived from the audited inventory at the end of the previous year).

Disclosures

The offering document will require significant disclosures that are not normally made by a private company. Executive compensation must be fully described; a complete description of the business covering three years must be given; the use of proceeds must be described, including the amounts for working capital, underwriters' fees (7% to 9%), and offering costs (legal, accounting, printing, blue sky—usually 5% to 7%); a management discussion and analysis (MD&A) section containing cash flow information, a liquidity section, material commitments, results since inception, and a pro forma presentation of any complex acquisitions must be provided. The MD&A is the most important part of the document.

> *Word of Caution:* The attorney selected should have experience with public offerings. The accountant and the underwriter selected should both have appropriate industry and IPO experience.

Underwriting Agreements

The investment banker or underwriter "takes the company public." The underwriter either acts as an agent for the company in offering and selling the securities or actually purchases the securities from the company and sells them to its own customers. There are three basic types of agreements.

Under a "firm commitment" agreement, the investment banker buys the complete offering at a discount from the public price and retains the spread on sale to the public. There may be several underwriters involved who may sell to other dealers at a price discount, or directly to the public. The company is guaranteed to receive its negotiated price. Firm commitments are rare and are available only to the strongest companies with important technology.

Under a "best efforts" agreement, the investment banker is an agent for the company, using its best efforts to sell as much of the issue as it can. The company receives the proceeds of whatever stock is sold, less the agent's commission to the underwriter. The agreement is exclusive, usually for 90 days. This type of agreement may also contain an "all or none" clause, wherein all the shares must be sold for the offering to be effective.

Under a "mini-maxi" agreement, the company and the underwriter agree that a certain minimum number of shares must be sold. Once the minimum is met, the underwriter may keep the offering open until the maximum is sold, within the agreed time period; or the offering may be closed at any time after the minimum is met if it appears that the maximum will not be reached. Here, too, the underwriter must use its best efforts.

Once the decision has been made to do an IPO and the accounting, legal, and investment banking team has been selected, the decision must be made on how many shares to sell and at what price. The investment banker will assess the demand for the company's stock. Market conditions and investor appetite for the industry are the main determinants of price. The investment bankers will consider historical and prospective financial statements, comparable recent IPO's, the percentage of the company's stock being sold, and the stock's total market float. When there are no directly comparable companies to provide pricing guidelines, an analysis of factors should be made as if the company were going to be acquired (see the checklist in Chapter 12), and an acquisition price—really a market value—should be determined. In addition to these specific numbers, the investment banker must make a subjective analysis to determine a price that will satisfy the underwriter, the company, and the investors. Too low a price will deny the issuer substantial monies and may produce a disgruntled and litigious issuer. Too high a price will result in poor after-issue stock price performance, criticism of the investment banker, and possible legal action by unhappy investors.

Once the size of the issue and the approximate price have been determined, the company and the underwriter must market the issue. The bankers usually arrange a "road show" in which the company makes presentations to institutional investors across the country. This promotes the offering and provides feedback as to market price and interest in the stock. At the same time, the investment banker's sales force approaches potential investors, both institutional and private, to determine their interest in participating in the offering and their perceptions of the price and number of shares that should be offered.

If the investment banker does its job well, in terms of price and number of shares offered, the stock will trade at a firm level for months following the IPO. Ultimately, the stock price will be based on a price/earnings ratio like the stock prices of established companies.

STRATEGIC BUSINESS EVALUATION

Strategic business evaluation is a method of providing feedback on the efficacy of corporate operating strategies. It is, in effect, an intelligence gathering action to enable the company to judge its performance compared to that of its competitors. Information about competitors is obtained from newspapers, trade magazines, annual reports, SEC filings, the Internet, and their former employees.

The information gathered is tailored to the company using it. Typical information by product line and/or for the entire company would be:

- ✧ Market share
- ✧ Profit margin
- ✧ Growth rate
- ✧ Service response time
- ✧ Delivery time
- ✧ Sales per sales representative
- ✧ Sales to net assets
- ✧ Customer complaints
- ✧ Customer satisfaction
- ✧ Customer expectations

SBE results in the company's measuring its performance not only against its other divisions or companies, but also against its competition. This will lead to revised goals and objectives and a new GOSPEL (see above).

ONLINE TREASURY WORKSTATIONS

From a global standpoint, a treasury workstation is defined as hardware and applications software working together with management applications to assume the treasury functions of managing cash, investments, and debt through a high-speed banking tie-line. This system will support access to capital markets, manage cash and portfolios, and create reports from both internal and external financial accounting systems. A working system will reduce data entry time and provide better rates on investments because the company can enter the market more quickly and will save on interest costs when it borrows. The system provides reconciliation and complex financial calculations to identify financial risk exposures, excellent tools for dealing with derivative financial instruments. If properly designed, the workstation will interface with the general ledger system.

Treasury operations are completely automated, are tied to a database, and provide for direct communication with banks and financial institutions. The workstation can be used by large companies with subsidiaries or divisions in many countries or by domestic companies with many branch offices or other locations. These systems can be stand-alone or a module in an overall ERP system (see Enterprise Resource Planning above). They are generally applicable to companies with revenues in the $50 to $100 million range, although off-the-shelf ERP software is available for smaller companies. A small, stand-alone system can cost about $30,000, with larger systems costing up to $300,000. Installation can be accomplished in 3 to 12 months, depending on complexity. Complexity increases with the addition of foreign exchange, debt, and investment functions. Vendors of workstations include large money-center banks like Citicorp and Chase, large accounting consulting firms like KPMG, and third-party software vendors like XRT-CERG, SunGard Treasury Systems, and Trema Group.

The key functions of treasury workstations are collecting bank data, cash forecasting, debt and investment analysis, and risk management. The workstation tracks investment purchases, maturity dates, and interest calculations; adjusts cash forecasts; and provides electronic funds transfers. It may access external databases to obtain online information on capital markets, customers, vendors, and financial institutions, in both domestic and global markets. It allows the treasurer to sweep cash from low-interest accounts to higher-yielding investments.

Lower-cost alternatives to complete treasury workstations are on-line banking arrangements with principal banks through the Internet. The bank may use a familiar partner like Microsoft or Intuit and interface with its software—Money or QuickBooks, respectively.

This all results in more efficient management of working capital. A tool for measuring this efficiency follows.

CASH SHORTFALL ANALYSIS (CSA)

A simple, big-picture approach to managing working capital concentrates on the major cash flow components of working capital. These are inventory, receivables, and payables. A cash shortfall is measured through the number of days between the company's payment for the merchandise and services it buys and its collection from customers for the merchandise and services it sells. Simply stated, the following formula indicates the cash shortfall that reduces working capital:

Days of inventory on hand + days required for receivables collection
  − accounts payable payment period = cash shortfall in days

Calculate the shortfall using these assumptions:

* Inventory on hand = 60 days. [To calculate this, find inventory turnover, using cost of goods sold (say, $156,000,000) for the year divided by the average inventory (say, $26,000,000) = 6 times per year. Then divide 365 days by the inventory turnover (365 / 6) = 60 days.]
* Days to collect receivables = 60 days. (Calculate this as described in Chapter 5, Forecasting Cash Requirements as a Basis for Maintaining Adequate Funds, in the section entitled Long-Range Forecasts). In effect, this equals the average outstanding accounts receivable divided by a day's sales.
* Accounts payable payment period = 30 days. (Calculate this as the average period from the time the vendor invoice is received until it is paid. As a shortcut, this may be estimated based on company policy. For more accuracy, test two or three months of payments, showing days outstanding before payment of each vendor invoice, and obtain an average payment period.)

Applying the formula,

  Cash shortfall in days = 60 + 60 − 30 = 90 days

Next, determine the cost of the cash shortfall based on the following assumptions:

Sales per day	= $1,000,000
Cost of goods sold per day	= $600,000 (say 60% of sales)
Interest cost	= 9% per year
Cash shortfall days	= 90 days

Cash shortfall per day =

  (cost of goods sold per day × cash shortfall days × 9%)/90 days

  Applying the formula,

Cash shortfall per day =

$$(\$600,000 \times 90 \times 9\%)/90 = \$54,000/\text{day}$$

CSA indicates that if the company can reduce the cash shortfall by even one day, income before income taxes will increase by $54,000. This can be accomplished by improving inventory turnover, shortening the receivables collection period, increasing the payment period for accounts payable, or any combination of these. In addition, increased sales at better margins will decrease the cash shortfall by decreasing the cost of goods sold. Using the numbers above, if inventory turnover were increased to 8 times a year (say, $156,000,000 cost divided by an average inventory of $19,500,000 instead of $26,000,000), then the inventory on hand would be reduced from 60 days to 46 days (365/8). The cash shortfall days would decrease from 90 days to 76 days (46 + 60 − 30), and the cash shortfall would be reduced by $756,000 (90 days − 76 days = 14 days × $54,000). This $756,000 would flow directly to the bottom line. Operating personnel can increase inventory turnover by arranging for just-in-time deliveries from vendors, by selecting alternative vendors, and by establishing e-purchasing systems to provide for more efficiency. The controller can lead in this effort by communicating the results of CSA to operating personnel and educating them on its implications.

The controller should also analyze the effects of budgeted changes in operations on the cash shortfall. For example, a 20% sales increase to $1,200,000 per day increases cost of goods sold per day to $720,000 and increases the cost of the cash shortfall per day to $64,800 [($720,000 × 90 × 9%)/90)] from $54,000. Given these figures, appropriate management personnel can make the necessary decisions to reduce the cash shortfall—change the mix of product sales to include (1) products with higher sales prices or lower costs, (2) products with a higher inventory turnover, and (3) products that are sold for cash or on shorter payment terms.

A related analysis, equally simple and easy for nonfinancial managers to understand, is the ratio of general and administrative (G&A) expenses to sales. This is perhaps the most significant indicator of the company's profitability or of its inefficiency during times of expansion. Each item of G&A expense should be divided between direct (variable) and period (fixed) costs. Certain expenses, such as office salaries and travel, may be part direct and part period. The direct expenses may be expected to increase in proportion to the increases in sales. The period expenses, such as bad debt expense, depreciation expense, insurance, nonincome taxes, officers' salaries, professional fees, rent, and utilities, should not increase. After the financial year is completed, G&A expenses, direct and period, should be computed. The expected ratio of G&A to sales should be compared to the actual ratio to determine whether an increasing ratio has caused a further cash shortfall, in which case additional analysis is needed.

Cash shortfall analysis can make a substantial contribution to increased earnings. Most importantly, it is a simple analytical method; the effect on profits of sales, cost of goods sold, inventory levels, and receivables and payables turnovers is easily understood by operating personnel, permitting them to take meaningful actions to increase profits and cash flow.

PRACTICAL POINTERS FOR USING TODAY'S MANAGEMENT TOOLS

The means to accomplish the stated objectives of the treasurer and controller, as set forth in Appendix A, have been enhanced with advances in technology. Customer relationship management, e-commerce, and enterprise resource planning are systems that provide financial and nonfinancial data on which to plan operations. Performance View and SysTrust are nonfinancial examinations of the overall business and its electronic systems that contribute directly to the performance and profitability of the enterprise. When these are coupled with a sound business plan and analysis of cash shortfalls, attainment of the performance objectives of the treasurer and controller is virtually assured.

Appendix A

Treasurer's and Controller's Functions Defined by the Financial Executives Institute

The major areas of responsibilities of treasurers and controllers have been defined by the Financial Executives Institute (FEI), the managing financial executives' major professional society. It is the voice of professional managers in the business and financial community and has established rules of practice and conduct for them. These defined responsibilities, as they appeared in *Financial Executive* magazine, are reproduced below.

CONTROLLERSHIP AND TREASURERSHIP FUNCTIONS DEFINED BY FEI

The first official statement of the responsibilities of the corporate treasurership function was approved in 1962 by the board of directors of the Financial Executives Institute (established in 1931 as Controllers Institute of America). For many years the institute and its predecessor body had published an established list of functions of controllership. The newly approved list of treasurership functions was developed coincident with the change of scope and name of the institute from Controllers Institute to Financial Executives Institute.

FINANCIAL MANAGEMENT

CONTROLLERSHIP

Planning for Control

To establish, coordinate and administer, as an integral part of management, an adequate plan for the control of operations. Such a plan would provide, to the extent required in the business, profit planning, programs for capital investing and for financing, sales forecasts, expense budgets and cost standards, together with the necessary procedures to effectuate the plan.

Reporting and Interpreting

To compare performance with operating plans and standards, and to report and interpret the results of operations to all levels of management and to the owners of the business. This function includes the formulation of accounting policy, the coordination of systems and procedures, the preparation of operating data, and of special reports as required.

Evaluating and Consulting

To consult with all segments of management responsible for policy or action concerning any phase of the operation of the business as it relates to the attainment of objec-

TREASURERSHIP

Provision of Capital

To establish and execute programs for the provision of the capital required by the business, including negotiating the procurement of capital and maintaining the required financial arrangements.

Investor Relations

To establish and maintain an adequate market for the company's securities and, in connection therewith, to maintain adequate liaison with investment bankers, financial analysts, and shareholders.

Short-Term Financing

To maintain adequate sources for the company's current borrowings from commercial banks and other lending institutions.

Banking and Custody

To maintain banking arrangements, to receive, have custody of and disburse the company's monies and securities, and to be responsible for the financial aspects of real estate transactions.

CONTROLLERSHIP

tives and the effectiveness of policies, organization structure, and procedures.

Tax Administration

To establish and administer tax policies and procedures.

Government Reporting

To supervise or coordinate the preparation of reports to government agencies.

Protection of Assets

To assure protection for the assets of the business through internal control, internal auditing, and assuring proper insurance coverage.

Economic Appraisal

To continuously appraise economic and social forces and government influences, and to interpret their effect upon the business.

TREASURERSHIP

Credit and Collections

To direct the granting of credit and the collection of accounts due the company, including the supervision of required special arrangements for financing sales, such as time payment and leasing plans.

Investments

To invest the company's funds as required, and to establish and coordinate policies for investment in pension and other similar trusts.

Insurance

To provide insurance coverage as may be required.

These functions are organized into position descriptions that delineate the specific route to performance of the various responsibilities. A position description for the treasurer and another for the controller follow.

POSITION DESCRIPTION
(Vice President Finance and Treasurer)

Effective Date:

TITLE: Vice President Finance and		
Treasurer	DIVISION:	President's
	DEPARTMENT:	N/A
President, Diversified	SECTION:	N/A
Equipment		
Leasing Corporation	UNIT:	N/A
(Divisional)		

REPORTS TO: The President

SUMMARY OF FUNCTIONS:

Corporate—Responsible to the president for all long-range financial matters and to establish companywide financial and administrative objectives, policies, programs, and practices that ensure the company of a continuously sound financial structure. As chief financial officer, controls the flow of cash through the organization and maintains the integrity of funds, securities, and other valuable documents. A member of the banking committee and the board of directors.

Divisional—As chief operating officer, conducts the affairs of the company, interprets and applies the policies of the board of directors; establishes policy; controls the operations and activities of the various departments; and conducts public relations.

MAJOR DUTIES AND RESPONSIBILITIES:

Corporate—Establishes and executes programs for the provision of the capital required by the business, including negotiating the procurement of capital and maintaining the required financial arrangements.

Coordinates the long-range plans (over three months) of the corporation, assesses the financial requirements implicit in these plans, evaluates the potential return on investment, and develops alternative ways in which financial requirements can be satisfied.

Establishes and maintains an adequate market for the company's securities and, in connection therewith, maintains adequate liaison with investment bankers, financial analysts, and shareholders (in conjunction with the president).

Maintains adequate sources for the company's current borrowings from commercial banks and other lending institutions.

Administers banking arrangements and loan agreements; receives, has custody of, and disburses the company's monies and securities; and is responsible for the financial aspects of real estate transactions, and executes bids, contracts, and leases.

Analyzes financial effects of proposals for acquisition of other companies and negotiates these acquisitions on behalf of the company.

Directs the granting of credit and the collection of accounts due the company, including the supervision of required special arrangements for financing sales, such as time payments and leasing plans.

Invests the company's funds as required, and establishes and coordinates policies for investment in pension and other similar trusts.

Provides insurance coverage as may be required.

Reviews and endorses or revises budget proposals received from those people reporting directly, according to corporate policy and procedure; submits budgets for assigned activities in accordance with the budget procedure; discusses proposed charges and significant revisions with those reporting directly.

Administers all stock option plans, incentive programs, and pension fund programs.

Establishes, coordinates, and administers, as an integral part of management, an adequate plan for the provision of capital. Such a plan provides, to the extent required in the business, programs for capital investing and for financing, together with the necessary controls and procedures to effectuate the plan.

Recommends financial policy affecting budgets and the expenditure of funds.

Analyzes the company's stockholder relations policies and recommends new or revised policies when needed.

Approves operating and administrative policies and procedures.

Compares performance with operating plans and standards, and reports and interprets the results of operations to all levels of management and to the owners of the business as they relate to his or her area of responsibility.

Continuously appraises economic and social forces and government influences, and interprets their effect upon the business.

Analyzes the company's stockholder information program covering such matters as the annual and interim reports to stockholders and recommends to the president new or revised programs.

Keeps abreast of new developments in the field of stockholder relations and advises the president of significant developments.

Ensures the execution of his or her functions at the lowest cost consistent with effective performance.

Establishes and issues the plans, policies, and procedures governing the performance of assigned activities.

Directs, reviews, and appraises the performance of the units immediately reporting, and provides the necessary coordination between the activities of such units.

Develops and presents matters requiring the decision of the president.

Provides advice on *all* matters to the president.

Provides other company units with information required by them to carry out their assigned responsibilities.

Establishes and implements a sound plan of organization of his or her assigned functions.

Coordinates activities of the assigned units with those of other company units; seeks material agreement on problems involving coordination.

Determines the necessary manpower required to perform his or her assigned functions; selects and maintains qualified personnel in all positions reporting directly, and recommends compensation for same.

Assists the president in the formulation of overall corporate objectives.

Keeps the president informed of the group's performance.

Divisional—Controls and coordinates operations and activities; approves operating plans; fosters economy throughout the company.

Ensures proper application of allotted funds, and fosters the best use of facilities in the interest of the company.

Approves operating and administrative policies.

Acts as the principal public relations officer of the company.

Reviews and analyzes qualitatively the company's efforts and results at regular intervals.

With the chairman of the board, reviews operations to enlarge the scope of the company through suitable acquisitions and other contractual arrangements.

Ensures overall company profitability.

Approves and enforces the organization plan of the company and any of its components, and changes therein.

Approves the addition, elimination, or alteration of management positions.

Approves salary and wage structures within corporate budgetary guidelines.

Recommends to the board of directors and stock option committee compensation for all officers of the company.

Sets the compensation of those (nonofficers) reporting directly.

Approves the hiring, appointing, releasing, and compensation of personnel reporting directly to his or her staff.

Coordinates personnel policies in conjunction with the corporate direction of personnel.

Ensures equitable administration of wage and salary policies and structures, employee benefit plans, and personnel rating programs, within the overall corporate policies.

Approves and submits the consolidated annual budget and proposed capital and extraordinary expenditure programs to the corporate president for final approval, making appropriate recommendations thereon.

Approves the initiation of any legal action within his or her limits of authority.

Sets the moral tone of the company by formulating policies that will govern the conduct of the business.

Promotes a climate for high motivation and dedication to corporate objectives.

ORGANIZATIONAL RELATIONSHIPS

Accountable to the president (corporate) for all phases of his or her activities and functions.

He or she is a member of the product development committee.

Credit and collection manager is accountable for all phases of his or her activities and functions.

Enlists the aid and cooperation of the vice president and controller:

> Executes programs for the provision of the capital required by Savin. Coordinates both long- and short-range financial planning. Maintains adequate sources for the company's borrowing from lending institutions.

Analyzes the financial effects of potential acquisitions of other companies or the sale of existing ones.

Provides insurance on recommended assets.

Aids and assists the executive vice president/market planning:

> Prepares, reviews, and analyzes financial projections with regard to the potential introduction of new products.

> Analyzes and is primarily responsible for negotiating the acquisition of companies brought to the corporation's attention by the executive vice president.

> Makes projections and forecasts on new products and distribution alternatives; estimates and projects royalty and licensing fees attrib-

utable to trademarks and patents; product line statistics and reports; budgets.

Aids and assists the vice president/marketing:

Develops and administers third-party leasing and rental programs designed to promote the sale of the corporation's products to the end user.

Budgets.

Takes part in the development of programs designed to promote the sale of the corporation's products to dealers, distributors, and licensees on a wholesale level.

Aids and assists the director of purchasing and distribution:

Financing and timing for fixed assets, capital expenditures, and leasehold improvements.

POSITION DESCRIPTION
(Vice President and Controller)

Effective Date:

TITLE: Vice President and Controller

DIVISION:	President's
DEPARTMENT:	N/A

REPORTS TO: President.

SECTION:	N/A
UNIT:	N/A

SUMMARY OF FUNCTIONS:

Directs the accounting and control functions, reporting the results of operations, providing chronological systems and data processing services.

MAJOR DUTIES AND RESPONSIBILITIES:

Coordinates all matters of business between the corporation and its stock transfer agents and registrars.

Prescribes the form of evidence and the manner of collection of loans to employees.

Forecasts short-range (3 months) cash requirements and obligations, as a basis for maintaining adequate funds.

Provides advice on *all* matters to the president.

Establishes, coordinates, and administers, as an integral part of management, an adequate plan for the control of operations. Such a plan provides, to the extent required in the business, profit planning, programs for capital investing and for financing, sales forecasts, expense budgets and cost standards, together with the necessary controls and procedures to effectuate the plan.

Reviews and endorses or revises budget proposals received from those people reporting directly; submits budgets for assigned activities in accordance with the budget procedure and discusses proposed changes and significant revisions with those reporting directly.

Directs, reviews, and appraises the performance of the units immediately reporting, and provides the necessary coordination between the activities of such units.

Compares performance with operating plans and standards, and reports and interprets the results of operations to all levels of management and to the owners of the business. This function includes the formulation of accounting policies, the coordination of systems and procedures, and the preparation of operating data and special reports as required.

Consults with all segments of management responsible for policy or action concerning any phase of the operation of the business as it relates to the attainment of objectives and the effectiveness of policies, organization structure, and procedures.

Provides for the control and editing of all company orders, to ensure conformity to established policies and procedures, and to facilitate data control and retrieval of records generated by these orders.

Establishes and administers tax policies and procedures.

Supervises or coordinates the preparation of reports to government agencies.

Ensures protection for the assets of the business through internal control, internal auditing, and ensuring proper insurance coverage.

Assists marketing in establishing and maintaining product pricing policies.

Serves as liaison between the company and legal counsel, and recommends the appointment of independent public accountants and the extent and scope of their audit work.

Provides other company units with information required by them to carry out their assigned responsibilities.

Establishes and implements a sound plan of organization of his or her assigned functions.

Coordinates the activities of the assigned units with those of other company units. Seeks mutual agreement on problems involving coordination.

Determines the necessary staffing required to perform his or her assigned functions. Selects and maintains qualified personnel in all positions reporting directly and recommends compensation for same.

Assists the president in the formulation of overall corporate objectives.

Keeps the president informed of the groups' performance.

Performs his or her functions at the lowest cost, consistent with effective performance.

Establishes and issues the plans, policies, and procedures governing the performance of assigned activities.

Develops and presents to the president matters requiring his or her decision.

Approves expense accounts of management reporting directly to him or her.

Coordinates plan and budget for the findings of the product development committee.

ORGANIZATIONAL RELATIONSHIPS:

Accountable to the president for all phases of his or her activities and functions.

He or she is a member of the product development committee.

The following are accountable for all phases of their activities and functions:

> Auditor manager
> Manager of accounting services department

Director of administrative operations (data processing)
National administrator (field administrator)
Manager of collection application
Director of purchasing

He or she advises, consults with, coordinates with, and provides administrative support, as follows:

Vice president/treasurer—Capital programs; insurance coverage; cash procedures; financial analyses.

Vice president/marketing—Compensation plans; product pricing; branch operating statements; control of field expenses; sales analyses by product and territory.

President, diversified equipment leasing corporation—Reports and analyses on leases by territory and product; financial statements preparation and analysis; credit and collection procedures; budgets.

Director of personnel and office services—Reports on payrolls and fringe benefits; compensation plans; planning of fixed assets, capital expenditures, and leasehold improvements (lease or buy and timing); office layout; budgets.

*   *   *   *   *

Observe that all of the FEI's defined functions appear in the position descriptions, in more detail to adapt them to the particular company using them. A summary of the overall function appears as the first paragraph of each position description and is worthy of repetition:

Treasurer—Responsible for all long-range financial matters and to establish companywide financial and administrative objectives, policies, programs, and practices that ensure the company of a continuously sound financial structure. As chief financial officer, controls the flow of cash through the organization and maintains the integrity of funds, securities, and other valuable documents.

Controller—Directs the accounting and control functions, reporting the results of operations, providing chronological systems and data processing services.

Appendix B
Index of Working Aids (Exhibits)

Index

About the Author

Daniel L. Gotthilf, a CPA, was Senior Vice President/Finance, Treasurer, Controller, and a Director of Savin Corporation. Mr. Gotthilf's areas of responsibilities with Savin over an eighteen-year period ranged from accounting services to data processing, personnel, budgeting and forecasting, and systems and procedures.

His early business years were spent in public accounting practice and as an internal operational auditor. Prior to joining Savin, he served as Controller for Universal Laboratories and as Treasurer and Controller for Technical Tape Corporation. He is presently engaged as a certified public accountant in his own practice and conducts peer reviews of other accountants under the AICPA Practice Monitoring Program.

Mr. Gotthilf was an honors graduate of the University of Michigan School of Business in 1948 and subsequently obtained a Certificate in Programming and Data Processing Analysis from New York University. The author has been a frequent lecturer before the American Management Association on a wide range of financial subjects and has written numerous articles for business and financial journals. He is a co-author of *Financial Analysis for Decision Making*, published by Prentice-Hall.